UNDERSTANDING CONTEMPORARY AFRICA

UNDERSTANDING

Introductions to the States and Regions of the Contemporary World

Donald L. Gordon, series editor

Understanding Contemporary Africa, 4th edition
edited by April A. Gordon and Donald L. Gordon

Understanding the Contemporary Caribbean
edited by Richard S. Hillman and Thomas J. D'Agostino

Understanding Contemporary China, 2nd edition
edited by Robert E. Gamer

Understanding Contemporary India
edited by Sumit Ganguly and Neil DeVotta

Understanding Contemporary Latin America, 3rd edition
edited by Richard S. Hillman

Understanding the Contemporary Middle East, 2nd edition
edited by Deborah J. Gerner and Jillian Schwedler

FOURTH EDITION

UNDERSTANDING CONTEMPORARY AFRICA

edited by
April A. Gordon
Donald L. Gordon

BOULDER
LONDON

Published in the United States of America in 2007 by
Lynne Rienner Publishers, Inc.
1800 30th Street, Boulder, Colorado 80301
www.rienner.com

and in the United Kingdom by
Lynne Rienner Publishers, Inc.
3 Henrietta Street, Covent Garden, London WC2E 8LU

Library of Congress Cataloging-in-Publication Data
Understanding contemporary Africa / edited by April A. Gordon and Donald L. Gordon.
—4th ed.
p. cm.—(Understanding)
Includes bibliographical references and index.
ISBN-13: 978-1-58826-466-4 (pbk. : alk. paper)
ISBN-10: 1-58826-466-1 (pbk. : alk. paper)
1. Africa—Politics and government—1960– 2. Africa—Social conditions—1960–
I. Gordon, April A. II. Gordon, Donald L.
DT30.5.U536 2006
960.3'2—dc22

2006020881

British Cataloguing in Publication Data
A Cataloguing in Publication record for this book
is available from the British Library.

Printed and bound in the United States of America

The paper used in this publication meets the requirements of the American National Standard for Permanence of Paper for Printed Library Materials Z39.48-1992.

5 4

Contents

Illustrations

Maps

Tables

Photographs

Preface

Since the first edition of *Understanding Contemporary Africa* was written fifteen years ago, much has changed in Africa. In 1990 South Africa was still under apartheid rule; many first- and second-generation autocratic leaders (such as Daniel arap Moi in Kenya and Mobutu Sese Seko of then Zaire) were still in power; civil war raged in Angola and Mozambique; and we were just beginning to realize the severity of the impact of HIV/AIDS on the continent. Now, nearly a decade into the twenty-first century, South Africa is free; almost all African countries have experienced substantial political liberalization; new generations of political leaders have come to power; and HIV/AIDS has exploded across sub-Saharan Africa, infecting close to 25 percent of Zimbabweans and more than 37 percent of the citizens of Botswana.

Many of the problems that were present in Africa twenty or so years ago remain or have intensified. Poverty abounds. Most of sub-Saharan Africa still depends on the production of cash crops or raw materials and remains an inconsequential part of the global economy. Population increases continue at a more rapid rate than job creation. And debilitating civil wars in countries such as Côte d'Ivoire and Sudan continue to plague the region.

Addressing these social, political, and economic problems provided the rationale for this book at the outset and continues to do so now. The success of the book confirms our belief that *Understanding Contemporary Africa,* with its broad scope, up-to-date and in-depth chapters, and attention to readability for undergraduate students, is a valuable text for both general African studies courses and discipline-based courses. It covers many of the most important topics and issues needed for a grasp of the reality of Africa in the early twenty-first century.

The information in each chapter of the book represents the best of the current research and thinking in various fields of study, providing students and professors with a useful background on Africa, and also presenting major issues in a way that students can understand. Although each chapter is designed to stand alone, the authors have produced a well-integrated volume, referring in their own chapters to complementary ideas discussed elsewhere in the book. This allows instructors to assign readings to meet their needs—by chapter or by topic—at the same time that the book helps students to see the connections among issues or events and reinforces what they may have read earlier.

In the introduction that follows this preface, the scope and themes of the book are discussed. Next, chapters on the geography and history of Africa provide the background necessary for understanding what follows. (Readers should refer to the maps in the geography chapter when reading later chapters of the book.) The remaining chapters cover major institutions and issues confronting Africa today. While each chapter provides historical background, the emphasis is on the vital concerns facing Africa now and in the future. Central among these concerns are African political and economic systems and issues, which are discussed in Chapters 4, 5, and 6. Tied closely to political and economic policies and trends are population growth, urbanization, AIDS, and environmental problems, as covered in Chapters 7 and 8. Next we address African family and kinship systems; without an awareness of how Africans understand kinship, issues like "tribalism" and corruption are difficult to comprehend and often misconstrued by outsiders. Women in Africa are the focus of Chapter 10; as this chapter shows, social change in Africa is affecting women much differently than it is men, and often to the disadvantage of women and Africa as a whole. In Chapters 11 and 12, on African religion and literature, the focus shifts to the ideological sphere—to how Africans explain and attempt to grapple with the complexities of their world and their place in it.

In the final chapter, turning to trends and prospects, we assess where Africa may be heading. While we do not attempt to predict any specific outcomes, we do note that many African countries are engaged in political and economic reform; some are making real progress while others are teetering on the brink of disaster. In all countries, new leaders are emerging, replacing those who assumed power at independence. Whether the new generation shaping the Africa of the future will improve on the record of the past remains very much an open question.

* * *

Writing and editing this book has left us indebted to a number of people.

Over time, our research has been aided by grants or other support from the University of Florida African Studies Center and the Institute of Development Studies at the University of Sussex, and both of us benefited from a Fulbright program in Cameroon under the direction of Mark DeLancey, then at the University of South Carolina.

We also received assistance from our respective universities—Furman and Winthrop—and from our departments. This included research funds, travel expenses, and staff support from patient and diligent secretarial staff. Over the years, as a result of the assistance we have received, we have been able to travel to at least ten African countries to learn firsthand what conditions and concerns exist in many parts of the continent.

In addition to Mark DeLancey, we wish to extend our appreciation to the late Bob Mundt of the University of North Carolina at Charlotte. For many students and scholars of Africa, both Mark and Bob have been catalysts for the careful study of the continent; this is true for us as well. Their love for Africa and their professionalism as social scientists have left an enduring legacy.

We are grateful to the chapter authors, without whose expertise and commitment to expanding an appreciation and understanding of Africa this book would not have been possible, nor would it have enjoyed such widespread success among classroom teachers and their students. Most of our authors have been with us since the first edition in 1992.

Thanks go to Michael Nwanze at Howard University, to Jack Parson at the College of Charleston, and to Erik Ching, codirector of Furman's study abroad programs in southern Africa. Their dedication to the education of undergraduate students and their insights on how best to teach undergraduates about Africa have helped us in the planning and revision of the book.

Since 1992, we have had important help from current and former graduate students. We want to acknowledge the work of Kevin Hill (at Florida International University), Beth Dotson (then at Indiana University), Mary Spear Prentice (then at St. Mary's College of Maryland), and Scott McPherson (a graduate student at the University of Florida). They created much of the content of the glossary, the list of acronyms, the basic political data, and some of the tables.

Finally, we extend our thanks to Mary Lou Ingram at the World Bank for her generosity in providing us with many of the photographs we have included.

—April A. Gordon,
Donald L. Gordon

UNDERSTANDING CONTEMPORARY AFRICA

1

Introduction

April A. Gordon and Donald L. Gordon

Africa is constantly in the media at the beginning of the twenty-first century. Almost every day, network and cable news programs feature some event or dilemma somewhere on the continent.

Yet, most Americans know very little about sub-Saharan Africa and its rich mosaic of peoples, cultural traditions, languages, political systems, and economies, or even about the geography of the continent. It is not uncommon to hear a college student refer to the "country of Africa" or for people to think about Africa as inhabited only by "tribes" of "savage" people living in "jungles."

The fact is that what most Americans, even college graduates, think about Africa is almost always only partially correct or based on stereotypes or an inadequate historical or conceptual framework for understanding and interpretation. The media tend to reinforce these misperceptions, especially with their almost exclusive focus on the exotic or on negative news such as drought and famine, civil war, and widespread poverty. While these phenomena certainly exist, there is far more to the continent and its people. Moreover, where Africa is suffering from problems like drought, civil war, and poverty, it is important to know why and what has been or should be done about such tragedies.

Understanding Contemporary Africa has been written to provide the basic concepts, theoretical perspectives, and essential information that are necessary for understanding the dynamic, as well as troubled, region that is Africa today. This book is mainly about sub-Saharan Africa, Africa south of the Sahara. While some mention is made of North Africa, Africa's Asiatic communities, and white settlers (especially in South Africa), those interested in these topics will need to consult additional sources. The authors have written in depth on the most important issues and institutions in Africa. Although these writers are from different disciplines and each chapter is more or less self-contained, a broad portrait of sub-Saharan Africa is discernible.

Geographically, Africa is a massive continent, roughly three and a half times larger than the United States. Africa's range of climates, topography, and physical beauty have created conditions conducive to the formation of an immense diversity of peoples and cultures. Africa is in fact the "home" of humankind, in which every means of livelihood from gathering and hunting to industrialism can be found. At the same time, the enormity of the continent and its often harsh ecological conditions, such as extremes of oppressive heat, vast deserts, marginal soils, and expanses of subtropical vegetation, left many groups relatively isolated from other parts of the world until the last few centuries and limited the concentrations of population and resources that led to the more technologically complex societies of the "old world" and industrial Europe. Despite this relative isolation, some societies had contact with regions as distant as North Africa, India, and even China. Regardless, all developed intricate cultures with rich religious and artistic traditions and complex social and kinship relations.

As is true of other areas of the world, sub-Saharan Africa's history is fraught with episodes of upheaval, violence, and cultural challenges generated by both internal and external forces. For instance, movements of people within the continent led to cross-cultural exchange of ideas, goods, and people as well as conflict. Foreign religions, mainly Christianity and Islam, were carried in by outsiders and resulted in challenges and conflicts not only with local religious beliefs but with long-established customs and ways of life. At the same time, these religions have been incorporated into African societies, changing both in the process. There have also been periods of peace and prosperity in which Africans could live out their lives in relative security and contentment, partly because most lacked the extreme class stratification and state structures that led to so much oppression and exploitation in so-called civilized areas of the world.

Beginning in the 1500s, Africa's history began to commingle with that of an expansionist West in pursuit of trade, booty, and exotic lands and people to conquer. This eventuated in the most cruel and disruptive period in African history, starting with the slave trade and culminating in colonial domination of the continent. This reached its most extreme form in South Africa, whose African majority was ruled until 1994 by the white descendants of its European colonizers.

Along with its other effects, the Western penetration of Africa exposed Africans to the material riches and culture of the West. As Bohannan and Curtin (1995:15) observe, Africans were not deprived before Western penetration of their societies. Many lived fulfilling lives of great dignity, content without the "trappings of Western civilization." However, once exposed to the possibilities of Western civilization, the lure has proven to be almost irresistible in Africa and elsewhere.

The influence of the West and Western culture is the major transformative force in Africa today. By responding to the promise of acquiring Western affluence, Africans across the continent, to varying degrees, are being integrated into the worldwide network of trade and productive relationships sometimes called "the global capitalist economy." This global economy is dominated for the most part by the few rich, politically and militarily powerful countries of Europe and by the United States—countries that initially gained much of their preeminence from the exploitation of Africans (and other non-Western people). As slaves or colonial subjects, Africans' labor and resources (usually obtained directly or indirectly by coercion) provided many of the low-cost raw materials for Western factories and affluent consumer lifestyles.

Since colonialism, African cash crops, minerals, and fuels have continued to be transported overseas, while Western manufactured goods, technology, financial capital, and Western lifestyles are imported to Africa. So far, the "integration" of Africa into the global economy has largely gone badly for most countries on the continent as the cost of Western imports compared to the prices of African exports has typically been unfavorable to Africa, leaving almost all countries in debt, their economies a shambles, and living standards spiraling downward. Only a minority of Africans have been able to acquire more than a few tokens of the promised life the West symbolizes.

Another import from the West is Western political systems. Like a hand-me-down suit never fitted to its new wearer, Western multiparty political systems, hastily handed over to Africans experienced mainly in colonial despotism, did not "fit." Most degenerated into one-party states or military dictatorships riddled with corruption and inefficiency. Opposition to the state was either co-opted or ruthlessly repressed. Expected to be the architects of development for their people, African states instead became largely self-serving, bloated bureaucracies alienated from the masses for whom "development" became a more remote prospect as economies began deteriorating from the 1970s on. These legacies have made it difficult for African states to democratize and to be able to benefit from the increasingly globalized world of the twenty-first century.

Making things worse has been the unprecedented growth of population in Africa and the rapid expansion of urban areas. In part, these two related trends both reflect and exacerbate economic and political problems. Certainly, agrarian societies like Africa's value large families. Nonetheless, African family sizes are considerably in excess of those found in most other developing regions. In Africa, inadequate investment in farming, especially in food crops grown mostly by women, keeps most agriculture highly "labor intensive" (dependent on labor rather than machines). Since mainly it is men who migrate to cities for work, women need children more than ever to help them with farm chores. Moreover, as patronage relationships based on ethnicity and kinship are often vital to gaining access to resources (such as jobs, schooling, or money), children are valuable assets even in affluent urban families. For many Africans, resources are shrinking because of mounting political and economic problems. Structural adjustment programs (SAPs), designed ostensibly to combat these problems, often compounded the hardships instead. The neglect of agriculture and lack of opportunity in rural areas along with the expansion of wage jobs in cities inevitably has attracted job seekers in numbers far greater than the capacity of cities to employ them or adequately service their needs. The resulting discontent of urbanites has frequently been the basis of political opposition to whatever regime is in power and contributed to the problems of political repression and instability.

The way Africans have tried to develop their economies, often on the basis of Western development advice, has indirectly promoted population growth and urbanization by favoring industry, export production, and cities over rural areas. It has also discriminated against women and neglected their interests as producers, mothers, and individuals, with detrimental effects on the economy and social welfare. It has also contributed to environmental degradation, especially soil erosion, deforestation, and desertification. Land scarcity is affecting growing numbers of poor farmers and pastoralists. Lack of resources or technology to improve methods of production, along with lack of opportunity to make a living elsewhere, leaves many people with little recourse other than cultivating or grazing their cattle on fragile or marginal land and destroying trees. Western multinational corporations and development agencies, often in league with African business or state elites, have also been guilty of pursuing economic "growth" and profits at the expense of the environment.

As gloomy as this picture of Africa looks, we must remember that African independence is less than fifty years old for most countries. Africans are a practical and adaptive people, as their history and cultures clearly show. Africans have not been locked in hopelessly outmoded traditions, as stereotypes sometimes suggest. Rather, they have always taken from other traditions and cultures what they perceived to be valuable for their own. African resilience and flexibility are in evidence now as in the past. Africans have been experimenting for well over a thousand years with Islam and Christianity and more recently with secular religions such as socialism, capitalism, and Marxism-Leninism, blending them in often quixotic stews with indigenous African practices. That such experimentation has produced mixed results should be expected. As Goran Hyden

(1983) noted in the title of his book on Africa, there are "no shortcuts to progress," a hard lesson being learned by many Africans whose expectations for quick development have been sharply downscaled as a result of chronic economic and political turmoil.

African cultures remain vibrant and are playing a leading role in the efforts to cope with and address the forces affecting African societies. Questions of personal and collective identity and meaning frequently come to the fore as well as discontent with political oppression, foreign exploitation, and economic inequality and poverty. These concerns are clearly manifested in new forms of religious expression, literature, and political movements for democratization and women's rights. The extended family remains a vital refuge for most Africans during these challenging times, but the spread of the Western nuclear family and other changes in African institutions reflect current adaptations to new realities.

Until recently, it was easy and convenient to blame Africa's problems on the West, and for the most part accurate. The negative legacy of colonialism has been especially profound. Many scholars still contend that the role Africa has been assigned in the global economy as a producer of cheap raw materials continues to prevent it from achieving its economic potential. At least partial blame for Africa's political problems such as coups d'état and authoritarian rule could be laid at the West's doorstep. After all, the West often has had a major role in deciding who came to power or stayed in power. Typically, Western interference in African politics has been determined mostly by geopolitical or economic interests rather than by such lofty goals as democracy or good government. During the Cold War, this was apparent in the support accorded dictators like former president Mobutu Sese Seko (now deceased) of what is now the Democratic Republic of Congo as well as Western complicity in maintaining the brutal apartheid system in South Africa.

As the colonial period recedes in time, more critical attention is being focused on Africans themselves, especially their leaders. This represents, for the most part, a growing awareness that Africans are not simply pawns in the machinations of self-interested Western multinational corporations, bankers, or governments. More Africans are acknowledging that they must address their own shortcomings and institute reforms, be they political, economic, social, or religious renewal. By themselves, such reforms are unlikely to overcome all the inequities of the global economic and political order over which Africa has little control; but only an enlightened and competent African leadership can hope to mobilize the energy and commitment of its people for the challenges that lie ahead.

One of the greatest of these challenges is the HIV/AIDS crisis sweeping many countries. Most of the world's victims of this dreadful disease are in Africa, and AIDS continues to spread. Even with a massive commitment of resources to combat AIDS (which currently does not exist), much of the improvement Africa has experienced economically and in extending the life and well-being of its people will be undermined as AIDS continues to run its relentless course.

As Africa moves through the first decade of the twenty-first century, we must keep some historical perspective to avoid the currently widespread "Afropessimism" about the continent's prospects. We must remember that profound societal transformations are under way and that such changes often entail considerable suffering, alienation, and disruptions that may take decades to resolve. Mao Zedong, the leader of postrevolutionary China, was once asked by author Edgar Snow what he thought was the significance of the French Revolution. Mao's sage reply was, "I think it's a little too early to tell" (in Whitaker, 1988:12). Despite the tragedies and disappointments Africans have experienced since independence, it is certainly "too early to tell" about Africa as well. The story of this immensely rich and diverse continent is still unfolding.

Bibliography

Bohannan, Paul, and Philip Curtin. 1995. *Africa and Africans.* Prospect Heights, IL: Waveland Press.

Hyden, Goran. 1983. *No Shortcuts to Progress.* Berkeley: University of California Press.

Whitaker, Jennifer Seymour. 1988. *How Can Africa Survive?* New York: Council on Foreign Relations Press.

2

Africa: A Geographic Preface

Jeffrey W. Neff

Of all the places of the world for which we can conjure up a mental map, Africa is frequently the "blankest." For this reason, some introduction to the geography of this vast and varied continent is needed (Map 2.1, at the end of this chapter). This chapter and the maps it includes will be useful reference sources as locations and features are mentioned in subsequent chapters.

A student of geography can appreciate the size of the United States (3.6 million square miles/9.5 million square kilometers) and the cultural diversity of its very large (275 million) population. Consider this, however: Three countries the size of the United States could fit into the landmass area of Africa, with a little room to spare! In addition, more than 900 million people live in Africa (over three-fourths of them in sub-Saharan Africa). Africa's population is not only three times larger than that of the United States, but it displays a greater degree of cultural complexity. Of all the world's known languages, over one-third are spoken in Africa (United States Bureau, 2005; deBlij and Muller, 1998:343). The perception of Africa as a wild, untamed land—vast herds of wild animals, spectacular gorges and waterfalls, towering mountains, trackless forests, great deserts—needs some revision in light of these basic population characteristics.

The Moving ITCZ

Most Africans are engaged in some form of agriculture or pastoralism, either at a subsistence level (the great majority) or in commercial agriculture (a very small minority). The African economy is further driven by other products harvested or extracted directly from nature, such as forest products and minerals.

Nature wields a much heavier hand in Africa in directly influencing the welfare of hundreds of millions of people than it does in the industrialized world where, at least up to now, people have been insulated to some degree from the effects of drought, flood, plagues, and other natural hazards. To understand contemporary Africa, the student of Africa needs a basic knowledge of natural phenomena and processes. In my estimation, the single most powerful environmental mechanism that affects life and survival in Africa south of the Sahara is something called the Intertropical Convergence Zone, or the ITCZ (Map 2.2).

The ITCZ represents a meteorological phenomenon whereby large-scale airflows from generally opposite directions converge or meet, creating a relatively constant updraft of displaced air. The vertical movement is supplemented by buoyant heated air from the sun-soaked, warm surface conditions of the tropical regions. This rising air cools off rapidly, causing atmospheric water vapor (if present) to condense into droplets first, then precipitation (Strahler and Strahler, 1979:100–111). At least, this is the ideal chain of events, and the ITCZ is the primary rainmaking mechanism not only in Africa but throughout the tropical world. Rainfall often occurs as daily thunderstorms and can be torrential during the rainy season.

World Bank

Pastoralists in the unpredictable environment of the Sahel move their cattle in search of food and water.

Note two very important features of Map 2.2. First, the ITCZ shifts pronouncedly from June to January. (The shift is caused by changing earth-sun relationships during the year and by the inclination of the earth's axis.) This motion is crucial for the delivery of rainfall to almost all of sub-Saharan Africa and gives most of Africa its wet-and-dry seasonality. When the ITCZ is stationed at its northward June position, the rainy season is on—or should be—and southern Africa is dry. The southward migration of the ITCZ signals rain for the south and the onset of the dry season in the north. And so it has gone, century after century. Some regions, such as the tropical forest belt, get longer rainy seasons and more rain than others, and some regions face greater unpredictability, or precipitation variation (the semi-arid Sahel). Sometimes the ITCZ "misbehaves" and does not shift when it's normally expected to or move where it usually should, bringing stress to the life that depends on it. Generally, though, farming societies throughout Africa continue to coordinate planting and harvesting with the ITCZ's rainmaking mechanism. Pastoralists move their cattle, and herds of wild animals migrate in similar response to seasonal moisture availability. Nature and people have adjusted to a life rhythm tied to this slow, unending, writhing dance of the ITCZ back and forth across the length and breadth of the continent.

Natural Regions

Map 2.2 also reveals, in a highly generalized rendition, the natural environments of Africa as depicted by vegetative patterns. The natural vegetation represents the long-term adjustment of complex plant communities to the conditions of the African climate. From a human perspective, these environmental regions possess very different capacities for life support (or carrying capacity). Awareness of the potentials and the problems of these life zones is crucial for survival; exceeding their carrying capacities promises serious penalties for the occupants, as Julius Nyang'oro details in Chapter 8.

Trouble spots abound in the drier margins. The semi-arid, grassy steppe of the Sahel and the East African desert (parts of Kenya, Somalia, and Ethiopia), plagued by an unpredictable ITCZ and burgeoning populations, have been the scenes of human misery periodically during the past two decades. The specter of mass starvation brought on by drought and desertification in the semi-arid regions of the Dry Savanna has been prominent and publicized but not surprising. Tropical wet-and-dry climates have always been problematic for their human occupants. By the twenty-first century, an exploding population had exceeded beyond all reason the ability of the more fragile, marginal zones to support it.

World Bank

The semi-arid Sahel is becoming increasingly vulnerable to drought and desertification, putting villages like this one in Burkino Faso at growing risk.

Even the "humid" tropical forest of Africa is not immune from trouble. Here, drought and desertification are removed as threats to be replaced by rampant deforestation, primarily for hardwood harvest and plantation expansion. At current rates of cutting, much of the easily accessible forests of coastal West and East Africa will be gone early in the twenty-first century. Probably only the relatively insulated interior forests of the eastern Congo Basin will survive the first several decades of the century. Without controls, they too could disappear by mid-century.

The "friendlier" Wet Savanna will come under increasing pressure as population growth and the movement of environmental refugees from the deteriorating Dry Savanna place undue strains on its carrying capacity. But almost all of tropical Africa is marked by poor, infertile, sometimes sterile soils, and the Wet Savanna has only limited agricultural potential. Only temperate South Africa is soil "rich"; however, it cannot sustain more than a fraction of Africa's future food needs.

Sub-Saharan Africa's natural regions are fragile and seem destined for continuing problems. If predicted global climatic changes affect the already erratic character and behavior of the ITCZ, the human carrying capacity of these natural regions could be reduced rapidly and massively. This is not a pleasant prospect to contemplate, but every student of Africa should be aware of the possibility. In the midst of the Sahelian drought of 1968–1974, for example, unusually large numbers of adult males in Upper Volta (now Burkina Faso) and Niger left their villages to search for jobs in more favored agricultural areas to the south or in large towns such as Abidjan and Lagos in the richer coastal countries. Such sudden movements placed heavy burdens on the meager support services and social balances of the destination areas (Caldwell, 1977:95–96).

Elsewhere, human suffering caused by drought was recently compounded by armed conflict over boundary alignments between Ethiopia and Eritrea. The dispute, commencing in 1998, severely reduced the ability of each country to respond effectively to the famine perpetuated by this lethal mix of natural and human factors.

Continents Adrift: Africa, the "Mother" of Landmasses

There is another geographic attribute crucial to the understanding of Africa, and most students who have had some earth science are aware of it. Until about 100 million years ago, the earth's landmasses were bound together as a supercontinent known as Pangaea. The southern landmasses constituted Gondwana, with present-day Africa the keystone. Through the phenomenon of plate tectonics, or continental drift, Africa's "children" began to leave the nest and scatter to their present positions: North and South America, Antarctica, Australia, and India all moved away from "mother" Africa, leaving her with her distinctive present-day shape and configuration. More important, it left her with relatively sharp, steep edges on all sides where the other plates tore away. (The presence of deep rift valleys in eastern Africa suggests that this continental separation process is not yet complete; Africa may be further fractured and split along the rift zone. The Red Sea is an expanding "rift," and eastern Africa could eventually pull away from the continent.) This steep edge is known generally as the Great Escarpment, and it is very prominent in eastern and southern Africa and somewhat less pronounced, but evident, in western Africa. It commences its sharp ascent just a few miles inland from the coast and, once topped, a high plateau-like landscape unfolds. Broad coastal lowlands are generally absent (Church et al., 1977:23, 26).

There are several interesting, important, and unique phenomena associated with this continental morphology that have had direct, powerful impacts on human history and activity in Africa.

Carriers and Barriers

"Carriers and barriers" refers to phenomena that influence, control, channel, restrict, or enhance various human spatial processes. An analysis of the pattern of railways and navigable waterways reveals the incomplete and unconnected nature of these linkages (Map 2.3). Oddly, except for the Nile River and the lower Niger River, most river transport does not connect with the coast. Why not? Primarily because of the barriers of falls and rapids created where major rivers fall over or break through the Great Escarpment in their escape to the sea. The most navigable stretches of water occur on interior sections of African rivers. Water access from the sea to Africa's interior is now and always has been physically restricted.

Nor does the Great Escarpment stimulate railway and road building between coast and interior. Some stretches of the escarpment tower 2,000 to 4,000 feet and more above the adjacent coastal lowland, especially in southern Africa (e.g., the Drakensberg). Construction is difficult and very expensive; some rail lines were built only where access to valuable raw

World Bank

The relative isolation of the African interior from the coast was reinforced during colonial times, when transportation links were determined by colonial interests. Improving infrastructure, such as roads, has been a major priority since independence.

materials warranted the effort. Note too the dearth of natural harbors and major ports along Africa's steep, smooth, and regular coastline, highlighting the difficulty of access to the interior. Movement *within* Africa has been easier, and in regions such as western Africa, a fairly lively intraregional trade developed over the centuries prior to European contact, as both Thomas O'Toole and Virginia DeLancey document in later chapters.

In fact, most of the significant states and empires that evolved within Africa through the centuries did so in the *interior* of the continent, not along the coastal margins (Map 2.4). By geographic edict, Africa's insular tendency was established long ago and was only slightly reoriented with the beginnings of the slave trade, first by the Arabs in eastern Africa, then more violently by the Europeans (sixteenth century) in western and equatorial Africa. Still, for three centuries European contact and interest remained peripheral; the walls of "Fortress Africa" were violated and permanently breached by these "invaders" only in the nineteenth century.

The Berlin Conference of 1884–1885 and the ensuing partitioning of Africa among the European powers symbolized the inevitable geographic reorientation of Africa and Africans and a wholesale dismantling of their states, societies, and livelihoods, to be replaced by European models (Betts, 1972). By the eve of World War I, a new type of fragmentation, as powerful in its own way as the Gondwana breakup 100 million years earlier, had changed the face of "the Mother of Continents" forever (Map 2.5). The historical and political dynamics of these periods are treated in great detail in Chapters 3 and 4.

The Resource Base

The huge, high block of mostly metamorphic rock that became post-Gondwana Africa may have hindered outside penetration, but geologic forces created some powerful attractions for European exploiters. The ancient metamorphic rock of Africa is highly "mineralized." Map 2.3 reveals the occurrence and location of some of these mineral resources, coveted by an industrial world.

In several categories of industrial raw materials and minerals production, Africa contains important countries and regions. The continent is famous not only for its annual yield of approximately one-fourth of the world's gold but also for over 50 percent of global diamond output. A copper-laden zone straddling the borders of Zambia and the Democratic Republic of Congo (DRC) and extending southward through Zimbabwe and South Africa accounts for about 4 percent of the world's production of that mineral. Africa provides about half of the world's cobalt, with mines concentrated in DRC and Zambia. (Cobalt is a critical ferroalloy in jet and rocket engines.) In 2000, the United States received about 25 percent of its cobalt from these two countries (USGS, 2000, 2004).

Guinea ranked third in the world in 2004 in bauxite production (for aluminum). South Africa and Zimbabwe together account for nearly half of the global output of chromite, a strategic metallic mineral crucial to steel manufacturing in the industrial world (USGS, 2004). And Nigeria is Africa's top petroleum producer and has consistently been among the top five exporters of crude oil to the United States (API, 2000, 2005). Intensive mineral exploration early in the twenty-first century is continuing as Africa's full potential in this sector has yet to be fully realized. Unfortunately, as is discussed in Chapter 13, Africa's raw materials blessings in many cases have been a curse rather than a boon to its own development.

As previously mentioned, many transportation lines exist primarily to provide access to these resources, not to interconnect Africa. Furthermore, many mineral sites were revealed only after the European partitioning process was completed and several mineral zones were divided between opposing states (e.g., the Copperbelt between Zaire and Zambia), contributing to tension and conflict in postcolonial Africa.

Although rich in metallic ores, Africa's geology yields only a few favored fossil fuel occurrences (coal, oil, and gas are normally associated with sedimentary rather than metamorphic rock), namely, the petroleum of the Niger River Delta, Gabon, Angola, and Algeria/Libya, and the coal of South Africa. Thus, Africa exports its metallic ores and imports much of its energy.

Another resource that exists in great potential abundance in Africa is directly related to the problematic topography of the landmass itself: water power. Although deficient in fossil fuel energy resources (Nigeria, Gabon, Angola, and South Africa are exceptions), sub-Saharan Africa is "rich" in hydroelectric potential. The specific sites of this potential are where major rivers experience impressive drops—and therefore rapids and falls—in their escape routes from the continent's interior. Electricity generation at these sites could conceivably enhance economic development over large regions. Several noteworthy projects have been completed for just this purpose: the Nile's Aswan High Dam in Egypt; the Zambezi's Kariba Dam, shared by Zambia and Zimbabwe; and the Volta's Akosombo Dam in Ghana. In fact, Africa possesses the greatest hydroelectric potential of any continent, and the intent of these projects has been to tap some of it.

More intriguing than the presence of such projects, however, is their small number in Africa. Most rivers are not being harnessed for power generation, and few hydroelectric facilities exist. Resource abundance, large "reserves" of power, and seemingly infinite potential have not been reconfigured into actual use for a very basic economic reason: lack of markets. Africans use very little electricity. They are predominantly farmers and laborers—and they are income-poor. Industry, a big potential user of electrical power, is not a significant part of Africa's economic mix. Cities are also viable concentrated electricity markets, but most Africans are village dwellers, not urbanites. A huge capital investment is required to build dams and generating facilities, to transport the electricity great distances, and to distribute it in regional grids. Achieving a reasonable return on such an investment in Africa would be extremely difficult; therefore, this particular component of the continent's resource base remains greatly underexploited.

The long exposure of the ancient African landmass to the tropical sun and rain—and to the force of gravity—has also removed much of the original surface material by erosion. The poor tropical soil that remains holds little fertility, and alluvial soils (the deep, rich, stream-deposited sediments found on floodplains and deltas) and rich volcanic soils are uncommon on the high plateau surface. (The fertile soils of the alluvial Inland Niger Delta between Segou and Timbuktu in Mali and the volcanically derived soils of Cameroon and the Kenya highlands are examples of exceptions to this generalization.) Many of the better coastal sites are held by large plantation operations geared to products for export.

As previously mentioned, nontropical southern Africa is richer in soil fertility and can be considered an exception to the African rule of low soil productivity. Cooler temperatures mark this projection of the African landmass into the middle latitudes of the Southern Hemisphere. Latitudinal position and the high elevation of South Africa's Highveld combine with lower rainfall to reduce the leaching of soil nutrients, while simultaneously allowing for a thicker accumulation of organic material (humus), which is a critical factor in soil fertility. The resulting greater productivity of South African soil has supported the development of a diverse agricultural economy that is relatively free of tropical disease vectors and is grain- and livestock–based (corn, wheat, sheep, and cattle). The shifting cultivation practices so typical of tropical Africa, described in Chapter 8 by Julius Nyang'oro, are replaced here by permanent and prosperous small family farms.

For most Africans, however, agriculture remains subsistence, and food supply problems have increased with the growing population, an issue treated more fully in later chapters on the economy, environment, and population.

Nature, history, and the global economic system have combined to deprive Africans of much potential wealth and well-being. In many instances, the artificially imposed unity of the colonial era exacerbated conflict. Supranationalism—i.e., multi-state political and economic cooperation to identify and promote shared objectives—remains highly elusive, frustrated by a disjointed transportation system, ethnic/tribal conflicts, and an illogical political geography of too many fragmented nation-states (Map 2.6). A problematic environment, an exploding population, and the political-geographic realities of early-twenty-first-century Africa may ultimately conspire to quickly drain this vast continent of the vitality and energy that is still there in the form of raw material wealth, food-production capacity, and resourceful human spirit. These issues and others will be addressed in the following chapters, which explore the political, economic, environmental, and social forces determining Africa's destiny.

Bibliography

API (American Petroleum Institute). 2000. "Energy Facts." Online at www.api.org/fags/ (April).

———. 2005. *Industry Statistics: U.S. Imports of Crude Oil by Country.* Online at www.api-ec.api.org/industry/ (January).

Best, Alan C. G., and Harm J. deBlij. 1977. *African Survey.* New York: John Wiley and Sons.

Betts, Raymond F. 1972. *The Scramble for Africa: Causes and Dimensions of Empire.* Lexington, MA: D. C. Heath.

Caldwell, J. C. 1977. "Demographic Aspects of Drought: An Examination of the African Drought of 1970–1974." Pp. 93–99 in D. Dalby, R. J. H. Church, and F. Bezzaz (eds.). *Drought in Africa.* London: International African Institute.

Church, R. J. H., John I. Clarke, P. J. H. Clarke, and H. J. R. Henderson. 1977. *Africa and the Islands.* New York: John Wiley and Sons.

deBlij, Harm J., and Peter O. Muller. 1998. *Geography: Realms, Regions, and Concepts.* New York: John Wiley and Sons.

Strahler, Arthur N., and Alan H. Strahler. 1979. *Elements of Physical Geography.* New York: John Wiley and Sons.

Udo, Reuben K. 1978. *A Comprehensive Geography of West Africa.* New York: Africana.

US Bureau of the Census. 2005. *International Data Base, International Programs Center, Washington, DC.* Online at www.census.gov.

US Central Intelligence Agency. 1999. "The World Factbook, 1999." Online at www.odci.gov/cia/publications/factbook/concopy.html (January).

USGS (United States Geological Survey). 2000. "Minerals Information." Online at http://www.minerals.usgs.gov/minerals.

———. 2004. "Commodity Statistics and Information." Online at www.minerals.usgs.gov/minerals.

Map 2.1

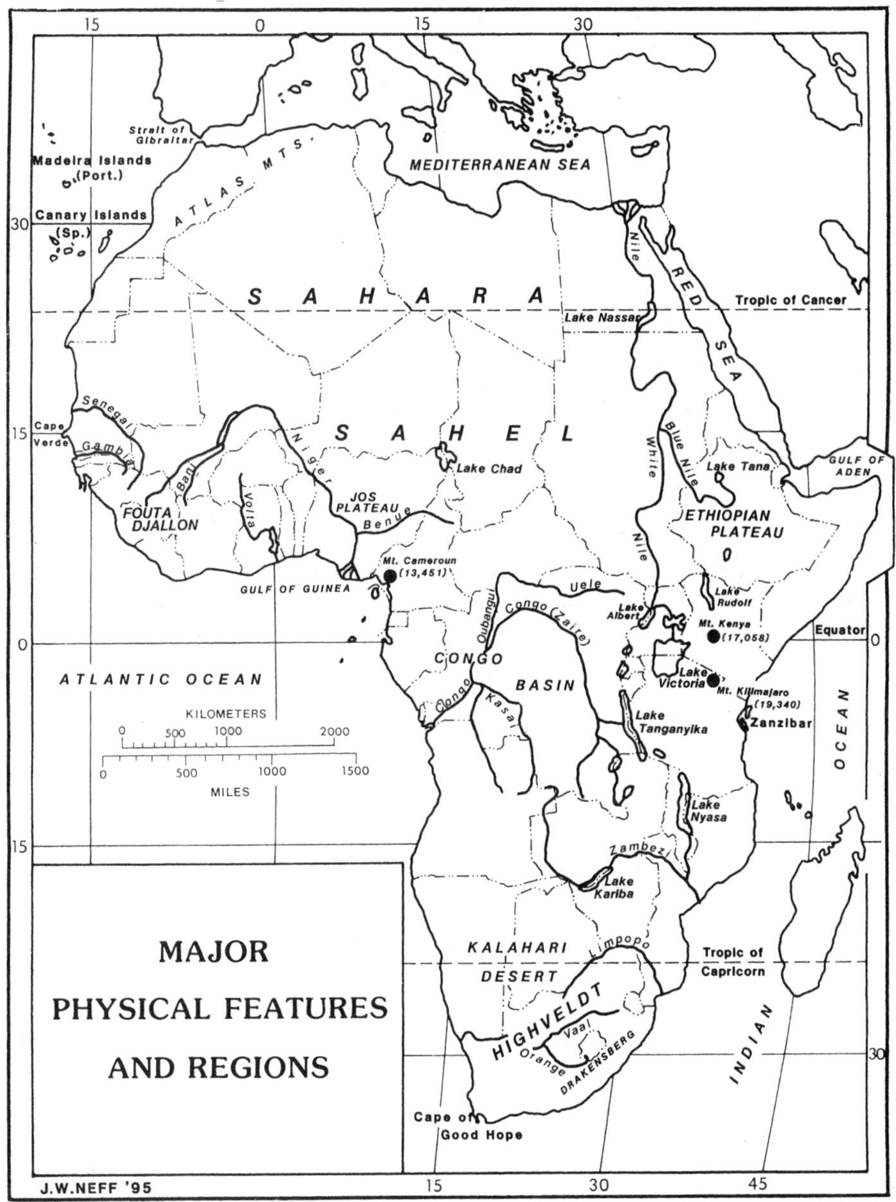
MAJOR
PHYSICAL FEATURES
AND REGIONS
J.W.NEFF '95
Strait of Gibraltar
Madeira Islands (Port.)
Canary Islands (Sp.)
ATLAS MTS.
MEDITERRANEAN SEA
SAHARA
Tropic of Cancer
Lake Nassar
Nile
RED SEA
SAHEL
Senegal
Cape Verde
Gambia
Niger
Bani
Volta
FOUTA DJALLON
JOS PLATEAU
Benue
Lake Chad
White Nile
Blue Nile
Lake Tana
GULF OF ADEN
ETHIOPIAN PLATEAU
Lake Rudolf
Mt. Cameroun (13,451)
GULF OF GUINEA
Uele
Congo (Zaire)
Oubangui
Lake Albert
Mt. Kenya (17,058)
Equator
CONGO
BASIN
Lake Victoria
Mt. Kilimajaro (19,340)
Zanzibar
ATLANTIC OCEAN
KILOMETERS
0 500 1000 2000
0 500 1000 1500
MILES
Kasai
Lake Tanganyika
Lake Nyasa
Zambezi
Lake Kariba
KALAHARI
DESERT
Limpopo
Tropic of Capricorn
HIGHVELDT
Vaal
Orange
DRAKENSBERG
Cape of Good Hope
INDIAN
OCEAN
15 0 15 30
30 15 0 15 30 45

Map 2.2

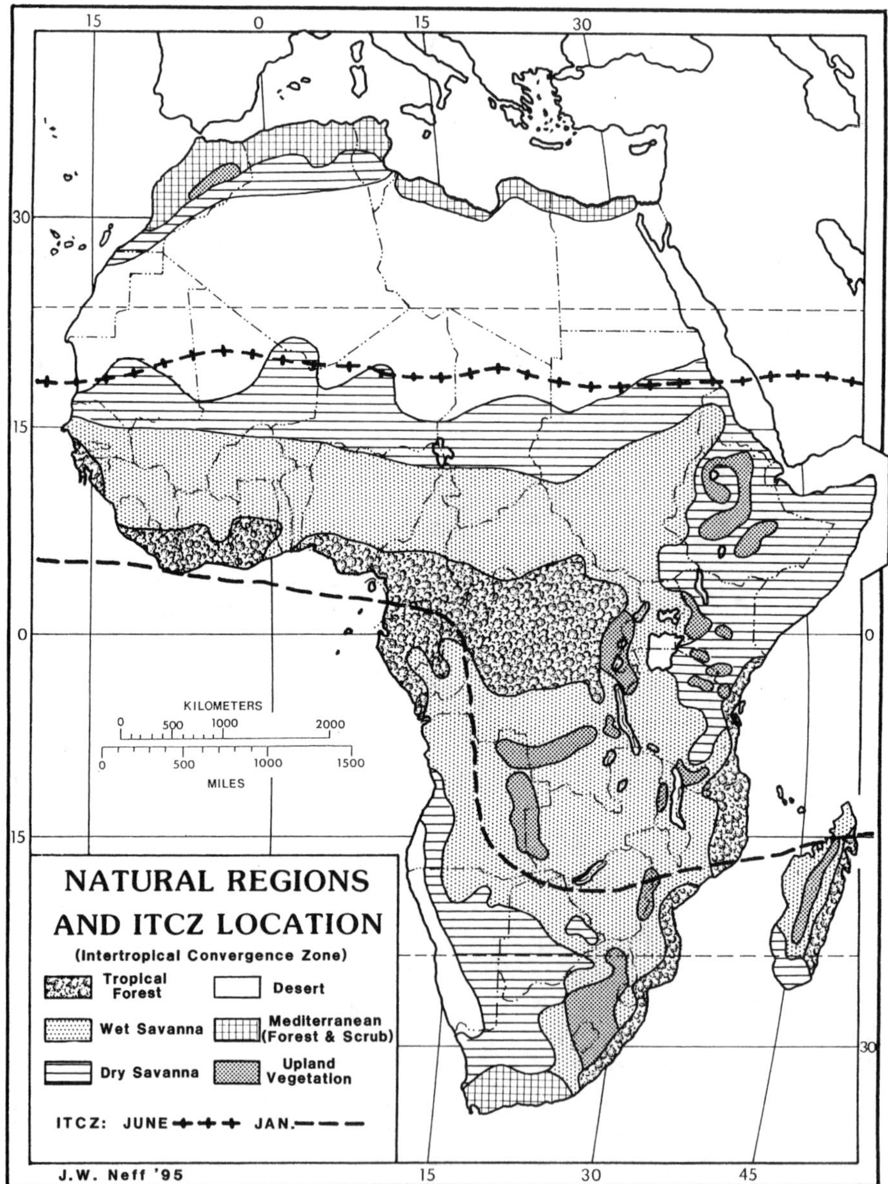

NATURAL REGIONS
AND ITCZ LOCATION
(Intertropical Convergence Zone)
Tropical Forest
Desert
Wet Savanna
Mediterranean (Forest & Scrub)
Dry Savanna
Upland Vegetation
ITCZ: JUNE
JAN.
KILOMETERS
0
500
1000
2000
MILES
0
500
1000
1500
15
0
15
30
30
15
0
15
30
45
J.W. Neff '95

Map 2.3

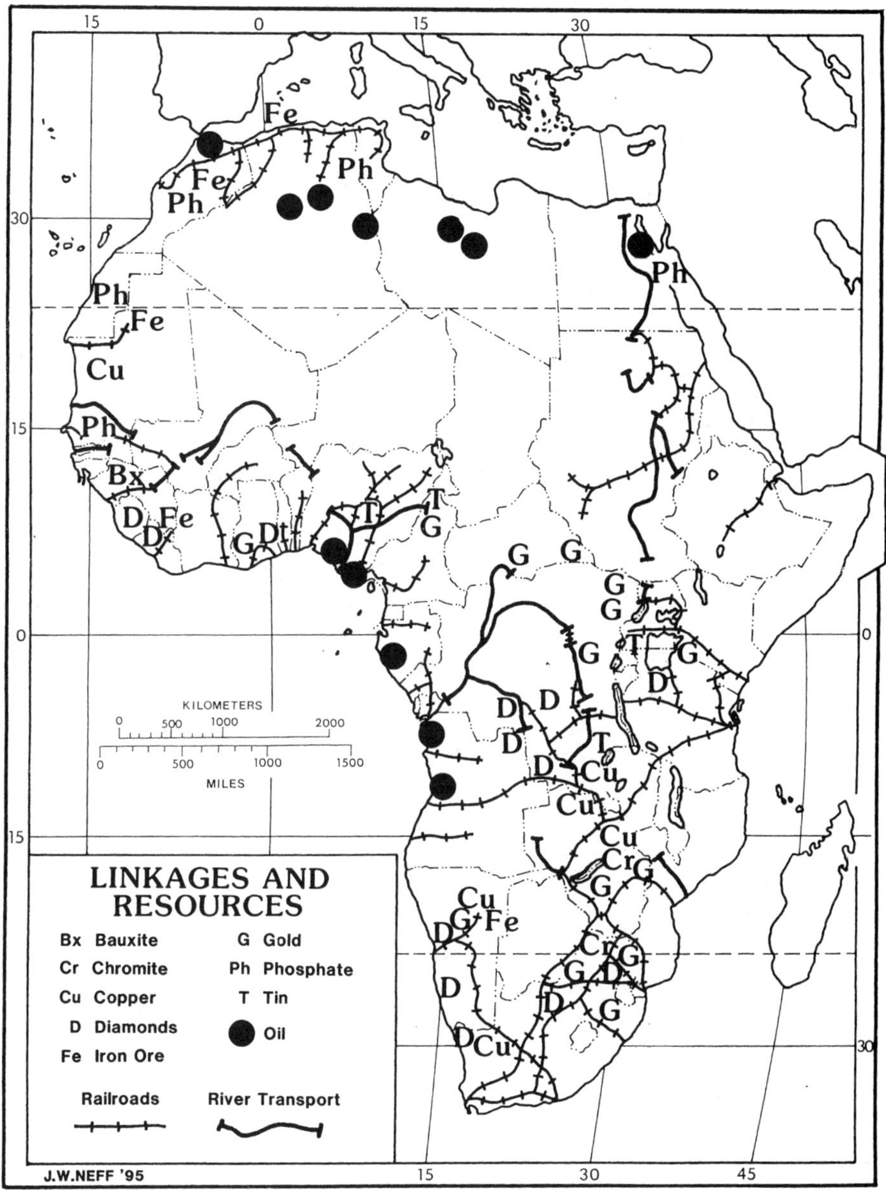
LINKAGES AND RESOURCES
Bx Bauxite
Cr Chromite
Cu Copper
D Diamonds
Fe Iron Ore
G Gold
Ph Phosphate
T Tin
Oil
Railroads
River Transport
KILOMETERS
0 500 1000 2000
0 500 1000 1500
MILES
J.W.NEFF '95

Map 2.4

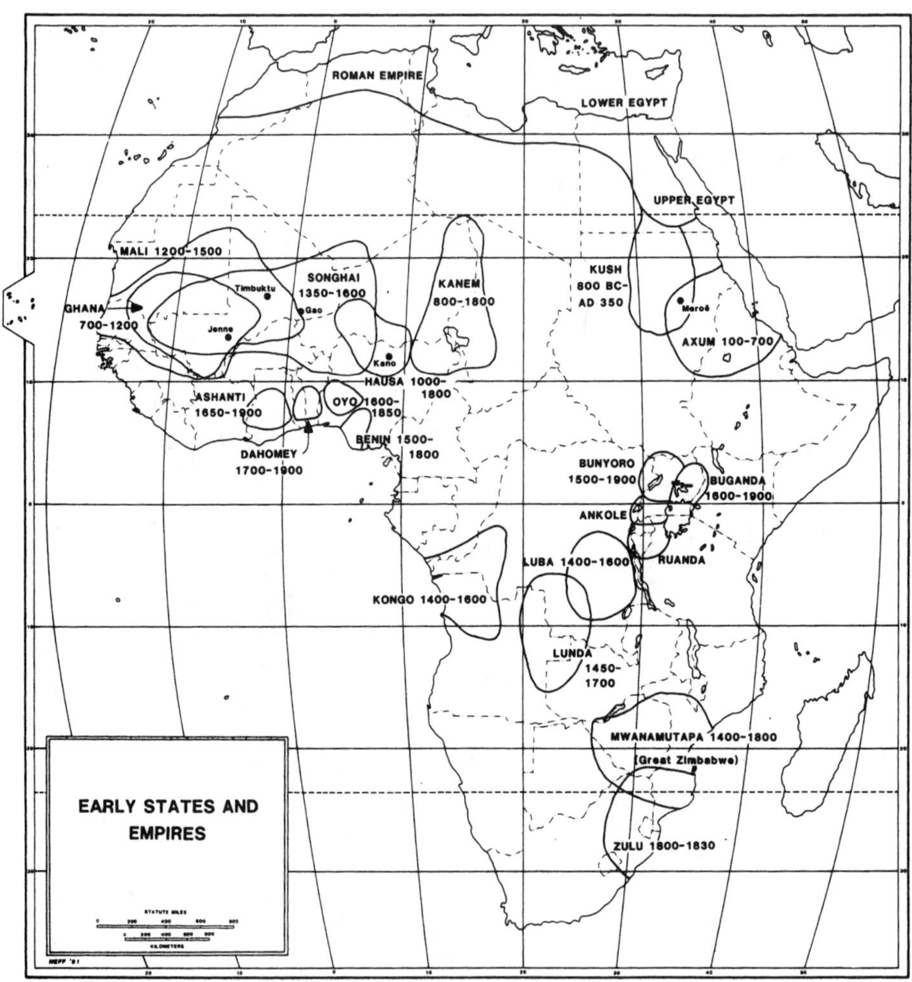

Adapted from Alan C. G. Best and Harm J. deBlij, *African Slavery* (New York: John Wiley and Sons, 1977), p. 64; and Reuben K. Udo, *A Comprehensive Geography of West Africa* (New York: Africana, 1978), p. xiv.

Map 2.5

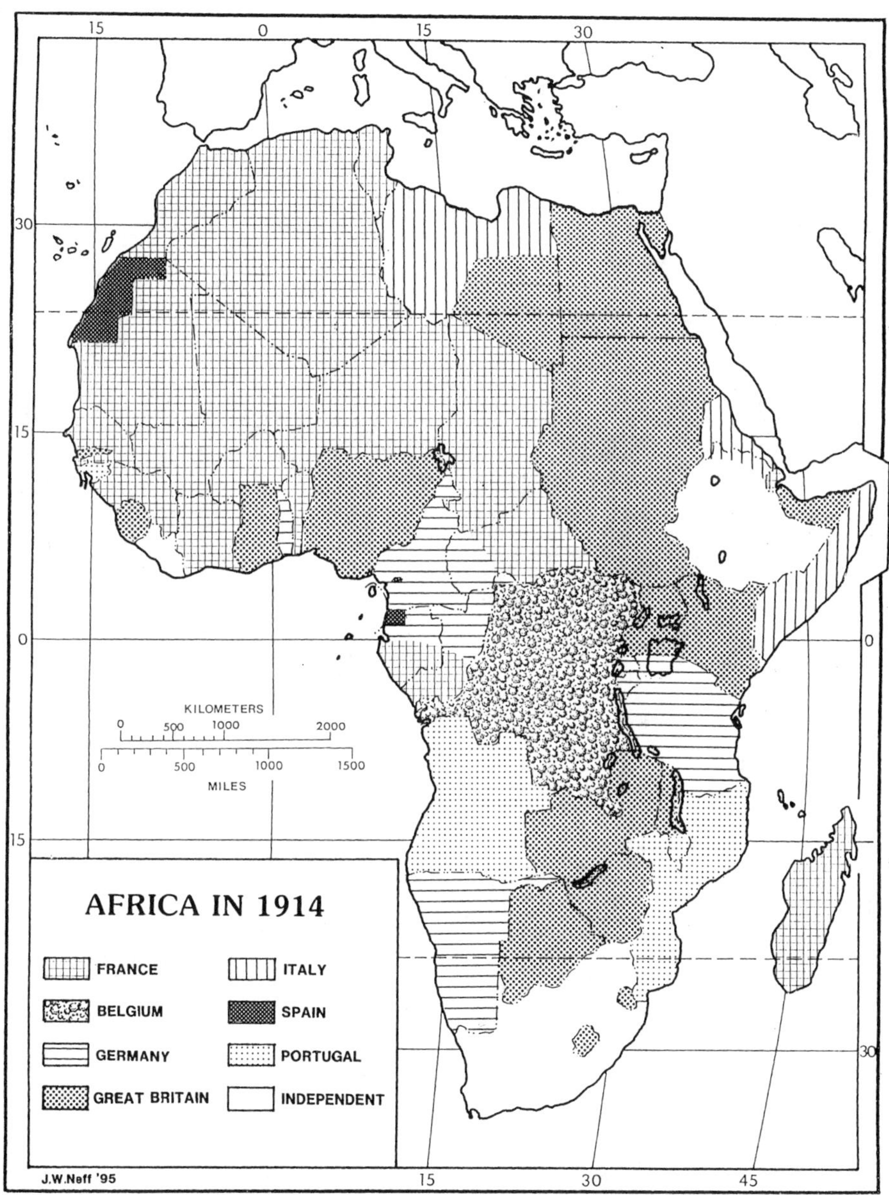

Adapted from R. F. Betts, *The Scramble for Africa: Causes and Dimensions of Empire* (Lexington, MA: D.C. Heath, 1972), p. xiv.

Map 2.6

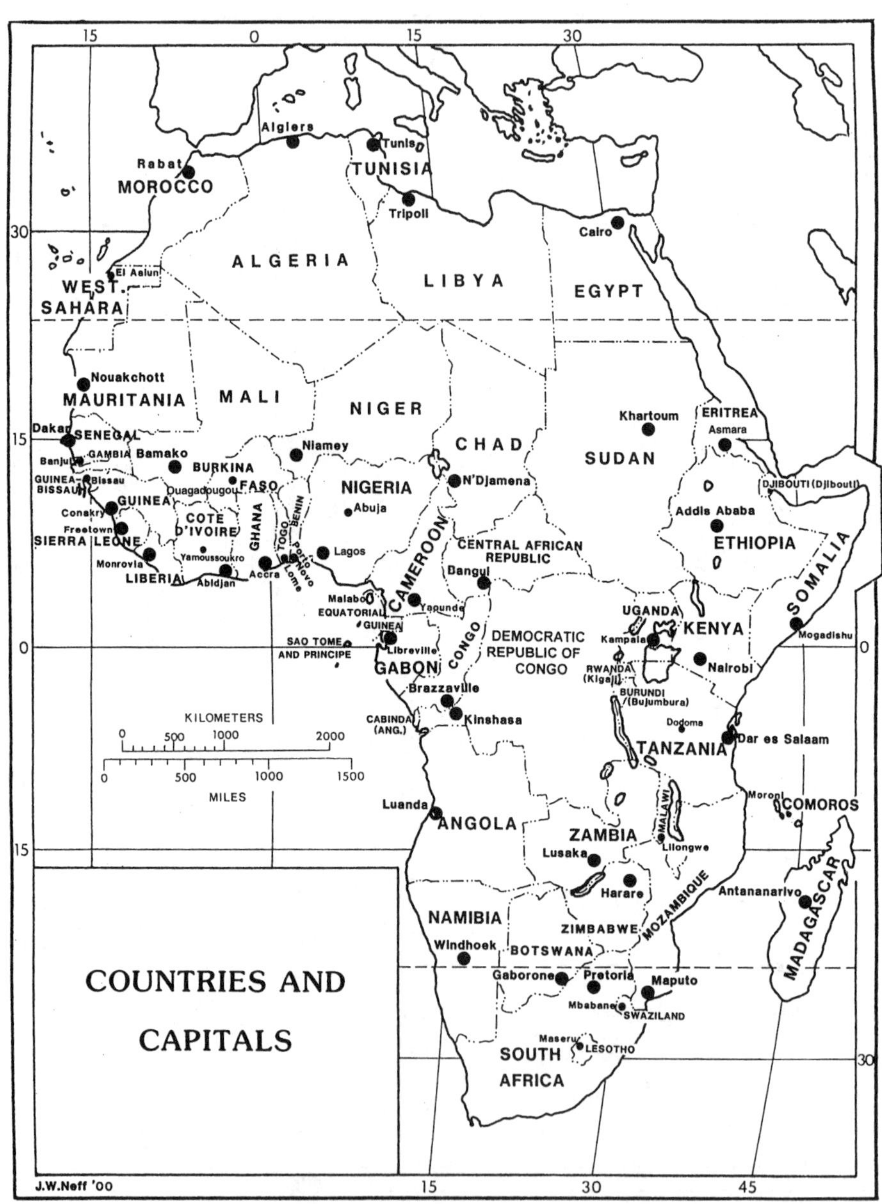

Although Abuja is the new legal capital of Nigeria and Yamassoukro is the new legal capital of Côte d'Ivoire, most government activities continue to be conducted and foreign embassies maintained in the traditional capital cities of Lagos and Abidjan. The official capital of Tanzania is Dar es Salaam, but some government offices have been moved to Dodoma, which is planned as the eventual capital city; the National Assembly now meets there on a regualar basis. US Central Intelligence Agency, *The World Factbook, 1999* (www.odci.gov).

3

The Historical Context

Thomas O'Toole

As was made clear in the previous chapter, Africa is a huge and geographically diverse continent over three times as large as the United States and several times larger than Europe. The continent's physical size, the scale of its human mosaic, and its geological and biological diversity defy both generalization and full coverage. In this chapter, I focus on the history of Africa south of the Sahara, though for thousands of years contacts between Mediterranean Africa and sub-Saharan Africa have been extensive. Because the histories of sub-Saharan Africa are distinctive in many ways from those of northern Africa, they warrant separate treatments (in the same way that South Asia and Southeast Asia are studied separately from other areas of the Asian continent). (See Map 2.1.)

I have also set some pragmatic limits on the time focus of this chapter. I begin about 200,000 years ago, since our species, *Homo sapiens,* was definitely present on the continent by then (Shillington, 2005:8). I conclude the chapter with the end of colonialism because the postindependence period is discussed thematically by other scholars in the remaining chapters of the book.

In this chapter, I present a general historical background on Africa to facilitate understanding of the issues treated in subsequent chapters. Many present-day conflicts and problems in Africa stem from economic, environmental, political, and social changes associated with the establishment of European colonial rule. However, as important as colonialism is, patterns and identities established over the millennia of precolonial African history influenced the colonial experience and continue to be a powerful force shaping postcolonial Africa. To see Africa in its historical context is to grasp the complexity of the continent and to appreciate the ingenuity and dynamism of its people as they respond to the challenges posed by history. Clearly, while Africans created and continue to create their own history, they did and still do under conditions that, in many cases, they do not control.

The Peopling of Africa

The Cradle of Humankind

The African savannas of mixed grasslands and scattered trees, which developed as part of a worldwide cooling and drying trend about 6 to 4 million years ago, are the ancestral homeland of all humankind. Before modern humans (*Homo sapiens*) appeared at least 130,000 years ago, the tool-making and fire-using genus *Homo erectus* emerged on these savannas around 2 million years ago. These early stone tool–using members of the genus *Homo*, to which all humans belong, were using cultural adaptations to adjust to growing savannah and shrinking forest environments. Living in small cooperative groups, maybe even family groups, they foraged the savannas for plant food and small animals, and occasionally, fed on the carcasses of large animals killed by predators. *Homo erectus* lived in East and South Africa, and according to most scientists, spread to northern Africa and beyond into Eurasia at least 1 million years ago.

April Gordon

Ancient ancestors to today's San people painted beautiful rock art in many parts of southern Africa, some dating back thousands of years.

Very early fossils of *Homo sapiens* have been found in Tanzania and Ethiopia. Many scholars suggest that between 130,000 and 90,000 *Homo sapiens* populations existed widely in Africa. Most scholars are convinced by the evidence that the descendants of these first true humans gradually spread out to other parts of the world beginning at least 60,000 years ago. In Africa, human groups developed regionally specialized cultural complexes and used sophisticated stone tools. By about 20,000 years ago, clusters of intensive fishing and hunting peoples were concentrated along the Nile. From approximately 18,000 years ago, these groups of people in the Nile Valley were collecting large numbers of tubers and, by 15,000 years ago, large quantities of wild cereals (Schick, 1995:63). By 10,000 years ago, groups of people making up two distinct gathering and hunting cultures were emerging on the southern border of the Mediterranean basin and in the savanna regions of eastern and southern Africa, with only slightly different adaptations to their savanna habitats. Peoples in a third cultural complex that was an adaptation to tropical forest environments probably were also to be found on the eastern and southern fringes of the central African forests.

Some scholars identify, in a general way, groups of people making up three major linguistic groups in Africa with the peoples making up these three cultural complexes. The humans in these linguistic groups had achieved clear linguistic difference about 12,000 years ago. Members of the Mediterranean cultural complex can be associated with the Afro-Asiatic language family, while the peoples of the eastern and southern savanna cultures generally spoke variations of the Khoisan ("click") language family. The people in the tropical rainforest cultural complexes can be linked to the Niger-Congo family. Humans speaking languages that can be grouped into a fourth major linguistic group, the Nilo-Saharan, can probably be associated with another cultural complex, highly adapted to fishing, which flourished in the entire central, south-central, and southeastern Sahara between 7,500 and 4,000 years ago, when the Sahara received far more rainfall than it does now (Ki-Zerbo, 1990:89–121).

Gathering and Hunting

In general, Africans, like all other humans, made their living by gathering and hunting for most of their history. Until about 7,000 years ago, when increasing populations and the climatic shift that would ultimately create the Sahara Desert made food cultivation and animal herding necessary, most sub-Saharan Africans were gatherers and hunters. Archaeological evidence and comparisons with surviving gathering and hunting peoples indicate that African gatherers and hunters adapted their tools and ways of life to three basic African environments: the moist tropical rain forests with hardwoods and small game; the more open savannas with a diversity of large game living in grasslands, woods, and gallery forests along the rivers; and riverbank and lakeside ecologies found along major water courses or around lakes and ponds.

I must point out, though, that rainforest, savanna, and waterside habitats differed greatly from place to place, and the societies found in them differed more among themselves and were far more complex than this general overview might imply. For each habitat, I could easily devote a whole chapter to pointing out differences in ways and styles of life that were the products of ceaseless change over millennia. The political, social, and economic histories of each specific society, along with its history of ideas, values, and ideology, could fill whole volumes. With such diversity it is obvious that savanna dwellers, rainforest dwellers, and people in water-focused societies were not so perfectly adapted to a single environment as to be incapable of leaving one for the other. These three environmental niches are simply explanatory categories. In the real world, environments merge gradually into others, as do the societies living within them.

Despite the myriad of habitats and diversity among their inhabitants as well as the internal differences that existed within these habitats, it still makes sense to generalize about rainforest societies. A few isolated forest dwellers, even in the twenty-first century, still live in bands of thirty to fifty individuals. Their pursuit of game and harvesting of a variety of insect, stream, and plant foods keep them on the move in a rather fixed cycle as various foods come into season at different locations in their foraging areas. Consequently, they construct only temporary shelters of leaves and poles, very functional for a life in which more permanent structures are useless. Drawing upon both vegetable and animal food sources, with the men most often specializing in hunting and the women generally specializing in gathering, they have little need for contact with outsiders or for exploration beyond the confines of their own regular territories. As in most gathering and hunting societies, women's economic functions along with childbearing are absolutely crucial. Women typically generate more food through gathering than the men, who hunt animals or look for game that has already been killed. Gathering and hunting societies appear to have developed delicately balanced social relationships that permitted necessary group decisions without the need for clearly defined leaders. Quite likely, their moral, ethical, and artistic sensitivities resembled those of their modern descendants, the Mbuti or M'Baka (so-called pygmies), who still live in the rainforests of equatorial Africa (Turnbull, 1983).

Savanna-dwelling gatherers and hunters, few if any of whom exist today, led similarly mobile lives but often specialized in the collection of wild cereals that grew on the grassy plains and the occasional hunting of large grass-eating animals—giraffe, zebra, warthog, and many species of antelope. In particularly favorable circumstances, savanna dwellers might congregate in groups of 300 or more during the rainy seasons, when vegetation was lush and game plentiful. They dispersed in groups of 30 to 100 during the dry months to gather and to hunt, first with sticks and game pits, and later with nets, bows and arrows, and poisons. As populations grew, their contacts with other groups intensified until relatively fixed territories were established, and exotic shells, stones, feathers, and other less durable items were passed in sporadic trade over distances of hundreds of miles. Their history consisted of the gradual refinement of gathering and hunting techniques, a slow spread of new inventions from one group to another, and, probably, the very slow growth of population. Historian John Iliffe offers an environmental thesis as an important element in the relatively slow growth of population and subsequently less pressure to turn to the more labor-intensive raising of crops. In his view, Africa's physical setting, climate, topography, and soils placed very real limits on human populations (Iliffe, 1995:1, 21).

Fishing

Major fishing communities in Africa probably predate the development of techniques of growing food crops and taming animals. Many settlements were clustered around the lakes and rivers of what are now the dry southern reaches of the Sahara. During the last great wet period in Africa's climate, from about 11,000 to 5,000 years ago, Lake Chad rose to cover a huge area many times its increasingly shrinking present size and may well have overflowed southwestward into the Benue-Niger rivers, which empty into the Atlantic Ocean. This huge lake was fed by rivers from the Tibesti Plateau in the central Sahara. Lake Nakaru in present-day Kenya may have overflowed into the Great Rift Valley, while Lake Turkana was 85 meters above its present level. The inland delta of the Niger in present-day Mali was far vaster and held enormous quantities of water in permanent lakes (Iliffe, 1995:13).

In these lands of lakes and rivers, people lived in thriving fishing communities. They carved intricate harpoon barbs and fishhooks out of bone, fired some of the earliest pottery in Africa, probably wove baskets and nets of reeds, and hunted crocodile, hippopotamus, and waterfowl. More important, these fishing peoples supported themselves without constant movement and at much higher population densities than gathering and hunting would allow. The need to cooperate in order to fish efficiently encouraged people to settle in larger and more permanent villages. The centralized coordination required in these larger settlements led to more formalized leadership structures than were necessary for gatherers and hunters. In these riverbank and lakeside villages, experienced elders or single arbitrators probably made the decisions. Some individuals could, for the first time, gain more wealth in the form of fishing equipment and houses than others in the village. These fishing peoples probably traded dried fish for plant and animal products offered by their gatherer-hunter neighbors. Local commercial networks developed, and new ideas spread more rapidly to larger areas. Fishing peoples probably played a crucial role in the transition from gathering and hunting to more settled ways of life.

Crop Raising and Herding

Most scholars overgeneralize when they suggest that the effect of the crop-raising revolution was a great step forward for humankind. Only with the invention of crop cultivation could the human species create the elaborate social and cultural patterns with which most people today would be familiar. Furthermore, it is in advanced hoe-farming and agricultural (those using animal traction) societies that the separation between rulers and ruled, inequality between men and women, and the institution of slavery evolved. In most of Africa, the shift to crop raising from fishing or gathering and hunting evolved much more slowly in most places than it did in southwest Asia, for example. And outside the Ethiopian highlands, there was no animal-drawn plow before contact with Europeans. A few very functional gathering and hunting societies continued into the twenty-first century in a variety of African natural environments. Though crop raising allows larger populations than gathering and hunting, the environmental realities of Africa limit agricultural potential in most places. Because of the continent's location on the equator, Africa generally has very fixed wet and dry seasons. This limits agricultural production and animal pasturing during the six or seven dry months. Three-fifths of the continent is desert, much of the rest has large areas of poor soils, and the more humid areas are home to the malaria-carrying mosquito and the parasitic infection-carrying tsetse fly. Africa's relatively light population density throughout history demonstrates the very real limits the continent's physical environment placed on the development of settled farming. In Africa, the rainfall and soils often meant that farming and herding peoples were more exposed to the dangers of famine caused by natural disasters such as drought or flood. In most African hoe-farming communities, gathering, hunting, and especially fishing have remained important sources of food and general livelihood (McCann, 1999:15–19).

Contrary to the Eurocentric view that agriculture was necessarily an improvement in the way of life for most people, agriculture was actually a much more difficult and tenuous way of life. For some scholars of Africa, a major question is why Africans ever turned to farming at all, given the effectiveness of the hunting and gathering lifestyles (Lee, 1993). Studies of

World Bank

Much African agriculture is hoe-farming. Agriculture was most likely invented thousands of years ago by women.

surviving gatherers and hunters, combined with archaeological evidence, convincingly refute any arguments about the short, nasty, and brutish lives of such people. Even in the harsh environment of the Kalahari Desert ecosystems, a larger percentage of people living there today are older "pensioners" and children than is typical in the crop-growing area of Africa. Gatherers and hunters in the Kalahari know agricultural techniques perfectly well, but have no reason or desire to adopt them. A logical, schematic reconstruction of what happened to cause many African people to adopt crop growing might be made based on several explanations, but none are based on direct knowledge. One, which I find quite persuasive, is given here as an example.

The fishing cultures, which evolved near lakes and rivers in the African savannas between the Sahara and the forests and in eastern Africa after the last Ice Age, allowed relatively large stationary settlements with new skills to grow. At the same time, these peoples began to domesticate animals, especially cattle, using skills acquired from hunting game that gathered near watering places. Five or six thousand years ago the Sahara was drying up, pushing to its margins large populations that could not adapt to the change without moving. Much African agricultural innovation apparently was forced upon people by the population pressures that grew along the waterways to the south and east of this expanding desert (Bohannan and Curtin, 1995:140–144).

How agriculture developed is much easier to guess at than it is to ascertain why it developed. Women, the gathering specialists, became aware of where particularly good food supplies, especially grains, grew, and they camped on sites where these foods were plentiful. Over time, the harvested seeds were planted, and larger and more firmly attached seed heads evolved. In the widespread African savanna, millets and sorghums were domesticated. In the Ethiopian highlands and the Futa Djallon, *teff* and *fonio,* grasslike grains with tiny kernels, became the respective staples. In the marshlands of the interior delta of the Niger River in present-day Mali, a type of rice was cultivated. Many East Africans probably planted *ensete,* a crop related to the banana, more than two thousand years ago (McCann, 1999:45–46, 94). Root crops and the native oil palm of western Africa enabled agriculturists to penetrate the forests (McCann, 1999, 114–128). Yet, for most gathering and hunting populations of southern and central Africa, there was little pressure to change from a way of life that had proven quite satisfactory for thousands of years. Likewise, fluctuating rainfall patterns, soils with ephemeral fertility, and relatively low populations allowed, and perhaps necessitated, swidden or slash-and-burn cropping techniques to persist into the present in many parts of Africa. With iron hoes and other iron tools, more efficient cropping techniques became possible. The growth of population, which accompanied the slow shift to agriculture, and later, the use of iron, set in motion another important process in African history.

Bantu Migrations

Early in the twentieth century, scholars were struck by the remarkable similarities in the languages and cultures of peoples living throughout the vast area stretching east from present-day Cameroon to Kenya and on south to the Republic of South Africa. All these peoples spoke languages having the word-stem *ntu,* or something very similar to it, meaning "person." The prefix *ba* denotes the plural in most of these languages so that *ba-ntu* means, literally, "people." The source of these languages and the farming and herding cultures associated with them and how they became so widespread in Africa were major questions by the mid-twentieth century.

One plausible—though still speculative—answer was based on linguistics, archaeology, and studies of plant origins. According to this account, about 3,000 years ago near the Benue River in the western African savannas, fairly large-scale settlements guided by councils of lineage elders evolved based on fishing with dugout canoes, nets, fishhooks, traps, and harpoons. Cultivating yams and oil palms and raising goats, these peoples, speaking Bantu languages, were better able to survive drought and misfortune than the small pockets of cultivators that might have developed by then in and south of the tropical rainforests of central Africa. Having long mastered the art of firing pottery, these Bantu speakers were smelting iron for spears, arrows, hoes, scythes, and axes more than 2,500 years ago. Population pressures grew along the Benue as Saharan farmers slowly moved south to escape the gradually drying desert. Pushed by growing populations, the Bantu fisherpeoples moved south and east. After reaching the Congo tributaries, they spread up the rivers of central Africa to the Zambezi and on south to the tip of Africa. Bantu-speaking groups intermarried with, conquered, or pushed out the Khoisan speakers and other populations they encountered. As they slowly migrated, these Bantu-speaking peoples learned to cultivate Asian yams and bananas, which had been introduced to eastern Africa by Malayo-Polynesian sailors who colonized the island of Madagascar about 1,800 years ago. In some cases, the Bantu-speaking migrants became large-scale cattle keepers. By 1,000 years ago, most of central and southern Africa was populated by iron-smelting, Bantu-speaking villagers who had virtually replaced all but scattered pockets of the original gathering and hunting peoples (Lamphear and Falola, 1995:86–94).

Political Patterns of the Past

Stateless Societies

Until the 1960s, most historians relied on written sources, so most history tended to be about societies with writing. Since most African societies did not develop writing, the historical record was sparse, gleaned from accounts of non-African travelers, usually Muslims, and archaeological remains. In the past forty years, specialists in African history have learned to use historical linguistics, oral traditions, and other sources to overcome the apparent lack of evidence and develop a far better understanding of African history.

Nevertheless, many writers of world history texts continue to treat human societies without writing as "prehistoric." This is rather ironic given that even in those complex urban-centered societies called civilizations, which have had written records for more than 5,000 years, only a small minority of people were literate and most people did not live in cities. Certainly in Africa this prehistoric-historic distinction has little value. Most historians of Africa realize that a focus on written sources alone would mean virtually ignoring the histories of the vast majority of Africa's peoples, who were able to achieve—through kinship, ritual, and other means—relatively orderly and just societies without centralized governments or states.

In fact, until about 2,500 years ago, virtually all Africans living south of the Sahara were able to avoid relying on bureaucratic organizations or "states" to carry out the political requirements of their societies. Even large groups created social systems based on lineage (kinship) with no single center of power or authority. Ideally, such systems could accommodate several million people. On the local level, lineage systems depended on a balance of power to solve political problems. People in these societies controlled conflict and resolved disputes through a balance of centers of cooperation and opposition, which appear to have been almost universal in human societies. (How these systems worked in practice is explained elsewhere in the text.) This human ethic of cooperation was especially crucial in herding and agricultural societies that existed in the often-challenging physical environments of Africa (Turnbull, 1973:233–255).

Variations of lineage systems also helped Africans resist European colonial domination. For example, colonial attempts to divide Africa into districts, cantons, and even "tribes" were doomed to failure when most of the continent south of the Sahara was really a kaleidoscope of lineage fragments, scattering and regrouping as the need arose. Through marriage alliances and various forms of reciprocal exchanges, these networks could expand almost indefinitely. As an example, European officials erroneously assumed that their control of an important African authority figure ensured the "pacification" of a given territory. The Africans, on the other hand,

World Bank

Most Africans have long relied on decentralized, kinship-based political systems. In Burkina Faso, male family heads meet to discuss a rural development project.

could simply turn to another member of a kinship linkage and continue their struggle against the outsiders.

Africa's past demonstrates the truly remarkable ability of African peoples to resist incorporation into state political and economic organizations right up to the present (Hyden, 1980). This represents one of the most unusual aspects of the history of this continent's peoples. Many Africans still rely on extended family organizations and call upon kinship behavior to maintain justice and cultural and territorial integrity, not only in domestic but also in wider spheres (see Mair, 1974). And, as in the past, many Africans see any state, without at least some symbolic lineage-based authority, as inherently tyrannical. The continuing desire to seek and find order in institutions other than the state is very understandable in the African context.

One important aspect of persisting kinship networks, still very important in Africa, is the degree to which people within such systems could mobilize women's labor and childbearing capacities. The formation of alliances between lineages was facilitated by marriage. This does not mean that women were simply pawns. In a good number of locations, women controlled many resources and could operate almost independently of their husbands' lineage. Quite often, though, especially where cattle keeping—almost always a male-dominated activity—was important, women had many of the crop-producing responsibilities as well as household and child-rearing duties. When colonial labor demands removed men even farther from household economies, this imbalance was often exacerbated (Coquery-Vidrovitch, 1997:9–20).

For those accustomed to state forms of organization, African social organization based on kinship seems chaotic, and nonstate societies are seen as less civilized or lacking in sociopolitical development. To dispel the notion that Africa lacked civilization, many dedicated Africanists have focused almost exclusively on the relatively unrepresentative centralized states when portraying Africa's past. This has sometimes obscured, however, the important role of local kinship relations in maintaining peace and harmony in most African societies. But since state societies as well as nonstate societies have a long history in Africa, I examine the significance of state societies in the history of Africa next.

State Societies

By the late 1960s, most scholars had rejected the essentially racial determinist views that Africans were incapable of organizing stable "civilizations" or states without external leadership. The once commonly accepted premise that the first states in Africa were the result of common patterns of "divine kingship" diffused from Egypt or elsewhere have been gradually abandoned by most knowledgeable scholars of African history. The equally misguided view that civilization originated in sub-Saharan Africa is also unacceptable to most scholars. The rigid distinction between state and stateless societies, though, continues to exist in many textbooks and other popular literature. Such categories were created by social anthropologists (mostly British) in response to colonial administrators' needs to classify the political structures of the peoples over whom they ruled. Most scholars now realize that African states, like states elsewhere in the world, arose from a variety of causes and most often resulted from internal forces present in various areas of the continent. (See Map 2.4 for early states and empires.) In many parts of Africa, control over long-distance trade was an important aspect of the origin of states. Control of military force for conquest and protection was also generally present. In most cases, African states or kingdoms typically retained an element of kinship-based social organization. In fact, the process of state-building was usually a long one in which rulers gradually established special privileges for their own lineages and created a superlineage basis for authority. This caused some elements of reciprocity or mutual obligations between the subjects and their rulers that persisted for generations in all but the most authoritarian states. Rulers brought prosperity to their people and organized the military to protect them, while the ruled supported their rulers with subsistence goods, labor, and even service in the military.

It is quite likely that the first regional states in Africa were those that united independent farming communities growing up below the first cataract in Egypt about 5,500 years ago. Here, the gradual drying of the Sahara Desert had forced together growing populations from the desert into a diminishing crop-growing area dependent upon the annual Nile floods. From this time until Egypt was conquered by the armies of Alexander the Great, the pharaohs, priests, and nobility of Egypt were able to extract surplus wealth from the cultivators of the valley and to war with, trade with, and interact with the Nubians south of the cataract as well as other peoples. The Egyptian ruling elite controlled irrigation and other public works and justified their rule through claims that the pharaoh was a god-king incarnate (Lamphear and Falola, 1995:79–80).

Farther to the south, in a land once called Kush by Egyptians, another independent political entity (though not continuously so) developed by about 3,800 years ago. Achieving its greatest power between 2,800 and 2,700 years ago, the history of Kush was closely linked to that of Egypt. In fact, Kushite kings ruled Egypt from about 700 to 500 B.C. Driven from Egypt about 2,500 years ago, the Kushite leaders pushed farther south into Meroe, where a vast iron industry flourished. The causes of the rise of Kush and the extent to which its political ideas and metallurgical techniques spread are still open to considerable discussion. Meroe's successor states adopted Coptic Christianity from Axum (the ancestor of today's Ethiopia) as a court religion in the first centuries of the Christian era, but this was replaced by Islam more than 1,000 years ago. Four hundred years ago, the Sennar kingdom imposed unity over much of this area, forcing peasants to pay heavy taxes to subsidize their rulers' households. A large, literate merchant class established itself in numerous towns and played a crucial role in deepening the Islamic cultural influence so important in the northern part of the present-day republic of Sudan (Leclant, 1980:295–314; Hakem, 1980:315–346).

Still farther south in the Ethiopian highlands, Axum, dating back more than 2,000 years, rose to challenge Kush. The founders of Axum migrated from southern Arabia as much as 2,100 years ago and later extended their authority over the northern half of what are now Ethiopia and eastern Sudan. Two thousand years ago they controlled ports on the Red Sea and maintained trade relations with merchants from the eastern end of the Mediterranean who came to buy ivory, gold, and incense from the African interior. Four hundred years later, Axum's rulers became Christians and expanded to control other lesser-known states that had also arisen in the central and southern highlands of Ethiopia. The leaders of a state led by Amharic-speaking peoples, which arose in the north-central area of the Ethiopian highlands about 700 years ago, claimed some ties to the long-collapsed Axum. This state was based on an expanding landowning class. It flourished 500 to 600 years ago, broke up, and was then substantially reunited in the eighteenth century (Shillington, 1995:68–71) and persisted into the present day.

State formation in the savannas of western Africa lagged after the Roman defeat of the Phoenician-founded city of Carthage (in Tunisia). This city-state had conducted a flourishing trans-Saharan trade with sub-Saharan Africans through Berber partners between 2,800 to 2,500 years ago. Gradually, kingdoms created by horse-mounted forces establishing control over small agricultural communities developed in the Senegambia and the middle Niger as early as 2,000 years ago. One of the first of these western African states was Tekrur on the Senegal River (mentioned by later travelers writing in Arabic). Eleven hundred years ago, Muslim traders from northern Africa also described Ghana, a state centered somewhat north and east of Tekrur. The location of Ghana's consecutive capitals, Kumbi Saleh and Walata, in southern Mauritania on the northern edge of cultivation, became crucial to the rulers of these cities. Serving as staging places to assemble and equip the members of caravans carrying gold shipments north, the leaders of these cities flourished as the gold trade between peoples in northern Africa and those farther south was reestablished. Archaeological evidence suggests that Ghana was already hundreds of years old when it was visited 1,000 years ago by Arab traders searching for profits, especially this gold. The writings of these traders and other travelers about Ghana and the subsequent western African savanna kingdoms of Mali and Songhai provide little knowledge of those crucial aspects of western African society not of direct interest to commercial travelers. Ghana's decline and ultimate sacking by Berber Muslims were part of a larger shift in sub-Saharan trade centers. Trade shifted south as the spreading desert made food production around Walata much more difficult, and Muslim groups pushing into the western desert prompted a shift eastward.

Trade and power passed first to Mali, a kingdom of Mande-speaking groups on the upper Niger River. Founded, according to oral traditions, between A.D. 1230 and 1235 by Sundiata Keita, the leaders of Mali not only extracted enough grain from local farmers to maintain a standing army, but also traded gold and other goods for the necessary salt from the desert and other commodities from the larger Muslim world. One of Mali's rulers, Mansa Musa, established a reputation for wealth as the result of the splendor of his pilgrimage to Mecca in 1324. From 1468 on, the power of the rulers of Mali passed to those of Songhai in a kingdom located yet farther east on the Niger, under Sonni Ali. The leaders of Songhai, who controlled the river by military canoes, were able to dominate the trading cities of Timbuktu, Jenne, and Gao until the Battle of Tondibi in April A.D. 1591, when Moroccan invaders decisively defeated an empire already in decline (Bohannan and Curtin, 1995:166–169).

With origins going back to a past almost as remote as that of Ghana, Kanem, a state near the desert edge in modern Chad, may have served as a trading entrepôt for centuries. Rulers of this state were in close contact with North Africa and, possibly, even with Southwest Asia by 1,500 years ago. Arabic sources of more than 500 years ago referred to a strong successor state called Bornu, southwest of Lake Chad in what is today northern Nigeria. This southward shift probably reveals a deepening control over a fixed population of cultivators. And though Bornu elites had no gold to sustain a large trade-based kingdom, they did exploit tin and copper resources (Lange, 1984:238–265).

Two very interesting savanna states, which actually prospered as the trade north declined, were the highly centralized non-Islamic kingdoms of Mossi (Mori-speaking) peoples in present-day Burkina Faso and the Bambara kingdoms of Segu and Kaarta (in the present nation of Mali). Though the Mossi kingdoms date back in some form more than 500 years, the leaders of both of these clusters of states probably drew on wealth generated by the slave trade to reach the height of their power (Izard, 1984:211–237).

By 400 years ago, the most dynamic political systems in the entire western African savanna were the Hausa city-states west of Bornu. In the area in which these states arose, a high water table and numerous river valleys permitted year-round irrigated cultivation. The resulting food supply permitted an exceptionally dense population, which established a thick network of walled settlements and an extensive, specialized, commodity-production economy by about 1,000 years ago. Influenced by Islamized people from the Mali Empire, one of the city-states, Kano, had become quite powerful 500 to 600 years ago. Other Hausa states, such as Gobir and Katsina and even Bornu, contended with Kano for dominance. Iron deposits, the availability of charcoal-producing woods, trade in kola nuts, slaves from the south, and surplus dyed textiles and leather goods supplied a substantial long-distance trade (Iliffe, 1995:73–74).

Elsewhere in Africa there were a number of major state clusters, few, if any, of which date back much more than 1,000 years. Sometime about 700 years ago, a process of state formation began in the region of the Great Lakes of eastern Africa. Though this process was long portrayed as the creation of Kushite- and Nilotic-speaking pastoralists imposing their rule over Bantu-speaking agriculturists, such a simplistic and essentially racist view (since the Kushite and Nilote speakers were said to have "Caucasian" features) is now largely rejected. It would appear that all of these states came into being as a conjuncture of the economic importance of salt, cattle, and iron and the demographic possibilities allowed by fertile soils and crops such as bananas. Unfortunately, the persistence of beliefs by an older generation of scholars contributed much to the twentieth-century suffering in Rwanda and Burundi. Clearly there were peoples whose ancestors came from the south, west, and east as well as the north into the Great Lakes regions in Rwanda and Burundi. Descending from ancestors speaking Kushite, Nilotic, and Bantu languages, the rulers of centralized kingdoms rose to power through a variety of factors, the least of which was their genetic heritage. A state such as Buganda, which occupied the fertile plains northwest of Lake Victoria Nyanza, is typical. In the eighteenth and nineteenth centuries, the *kabaka*, the ruler of the Buganda, extended his authority over much of modern Uganda by gradually taking over the prerogatives of all the Ganda lineages. Besides plentiful supplies of bananas, a very important food staple, the economic base of this state also appeared to be a lively trade in handicraft production (Lamphear and Falola, 1995:91–94).

Other states have existed south of the equator for centuries. Near the mouth of the river of the same name lay the Kongo kingdom. When the Portuguese first arrived in the late fifteenth century, this kingdom, ruled by Nzinga Nkuwu, had already existed for several generations. In 1506, Nzinga Nkuwu's son Affonso, who had converted to Catholicism, defeated his brother to become *manicongo* (ruler) of this kingdom. His ascension to power marked the beginning of decline for the kingdom, since much of the ruler's authority depended upon local religious values (which were undermined by his conversion). The missionaries who surrounded him, and the expanding Portuguese influence as slave traders, further reduced his authority (Iliffe, 1995:80). In recent years, a number of scholars have pointed out the widespread influence of Christianity all along the west and west-central coast in precolonial Africa and its subsequent influence on people of African ancestry in the Americas (Thornton, 1998:262–271).

Another cluster of centralized polities lay far inland east of Kongo in a basin where salt and iron deposits assisted the development of long-distance trade. In the present-day Shaba province of Congo, a huntsman hero, Ilunga Kalala, had founded a dynasty among the Luba in the early 1400s. Other states of the southern savanna in what are now the DRC, Zambia, and Angola established the superiority of their ruling lineages by associating their founding legends with the Luba. The Lozi state in the upper Zambezi floodplain of western Zambia, which unified only in the nineteenth century, is one such example (Shillington, 2005:141).

Great Zimbabwe (in the modern country of the same name), the center of extensive and complex archaeological remains, dates back at least 800 years. The impressive stone ruins called Zimbabwe (Great House) were built by people ancestral to modern-day Shona speakers. This complex probably served as a capital for an empire that stretched from the Zambezi to the Limpopo, had linkages with widespread Indian Ocean trade networks, and encompassed an area of rich gold works. The sophisticated stone architecture of this state indicates a complex economic and political system. The organization of the necessary labor to build these structures suggests a sophisticated and complex social, economic, and political organization. Oral histories and firsthand descriptions of early Portuguese visitors to the area also confirm the existence of a strong centralized political system. Though the original Shona state probably broke up because of intergroup warfare after Indian Ocean traders found alternative African partners in the Zambezi valley, a successor state was established by 1420 or so under a northern Shona, Nyatsimbe Mutota, using the title *Mwene Mutapa* (Iliffe, 1995:101–103).

As elsewhere in the world, many African states derived great stimulus from outside forces. The oldest and best examples of these externally influenced states were the trading states of the coast of eastern Africa. Evolving from previously existing coastal fishing towns linked to farming peoples in the interior, these trading entrepôts had contacts with the Greco-Roman world as early as A.D. 100 (Iliffe, 1995:53–55). Beginning gradually in the ninth century, these city-states rose and fell in concert with both the Islamized maritime cultures of the Indian Ocean and the African political systems that supplied the ivory, gold, and slaves for trade. By A.D. 1000, merchants in these local African towns, from Mogadishu (Somalia) to Sofala (Mozambique), were deeply involved in overseas commerce. Some, like Kilwa in southern Tanzania, which drew upon the Shona-controlled goldfields of Zimbabwe, traded extensively with China, India, and the Islamic world. These city-state–based, coastal-trading societies were influenced by Arab and Persian immigrants and developed a unique Swahili culture derived from both African and southwest Asian sources (Connah, 1987:150–182).

The kingdoms of Benin and Oyo in present-day Nigeria have historical origins dating back hundreds of years. Yet, it was not until 1500, when trade with Europeans on the coast contributed to the increase in the scale of organization, that other centralized political systems developed in the forests and savannas closer to the Atlantic coast of western Africa. For example, the Asante of modern Ghana rose to power after 1680 when the Asantehene (king of the Asante) Osei Tutu and his adviser and priest, Okonfo Anokye, forcefully united three smaller states into a confederation dominated by Akan-speaking peoples. The rise of the Asante state owed much to the control of the goldfields in central Ghana. The major factor in the success of the Asante leaders, though, was the growth of military activity connected with the slave trade and the imported guns that came with this trade. The Asante fought to protect the trade to the coast in much the same way that the leaders of the United States intervened in Kuwait to maintain control of the oil, which they considered a vital resource (Shillington, 2005:192–194).

Four hundred years ago, the dominant state behind the coast in western Africa was the savanna-based Yoruba state of Oyo. With far-ranging cavalry, Oyo leaders were poised to respond to the growing demand for slaves by French, English, Portuguese, and other traders at ports such as Whydah, Porto Novo, and Badagry. By 1730, Dahomey, a tributary state of Oyo, became a major slave-trading power in its own right under King Agaja and dominated the major routes to the sea until the slave trade declined in the nineteenth century. Faced with the rise of the Muslim Sokoto caliphate to the north and the breaking away led by leaders of Yoruba satellite states to the south who were able to obtain guns from coastal traders, the leaders of Oyo lost power (Shillington, 2005:189–192).

A very different series of events, the jihads (holy wars) of the western Sudan in the eighteenth and nineteenth centuries, was directly inspired by Islamic reforming movements introduced from northern Africa and the Arabian peninsula and by the large-scale shift in trade and production brought about by European commercial interests pressing in from the coast. The jihads of western Africa began in the highlands of the Futa Djallon in present-day Guinea when Fulbé (Fulani) pastoralists, supported by Muslim traders, revolted against their farming rulers and created a Fulbé-dominated Islamic state by about 1750 under the leadership of Ibrahima Sori. By 1776, the Fulbé had produced a *shari'a*-ruled (based on Islamic law) state on the lower Senegal led by Abd al-Qadir. In the early nineteenth century, a similar Fulbé-inspired revolution launched by Uthman dan Fodio against the Hausa kingdoms farther east created the Sokoto caliphate with a population of about 10 million people and the Ilorin emirate, Oyo's rival, in the 1830s. This jihad was extended into northern Cameroon by other Fulbé leaders. Another Fulbé jihad, inspired by that of Uthman dan Fodio, was led by Seku Ahmadu in Macina in present-day Mali. Beginning in 1852, al-Hajj Umar formed another empire on the upper Niger that united previously existing Bambara kingdoms until it fell to the French in the 1890s (Shillington, 2005:224–230).

Several other state-building processes, the result of both indigenous and external forces, occurred in the past 300 years. A formidable state was developed by the notorious nineteenth-century Zulu leader, Shaka. This Zulu state-building process in South Africa set in motion the Mfecane, a period of wars and disturbances that led to migrations and conquest of thousands of people. The Mfecane, which in the Zulu language means "the era of the crushing or breaking," may have been directly influenced by the presence of expanding white settlement in South Africa. But the conditions making the rise of the Zulu kingdom possible were the result of more profound changes, such as long-distance trade in slaves and ivory, and the introduction of maize (corn) by the Portuguese centuries before, which enabled populations to expand greatly.

Until the nineteenth century, the necessities of defense, irrigation, trade, and other factors, which led to the creation of states elsewhere in Africa, were apparently not as important farther south. Ecological pressures and perhaps the activities of Portuguese and Cape Colony slave traders caused an intensification of rivalries between small political groupings in the region between the Drakensberg Mountains and the Indian Ocean about 200 years ago. In that struggle for power, the most successful leader to emerge was Shaka. He refined and improved local warfare techniques and consolidated authority so effectively that between 1819 and 1828 he was able to create a military state that set in motion a series of migrations and conquests resulting in the creation of many kingdoms throughout southern Africa. This extraordinary individual trained an army that was very effective and able to expand rapidly. He was able to do this by transforming the existing system of initiation groups (an age-grade system) into cross-lineage groups that he then was able to centrally control. This revolutionary social organization allowed him to mobilize an entire generation of young men to fight for him while the women worked to produce food to support them.

This forging of a Zulu nation pushed other peoples, desperate to replace cattle stolen by the Zulu, into the interior grasslands of modern-day South Africa and far beyond, creating new political formations in what are now Zimbabwe, Malawi, Mozambique, Zambia, and Tanzania. The Sotho kingdom of present-day Lesotho and the Ndebele kingdom of modern Zimbabwe were among the results of the Mfecane (Omer-Cooper, 1994:52–81).

Trade, Exploration, and Conquest

Slavery

Apologists for the slave trade in the eighteenth and nineteenth centuries argued that slavery was intrinsic in backward African societies. They also claimed that slavery in the "Christian" Americas was probably better for Africans than their situation had been in their "pagan" homelands. Abolitionists essentially agreed with these negative stereotypes about indigenous African societies. Most abolitionists supported "legitimate" trade, missionary activities, and ultimately colonialism, because these intrusions would put an end to slavery and the slave trade and begin the process of redeeming this "pagan" continent. Some African nationalists and defenders of African culture in the twentieth century argued that African civilizations, extending back to the glories of ancient Egypt, had been deformed and barbarized by the effects of the Atlantic slave trade. It was supposed by most Africans and the supporters of Africans that the Atlantic slave trade had enriched the West at the expense of Africa and was largely responsible for Africa's relative economic backwardness (Manning, 1990:8–26).

It should be noted that slavery in Africa, as elsewhere, is as old as civilization. From the Egyptian dynasties through the Carthaginian and Greek trading states to the Roman Empire, a small number of black Africans were always part of trans-Saharan commerce. By the time the Arabs overran northern Africa in the middle of the seventh century, bondage and the slave trade were already fixtures of this part of the world as elsewhere. War prisoners from the Sudan, in Arabic *bilad al-Sudan,* "the land of the blacks," were sold north from at least 1,300 years ago. The demand for slaves in the Mediterranean world kept a persistent and substantial movement of black humans as trade goods flowing across the desert (with many more dying on the journey) well into the twentieth century (Manning, 1990:27–37, 149–164).

Clientship, pawning, and sale of individuals to pay for food in times of famine have existed in human societies—in Africa and elsewhere—from at least the beginning of crop production. Conquered peoples were absorbed into the victors' societies, often serving in a lowly status with few rights and privileges for generations before prerogatives and status distinctions

April Gordon

The Slave House on Senegal's Gorée Island, with its notorious "door of no return," is one location where slaves were held before being shipped to the Americas in the Atlantic slave trade.

between slave and free blurred. In some African states, plantation, quarry, mining, and porterage slavery were important parts of the economic base. Slave-soldiers were found in the Cayor kingdom of Senegal in the fifteenth century (Meirs and Kopytoff, 1977:3ff; Shillington, 1995:172–180). In Sudan and elsewhere in Africa, slavery is still present.

While recent historical research no longer maintains, as serious scholars once did, that as many as 50 million Africans were taken from western Africa as part of the Atlantic slave trade, the economic and human loss to Africa of the 10 million or more slave immigrants who reached the New World was serious enough (Manning, 1990:5). More important to understand are the broader negative effects that the slave trade, the conflicts connected with it, and the rise of slavery within Africa associated with the trade had on African culture. At a time when European and American populations were growing rapidly, Africa's was in decline. While Europe and North America were industrializing, Africa, largely as a result of the slave trade, was involved in an exploitative and unproductive system of trade (Bah, 1993:79–84).

Focus on the Atlantic slave trade should not result in less attention being paid to the Indian Ocean slave trade. This trade, though it never matched the massive numbers of the Atlantic slave trade, had disastrous consequences as far inland as the shores of Lake Malawi and those areas of the DRC west of Lake Tanganyika. The centuries-old, though relatively small, trade in African humans to south and southwest Asia for plantation and mine workers, soldiers, and concubines reached substantial proportions beginning in the middle decades of the eighteenth century as demand for slaves grew on the French plantations on Mauritius and Réunion. This trade continued very actively into the nineteenth century, supplying slaves for Brazil, for the clove plantations on the islands of Pemba and Zanzibar off the coast of eastern Africa, as well as for the sugar plantations on the Indian Ocean islands. The nineteenth-century Afro-Arab slavers and ivory hunters penetrated swiftly and deeply inland, causing proportionately as great a loss of life and disruption in eastern African societies as the Atlantic slave trade did at its height (Alpers, 1975). The slave trade from Kilwa and the offshore island of Zanzibar reached tremendous proportions in the late eighteenth century, furnishing labor to the French plantations on the fertile and previously unpopulated islands of Mauritius and Réunion in the Indian Ocean.

Clearly the various slave-trading patterns had economic, political, and social impacts on both African and other Atlantic societies. The profits of European merchants in the Atlantic slave trade from the mid-seventeenth century on to the early nineteenth century were immense. It should be noted, though, that these profits diminished considerably for Europeans as African traders established a dominant position in the trade. The profits from the Atlantic slave trade may well have helped lay the foundation for the Industrial Revolution and the expansion of capitalism in Europe and North America, but it also enriched many Africans and Afro-Europeans in Africa as well (see Klein, 1999, and Eltis, 2000). The various slave trades turned African enterprise, over wide geographic areas, from more productive pursuits and influenced the rise of more authoritarian rulers. By the end of the eighteenth century, slaves were being delivered by Africans to the coast from regions as far away as the Hausa states and Katanga (Shaba) in the Congo (once called Zaire; Iliffe, 1995:127–158).

"Legitimate" Trade

By the end of the eighteenth century, the world price of sugar was declining because of overproduction. At the same time, the price of slaves was rising because of stiffer competition among African suppliers in western Africa. As a result, the power and influence of plantation owners from the British West Indies was declining in the British Parliament. The Industrial Revolution was spawning a new dominant class of industrialists in Great Britain who were finding it increasingly necessary to seek new markets abroad for the clothing, pottery, and metal goods they were producing in growing quantities. These industrialists saw that Africans in Africa could provide European producers with both necessary raw materials and new markets for their cheaply produced manufactured goods (Bohannan and Curtin, 1995:213–214).

The Haitian revolution where people of African descent overthrew European domination, the abolition movement, the French presence in the sugar industry, and, perhaps, some growing acceptance of the egalitarian principles of the French Revolution and the US War of Independence led the British, with the strongest navy in the world, to abandon the slave trade. Having transported half the captives from western Africa at the end of the eighteenth century, the British government set up an "anti-slavery squadron" and began using force to stop the trade by 1807 (Manning, 1990:149–157).

Beginning in the 1790s, trade in palm oil for use in soap, candles, cooking products, and lubricants for looms in return for goods produced in Europe had begun in western Africa. By the 1830s, the commercial production of peanuts for the European market was well under way in western Africa. Though slaving and the "legitimate" trade in these commodities, as well as gold, timber, gum arabic, skins, and spices, coexisted through mid-century, it became apparent that greater profits existed in "legitimate commerce" than in slaves after the markets in the United States were closed in the first decade of the nineteenth century. The Brazilian and Cuban markets dried up by the 1870s.

Large European trading firms were soon to squeeze out a number of smaller-scale entrepreneurs in Africa. Among those squeezed out were Afro-Europeans, groups of people of mixed European and African ancestry from the Senegambia who had promoted the peanut trade and other trades along the coast to the south and other Eurafricans and former African slavers from Liberia to Cameroon who had become increasingly involved in palm oil commerce. Arab, Indian, and Luso-African (of Portuguese and African ancestry) intermediaries from Angola to Somalia, who had switched from trading slaves to trading ivory, gum arabic, copra, cloves, and other commodities, also suffered. Some of these intermediaries were reduced to becoming agents for the European companies, while others were simply driven out of business. The cloth, alcohol, tobacco, and firearms imported by the European trading houses did little to strengthen African economies, and as competition grew fiercer, European trading monopolies backed by their governments fought even harder to cut out all the African intermediaries and their European competitors. This growing European trading competition played a major role in the European "scramble for Africa" in the 1870s and 1880s (Azevedo, 1993:103–110).

Exploration

It is ironic that people continue to credit European explorers of the nineteenth century with the "discovery" of rivers, waterfalls, and such in Africa when it is obvious that Africans living there already knew these things existed. Obviously, discovery simply meant that a European had verified in writing the existence of something long known to others.

With the exception of the Portuguese and perhaps a few Afrikaans-speaking people, the systematic exploration of Africa between the Limpopo River and the Sahara Desert by Europeans can be dated to Mungo Park's first expedition to the Niger in 1795. By 1885, crossings of the continent from east to west had been thoroughly documented, the extent of the Sahara was known to the European and North American public, and the major rivers in Africa had been followed and mapped by Europeans. To most Africans, though, this was of little importance, and most African rulers by the latter part of the nineteenth century were ceasing to welcome wandering white men. These rulers had begun to fear the outside influence and rivalry that might weaken their control over trade or, as in the case of the Afro-Arab slave traders in central and eastern Africa, bring it to an end.

Mungo Park, for example, traveled up the Gambia River in 1795 to determine if it was linked to the Niger River, which appeared on some maps of the period as rising near Lake Chad and flowing west to the Atlantic. He did find the Niger and determined that it flowed eastward, not westward, thereby disproving the Gambia-Niger connection. Since he was then unable to follow the river to its mouth, he returned in 1805 bent on proving that the Niger actually was the Congo River. He died on this expedition, and only in 1830 did Richard Lander demonstrate that the Niger flows into the Gulf of Guinea.

In the first half of the nineteenth century, other explorers, like René Caille, Hugh Clapperton, and Heinrich Barth, traversed the western parts of Africa recording information that might be of interest to the governments, scientific groups, and missionary organizations that sponsored them. Not until the second half of the century were the sporadic efforts of Portuguese and Arab explorers penetrating equatorial Africa really taken up by Europeans. The first of these explorers, I presume, was the most famous of all, David Livingstone.

Livingstone was sent to Africa by the London Missionary Society. He arrived in Cape Town, South Africa, in 1841 and then traveled north. He roamed the interior for years, reaching the Okavango swamp and delta complex in Botswana in 1849, crossing Angola to Luanda in 1854, and reaching Victoria Falls in 1855. In 1858, he traveled up the Zambezi from its mouth and then turned north up the Shire River to Lake Malawi. His death south of Lake Bangweulu in 1873 inspired a great deal of European interest in this part of Africa, especially because of the writings of Henry Morton Stanley, who had "found" Livingstone in 1871.

For the majority of peoples in Europe and North America, the exploits of these explorers meant little more than excitement and drama set on an exotic stage. For small minorities, the diaries of these explorers and those of others, such as Richard Burton and John Speke who sought the source of the Nile, did much to arouse their interest. Church groups and members of missionary societies were interested in "saving" the Africans. Also interested were the new monied classes spawned by the Industrial Revolution in Europe and North America. These entrepreneurs and investors urged their respective governments to act in their behalf to establish control of the "newly found" riches and regions (Shillington, 2005:293–300).

African Americans in Africa

During the 1800s, as European expansion into Africa increased, many former African slaves and their descendants were reestablishing ties with their African homeland in western Africa. While most attention has been paid to the activities of whites in Africa, attention should also be given to the role of African Americans as missionaries, explorers, settlers, and political opponents of colonialism.

Many ex-slaves from the Americas and some who never reached the Americas returned to Africa. For example, ex-slaves from Brazil began arriving in what are now Nigeria, Benin, and Togo in the 1840s. They became active in commerce and the skilled trades and, by the 1880s, dominated the inland trade from the French post in Dahomey (now Benin). The Brazilian architectural styles they brought with them can still be seen in some older homes in western Nigeria. In Freetown, Sierra Leone, Africans freed from slavery by British antislavery patrols were released. They were joined by African Americans returning from Jamaica and British North America. These Africans of many origins eventually formed a mixed African-Western "Krio" (Creole) culture. They too specialized in trade both along the coast and into the interior. Many people of Yoruba ancestry returning from Brazil moved to Lagos and Badagry in western Nigeria. When the British annexed Lagos in 1861, many Krios became officials in the new colony (Bohannan and Curtin, 1995:215–216).

Liberia was another refuge for people of African ancestry, in this case from the United States. In 1822, the American Colonization Society transported freed slaves from the Carolinas to Monrovia, named after then-president James Monroe. Alexander Crummell, a leading nineteenth-century African American intellectual, migrated to Liberia in the 1850s, and Bishop H. M. Turner was one of the leading black advocates of immigration to Africa for African Americans at the turn of the century.

All along the Guinea coast—especially in Nigeria, Sierra Leone, and Liberia—Africans and African Americans joined the Christian missionary effort. Many were Krios from Sierra Leone or Nigeria. African American missionaries also met with considerable success in other parts of western Africa, the Congo, and as far as South Africa.

African Americans helped to explore the continent. Notably, the National Emigration Convention of Colored Men sent out an all-black exploring party headed by Martin Delany, a physician, to explore the Niger valley from the coast shortly before the American Civil War (Ohaegbulam, 1993:219–231).

The combined activities of African Americans and Westernized Africans were, in fact, slowly transforming many areas of Africa before European conquest and rule were imposed. As Bohannan and Curtin point out, many progressive changes that had been occurring in Africa during the 1800s were reversed during the colonial period.

> With the colonial period, Europeans reasserted their authority over the missionary movement. Europeans replaced most of the Africans who had held high posts in government administration, medical services, and the like. The African middle class of traders in Senegal, Sierra Leone, Liberia, and elsewhere found it increasingly hard to compete with large European firms in the export trade to Europe, though Africans continued to fill the role of middlemen between the African producers and the European firms. In the colonial setting, Western impact increased immensely, but with Africans playing a diminished role as responsible participants in the process. (Bohannan and Curtin, 1995:218)

Finally, the role of African Americans in the anticolonial struggle should be mentioned. The "back to Africa" movement in the United States in the early 1800s later spawned the idea that all people of African descent should unite to promote their common interests and fight racism. Leaders of the pan-African movement in the late 1800s and early 1900s protested the abuses and racism affecting Africans in such areas as Rhodesia and South Africa. While lacking the power to change colonialism, those involved in such movements publicized alternative perspectives on colonialism to the people of the world. African Americans influential in the pan-African movement included the West Indian, and later Liberian, diplomat Edward Wilmot Blyden and Jamaican-born Marcus Moziah Garvey. In 1914 in New York, Garvey founded the Universal Negro Improvement Association, whose influence was widespread in Africa, the Caribbean, and Central America. Perhaps the most famous member of the pan-African movement was W. E. B. Du Bois, who was a founder of the National Association for the Advancement of Colored People (NAACP). Du Bois's ideas on pan-Africanism influenced many Africans, including US-educated Kwame Nkrumah, the first president of Ghana. A great student of African history, Du Bois became a citizen of Ghana and was buried in Accra (Ohaegbulam, 1993:226–232).

Conquest and Resistance

Aided by missionaries who appealed to their home governments for various degrees of political or military "protection," by explorers who touted the riches to be found in the interior of Africa if only the local inhabitants could be "pacified," and by the owners of trading companies who wanted to eliminate competition, the support of political and military authorities for the takeover of Africa was not difficult to find in most European countries by the last decades of the nineteenth century. By 1884, at the Berlin Conference, the leaders of most European states came together and agreed on ground rules for dividing up Africa. Unfortunately, the political boundaries they drew on their largely inaccurate maps cut apart ethnic groups, kingdoms, and historically linked regions in ways that continue to cause conflicts in Africa today (Freund, 1998:73–90).

The push of the British, French, German, and other European powers into Africa in the last quarter of the nineteenth century required considerable effort. A good majority of the people of Africa, whether living in states or small-scale lineage-based societies, opposed European occupation through force of arms or nonviolently (Freund, 1998:91–96). Well-organized, if poorly armed, Muslim armies filled with a spirit of jihad resisted British advances in Sudan, and the full subjugation of the region was not completed until the late 1890s. In western Africa, Ahmadu Seku, the leader of the Tukolor state, and the Maninka leader, Samory Touré, fought the French into the 1890s. Rabih, a Muslim leader from the upper Nile, resisted French expansion in what are today Chad and the Central African Republic until 1900 (O'Toole, 1986:18–20).

Dahomey, a kingdom in present-day Benin, was not conquered by Europeans until 1894. And even then the French were only able to do it with the help of Senegalese troops. Leaders of numerous groups in the forests of Côte d'Ivoire resisted the French for twenty years. The British had to invade the Asante in Ghana in 1874 and 1895–1896 and again in 1900 before they could establish the Gold Coast colony. In Nigeria, the British had to launch major offensives to defeat the various peoples: Ilorin in Yorubaland held out until 1897 as did the *oba,* or leader, of Benin City; and the Sokoto caliphate was not completely overcome until 1903. In Uganda, the Bunyoro used guerrilla warfare against the British until 1898; Swahili speakers on the coast of Kenya successfully resisted the British for most of 1895 and 1896; Nandi and other Kenyan peoples fought the British well into the 1900s (Shillington, 1995:305–316).

Farther south in Nyasaland (Malawi), Yao, Chewa, and Nguni forces fought the British in the 1890s; the Gaza empire and the Barwe kingdom fought the Portuguese in Mozambique; and the Nama resisted the Germans in South-West Africa (Namibia). South African groups resisted the imposition of British control as well.

Even after the colonial regimes seemed to have been well established, attempts to reassert independence broke out throughout Africa. In the 1890s, the Shona and Ndebele rose up against the British in Southern Rhodesia (Zimbabwe); the people of Tanganyika (Tanzania) fought the Germans in the Maji Maji resistance in 1905–1906; and the Herero and Nama peoples launched open warfare against the Germans in South-West Africa in 1904–1907. Throughout colonial Africa, these and other struggles, such as the Kongo War in the present-day Central African Republic (then part of French Equatorial Africa), continued as late as the 1930s (O'Toole, 1984:329–344; Freund, 1998:140–142).

In the end, though, the superior military technology, logistic and organizational skills, and resources of the Europeans won out. All too often, African leaders found that their inability to unite various ethnic groups and factions against their common European enemies led to defeat. Most of Africa north of the Limpopo River fell under European rule between 1880 and 1905.

The Colonial Period

Colonial Rule

The two major European powers to establish colonial systems in Africa were Britain and France. After World War I, the limited amount of German territory in Africa was redistributed, in most cases to France or Britain, while the Belgians and Portuguese maintained smaller areas under their nominal control. Wherever and whenever the colonial rule was established, it was essentially a paternalistic, bureaucratic dictatorship. Yet, given the vast areas occupied and the variety of African communities encountered, the colonialists were forced to recognize or to create a class of intermediaries to assist them. Considerably oversimplified, colonial policies can be divided into direct and indirect rule, with the British portrayed as indirect rulers and the French as direct rulers (Shillington, 2005:354–358). Colonial rule from the standpoint of colonial economic interests in different regions of Africa is discussed by the authors of other chapters.

The British, in particular, were often convinced that ruling through "traditional tribal" authorities was the most efficient way to govern and to extract whatever revenue possible. This indirect-rule policy, theoretically, interfered as little as possible so that Africans could advance along "their own lines." In reality, even in northern Nigeria, one place where this form of colonialism came quite close to working, the "traditional" authorities could often use their positions to extort substantial incomes, though their freedom to rule was very circumscribed. They often faced resistance from their own subjects. And any "traditional" ruler not acceptable to the colonial power was deposed and replaced by British appointees who were more amenable to the colonial regime.

The British tried to use indirect rule in several other places by reintroducing monarchy to Benin (in southern Nigeria), by restoring the Asantehene in central Ghana (Gold Coast), and by attempting to reestablish the Oyo empire among the Yoruba in Nigeria. They also were instrumental in maintaining monarchies in Swaziland, Lesotho, Uganda, and "Barotseland" in what was then Northern Rhodesia.

The French were relatively disinterested in indirect rule, though they too utilized the old ruling classes when it seemed advantageous. The French typically established administrative units that cut across traditional boundaries, created a trans-ethnic elite, and used the French language at all levels of administration. At its extreme, French policy held that all Africans were to be completely assimilated and made equal citizens of France. More often, the highly centralized French administration maintained the necessity of deliberately creating an African elite who would accept French standards and then become "associated" with French rulers in the work of governing the colonies.

The authors of Belgian policy, like the French and the Portuguese, never displayed a great interest in indirect rule. Initially, the Belgians ruled through private companies whose owners were granted control of the people in their areas of interest. This was changed to direct rule by the 1910s because of the gross abuses committed by the owners and participants in companies against the local people under their control. The Belgians, unlike the French, deliberately limited African education to the primary levels and geared it entirely to semiskilled occupational training. Rather ironically, local political realities, coupled with a lack of finance for developed systems of bureaucratic control, meant that the French, Belgians, and Portuguese were often forced to rule through traditional elites in ways little different from the British.

Overall, the French colonies were as despotically ruled as any, but they did have the anomaly of the *quatre communes,* the four towns of Senegal—Dakar, Saint Louis, Gorée, and Rufisque—where all locally born residents had the legal rights of French citizenship from the time of the French Revolution and were represented, after 1848, in the French chamber of deputies. Likewise, from 1910 to 1926, the Portuguese allowed a few Portuguese-speaking African Catholics from Angola, Mozambique, and Guinea-Bissau to be represented in the Portuguese parliament.

The major differences in colonial policies were regionally based rather than based on the particular colonial power that controlled the land. In most of western Africa, both the French and British refused to allocate land to European settlers or companies since local suppliers produced enough materials for trade. By contrast, in parts of British East and

Central Africa, as well as in French Equatorial Africa and the Belgian Congo, land was taken from Africans and sold to European settlers and companies to ensure sufficient production for export. This difference caused a number of grave political problems in the nationalist era (Freund, 1998:97–144, 217–232).

Toward Independence

As the authors of other chapters point out, Africans became increasingly involved in the world economy during the colonial period. For the seventy-plus years that countries of Europe held both political and economic control in Africa, the economies of African countries were shaped to the advantage of the colonizers. Cash crops such as coffee, rubber, peanuts, and cocoa were grown for the European markets. Mining also increased during colonial times. Most cash crop economies benefited the European owners of large plantations rather than African farmers, and almost all mines produced for European companies.

In both the French- and the British-ruled areas of Africa, Western-educated African elites were active participants in some form of local government from the early decades of the twentieth century. In the 1920s, reform movements developed in British West Africa, which, apart from activity in South Africa, were probably the earliest nationalist movements in Africa (unless one includes Liberia and Ethiopia, where European colonial rule was never fully established). These movements, like those led earlier by such men as J. E. Casely Hayford and John Mensah Sarbah in the Gold Coast and Samuel Lewis in Sierra Leone, originated among urban, highly Westernized populations in the cities of the coast and were directed primarily at abuses of the rights of these elites caused by the colonial system. Nowhere before World War II did the idea of actual political independence from colonial rule gather much momentum (Bohannan and Curtin, 1995:240–250).

World War II, though, helped to raise African political consciousness. African soldiers fought in most of the same areas as their European masters. In cooperation with Charles de Gaulle and his "Free French," French West Africans and French Equatorial Africans joined in the fight against Nazi racialism. During the war, the Atlantic Charter was proclaimed and the United Nations created. The ideas therein contributed to the new visions of the right to freedom from colonial rule that Africans began to voice. After the war, national political parties took hold all over Africa. Initially, the strongest parties to emerge were those in West Africa, where no large European settler class blocked demands. From 1945 to 1960, African nationalist parties under men such as Kwame Nkrumah, Sékou Touré, Nnamdi Azikiwe, Leopold Senghor, and Félix Houphouët-Boigny developed mass support, won local elections, and pressured for more political rights and ultimately for independence (Freund, 1998:167–203).

In 1957, Ghana became the first black African nation to become independent in the twentieth century. From the capital, Accra, Ghana's first president, Kwame Nkrumah (1909–1972), set about creating a nation from the former British colony of Gold Coast. He was faced with a cocoa monoculture export economy and Asante nationalism dating back to the resistance against British imperialism by the Asantehene Prempeh I in the nineteenth century. Nkrumah's advocacy of pan-African unity was never sufficient to overcome the influences of competing nationalisms and economic dependency that worked against unity (Shillington, 1995:374–377).

In eastern Africa, the presence of European settlers made the struggle for independence even more difficult. In Kenya, colonized by the British between 1895 and 1963, a peaceful evolution to independence was ruled out by white settler opposition. Waiyaki Wa Hinga, a Gikuyu leader, initially welcomed Europeans and even entered into "blood brotherhood" with one early colonial administrator in 1890. Waiyaki was killed in 1892 by officials of the Imperial East African Company when he objected to the building of an unsanctioned fort in his area. Harry Thuku, Kenya's pioneer nationalist, also tried peaceful means to resist British colonialism. Concerned with improving the economic lot of Africans, he founded in 1921 a broad-based organization known as the East African Association. Advocating civil disobedience as a political weapon, he was arrested for disturbing the peace in February 1922. His arrest led to riots and the deaths of several Africans (Freund, 1998:145).

Independence for most settler colonies was won only through armed struggle. Like the Algerians, who fought a bitter eight-year freedom struggle against the French, Kenyans too found it necessary to resort to arms to achieve independence. The national liberation struggle in Kenya, called Mau Mau by the British, began in the late 1940s and was most strongly supported by the Gikuyu. Jomo Kenyatta (a London-educated anthropologist married to a white Englishwoman) was imprisoned by the British between 1953 and 1961 as the alleged brains behind the movement, though the actual fighting was done by such "forest fighters" as Dedan Kimathi, who was captured and executed in 1957. During the struggle, as many as 10,000 Africans (mostly Gikuyu) were killed. A growing sense of national unity against the British resulted from this conflict, and the British finally granted independence to Kenya in 1963 (Shillington, 2005:391–393).

Among the last African nations to achieve independence north of the Limpopo were the former colonies of Portugal: Angola, Guinea-Bissau, and Mozambique. After more than two decades of armed struggle, independence for the three colonies came quickly when the Portuguese government was overthrown by a military coup in 1974. Faced with South African– and US-backed guerrilla oppositions, the people of Angola found the goal of a peace settlement very difficult. The people of Mozambique also faced armed opposition financed by South African and ultraconservative groups from the United States well into the 1990s (Freund, 1998:231–234).

Both Zimbabwe and Namibia achieved black majority rule even later. The people of African ancestry in Zimbabwe defeated the white settler government after a long liberation war, and Zimbabwe became an internationally recognized independent state in 1980. With the support of the United Nations, Namibia achieved its independence from South African control in 1990 after a protracted armed struggle. In 1994, Africa's last "colony," South Africa, finally attained black majority rule after Nelson Mandela was elected president in the country's first racially inclusive democratic elections (Freund, 1998:234–236).

Independence did not usher in a golden era. In almost all countries, the bright hopes of democracy soon degenerated into authoritarianism. Throughout the continent, economic decline is almost universal, and population, health, and environmental problems persist. These and other issues will be discussed in the chapters that follow. Virtually all of Africa's post-colonial "nation-states" began their existence with arbitrarily drawn borders. Few of the descendants of the people who were colonially dominated little more than a century ago live in nations with popular legitimacy today. Yet the past does not determine the future, and I have always questioned the utility of simply blaming the political turmoil in present-day Africa on colonialism alone. In fact, the present problem of "warlord" conditions in Africa may well represent a global future rather than historical hangovers in Africa. As the nation-state gives way to global entrepreneurs who have no allegiance to any institutions beyond their own interests, more countries in the world may become pawns in global power games. In this case, *ex Africa semper ali quid novi* (out of Africa always something new) may be that the collapse of weak nation-states in Africa represents a foreshadowing of the future of much of the rest of the world.

Yet, while the present appears bleak in many respects, most historians of Africa are wise enough to avoid hazarding too many predictions about the future. As Coquery-Vidrovitch stated so well:

> In twenty years every aspect that defines Africa today will have undergone an alteration that cannot be foretold by our present means of analysis. The pessimism undeniably called for in the short term, then, cannot validly be extended to the longer term. (Coquery-Vidrovitch, 1988:318)

Conclusion

African history in the first decade of the twenty-first century is quite different from what it was when African studies was expanding rapidly in the early 1960s. It is no longer necessary to prove that Africans have histories.

The racist and antihistorical synthesis that Africa was "discovered" or "saved" by Europe, or that Caucasians were the original rulers of some African states, though still reflected in much so-called common knowledge, has been eliminated as an acceptable view by most respectable scholars of Africa. Professional historians have written hundreds of works about virtually every part of the continent. There are specific studies of individual African nations; regional introductory histories of eastern, western, central, and southern Africa; and general histories of the whole continent.

In this chapter, I discussed four basic concept-centered goals that I have evolved through my teaching, reading, and writing on the broad subject of African history. The first goal is to enhance the long time span and wide geographical area involved in African history. The second goal is to increase understanding of the great diversity of Africa's past. The third is to make clear that both change and continuity have been integral parts of the human experience in Africa. The fourth goal I have sought to weave into this chapter is a heightened awareness that all events of history have more than one cause and that the interwoven happenings that produce a given outcome are the result of complex chains of events.

You, as students of Africa, ought personally to pursue a fifth goal—not explicitly focused on in this chapter—as you read the other chapters in this text. That goal is to sharpen your awareness of the role Africa has played in world history. To deal with today's global realities, a marriage between the past and the present is needed. On the one hand, one needs to be introduced to humanity's collective memory, a large part of which flows from Africa. On the other hand, one needs to be sensitized to the current world. People must realize that what happens in Africa is linked to what happens to them and vice versa. As was true hundreds of thousands of years ago, everyone on earth shares a common humanity as members of one race—the human race. And, while only a few of us were actually born in Africa, our destinies are still linked.

Bibliography

Alpers, Edward. 1975. *Ivory and Slaves in East Central Africa*. London: Heinemann.

Azevedo, Mario. 1993. "European Exploration and Conquest." Pp. 103–116 in Mario Azevedo (ed.). *Africana Studies*. Durham, NC: Carolina Academic Press.

Bah, M. Alpha. 1993. "Legitimate Trade, Diplomacy, and the Slave Trade." Pp. 65–85 in Mario Azevedo (ed.). *Africana Studies*. Durham, NC: Carolina Academic Press.

Bohannan, Paul, and Philip Curtin. 1995. *Africa and Africans*. Prospect Heights, IL: Waveland Press.

Connah, Graham. 1987. *African Civilizations.* Cambridge: Cambridge University Press.

Coquery-Vidrovitch, Catherine. 1988. *Africa: Endurance and Change South of the Sahara.* Berkeley: University of California Press.

———. 1997. *African Women.* Boulder, CO: Westview Press.

Eltis, David. 2000. *The Rise of African Slavery in the Americas.* Cambridge: Cambridge University Press.

Freund, Bill. 1998. *The Making of Contemporary Africa.* Boulder, CO: Lynne Rienner Publishers.

Hakem, A. 1980. "La civilisation de Napata et de Meroé." Pp. 315–346 in G. Mokhtar (ed.). *Histoire Générale de l'Afrique.* Vol. 2. Paris: UNESCO (Jeune Afrique).

Hyden, Goran. 1980. *Beyond Ujamaa in Tanzania: Underdevelopment and an Uncaptured Peasantry.* London: Heinemann.

Iliffe, John. 1995. *Africans: The History of a Continent.* Cambridge: Cambridge University Press.

Izard, M. 1984. "The Peoples and Kingdoms of the Niger Bend and the Volta Basin from the 12th to the 16th Century." Pp. 211–237 in D. T. Niane (ed.). *General History of Africa.* Vol. 4. London: Heinemann.

Ki-Zerbo, J. 1990. *General History of Africa.* Vol. 1. *Methodology and African Prehistory.* Berkeley, CA: University of California Press.

Klein, Herbert S. 1999. *The Atlantic Slave Trade.* Cambridge: Cambridge University Press.

Lamphear, John, and Toyin Falola. 1995. "Aspects of Early African History." Pp. 73–96 in Phyllis M. Martin and Patrick O'Meara (eds.). *Africa.* Bloomington: Indiana University Press.

Lange, D. 1984. "The Kingdoms and Peoples of Chad." Pp. 238–265 in D. T. Niane (ed.). *General History of Africa.* Vol. 4. London: Heinemann.

Leclant, J. 1980. "L'empire de Koush: Napata et Meroé." Pp. 295–314 in G. Mokhtar (ed.). *Histoire Générale de l'Afrique.* Vol. 2. Paris: UNESCO (Jeune Afrique).

Lee, Richard G. 1993. *The Dobe Ju/'hoansi.* Fort Worth, TX: Harcourt Brace College Publishers.

Mair, Lucy. 1974. *African Societies.* Cambridge: Cambridge University Press.

Manning, Patrick. 1990. *Slavery and African Life.* Cambridge: Cambridge University Press.

McCann, James C. 1999. *Green Land, Brown Land, Black Land.* Portsmouth, NH: Heinemann.

Meirs, Suzanne, and Igor Kopytoff (eds.). 1977. *Slavery in Africa.* Madison: University of Wisconsin Press.

Ohaegbulam, F. Ugboaja. 1993. "Continental Africans and Africans in America." Pp. 219–240 in Mario Azevedo (ed.). *Africana Studies.* Durham, NC: Carolina Academic Press.

Omer-Cooper, J. B. 1994. *History of Southern Africa.* Portsmouth, NH: Heinemann.

O'Toole, Thomas. 1984. "The 1929–1931 Gbaya Insurrection in Ubangui-Shari: Messianic Movement or Village Self Defense?" *Canadian Journal of African Studies* 18:329–344.

———. 1986. *The Central African Republic: The Continent's Hidden Heart.* Boulder, CO: Westview Press.

Schick, Kathy D. 1995. "Prehistoric Africa." Pp. 49–72 in Phyllis M. Martin and Patrick O'Meara (eds.). *Africa.* Bloomington: Indiana University Press.

Shillington, Kevin. 1995. *History of Africa,* rev. ed. New York: St. Martin's Press.
———. 2005. *History of Africa.* Oxford: Macmillan Publishers Press.
Thornton, John. 1998. *Africa and Africans in the Making of the Atlantic World, 1400–1880.* Cambridge: Cambridge University Press.
Turnbull, Colin (ed.). 1973. *Africa and Change.* New York: Alfred A. Knopf.
———. 1983. *The Mbuti Pygmies: Change and Adaptation.* New York: Holt, Rinehart, and Winston.

4

African Politics

Donald L. Gordon

Deep into the first decade of the twenty-first century, sub-Saharan Africa is the poorest region on earth. Most of its more than 700 million citizens are trapped in a seemingly intractable economic circumstance that "constitutes the core of the worldwide development challenge for the foreseeable future" (Lancaster, 2005:222). Data from the 2004 UN *Human Development Report* indicate that forty of the world's fifty least developed countries are in Africa and that the twenty-seven least developed countries in the world are African (UNDP, 2004). With average per capita incomes no better today than three decades ago, almost half of all Africans south of the Sahara live on less than a dollar a day, and the average income of the extremely poor is actually declining (UN, 2005:7). It is this "dehumanizing" poverty that led South African President Thabo Mbeki to issue a blunt challenge to African leaders at the dawn of the new millennium.

> An ill wind has blown me across the face of Africa. I have seen the poverty of Orlando East and the wealth of Morningside in Johannesburg. In Lusaka (Zambia) I have seen the poor of Kanyama township and the prosperous residents of Kabulonga. I have seen the slums of Sirulere in Lagos (Nigeria) and the Opulence of Victoria Island. I have seen the faces of the poor in Mbare in Harare (Zimbabwe) and the quiet wealth of Borrowdale.
>
> And I have heard the stories of how those who had access to power, or access to those who had access to power, of how they have robbed and pillaged and broken all laws and all ethical norms to acquire wealth. It is out of this pungent mixture of greed, dehumanizing poverty, obscene wealth, and endemic public and private corrupt practice, that many of Africa's *coups d'état,* civil wars, and situations of instability are born and entrenched.
>
> Surely there must be politicians and business people, youth and

> women activists, trade unionists, religious leaders, artists and professionals from the Cape to Cairo, from Madagascar to Cape Verde who are sufficiently enraged by Africa's condition in the world to join the mass crusade for Africa's renewal. It is to these that we say, without equivocation, that to be a true African is to be a rebel in the cause of the African Renaissance, whose success in the new century and the millennium is one of the greatest challenges of our time. (le Pere and van Nieuwkerk, 1999:205)

The "ill wind" blowing at the end of the last decade of the twentieth century contrasts sharply with the "winds of political change" that swept through Africa at the beginning of the 1990s. Because then, after more than thirty years of predominantly authoritarian rule, a period of massive political reform virtually exploded across the continent, changing the political landscape and electrifying the imagination of the African people. Beginning with Benin in 1989 and gathering momentum throughout the early 1990s, African citizens moved to challenge autocratic rule. Motivated by stifling, deteriorating economies, and domestic revolutions in the former Soviet Union and Eastern Europe (among other circumstances), Africans demanded multiparty political systems, expanded civil liberties, accountable political officials, and free elections. In a wide variety of countries across the continent, existing regimes allowed opposition parties to form and open national elections to take place. By the end of 1997, only four of the forty-eight states in sub-Saharan Africa had not held a competitive, multiparty national election (Diamond, 1999:xi). Indeed, "Africa in the early 1990s appeared poised to join fully the apparent 'wave' of democratization sweeping the globe" (Villalón, 1998:1). The extent of the political transformation is marked by the fact that by 1994 not a single de jure (created by law) one-party state remained on the continent (Bratton and van de Walle, 1997:8).

Yet by the middle of the 1990s, this wave had crested (Bratton, 1999:18). And as the twentieth century came to an end, the promises of immediate and sustained democratization were ended for many African countries as powerful incumbents armed with superior resources moved to regain control of African states. As Leonardo Villalón points out,

> In country after country efforts to restructure political systems along democratic lines quickly found themselves entangled in power struggles as incumbent elites struggled to preserve what they could of their privileges. Even in those cases where autocratic incumbents were dislodged in the initial wave of change, ensuing struggles demonstrated clearly that there was little consensus on how power should be distributed or on the democratic processes contesting it. Democracy was not to come easily in Africa. (Villalón, 1998:1)

For many who study Africa, the beginning of the 1990s—marked by moves toward political liberalization, reform, and apparent democratization and the energy, euphoria, and hope that accompanied them—were highly reminiscent of the anticolonial struggle and the early days of independence from colonial rule. For then as in the early 1990s, there were expectations of immediate and substantial changes not only in the political systems but also in the daily lives of Africans. The transfer of power to African decisionmakers was expected to end political repression and allow the perceived wealth of the former colony, siphoned off to Europe, to bring quick relief and instant economic progress to African professionals, businesspeople, artisans, and the huge ranks of the poor. However, this joyous anticipation that marked the late 1950s and early 1960s soon disappeared as the new leadership grappled with the sobering aftermath of colonial rule.

Over time, more than fifty independent African states emerged. The variety of government structures and regimes virtually covered the scope of possibilities. By the 1980s in Africa, one could find monarchies and dictatorships, military regimes and civilian governments, revolutionary systems and democracies, populist administrations, and authoritarian modes of rule (Chazan et al., 1988:3–4). Yet, notwithstanding the diversity of structures, variations in political style, and professed ideological differences (from Marxism to capitalism), the political evolution of African states since independence was characterized by patterns that were strikingly similar.

With some exceptions, African governments became increasingly authoritarian. This trend was marked by the concentration of power in single political parties and, in many cases, in personal rule by the national president. Centralization of power was accompanied by the elimination of competitive elections, greater reliance on administrative bureaucracies, and intolerance of dissent. These systems of rule were often unstable and subject to coups d'état. Stable or unstable, most were also characterized by inefficiency, mismanagement, and corruption.

How and why did all of this develop? Why were most African states unable to sustain democratic, multiparty political systems? What consequences did this have on Africa's people and on economic development? Are Western style democratic states possible in Africa now? These are some of the central questions to be examined in this chapter. And as I will demonstrate, the structures and problems of African societies have not only been shaped by the systems of politics that have evolved, but they, in turn, have also been shaping the changes in the politics of Africa that we are now observing.

Before proceeding, however, readers need to be aware of what this chapter does not discuss as well as what it does. First, my remarks are of necessity relatively abstract and general, as it is a difficult task to synthesize given the variation and complexity of Africa's many countries. Moreover, although an attempt has been made to examine and link together the most important processes and trends, significant issues are inevitably bound to be left out or to be insufficiently detailed. Perhaps the most important issue I have not discussed in more length is the role of foreign political and economic interests in shaping—or misshaping—African political regimes and processes since independence. Although foreign governments have regularly intervened to topple or support African rulers or to influence their policies, I have chosen to focus on Africans as political actors rather than as pawns of, say, superpower politics, multinational corporations, or Western development agencies. I have also largely omitted Africans' political dealings both with each other, through such organizations as the African Union (formerly the Organization of African Unity), and with the international community outside Africa. The reader should refer to Chapter 6 for a discussion of these topics. In sum, this chapter is an introduction to African politics rather than an exhaustive survey.

The Impact of Colonialism

It is surprising to many students that most of Africa was under European control for less than a century and that the Berlin Conference of 1884–1885, which initiated the European scramble for Africa, took place just over a century ago. Yet, in that relatively short period massive changes took place on the continent that not only established the immediate context for African politics but also continue to constrain and shape its future.

To begin, the political map inherited by the new states of Africa was based largely on the expedient economic and political strategies of imperial Europe. Superimposed over the continent were highly divergent and artificial geographical forms and the distortion of traditional social and economic patterns. For one, the physical map of Africa contrasts such sprawling giants as Sudan, the Democratic Republic of Congo (formerly Zaire until 1997), and Algeria with the mini-states of Djibouti and Gambia (see Map 2.6). Diminutive, Gambia (4,127 square miles) could fit into Sudan more than 240 times! Substantial diversity was and is also apparent in population sizes. Nigeria, now estimated at over 130 million people, and Equatorial Guinea, with only about 500,000, provide extreme examples (World Bank, 2005; Sullivan, 1989). With the creation of these artificial boundaries, cohesive social groups were separated, and logical and well-established trading areas were divided. Geographical units were developed that were landlocked or contained few if any resources or enveloped existing diverse and highly competitive cultural and political systems. As a result of these and other circumstances, the political map inherited at independence created huge differences among the various African countries in their potentials for nation-building, economic development, and stability.

While the colonial economic history of Africa and its contemporary impact is complex and variegated, European strategies and actions during the period were generally quite similar. African colonies were made politically and economically subordinate to European needs. The recently industrialized states of Europe, particularly Britain and France, required cheap raw materials and desired captive markets for manufactured goods. Over time, these governments integrated their African colonies into what many call the "international capitalist system." African territories supplied inexpensively produced agricultural commodities such as palm oil, rubber, and cotton, and such minerals and metals as copper and gold to the industries of Europe. Manufactured textiles, household goods, and farm implements sold to Africans at high profit completed the integrated economic system.

But there were differences as well as similarities in the forms colonialism took to extract Africa's wealth. Samir Amin (1972:503–521) argues that regional differences in colonial political and economic policies were determined by the nature of exploitable resources.

For instance, in the coastal territories of French and British West Africa, Amin's "Africa of the colonial trade economy," the colonial state attempted to pay for itself and to satisfy the needs of European industry by promoting cash cropping among the indigenous population. In Senegal, the Ivory Coast (Côte d'Ivoire), the Gold Coast (Ghana), and Nigeria, many traditional subsistence farmers (growing food crops for their own use) switched to producing such export crops as palm oil, rubber, cotton, cocoa, and peanuts.

Amin's "Africa of the labor reserves" describes such colonial territories as Malawi, Mozambique, and Upper Volta (Burkina Faso), which had few easily tapped material resources or had limited potential for peasant- or settler-produced agricultural exports. As a result, these colonies rather quickly became reservoirs of labor migrants, primarily for the mines of the Belgian Congo (Democratic Republic of Congo, or DRC), Northern Rhodesia (Zambia), and South Africa, and for the white settler plantations of sections of Kenya, Tanganyika (Tanzania), and Southern Rhodesia (Zimbabwe).

The former French colonies of Gabon, Congo, and the Central African Republic and the Belgian Congo are labeled by Amin as "Africa of the concession-owning companies." Environmental constraints and low population densities that prohibited profitable cash cropping prompted transfer of most of these areas to concessionary companies. Exploitation of available resources in the concession areas was characterized by low investment and brutality.

A fourth macro-region, "white settler Africa" (parts of Kenya,

Tanganyika until 1918, and Southern and Northern Rhodesia), was, like western Africa, characterized by colonial concentration on the production of agricultural exports. Aided by colonial authorities, Europeans quickly expropriated most of the region's fertile land, displacing traditional African farming groups such as the Gikuyu in Kenya, the Chagga in Tanganyika, and the Shona in Southern Rhodesia. Peasant farmers were either legally shut off from growing most cash crops as in Kenya or deprived of suitable land.

No matter what specialized impact colonial economic decisions had on particular geographical areas, the profit-centered activities of European industrial and commercial firms, settlers, and supportive colonial administrators clearly disregarded *African* development. In no case, even after World War II, when the pressures of world opinion and decolonization were heavy, did European colonizers invest in cogent, rational programs of development designed to make African states self-sufficient. Without joining the debate about whether Europe actually "underdeveloped" Africa, it is obvious that colonial policies worked to handicap independent Africa's economic future.

On departure, colonial administrations left Africa with weak, mal-integrated, severely distorted economies. These realities and others placed most of Africa into a multifaceted and tenacious dependency relationship with more economically advanced states. The decisions, strategies, and even sovereignty of emergent Africa would be contingent on *foreign* markets, industry, finance, and expertise. (See Chapter 5 for more on colonial economies.)

It is important to note that the end of colonial rule by the British and French was accomplished with almost the same speed that had characterized its initial imposition. The achievement of independence by Ghana in 1957 and Guinea in 1958 came quickly and was for many observers unexpected (Liebenow, 1986:21). With very few exceptions, British, French, and Belgian colonies had been granted independence by 1966, over twenty between 1960 and 1964.

Independence, therefore, was not the culmination of a long process of preparation in which the end was long known and the means carefully developed. Among the colonizing powers, only the British and French made attempts to bequeath to Africans the administrative and executive skills requisite for governing the new states (Hodder-Williams, 1984:84). Furthermore, decisions allowing Africans the possibility of more participation in voting for legislative councils with relatively significant power came almost entirely after 1950 (Hayward, 1987:7).

Within this context, the democratic governmental models developed by the French and British for their colonies were essentially alien structures hastily superimposed over the deeply ingrained political legacies of imperial rule. The real political inheritances of African states at independence were the authoritarian structures of the colonial state, an accompanying political culture, and an environment of politically relevant circumstances tied heavily to the nature of colonial rule. Imperial rule from the beginning expropriated political power. Unconcerned with the needs and wishes of the indigenous population, the colonial powers created governing apparatuses primarily intended to control the territorial population, to implement exploitation of natural resources, and to maintain themselves and the European population. For all European colonizers—British, French, Belgian, Portuguese, German, Spanish, and Italian—power was vested in a colonial state that was, in essence, a centralized hierarchical bureaucracy. Specifically, colonial rule was highly authoritarian and backed by police forces and colonial troops. Under this circumstance, power did not rest in the legitimacy of public confidence and acceptance. There was no doubt where power lay; it lay firmly with the political authorities.

Long-term experience with the colonial state also shaped the nature of ideas bequeathed at independence. Future African leaders, continuously exposed to the milieu of authoritarian control, were accustomed to government justified on the basis of force. The idea that government was above self-interested political activity (which only served to subvert the public's welfare) was communicated by colonial administrators. As a result, notions that authoritarianism was an appropriate mode of rule were part of the colonial political legacy (Kasfir, 1983:34).

Furthermore, at independence the politics of the new states would be shaped by at least four heavily influential societal circumstances either set in motion or amplified by colonial political decisions. First, virtually all colonial territories experienced growing inequalities between social classes as both the actions of and the location of colonial administrations created opportunities for some and obstacles for others. (For the impact of colonial policies on postcolonial domestic politics in West Africa, see Boone, 2003.) Second, in most colonies, particularly those under the British model of "indirect" rule through so-called tribal rulers, heightened identification with and competition between ethnic, language, and other groups took place. (For an excellent analysis of how colonial policies shaped social cleavages in Zambia along ethnic and language group lines, see Posner, 2005, and for a comparison of direct and indirect rule, see Chapter 3.) This "tribalism" would especially mark the politics of the early independence period. Third, the context of postcolonial politics in many new states would include dramatic shifts of population from rural areas to the primary administrative city. Finally, as a result of discriminatory colonial educational policies that provided little money for or access to education for most Africans until after World War II, African countries entered independence ill-equipped to staff either the agencies of government or private business and development organizations. (For one of the best accounts of the colonial state in Africa, see Young, 1994; 2000:23–39.)

Nationalism and the Politics of Independence

For most African states, freedom from colonial rule has come only within the past forty years. For some, it is far more recent. The former Portuguese colonies of Guinea-Bissau, Angola, and Mozambique achieved independence in 1974–1975, the former French colony of Djibouti in 1977, and Zimbabwe in 1980. After years of illegal subjugation by South Africa, Namibia became independent in 1990. And while not a colony, South Africa attained majority black rule only in 1994. African states are thus very young.

The nature of the imperial response to African nationalism and the way in which power was eventually transferred to Africans influenced the ideological orientations, political practices, and economic possibilities of the new African states. Especially important here is whether the transfer of power came as a result of peaceful confrontation or whether independence was achieved only after a violent armed struggle. Our understanding of contemporary African politics requires us to look, if only briefly, at nationalism in Africa and at the politics of the independence period.

To begin, the term *nationalism* widely applied to African struggles for

Jason Lauré, Impact Visuals

An independence rally in Luanda, Angola.

independence is somewhat misleading. The term was borrowed from European history, where it referred to nineteenth-century political movements in which people with a common culture, language, and historical tradition claimed the right of self-determination. As Bohannan and Curtin (1995:240–242) further state, "Europeans began with the nation which then wanted to become an independent state. The Africans had states—the existing colonial units through which the Europeans ruled—and they wanted independence for the units so that they could become nations." Yet, it is important to note that, at least initially, very few Africans pushing for autonomy from the European colonizers thought in terms of building a nation. The struggle that would become known as African nationalism was essentially an anticolonial struggle, and its intensity was a reflection in large part of the degree of colonial impact on groups and individuals.

Anticolonial feelings and criticism of and actions against imperial rule were present in Africa from the very beginnings of colonialism. Where European economic and political penetration was deepest—the white settler areas and mining centers of eastern and southern Africa—worker-initiated petitions, strikes, and minor sabotage began in the early 1900s. For the most part, however, these work actions were localized attempts to protest low wages, hard work, and harsh discipline. They were not part of a nationalist independence movement (Tangri, 1985:4–9).

In nonsettler Africa, especially in the British territories of western Africa, objections to colonial rule were primarily articulated by a small core of educated and professional Africans kept from good jobs and access to political power by the racially discriminatory practices of colonial rule. In fact, until what Freund (1984:191) refers to as the "second occupation of Africa," beginning mainly after World War II, most objections and actions against colonial rule were attempts to reform the system, to open it to participation by Africans. The great masses of Africans, mostly engaged in subsistence agriculture and relatively unaffected by colonial authority, were virtually uninvolved in anticolonial activity.

The end of the Great Depression and World War II marked the beginning of a period of rapid change and intense pressure on Africa. Unable to provide for their industrial and food requirements because of the war, Europeans turned to their colonial holdings. At war's end, and even more so by the late 1940s, food crop and cash crop agriculture would be dramatically increased; roads, bridges, railways, and ports would be improved and expanded; and large numbers of additional bureaucrats would be added to the rolls of African colonial administrations. These extraordinary changes in African society set the stage for expanded anticolonial activity. The changes greatly influenced the creation of new groups and classes among Africans and helped shape the conditions, opportunities, and relationships from which the new nationalist leadership emerged.

Increased colonial activity in Africa after World War II took place in a changed international environment and among the changing expectations of a growing number of Africans. A substantial number of African soldiers from such British and French colonies as Senegal, the Gold Coast, Kenya, and the Rhodesias had fought in the war. Their experiences in battle and knowledge of Japanese successes against Western forces in the Asian theater challenged ideas of white superiority. The war itself had been justified on the grounds of rejection of racial superiority and the rights of national independence. Furthermore, many Africans were aware of the new UN Charter, which advocated political self-determination.

Within this atmosphere of new expectations, European colonial administrators began to push new rules and regulations, especially into rural areas of Africa. In eastern Africa, particularly, a series of new regulations imposing Western-oriented agricultural methods were forced on rural farmers and cattle herders. Ostensibly imposed to protect resources, these alien measures, such as contour plowing and cattle destocking, were often coercively enforced. Though less affected, western, central, and southern African farmers were subject to new agricultural orders that provoked considerable discontent. In the Gold Coast (Ghana), the "swollen shoot program" required the cutting of huge numbers of cocoa trees. In the Belgian and Portuguese colonies, forced crop production and resettlement of farmers took place. These and other new colonial operations caused mass rural discontent across much of sub-Saharan Africa (Tangri, 1985:18).

This watershed period immediately after World War II marked the beginning of true African nationalism. The nature and pace of political activity was dramatically transformed. Anticolonial activity focused on influencing policies within the colonial system rapidly became efforts aimed at political liberation.

The prewar associations of African elites (owners of small businesses, physicians, lawyers, and other professionals in West Africa, teachers and clerks in East Africa) were limited in size and scope. Composed mainly of Western-educated "notables" with some access to colonial authorities, these groups were mainly confined to urban administrative centers such as Lagos (Nigeria), Accra (Ghana), and Nairobi (Kenya). Their central concerns were the common interests of a relatively privileged minority.

New and more militant groups were formed by younger activists from among what Marxist analysts refer to as the "petty bourgeoisie"—traders, farmers, and low-level civil servants. Stimulated by the enthusiasm of those in the new movements, many of the old prewar elite associations were themselves transformed into nationalist organizations (Tangri, 1985:15–17).

The combination of bourgeoisie (the elites) and petty bourgeoisie groups was central to the eventual attainment of independence. To become formidable opponents of colonial rule, embryonic elite-led nationalist organizations had to tie themselves to the rural (and increasingly urban) masses of Africans. As Roger Tangri (1985:18) indicates, a litany of complaints was tapped by the nationalist politicians. These included not only the disgust of subsistence and cash crop farmers over onerous new agricultural rules but also worker unrest, complaints against colonial restrictions on small businesses and cooperatives, anti–poll tax agitation, and the general revulsion over the white man's racist behavior and racial discrimination.

It must be noted that in very few instances were nationalist groups part of a unified and highly integrated movement. In fact, in most colonies the African nationalist campaign was a relatively loose linking of "different elements representing sometimes interrelated, but often diverse, economic, ethnic, and regional interests temporarily united in a struggle for independence" (Tordoff, 1984:53).

During the late 1940s and early to middle 1950s, a series of circumstances led the French and British to consider and then begin the process of decolonization. The decade of the 1950s saw substantial shifts in colonial policies over much of the continent. Among other factors, rising costs of administering the territories, pressure from the UN, and the growth of nationalism influenced policymakers, especially in France, England, and Belgium. In 1956, the French granted independence to the North African territories of Morocco and Tunisia and instituted the Loi-Cadre for colonies in sub-Saharan Africa. The Loi-Cadre allowed for domestic autonomy but not independence. In 1957, the British granted independence to the Gold Coast; and by 1959, along with the Belgians, they had accepted the imminence of African self-rule for all territories (Young, 1988a:52–53).

As colonial authorities began to allow consultative forums and African-elected councils to form before independence, many of the nationalist organizations placed emphasis on expanding their influence. Many, if not most, became full-fledged political parties bent on mobilizing mass support and promoting agitational politics. "As independence neared, demonstration of numerical strength became indispensable to validate the claims of a nationalist party to succeed to power" (Young, 1988b:516). It should be noted that the ideas, characteristics, and activities of politicians leading the nationalist organizations would have a significant impact on the nature of African governments after independence. Their position in the social and economic hierarchy, the methods used to recruit support, and indeed the personal goals of Africa's new nationalist leadership would all set patterns for future political activity.

Remember that only a few Africans lived outside the bounds of poverty and material deprivation during the colonial period. Although most of the nationalist leaders, especially in West Africa, were educated and somewhat better off than the masses, they were poor compared to low-level European administrators and settlers. Many were low-salaried teachers or clerical employees of the colonial government or foreign business. Others were small-time traders, contractors, or shopkeepers. Given these circumstances, a significant number of the new leaders from this economic class hoped to convert their leadership positions into social and economic gain. Common among these were, as Wolpe (1974:118) says, "men on the make," their political activities motivated by freedom from colonial domination and the desire for individual mobility. Those that rose to the top were usually charismatic, fluent speakers with organizational skills. After independence, many nationalist leaders, recognizing that political office was the only vehicle available to escape poverty, would not easily relinquish such powerful positions (see Kasfir, 1987; Tangri, 1985).

Political parties and individual politicians recognized that mass protest and wide support would not only hasten independence but also work to secure political advantage or even to ratify leadership positions at independence. Securing mass support in the circumstances African nationalists faced was not easy. Lack of money, poor communications facilities, transportation problems, and widely spread populations were obvious obstacles. Partly as a result, but more so because of familiarity and social access, politicians appealed for support from individuals and groups from their home villages and regions and from their ethnic groups. (Perhaps the best discussion of political parties in the nationalist period is found in Hodgkin, 1957.)

The networks of political affiliation that resulted would have at least two important consequences for the postindependence period. For one thing, in most of Africa this pattern of political recruitment and support worked to create political parties along "natural" lines of social cleavage. Perhaps the most blatant example of this pattern was Nigeria, where the three main parties were sharply divided along ethnic and regional lines: the Northern People's Congress (NPC) in the predominantly Hausa-Fulani north, the National Council of Nigeria and the Cameroons (NCNC) in the heavily Ibo east, and the Action Group in the mainly Yoruba west (Diamond, 1988:33–39). A second result of this form of "linkage" developed during the preindependence period. Promises of material aid to supporters for their backing or for votes created the basis for patronage relationships after independence. Called "patron-client networks" by social scientists, these political webs would become the major form of political interaction for many African countries in the postcolonial era.

The Transfer of Power

When the British, French, and Belgians decided to relinquish power to their African colonies, they did so with deliberate speed. In part, the rapidity of transition reflected practical difficulties of control. Riots in the Gold Coast (Ghana) in 1948, the Mau Mau rebellion in Kenya in the early 1950s, and a breakdown of law and order in Nyasaland (Malawi) in the mid-1950s were strong hints to the British that containing nationalism would be very expensive. For the French, the defeat at Dien Bien Phu (in Vietnam) in 1954, the failure at Suez in 1956, and the Algerian rebellion were most influential (Hodder-Williams, 1984:78–79).

Many observers, however, point to more politically advantageous reasons for the colonial powers' quick exit. The main goal was to retain as much political and especially economic control as possible. Rapid decolonization lowered the level of conflict between the colonial rulers and nationalist leaders. By creating a basically smooth transition to independence (especially in West Africa), the British and French prevented the creation of radicalized political leaders and the formation of segregated, militant, and broadly based nationalist organizations. While not having complete freedom during the transfer period, the imperial powers were the dominant actors (Hodder-Williams, 1984:80–83). Essentially, they maneuvered to exclude elements of the nationalist movements perceived to be dangerous and to aid those leaders and parties friendlier to European economic interests (see Freund, 1984:202–224; Tangri, 1985:20–23). One example is Cameroon, where the French essentially eliminated the Union des Populations Camerounaises (UPC), a radical movement that played a leading role in the Cameroonian nationalist struggle. The politicians who eventually inherited power in Cameroon were moderate and conservative leaders whose roles in the struggle were insignificant (Joseph, 1977:2–3).

This strategy of a quick transition coupled with active promotion of moderate nationalist leaders had generally favorable results for the British and French. Influenced heavily by their own class and personal goals, most nationalist leaders endorsed the legitimacy of private property and other tenets of capitalism. As a consequence, in most countries the economic interests of the European powers were largely preserved (see Young, 1988b:53–55; Tangri, 1985:23).

In contrast, during the 1960s and early 1970s, Portuguese refusal to grant independence to Angola, Guinea-Bissau, and Mozambique led to armed revolt. A protracted liberation struggle provoked mass mobilization of farmers and urban workers. A revolutionary consciousness evolved that rejected most elements of Portuguese colonialism, including the capitalist economy. In addition, mass involvement of destitute populations in FRELIMO (Frente de Libertação de Moçambique) and the MPLA (Movimento Popular de Libertação de Angola) presented obstacles to leaders bent on personal gain through entrepreneurial activity (Saul, 1975:330; Tangri, 1985:24).

For the first wave of African countries to receive independence, a final legacy of colonial rule was bequeathed at independence—formal structures of democratic rule. British colonies received negotiated variations of the basic Westminster parliamentary type of government in which a prime minister is chosen from elected members of parliament and in which executive and legislative powers are fused. The French model was a president-centered form in which the legislative and executive branches are separate. Both instituted a democratic election process, political parties, separate judiciaries, and protection for citizens' rights.

The first period of decolonization, roughly 1957–1969, which saw more than thirty new African states obtain sovereignty, came at the end of more than a decade of rising commodity prices. In the words of Crawford Young (1988a:56), "The extraordinary prosperity of the 1950s contributed heavily to [a] mood of optimism and good feeling. . . . The metropolitan states looked forward to fruitful continuing partnerships with their erstwhile appendages and turned over the keys to the kingdom in a veritable orgy of self-celebration."

Independence

The early days of freedom from colonial rule were charged with excitement and full of hope. The immediately obvious burdens of racist imperial rule were gone. New flags flew over government offices, Africans rather than Europeans held political control, and the world recognized the new states as sovereign. Yet, the excitement of independence masked an enormous set of problems the leadership had to confront promptly.

From the beginning, internal conflict plagued the parties that assumed leadership at independence. The anticolonial organizations that the nationalist movements comprised differed along ethnic, regional, and ideological lines. At independence, with the overarching bond of opposition to colonial oppression weakened or removed, intraparty and interparty conflicts emerged. One divisive issue was access to positions of power in the government and ruling political party. Offices in government (whether at the national or local level) meant access to influencing decisions, to power over resources, and to personal profit (Tangri, 1985:28–33).

The anticolonialist leaders who became the national leaders in the elections of the decolonization period faced a fragile national unity. The geographical areas ruled by the colonizers were superimposed over diverse cultures, language groups, political entities, and trading areas. During the colonial period, little attempt was made to integrate or unify peoples within the colonies. Rather, as a method of control, ethnic groups were often pitted against each other.

The reality of African life, heavily oriented toward subsistence farming and tied to the land, was that most Africans identified primarily with their village and clan and secondarily to a "tribal" or ethnic group. At independence, subnational loyalties were far more important than the new state, for which there were no national traditions, no national symbols, and no national consciousness. While Africans did not necessarily identify with the new state or its leadership, their expectations about what should come from the end of colonialism were high. They wanted education for their children, hospitals and health care, drinkable water, farm-to-market roads, better prices for their crops, and an instantly better life.

No matter what policy orientations the new leadership pursued, all faced bleak economic circumstances and little available capital. Most of the new states had an underdeveloped industrial structure, if any at all. Almost all states would depend on the sale of one or a very limited number of export commodities to make up their treasury. But many of the new states had few natural resources. And all were in an economically dependent relationship with Europe and the industrial countries (Ake, 1981:90–114).

In addition to this environment of meager economic resources, external vulnerability, high demands and expectations, and a political arena in flux, the new governments were shackled with inexperience. "Localization," the placing of Africans into civil service clerical positions, increased (rapidly in parts of nonsettler West Africa) immediately prior to independence. Yet, in areas of technical expertise (accounting, engineering, health), on which the new states would heavily depend, the colonial powers had provided Africans with little training. Furthermore, "the new leaders themselves had earned their positions as a result of their ability to organize and capitalize upon colonial protest. They had little, if any, experience in governing even a small area, let alone an entire country" (Chazan et al., 1999:42–44).

The Centralization of State Power

From the outset, the leadership of most new states felt—and indeed were—politically insecure. With some exceptions (such as Tanzania), most of the new governments had only a thin base of support after the unraveling of the anticolonial alliances left those in power with limited backing (often of only their own ethnic groups and regions). Any expansion of support would have to come from a quick and meaningful response to the high expectations and deep social and economic needs of the population.

The fact is that most states simply did not have the revenues to meet social needs. While most commodity prices remained relatively high during the early independence period, the enormous neglect of Africans during the colonial era would require decades for substantial improvement. Extreme poverty and the high expectations of most Africans led to enormous demands on the leadership.

Formed or heavily expanded during the openness of the waning colonial period, organized interest groups (especially trade unions, rural cooperatives, and student organizations) became increasingly vocal and insistent on government help and action. In many countries, demonstrations and strikes among an increasing number of associational groups soon followed. In reality, many of the new governments were forced to spend much of their time, energy, and money on simply maintaining order (Chazan et al., 1999:46–47).

Most threatening to the new state rulers during the early independence period were organizations based on the mobilization of regional, religious, generational, class, commercial, and (especially) ethnic interests. During the colonial period, economic and social disparities were created in a variety of ways. People living close to colonial administrative centers, European mercantile centers or plantations, or shipping and port facilities had opportunities for wage labor or low-level public or private clerical positions or as low-ranked foot soldiers in the colonial military. Close proximity and employment also led to facility in European languages. For some, especially after World War II, it led to education in government- or mission-sponsored schools. Such circumstances not only created an embryonic political elite with tremendous advantages to gain office at independence but also left most other individuals and groups disadvantaged. Whatever group or coalition of anticolonial groups attained power at independence, either as a dominating single party such as the Tanganyika African National Union or a winning party among several contenders, winners and losers were created. Debilitating poverty and the understanding that the only mechanism for economic development and personal gain was the state itself had prompted the politicization of ethnicity during the preindependence election period. The rapidly forming structures of power after independence, in which the ascendant leadership was easily identifiable by group and region, were perceived generally to bring instant economic and political power for particular ethnic groups. At the same time, those groups not represented in the leadership group or on its periphery felt immensely threatened with the loss of "their" share of the government pie. Such conditions caused tumultuous political activity. Groups jockeyed for power within the ruling party, and often new parties were formed representing specific ethnic or regional interests (see Rothchild, 1981; Horowitz, 1985).

Under the circumstances, the choices confronting the governing elites were limited. They could use their positions to strengthen themselves politically, or they could operate within the colonially positioned democratic political structures and risk electoral defeat. No matter what motivations prevailed among the political elites of the continent—personal greed or selfless nationalism or some combination—there was no option. With few exceptions, the independence leadership quickly moved to consolidate power and expand political control. Across the continent, the early years of independence witnessed a strikingly similar transformation of inherited governmental and political structures. Concentration of political power and control was achieved primarily through (1) limiting or eliminating opposition; (2) expanding the bureaucratic agencies and the security (military and police) organizations, which passed to the new leadership at independence; and (3) maintaining and expanding systems for taxing rural cash crop producers on which the colonial regimes depended for revenue. (The works of Zolberg, 1966; Wunsch and Olowu, 1990; Chazan et al., 1999:46–54; and Boone, 2003, are particularly instructive.)

A variety of justifications for centralizing state power was offered by African independence leaders. Fundamentally, most leaders believed that a strong central government was essential to national unity and economic development. If political competition along the ethnic, regional, and religious (in areas of heavy Islamic concentration) fault lines of society were not eliminated, the resulting antagonisms would "shred the precious fabric of national accord" (Young, 1988b:495). James Wunsch and Dele Olowu (1990:44) point to other influential factors in the movement toward centralization:

1. It was part of the colonial legacy of an administrative state.
2. Outside development consultants from both Western countries and the Eastern bloc were heavily emphasizing central direction and long-term planning.
3. It complemented the expectation of potential donor agencies for "rational" planning and management of assistance programs.
4. It provided a possible solution for the very real challenges African leaders faced.

The manner in which opponents to regimes lost power and access to government involved a variety of actions and mechanisms, with regimes differing on the emphasis and degree of restrictiveness. At the outset, the main targets of government moves to eliminate political competition were rival political parties. Some states, such as Guinea and Ghana, simply declared local political parties illegal and contrary to the national interest; others (e.g., Cameroon) made it virtually impossible for opposition parties to exist. In Uganda, Angola, and Mozambique, coercive force was used to eliminate opposition parties. In any event, as Astride Zolberg's (1966:66–76) classic work *Creating Political Order* points out:

1. Competing political parties were eliminated and the government party fortified.

2. Political opponents were co-opted (drawn in by various inducements), intimidated, detained, or otherwise eliminated (imprisonment, exile, or, much more rarely, murder).
3. Electoral systems were modified to make competition unlikely or impossible.
4. Constitutions were changed to give wide authority to restrict the power of representative assemblies, including national parliaments and provincial and local assemblies.

By the late 1960s, the most common political organization of the new states was the single-party state. Arguably, only Botswana and Gambia were true multiparty exceptions. But transformation of the democratic political structures bequeathed by European political powers involved considerably more than the systematic dismantling of institutions of representation and interest expression—opposition parties, parliaments, provincial and state assemblies, and local district and city councils. Motivated by the desire for more comprehensive political control, for regime security, and for implementation of government policies, ruling groups moved hastily to fortify three main structures of government: administrative bureaucracies, the military and police, and the executive. Building on the legacy of effective colonial bureaucracies and security forces (passed on virtually intact in many instances and containing the main reservoir of skilled personnel in all African countries), the new regimes expanded both the size and function of administrative agencies (Chazan et al., 1999:54–58). While the number and size of almost all administrative bodies increased during the immediate postindependence years, the most dramatic increases were created in the ministries of economic planning, transportation, education, and social services, especially the latter two. Greatly expanded too were government bureaucracies and parastatals (relatively autonomous, state-owned corporations) involved in buying and marketing agricultural and mineral commodities, producing beer and cigarettes, and controlling railroads, airlines, and electric power.

Kept small and under heavy European control (all officers and many noncommissioned officers were European) during the colonial period, the police and especially the military were expanded. In Nigeria, Kenya, Uganda, Sudan, and what is now the Democratic Republic of Congo, where particularly strong regional or ethnic interests either challenged the government or were perceived to be an immediate threat to the regime, the growth of coercive elements was most rapid.

Perhaps most important in the transformation and augmentation of administrative institutions was the concentration of legitimate authority in the executive. Virtually all new states in the first decolonization wave were left with mechanisms to limit, disperse, or check executive power. Yet, beginning in the early postindependence period, strong executive presidencies (supported by the creation of single-party states and the preemption of regional and local politics by bureaucracies) began to displace all independent legislative authority (Wunsch and Olowu, 1990:55–56). By the late 1960s, in governments such as Malawi, Cameroon, Mali, Tanzania, Togo, Zaire (now the Democratic Republic of Congo), and Zambia, presidential decree had replaced meaningful legislative debate.

The relative ease with which early postindependence African leaders consolidated power through shutting off avenues of access to government, gutting representative bodies, and extending the hold on society of the administrative branches came as a surprise to many Western observers. After all, in the 1950s Europeans had expanded social services to Africans; opened the lower branches of colonial government to African clerks; allowed trade unions, political parties, and other associations to flourish; and "given" the gift of democracy to Africans. Critics blamed (among other things) the "intelligence of Africans" and the "incomplete job of 'Europeanization' of Africans." Others saw in the anti-imperial slogans of the nationalist period and in the extension of the state an anticapitalist bias. When coupled with the "abandoning" of democratic institutions and heavy expansion of the state, many, Americans especially, saw the specter of socialism (easily equated in the Cold War period with communism). Ironically, while lamenting the antidemocratic trend in Africa, the United States was at the same time supporting such dictators as Mobutu Sese Seko in Zaire, the white-ruled repressive apartheid government in South Africa, and other nondemocratic regimes so long as they were avowedly anticommunist.

In reality, the ease and speed with which authoritarian regimes were created were heavily rooted in the social and economic by-products of colonial rule. Long-term colonial economic policies oriented toward commodity production and keeping labor cheap left most African states with huge peasant farmer populations overlaid by very small middle classes and minuscule upper classes. Effective opposition to the monopolization of power by political elites is most often associated with a strong middle class with investments to protect and with sources of economic and political power independent of the state. Only a large middle class would have the educational and organizational skills, the motivation, and the monetary resources to successfully challenge government actions. Furthermore, the colonial system, highly capitalistic in an international context, created conditions that made accumulation of wealth by local individuals and groups virtually impossible. Without considerable amounts of savings, significant private investment in production of new resources and goods for society cannot take place. In effect, colonial rule thwarted local capitalism; consequently, independent centers of economic and political power were severely limited. Only the new African state itself, through its taxing and revenue-creating powers, could aggregate money to finance development of the country. Those who controlled the state, therefore, not only had little effective political opposition but controlled the only viable source for the attainment of wealth.

Patronage, the Patrimonial State, and Personal Rule

The rulers and their associates who dismantled the democratic structures left at independence were attempting to stay in power. The creation of centralized single-party systems of governance was an attempt to consolidate control over the political actions of rival interest groups. By centralizing power under the executive, the regimes also were acting to obtain compliance with government policies.

Yet, the constriction of the political arena, the often ruthless manner with which single-party governments were imposed on the populations, and the fact that the party and the central organs of government were usually closely tied to the ethnic and regional support base of the ruling elite did little to dampen opposition. Politicians who lost out in the moves that restricted access to decisionmakers and limited participation in the political process found it relatively easy to mobilize ethnic and other groups not associated with or favored by the ruling elite. As Sandbrook (1985:77–81) makes clear, ethnic politicization, or "tribalism," increased throughout the first decade of independence as ethnicity became one of, if not the main, vehicle for expressing grievances by those outside the system.

To maintain themselves in power, therefore, African leaders had to construct stronger bases of social support. Given the virtual monopolization of scarce economic resources by the new regimes and the elimination of restrictions on the leaders of most African countries, the answer lay in the discretionary distribution of patronage and the development of "clientelistic" ties to key individuals and groups (see Eisenstadt and Lemarchand, 1981; Fatton, 1986; Chazan et al., 1999:185–187). While patron-client relations quickly became the main form of political exchange in postindependence Africa, "clientelism" and the swapping of favors for support were rooted in the politics of anticolonialism. Local leaders were drawn into various nationalist movements with promises of personal office and gain of aid to their villages and regions at independence.

In any event, most African rulers moved to build support and defuse opposition by a wide variety of patronage devices made possible by their control of the state. Key figures were co-opted into government by appointment to high political offices or important positions in the administrative branch or in parastatals. Among other kinds of patronage used to bind support for the regimes and rulers were import-export licenses, government contracts, monopolies over certain kinds of business, tax exemptions, the use of government houses and automobiles, and subsidizing of university educations.

The fact is that patron-client relationships permeate most African governments. Citizens "tie" themselves to patrons (from their kinship line, village, or ethnic, language, or regional group) in government who can help them in some way. Lower-level patrons invariably are clients themselves to a more important patron who may have been responsible for securing his ethnic "brother's" job in the first place. At the upper end of patron-client networks are "middlemen" clients of the ruling elite. Using political clout, powerful positions, and access to government monetary resources made available by the rulers, these middlemen-patrons not only supply jobs in government but money for schools, health clinics, wells, storage facilities, roads, and other favors to their ethnic groups and regions. Patronage binds local constituencies not only to their network of patronage but also to support for the regime itself. Emanating from the country leader may be literally hundreds of patron-client linkages that fix support of other elites to the country's leadership and create substantial support for the regime. Acting also as a system of control, state patronage and "clientelism" served to consolidate regimes by offering access to state resources in exchange for political acquiescence (Boone, 1990b:37).

Following Max Weber, social scientists generally refer to the political process in which government office is bestowed in return for political support and personal loyalty and service as "patrimonialism" (Bendix, 1962:334–335). The essence of patrimonial rule is the personalization of power by a country's ruler. By the end of the first decade of independence, most African political systems were characterized by varying degrees of personal authoritarian rule. In some countries, such as Zaire under Mobutu in the early to mid-1970s, the personal authority of a strongman ruler became virtually synonymous with government itself. (For Zaire, see Callaghy, 1984; Young and Turner, 1985:166–184; Leslie, 1993; for personal rule generally, see Jackson and Rosberg, 1982, and Chabal and Daloz, 1999.) A most illustrative "portrait" of a personal authoritarian ruler is one described by Richard Sandbrook:

> The strongman, usually the president, occupies the center of political life. Front and center stage he is the central force around which all else revolves. Not only the ceremonial head of state, the president is also the chief political, military and cultural figure; head of government, commander-in-chief of the armed forces, head of the governing party (if there is one) and even chancellor of the local university. His aim is typically to identify his person with the "nation." His physical self is omnipresent: as in Orwell's *1984,* Big Brother is plastered on public walls, billboards and

> even private homes. His portrait also adorns stamps, coins, paper money and even T-shirts and buttons often distributed to the party "faithful." Schools, hospitals and stadiums are named after him. The mass media herald his every word and action, no matter how insignificant. (Sandbrook, 1985:90)

Personal rule, of course, depends on the combination of patronage and coercion. Regimes varied in the degree of repressiveness and in the size of those sharing the resources of government. In Cameroon under Ahidjo and Côte d'Ivoire under Houphouët-Boigny, broad and relatively genuine ethnically balanced elite networks created long periods of stability. The more autocratic the personal ruler, the more likely the spoils were to be distributed only among the politically important: top bureaucrats, party officials, local notables, national and regional politicians, military officers, and trade union officials (Sandbrook, 1985:94–95). In Idi Amin's Uganda, patronage was limited to the ruler's band of close associates and his numerically small cultural group, and violent repression became virtually the only method of political and social control. In any event, what must be understood is that maintaining patronage networks and forces of coercion requires a huge amount of money. And in short order, African rulers found that to keep clients secure and the system stable, governments had to commit increasing amounts of money to patronage or allow increasing opportunities for those in government to use their positions for personal gain.

Military Intervention

As African leaders shut down rival political parties and representational bodies and closed off access to government for the vast majority of their citizens, they also increased the size of their armed forces. First used as symbols of national sovereignty and independence throughout the 1960s and 1970s, the military increasingly became a part of the ruling group's enforcement apparatus. Although the actual growth of the military and its relationship to African rulers varied, the armed forces in most countries became politically powerful entities (Chazan et al., 1999:58–61). As a result of their organization and control of weaponry, the armed forces were uniquely positioned to overthrow civilian regimes. As the good feeling and political openness of the nationalist period quickly disappeared in the actuality of single-party government, a variety of factors created conditions that "justified" military intervention in politics. Certainly, the amount and speed of economic improvement was not even close to public expectations. Animosity toward the government grew among those touched by increasingly repressive personal rule. Furthermore, conspicuous spending on palaces, airplanes, and personal luxury items by many of the ruling elite,

Hollandse Hoogte/Jan Bogaerts, Impact Visuals

The military is an important political actor in most African states.

contrasting with the general poverty of the masses of citizens, created resentment. While military takeovers have occurred to rid countries of unpopular and corrupt regimes, most are probably better explained by other factors such as the personal ambitions of military officers or attempts by the military to deal with low pay, poor conditions, or neglect (see Decalo, 1976; Cox, 1976).

In any event, between the 1952 overthrow of King Farouk by Egyptian colonel Gamal Abdel Nasser and 1984, seventy successful coups took place in thirty African countries (McGowan and Johnson, 1984:633–666). According to Samuel Decalo (1989:547–548), "If during the 1960s the coup d'état emerged as the most visible and recurrent characteristic of the African political experience, by the 1980s, quasi-permanent military rule, of whatever ideological hue, had become the norm for most of the continent. At any one time, 65 percent of all of Africa's inhabitants and well over half of its states are governed by military administrations."

Since independence, Benin, Burkina Faso (formerly Upper Volta), Ghana, and Nigeria have had five or more successful coups d'état, and just twelve African states have never had civilian rule disrupted by military intervention. In fact, as late as 1996, only Côte d'Ivoire and Malawi had not yet experienced an attempted or successful coup d'état (see Chazan et al., 1999:225–230). Then, just three years later, only Malawi remained following the successful overthrow of Ivoirian President Konan Bedie on December 24, 1999.

While military regimes have normally claimed to be "caretakers" who would "clean up the mess" and "return to the barracks," most instead have moved to consolidate power. It is important to note that almost invariably military regimes have tended to operate much like the civilian regimes that preceded them (Ball, 1981:576–580; Young, 1988a:496–497; Meroe, 1980). Most have adopted the single-party political organization, and, usually from a small ruling group, a single ruler emerges. Furthermore, and highly important for an understanding of the continent, most military rulers share with their civilian counterparts both the use of patronage as a mechanism for gathering political support and the use of coercion to control or eliminate opposition. They also share an overall preoccupation with increasing their own economic position. Nigeria's military ruler from 1993 to 1998, General Sani Abacha, is a case in point. Along with crushing all political opposition, Abacha and his corrupt military cronies diverted vast oil revenues for patronage and their own aggrandizement. Abacha is alleged to have stolen a $6 billion fortune for himself (Gordon, 2003: 195–196). Finally, while military and civilian rulers alike have pursued almost identical economic development policies and have reaped similar results, the Afrobarometer Project has found that military rule is by far the least popular form of rule in Africa (Bratton et al., 2006:78). (For an exhaustive review of the military in Africa, see Luckham, 1994:13–75.)

The Political Economy of Decline

For ordinary Africans, development is seen in personal terms. It means additional money for children's schoolbooks, usable roads that allow farmers to get their produce to market, electric lights in the village, affordable rice and flour, or a health clinic within walking distance. Development too is measured by access to land, jobs, and better housing. But most Africans experienced little real economic progress in the postcolonial period. Resources needed for effective, broad-scale development were drained away, among other reasons, to support regime efforts to consolidate power.

As we have seen, attempts by African regimes to enhance control over the political arena and to strengthen and extend bases of support led to remarkably similar actions. State patronage and clientelism emerged as the main methods of political control and governance. State resources that could have been committed to development were used to pull into the system the elite from a variety of politicized factions (ethnic, regional, workers' groups, student associations, women's groups). In reality, private appropriation of state resources and the use of government money to build and expand personal rule lay at the very heart of the process by which most postcolonial regimes sought to govern (Boone, 1990b:36–37).

In large part because of patronage-based rule, the 1960s and 1970s (and beyond) were marked by the rapid growth of the political branch, the bureaucracies, and the parastatals. In fact, during the 1960s, the civil service in Africa grew at a rate of 7 percent per year, a rate that doubled the number of employees in ten years. The result was that by 1970 over 60 percent of all African wage earners were government employees. By 1980, at least half of *all* African government expenditures were allocated simply to pay the salaries of government employees. Furthermore, the expansion of government corporations during the first two decades borders on phenomenal. Parastatals were developed to deal with a broad range of government activities. For example, state-owned companies were created to handle the control and marketing of agricultural products, provide banking services, run airlines and railroads, manufacture products, and manage retail stores. As an extreme example of their number and range in a particular country, Nigeria (in the mid-1970s) had over 250 state-owned corporations (Chazan et al., 1999:56).

The patronage-based elaboration of the state, the expansion of the armed forces, and economic development of a country depended on the availability of substantial amounts of money. Especially needed was foreign exchange to purchase petroleum, trucks, buses, industrial parts, and a vast menu of items Africans could not produce. While some money began to flow from donor nations, most government activities would depend on money aggregated locally. Given the scarcity of indigenous private savings from which to borrow, the lack of established middle- and upper-income groups on which income taxes could be levied, the absence of an industrial base, and a heavy dependency on technologically advanced countries, most African regimes turned to the profits to be made from the export of mainly agricultural commodities. Catherine Boone's description of how African regimes moved to control highly productive areas of post-colonial commerce is highly relevant. "Building on the regulatory apparatus of the colonial state, post-colonial governments licensed wholesalers and importers, controlled imports through tax and tariff regimes and fixed the process of agricultural commodities, agricultural imports, and staple consumer goods" (Boone, 1990b:26). While the process of sustaining revenues from taxes on rural commercial farmers developed by the colonial power or intensifying (raising) them was complicated and varied considerably depending on the political and economic resources of local farmers, the result was that throughout most of the continent, substantial profits were "earned" by African regimes by paying rural agricultural commodity producers low prices and marketing the commodities at considerably higher prices (Bates, 1981; Boone, 2003). The consequence for farmers and rural areas of Africa was that the promise of development turned into the harsh reality of subsistence living. For increasing numbers, the hope for a better life centered on the already well-traveled path of migration to the cities.

In fact, government economic policies that handicapped farmers were heavily reinforced by the reactions of rulers to major population growth in urban areas. By the early 1960s, "primate cities" (capitals and ports) often were growing at rates as high as 10 percent per year. For example, between 1958 and 1970, the population of Kinshasa in what is now the Democratic Republic of Congo increased from 389,000 to 1,323,000 (Young and Turner, 1985:81), and Douala, Cameroon, grew from 54,000 in 1957 to over 313,000 in 1976 (Government of Cameroon, 1977). Early within the first decade of independence in most African capitals, massive conglomerations of under- and unemployed Africans existed in sprawling squatter settlements with no city services. In some instances, they already formed the bulk of cities' populations. (More on urbanization and population growth in Africa is found in Chapters 5 and 7.)

From the earliest days of independence, African leaders were aware of the potential danger of large urban concentrations of the poor and unemployed. Many regimes had experienced urban-based strikes, demonstrations, and even violence during moves to centralize the state or as disappointment grew over slow progress toward meeting the needs and expectations of various interest groups. As a result, most leaders acted to cut the potential of "instability" of large concentrations of urban poor by holding down food prices in the cities. In effect, urban areas were subsidized by requiring food crop farmers (mostly women) to accept low prices from government monopoly wholesalers or by setting price caps on food sold in urban areas.

In order to extract profits from rurally produced agricultural commodities and to keep food costs low for urban residents, government policies caused the deterioration of rural economies, pushed the rate of rural to urban migration dramatically upward, and added to the growing inequality between rural and urban areas. Furthermore, farmers, in large numbers where access was available, began to sell their crops in the black market economy outside government control (see Bates, 1981).

For much of Africa, then, development of the rural areas was sacrificed to finance patrimonial states. These patronage-based systems created opportunities for all those connected to government through patron-client networks. For the elite, appointed by rulers to the highest party, administrative, and parastatal positions, state office and political influence created amazing legal and illegal advantages for personal gain. And in virtually all states, those in positions of power (and their patrons) moved to use their influence for economic profit (Young, 1988b:503).

It is the way in which the state-based elite used their profits that is most important for an understanding of a political economy of decline. For the most part, money legally or illegally secured from government position was either used to buy luxury import items or placed into speculative real estate development, taxis and trucks, or retail and wholesale commercial ventures (Boone, 1990a:427). For a variety of reasons, very little investment took place in ventures that created substantial employment, boosted industrial capacity, or generally helped develop the country (see Sandbrook, 1985).

Given the circumstances of government economic policies that virtually devastated rural areas and pushed urbanization, the expansion of the state and the huge costs of personnel and patronage, and the essentially nonproductive and wasteful use by the elite of public resources, almost all African states were in economic decline by the early 1970s. During the mid- to late 1970s, a combination of external and internal political, economic, and social factors moved the continent from decline into crisis.

State and Society in Crisis

The political agendas that created costly government superstructures and siphoned money into the hands of a relatively nonproductive elite class inhibited the development of most African countries. In many regimes, inefficiency, mismanagement, and corruption wasted public resources. Moreover, most of the wealth that flowed to the dominant classes was not spent on capital investments, investments that help a country to produce more and that ultimately promote development.

As a result of these and other factors, the economic growth rate of the continent declined. Data taken from Nafziger (1988:16–34) help chart the path of African economic stagnation and descent in the 1970s and 1980s. From a growth rate of approximately 1.3 percent per year in the decade prior to independence, economic growth dropped to 0.2 percent yearly for the period from 1965 through 1984. Between 1980 and 1985, Africa's real gross domestic product (GDP) per capita fell an average of 2.3 percent yearly. By the mid-1980s, the "great descent" had become an internationally recognized tragedy of crisis proportions. While the economic impact of political decisions by African rulers was a major factor in creating crisis conditions, other factors generally outside the control of rulers contributed substantially.

The relatively high prices that commodities brought in the waning colonial years began to drop in the early independence period. During the 1970s, and continuously since, prices for virtually all of the continent's main agricultural and mineral commodities have declined. At the same time, costs of goods imported from the more technologically sophisticated countries have risen steadily. Machine parts, automobiles and trucks, industrial tools, and luxury items have become increasingly more expensive.

Even more disadvantageous changes in the "terms of trade" for African states were caused by the oil shocks from the mid-1970s to the early 1980s. With the exception of oil producers such as Nigeria, Angola, and Gabon, sub-Saharan African states were staggered by the high costs of petroleum products.

While changes in the international economy placed most African countries in increasing jeopardy, population changes within Africa created conditions that would hinder any hope of economic progress. From the relatively slow population increases of the colonial period, population growth rates in independent Africa simply exploded. By the mid-1980s, the continental population growth average rose to a yearly rate of over 3.0 percent. At this rate of growth, populations double in size in little more than twenty years (World Bank, 1990a:229).

The scope of the crisis can be understood by the number of Africans relegated to absolute poverty (living on one dollar per day or less). By 1985, the number of absolute poor had grown to 180 million people—47 percent of the population. By 1998, rapid population growth and slow economic growth combined to increase the number of poor by an additional 111 million. This means that at the dawn of the twenty-first century Africans constituted 25 percent of all the poor in the developing world as compared to only 16 percent in 1985 (World Bank, 1990b:5, 29; 2001:4, 23). (A comprehensive discussion of the current economic crisis is found in Chapter 5. See Chapter 13 for more on poverty.)

In any event, the fact is that by the early 1980s most African states simply did not have the capacity to meet rapidly growing budgetary requirements. Most often, among other results, there was an overall weakening of the government's ability to carry out essential public services. Over time, roads and rail systems deteriorated. Services to agriculture were abandoned. School systems (already shocked by huge increases in the under-fifteen population) found little money available for school construction or teacher salaries. Furthermore, as the state "softened" (Hyden, 1983:60–63), even the most essential government tasks, such as tax collection, became problematic. As Goren Hyden (2006:8) makes clear, "in the absence of a welfare state that would provide Africans with a measure of social security, citizens have always relied on informal social and economic support systems such as extended families, neighbors, or the community at large." During the period of economic and political decline and now, Africans increasingly had to rely on the "informal economy," which forms the majority of income for most people across the continent and which almost entirely escapes the taxing arm of most African countries.

As the administrative capacity of governments decreased, decay within regimes increased. In many states, corrupt practices among strategically placed politicians and bureaucrats became so habitual as to be institutionalized. Under these circumstances, citizens expected to pay bribes, and they viewed politicians' raiding of government treasuries as simply "the way things are done." The term *kleptocratic* has been applied to states such as the former Zaire, where corruption was systematically practiced at all levels (Young and Turner, 1985:183). Yet, even in countries with a traditionally professional civil service, the economic crisis created conditions or "structured" incentives for corruption. In Ghana, for example, "where hyper-inflation rapidly outran increases in salaries, demanding a bribe (or a higher one than previously) was an understandable reaction of junior or middle-ranking government officials to the problem of feeding their families" (Jeffries, 1989:80).

For individual Africans, strategies for survival are registered in such rational acts as the following: a decision to sell cocoa not to the official government agency but on the black market for twice the government price; a move to avoid the possibility of losing money on an export peanut crop by "retreating" into subsistence agriculture (for one's own use); or the decision (made by many) to invest time and work in one or a variety of mutual aid organizations that operate to help finance a farmer's seeds, repair a road, build a school, or even protect a village from thieves.

Since the early 1980s, the actions of individual Africans combined to have a substantial impact on African regimes. Basically, two major patterns emerged. First, although varying by country and regime, large numbers of Africans disengaged from the state or were at least partially successful in avoiding state laws and officials (see Rothchild and Chazan, 1988). Second, a resurgence and expansion of voluntary organizations and associations occurred, even within coercive states (see Bratton, 1989b; Fatton, 1992; and Harbeson, Rothchild, and Chazan, 1994). While both developments had significant ramifications for African regimes, withdrawal from the state and its power to tax was most difficult for rulers to control and added most immediately to the state in crisis.

Disengagement from the state denies regimes their expected revenues in two significant ways. First, the economic foundation of most African states rests on revenues produced from selling agricultural exports. When farmers simply stop growing export crops, the fiscal base of regimes (already weakened by a continuing slide in commodity prices) is further eroded. Certainly, less foreign exchange is accrued and the economic crisis deepens. Disengagement from the state also takes place when people turn to clandestine economic transactions for survival or profit. These black market activities are remarkably alike throughout the continent and primarily involve:

1. Hoarding and exchanging scarce goods above both official and justified market prices;
2. Smuggling lucrative cash crops, precious metals, or manufactured foods either into or out of the country; and
3. Engaging in illegal currency transactions to avoid monetary exchange controls or exchange rates.

These and other activities are a major part of the parallel or informal economy, which creates incomes and assets that largely escape government regulations and taxes. African governments lose huge amounts of money in this manner, weakening the fiscal basis of the state even further (MacGaffey, 1988:177–185; Lemarchand, 1988:160–166; Sandbrook, 1985:139–149).

In any event, as revenues stagnated or declined, as treasuries were drained, and as terms of trade for imported goods and services became increasingly disadvantageous, African governments borrowed heavily to maintain themselves. Unfortunately, many commercial loans were secured when rates were high. Because of Africa's heavy dependence on Europe, Japan, the United States, the Soviet Union, and other industrial nations for money, sub-Saharan Africa had by 1990 compiled debts so huge that over 40 percent of export earnings needed to be spent each year simply to pay interest (World Bank, 1990b). Economists generally agreed that with economies further deteriorating, few African states would have the ability to ever pay debt principal, and a significant number could not meet interest payment schedules. Under these circumstances, economic credit from virtually all major lenders dried up, which left only the World Bank/International Monetary Fund loan packages with their grinding austerity measures to ward off the virtually complete economic collapse of many (if not most) African governments.

Structural Adjustment and the Reordering of the State

For the first twenty to twenty-five years, independent rule in most African states was based on a relatively standard political and economic structure. In the most simple terms, an autocratic leader emerged and consolidated political control through patronage and a heavily expanded state. As a result of government employment and opportunities, connections, and favors, a dominant group formed. Over time, as this urban-based group coalesced, government policies increasingly focused on maintaining their support.

Patronage networks, massive bureaucracies, and the economic needs of a dominant class require a large and steady stream of money. As the economic crisis of the late 1970s reached "almost cataclysmic proportions" in the mid-1980s, most African regimes were forced into the desperate gamble of "structural adjustment" loans from the International Monetary Fund (IMF).

What must be understood is that African regimes had consistently avoided IMF loans. Conditions tied to them require countries essentially to reorder society by adjusting the structure of internal economic relationships. Structural adjustment was and is controversial in Africa, as Virginia DeLancey discusses in Chapter 5, and for authoritarian patrimonial states, they seemed truly last-ditch agreements. Most structural adjustment agreements required countries to:

1. Devalue currencies so that exports will be cheaper to foreign buyers.
2. Reduce deficits by freezing government salaries.
3. Stop setting agricultural prices and eliminate subsidies to urban consumers.
4. End import restrictions.
5. Privatize state-owned enterprises.
6. Increase bank interest rates to encourage savings to generate capital investment.

Countries that received these loans accepted close surveillance of their economies by the Bank. Lofchie (1989:122) states that "at the level of government officer, structural adjustment transferred effective operational authority from African civil servants to staff members of these international lending agencies." By 1989, all but five of forty-four sub-Saharan African states were borrowers from the IMF (Kraus, 1991:211–212).

From a political standpoint, the significance of these developments should not be underestimated, because for most countries the sweeping economic reforms required to receive IMF monies change the context of political relations not only between the rulers and the ruled but within regimes themselves.

At the outset, structural adjustment policies had a major impact on the urban areas, which rulers often pacified by subsidizing foodstuffs. Deregulating agricultural prices caused food costs to rise dramatically. In the major cities, where relatively little food is grown for personal use, price increases for such staples as rice, flour, and meal are often devastating. While the vast urban population made up largely of nonsalaried, underemployed, or unemployed poor feels the full effect of structural adjustment austerity, lower- and middle-range government employees are also affected substantially. Across the continent, opposition to food price increases was especially bitter and led to demonstrations and riots in many countries.

While allowing agricultural prices to rise and eliminating subsidies increased the scope and intensity of opposition to many African regimes and further undermined any remaining legitimacy, other austerity measures associated with structural adjustment threatened to unravel the very basis of regime existence. As governments froze salaries and sold off government corporations, money for patronage was drastically reduced, and positions connected to the system were eliminated. Furthermore, virtually bankrupt regimes slashed services and were increasingly unable to meet the pay schedules of teachers, public health workers, and other low- and medium-level civil servants. In other words, the patronage systems that in most African states tied together and supported an essential socioeconomic-political elite were either substantially weakened or began to break apart. (See Chakoadza, 1993; Olukoshi, 1993; Onimode, 1989; and Ponte, 1994, for the social and political impact of SAPs.)

In many African countries by the late 1980s, regimes in political and economic retreat faced variations of an increasingly common scenario:

1. Associational groups such as self-help organizations, cooperatives, churches, vigilante groups, and professional organizations, which had increased as the economic crisis worsened, expanded further under structural adjustment. Deeply rooted in society, these groups formed the basis of popular dissent toward the regime (see Bratton, 1989a, 1989b:29–33; Hyden, 1989:4–5; Shaw, 1990).
2. Civil servants and trade union members—whose living standards and incomes were most threatened by the economic crisis and austerity measures—began demanding political reforms ("A Chance for Africa," 1991:2; Neavoll, 1991:40; Press, 1991:4; Henry, 1991).
3. College students, graduates, and professors facing cutbacks and poor job prospects actively worked against the regime (Morna, 1990, 1991). They, along with civil servants and trade unionists, led popular demonstrations against the government.

As autonomous centers of power formed and opposition to regimes increased, many regimes faced additional pressures from outside the continent as well. The extraordinary political upheaval that brought democratization to the Soviet Union and Eastern Europe resulted in political accord between the superpowers and ended the Cold War. Under these new conditions, the strategic importance of Africa was greatly diminished. Among the consequences, the United States and the Soviet Union began to cooperate in foreign policy and to reduce both military and economic aid. (See Chazan et al., 1999:449–451.) Countries tied to the Soviet Union and Eastern European states for aid and technology (such as Mozambique, Ethiopia, and Angola) had monies cut off and were pressured to accommodate political change. For client states of the United States (especially Zaire and

Kenya), cutbacks in US aid and the consequent new attention paid by the United States to human rights abuses brought new and heavy pressure on rulers (see Hull, 1991:193–196, 233–234). As Young points out, "By 1990 US policy was aggressively promoting democratization, aided by the efforts of unusually outspoken ambassadors in Cameroon, the Central African Republic, Zaire, and Kenya" (Young, 1999a:69). In West Africa, former French colonies (Benin, Gabon, Côte d'Ivoire, and Chad) long dependent on French aid and French troops to support single-party states and authoritarian rulers were subject to change in the foreign policy of France. New assistance from France apparently required regimes to be responsive to citizens' demands for political reform (Whiteman, 1991; Clark, 1997:2; see also Chapter 6). During 1991, the United Kingdom, the European Community, and Japan linked future aid to African countries to such "political conditionalities" as respect for human rights, a free press, democratization, and "honest" government (Clapham, 1996:194–195; Khadiagala, 2000:93). More important for some countries, influential voices within the World Bank began to call for political reform as a necessary component to economic aid (Young, 1999a:69).

All of these events created an atmosphere for change and heightened expectations Africans had for political transformation. Under these circumstances, the last decade of the twentieth century began.

Beyond Autocracy: Political Liberalization and Democratization

By late 1989, in countries as different as Algeria and Zaire, Gabon and Madagascar, and Benin and Togo, open challenges to incumbent regimes became commonplace. At first, spontaneous demonstrations, strikes, and riots were focused on government austerity measures. Shortly thereafter, protest escalated rapidly into widespread and strident demands for the end of single-party rule, for accountable political officials, and for free elections (Bratton and van de Walle, 1992:27–38).

Most African regimes responded first with repression. However, shaken by the scope and intensity of protest and pressured by conditions and countries outside the continent, many African rulers moved reluctantly to actual or promised reform (see Kraus, 1991).

Beginning approximately with the new decade (1990), a period of remarkable political change began to take place. Within eighteen months, a large number of states had either publicly committed to a multiparty political system or allowed opposition parties to form. Among those that had legalized multiple political parties by late 1991 were Angola, Burkina Faso, Cameroon, Republic of Congo, Guinea, Mozambique, Niger, Sierra Leone,

Under President Robert Mugabe, Zimbabwe has descended into being an autocratic state with its economy in shambles.

Togo, Zaire, and Zambia. Two others, Côte d'Ivoire and Gabon, had allowed competitive elections with opposing parties to take place by late 1990. Also during this period, President Robert Mugabe retreated from his attempts to impose one-party rule on multiparty Zimbabwe, and the Nigerian military government announced the formation of a two-party system (though initial presidential elections were annulled) (*African Demos,* 1991:vols. 1, 2, 4; Diamond, 1995:458).

During 1990 and 1991, several authoritarian regimes fell as the result of either wars of liberation or peaceful elections. For example, after decades of illegal occupation and rule by South Africa and a bloody liberation struggle, Namibia (formerly South-West Africa) received independence in March 1990. And in the Horn of Africa, the highly repressive regimes of Siad Barre in Somalia and Mengistu Haile Mariam of Ethiopia fell to liberation movements during the first half of 1991. In West Africa, political pressures led to open democratic presidential elections in February and March 1991 in Cape Verde, São Tomé and Principe, and Benin. In each case, a new president was elected over the former ruler, and a peaceful transfer of power took place (*African Demos,* 1991:vol.4:8). In November 1991, Kenneth Kaunda, leader of Zambia since independence, was soundly defeated in a relatively problem-free presidential election by trade union leader Frederick Chiluba. And, most remarkably, on May 10, 1994, Nelson Mandela, leader of the African National Congress (ANC), was sworn in as

South Africa's first black president. Altogether between 1990 and 1995, over thirty competitive national elections were held across the continent, fourteen of which resulted in peaceful transfers of power (Doro, 1995:245).

Clearly, by the end of 1994 significant political changes had taken place on the African continent. In a wide variety of states, power was decentralized, political liberties expanded, and new individuals and groups entered the political arena. This thrust toward political reform and democratization was strengthened by the loss of credibility of ideologies that legitimated autocracy (particularly by the Leninist version of Marxism); by the growth of local African and international human rights movements; and by expectations and the will to act prompted by democratic revolutions elsewhere in the world. These were heady days across the continent; the world was democratizing, and, to many, the continent of Africa seemed destined to fulfill a global democratic imperative.

The Political Trajectory of Democratic Reform

Despite the democratic impulse, the social and economic context that shaped the political trajectory of Africa over the past forty years remains substantially intact. Illiteracy and disease abound, unemployment and poverty continue unabated, and inequalities between classes are far worse than at independence. Furthermore, in many, if not most, countries, divisive ethnic, regional, religious, and even subethnic cleavages tear at the social fabric (see Adediji, 1995:134). Civil war in Côte d'Ivoire("A General Emerges from Hiding," 2005:40), genocide or mass killing in Darfur (Sudan) (Kasfir, 2005:195), religious and regional tensions in Nigeria (Okonta, 2005:203; Gordon, 2003), and smoldering rebellions in the Democratic Republic of Congo and Uganda are notable cases in point. (For the DRC, see Clark, 2002, and for Uganda, see "Lord's Resistance Army," 2006). Therefore, as promising as these movements toward democratization in Africa might appear, it is premature to conclude that genuinely competitive multiparty democracies can easily be built or, with Africa's myriad problems, that they can survive.

To understand the problems associated with achieving democracy in Africa, it is important to be clear on what is meant by *democracy* and how we determine if a country is democratic. Many political scientists, especially from Western industrial democracies such as the United States, broadly define democracy to describe a government chosen in open and fairly conducted elections, where citizens of the country are protected by a code of civil liberties, and where election results are accepted as legitimate by all contestants. The term *consolidated democracy* is used to indicate the widespread acceptance (by both political elites and by ordinary citizens) of rules guaranteeing political participation, open competition, and human rights (Bratton, 1999:18).

In reality, by the beginning of the twenty-first century it became quite apparent that the democratic gains of 1990 to 1994 were eroding (Bratton and van de Walle, 1997). Writing in 1999, Young observed that "the euphoria that marked the early 1990s has long since evaporated and even the most optimistic observers concede that democratization in Africa will be gradual, messy, fitful, and slow with many imperfections along the way" (Young, 1999b:25).

While in many African states political reforms were substantial and real, movement toward democracy was decidedly uneven across the continent. Indeed, for many Africans gains in political freedom were very limited or nonexistent. In 1997, only sixteen of Africa's fifty-three states were categorized as "relatively democratic," a term that indicates a multiparty state in which elections are relatively fair and that at least one change in the national leadership has taken place (Young, 1999b:27). Michael Bratton and Nicolas van de Walle note that while almost all African regimes "opened up" to some degree in the flurry of reform between 1990 and 1994, the paths of political change were distinctive and divergent. About 40 percent of the forty-four sub-Saharan African states became relatively democratic, but the majority did not (Bratton and van de Walle, 1997:116). In twelve countries (including Cameroon, Kenya, Gabon, and Ghana), regime incumbents allowed the formation of opposition parties but "exploited the powers of incumbency to dictate the rules of the political game by manipulating electoral laws, monopolizing campaign resources, or interfering with the polls. In an additional twelve countries (such as Uganda, Guinea, and Zaire) incumbent strongmen made insincere and tactical concessions while under pressure to reform, but never intended to give up power" (Bratton and van de Walle, 1997:121).

The Political Economy of Democratization

Africa's divergent transitions toward political reform and democratization are the result of a variety of factors that have an impact on the actions and policies of those in power in African states at the beginning of the twenty-first century. The general context within which domestic politics takes place in Africa includes the colonial legacies of poverty and dependent economies, patron-client–based political systems, and the increasing impact of external political and economic forces (such as the World Bank/IMF). It is to the changing circumstances of Africa's external environment that we now turn.

To begin, African states and their political systems operate within an international environment in constant transition. The favorable combination of factors that formed the context of dramatic political change in the early 1990s changed. As a result, many African leaders seeking to remain in power took advantage of the new circumstances and were able to halt what seemed to be a democratic destiny across the continent.

Almost from the start of Africa's precipitous economic decline that began in the late 1970s and early 1980s, African economic and political systems have been increasingly influenced by donor nations and especially by the World Bank and the IMF. Operating on assumptions that only a major restructuring of the economic (and later) political systems of African countries would save them from complete economic destitution, these lenders required variations of structural adjustment programs outlined above. These assumptions centered on the belief that African countries could only build strong economies by focusing on increased export sales of primary products (unprocessed raw agricultural and mineral products). Sale of export crops and minerals would give African countries a comparative advantage over other states in that low labor costs would allow African states to export these products at very competitive prices, especially to industrial states. A second goal of the World Bank/IMF lending agencies was to open African states to investment from the outside and particularly from the wealthy industrial states, such as the United States, Japan, and Germany. Removal of tariffs (developed in part to protect fragile African industries) and other obstacles to investment would lure companies from the industrialized world to the low labor costs and cheap raw materials of Africa. Additional investment would be secured as government corporations (state-owned enterprises) were sold to either domestic or foreign businesses or individual investors. (For information on trade and investment, see Chapters 5 and 13.)

According to the World Bank/IMF, the benefits of structural adjustment would move to quickly revive and "modernize" African economies and, indirectly, would promote the development of business and civic groups, which would provide a check on government and help contain or prevent autocratic regimes. In other words, political reform and democracy would be promoted. The reality was decidedly different.

To work as anticipated, the World Bank/IMF economic reforms depend on ready markets for exports and substantial investment from industrial countries. For the most part, neither happened. As the Cold War ended and Russia and the new states of Eastern Europe democratized, Western industrial states and their huge multinational corporations looked east rather than south for profitable investment. Eastern Europe and Russia, with their more highly educated populations, relatively well-off domestic markets, and better infrastructure (roads, railroads, and communications technology), provided a superior investment opportunity with less risk and more chance for profit than any African state (with the exception of South Africa). With the addition of Russia and such states as the Czech Republic and Poland to newly industrializing democratic states in Latin America (Brazil,

Argentina, and Chile, for example) and the so-called Asian Tiger states (including Singapore, Taiwan, South Korea, and Thailand), little attention was paid to Africa.

Nor was the anticipated huge increase in export revenues available to African states. The "comparative advantage" formula for driving African economies was used as a model for economic growth not only among the developing countries of Africa, but also for other nonindustrial states around the world. For African states and economies, the results were reminiscent of the days after independence when the new states of Africa with huge needs rapidly expanded their export crops. The result then and during the 1990s was to flood the world markets, resulting in falling prices for many cash crops.

Under these circumstances, economic stagnation and decline continued for most African states throughout the 1990s. As John Clark points out,

> Currency devaluation, the revocation of government subsidies, and privatization [of government-owned corporations] whatever their long term merits, lead to job losses, declining standards of living, and economic despair in the short term. Ironically, though these social costs can be the source of huge opposition to autocratic regimes, they make consolidation of democratic regimes that follow them difficult. For besides creating outright antipathy for new governments, economic concentration quite often creates class and ethnic conflicts as people vie for scarce goods, which in turn undermines the consolidation of democracy. (Clark, 1997:29)

Already poor and unable to provide basic services to most citizens outside the capital cities, African governments were required by World Bank/IMF retrenchments to become even smaller or "weaker," further diminishing their capacity to promote and sustain economic development (van de Walle, 2001:81–83). In addition, structural adjustment programs pushed African states into "rapid and premature trade liberalization" which "exposed the vulnerabilities of African farmers and manufacturers who could not compete against the mass produced or subsidized products from Europe and America that soon flooded the markets." "Jobs were lost as farms cut production and factories closed" and "because there were no 'safety nets' in place, those who lost their jobs were forced into poverty" (Stiglitz, 2002:17; Bratton, Mattes, and Gyimah-Boadi, 2006:21). (See also Englebert, 2000, and Rapley, 2002.)

As the 1990s progressed, Africa would be further marginalized. During the Cold War, Africa's location near the Middle East and the sea lanes of the South Atlantic and Indian Oceans and its mineral resources created what political scientists refer to as "geostrategic" importance for the continent. A considerable portion of aid and grants to Africa (both economic and military) had come from the United States and, to a much lesser extent, from the Soviet Union. With the breakup of the Soviet Union and the end of Soviet control of Eastern Europe, Africa was far less important. Aid was cut not only to US client states, such as Zaire and Kenya, but to other African states as well. The end of the Cold War also reduced the demand for Africa's strategic minerals, while making alternative sources of supply available from Russia and Eastern Europe, further intensifying the economic marginalization of the continent (Clapham, 1996:164).

As Tom Callaghy makes clear (2000:44–45), "Africa generates a declining share of the world output. The main commodities it produces are either becoming less important or being more effectively produced by other developing countries." And as Africa becomes increasingly marginalized, it becomes increasingly dependent on the industrial countries. These unfavorable economic circumstances formed the background for an evolution in the international political arena taking place in the second half of the 1990s.

Since the "global conjuncture" (1988–1990) that helped create conditions for explosive political reform in Africa, the international political arena has evolved in significant ways (Young, 1999a:28). And, despite successful transitions to more politically liberalized and relatively democratic governments for many African states during the early 1990s, the second part of the decade was marked by a drop in international pressure on African states to democratize. As early as November 1991, French president François Mitterrand had already retreated from the strong support he had given to African democratization at the Franco-African Summit at La Baule, France, in June 1990 (Clark, 1997:3, 34). Benin, which led the move to democracy in Africa in 1989, actually saw a decline in French aid the year following its transition, while continuing authoritarian regimes in Togo, Cameroon, and Zaire all benefited from French aid increases during the same period (Clapham, 1996:241). Though largely sponsoring attempts to promote political liberalization in Africa, the United States was decidedly uneven in its attempts to promote democracy on the continent. At the same time as the United States expanded its Agency for International Development (USAID) to include democracy and governance officers, other US efforts toward political reform and democratization were at once limited and "contradictory." Pressures for democratization were not applied toward Egypt, where security and strategic concerns ranked high, or toward Algeria, where the cancellation of elections that would have put the Islamic Salvation Front in power drew no protests from the United States.

Furthermore, little pressure toward democratic reform was applied to such countries as Uganda and Ghana, which were getting high marks for economic liberalization from the United States through moves toward "freer markets" (Young, 1999b:28). Where they have commercial interests, Western industrial democracies appear less likely to push heavily (if at all) for political reform. As examples, Bratton and van de Walle (1997) point to the British and French giving in to questionable elections in Kenya and Cameroon, where incumbent regimes used state power to return Presidents Daniel arap Moi (Kenya) and Paul Biya (Cameroon) to power in 1997. Indeed, it seems clear that whatever their level of commitment to political liberalization and democratic rule in Africa, all Western governments have other interests and priorities on the continent. Of these, the most important are political stability and economic interests such as oil. (For the importance of oil in Nigeria to Western companies and governments, see Okonta and Douglas, 2003.) If they have to make a choice, the Western industrial democracies will apparently choose stability for an African state rather than democratic rule (Bratton and van de Walle, 1997:114, 241–242). (For a more detailed analysis of Africa's international relations, see Chapter 6.)

As Western democracies backed away from earlier positions, many African leaders were able to stay in power by allowing the emergence of "semi-democracies" or "virtual democracies" (Young, 1999b:35; Joseph, 1999:60–61). In less than a decade after Western democracies pushed African states to democratize or risk having aid cut off or reduced, many of these "liberalized autocracies" (Diamond, 2002) were seen as exhibiting satisfactory progress by the United States, Great Britain, France, and other Western states. In these systems, political parties were allowed to form but not compete for office (Uganda) or were restricted or intimidated in such a way as not to be a factor in elections (Zimbabwe); independent newspapers were published but were subjected to restrictions (Zambia); and while elections were held, results were apparently falsified, as in Cameroon, Togo, and Niger (Joseph, 1999:62).

In some African states, such as Sierra Leone, Liberia, and the DRC, politicians used far more drastic strategies and actions to stay in power. In these already administratively weak and economically destitute states, where to remain in power required using resources to retain important allies, the political leader simply shut down "costly" government agencies (such as health and education) and, using valuable resources such as diamonds, financed private armies to control either all or parts of the country. In areas where government control was either weak or nonexistent, other political leaders with armies financed through similar means often took control. Known as "shadow" states controlled by "warlords," they along with Somalia were essentially collapsed states, neither interested in nor accountable to those living under their control (see Reno, 1998; Clapham, 1996:249–252; and Zartman, 1995).

Prospects for Democracy in Africa

It was within this context of economic decline, weakened capacity (for states to foster or sustain development), decreased political importance in the global community, and political instability that domestic politics in African countries took place at the dawn of the new millennium. Efforts by African citizens to achieve further liberalization and democratization in many states had been stalled by powerful elites, while in other states, previously gained liberties were lost. At the beginning of the new century, only about 40 percent of sub-Saharan countries had become "relatively democratic," a percentage virtually unchanged from 1994. Yet, as I will discuss later, despite these circumstances popular support for democracy is widespread across Africa, with Africans valuing democracy as an end in itself and as a means to improved governance and welfare (Bratton, Mattes, and Gyimah-Boadi, 2006:65–66). In this regard, at what point are African states now, over a decade after the "wave of political liberalization" that swept the continent in the early 1990s, and what are the prospects for democracy in Africa?

In Table 4.1, I categorize the political "location" of regimes in sub-Saharan Africa in 2006, using a typology based on data about political freedom and civil rights collected by Freedom House (2006). Originally developed by Larry Diamond (2002:2) and revised by Bratton, Mattes, and Gyimah-Boadi (2006:17), sub-Saharan African countries are divided into five categories along a continuum from "unreformed autocracies" (where governments make no pretense at legitimizing themselves through democratic elections) to "liberal democracies" (where governments came to power peacefully in free multiparty elections and subsequently held regular elections at intervals prescribed by national constitutions). In between are "electoral democracies" (which are constitutionally based civilian governments that meet minimal democratic standards by holding free and fair elections for the executive and legislative office, but where civil and political liberties are not universally secure) and "liberalized autocracies" where leaders from previously military and one-party–ruled states maintain power by manipulating the rules of the democratic game and "stage manage" elections to their own advantage.

It should be clear from the above typology that the trajectories of African countries diverge remarkably in their commitments to political rights and civil liberties. In 2006, five countries (Cape Verde, Mauritius, South Africa, São Tomé and Principe, and Botswana) can now be considered liberal democracies and another four (Ghana, Mali, Namibia, and Benin) appear to meet the qualifications for that category. Nine countries, while allowing democratic elections, still have substantial restrictions on the civil liberties and "human rights" of their citizens. But most, approximately 60 percent, while varying in the calculus of restrictions on political liberties and rights, are still nondemocratic states. And of these, five (the DRC, Swaziland, Eritrea, Somalia, and Sudan) are, simply put, unreformed autocracies.

Table 4.1 Political Regimes in Sub-Saharan Africa, 2006

Liberal Democracy	Electoral Democracy	Ambiguous	Liberalized Autocracy	Unreformed Autocracy
Consolidating democracies	Senegal (2,3)	Mozambique (3,4)	Burkina Faso (5,3)	Democratic Republic of Congo (6,6)
Cape Verde (1,1)	Lesotho (2,3)	Guinea-Bissau (3,4)	Central African Republic (5,4)	Swaziland (7,5)
Mauritius (1,1)	Madagascar (3,3)	Sierra Leone (4,3)	Gambia (5,4)	Eritrea (7,6)
South Africa (1,2)	Kenya (3,3)	Nigeria (4,4)	Uganda (5,4)	Somalia (6,7)
São Tomé and Principe (2,2)	Niger (3,3)	Zambia (4,4)	Republic of Congo (5,5)	Sudan (7,7)
Botswana (2,2)	Tanzania (4,3)	Djibouti (5,5)	Ethiopia (5,5)	
	Malawi (4,4)	Burundi (5,5)	Gabon (6,4)	
In transition	Liberia (4,4)		Mauritania (6,4)	
Ghana (1,2)			Togo (6,5)	
Mali (2,2)			Chad (6,5)	
Namibia (2,2)			Guinea (6,5)	
Benin (2,2)			Angola (6,5)	
			Côte d'Ivoire (6,6)	
			Cameroon (6,6)	
			Equitorial Guinea (7,6)	
			Zimbabwe (7,6)	

Source: Adapted from Larry Diamond, "Thinking About Hybrid Regimes," *Journal of Democracy* 13 (2) (2002): table 2; and from Michael Bratton, Robert Mattes, and E. Gyimah-Boadi, *Public Opinion, Democracy, and Market Reform in Africa* (Cambridge: Cambridge University Press, 2006): table 1.1.

Note: Figures in parentheses are Freedom House political rights and civil liberties scores for 2006 on a scale of 1 (high) to 7 (low).

Why have some African countries been able to implement and sustain democratic reforms and others not? While it is difficult to generalize, certain patterns appear to be associated with political reforms leading to political liberalization, democratic elections, and, at least for now, to relatively democratic governments in Africa. Two very important studies give us both information about and insight into how ordinary Africans view democracy and why the trajectories of political reform in Africa are decidedly different (see Bratton and van de Walle, 1997; Bratton, Mattes, and Gyimah-Boadi, 2006; and information from the Afrobarometer project at www.afrobarometer.org).

The context for political reform in Africa is directly influenced by those in power, the rulers, and by the ruled, ordinary Africans seeking a better life for themselves and their children. For most of sub-Saharan Africa, "the top stratum of political leaders remains wedded to a political economy in which wealth and power derive from personal control of the resources of the state and incumbent elites are pre-disposed to resist reforms in systems that have served them well in the past." This is a main reason that political reforms "have been tentative and incomplete, leaving Africa with hybrid regimes that awkwardly mix old and new principles of organization" (Bratton, Mattes, and Gyimah-Boadi, 2006:14). And at the bottom are the African people, subsistence and cash crop farmers, small businessmen and women, students, and others whose lives are marked by unemployment and poverty. "They address their daily needs by hoping and coping—piecing together eclectic livelihoods in an array of formal and informal economic activities" (Bratton, Mattes, and Gyimah-Boadi, 2006:346).

As I mentioned much earlier in this chapter, Africans, no matter their level of formal education, look at the world in which they live as rationally as people in other parts of the world. "They pass judgment on public affairs (and political regimes and leaders) based on their own circumstances and on how well they believe their country is doing." In other words, people in Africa arrive at opinions on the basis of "knowledge, reasoning, experience, and on their own self-interest" (Bratton, Mattes, and Gyimah-Boadi, 2006:222, 248). Under these circumstances, "where Africans believe that corrupt and weakened incumbent regimes cannot generate employment, deliver services, or protect their interests," it is not surprising that support for political reform and democracy is widespread (Bratton, Mattes, and Gyimah-Boadi, 2006:345).

While support for democracy (as a perceived mechanism to change the circumstances under which most Africans live) may be widespread, it is also shallow (Bratton, Mattes, and Gyimah-Boadi, 2006:65). Low levels of educational attainment and lack of awareness of public affairs leave most Africans with little knowledge of the procedures through which democratic regimes operate and the theoretical concepts on which democracy is based. So what strengthens support for democracy among ordinary Africans and what factors work to create diverging paths to political reform across sub-Saharan Africa?

As pointed out by Bratton and van de Walle (1997) and Bratton, Mattes, and Gyimah-Boadi (2006), "political legacies matter." "Past episodes of multi-party rule, however brief, are extremely helpful." Successful transitions (from authoritarian regimes) toward democratization were found to be highly influenced by the degree of freedom allowed by the preceding authoritarian regime. Those authoritarian regimes that allowed relatively more political freedom (participation and competition) were more likely to have more frequent political protests that would lead to regime transitions in the early 1990s. Furthermore, these transitions were more likely to lead to political liberalization than in countries whose regimes were more autocratic. Finally, higher levels of participation (even if just to vote for handpicked government candidates) and competition (as measured by the amount of opposition tolerated by the authoritarian regime) were associated with higher levels of democratization after the fall of the authoritarian government (Bratton and van de Walle, 1997). It is interesting to note that countries that sustain multiparty rule after independence or reinstalled multiparty rule after an authoritarian episode are three times more likely to consolidate democracy as countries that emerged from settler colonial states (The Afrobarometer Project, 2005, www.afrobarometer.org).

We know, too, that education has an impact on support for democracy in Africa. "Education induces support for democracy and it does so at the expense of attachments to nondemocratic alternatives. As individuals gain formal education, they disengage from loyalties to old political regimes" (Bratton, Mattes, and Gyimah-Boadi, 2006:205). The combination of more formal education and the informal education of experience with democratic procedures buttresses support for democracy among Africans and helps explain the diverging paths of political reform among African countries.

Despite successful transitions to relatively democratic governments for many African states since the great wave of democratic reform between 1990 and 1994 and the move by as many as nine into the category of "liberal democracies," in 2006 most African states were nondemocratic. The quick and dramatic political changes that marked the beginning of the 1990s have slowed or stopped. Moves toward further political liberalization have ended for many African countries, and for most, real "consolidated" democracies appear unlikely. Furthermore, in a variety of countries, leaders determined to stay in power have been able to reverse democratic gains made earlier. It was within this context that a frustrated but hopeful President Thabo Mbeki issued his call for Africans to recapture the twenty-first century from those whose personal greed would block an "African Renaissance."

Yet, notwithstanding the apparent end of movement toward political reform in many countries (or even erosion in some), for many Africans remarkable political changes have taken place since 1989. While obstacles to democratization abound, there have been fundamental reforms made in the structures of politics at all levels in most African states. Across the continent, virtually all countries have undergone political liberalization, and with rare exceptions the single-party state has disappeared. While most Africans could only read state-owned newspapers a decade ago, most countries now have a variety of independent newspapers available to citizens. The number of independent radio stations has increased across much of the continent, and computer usage, though in its infancy, is increasing (see Chapter 13). Since independence, and especially over the past decade, literacy rates have risen across Africa. It is clear, however, that the main social impact of liberalization in Africa has been in the large number of associations and groups that have formed in virtually all countries across the continent. The rapid proliferation of groups (civil society) in response to political openings may be the most noteworthy legacy of the early 1990s (Young, 1999b:35). In fact, in the twelve countries studied by the Afrobarometer project, almost seventy-five percent of those interviewed claimed membership or activity in a voluntary association of some kind (Bratton, Mattes, and Gyimah-Boadi, 2006:251).

To set in motion the processes of political liberalization and democratization in Africa did not require a particular level of economic achievement or class structure. Per capita incomes in most African states are among the lowest in the world, and the number of Africans with personal incomes and education levels high enough to be categorized as middle or upper class is very small. But, once democracies are established, economic constraints substantially shape the prospects for consolidation (sustaining the democracy). The chances of a democracy surviving are greater the better off the country is economically (Young, 1999b:34; Przeworski et al., 2000:78–139). As William Reno says, "the current wealth of a country is not entirely decisive. . . . If they succeed in generating development, democracies may survive in even the poorest countries" (Young, 1999b:34). And both education and a balance of power between political groups may help them survive independently of income (Przeworski et al., 2000:137).

It is important to remember that political liberalization in Africa is little more than a decade old. While the new democracies on the continent are both very young and unconsolidated, they are not necessarily doomed to failure by poverty and backwardness. They need "time to work with and become habituated to democratic institutions, to shape them to fit particular cultural and political circumstances, and to allow them to sink deep roots of commitment among all the major players and the public at large" (Diamond, 1999:xxv–xxvi). (See also Widner, 2005.) Democratic or not, however, no African state will long survive without a measurable and sustainable improvement in economic development for its long-suffering people.

Bibliography

"A Chance for Africa." 1991. *Africa News* 34 (May 20):2.

"A General Emerges from Hiding." 2005. *The Economist* (August 27):40.

Adediji, Adebayo. 1995. "An Alternative for Africa." Pp. 126–139 in Larry Diamond and Marc F. Plattner (eds.). *Economic Reform and Democracy.* Baltimore: Johns Hopkins University Press.

African Demos. 1991. Vols. 1, 2, and 4 (January, March, and May).

Ake, Claude. 1981. *A Political Economy of Africa.* Burnt Mill, Harlow (Essex), England: Longman.

Amin, Samir. 1972. "Underdevelopment and Dependence in Black Africa: Origins and Contemporary Forms." *Journal of Modern African Studies* 4:503–521.

Ball, Nicole. 1981. "The Military in Politics: Who Benefits and How." *World Development* 9 (6):569–582.

Bates, Robert. 1981. Markets and States in Tropical Africa. Los Angeles: University of California Press.

Bendix, Reinhard. 1962. *Max Weber: An Intellectual Portrait.* Garden City, NY: Doubleday.

Bohannan, Paul, and Philip Curtin. 1995. *Africa and Africans.* Prospect Heights, IL: Waveland Press.

Boone, Catherine. 1990a. "The Making of a Rentier Class: Wealth Accumulation and Political Control in Senegal." *Journal of Development Studies* 26:425–449.

———. 1990b. "States and Ruling Classes in Post-Colonial Africa: The Enduring Contradictions of Power." Paper presented at the thirty-third annual meeting of the African Studies Association, Baltimore, November 1–4.

———. 2003. *Political Topographies of the African State: Territorial Authority and Institutional Choice.* Cambridge: Cambridge University Press.

Bratton, Michael. 1989a. "Beyond Autocracy: Civil Society in Africa." Pp. 29–33 in *Beyond Autocracy in Africa.* Atlanta: The Carter Center of Emory University.

———. 1989b. "Beyond the State: Civil Society and Associational Life in Africa." *World Politics* 41:407–430.

———. 1999. "Second Elections in Africa." Pp. 18–33 in Larry Diamond and Marc F. Plattner (eds.). *Democratization in Africa.* Baltimore: Johns Hopkins University Press.

Bratton, Michael, Robert Mattes, and E. Gyimah-Boadi. 2006. *Public Opinion, Democracy, and Market Reform in Africa.* Cambridge: Cambridge University Press.

Bratton, Michael, and Nicolas van de Walle. 1992. "Towards Governance in Africa: Popular Demands and State Responses." Pp. 27–55 in Goran Hyden and Michael Bratton (eds.). *Governance and Politics in Africa.* Boulder, CO: Lynne Rienner Publishers.

———. 1997. *Democratic Experiences in Africa.* Cambridge: Cambridge University Press.

Callaghy, Thomas M. 1984. *The State-Society Struggle: Zaire in Comparative Perspective.* New York: Columbia University Press.

———. 2000. "Africa and the World Economy: Caught Between a Rock and a Hard Place." Pp. 43–82 in John W. Harbeson and Donald Rothchild (eds.). *Africa in World Politics: The African State System in Flux.* Boulder, CO: Westview.

Chabal, Patrick, and Jean-Pascal Daloz. 1999. *Africa Works: Disorder as Political Instrument.* Oxford: James Curry.

Chakoadza, Austin M. 1993. *Structural Adjustment in Zambia and Zimbabwe: Reconstruction or Destruction?* Harare, Zimbabwe: Third World Publishing House.

Chazan, Naomi, Peter Lewis, Robert A. Mortimer, Donald Rothchild, and Stephen John Stedman. 1999. *Politics and Society in Contemporary Africa.* Boulder, CO: Lynne Rienner Publishers.

Chazan, Naomi, Robert Mortimer, John Ravenhill, and Donald Rothchild. 1988. *Politics and Society in Contemporary Africa.* Boulder, CO: Lynne Rienner Publishers.

Clapham, Christopher. 1996. *Africa and the International System.* Cambridge: Cambridge University Press.

Clark, John F. 1997. "The Challenge of Political Reform in Sub-Saharan Africa." Pp. 23–39 in John F. Clark and David Gardinier (eds.). *Political Reform in Francophone Africa.* Boulder, CO: Westview Press.

———. 2002. *The African Stakes of the Congo War.* New York: Palgrave MacMillan.

Cox, Thomas S. 1976. *Civil-Military Relations in Sierra Leone: A Case Study of African Soldiers in Politics.* Cambridge: Harvard University Press.

Decalo, Samuel. 1976. *Coups and Army Rule in Africa: Studies in Military Style.* New Haven: Yale University Press.

———. 1989. "Modalities of Civil-Military Stability in Africa." *Journal of Modern African Studies* 27:547–578.

Diamond, Larry. 1988. "Nigeria: Pluralism, Statism, and the Struggle for Democracy." Pp. 33–91 in Larry Diamond, Juan J. Linz, and Seymour Martin Lipset (eds.). *Democracy in Developing Countries: Africa.* Boulder, CO: Lynne Rienner Publishers.

———. 1995. "Nigeria: The Uncivic Society and the Descent into Praetorianism." Pp. 417–491 in Larry Diamond, Juan J. Linz, and Seymour Martin Lipset (eds.). *Politics in Developing Countries: Comparing Experiences with Democracy.* Boulder, CO: Lynne Rienner Publishers.

———. 1999. "Introduction." Pp. ix–xxvii in Larry Diamond and Marc F. Plattner (eds.). *Democratization in Africa.* Baltimore: Johns Hopkins University Press.

———. 2002. "Thinking About Hybrid Regimes." *Journal of Democracy* 13 (2): 22.

Doro, Marion E. 1995. "The Democratization Process in Africa." *Choice* (October):245–257.

Eisenstadt, Stuart N., and René Lemarchand. 1981. *Political Clientelism, Patronage and Development.* Beverly Hills, CA: Sage Publications.

Englebert, Pierre. *State Legitimacy in Africa.* 2000. Boulder, CO: Lynne Rienner Publishers.

Fatton, Robert, Jr. 1986. "Clientelism and Patronage in Senegal." *African Studies Review* 29:61–78.

———. 1992. *Predatory Rule: State and Civil Society in Africa.* Boulder, CO: Lynne Rienner Publishers.

Freedom House. 2006. *Freedom in the World 2006.* Online at www.freedomhouse.org.

Freund, Bill. 1984. *The Making of Contemporary Africa: The Development of African Society Since 1800.* Bloomington: Indiana University Press.

Gordon, April. 2003. *Nigeria's Diverse Peoples: A Reference Sourcebook.* Santa Barbara: ABC-CLIO.

Government of Cameroon. Central Bureau of the Census. 1977. *Main Results of the April 1976 General Population and Housing Census.* Yaounde: Ministry of Economic Affairs and Planning.

Harbeson, John W., Donald Rothchild, and Naomi Chazan (eds.). 1994. *Civil Society and the State.* Boulder, CO: Lynne Rienner Publishers.

Hayward, Fred M. 1987. "Introduction." Pp. 1–23 in Fred M. Hayward (ed.). *Elections in Independent Africa.* Boulder, CO: Westview Press.

Henry, Neil. 1991. "Will Freedom Finally Follow Independence?" *The Washington Post National Weekly Edition* (June 3–9):18.

Hodder-Williams, Richard. 1984. *An Introduction to the Politics of Tropical Africa.* London: George Allen and Unwin.

Hodgkin, Thomas. 1957. *Nationalism in Colonial Africa.* New York: New York University Press.

Horowitz, Donald L. 1985. *Ethnic Groups in Conflict.* Berkeley: University of California Press.

Hull, Richard. 1991. "The Challenge to the United States in Africa." *Current History* 90:193–234.

Hyden, Goran. 1983. *No Shortcuts to Progress.* Berkeley: University of California Press.

———. 1989. "Community Governance and 'High' Politics." Pp. 2–7 in *Beyond Autocracy in Africa.* Atlanta: The Carter Center of Emory University.

———. 2006. *African Politics in Comparative Perspective.* Cambridge: Cambridge University Press.

Jackson, Robert H., and Carl J. Rosberg. 1982. *Personal Rule in Black Africa.* Berkeley: University of California Press.

Jeffries, Richard. 1989. "Ghana: The Political Economy of Personal Rule." Pp. 75–98 in Donald B. Cruise O'Brien, John Dunn, and Richard Rathbone (eds.). *Contemporary West African States.* Cambridge: Cambridge University Press.

Joseph, Richard A. 1977. *Radical Nationalism in Cameroon: Social Origins of the UPC Rebellion.* Oxford: Oxford University Press.

———. 1999. "The Reconfiguration of Power in Late Twentieth Century Africa." Pp. 57–80 in Richard Joseph (ed.). *State, Conflict, and Democracy in Africa.* Boulder, CO: Lynne Rienner Publishers.

Kasfir, Nelson. 1983. "Designs and Dilemmas: An Overview." Pp. 25–47 in Phillip Mawhood (ed.). *Local Government in the Third World: The Experience of Tropical Africa.* Chichester, England: John Wiley and Sons.

———. 1987. "Class, Political Domination, and the African State." Pp. 35–61 in Zaki Ergas (ed.). *The African State in Transition.* New York: St. Martin's Press.

———. 2005. "Sudan's Darfur: Is It Genocide?" *Current History* (May):195–208.

Khadiagala, Gilbert M. 2000. "Europe in Africa's Renewal: Beyond Post-Colonialism." Pp. 83–109 in John H. Harbeson and Donald Rothchild (eds.). *Africa in World Politics: The African State System in Flux.* Boulder, CO: Westview Press.

Kraus, John. 1991. "Building Democracy in Africa." *Current History* 90:209–212.
Lancaster, Carol. 2005. "Development in Africa: The Good, the Bad, and the Ugly." *Current History* (May):222–227.
Lemarchand, René. 1988. "The State, the Parallel Economy and the Changing Structure of Patronage Systems." Pp. 149–170 in Donald Rothchild and Naomi Chazan (eds.). *The Precarious Balance: State and Society in Africa.* Boulder, CO: Westview Press.
le Pere, Garth, and Anthoni van Nieuwkerk. 1999. "Making Foreign Policy in South Africa." P. 205 in Philip Nel and Patrick J. McGowan (eds.). *Power, Wealth, and the Global Order.* Cape Town: University of Cape Town Press.
Leslie, Winsome J. 1993. *Continuity and Change in an Oppressive State.* Boulder, CO: Westview.
Liebenow, Gus J. 1986. *African Politics: Crisis and Challenges.* Bloomington: Indiana University Press.
Lofchie, Michael F. 1989. "Reflections on Structural Adjustment in Africa." Pp. 121–125 in *Beyond Autocracy in Africa.* Atlanta: The Carter Center of Emory University.
"Lord's Resistance Army." 2006. Online at www.globalsecurity.org.
Luckham, Robin. 1994. "The Military, Militarization and Democratization in Africa." *African Studies Review* 37:13–75.
MacGaffey, Janet. 1988. "Economic Disengagement and Class Formation in Zaire." Pp. 171–188 in Donald Rothchild and Naomi Chazan (eds.). *The Precarious Balance: State and Society in Africa.* Boulder, CO: Westview Press.
McGowan, Pat, and Thomas H. Johnson. 1984. "African Military Coups d'Etat and Underdevelopment: A Quantitative Historical Analysis." *Journal of Modern African Studies* 22:633–666.
Meroe, Isaac J. 1980. *The Performance of Soldiers as Governors.* Washington, DC: University Press of America.
Morna, Colleen Lowe. 1990. "Africa's Campuses Lead Pro-Democracy Drive." *The Chronicle of Higher Education* (November 28):A1, 40.
———. 1991. "Cutting Back on Campus." *Africa Report* 36 (March-April):61–63.
Nafziger, Wayne F. 1988. *Inequality in Africa.* Cambridge: Cambridge University Press.
Neavoll, George. 1991. "A Victory for Democracy." *Africa Report* 36 (May-June): 39–40, 42.
Okonta, Ike. 2005. "Nigeria: Chronicle of a Dying State." *Current History* (May):203–208.
Okonta, Ike, and Oronto Douglas. 2003. *Where Vultures Feast: Shell, Human Rights, and Oil.* London: Verso.
Olukoshi, Adebayo (ed.). 1993. *The Politics of Structural Adjustment in Nigeria.* Portsmouth, NH: Heinemann.
Onimode, Bade (ed.). 1989. *The IMF, the World Bank and the African Debt: The Social and Political Impact.* Vol. 2. London: Zed.
Ponte, Stefano. 1994. "The World Bank and Adjustment in Africa." *Review of African Political Economy* 22, no. 66 (December):539–558.
Posner, Daniel. 2005. *Institutions and Ethnic Politics in Africa.* Cambridge: Cambridge University Press.
Press, Robert M. 1991. "Africa's Struggle for Democracy." *The Christian Science Monitor* (March 21):4.
Przeworski, Adam, Michael Alvarez, José Antonio Cheibub, and Fernando

Limongi. 2000. *Democracy and Development.* Cambridge: Cambridge University Press.

Przeworski, Adam, and Fernando Limongi. 1997. "Development and Democracy." Pp. 155–183 in A. Hadenious (ed.). *Democracy's Victory and Crisis.* Cambridge: Cambridge University Press.

Rapley, John. 2002. *Understanding Development: Theory and Practice in the Third World.* Boulder, CO: Lynne Rienner Publishers.

Reno, William. 1998. *Warlord Politics and African States.* Boulder, CO: Lynne Rienner Publishers.

Rothchild, Donald, and Naomi Chazan (eds.). 1988. *The Precarious Balance: State and Society in Africa.* Boulder, CO: Westview Press.

Rothchild, Joseph. 1981. *Ethnopolitics.* New York: Cambridge University Press.

Sandbrook, Richard. 1985. *The Politics of Africa's Economic Stagnation.* Cambridge: Cambridge University Press.

———. 1993. *The Politics of Africa's Economic Recovery.* Cambridge: Cambridge University Press.

Saul, John. 1975. "The Revolution in Portugal's African Colonies: A Review Essay." *Canadian Journal of African Studies* 9:321–340.

Shaw, Timothy M. 1990. "Popular Participation in Non-Government Structures in Africa: Implications for Democratic Development." Pp. 5–22 in *Africa Today.* Denver: Africa Today Associates.

Stiglitz, Joseph. 2002. *Globalization and Its Discontents.* New York: Norton.

Sullivan, Jo. 1989. *Global Studies: Africa.* Guilford, CT: Dushkin Publishing Group.

Tangri, Roger. 1985. *Politics in Sub-Saharan Africa.* London: James Currey and Heinemann Educational Books.

Tordoff, William. 1984. *Government and Politics in Africa.* Bloomington: Indiana University Press.

UN. 2005. *Millennium Goals Development Report.* Online at www.un.org/summit2005/MDGBook.

UNDP (United Nations Development Programme). 2004. *Human Development Report.* Online at www.undp.org.

van de Walle, Nicolas. 2001. *African Economies and the Politics of Permanent Crisis, 1979–1999.* Cambridge: Cambridge University Press.

Villalón, Leonardo A. 1998. "After the Wave: The Democratic Question and State Reconfiguration in the Francophone Sahel." Paper presented at the forty-first annual meeting of the African Studies Association, Chicago, October 29–November 1.

Whiteman, Kaye. 1991. "The Gallic Paradox." *Africa Report* 36 (January-February):17–20.

Widner, Jennifer. 2005. "Africa's Democratization: A Work in Progress." *Current History* (May):216–221.

Wolpe, Howard. 1974. *Urban Politics in Nigeria: A Study of Port Harcourt.* Berkeley: University of California Press.

World Bank. 1990a. *World Debt Tables, 1989–1990: Supplemental Report.* Washington, DC: World Bank.

———. 1990b. *World Development Report.* New York: Oxford University Press.

———. 2001. *World Development Report.* New York: Oxford University Press.

———. 2005. *World Development Report.* New York: Oxford University Press.

Wunsch, James S., and Dele Olowu. 1990. *The Failure of the Centralized State: Institutions and Self-Governance in Africa.* Boulder, CO: Westview Press.

Young, Crawford. 1988a. "The African State and Its Colonial Legacy." Pp. 25–66 in Donald Rothchild and Naomi Chazan (eds.). *The Precarious Balance: State and Society in Africa.* Boulder, CO: Westview Press.

———. 1988b. "Politics in Africa." Pp. 487–538 in Gabriel Almond and G. Bingham Powell, Jr. (eds.). *Comparative Politics Today: A World View.* Glenview, IL: Scott Foresman.

———. 1994. *The African Colonial State in Comparative Perspective.* New Haven: Yale University Press.

———. 1999a. "Africa: An Interim Balance Sheet." In Larry Diamond and Marc F. Plattner (eds.). *Democratization in Africa.* Baltimore: Johns Hopkins University Press.

———. 1999b. "The Third Wave of Democratization in Africa." Pp. 15–38 in Richard Joseph (ed.). *State, Conflict, and Democracy in Africa.* Boulder, CO: Lynne Rienner Publishers.

———. 2000. "The Heritage of Colonialism." Pp. 23–42 in John W. Harbeson and Donald Rothchild (eds.). *Africa in World Politics.* Boulder, CO: Westview Press.

Young, Crawford, and Thomas Turner. 1985. *The Rise and Decline of the Zairian State.* Madison: University of Wisconsin Press.

Zartman, I. William (ed.). 1995. *Collapsed States.* Boulder, CO: Lynne Rienner Publishers.

Zolberg, Aristide R. 1966. *Creating Political Order: The Party-States of West Africa.* Chicago: Rand McNally.

5

The Economies of Africa

Virginia DeLancey

Precolonial Economies

The earliest economies in sub-Saharan Africa were based on hunting, fishing, and gathering food. Economic activity varied, however, depending upon geographic location. In some regions of the continent, populations moved continually to search for food as the seasons changed. In regions where conditions were favorable year-round, populations were relatively sedentary (Clark, 1962:211–214). (See Chapter 2 for more on the relationship between Africa's geography and economic activities.)

Hunting and gathering societies persist today, such as the San of the Kalahari Desert in southern Africa and the Mbuti and the M'Baka of equatorial Africa. Pastoral societies are even more prevalent, particularly in the Sahel (areas bordering the Sahara Desert) and the savanna lands (grasslands) throughout the continent. The Fulani (Fulbe) of West Africa and the Maasai, the Somali, and the Turkana of East Africa are examples of pastoral peoples. Nevertheless, over time, populations became increasingly sedentary. As livestock and crops, especially cereals such as millet and sorghum, became domesticated, populations began to permanently occupy lands that previously could support only temporary settlements. Their economies became based upon agriculture or on agro-pastoralism (Wickins, 1986:33–36).[1]

Although societies became more sedentary over time, they did not necessarily become more isolated. On the contrary, the change to crop cultivation and/or livestock management meant that it was no longer necessary to search constantly for food. It provided both the opportunity to produce surplus food and the possibility to specialize in the production of food or other commodities for exchange in the market. It also allowed time to develop commercial networks. As a result, although many economies were basically self-sufficient—producing all necessary food, clothing, household objects, and farm equipment—many economies also included trade.

Markets developed for the exchange of food crops and livestock as well as for household and farm equipment within local economies and among neighboring communities. Trade developed over very great distances as well. Gold from western Africa was traded internationally beginning as early as the eighth century (Fage, 1959:15, 47; Herskovits and Harwitz, 1964:299–300). Spices and tropical products were traded between eastern Africa and the Middle East. During the Middle Ages, gold, salt, and slaves, as well as many other products, continued to be traded along the trans-Saharan caravan routes that connected sub-Saharan Africa, especially western Africa, with northern Africa (Neumark, 1977:127–130). Clearly, African economies were interdependent and based on long-distance trade long before contact with the Europeans (Davidson, 1972:84). It was not until the 1400s, when Europeans began to explore the coasts of Africa, that African economies began to have major interaction with the economies of Europe.

Precolonial contacts with the international economy beyond the continental borders developed in eastern Africa as a result of trade along the perimeter of the Indian Ocean with the Middle East and Asia. Some of the earliest references to this trade occurred about A.D. 150. Because of the use of sea transport rather than camels, the products traded were less restricted to luxuries, although ivory was the most important commodity until the end of the nineteenth century. Other African commodities that entered the trade were slaves,[2] mangrove tree poles for house construction, iron, and gold (Austen, 1987:59).

Beginning about 1500, first the Portuguese and then the Omani attempted to control the Indian Ocean trade along the coast of eastern Africa, although other countries continued to trade as well (Austen, 1987:60–62).

In the nineteenth century, the British succeeded in gaining political dominance over the coast of eastern Africa. They attempted to destroy the slave trade but were not successful immediately. However, ivory, resins, cloves, and other "legitimate" products were also exported from as far south on the continent as Mozambique through Zanzibar in exchange for manufactured goods from Britain, France, and the United States. During this time, there was considerable expansion of trade far into the interior of the continent in commodities such as foodstuffs, iron (and iron implements), copper, salt, and other export goods such as cloves, cowries, gum copal, copra, and cereals (Austen, 1987:60–63).

In western Africa, the Portuguese voyages of exploration, beginning in the fifteenth century, brought the coastal societies into contact with the international economy. Over time, economic relations increased from Senegal to Angola, although Europeans seldom settled on this part of the continent because of the harsh climate and the associated health risks. Instead, European traders, who relied on African intermediaries to reach the hinterland, established permanent trading posts, called "factories," on shipboard (Austen, 1987:81–84).

Although certain commodities such as ivory, timber, gum, and wax were staple exports from the African continent, there were other commodities that were especially important at different periods of time. The Portuguese, then later the Dutch, British, and the Danish, came to search for gold. The trade in gold reached its peak in the sixteenth and seventeenth centuries and then declined, either because of the inability to mine additional gold with the technology of that era or because of the increase in demand for slaves.

The demand for slaves arose with the development of European-owned sugar plantations. After 1600, as the Dutch, British, and French opened plantations in the New World, the demand for slaves increased rapidly, reaching its peak in the 1800s. Between 1810 and 1870, the slave trade was declared illegal for Europeans and North Americans, although it continued for many more years.

The most immediate economic impact of the slave trade was the loss of an enormous source of productive human labor and the resultant redistribution of the population of the continent. The civil disruption associated with slaving also had economic effects. Many of those who were not captured died during the raids or went into hiding to escape being caught. Agricultural production must have decreased, in part because of the difficulty of farming during the raids. In addition, the strongest young men and women were forced to leave their farms or disappeared on their own initiative until danger subsided. Health was also affected as a result of new diseases such as cholera and smallpox, which were introduced by the movement of peoples through the continent. Susceptibility to disease also increased, resulting from the poor diets and reduced food consumption that occurred with the disruption of agriculture. This surely lowered productivity for physical reasons as well as for psychological reasons.

"Legitimate" trade of vegetable oils such as palm oil, palm kernels, and peanuts began to increase from the beginning of the nineteenth century, while trade of wild rubber developed later in the century. The Industrial Revolution continuing in Europe during the nineteenth century provided the opportunity for shifting from the illegal trade in slaves to trade in the raw materials that were needed for European industry (Austen, 1987:85–87).

The Influence of Colonialism

The partition of Africa among the European powers in the late 1800s had both economic and political origins. Although imperialism may have spread to protect strategic transport routes and to demonstrate national power and prestige, perhaps its most immediate purpose was to protect economic interests that had been developing over the past several centuries. The Berlin Conference of 1884–1885 marked the beginning of this new era of economic as well as political relationships between Europe and Africa.

The economic impact of colonialism was significant and varied. It affected production, distribution, and consumption on the continent. As the Industrial Revolution spread throughout Europe, increased quantities of raw materials were required for the growth of production in the recently established factories. The trade in primary commodities that had begun earlier in the century expanded to include other commodities as a result of successful experimentation with crops introduced from other parts of the world. Among these were cotton and other fibers introduced for export to the new European textile mills. Coffee, tea, and cacao were introduced for the production of beverages and sweets for wealthy Europeans. Cultivation of these export crops brought many African farmers into the cash economy either as smallholders or as wage employees on plantations.

Following the European assumption that only men were farmers, production of these crops was introduced mainly to men, even though African women have always been important farmers. As a result, African men became the most important export crop producers, while women continued to produce food crops to sustain their families. However, when women were able to produce a surplus of food crops, they often sold them in local markets to earn extra cash. This pattern has persisted until today and has continued to affect the gender-based division of labor in African agriculture, as April Gordon discusses in Chapter 10.

Where climate and other conditions were favorable, some Europeans migrated to Africa. They established their own farms or plantations, settling some of the best, most fertile land, particularly in eastern, central, and southern Africa. This has had both economic and political repercussions with South Africa representing the extreme.

The European factories craved not only agricultural crops but also minerals. Copper, diamond, and gold mines, as well as mines for cobalt, manganese, and other minerals, were established, mainly in central and southern Africa. The demand for labor in these mines led to distinct patterns of migration to supply that labor.

Young men left home and even migrated across borders to work in the mines of the Rhodesias and South Africa. Many young men also migrated from the poor, landlocked hinterland to work for wages on the coastal plantations in western Africa. They went either permanently or for long periods of time alternating with short visits home. This changed the role of the wives and families who were often left behind. The women attempted to farm without the assistance of their men, often taking over the agricultural tasks formerly done by men. Sometimes they received seasonal assistance from the men when they were able to take leave from their wage employment to return home to help with the heaviest work of preparing the land for the next farming season or harvesting the crops.

Where migration did not occur naturally, the movement of people was sometimes "assisted." Forced labor was not uncommon; it was often demanded by colonial governments to build roads and railroads or to work on the plantations.

The increased production of export commodities not only caused population movement but also affected the infrastructure of the continent. It led to the development of new distribution systems. Roads and railroads were built to evacuate the commodities from the hinterland to the coast for export to Europe. However, they did not connect and integrate countries on the continent. This too is a pattern that persists today and has been a constraint upon the ability of countries to implement regional economic integration. (See Map 2.3.)

Colonialism affected consumption as well. The new industries of Europe sought not only sources of raw materials from their colonies but also markets for the products they produced. Colonies provided "captive consumers"; the special trade preferences that were often set up between the colonial powers and their colonies remain strong today. As African workers entered the money economy, they began to desire imported consumer goods that were not produced domestically or luxuries such as bicycles and radios. Increasing numbers of Africans entered the money economy during the colonial years either as cash crop farmers or as wage earners. They worked to earn income not only to purchase goods but also to pay required taxes. Because colonial administrations were responsible for financing much of their budget in each country, they had to find sources of revenue. As a result, various forms of taxation were instituted, including taxation of individuals as well as taxation of export production and imports.

In sum, colonialism did not originate to assist African countries to develop economically. It originated to benefit European countries. That is not to say that African countries did not receive any benefits, but the growth or development that occurred in those countries was mainly peripheral to the growth and development of Europe. Only as it became clear that the colonies would soon seek independence did European countries begin to guide some of their colonies toward the goal of developing their own economies. In doing so, they began to establish a few domestic industries (usually fledgling import-substitution industries for simple-to-produce goods such as matches, plastic shoes, beer and soft drinks, and textiles) in addition to continuing production of primary commodities for export. These efforts were minimal, however, and did little to make African economies self-sufficient. By the 1960s, the colonial administrations were being dismantled rapidly across the continent—but many economic ties to the former colonial powers remained.

Postcolonial Development Strategies

In the years following World War II, European countries realized that soon they would have to grant their colonies independence and began to take definite steps toward the conclusion of their political rule. Britain and France especially began to draw up long-term development plans for their colonies. Following independence in the 1960s, nearly every sub-Saharan African country continued to prepare (with mixed success) medium- to long-term economic development plans, usually covering time spans of three to five years.

In the early days of independence, Africans were optimistic that the plans would succeed in achieving the objective of promoting rapid economic growth as well as economic development within a few years. Alas, as the First Development Decade ended at the close of the 1960s, it was clear that the objective was not much closer to being achieved than at the beginning of the decade. This was especially difficult to accept, as it had been widely believed at the time of independence that as soon as the colonial powers left the continent and countries were able to take charge of their own economies, they would prosper. It was difficult to deal with rising aspirations that were not being satisfied.

There were several reasons why initial development efforts failed to bring about the desired results. Recent experience in rebuilding Europe after World War II showed the success of the Marshall Plan in channeling large quantities of foreign aid to the European countries, but Europe had already been developed prior to its destruction. The infrastructure and capital had already existed. There was an educated, skilled labor force and experienced management. Foreign aid was used simply to rebuild and replace what had already existed. In Africa the situation was different. The physical infrastructure during colonial days was minimal and was designed mainly to produce and export primary commodities to Europe and to support the colonial administration. Thus, new road systems had to be built as well as water, electric, and telephone networks. Furthermore, appropriate educational systems had to be designed and human resources trained. Not only was the literacy level low, but the educational system that existed then, and that exists in many countries even today, was not relevant to the needs of society. In addition, few Africans had been trained in management or public administration, and few had much experience in the practical aspects of running a government or operating a large-scale business or industry.

At independence, most countries were still agrarian. However, it was widely believed at that time that industrialization was the best strategy to achieve development. As a result, the agricultural sector was ignored in many development plans and emphasis was placed upon building industries. Most of the initial attempts were aimed at setting up import-substitution industries to produce previously imported goods. It was believed that this would be beneficial because it would save foreign exchange. It was forgotten, however, that if these industries took the place of industries that could produce for export, the countries would lose the opportunity to earn foreign exchange, which was required to import necessary capital (e.g., technology) for development. In addition, import-substitution industries do not always save foreign exchange as planned, because they often must import the required production equipment, spare parts, and sometimes even the raw materials to go into the production process. Consequently, the emphasis on industrialization did not necessarily improve the economies of Africa.

The drive to industrialize, in fact, hurt the economies of many countries, particularly the agricultural sectors. It stimulated rural-urban migration, yet there were insufficient jobs in the cities to absorb those who had left the countryside. And, as will be discussed in greater detail below, the net emigration rate from the rural areas was one of the causes of the decrease in food production that has led to the continent-wide food crisis.

During the Second (1970s) and Third (1980s) Development Decades, African countries began to recognize that there were problems in the agricultural sector, but few of them invested heavily in that sector. During those decades, many African countries also recognized that political independence was a necessary, but not a sufficient, condition for taking control of their destiny. They realized that it was necessary to have economic independence but that they had not been able to achieve it.

Latin American economists had been the first to develop the theory of economic "dependency," but African countries soon discovered that it was applicable to them as well. For example, they were still tied to their former colonial powers through preferential trade agreements and bilateral aid. That is, their exports continued to be primary commodities, and trade (both exports and imports) was still directed toward the former colonizers. In addition, many countries had monocrop economies, where they depended primarily on one commodity for their export earnings; this continues even today. For example, in 2002–2003, Mali received 73 percent of the value of its exports from cotton, Malawi received 55 percent from tobacco, Rwanda received 53 percent from coffee and tea, and Mauritania received 50 percent from fish. Other countries gained most of their foreign earnings from a single mineral export. Algeria, Equatorial Guinea, Libya, and Nigeria, for example, received more than 90 percent of their export earnings from crude petroleum, gas, and petroleum products. Mozambique received 54 percent of export earnings from aluminum, Zambia received 52 percent from copper, and Niger received 50 percent from uranium (UNCTAD, 2005:160–179).

Such undiversified economies left many African countries at the mercy of not only their former colonial masters but also the whims of the international market. When the international price of their main export product dropped, the revenues for their development plan suffered. In addition, over time the international "terms of trade" for their exports deteriorated. That is, many African countries found that they had to export more and more of their primary commodities simply to earn enough foreign exchange to purchase the same quantity of manufactured goods as in the past.

Not only did these former colonies remain dependent upon their former colonizers, but they also became dependent upon the wealthy, developed nations in general. Because of the unequal and exploitative power relationships in the international capitalist system that dominates the world, according to dependency theory or center-periphery models of development, the wealthy, developed countries (the "center") prevent the poor countries (the "periphery") from developing. Instead, the gap between the rich and poor countries remains or even widens as most of the benefits of trade go to the already developed countries.

Moreover, within the peripheral countries, the members of certain elite groups, especially government officials, military leaders, and certain entrepreneurs, cooperate with the institutions of the powerful center, such as multinational corporations and bilateral and multilateral foreign aid donors. In doing so, the elite promote their own interests, especially financial interests, but they also help to maintain themselves and their country in a dependent relationship with those powerful international institutions.

As the 1980s began and African countries entered the Third Development Decade without much progress toward achieving their goals, considerable controversy arose as to the direction that renewed development efforts should take. Determined to take the initiative for their continent's development and to have some input into the development strategy for the next UN Development Decade, the Assembly of Heads of State and Government of the Organization of African Unity (OAU) adopted the Monrovia Declaration in 1979. The strategy emphasized self-reliant development.

In April 1980, the UN Economic Commission for Africa (UNECA) and the OAU adopted the Lagos Plan of Action (LPA). It identified actions that needed to be taken to implement the objectives of the Monrovia

Declaration. More specifically, the LPA set food self-sufficiency as its primary goal. It also urged self-reliance in industry, transport and communications, human and natural resources, and science and technology. The Final Act of Lagos (FAL) pressed for subregional economic integration with the goal of establishing an African Economic Community by the end of the century.

In the fall of 1979, while the LPA was being finalized, the African finance ministers, in their capacity as the African governors of the World Bank, sent a memorandum to the president of the World Bank. They requested that a special report be written on the economic problems of sub-Saharan African countries—a report that would include suggestions for solving those problems. The result was the preparation of *Accelerated Development in Sub-Saharan Africa: An Agenda for Action* (World Bank, 1981), more commonly known as the Berg Report (after Elliot Berg, the coordinator of the group that wrote the report).

The Berg Report stated that it accepted the long-term objectives of African development as expressed in the Lagos Plan of Action (based on the Monrovia Declaration); however, it foresaw the need for alternative short- and medium-term action to respond to Africa's economic difficulties. One of its most important recommendations urged that aid in real terms be doubled in order to stimulate a renewal of economic growth.

The central theme of the Berg Report stressed that more efficient use of scarce resources—human and capital, managerial and technical, domes-

April Gordon

Farmers bring tobacco, a major cash crop, to market in Zimbabwe.

tic and foreign—was essential for improving economic conditions in most African countries. It pointed out that public sector organizations would have to build the infrastructure and provide education, health care, and other services. That would create enormous demand for capable administrators and managers, the scarcest resources in those countries; therefore, the report recommended that African governments seek ways to make public sector organizations more efficient and place greater reliance on the private sector to fulfill those needs.

The report also emphasized the interdependency of countries throughout the world and maintained that African countries should pursue their "comparative advantage" by striving to improve production of their export products. In effect, this meant that African countries should continue to export primary commodities like coffee and use their foreign exchange earnings to import essential manufactured goods and even their food requirements. This was unacceptable to African governments, and it initiated a heated debate. African governments believed that implementation of such a policy would most certainly leave their countries in a permanent state of dependency and poverty and prevent them from solving their ever-increasing problems of feeding their rapidly growing populations. Pursuing their comparative advantage in production and export of primary commodities would make them dependent upon the developed world for their food supplies as well as for capital goods (e.g., technology) and many manufactured consumer goods. Even worse, those capital and other manufactured goods were becoming increasingly expensive as long-term deterioration in the terms of trade between manufactured goods and primary commodities occurred. Even the cost of imported food requirements, such as wheat, was becoming increasingly expensive.

In response to criticism of the Berg Report by African governments, the World Bank issued several follow-up reports,[3] including *Sub-Saharan Africa: From Crisis to Sustainable Growth* (World Bank, 1989b:xi–xii). The latter affirmed:

1. Most African countries have embarked upon structural adjustment programs designed to transform their economies and make them more competitive.
2. To achieve food security, provide jobs, and improve living standards, African economies must achieve an annual growth rate of 4–5 percent.
3. For growth to be sustainable, major efforts must be made to protect the environment.
4. Economic growth must be based upon agriculture for at least the next decade.
5. Agriculture must expand twice as fast as at present in order to feed the rapidly growing population and decrease malnutrition.

6. The key to food security is to develop and apply new technology while slowing population growth rates.

An important theme of the report was that sound macroeconomic policies and an efficient infrastructure are necessary for the productive use of resources, but that they are not sufficient to transform the structure of African economies. Major efforts are needed to build African capacities; to produce a better-trained, healthier population; and to strengthen the institutional framework within which development can take place. The report supported the call made by the UNECA, the UN Development Programme (UNDP), and the UN International Children's Emergency Fund (UNICEF) for a human-centered development strategy.

The report also stressed that good governance is important, that there must be an efficient public service, a judicial system that is reliable, and an administration that is accountable to its public. There must be a better balance between the government and the governed. (Donald Gordon explains in Chapter 4 how African political systems have hindered economic development.) The report contained proposals to give ordinary people, and especially women, greater responsibility for improving their lives. This can be achieved best through grassroots organization that nurtures rather than obstructs informal sector enterprises and that promotes nongovernmental organizations (NGOs) and intermediary bodies. In other words, development must be more bottom-up and less top-down; it must include more participation, particularly in the planning stages, by those who will benefit from it.

The report encouraged joint action among all the partners in development—African governments and multilateral institutions, the private sector and the donors, official and nongovernmental organizations. It maintained that by working together, African governments would be able to achieve more rapid progress toward regional cooperation and integration, the central theme of the Lagos Plan of Action as well as the African Development Bank.

The earlier World Bank reports as well as this one called for increased aid. They noted, however, that aid must be accompanied by improved policies because, in the long run, dependency on aid must be reduced and eliminated. Moreover, ways must be found to mobilize resources, including measures to reduce African debt (World Bank, 1989b:xii).

Current Issues

Since the 1960s, when most sub-Saharan African countries gained political independence, the continent has experienced persistent economic problems. These economic problems, in turn, have affected the social aspects of development, that is, the health, education, and general quality of life.

Throughout the continent, economic growth[4] has occurred, but the rate of growth has varied by country. The existence of economic growth, even rapid economic growth, however, does not mean that economic development is also occurring. For example, economic growth may increase income inequality within countries if the wealthy control the resources and reap the benefits of increased production. Economic growth may also result in environmental degradation in the race to increase production. Neither of these consequences of economic growth can be considered economic development. Neither of these consequences improves the overall quality of life of the people in terms of reducing poverty, increasing the equality of income distribution, and decreasing unemployment, some of the most important goals of economic development. Yet, if economic growth is slow, it is more difficult to achieve the goals of development. This is particularly true if population growth is also rapid. It would be extremely difficult to achieve development if population growth is more rapid than economic growth, because this would cause the gross national product (GNP) per capita to actually decline. In fact, the worst scenario has occurred in sub-Saharan Africa; overall economic growth stagnated or became negative for several decades after independence, while the population growth rate increased and remained high during those same years. Although the rate of economic growth has now increased, it remains slower than other regions of the world, and although the rate of population growth has declined, it remains higher, on average, than all other regions of the world.

Economic growth in sub-Saharan Africa has also varied over time. From 1961 to 1972, per capita income increased. Those were optimistic years immediately after independence when there was a net positive inflow of foreign investment and assistance. From 1973 to 1982, economies stagnated, at least partly from the impact of adverse external factors. For example, in 1973 when the Organization of Petroleum Exporting Countries (OPEC) agreed to a dramatic increase in oil prices, it immediately affected the supply of foreign exchange of African countries. The increased prices benefited the few African petroleum exporters (Nigeria, Gabon, Angola, and Republic of Congo) by increasing their supply of foreign exchange. However, it was an economic disaster for most African countries. It severely depleted their reserves of foreign exchange or increased their already heavy burden of debt as they attempted to continue to maintain imports of petroleum necessary for continuing their previously determined development plans.

The impact of the oil crisis was compounded by a severe drought that stretched across the entire Sahelian region in 1972–1973. Hundreds of thousands of refugees fled the drought-stricken areas, flocking to the cities or seeking new pastures, often crossing borders into other countries. Agricultural production decreased drastically, and livestock starved to death. The affected countries required immediate supplies of imported food and food aid to prevent mass starvation of their populations. This put a further burden on foreign exchange reserves and increased the debt of many countries.

These mainly external factors in combination with domestic policy shortcomings resulted in a slowing of economic growth. A similar oil crisis in 1978 and declining world prices for the primary commodity exports of Africa, along with continued domestic policy deficiencies, led to a period of actual economic decline in the 1980s and the first half of the 1990s as annual growth of GNP per capita became negative from 1980 to 1993 (Katsouris and Bentsi-Enchill, 1995:1, 10; World Bank, 1995:163; UNDP, 1995:195).

In 1994, sub-Saharan Africa began to recover, and by 1995, the region achieved positive growth of per capita income for the first time in many years. This was repeated in 1996 and again in 1997—a result of better weather conditions, fewer armed conflicts in a number of countries, and strong growth in export earnings that improved the trade and current

April Gordon

Not all Africans are poor. In South Africa, for example, since the end of apartheid in 1994, the black middle class is growing and enjoying the affluence once restricted to the white minority. The development challenge is to make such prosperity more widespread.

account balances, as well as debt and debt servicing ratios (UNCTAD, 1998:124). In 1998, however, per capita income declined once again. This setback was due mainly to the Asian crisis that occurred during those years. The value of exports fell because commodity prices collapsed, and export volumes also declined. In addition, industrial growth rates dropped, and fiscal budget deficits rose. Per capita income continued to decline each year until 2003 when it began once again to increase (UNCTAD, 1999b:6; World Bank, 2000a:table 2.19; 2000b:230–231; 2005a:33).

In September 2000, at the UN Millennium Summit, world leaders agreed to the Millennium Development Goals (MDGs), a set of goals and targets to be achieved by the year 2015 in order to attain peace and security, human rights, and sustainable development throughout the world. Those goals have provided a framework for the entire UN system to work together, with members of the developed world providing direct support to developing countries in the form of aid, trade, debt relief, and investment, while the developing countries undertake sustained political and economic reforms. The eight goals, with the specific targets to be reached by 2015, include:

1. Eradicate extreme poverty and hunger
   Target: Halve the proportion of people living on less than a dollar a day and those who suffer from hunger.
2. Achieve universal primary education
   Target: Ensure that all boys and girls complete primary school.
3. Promote gender equality and empower women
   Target: Eliminate gender disparities in primary and secondary education preferably by 2005 and at all levels by 2015.
4. Reduce child mortality
   Target: Reduce by two-thirds the mortality rate among children under five.
5. Improve maternal health
   Target: Reduce by three-fourths the ratio of women dying in childbirth.
6. Combat HIV/AIDS, malaria, and other diseases
   Target: Halt and begin to reverse the spread of HIV/AIDS and the incidence of malaria and other major diseases.
7. Ensure environmental sustainability
   Targets: Integrate the principles of sustainable development into country policies and programs and reverse the loss of environmental resources; reduce by half the proportion of people without access to safe drinking water; and achieve significant improvement in the lives of at least 100 million slum dwellers by 2020.
8. Develop a global partnership for development

> *Targets:* Develop further an open trading and financial system that includes a commitment to good governance, development, and poverty reduction—nationally and internationally; address the least developed countries' special needs, and the special needs of landlocked and small island developing states; deal comprehensively with developing countries' debt problems; develop decent and productive work for youth; in cooperation with pharmaceutical companies, provide access to affordable essential drugs in developing countries; and in cooperation with the private sector, make available the benefits of new technologies—especially information and communications technologies. (UN, *Implementing the Millennium Declaration,* 2002; UNDP, 2003)

Progress on achieving the goals and specific targets has been slow throughout the world, but it has been particularly slow for sub-Saharan Africa. In general, the progress report of 2005 found that the region as a whole has made little or no progress in achieving most targets. Poverty remains high; the percentage of people in sub-Saharan Africa whose income is less than $1 per day has risen, increasing the number of poor Africans from 227 million to 313 million. Child and maternal mortality rates remain high. The risk of disease is high, including high prevalence of HIV/AIDS and malaria, high mortality from tuberculosis, and high risk of contracting measles because of low coverage of inoculations. There is also little positive progress in ensuring environmental sustainability. Overall, it is not expected that sub-Saharan Africa will meet any of the targets by the year 2015. One UN report maintains that at its current pace, Africa will not reach the MDG goals until 2169, and that would mean that the region had still only reduced poverty by half (UN Department of Economic and Social Affairs, 2005; Colgan, 2005). (See also Chapter 13.)

As the year 2005 neared, and progress toward achieving the MDGs was being analyzed, British Prime Minister Tony Blair brought together seventeen people to form the Commission for Africa to define the challenges facing Africa and to provide recommendations on how to support the changes needed to accelerate economic growth and reduce poverty in Africa. The recommendations included increasing aid, especially on infrastructure; identifying the obstacles to a favorable investment climate; fostering small enterprises through ensuring better access to markets, finance, and business linkages, with a particular focus on youth and women, as well as family farms; encouraging action by the business community to contribute in each of the areas recommended by the report; and taking action to ensure that environmental sustainability is integral to donor interventions and to manage and build Africa's resilience to climate change. The recommendations were incorporated into what is commonly referred to as the

Commission for Africa Report and were used in deliberations during the Gleneagles G8 summit in summer 2005 (Commission for Africa Report, 2005, www.commissionforafrica.org).

Although the prognosis for the Millennium Development Goals in Africa is not good, economic growth has continued. In 2005, the growth of gross domestic product (GDP) was estimated at 4.6 percent, the sixth consecutive year of growth in excess of 3 percent. This growth occurred even as oil prices rose rapidly, growth slowed in Europe, a severe locust infestation occurred, drought spread throughout southern and eastern Africa, the price of cotton declined, and the terms of trade of oil importers deteriorated. Growth of oil-exporting countries was higher than that of oil-importing countries, although growth of the oil exporters slowed somewhat due to capacity constraints in the oil sectors and disruption in Nigeria resulting from unrest in production locations. Growth of GDP per capita in 2005 was estimated at 2.6 percent, lower than growth of GDP, as population growth, estimated at 2.0–2.5 percent, took its toll (IMF, 2005b:3; World Bank, 2005b).

Today, sub-Saharan Africa is at a turning point. Economic growth has become positive and has increased, although population growth still consumes much of it and slows the growth of GDP per capita. Some of the previous problems have improved, although many of them remain. Thus, many of the economies are characterized by food insecurity, weak agricultural growth, unsupportable levels of debt, deteriorating social indicators and related sectors (especially education, public health and sanitation, and housing), destruction of the environment, and the impact of the HIV/AIDS pandemic. As a result of these problems, the standard of living of most Africans has declined, and there is increased poverty throughout the continent.

Some of the most important issues that have affected sub-Saharan African economies in the 1980s and 1990s, and which continue to have an impact in the new millennium, include the following:

- The impact of HIV/AIDS, tuberculosis, and malaria
- The debt crisis
- Foreign aid
- International trade
- Rapid population growth and economic growth
- Food insecurity
- Urbanization and unemployment
- Deforestation and environmental degradation
- The marginalization of women in the development process
- Domestic and international conflicts
- Structural adjustment and African development plans: the role of

the World Bank, the IMF, the UN, the OAU, and the African Union (AU)

While some of these topics are discussed in other chapters (see especially Chapters 4, 6, 7, 8, and 10), each will be discussed briefly below to emphasize its economic significance.

The Impact of HIV/AIDS, Tuberculosis, and Malaria

In Chapter 7, April Gordon discusses the impact of AIDS on Africa's population. AIDS exerts one of the most important negative impacts on the economies of sub-Saharan African countries today. The most recent data from UNAIDS, the Joint UN Programme on HIV/AIDS, indicate that there are currently 40.3 million adults and children living with HIV/AIDS worldwide, of which 25.8 million (64 percent) are living in sub-Saharan Africa. Nearly all of those who have contracted the infection are in the fifteen to forty-nine age group, the most economically productive age group, with women representing more than 57 percent (13.5 million) of the total. Approximately 1.9 million children under the age of fifteen are infected, and 12.1 million have become orphans over the years (UNAIDS, 2004; UNAIDS and WHO, 2005). These infection rates have profound current and future economic consequences for Africa.

The economic impact of HIV/AIDS is broad and multifaceted. Initially, the greatest impact was at the micro (household) level, but the impact has now reached the macro (national) level in many countries.

1. Initially, those who are HIV positive may have to deal with the stigma of the infection and subsequent disease, not only affecting friendships and familial relationships, but also making it difficult or impossible to obtain employment.

2. Within the household, the death of a spouse may cause family income to decrease dramatically, and it may also alter the division of labor, requiring the remaining spouse either to take over the household duties of the deceased spouse her/himself or find a substitute. The latter may be a paid household laborer or a member of the extended family, who must still be compensated in some way, which will increase the expenses of the surviving spouse.

3. Also within the household, women and girls take on additional burdens of caring for family members. Girls care for parents or siblings. Older women care for adult children and later their orphaned grandchildren, often while continuing to be responsible for earning a living or growing food crops (UNAIDS, 2004).

4. Because of the heterosexual transmission, there is a strong likeli-

hood of both husband and wife dying, leaving increasing numbers of orphans. This has a further impact on the children's standard of living and chances for education, and it places an increased burden on the family members who absorb them into their households.

5. As the number of infected women increases, the percentage of children born HIV positive is increasing, and the number of children dying as a result of this is increasing.

6. The largest numbers of AIDS cases tend to be among men and women in the most productive age groups. As the disease continues to spread, it has begun to have a profound impact on the supply of labor, reducing the size and productivity of the labor force, including the highly trained sector. In Zimbabwe, for example, businesses have gone bankrupt because of the deaths of skilled, educated staff members (UNAIDS, 2000).

7. In the education sector, AIDS is claiming the lives of thousands of teachers, leading to school closures. In Kenya, Uganda, Swaziland, Zambia, and Zimbabwe, the epidemic is expected to lead to future shortages of primary school teachers, causing a decline in the quality of education. Children, especially girls, from AIDS-affected families are often withdrawn from school to take care of sick relatives and look after the home, or because the family cannot afford school fees (UNAIDS, 2004; Global Fund, "Fighting AIDS").

8. In the health sector, hospitals are overwhelmed by AIDS patients. Many have inadequate supplies of even basic antibiotics to fight the pneumonia, tuberculosis, or opportunistic diseases that accompany AIDS, let alone the sophisticated drugs that have eased suffering in wealthy countries. Thus, the increased costs of hospital or outpatient care and medicine and the cost of education campaigns are driving up the health care costs of individuals as well as the national budget requirements of many countries. In addition, essential medical staff are being lost to sickness and death related to AIDS. Between 19 percent and 53 percent of all government health employee deaths in Africa are caused by AIDS. In some countries, the supply of health sector workers cannot keep up with the number of deaths of such workers (UNAIDS, 2000, 2004).

9. In rural areas, there may be a reduction of the number of adults who can produce food, and there may be a significant change in the gender-based division of labor on the farm. The death of a spouse makes it difficult for either remaining spouse to farm by her/himself. Agricultural production may decline because of reduced investments in irrigation, soil enhancement, and other capital improvements. In some countries in sub-Saharan Africa, aggregate agricultural production has already fallen (UNAIDS, 2000; Global Fund, "Fighting AIDS").

10. In general, the age distribution of the population in some countries is changing, with more people in their sixties and seventies than there are in

their thirties and forties. This is altering the overall dependency ratio, requiring a smaller percentage of the productive population to support a larger proportion of the elderly who are beyond normal retirement age (UNAIDS, 2000).

11. The World Bank declared AIDS a development crisis in 2000. It has been estimated that per capita growth in half of the countries in sub-Saharan Africa is falling by 0.5–1.2 percent each year as a direct result of AIDS. By 2010, per capita GDP in some countries may decline by 8 percent, and per capita consumption may fall by even more (Global Fund, "Fighting AIDS").

Other diseases also have a negative impact on the economies of sub-Saharan Africa. Tuberculosis (TB) is on the rise, with more than 1.5 million cases each year, and the number is rising rapidly, due to the high prevalence of HIV. TB and HIV/AIDS form a lethal combination, with each one speeding the other's progress. One-third of people infected with HIV will develop TB, and TB is a leading killer of people living with HIV/AIDS.

More than 75 percent of TB-related disease and death occurs among people between the ages of fifteen and fifty-four, the most economically active segment of the population. This has a strong impact on the economy, as the average TB patient loses three to four months of work time as a result of the disease. This can lead to lost earnings equal to 30 percent of annual household income, while some families lose up to 100 percent of their income (The Global Fund, "Fighting Tuberculosis").

Malaria is another disease that has a strong negative impact on sub-Saharan Africa. It is prevalent in forty-five countries in the World Health Organization's African Region. Each year, malaria causes at least 1 million deaths and an additional 309 to 500 million clinical cases throughout the world. Ninety percent of malaria deaths occur in sub-Saharan Africa, approximately 3,000 people each day, mostly children.

Malaria has a strong impact on the economy, increasing poverty by significantly reducing productivity. In rural areas, the infection rates are highest during the rainy season, a time of intense agricultural activity, causing families to clear 60 percent less crops than other families. It has been estimated that malaria costs Africa $12 billion every year in lost GDP, even though it could be controlled at relatively low cost (The Global Fund, "Fighting Malaria").

The Debt Crisis

Along with AIDS, the debt crisis perhaps has the greatest negative impact on development in Africa today. The debt crisis is not unique to African countries; however, it has affected their economies particularly severely.

The actual amount of debt has increased rapidly and by a significant amount. Debt in sub-Saharan Africa increased from $6 billion in 1970 to $60.9 billion in 1980, $176.9 billion in 1990, and $231.4 billion in 2003. The latter is equal to 63 percent of sub-Saharan Africa's GDP in that year and 167 percent of its export earnings. The debt-export ratio varied significantly for individual countries, however, ranging from a low of 0 for Gabon, Madagascar, and São Tomé and Principe, to a high of 2,111 for Burundi. Twenty-eight countries had debt-export ratios of over 200:1 by the end of 2003 (World Bank, 2005a:28, 30, 176).

Most sub-Saharan African countries have had great difficulty servicing their debt.[5] Despite the problem, creditors have not taken much action until recently. This is because much of the debt is public debt, owed to other governments or international organizations. It is also because Africa's commercial debt is only a small percentage of that of total developing country debt, too little to threaten the international banking system. Overall, debt service payments were 10 percent of export revenues in 2003.[6] That is, about 10 percent of the income earned from exports was used simply to make annual payments of principal and interest on the debt. The debt service ratio also varied significantly among individual countries. For example, debt service (ex post) as a percentage of the value of the export of goods and services ranged from a low of 2 percent for Togo to 83 percent for Burundi. These percentages are misleading because they indicate actual, rather than required, transactions; countries have been accumulating arrears rather than meeting their entire debt service obligation each year. By 1998, they had accumulated arrears of $18.3 million on interest payments and $37.9 million on principal payments (World Bank, 2005a:28, 30, 176).

The debt of African countries originated in the same way as that of other highly indebted countries. It resulted from a complex combination of events:

1. In 1973–1974 and again in 1979–1980, OPEC members announced unexpected, sharp increases in the price of oil. As mentioned above, these price increases were beneficial to the few oil-exporting countries of sub-Saharan Africa; however, they were a catastrophe for the majority of countries that are oil importers. For those few petroleum exporters on the continent, the increase in the price of oil led to balance of payments surpluses; however, it led to huge balance of payments deficits for most of the countries that had to continue to import oil to keep their economies on a growth path.

2. The economies of the oil-importing countries slowed down. These included the economies of some of the industrialized countries. As the latter countries sought to restructure their own economies to reduce the balance of payments and inflationary impacts of the oil price increases, they

reduced expenditures on nonessential imports, foreign travel, and foreign aid. These cutbacks had repercussions on the economies of sub-Saharan Africa.

3. As foreign aid from the oil-dependent developed countries was reduced, commercial bank credit was made readily available. This resulted from a large portion of the oil profits of the oil exporters being deposited into bank accounts; those funds were then recycled as "petrodollar" loans, particularly to less developed countries (LDCs). During the 1970s, African countries turned to such commercial loans, at market rates of interest. This was not much of a problem during the late 1970s because interest rates were low, often negative in real terms.[7]

4. Some of those loans were used for nonproductive purposes such as the import of nonessential consumer goods or for investment in projects with low rates of return, especially public sector investments. This use of the loans failed to generate the foreign exchange required to service the debts.

5. In addition, during the 1980s the terms of trade of sub-Saharan African countries declined as a result of both low world market prices for the primary commodities exported by African countries and rising import prices.[8] Overall, by 1986 the terms of trade (using 1980 as the base year) had declined from 100 to 72. By 1988 they had declined to 65, and by 1993 they were down to an estimated 58 (UNCTAD, 1994:46). The significance of the declining terms of trade is that it began to take a greater and greater quantity of African exports (usually primary commodities such as agricultural products and minerals) to pay for their imports. Those imports included petroleum products, manufactured goods, and capital goods required for further development. Facing low or negative real interest rates, African countries continued to succumb to the temptation to borrow from commercial sources that were actively competing for their business.

6. The economic stabilization policies of developed countries continued to affect African countries during the 1980s. By 1984, foreign aid had stagnated at $7 billion. During that same year, net private investment decreased by $480 million (Todaro, 1989:596). As a final blow, interest rates rose, causing the debt service burden of borrowers to increase. This was significant for African countries because, by that time, they had a much greater proportion of their debt from commercial and other private sources. Since banks operate on the principle of profits, they required regular debt service payments. The combination of increased debts and increased debt service burdens led rapidly to a debt crisis. Sub-Saharan African countries, along with other LDCs, suddenly found that they were unable to continue to make their scheduled payments. Mexico was the first to announce the inability to service its debt in 1982, but African countries followed soon after. Unable to pay their debts, most African countries were

compelled to seek various forms of debt relief and to implement structural adjustment programs (SAPs).

Over the years, various forms of debt relief have been proposed by the international community, including the Toronto terms, the London terms (enhanced Toronto terms), the Naples terms, and the Lyon terms, as improvements implemented in each form of relief proved inadequate to resolve the problem. One of the reasons is that the above proposals excluded multilateral debt from debt reduction and concentrated on bilateral debt. Yet multilateral debt accounted for an increasing proportion of total debt because countries began to borrow heavily from multilateral sources in the 1980s in order to finance debt servicing to private creditors and also to support IMF/World Bank structural adjustment programs. Economic performance did not improve for many countries under the SAPs; thus much of the borrowing was not repayable.

The Heavily Indebted Poor Countries (HIPC) Initiative launched in 1996 by the World Bank and the IMF was designed to relieve the debt burdens of the poorest countries. Initially, there were so many conditions to be met in order to qualify under the HIPC Initiative that by July 1999 only four countries had been granted actual debt reduction, two of which were African (Uganda and Mozambique), and only three more (including Burkina Faso, Mali, and Côte d'Ivoire) were to benefit by 2001. Thus the major creditor countries agreed to the Cologne Initiative in 1999 as an enhanced HIPC package, designated HIPC-2, which relaxed the strict criteria for eligibility and made a clearer link between debt relief followed by poverty reduction programs. As of 2006, eighteen countries, including fourteen African countries, had implemented required macroeconomic reforms under HIPC-2 to reach the "Completion Point" and were receiving irrevocable debt relief. Eleven other countries, all of which are African countries, had implemented reforms required to reach the "Decision Point" and were receiving debt relief on a provisional basis under the initiative.

While progress was made toward granting debt relief through HIPC-1 and HIPC-2 and by some bilateral creditors (Paris Club), the process was slow and incomplete, and it did not resolve the debt crisis. As a result, Jubilee 2000, an international coalition of NGOs, called for the total cancellation of poor country debt. Because thirty-three of the original HIPC countries were African, Jubilee 2000 made sub-Saharan Africa's debt burden its major focus. Other NGOs and pressure groups, such as the American Friends Service Committee, Oxfam, and Africa Action, as well as some governments, joined the campaign to cancel the debt of African countries, especially as much of the current debt is considered to be illegitimate, odious debt—debt resulting from irresponsible loans made to former regimes, without the consent of the people and not for the benefit of the people who must now make the repayments.

In July 2005 at a summit in Gleneagles, Scotland, G8 leaders (Canada, France, Germany, Italy, Japan, Russia, UK, and the United States) pledged to cancel the debt of the world's most indebted countries, most of which are in Africa. Debt cancellation would be provided by the International Development Association of the World Bank, the IMF, and the African Development Fund. Countries that have reached the "Completion Point" of the HIPC-2 initiative would be eligible for 100 percent debt cancellation. Donors agreed to a financing package that provides additional donor contributions over time as resources for poverty reduction initiatives by the recipient countries. In September 2005, the IMF and the World Bank approved the G8 plan, providing an important precedent for 100 percent debt cancellation, although it still excludes the majority of African countries and continues the precedent of future debt relief being tied to the implementation of World Bank/IMF-imposed economic conditions. Final approval of this Multilateral Debt Relief Initiative was announced in April, 2006.

Foreign aid. While debt cancellation is extremely important, foreign aid is equally important. At the UN Millennium Summit in 2000, developed countries promised to support the efforts of developing countries to reach the specific targets of the MDGs by providing additional foreign assistance. The UN maintains that developing countries would require a doubling of annual development assistance from developed countries, to $135 billion in 2006, and to $195 billion in 2015, in order to achieve the MDGs.

In summer 2005, at the summit meeting in Gleneagles, Scotland, G8 leaders noted that sub-Saharan African countries would need not only debt relief, but also additional foreign aid in order to develop and to achieve the MDGs. Thus, in addition to proposing cancellation of 100 percent of outstanding debts of eligible HIPC countries, most of which are in Africa, and to writing off $17 billion of Nigeria's debt (an effort that was concluded in April 2006), G8 leaders agreed to increase official development assistance to Africa by $25 billion a year by 2010, more than doubling aid to Africa compared to 2004 (G8, 2005).

The United States pledged to double its aid to sub-Saharan Africa between 2004 and 2010. To accomplish this, the administration launched the Millennium Challenge Account (MCA) with the aim of providing up to $5 billion a year; the $15 billion President's Emergency Plan for AIDS Relief (PEPFAR), an initiative to provide more than $2 billion in 2005 for initiatives in Africa; and a new $1.2 billion malaria initiative (G8, 2005). The United States has committed less than it pledged, however. In 2004, $1 billion was appropriated for the MCA account, and in 2005, $1.25 billion was appropriated. For the 2007 budget, the president requested only $3 billion for the MCA, and by 2006 only three African countries (Benin, Cape Verde, and Madagascar) had received any funds from it. While European Union countries have pledged to commit 0.7 percent of gross national income (GNI) to development assistance by 2015 (including an interim goal of 0.56 percent of GNI), with at least 50 percent of this increase going to Africa, the United States refused to make a similar commitment, and it has fallen short of the commitment that it did make (see Chapter 13 for further discussion).

African countries need additional aid to meet the MDGs, as well as other development requirements, but much of the aid that is provided is related to the geopolitical priorities of the donors, and it does not always go to those countries that need it most. In the past, aid also has been used to tie recipients to the donor country, and this still continues. For example, about 70 percent of US aid is tied to purchases of US goods and services. Sub-Saharan Africa could benefit much more from increased aid if strings were not attached to it.

International trade. Many developed countries maintain that integrating developing countries into the global economy through trade and investment is a more effective way of reducing poverty than is the provision of aid or debt relief. Yet, African countries claim that they are too often blocked from access to the markets of the wealthy countries. Within the continent, African countries have organized some thirty regional trade associations (RTAs), and each country belongs to an average of four.[9] These RTAs have four key objectives: (1) promote intraregional trade; (2) improve regional competitiveness; (3) prevent and resolve conflicts in Africa; and (4) strengthen Africa's bargaining power in international trade negotiation through collective action. Although the RTAs may have had a positive effect on intraregional trade, the overall effect thus far has been rather small. Trade within Africa, as a share of the continent's global trade, remains low (about 10 percent) (IMF, 2005a:40).

Internationally, African countries have participated in the Doha Round of trade negotiations initiated by the World Trade Organization in November 2001 in Doha, Qatar. Negotiations have continued over the years and are expected to end in 2006. African countries, along with other developing regions, were opposed to the Doha Round, on the grounds that they had not seen any benefits from the agreements that they had signed as part of the 1994 Uruguay Round. Some 70 percent of gains from the Uruguay Round went to industrialized nations, and the remainder mostly to a few large export-oriented developing countries, according to studies by the UN Development Programme. However, the wealthy countries promised that the Doha Round would be a "Development Round" with the specific aim of boosting the participation of poor countries in international trade.

Talks came to a halt in Cancún, Mexico, in September 2003 as several West African countries demanded the elimination of subsidies on cotton exports from the North and other developing countries made similar demands on other key agricultural exports such as sugar, while developed countries introduced new areas for negotiation. Developed countries provide around $300 billion in farm subsidies annually, which promote excess production, depress world market prices, and give an unfair advantage to farmers in wealthy nations.

As the talks resumed in December 2005 in Hong Kong, the United States offered to eliminate all agricultural tariffs within ten years, with most reductions coming in the first five years, and to eliminate all agricultural export subsidies by 2010 as well as a 60 percent reduction in domestic agricultural subsidies within five years. Europe did not agree to make similar concessions, although the developed countries did agree to eliminate agricultural export subsidies by 2013. However, tariffs and quotas are now being replaced with technical regulations that allow countries to bar products from entering their markets if the products do not meet certain standards. These nontariff barriers, called sanitary and phytosanitary measures, are meant to protect people from food hazards, but they can also be used arbitrarily to limit imports of certain goods (Kahn, 2006; Mutume, 2006).

As the Doha Round comes to a close in 2006, some of the issues yet to be resolved include the dumping by developed countries of products of interest to African countries, such as cotton; the lack of duty-free, quota-free access to rich-country markets for developing countries; and the existence of nontariff barriers, which limit access to markets. Yet, on the import side, although developing countries are largely exempt from tariff reductions, some African countries are being asked to reduce their tariffs, with potentially negative consequences. And requests for "Aid for Trade" to help developing countries implement the Round are not likely to be fully provided. Thus, African countries do not consider the Doha Round to be the "Development Round" that was promised. Talks were to continue in April 2006, and it is yet to be determined whether the Doha Round will be completed by the end of 2006 (Mutume, 2001:3; Oxfam, 2005).

While Doha Round negotiations continued, the United States implemented a special law for African trade, the African Growth and Opportunity Act (AGOA). It was initially signed into law by President Bill Clinton on May 18, 2000, in order to expand Africa's access to US markets. It has been extended through enactment of AGOA III, which will extend preferential access for imports from beneficiary sub-Saharan African countries, until September 30, 2015. At the time, sub-Saharan Africa accounted for barely 1 percent of total US exports, imports, and foreign direct investment.

Total two-way trade amounted to less than $20 billion, of which South Africa and the petroleum exporters Nigeria, Angola, and Gabon accounted for $15 billion (AGOA, n.d.).

One of the provisions of the Act was to remove all quotas on textile and apparel products from Africa. Critics said that such benefits would be fleeting, as such quotas would be phased out in 2005 under the World Trade Organization rules. Beyond that, the legislation was to increase the number of products eligible for duty-free access from 4,000 to 5,000, but many of those items are either not currently produced in Africa or they have a limited potential US market. In addition, critics pointed out that the bill failed to provide trade preferences for many African products, including agricultural and mining commodities. The US government counters the criticisms with a list of accomplishments of the law, including the desired increase in trade (Lobe, 2000; AGOA, n.d.). Chapter 13 also discusses the limited impact of AGOA.

Rapid Population Growth and Economic Growth

In precolonial and colonial days, birth rates were high in Africa, as they were in Europe and the United States when the latter economies were still mainly agrarian. Since World War II, and especially since independence, many new medicines have been developed, public health measures have been expanded (such as providing clean water), and African populations have slowly gained greater access to trained health officials and medical facilities. As a result, death rates dropped dramatically across the continent, although this was more true in urban than in rural locations. Birth rates have remained high, however, producing increased population growth rates in some countries until confounded by the impact of AIDS-related deaths, which have increased relentlessly in recent years.

One of the important economic implications of high population growth rates is that it is difficult for countries to maintain or increase the amount of food production per person. That is, if population grows at a rate faster than that of food production, people will experience a decrease in the amount of food they can consume unless countries begin to import food or resort to food aid. If countries attempt to close the food gap by importing food, they must pay for it with foreign exchange, which presents further problems, because most African countries already suffer from severe balance-of-payments problems and thus shortages of foreign exchange. In addition, if countries resort to food aid, they increase their dependency on other countries.

A second economic implication of high population growth rates is that they require an expansion in services and infrastructure such as schools, hospitals, and roads as well as supplies of water and electricity. Yet, African governments have had difficulty maintaining the services and infrastructure that now exist.

A third economic implication of high population growth rates is that GNP must be divided among an increasing number of people if the growth rate of the population is greater than that of the GNP. Although a declining GNP per capita does not necessarily mean that development is decreasing, it suggests that development may be increasingly difficult to achieve. For example, if one goal of development is to increase the equality of incomes throughout the economy, then it may be necessary to redistribute income from the rich to the poor if national income is not growing, a politically difficult task. Similarly, if another goal is to decrease unemployment, it may be difficult to find new jobs for individuals if production is not increasing. In general, it will be more difficult to eradicate poverty in a stagnant or declining economy. In fact, from 1988 to 1998, twenty of the forty-five sub-Saharan African countries for which data are available showed negative growth rates of GNP per capita, and eight others had growth rates lower than 1 percent. Thus, nearly two-thirds (62 percent) of the countries had either stagnant or declining economies on a per capita basis during that time period. It should not be unexpected, then, that the average growth rate of GNP per capita from 1988 to 1998 for sub-Saharan countries was also negative (–0.6 percent) (World Bank, 2000a:table 1.1).

In recent years, population growth rates in sub-Saharan Africa have begun to decline, for various reasons, from an average of 2.8 percent to an estimated average of 2.5–2.1 percent per annum, while the growth rates of GDP have improved for most countries. Fewer countries registered negative rates of GDP growth, and many more countries registered positive rates of growth, rates that exceeded the growth rate of population, to provide an increasing GDP per capita. The IMF indicated that the growth rate of GDP per capita in 2004 was 3.4 percent, although it also estimated that the per capita growth rate would slow in 2005 to 2.5 percent (IMF, 2005b: 23, 25).

Food Insecurity

Although the economies of most sub-Saharan African countries remain based upon agriculture, their agricultural sectors are not healthy. They have recorded weak growth rates of agricultural production, in general, and of food production, in particular. The food production per capita index for sub-Saharan Africa in 2003 was 98 (1999–2001 = 100). Thus, on the average, individuals had access to only 98 percent as much food in 2003 as they did during the base years of 1999–2001. The average annual percentage growth of food production per capita was –1.5 percent from 1975 to 1984. It improved to 0.8 percent between 1985 and 1994, but then decreased again to –0.1 percent from 1995 to 2004. The growth rate in the latter period was negative for twenty-six countries, zero for two countries, and positive for only twenty countries (World Bank, 2005a:table 8.5; UN FAO, 2005a:table A3). As a result of poor performance in the sector and other factors, there were 203.5 million undernourished people in sub-Saharan Africa during the period 2000–2002, 33 percent of the population. Moreover in 2005, twenty-seven countries required urgent external assistance as a result of overall food shortages, generalized lack of access to food, or severe localized food insecurity. These conditions were brought on by drought, locusts, civil strife, existence of internally displaced persons, settlement of refugees, resettlement of returnees, economic crisis, or high food prices (UN FAO, 2005b:Intro.).

In the United States, only 2 percent of the labor force produces enough food to feed the US population, sell large quantities on the world market, and still supply food aid to other countries, including many in Africa. The percentage of the labor force working in agriculture in Africa has decreased from 78 percent in 1965 to 60 percent in 2005 (UNDP, 1995:177; World Bank, 2000a:table 11.14; UN FAO, 2005a:table A4). This is a problem, however, because those remaining have been unable to produce enough to feed the populations of their countries. Every country in sub-Saharan Africa imported cereals in the 2004–2005 or 2005 marketing year. The anticipated commercial imports of cereal during that time period were 21,442,000 metric tons, more than five times the amount imported in 1974. Furthermore, many of those countries also required food aid, a total of 3,284,000 metric tons, one-third more than in 1994–1995 (World Bank 1990:184; 2000a:table 5.36; UN FAO, 2005b:tables 1, 2, 3).

There are many reasons why agricultural production is weak. Rural-urban migration, discussed below, is only symptomatic of deeper problems that exist in the agricultural sector. Reasons for weak agricultural production include low levels of rural services, such as access to water, cooking fuel, and electricity, and deficient infrastructure, particularly farm-to-market roads and other marketing channels. Other reasons for low agricultural production include lack of sufficient and relevant agricultural research and extension of the results of that research, especially new agricultural methods and technology. The reasons include, as well, uncertainty brought about by recent changes in land tenure legislation and the subsequent reluctance to invest in the land. Finally, they include continued lack of attention to the important role of women in African agriculture, especially in food production for domestic consumption, and consequent failure to adequately assist women farmers to increase their production.

Government macroeconomic policies have also hurt the agricultural sectors of African countries. Development policies in the past have emphasized other sectors of the economy to the neglect of agriculture. Recall that in the 1960s, development policies emphasized industrialization. When it was realized that industrialization did not necessarily lead to development, governments began to pay lip service to promoting the Green Revolution in agriculture, though they continued to initiate development projects in the cities.

It is not uncommon for the agricultural sector in many developing countries to contribute a higher percentage of GNP than is invested in that sector. In sub-Saharan Africa, agriculture on the average contributed 16.8 percent of gross domestic product in 2003, although it ranged as high as 68.8 percent in Guinea-Bissau, 60.8 percent in the Central African Republic, and 52.7 percent in Sierra Leone. Yet in the past, national investment in agriculture did not approach that percentage. Available evidence indicates that the percent of government expenditure going to agriculture has remained under 10 percent, on average (UN FAO, 2005a:table A7; UNCTAD, 1998:171).

Government control over prices paid to farmers has been a major factor in declining food and export crop production.

World Bank

In sum, throughout sub-Saharan Africa, rural areas have often been exploited for the benefit of the urban areas, not only during colonial times but also since independence.

Investing heavily in the urban areas makes political sense. It is difficult for farmers who are physically separated from each other and distant from the urban-based politicians to form a united front to lobby for improved services and infrastructure and for higher prices for their products. The ever-increasing numbers of urban constituents have immediate access to the government to pressure for their interests, including low food prices.

Government policies to regulate the prices and marketing channels of agricultural products, especially for export crops and domestic staples, have affected production as well. In colonial days, government marketing boards were set up for individual crops to consolidate the export production of individual producers for sale on the international market. The marketing boards were designed to serve a price stabilization function as well. That is, when prices were high on the world market, they paid farmers a fixed price for their crop that was lower than the world market price. The difference between the producer price and the world market price was to be invested in the development of that crop and its marketing channels, and some was to be set aside in a price stabilization fund. When world market prices were low, the stabilization fund was to be used to maintain the prices paid to the farmers by supplementing the world market price. These marketing boards were maintained after independence, but their price stabilization function seldom worked well. The prices paid to farmers have nearly always been below the world market prices for the products, even when world market prices were low. Large proportions of the resources received from export sales have often been channeled into the development of urban areas rather than into the stabilization fund or into rural development in general. Many of these marketing boards have now been dismantled.

It has also been common to regulate prices and marketing channels for domestic staples such as rice and maize. Governments know that farmers must receive prices that are high enough to provide the incentive to produce. They also know that if those higher prices are passed on to the consumers, a small increase in urban food prices might touch off riots that could topple the government. Heavy pressure in the urban areas to maintain low food prices has generally been translated into low incomes for the farmers (often women) who produce that food, and the farmers have responded.

Farmers are rational, price-responsive human beings. When they fail to receive prices for their crops that will provide them with a minimal standard of income, they refuse to produce those crops. Some alter their production and plant other crops that are more lucrative. Government price policies may even encourage a trade-off of production from domestic food crops to export crops, even though producer prices for exports are also exploitative. The trade-off may occur if the prices paid for export crops are raised relative to those paid for domestic food crops. However, feeling exploited in general, some farmers simply give up farming altogether and try to find other ways of earning a living, or they migrate to the city.

These are some of the important reasons why there is food insecurity throughout Africa today, why insufficient food is being produced to feed African populations, and why there has been increasing dependence on food imports and food aid. The situation has become even more severe as a result of the droughts and the decimation of crops by locusts that have occurred in recent years, the migration to the cities by the young and educated, the reduction in the agricultural labor force as a result of HIV/AIDS, and the disruption of agricultural activity and the massive movements of people that have resulted from civil strife.

Urbanization and Unemployment

Young people, especially educated young men, have been leaving the rural areas and moving to the cities in increasing numbers. By 2003, 36.2 percent of the population of sub-Saharan Africa lived in urban areas, and the urban population has been increasing at an annual rate of at least 4.2 percent since 1990 (World Bank, 2005a:311). This is not only because life is difficult and incomes are low in the countryside, but also because the migrants expect that conditions will be better in the city. Development strategies emphasizing industrialization have caused many to leave the countryside in hopes of finding employment in industry, which is usually located in or near the cities. But industry has not succeeded in providing employment for all the hopeful applicants. In fact, it has been found that a small increase in the number of jobs available may stimulate migration to such an extent that unemployment actually increases as a result. In sum, providing employment for labor-abundant economies is particularly difficult when capital-intensive (highly mechanized) industrialization strategies are pursued. Not only does migration to the cities not always provide the migrants with anticipated benefits, but it has often exacerbated the problems in the agricultural sector.

As urbanization has interacted with high rates of population growth, economies have been unable to create sufficient jobs in the cities. For lack of other formal wage employment opportunities, uncounted numbers have looked for survival to the informal sector, where petty trading, commodity production, or services afford a typically meager income. Many have also migrated to other countries. This may be beneficial if it relieves unemployment at home, increases the standard of living of those who migrate, and provides remittances to family members who remain at home. But it may also be detrimental, particularly if those who migrate are the most skilled or the most educated, thus creating an international brain drain. It may also be a disaster if external events, such as wars, cause the migrants to flee back to their country of origin, causing an immediate unemployment crisis.

Many of those who are unemployed in the cities are those who have migrated from the rural areas. Although they may have migrated because they concluded that their expected income in the city would exceed that in the rural areas, according to one prominent theory of migration,[10] they now find themselves without an income, unable to produce their own food, and required to purchase food from the rural areas. But it is becoming increasingly difficult for those who remain in the rural areas to maintain food production, as the most able young people are the ones who departed for the cities, leaving the farming to their aging parents or to wives who remain behind. Consequently, while there is an increasing need for food in the cities, there are fewer people remaining in the countryside to produce it, and many of those who continue to farm are becoming older and potentially less productive.

Deforestation and Environmental Degradation

As population increases, forests are cut down for urban expansion and industrialization, new farmlands, household uses such as cooking fuel, and as a result of intensive livestock grazing. Drought, civil wars, and bush fires also contribute to forest degradation, as do agricultural systems such as the *chitemene* system of shifting cultivation practiced in parts of Southern and Central Africa and slash and burn agriculture practiced in Madagascar and other parts of the continent. But in sub-Saharan Africa, deforestation is also taking place in many countries because of the economic crisis. In an effort to increase exports to earn foreign exchange, to reduce the international debt burden, and to maintain imports, forests are being slashed, and rough unprocessed timber is being exported, with little enforcement of reforestation laws where they exist. While estimates indicate that the rate of deforestation has been declining in recent years, from 0.8 percent during 1980–1990 to 0.7 percent during 1990–2000, it remains significant. The highest rates from 1990 to 2000 were in Burundi (21.9 percent) and in Rwanda (15.2 percent), but rates in sixteen other countries for which data existed exceeded 1 percent. Between the years 1990 and 2000, total forest land on the continent of Africa declined by 52.6 million hectares, from 702.5 million hectares to 649.9 million hectares (UNEP, 2000, 2002; World Bank, 2005a:343).

The destruction of the forests has multiple repercussions on the economies of countries. The trees that are most valuable are the tropical hardwoods. Once gone, they cannot be replaced in the near future.

Moreover, removal of the forests leads to problems of soil erosion and general degradation of the land, as well as to changes in climate, which in turn affect agriculture. Deforestation also affects rural dwellers, who may depend on the forests for subsistence products such as cooking fuel, food, medicines, and building materials.

In addition to deforestation, there are also other environmental concerns. One of the most important in some countries, such as Nigeria, has been the pollution of land and water resulting from production of petroleum, and the threat of pollution continues, for example, with the completion of the Chad-Cameroon pipeline. These and other environmental issues are examined by Julius Nyang'oro in Chapter 8. While current disregard for the environment often reflects short-term economic interests, in the long run, environmental degradation will be ruinous for Africa's future. In its 1992 Development Report, the World Bank (1992:178) argues that economic efficiency and sound environmental management go hand in hand. The Bank and other agencies, such as the US Agency for International Development (USAID), recognize, however, that economic pressures on governments, poverty, and rapid population growth are the root problems that must be addressed if Africa's environment is to be preserved to sustain the economic needs of future generations (see Green, 1994).

The Marginalization of Women in the Development Process

Women's economic productivity and independence is a long-established tradition in much of Africa. Not only do women grow most of the food and assist with cash crops, they are also actively involved in marketing foodstuffs. In the informal sector, where many nonagricultural workers pursue their livelihood, women can be found providing valuable economic services and products. In the markets of West Africa, for instance, some women have become wealthy as cloth merchants, and some of them have used their profits to become owners of vehicles for long-distance transport services. In wage jobs in the formal economy, women help support themselves and their families.

Despite the important contributions women have made to African economies, the role of women is often underrated in official economic statistics, and women's interests are ignored, if not purposely undermined, by African governments and the international financial and donor community. The neglect of women has especially hurt agricultural production, but it also negatively affects other areas of the economy, as discrimination lessens women's opportunities to contribute their talents and skills to the development effort.

The UNDP calculates the Human Development Index (HDI) each year

April Gordon

African women work hard, often in the informal sector of the economy, selling their produce to support their families.

for 177 countries to try to indicate the level of development of countries more accurately than by simply using the size of GNP. The HDI measures average achievements in life expectancy, educational achievement, and income, but it does not disaggregate these indicators to reflect gender differences in human development. To address this deficiency, the UNDP developed two new indices in 1995 to capture gender inequalities.

One of the indices is the Gender-Related Development Index (GDI). It measures development in the same way as the HDI, but it adjusts the results for gender inequality. The closer a country's GDI is to its HDI, the less gender disparity there is; however, the data show that the GDI for each country is lower than its HDI, implying that there is gender inequality in every society.

The HDI for all countries of sub-Saharan Africa is .515 (compared to .911 for high-income OECD countries, with Norway having the highest score of .963). For sub-Saharan Africa, the scores ranged from a high of .821 for Seychelles, .791 for Mauritius, and .721 for Cape Verde, to a low of .298 for Sierra Leone and .281 for Niger (UNDP, 2005:219–222).

The GDI scores ranged from a high of .781 for Mauritius, and .714 for Cape Verde (there is insufficient information to calculate the GDI for Seychelles), to a low of .139 for Sierra Leone and .271 for Niger. Overall, in sub-Saharan Africa, life expectancy is greater for women than for men, but the other measures comprising the GDI (adult literacy rate, gross enrollment rate for all levels of education, and estimated earned income) reveal the inequalities (UNDP, 2005:219–222).

The second of those indices is the Gender Empowerment Measure (GEM). It attempts to capture gender inequality in key areas of economic and political participation and decisionmaking, focusing on women's opportunities rather than capabilities as in the GDI. The GEM measures these opportunities in terms of women's share of parliamentary seats, professional jobs, administrative positions, and income.

Of the 102 countries throughout the world for which the GEM was calculated, Norway achieved a score of .928, the only country to earn a score greater than .900. In sub-Saharan Africa, only four countries provided enough data for the most recent calculations of the GEM. Namibia earned a score of .603, while Tanzania earned .538, Botswana earned .505, and Swaziland earned .492. In Rwanda, a woman has become the president of the Supreme Court and women hold 45.3 percent of the seats in Parliament, the highest percentage throughout the world, though a victory which came partly as a necessity following the 1994 genocide, which left women greatly outnumbering men in the population. In Tanzania, 49 percent of the legislators, senior officials, and managers are female. In Swaziland, 61 percent of the professional and technical workers are women. In Kenya, the ratio of female to male earned income is .93. And in Liberia, a woman was elected president of her country in 2005. While there remain many inequities, women are beginning slowly to gain empowerment. (UNDP, 2005:303–306; Hammer, 2006).

In general, however, the World Bank's summary of the economic plight of women in sub-Saharan Africa remains valid:

> "Modernization" has shifted the balance of advantage against women. The legal framework and the modern social sector and producer services developed by the independent African nations (and also most externally sponsored development projects) have not served women well. Legal systems have discriminated in land titling. . . . It is often more difficult for women to gain access to information and technology, resources, and credit. Agricultural extension and formal financial institutions are biased toward a male clientele. . . . There is a wide gender gap in education. . . . As a result, women are less well equipped than men to take advantage of the better income-earning opportunities. . . . In industry and trade women have been confined to small-scale operations in the informal sector; . . . despite the trading empires built up by the most successful female entrepreneurs, women's average incomes are relatively low. Women are also handicapped in access to formal sector jobs by their lower educational attainments, and those who succeed are placed in lower-grade, lower-paid jobs. (World Bank, 1989b:86–87)

Domestic and International Conflicts

Much of the progress toward development in many sub-Saharan African economies and much of the potential for progress has been destroyed as a result of domestic and international conflicts. Major conflicts have occurred in recent years in Angola, Burundi, Democratic Republic of Congo, Eritrea, Ethiopia, Liberia, Rwanda, Sierra Leone, Somalia, and Sudan, to name a few, and at the time of writing, other countries such as Nigeria and Zimbabwe are on the verge of civil strife over religious, land, and natural resource issues.

Domestic and international conflicts impose many negative impacts on a country. For example, the national budget is drained for military purposes rather than invested in development or used to service the international debt. Cities may be destroyed along with industrial complexes, and environmental degradation may occur in the countryside where battles take place. Agriculture suffers, as it becomes difficult for farmers to anticipate whether it will be possible to harvest crops if they plant them, or whether harvested crops might be destroyed in battle, confiscated by the military, or even stolen by scavenging soldiers in the countryside. Thus farmers become reluctant to invest in their farms. In the social sector, children often find their education terminated and hospitals become overwhelmed with the sick and the injured. Even the incidence of HIV/AIDS increases, as the military in most countries incurs a higher rate of infection than other sectors of the population. Also, it becomes almost impossible to restructure the economy in any meaningful way to promote economic efficiency and support growth and development. Finally, the negative impact of domestic and international conflict lasts long after the conflict ceases, while countries struggle to rebuild what they previously destroyed.

Structural Adjustment Programs and African Development Plans: The Role of the World Bank, the IMF, the United Nations, the OAU, and the AU

The World Bank, supported by bilateral and multilateral foreign aid donors, has stressed that the solutions to sub-Saharan Africa's economic problems must be solved by long-run structural adjustment programs. Moreover, most donor organizations have required implementation of structural adjustment policies prior to negotiations for various forms of debt relief and before provision of increased loan support. The main objectives of World Bank SAPs have included the following:

- Reduction in the size of the public sector and improvements in its management.
- Elimination of price distortions in various sectors of the economy.
- Increasing trade liberalization.
- Promotion of domestic savings in the public and private sectors.

The main policy instruments the World Bank and the IMF have used to achieve the above objectives are:

- Exchange rate adjustment, especially devaluation.
- Interest rate policies to encourage domestic savings and achieve appropriate allocation of resources.
- Control of money supply and credit.
- Fiscal policies to reduce government expenditures and deficit financing.
- Trade and payments liberalization.
- Deregulation of the prices of goods, services, and factor inputs.

Most African countries have recognized the problems that such policies create, at least in the short run. These include increased costs for imports, including essential imports of resources, supplies, and capital to promote economic growth. They also include increased prices of domestic goods after subsidies are removed and prices are deregulated. The increased prices of domestic goods often have immediate impact on the welfare of the poorest members of society—especially if they affect food prices, costs of education, and payment for medical services—and they have an especially negative impact on women, who most often deal with such domestic issues. In many cases, price increases have led to political instability as citizens express their dislike of the changes. African countries fear that they may never have the opportunity to enjoy the promised long-term benefits of SAPs if they are unable to survive the short-run problems that are certain to occur. They believe, therefore, that they must move at a deliberate pace if they agree to proceed with structural adjustment, because their constituencies generally will not allow such extensive changes at one time.

In March 1989, a World Bank–UNDP report concluded that the more than thirty sub-Saharan African countries that adopted SAPs were performing better than those that had not (World Bank, 1989a:iii). African countries disagreed. They believe that the World Bank used a biased analysis to push through "doctrinaire privatization" and promote "excessive dependence on market forces." Moreover, they believe that the SAPs have been unduly harsh in effect and that they have not been producing the desired results. They complain that World Bank SAPs as well as IMF stabilization programs follow only one formula, rather than individualizing programs for each country. As a result, SAPs do not meet the needs of the people or the differing conditions of their economies. They believe that many World Bank policy prescriptions are not appropriate and that they will never lead to self-sustained growth and development but only to continued marginalization and dependency.

On the basis of these criticisms, African countries have jointly prepared programs that counter the policy prescriptions and provide alternatives to those of the World Bank. The first of those major programs was the

Lagos Plan of Action, discussed earlier, which emphasized self-reliant development. In 1985, African countries devised another alternative, Africa's Priority Programme for Economic Recovery 1986–1990 (APPER), which was adopted by the OAU. In APPER, Africans took some of the responsibility for their economic failures and stressed the need for economic policy reforms, but of their own design. This was the African contribution to the more general UN Programme of Action for African Economic Recovery and Development (UNPAAERD), under which developed countries agreed to support African efforts, especially with increased aid (approximately $46 billion) and greater debt relief. UNPAAERD initially was considered by donors and African countries alike to be a major breakthrough in providing increased development assistance for Africa. Economic performance, however, continued to be poor, and the final reviews of UNPAAERD determined that it was a failure. It had little impact on African economies, and Africans were poorer in 1991 than they were in 1986.

In 1989, under the auspices of the UNECA, African countries prepared yet another document, this one entitled *African Alternative Framework to Structural Adjustment Programmes for Socio-Economic Recovery and Transformation (AAF-SAP).* It looked beyond short-term adjustment and proposed a long list of policy intended to direct countries eventually toward long-term, balanced development and fulfillment of human needs. It recommended, for example, greater limits on debt service payments, multiple exchange rates, selective subsidies and price controls, and a decrease in defense expenditures. It also advocated differential export subsidies and limited use of deficit spending for productive and infrastructural investments. As in the earlier documents, it emphasized that African governments must take responsibility for determining their own economic programs rather than allowing donor agencies to dictate them (UNECA, n.d.).

Another attempt by sub-Saharan African countries to solve their own problems developed at a conference organized by the UNECA and NGOs in Arusha, Tanzania, in February 1990. Participants unanimously agreed that the absence of full democratic rights was the primary cause of Africa's decade-long economic crisis (Lone, 1990:1). Thus, the African Charter for Popular Participation in Development and Transformation, which was adopted at the conference, states that "there must be an opening up of political processes to accommodate freedom of opinion, and tolerate differences. In this regard, it is essential to establish independent people's organizations that are genuinely grassroot and democratically administered."

On December 18, 1991, the international community renewed the commitment to Africa it made five years earlier in the UNPAAERD by entering into a stronger accord, the UN New Agenda for the Development of Africa in the 1990s (UN-NADAF). The agenda set specific goals, including:

- Average real growth rate of GDP of 6 percent per year.
- Provision of $30 billion in net Official Development Assistance (ODA) in 1992, with 4 percent growth of that amount in each succeeding year.
- Preparation of a study on the need for and feasibility of a "diversification fund" to help free African economies from heavy dependence on exports of primary commodities.
- Solution to the African debt crisis by commitment of creditors to further cancellation or reduction of ODA debt, additional relief for official bilateral debt, and encouragement to write off or swap commercial debt.

For their part, African countries promised to transform the structure of their economies by continuing with necessary reforms and pursuing improvement of domestic economic management, including effective mobilization and utilization of domestic resources. They would do the following (Lone, 1991:1, 18–23):

- Pursue regional and subregional economic cooperation and integration with the ultimate goal of establishing the African Economic Community.
- Intensify the process of democratization.
- Create an enabling environment to attract foreign and domestic investment and promote the participation of the private sector.
- Protect the environment through sustainable development.
- Continue to integrate population factors into development programs.
- Improve policies to support agriculture, rural development, and food security.

Subsequently, in the midst of generally discouraging economic indicators for Africa, the World Bank (1994a) published another study of Africa, *Adjustment in Africa.* That study focused on twenty-nine sub-Saharan African countries that had adjustment programs in place during 1987–1991. It concluded that in the countries that had undertaken and sustained major policy reforms, adjustment was working; of the twenty-nine countries, the six with the most improvement in macroeconomic policies during the periods 1981–1986 and 1987–1991 (Ghana, Tanzania, Gambia, Burkina Faso, Nigeria, and Zimbabwe) enjoyed the strongest resurgence in economic performance in terms of GDP per capita growth. The countries were more successful in improving their macroeconomic, trade, and agricultural policies than their public and financial sectors, and no African country had achieved a sound macroeconomic policy stance—meaning inflation under 10 percent, a very low budget deficit, and a competitive exchange rate. Moreover, the reforms that were undertaken were fragile and were merely returning Africa to the slow-growth path of the 1960s and 1970s. Finally, the report maintained that while adjustment can work in Africa, adjustment alone will not put countries on a sustained, poverty-reducing growth path, because long-term development also requires more investment in human capital (i.e., people), infrastructure, and institution building, along with better governance (World Bank, 1994a:1–2).

At nearly the same time, at a May 1994 conference of the UNECA, the African ministers of economic and social development and planning approved a "Framework Agenda for Building and Utilizing Critical Capacities in Africa," and mandated the preparation of a financing plan for the 1995–2005 first phase of an action program at national, subregional, and regional levels. The Framework Agenda identified eight priority areas that have been integral to previous development strategies over the past two decades. These include building critical capacities that support good governance, human rights, and political stability; creating capacities for effective socioeconomic policy analysis and management; developing entrepreneurship for public and private sector management; building and utilizing physical infrastructure; building capacities to exploit natural resources and diversify African economies into processing and manufacturing; strengthening food security and self-sufficiency; and mobilizing and efficiently allocating domestic and external financial resources (Harsch, 1994:1, 30).

By mid-1995, action to support the commitments of the international community for the earlier UN-NADAF was very weak. As a result, in March 1996, the UN agencies and the Bretton Woods institutions launched the System-Wide Special Initiative on Africa, a decade-long effort to operationalize, rather than replace, the UN-NADAF. This is a multibillion dollar program of concrete actions to accelerate African development. The bulk of the resources are to be devoted to expanding basic education and improving health care, promoting peace and better governance, improving water and food security, increasing the continent's competitiveness in world trade, and making available new information technology. These components are also based on themes reflecting Africa's development priorities as expressed in the OAU's 1995 Cairo Agenda for Action (Novicki, 1996:8–9).

The most recent plan to address the current challenges facing the African continent and promote a "made-in-Africa" development strategy is the New Partnership for Africa's Development (NEPAD), launched by a summit of the OAU in October 2001 (now the AU). Initially called the New African Initiative, it incorporated two earlier draft plans, the Millennium Partnership for the African Recovery Programme and the Omega Plan. Its

NEPAD

The Priorities of NEPAD

1. Establishing the conditions for sustainable development by ensuring:
   - Peace and security
   - Democracy and good political, economic, and corporate governance
   - Regional cooperation and integration
   - Capacity building
2. Carrying out policy reforms and increasing investment in the following priority sectors:
   - Agriculture
   - Human development with a focus on health, education, science and technology, and skills development
   - Building and improving infrastructure, including information and communication technology (ICT), energy, transport, water, and sanitation
   - Promoting diversification of production and exports, particularly with respect to agro-industries, manufacturing, mining, mineral beneficiation, and tourism
   - Accelerating intra-African trade and improving access to markets of developed countries
   - The environment
3. Mobilizing resources by:
   - Increasing domestic savings and investments
   - Improving management of public revenue and expenditure
   - Improving Africa's share in global trade
   - Attracting foreign direct investment
   - Increasing capital flows through further debt reduction and increase of Official Development Assistance (ODA) flows

Key Priority Action Areas of NEPAD

- Operationalizing an African Peer Review Mechanism to ensure that the policies and practices of participating states conform to the internationally agreed governance values, codes, and standards
- Facilitating and supporting implementation of short-term regional infrastructure programs covering transport, energy, ICT, water, and sanitation
- Facilitating implementation of the food security and agricultural development program in all subregions
- Facilitating the preparation of a coordinated African position on market access, debt relief, and ODA reforms
- Monitoring and intervening as appropriate to ensure that the Millennium Development Goals in the areas of health and education are met

---

Source: NEPAD, *NEPAD in Brief* (2005), available online at www.nepad.org/2005/files/inbrief.php.

strategic framework document arose from a mandate given to five initiating Heads of State (Algeria, Egypt, Nigeria, Senegal, and South Africa) by the OAU to develop an integrated socioeconomic development framework for Africa. The overall goal of the organization is to achieve "human-centered and sustainable development" while also ensuring that Africa becomes more than a marginal player in the world economy. It calls for "a new relationship of partnership between Africa and the international community, especially the highly industrialized countries, to overcome the development chasm that had widened over centuries of unequal relations." The president of the World Bank praised the initiative and recognized that top-down development imposed from Washington or London or Geneva would not work.

In summary, African countries have made a critical examination of their constraints on development and have evaluated the recommendations or demands made by international donors. While recognizing the external causes of underdevelopment and admitting their own responsibility for lack of development, they continue to propose strategies for achieving it. By doing so, they hope to promote economic development of their own countries on their own terms. We must now look to the future to observe whether such initiatives will be successful.

Notes

1. Agro-pastoralists cultivate crops during the growing season but move with their livestock during the dry season, in sometimes well-established patterns of transhumance, in search of pasturage.

2. It has been estimated that about 5 million slaves were exported from eastern Africa between the years 650 and 1500 (Austen, 1987:59).

3. *Sub-Saharan Africa: Progress Report on Development Prospects and Programs,* 1983, and *Toward Sustained Development in Sub-Saharan Africa: A Joint Program of Action,* 1984.

4. Growth of GNP, measured by growth of the value of all goods and services produced by a country within a year.

5. Debt service is a combination of the periodic (a) repayment of principal (amortization) of a loan, as well as (b) payment of interest on it.

6. Debt service is the required repayment of principal and interest on a loan.

7. The real interest rate is equal to the market rate of interest minus the rate of inflation.

8. The "terms of trade" for a country usually refers to the ratio of an index of its export prices to an index of its import prices. Therefore, if the terms of trade decline, it means that the ratio decreases as a result of either the index of export prices declining and/or the index of import prices rising.

9. Many attempts at regional integration in Africa have been made over the years, some more successful than others. The major groups at this time are:

Arab Common Market: Egypt, Libya, Mauritania, Iraq, Jordan, and Yemen

CEMAC: Communauté Economique et Monétaire de l'Afrique Centrale (Central African Economic and Monetary Union), formerly UDEAC (Union Douanière et Economique de l'Afrique Centrale [Central African Customs and Economic Union]): Cameroon, Chad, Republic of Congo, Equatorial Guinea, Gabon

CEPGL: Communauté Economique des Pays des Grands Lacs (Economic Community of the Great Lakes States [ECGLS]): Burundi, Democratic Republic of Congo, Rwanda

COMESA: Common Market for Eastern and Southern Africa (Marché Commun d'Afrique de l'Est et d'Afrique Australe): Angola, Burundi, Comoros, Democratic Republic of Congo, Djibouti, Egypt, Eritrea, Ethiopia, Kenya, Madagascar, Malawi, Mauritius, Namibia, Rwanda, Seychelles, Sudan, Swaziland, Tanzania, Uganda, Zambia, Zimbabwe

Conseil de l'Entente: Council of the Entente: Benin, Burkina Faso, Côte d'Ivoire, Niger, Togo

Cross Border Initiative: Burundi, Comoros, Kenya, Madagascar, Malawi, Mauritius, Namibia, Rwanda, Seychelles, Swaziland, Tanzania, Uganda, Zambia, Zimbabwe

EAC: East African Community: Kenya, Tanzania, Uganda

ECCAS: Economic Community of Central African States (Communauté Economique des Etats de l'Afrique Centrale [CEEAC]): Angola, Burundi, Cameroon, Central African Republic, Chad, Democratic Republic of Congo, Equatorial Guinea, Gabon, Republic of Congo, Rwanda, São Tomé and Principe

ECOWAS: Economic Community of West African States (Communauté Economique des Etats de l'Afrique de l'Ouest [CEDEAO]): Benin, Burkina Faso, Cape Verde, Côte d'Ivoire, Gambia, Ghana, Guinea, Guinea-Bissau, Liberia, Mali, Mauritania, Niger, Nigeria, Senegal, Sierra Leone, Togo

GAFTA: Greater Arab Free Trade Area: Egypt, Libya, Morocco, Somalia, Sudan, Tunisia, as well as Bahrain, Iraq, Jordan, Kuwait, Lebanon, Oman, Qatar, Saudi Arabia, Syria, United Arab Emirates, West Bank and Gaza, Yemen

InOC: Indian Ocean Commission: Comoros, France (for Réunion), Madagascar, Mauritius, Seychelles

MRU: Mano River Union: Guinea, Liberia, Sierra Leone

SACU: Southern African Customs Union: Botswana, Lesotho, Namibia, South Africa, Swaziland

SADC: Southern African Development Community (Communauté de Développement de l'Afrique Australe): Angola, Botswana, Democratic Republic of Congo, Lesotho, Malawi, Mauritius, Mozambique, Namibia, Seychelles, South Africa, Swaziland, Tanzania, Zambia, Zimbabwe

UEMOA: Union Economique et Monetaire Ouest Africaine (West African Economic and Monetary Union [WAEMU]): Benin, Burkina Faso, Côte d'Ivoire, Guinea-Bissau, Mali, Niger, Senegal, Togo

UMA: Union du Maghreb Arabe (Arab Maghreb Union [AMU]): Algeria, Libya, Mauritania, Morocco, Tunisia

10. According to the Todaro theory, the decision to migrate depends upon expected urban-rural real wage differentials, where the expected differential is determined by the interaction of two variables, the actual urban-rural wage differential and the probability of successfully obtaining employment in the urban sector (Todaro, 1989:278–281). That is:

Expected income = (actual wage or salary) X (probability of finding a job).

Bibliography

AGOA. N.d. *AGOA Legislation—Summary of AGOA III*. Online at www.agoa.gov/agoa_legislation/agoa_legislation//agoa_legislation3.html.

Austen, Ralph. 1987. *African Economic History: Internal Development and External Dependency.* London: James Currey; Portsmouth, NH: Heinemann.

Clark, J. Desmond. 1962. "The Spread of Food Production in Sub-Saharan Africa." *Journal of African History* 3. Reprinted in Z. A. Konczacki and J. M. Konczacki (eds.). *An Economic History of Tropical Africa.* Vol. 1. Pp. 3–13. London: Frank Cass, 1977.

Colgan, Ann-Louise. 2005 (January). *Africa Policy Outlook 2005.* Silver City, NM and Washington, DC: Foreign Policy in Focus. Online at www.fpif.org/papers/2005africa.html.

Davidson, Basil. 1972. *Africa: History of a Continent.* New York: Macmillan.

Fage, J. D. 1959. *Ghana: A Historical Perspective.* Madison: University of Wisconsin Press.

G8. 2005. "G8 Gleneagles 2005." Online at www.g8.gov.uk.

Green, Cynthia P. 1994. *Sustainable Development: Population and the Environment.* Washington, DC: USAID.

The Global Fund to Fight AIDS, Tuberculosis, and Malaria. N.d. "Fighting AIDS." Online at www.theglobalfund.org/en/about/aids/default.asp.

———. N.d. "Fighting Malaria." Online at www.theglobalfund.org/en/about/malaria/default.asp.

———. N.d. "Fighting Tuberculosis." Online at www.theglobalfund.org/en/about/tuberculosis/default.asp.

Hammer, Joshua. 2006. "Healing Powers." *Newsweek* (April 3):30–39.

Harsch, Ernest. 1994. "Building Africa's Economic Capacity." *Africa Recovery* 8 (April-September):1, 30–31.

———. 2003. "Africa Beyond Famine." *Africa Recovery* 17 (May):1, 10, 22.

Herskovits, Melville J., and Mitchell Harwitz. 1964. *Economic Transition in Africa.* Chicago: Northwestern University Press.

IMF (International Monetary Fund). 2005a (May). *Regional Economic Outlook: Sub-Saharan Africa.* Washington, DC: IMF.

———. 2005b (October). *Regional Economic Outlook: Sub-Saharan Africa, Supplement.* Washington, DC: IMF.

Kahn, Jeremy. 2006. "Can the WTO Get to the Next Stage of Global Trade?" *World Trade Magazine* (May).

Katsouris, Christina, and Nii K. Bentsi-Enchill. 1995. "Africa Under Pressure from Falling Aid, Rising Debt." *Africa Recovery* 9 (June):1, 10, 12.

Lobe, Jim. 2000. "New Law to Boost US-Africa Trade." *Africa Recovery* 14, no. 2 (July):11.

Lone, Salim. 1990. "Africans Adopt Bold Charter for Democratization." *Africa Recovery* 4 (April–June):14–17.

———. 1991. "New Africa Agenda Adopted at U.N." *Africa Recovery* 5 (December):1, 18–23.

Mutume, Gumisai. 2001. "What Doha Means for Africa." *Africa Recovery* 15, no. 4 (December):3.

———. 2006. "New Barriers Hinder African Trade." *African Recovery* 19, no. 4 (January):19.

Neumark, S. Daniel. 1977. "Trans-Saharan Trade in the Middle Ages." Pp. 127–131 in Z. A. Konczacki and J. M. Konczacki (eds.). *An Economic History of*

Tropical Africa. Vol. 1. London: Frank Cass. Reprinted from Daniel Neumark. *Foreign Trade and Economic Development in Africa: An Historical Perspective.* Stanford: Food Research Institute, Stanford University, 1964.

Novicki, Margaret A. 1996. "A New Impetus for African Development." *Africa Recovery* 10 (May):8–9.

Oxfam. 2005. *Africa and the Doha Round. Oxfam Briefing Paper* (November).

Todaro, Michael P. 1989. *Economic Development in the Third World.* New York: Longman.

UN. 2002 (October). *Implementing the Millennium Declaration. The Millennium Development Goals and the United Nations Role.* Fact Sheet. New York: UN Department of Public Information.

———. 2005. *The Millennium Development Goals Report, 2005.* New York: United Nations.

UNAIDS (Joint United Nations Programme on HIV/AIDS). 2000 (June). *Report on the Global HIV/AIDS Epidemic.* Online at www.unaids.org/epidemic_update/report/Epi_report.htm.

———. 2004. *2004 Report on the Global AIDS Epidemic.* Geneva, Switzerland: UNAIDS.

UNAIDS and WHO (World Health Organization). 2005 (December). *AIDS Epidemic Update: Special Report on HIV Prevention.* UNAIDS/05.19E. Geneva, Switzerland: UNAIDS.

UNCTAD (United Nations Conference on Trade and Development). 1994. *Handbook of International Trade and Development Statistics 1993.* New York and Geneva: United Nations.

———. 1998. *Trade and Development Report, 1998.* New York: United Nations.

———. 1999a. *Handbook of International Trade and Development Statistics 1996/1997.* New York: United Nations.

———. 1999b. *The Least Developed Countries 1999 Report.* New York: United Nations.

———. 2005. *UNCTAD Handbook of Statistics 2005.* New York: United Nations. Online at www.unctad.org/Templates/webflyer.asp?docid=6558&intItemID=1397&lang=1.

UN Department of Economic and Social Affairs. 2005 (September). *Millennium Development Goals: 2005 Progress Chart.* DPI/2363/Rev.2. New York: UN Dept. of Economic and Social Affairs and UN Dept. of Public Information. Online at unstats.un.org/unsd/mi/pdf/MDG%20Chart%20Sept.pdf.

UNDP (United Nations Development Programme). 1995. *Human Development Report 1995.* New York: Oxford University Press, for the UNDP.

———. 2003 (September). *Why Do the Millennium Development Goals Matter?* New York: UN Development Programme and the UN Department of Public Information.

———. 2005. *Human Development Report 2005.* New York: Oxford University Press, for the UNDP.

UNECA (UN Economic Commission for Africa). N.d. *African Alternative Framework to Structural Adjustment Programmes for Socio-Economic Recovery and Transformation (AAF-SAP).* E/ECA/CM.15/6/Rev. 3. Addis Ababa, Ethiopia: UNECA.

UNEP (United Nations Environment Programme). 2000. *Global Environment Outlook 2000.* Nairobi, Kenya: UNEP.

———. 2002. *Global Environment Outlook 3: Past, Present and Future Perspectives.* Nairobi, Kenya: UNEP.

UN FAO (Food and Agriculture Organization). 2005a. *The State of Food and Agriculture 2005.* Rome, Italy: FAO.

———. 2005b (December). *Food Supply Situation and Crop Prospects in Sub-Saharan Africa*, No. 3. Rome, Italy: FAO Global Information and Early Warning System.

Wickins, Peter. 1986. *Africa 1880–1980: An Economic History.* Cape Town: Oxford University Press.

World Bank. 1981. *Accelerated Development in Sub-Saharan Africa: An Agenda for Action.* Washington, DC: World Bank.

———. 1989a. *Africa's Adjustment and Growth in the 1980s.* Washington, DC: World Bank.

———. 1989b. *Sub-Saharan Africa: From Crisis to Sustainable Growth: A Long-Term Perspective Study.* Washington, DC: World Bank.

———. 1990. *World Development Report.* New York: Oxford University Press.

———. 1992. *World Development Report.* New York: Oxford University Press.

———. 1994a. *Adjustment in Africa: Reforms, Results, and the Road Ahead.* A World Bank Policy Research Report. New York: Oxford University Press.

———. 1994b. *World Debt Tables 1994–95.* Vol. 1. Washington, DC: World Bank.

———. 1995. *World Development Report.* New York: Oxford University Press.

———. 2000a. *World Bank Africa Data Base 2000.* African Development Indicators. CD-ROM. Washington, DC: World Bank.

———. 2000b. *World Development Report 1999/2000.* New York: Oxford University Press for the World Bank.

———. 2005a. *African Development Indicators 2005.* Washington, DC: World Bank.

———. 2005b. *Prospects for the Global Economy*, November 16, 2005. Online at www.web.worldbank.org.

———. 2005c. *World Development Indicators 2005.* Washington, DC: World Bank.

6

African International Relations

Peter J. Schraeder

Several watershed events have influenced the evolution of African international relations since the late nineteenth century. In the aftermath of the Berlin Conference of 1884–1885, independent Africa (except for Ethiopia and Liberia) ceased to exist, and African international relations were controlled by the European colonial powers. A second watershed event—the extended global conflict of World War II (1935–1945)—heralded the decline of Europe as the most powerful region of the world and the emergence of African nationalist movements intent on achieving independence from colonial rule. This period marked the beginning of the end of colonial rule and the return of control over African international relations to Africans. The outbreak and intensification of the Cold War (1947–1989) transformed the newly independent African countries into proxy battlefields between the United States and the former Soviet Union, the unparalleled superpowers of the post–World War II era. African conflicts often having little, if anything, to do with the ideological concerns of communism or capitalism threatened to become East-West flashpoints in the face of growing US-Soviet involvement. A fourth watershed event, the fall of the Berlin Wall in 1989, signaled the end of the Cold War but not the end of international rivalry in Africa. The ideologically based Cold War between the United States and the former Soviet Union was replaced by a Cold Peace, in which the major northern industrialized democracies struggled for economic supremacy in a highly competitive economic environment of the 1990s. The security dimension of this cold peace became evident in the aftermath of the September 11, 2001, terrorist attacks against the World Trade Center in New York and the Pentagon in Washington, D.C., as the United States sought to enlist its African allies in a global war on terrorism. As African leaders continue to guide their countries toward the second decade of the new millennium, they must manage international relations in an environment marked by the growing competition among today's economic superpowers: China, Germany, Japan, and the United States.

This chapter is devoted to exploring African international relations in the aftermath of Europe's partition and eventual granting of independence to the fifty-three countries that currently constitute the African continent. After briefly outlining the major themes of what has been called the dependency-decolonization debate, I explore in the remainder of the chapter six topics that are critical to understanding the evolution of African international relations: (1) the formulation and implementation of African foreign policies; (2) pan-Africanism and the African Union; (3) regional economic cooperation and integration; (4) the role of foreign powers in African international relations; (5) the UN and international financial institutions; and (6) emerging trends related to military intervention on the African continent.

The Dependency-Decolonization Debate

Although the independence of Libya in 1951 marked the beginning of the end of formal colonial rule—a process largely culminating in 1994 when elections in South Africa led to black majority rule[1]—both African and foreign observers began an ongoing debate over the degree to which these newly independent countries truly control their international relations (see Shaw and Newbury, 1979). According to one group of observers who belong to what has become known as the *dependency school of thought,* the granting of legal independence that began in the 1950s did little to alter the constraining web of economic, political, military, and cultural ties that continued to bind African countries to the former colonial powers (Amin, 1973). This conceptualization of African international relations, often referred to as neocolonialism (Nkrumah, 1965), is especially prominent in writings about the relationship between France and its former colonies, primarily due to policies designed to maintain what French policymakers refer to as their *chasse gardée* (literally, an exclusive hunting ground) in francophone Africa (Suret-Canale, 1975). Even in those former colonies where the European power was either too weak (e.g., Spain) or uninterested (e.g., Britain) to preserve privileged ties, the rise of the Cold War and superpower intervention are said to have ensured the gradual replacement of European neocolonial relationships with a new set of ties dominated by Moscow and Washington (Laïdi, 1990). According to this perspective, direct colonial rule has been replaced by a series of neocolonial relationships that perpetuates external domination—albeit in a more subtle form—of African international relations.

Scholars of the *decolonization school of thought* argue instead that legal independence was but the first step of an evolutionary process permitting African leaders to assume greater control over their countries' international relations (Zartman, 1976; see also Bayart, 2000). According to this perspective, although external influences were extremely powerful in the immediate postindependence era, layer upon layer of this foreign control is slowly being "peeled away" with the passage of time. While carefully underscoring that individual African countries can follow different pathways, proponents of the decolonization school argue that the most common pattern begins with legal independence, followed by efforts to assure national sovereignty in the military, economic, and cultural realms. "In this view, each layer of colonial influence is supported by the others, and as each is removed, it uncovers and exposes the next underlying one, rendering it vulnerable, untenable, and unnecessary," explains I. William Zartman (1976:326–327), one of the most prominent proponents of the decolonization school. "Thus, there is a natural progression to the removal of colonial influence: its speed can be varied by policy and effort, but the direction and evolution are inherent in the process and become extremely difficult to reverse."

The end of the Cold War ushered in a radically changed international environment with important implications for the dependency-decolonization debate. Donald Gordon discusses in Chapter 4 how the fall of communist regimes in the former Soviet Union and Eastern Europe—the intellectual heartland of single-party rule—reinforced a democratization trend in Africa. In many cases this led to the replacement of authoritarian regimes with newly elected democratic leaders less enamored of their former foreign patrons (see Schraeder, 1994b). According to optimistic interpretations of the impact of this transforming event, Africa is undergoing a "second independence" or a "second national liberation" in which a second generation of African leaders will assume greater control over the international relations of their respective countries. However, observers associated with the dependency school equate the end of the Cold War with the rising marginalization of African international relations. They imply that African leaders enjoy less, rather than more, options in the post–Cold War international system (e.g., Shaw, 1991). Focusing on aggressive foreign efforts to promote democratization and economic reform, some observers have even suggested that the "recolonization" or "second scramble" for Africa is occurring (Ake, 1995). Although the dependency-decolonization debate is far from being resolved, the year 2018 will mark a symbolic turning point as the contemporary independence era (1951–2018) will have then lasted as long as the colonial era (1884–1951).

The Formulation and Implementation of African Foreign Policies

The principal theme of early studies of African foreign policy is that foreign policy begins and ends with the desires of African presidents (Korany, 1986; see also Wright, 1998). The primary reason for what has become known as the "big man" syndrome of African foreign policy is that the majority of the first generation of African presidents systematically suppressed and dismantled centers of power capable of challenging the foreign policy supremacy of the presidential mansion. The various efforts undertaken by this first generation included the stifling of a free press, the suspension of constitutions, the banning of opposition parties, the jailing of vocal political opponents, the dismantling of independent judiciaries, and, finally, the co-optation or jailing of legislative opponents to create "rubber stamp" parliaments (Chazan et al., 1999; see also Clapham, 1996; Schraeder, 2000a:217–243). In short, the institutional actors typically associated with making their voices heard in the foreign policy making processes of democratic polities were often marginalized in the name of creating single-party regimes capable of promoting unity and development.

The net result of what in essence constituted a highly centralized foreign policy machinery was the promotion of a "personalized" foreign policies derivative of the interests and idiosyncrasies of individual presidents (Jackson and Rosberg, 1982). In the case of the Democratic Republic of Congo (formerly Zaire), for example, Mobutu Sese Seko assumed power in 1965 through a military coup d'état supported by the US government and gradually concentrated all power around the office of the president (Young and Turner, 1989). Often unwilling to listen to his foreign policy experts within the Ministry of Foreign Affairs and having effectively silenced other potential centers of opposition, most notably by disbanding the Zairian National Assembly, Mobutu was known for declaring policies that created international controversy. During a presidential visit to the United States during 1973, for example, Mobutu made a speech before the UN General Assembly in which he announced his decision to rupture all diplomatic ties with Israel. This decision was notable in that it was made without any warning to the Nixon White House and effectively derailed State Department efforts to win congressional passage of a Zairian foreign aid bill (Schraeder, 1994b:82).

A second outcome associated with the centralization of the foreign policy apparatus is that the first generation of African presidents often pursued foreign policies strongly tied to those of the former colonial powers. In addition to the variety of formal ties (e.g., military treaties) that bound the newly independent countries to the former colonial powers, the primary reason for what proponents of the dependency school would characterize as "dependent" foreign policies (e.g., Shaw and Aluko, 1984) was the shared culture and political values of colonially trained African presidents and their European counterparts. Moreover, although they had actively campaigned for political independence, several first-generation presidents benefited from colonial efforts designed to ensure the victory of leaders sympathetic to European concerns. In the case of Senegal, for example, former president Léopold Sédar Senghor, sometimes described by his critics as more French than Senegalese, married a Frenchwoman, retired to a home in France, and carries the distinction of being the only African to be inducted into France's highly prestigious and selective Académie Française, the national watchdog of French language and culture (see Markovitz, 1969).

The most important outcome of the rise to power of the first generation of African presidents is that these leaders would often be more responsive to the foreign policy concerns of their external patrons than to the popular demands of their own peoples. Especially in the case of francophone Africa, the first generation of African presidents signed a variety of defense agreements with France that, rather than ensuring protection from threats from abroad, in reality were designed to ensure their political longevity. From 1963 to 1993, France intervened militarily at least thirty times in its former colonies, often at the request of presidents either under threat from internal opposition movements or seeking to be reinstated in power after being overthrown. Even in cases where pro-French leaders were overthrown by military coups d'état during the decade of the 1960s, the guiding principle of French involvement was the willingness of a particular leader to support French foreign policy objectives. For example, when asked why France did not militarily intervene when David Dacko, the democratically elected president of the Central African Republic, was overthrown in a military coup d'état in 1966, Jacques Foccart (1995:287), architect of France's policies toward francophone Africa under Presidents Charles de Gaulle and Georges Pompidou, noted in his memoirs that the new leader, Jean-Bedel Bokassa, "after all was a very pro-French military man."

The combination of the Cold War's end and the rising strength and intensity of prodemocracy movements is contributing to the "democratization" of African foreign policies (Adar and Ajulu, 2002; see also Schraeder and Gaye, 1997). The importance of this democratization trend—especially in the countries where multiparty elections have ensured a relatively peaceful transfer of power from one ruling elite to another—is its reinforcement of the rise to power of a new generation of African presidents less tied to their former foreign patrons and more willing to pursue increasingly independent foreign policies. In the case of Senegal, for example, President Abdou Diouf (1981–2000), like many of his second-generation counterparts, took advantage of growing economic competition among the industrialized Western democracies in the post–Cold War era to lessen his country's foreign policy dependence on France (Diop and Diouf, 1990). In a sharp departure from past policies, President Diouf withstood intense French pressures and signed contracts with South African and US companies in 1995 to exploit oil fields discovered off the southwestern coast of Senegal. This trend toward diversification of Senegalese foreign policy ties has been strengthened under the democratically elected administration of President Abdoulaye Wade (2000–present).

The democratization process has also significantly altered the centralized foreign policy structures in several African countries. In some cases, democratization has been accompanied by the implementation of policies designed to decrease both the size of the military establishment and its involvement in governmental affairs, including in the realm of foreign policy. In South Africa during the 1980s, for example, the military strongly argued in favor of the Afrikaner regime's decision to undertake destabilization policies against its immediate neighbors (Grundy, 1986). In the wake of the country's first multiparty elections in 1994, however, the new government headed by Nelson Mandela undertook a series of reforms designed to restore greater government control over a military force that had become too prominent in both domestic and foreign policies (Bischoff and Southall, 1999).

The democratization process has also led to the strengthening of institutional actors, most notably increasingly independent and vocal national legislatures, capable of challenging the presidency in the foreign policy realm. The primary reason behind this newfound legislative role is the creation of democratic political systems that embody the concept of separation of powers between the various branches of government. In the case of Benin, one of the democratic leaders of francophone West Africa, the National Assembly in December 1995 refused to ratify highly unpopular legislation that would have permitted the launching of a third structural adjustment program (SAP) promoted by both the administration of President Nicéphore Soglo (1991–1996) and the International Monetary Fund (IMF) and the World Bank. President Soglo's subsequent attempts at breaking the political stalemate between the legislative and executive branches of government (he announced his intention to launch the SAP through the "exceptional power" granted to the executive under Article 68 of the Constitution) was one of the critical factors that strengthened popular discontent to such a degree that he lost the 1996 presidential elections to his autocratic predecessor, President Mathieu Kérékou (1996–present; previously ruled 1972–1991) (Adjovi, 1998:107–139). Soglo had severely underestimated the power of his legislative opponents and their ability to translate deep-seated popular resentment of foreign-imposed SAPs into electoral defeat at the ballot box. For perhaps the first time in African political history, a democratically elected National Assembly played a critical role in ensuring the defeat of a previously popular and democratically elected president.

The democratization process also portends greater popular input into the foreign policy making process as the policies of the second generation of African leaders are increasingly held accountable to public opinion (e.g., see Bratton, Mattes, and Gyimah-Boadi, 2005). Even during the Cold War era, public opinion played an influential, albeit intermittent, role in African foreign policies. For example, it has been argued that public opinion, fueled primarily by radio broadcasts by Radio France Internationale, was the primary factor that led to bloody clashes between Senegal and Mauritania in 1989 (Parker, 1991; see also Pazzanita, 1992). Despite the fact that this conflict was neither desired nor promoted by President Diouf of Senegal or President Ould Taya of Mauritania, and despite their best efforts to contain public passions, both these leaders were confronted by violent clashes that spiraled out of control. In a sense, both leaders, as well as the foreign policies of their respective countries, became "prisoners" of public opinion.

One must also consider the impact of religious groups and leaders, especially Islamist movements, on African foreign policies. Sudan, Egypt, and Algeria are three countries in which Islamist movements play a key role either in supporting or opposing government policies in the post–Cold War era. Even during the Cold War, however, religion played a key role in African foreign policies in many countries. In the case of Senegal, Islamic leaders known as *marabouts* constitute an integral part of the domestic political system and play both informal and formal roles in the making of foreign policy (Villalón, 1995). The *marabouts* played a critical role in reducing tensions between Senegal and Mauritania in the aftermath of the 1989 border conflict by shuttling back and forth across the river that separates the two countries. A equally dramatic case occurred in the mid-1980s, when the Diouf administration was forced to withdraw an invitation to Pope John Paul II to visit the country due to the threats of leading *marabouts* to call upon their *taalibe* (disciples) to occupy the runways at the international airport. Although the Pope was subsequently reinvited and visited Senegal several years later in 1991, to the wide acclaim of both Muslims and Christians, the *marabouts* have clearly served notice that sensitive issues had to be raised with them in advance if the president wished to avoid embarrassing public confrontations. In short, if one wants to completely understand the formulation and implementation of Senegal's foreign policy, as well as that of other African countries with sizable Muslim populations, one must take into account the role of religion. (See Chapter 11 for more on the role of Islam in African politics.)

Finally, one must take into account the foreign policy impact of guerrilla groups that are opposed to the central authority of their countries and that create parallel diplomatic networks to promote their guerrilla causes.

Such networks are typically limited to neighboring countries that provide economic and military support and that serve as the bases of military operations. The most extensive diplomatic network maintained by an African guerrilla insurgency was that of the African National Congress (ANC). From 1960, the year that the ANC was banned by South Africa's apartheid regime, to 1994, the year that Nelson Mandela emerged victorious in South Africa's first multiracial, multiparty democratic elections, the ANC established forty-three diplomatic missions in Africa, Asia, Europe, and the Western Hemisphere, each of which was maintained during various lengths of time (Pfister, 2003).

Pan-Africanism and the Organization of African Unity

Inspired by the anticolonial activities of peoples of African descent living in North America and the West Indies during the nineteenth and twentieth centuries, African nationalists sought to promote a unified African front against colonial rule. What subsequently became known as the pan-African ideal was most forcefully enunciated for the first time at the 1945 meeting of the Pan-African Congress held in Manchester, England. At the conference, participants adopted a Declaration to the Colonial Peoples that affirmed the "rights" of all colonized peoples to be "free from foreign imperialist control, whether political or economic," and "to elect their own governments, without restrictions from foreign powers" (Ajala, 1988:36). In a separate Declaration to the Colonial Powers, participants underscored that if the colonial powers were "still determined to rule mankind by force, then Africans, as a last resort, may have to appeal to force in the effort to achieve freedom" (Ajala, 1988:36).

The pan-African ideal gained momentum during the heady independence era of the late 1950s and early 1960s. In an opening address to the first gathering of independent African nations on African soil, held in 1958 in Accra, Ghana, President Kwame Nkrumah proclaimed: "Never before has it been possible for so representative a gathering of African Freedom Fighters to assemble in a free independent African state for the purpose of planning for a final assault upon imperialism and colonialism" (in Ajala, 1988:39). According to Nkrumah, the realization of the pan-African ideal required a commitment between African leaders and their peoples to guide their countries through four stages: (1) "the attainment of freedom and independence"; (2) "the consolidation of that independence and freedom"; (3) "the creation of unity and community between the African states"; and (4) "the economic and social reconstruction of Africa" (Ajala, 1988:30).

Despite overwhelming agreement among African leaders that pan-

Africanism constituted a worthy foreign policy goal, sharp disagreement existed over the proper path to ensure such unity. One group of primarily francophone countries known as the Brazzaville Group (named after the capital of the Republic of Congo) sought a minimalist approach: the coordination of national economic policies through standard diplomatic practices. Little consideration was given to the possibility of creating continent-wide institutions. In sharp contrast, Nkrumah and other leaders, who belonged to what became known as the Casablanca Group (named after the Moroccan city), argued instead that the success of pan-Africanism required a political union of all independent African countries, patterned after the federal model of the United States. In speech after speech, Nkrumah promoted two themes that became the hallmark of this international vision: "Africa must unite!" and "Seek ye first the political kingdom!" (see Rooney, 1988).

A third group of African leaders, who belonged to what became known as the Monrovia Group (named after the capital of Liberia), rejected the idea of political union as both undesirable and unfeasible, primarily due to the assumption that African leaders would jealously guard their countries' newfound independence. They nonetheless sought a greater degree of cooperation than that espoused by the Brazzaville Group. Led by Alhaji Abubakar Tafawa Belewa, prime minister of Nigeria, the Monrovia Group called for the creation of a *looser organization* of African states. According to this vision of African international relations, African countries would guard their independence but promote growing cooperation in a variety of functional areas, most notably economic, scientific, educational, and social development. An important component of the Monrovia Group approach was a desire to create continent-wide institutions that would oversee and strengthen policy harmonization.

On May 25, 1963, thirty-one African heads of state largely embraced the Monrovia vision of African international relations by launching the Organization of African Unity (OAU), the first pan-African, intergovernmental organization of independent African countries based on African soil. Addis Ababa, Ethiopia, was chosen as the site for the OAU headquarters, and all major decisions and resolutions were formally discussed at the annual Assembly of Heads of State and Government. The sovereign equality of all member states was an important guiding principle of the organization, which differed significantly from the Great Power domination of the UN, given the special powers conferred upon the five permanent members (Britain, China, France, Russia, and the United States) of the UN Security Council.

Although the OAU's thirty-nine-year existence, which came to an end in 2002 with the launching of the African Union (discussed further below), has been correctly described as a "victory for pan-Africanism" (Olusanya, 1988:67), both critics and sympathetic observers questioned the organization's ability to play an effective role in African international relations (see also Amate, 1986; El-Ayouty, 1994). In a special issue of the *Nigerian Journal of International Affairs,* which assessed the OAU's continued relevance on the "Silver Jubilee" (twenty-five-year) anniversary of the organization's creation, one Nigerian scholar expressed "sadness" over the fact that, despite the best of intentions, the OAU had failed to live up to the expectations of its original framers (Olusanya, 1988:70). The OAU's effectiveness can be assessed by exploring several elements of the OAU Charter, each of which holds important implications for the dependency-decolonization debate.

The most important theme of the OAU Charter was support for the *inviolability of frontiers* inherited from the colonial era. Due to the multiethnic nature of most African countries, African leaders were concerned that changing even one boundary would open a Pandora's box of ethnically based secessionist movements and lead to the further Balkanization of the African continent into ever smaller economic and political units (see Davidson, 1992). In the case of the Nigerian civil war (1967–1970), for example, the OAU not only refused to sanction aid provision to Biafra (the secessionist southeast portion of the country), but voted a series of resolutions that underscored official support for the Nigerian federal government (Bukarambe, 1988:98). This decision upset international human rights activists, as well as several African countries aiding the secessionist government, because the military-dominated Nigerian government was using very effective starvation methods designed to bring the Biafrans—government and general population alike—to their knees (see Gordon, 2003: 141–142; Stremlau, 1977).

As ethnic tensions and separatist movements intensified in the post–Cold War era, African leaders remained firmly committed to maintaining borders inherited from the colonial era. Although the OAU recognized the sovereignty of Eritrea in 1993, after a UN-sponsored referendum in that country resulted in overwhelming popular support for independence, African leaders subsequently noted that this process did not question the hallowed concept of the inviolability of frontiers. Unlike most African countries, Eritrea was federated to Ethiopia after independence from colonial rule and therefore enjoyed the legal right to withdraw from that voluntary union (see Iyob, 1995). However, in similar cases of voluntary federation that have unraveled in the post–Cold War era, such as northern Somalia's 1991 unilateral declaration of independence as the Somaliland Republic, as well as other cases where a disgruntled region, such as the southern Sudan, has affirmed the right of self-determination, the OAU continued to affirm the concept of territorial integrity (see Omaar, 1994).

A second guiding principle of the OAU Charter was *noninterference in the internal affairs* of member states. In the early years of the organization,

African leaders debated whether to allow military leaders who had illegally deposed their civilian counterparts to maintain their OAU seats. This debate was resolved in favor of recognizing whatever group controlled the reins of power in a particular country (Akindele, 1988b:82–85). More significant was the silence among African leaders concerning human rights abuses in OAU member states. "Increased repression, denial of political choice, restrictions on the freedom of association, and like events occurred, with rare murmurs of dissent," explains Claude Welch, Jr., a specialist on human rights in Africa. "The OAU seemed to function as a club of presidents, engaged in a tacit policy of not inquiring into each other's practices" (Welch, 1991:537). During the 1970s, for example, Ugandan dictator Idi Amin was elected OAU chair despite his personal involvement in "politically sanctioned repression and murders" in Uganda (Welch, 1991:538).

Although still highly reluctant to criticize their counterparts, African leaders began to accept a growing role for the OAU in addressing human rights abuses at the beginning of the 1980s. In 1981, the annual Assembly of Heads of State and Government held in Banjul, Gambia, adopted the African Charter on Human and People's Rights (popularly called the Banjul Charter). This human rights code officially went into effect in October 1986 and has served as the guiding principle for a variety of human rights groups that emerged during the 1980s (Welch, 1991). In addition to encompassing first-generation rights (civil and political liberties) usually associated with the Western world and second-generation rights (economic and social rights) usually associated with the socialist world, the Banjul Charter has been described as "breaking some new ground" through the adoption of third-generation rights intended to protect the rights of individual peoples or ethnic groups (Welch, 1991:538–539; see also Shivji, 1989).

Despite the ratification of the Banjul Charter, however, the OAU's response to events in Nigeria during 1995 demonstrated the continued difficulty of translating human rights rhetoric into policy action. In response to disturbances among the Ogoni ethnic group in southeastern Nigeria, which began in 1990 over control of that region's vast oil resources, Nigeria's military regime unleashed a brutal campaign of repression that included the November 1995 execution of Nobel Peace Prize candidate Ken Saro-Wiwa and eight other Ogoni activists on trumped-up murder charges (French, 1995:E3; see also Osaghae, 1995). Although OAU Secretary General Salim Ahmed Salim expressed "disappointment" over the fact that the Nigerian generals failed to "respond positively" to OAU appeals for clemency, the organization did not adopt concrete, comprehensive measures to punish or to internationally isolate the Nigerian regime (quoted in French, 1995:E3).

The *peaceful settlement of all disputes* by negotiation, mediation, conciliation, or arbitration constituted a third guiding principle of the OAU.

Yet strict adherence to the first two principles—support for territorial integrity and noninterference in internal affairs—historically impeded the OAU's ability to mediate either internal conflicts or conflicts between two or more member states. In the case of the 1967–1970 Nigerian civil war, almost reflexive support for the territorial integrity of Nigeria seriously called into doubt, at least from the viewpoint of the secessionist Igbos, the OAU's ability to serve as an impartial negotiator. For this reason, the OAU Commission of Mediation, Arbitration, and Conciliation was "stillborn" (Zartman, 1995b) and most African-initiated arbitration efforts were carried out ad hoc by African presidents. For example, Djiboutian president Hassan Gouled Aptidon used his country's stature as the headquarters for the Intergovernmental Authority on Development (IGAD) to mediate the conflict between Ethiopia and Somalia. According to Zartman (1995a:241), a specialist of conflict resolution, such efforts led to success in only 33 percent of roughly twenty-four cases, and this success was often only temporary in nature as warring parties returned to the battlefield.

The ability to dispatch peacekeeping or peacemaking forces once a conflict has broken out is a critical aspect of conflict resolution. The OAU founding fathers attempted to prepare for this eventuality by planning the creation of an African High Command, a multinational military force comprised of military contingents from OAU member states. The African High Command never made it beyond the planning stage, however, leading once again to a variety of ad hoc measures. In 1981, the OAU sponsored the creation of a short-term, all-African military force designed to resolve an expanding civil war in Chad. Composed of approximately 4,800 troops from Zaire, Nigeria, and Senegal, the OAU force "failed to achieve any concrete solution" due to financial, logistical, and political difficulties and within a few months was "forced to withdraw" (Gambari, 1995:225).

An important outcome of the lack of OAU coordination in the military realm has been a variety of military interventions by individual countries and intergovernmental organizations. Four sets of actors periodically have intervened in African conflicts: (1) the UN, as demonstrated by its approval of more than fifteen peacekeeping missions in Africa since 1989; (2) African regional organizations, such as the decision of the Economic Community of West African States (ECOWAS) to sponsor a series of Nigerian-led military operations in Liberia; (3) foreign powers, most notably France, the United States, and, to a lesser degree, the United Kingdom, as witnessed by the dispatch of British troops to Sierra Leone; and (4) African powers, as demonstrated by South Africa's military intervention in neighboring Lesotho. From the perspective of pan-Africanists, such ad hoc interventions, especially those undertaken by foreign powers without the consent of either the local or international communities, are ultimately undesirable; rather than representing an African consensus opinion, such interventions are theoretically driven by the self-interests of the intervening country.

Two developments underscored the OAU's desire to take a more proactive role in African conflicts in the post–Cold War era. In 1993, the OAU Assembly of Heads of State and Government adopted a resolution creating the Mechanism for Conflict Prevention, Management, and Resolution, a formal consultative process ideally designed to prevent the outbreak and further spread of conflicts on the African continent (Zartman, 1995a:243). The inspiration for this consultative process was a forward-thinking document, "Toward a Conference on Security, Stability, Development and Cooperation in Africa," popularly called the Kampala Document, which was the result of a 1991 conference convened by former Nigerian president Olusegun Obasanjo (see also Zartman, 1999).

The most important development, however, revolved around the possibility of creating a multinational African Defense Force, able to respond militarily to African crises. In May 1997, African leaders agreed that such a force should be comprised of existing military units of contributing OAU member states and that these units would be equipped with the aid of foreign powers, most notably the United States and France. The African Defense Force would remain under the operational command of the OAU. Unresolved issues included which countries should be eligible to contribute forces (e.g., should involvement be limited to democratic countries?) and what type of decisionmaking body should be capable of authorizing when and where to intervene (e.g., should intervention be based on the consensus of all OAU member states or should a smaller body of representative members be responsible?). Discussions concerning the African Defense Force nonetheless remained at an exploratory stage, and the Mechanism for Conflict Prevention, Management, and Resolution remained largely untested.

The final and most successful principle embodied within the OAU Charter was the *unswerving opposition to colonialism and white minority rule.* Principally concerned with the past existence of minority white-ruled regimes in Namibia, South Africa, Zimbabwe, and the former Portuguese-controlled territories of Angola, Mozambique, Guinea-Bissau, and São Tomé and Principe, the OAU established a Liberation Committee based in Dar es Salaam, Tanzania, to aid liberation movements with both economic and military assistance (see Akindele, 1988a). Although disagreements often arose over which tactics would best ensure transitions to majority-ruled governments (e.g., should one support dialogue with a white regime or fund a guerrilla insurgency?), every OAU member expressed public opposition to the continued existence of minority white-ruled regimes. The work of the Liberation Committee largely came to an end in 1994, when South Africa transitioned to a multiracial, multiparty democracy.

The OAU entered the history books July 8–10, 2002, as leaders from more than forty African countries met in Durban, South Africa, to launch the African Union, a pan-African organization designed to build on the successes of the OAU in the continuing search for African unity. Amara Essy, a distinguished statesman from Côte d'Ivoire, was chosen to serve as interim chairperson of the African Union's Commission and Thabo Mbecki, president of South Africa, hosted the summit. Like its OAU predecessor, the African Union holds an Annual Summit of Heads of State and Government, adopts official positions on a wide array of diplomatic topics affecting the African continent, and counts on a number of offices and institutions designed to strengthen African cooperation. It is led by a ten-member executive body—the African Commission—that is composed of a chairperson, deputy chairperson, and eight commissioners who are responsible for the following eight portfolios:

- *Political affairs,* such as democratic elections and human rights
- *Peace and security,* most notably efforts devoted to conflict resolution
- *Economic affairs,* inclusive of promoting regional integration
- *Infrastructure and energy,* such as the development of the transportation and telecommunications sectors
- *Social affairs,* ranging from sports and migration to health issues and anti-drug efforts
- *Human resources, science, and technology,* such as education and new information technologies
- *Trade and industry,* most notably efforts devoted to trade and investment
- *Rural economy and agriculture,* inclusive of food security and protection of the environment

Several guiding principles of the organization clearly indicate a new path in African regional cooperation that builds on both the successes and failures of the OAU. In sharp contrast to the OAU, the African Union has not enshrined in its founding charter the concept of inviolability of frontiers inherited from the colonial era. Despite its commitment to the territorial integrity of African countries, the African Union maintains a greater amount of flexibility in dealing with both ongoing and future conflicts by not including such a rigid and restrictive principle in its founding document. Especially noteworthy is the African Union's rejection of the OAU principle of noninterference in the domestic affairs of member countries. Member states have instead agreed that the African Union has the right to intervene in the domestic affairs of member states in cases of gross violations of human rights and genocide and war crimes. In addition, all member states commit themselves to strengthening democratic practices, most notably holding free and fair elections and ensuring freedom of expression. In the international realm, an important African Union–sponsored initiative is the New Partnership for Africa's Development (NEPAD), designed to strengthen Africa's position in the global economy and attract greater levels of foreign aid and investment (discussed further below). Together these principles have reignited a sense of African optimism in the pursuit of the cherished goal of pan-Africanism.

Regional Economic Cooperation and Integration

Inspired by the success of the European Union (EU) and encouraged by the UN-sponsored Economic Commission for Africa (ECA), based in Addis Ababa, Ethiopia, the first generation of African leaders sought to create regional entities capable of promoting regional cooperation and integration. This vision of African international relations was best captured by the OAU's publication in 1981 of a document, *Lagos Plan of Action for the Economic Development of Africa, 1980–2000,* which proposed the establishment of an African Economic Community (AEC) that would be based on an African Common Market (ACM). The guiding logic of the *Lagos Plan of Action* is that the creation of intergovernmental economic organizations in each of Africa's five major regions—North, East, West, Southern, and Central Africa—is the best means for ensuring the ultimate creation of a continent-wide AEC. (See Chapter 5 for information on the economic crises that have inspired these efforts.)

The flourishing of experiments in regional cooperation and integration throughout the contemporary independence era demonstrated the firm commitment of the first generation of African leaders to the economic dimension of the pan-African ideal. By the end of the 1980s, it was estimated that at least 160 intergovernmental economic groupings existed on the African continent, with thirty-two such organizations in West Africa alone (Seidman and Anang, 1992:73). Among the most notable and far-reaching economic groupings in each of Africa's major regions (including dates of launching) are the Economic Community of West African States (ECOWAS, 1975); the Union of the Arab Maghreb (UAM, 1989); the Southern African Development Community (SADC, 1980); the Economic Community of Central African States (ECCAS, 1983); and the Intergovernmental Authority on Development (IGAD) in northeast Africa (1986). These regional organizations are complemented by a few larger groupings, such as the Lomé Convention, which promotes preferential trade links between the European Union and dozens of countries from Africa, the Caribbean, and the Pacific (see Ojo, 1985:146–150).

African leaders offer several rationales for seeking regional cooperation and integration. The simplest reason is the firm belief that there is strength in numbers. In order to effectively compete within an increasingly competitive international economic system, dominated by economic superpowers (e.g., the United States and Japan) and powerful regional economic entities (e.g., the European Union and the North American Free Trade Agreement [NAFTA] zone), African countries must band together and pool their respective resources. Second, African leaders desire to promote self-sustaining economic development and particularly the industrialization of the African continent. Struggling with the reality that many of their countries are economically impoverished and lack the tools for the creation of advanced industries, African leaders believe that they can build upon the individual strengths of their neighbors to forge integrated and self-sustaining regional economies.

Most important, regional economic schemes are perceived as the best means of creating self-reliant development, thereby reducing and ultimately ridding the African continent of the ties of dependency inherited from the colonial era (Asante and Chanaiwa, 1993:741–743). For example, African leaders are rightfully concerned that national control over the evolution of their respective economies is constrained by Africa's trade dependency on Europe, at the expense of intraregional trade links with African countries. For this reason the primary objective of early regional economic schemes was to promote intraregional trade with neighbors who theoretically share a common set of development objectives—either due to special geographic features, historical ties, or a shared religion, such as Islam in North Africa (e.g., see Grundy, 1985). By strengthening these ties with like-minded neighbors, a stronger African economic entity is expected to emerge that will be capable of reducing foreign influence and strengthening Africa's collective ability to bargain with non-African powers on a more equal basis.

Early optimism began to wane in the aftermath of the launching of several regional integration efforts, which included the creation of supranational authorities and formal economic unions designed to promote intraregional trade and investment. In the case of the East African Community (EAC), the 1967 decision of Kenya, Tanzania, and Uganda to create a common market with common services, coordinated by a supranational governing body, collapsed less then ten years later, and was followed in 1978–1979 by Tanzania's military intervention in Uganda to overthrow the dictatorial regime of Amin (Potholm and Fredland, 1980). As explained by Olatunde Ojo (1985), a specialist of regional cooperation and integration in Africa, several factors that contributed to the EAC's decline clarify why other similar efforts, from the 1960s to the 1980s, either failed or demonstrated minimal progress.

An initial problem was the *polarization of national development and the perception of unequal gains* (Ojo, 1985:159–161). As typically occurred in other cases in Africa where the creation of a common market served as the cornerstone of the regional grouping, the most industrialized country (Kenya) usually reaped the benefits of economic integration at the expense of its partners (Uganda and Tanzania). For example, Kenya's share of intracommunity trade increased from 63 percent in 1968 to 77 percent in 1974, whereas Uganda's share decreased from 26 to 6 percent during the same period. In addition, despite the fashioning of a common policy toward the establishment of new operations by multinational corporations (MNCs), the majority of these firms decided to locate their bases of operations in Kenya due to its more advanced economy and workforce, as well as its extensive infrastructural network of roads, railroads, ports, and airports.

The EAC also foundered due to the *inadequacy of compensatory and corrective measures* (Ojo, 1985:161–166). In every integration scheme, some countries inevitably benefit more than others. As a result, policymakers can implement measures, such as the creation of regional development banks or the disproportionate sharing of customs revenue, to correct the imbalance and compensate those countries expected to lose out in the short term. In the case of the EAC, a regional development bank was created to disburse funds in the following manner to the three members: Kenya (22 percent), Tanzania (38 percent), and Uganda (40 percent). However, in this and other cases of integration in Africa, even the richest members are usually incapable of subsidizing bank operations. The actual finances provided to the most needy members therefore never even begin to approach true development needs or completely compensate for losses incurred.

A third stumbling block to successful regional integration of the EAC was *ideological differences and the rise of economic nationalism* (Ojo, 1985:168–169). Simply put, ideological differences often ensure a radically different approach to development projects, which in turn can significantly hinder regional integration. In the case of Kenya, a pro-West capitalist regime was very open to private enterprise and foreign investment, particularly the opening of local offices of MNCs. The socialist-oriented regime of Tanzania, however, opted for a self-help strategy known as *ujamaa* (the Kiswahili term for brotherhood), which not only denounced private enterprise as exploitative, but also restricted the flow of foreign investment, and strongly controlled the MNCs. When combined with the growing public perception of unequal gains between the two countries, these ideological differences led to often acrimonious public debate between President Jomo Kenyatta of Kenya and President Julius Nyerere of Tanzania, and to the rise of economic nationalism in both countries.

A final element that contributed to the EAC's decline was the *impact of foreign influences* (Ojo, 1985:169–171). Whereas Kenya developed close relationships with the Western-bloc nations (e.g., the United States and Great Britain), Tanzania pursued close links with the socialist bloc (particularly the People's Republic of China), and Uganda sought links with the former Soviet Union and the Arab world. These links ensured that the EAC became embroiled in the Cold War rivalry of the 1960s and the 1970s and contributed to the creation of an outwardly directed "strategic image" that prompted EAC member states to look "outward" toward their foreign patrons rather than "inward" toward their natural regional partners.

Beginning in the 1980s, the failure and stagnation of classic integration schemes prompted African leaders to undertake looser forms of regional *economic cooperation* in a variety of functionally specific areas, such as transportation infrastructure (e.g., regional rail links), energy (e.g., hydroelectric projects on common rivers), and telecommunications (see Onwuka and Sesay, 1985; Aly, 1994; Lavergne, 1997; Oyejide, Elbadawi, and Collier, 1997). The logic behind pursuing this form of regionalism is that it does not require the creation of supranational authorities, nor does it require policymakers to sacrifice national control over the sensitive areas of foreign trade and investment. This looser form of economic cooperation is gathering strength in the post–Cold War era, particularly as democratically elected elites increasingly assume power and seek to promote cooperation with other democracies in their regions.

The 1992 transformation of the Southern African Development Coordination Conference (SADCC) into the SADC is a good example of this growing trend in African regional relations. Originally conceived as a vehicle for reducing the economic dependence of the Frontline States[2] on South Africa during the apartheid era, the transformed SADC now counts South Africa among its members and is seeking to enhance traditional cooperation in a variety of functional realms, most notably transportation (Khadiagala, 1994; see also Love, 2005). The new SADC stands poised at "the threshold of a new era," according to several reports published by the African Development Bank in conjunction with the World Bank and the Development Bank of South Africa. "Although its effects and the inequities it has embedded will linger for a long time to come, the demise of apartheid opens up prospects unimaginable even a few years ago," explains one report. "New opportunities have emerged in every sector of economic activity for expanded trade and mutually beneficial exchanges of all kinds among the countries of southern Africa" (Morna, 1995:65).

Several factors are essential to understanding the optimism surrounding SADC's newfound status as a model for economic cooperation in Africa, particularly in terms of reducing southern Africa's dependence on foreign economic interests and creating the basis for self-sustaining development in the post–Cold War era (see Blumenfeld, 1992; see also Gibb, 1998). First, the inclusion of a highly industrialized South Africa provides

SADC with an engine for economic growth that will potentially reinvigorate the entire region. In this regard, South Africa may play a leadership role similar to that enjoyed by Germany in the EU, the United States in NAFTA, and Nigeria in ECOWAS. The majority of SADC members (seven out of ten) also share a common British colonial heritage. Although a shared colonial past is not a precondition for effective regional cooperation, it facilitates such technical matters as which language should serve as the official language of communication (in the case of SADC, English).

A third facilitating factor is the decline in ideological differences between SADC member states that accompanied the end of the Cold War. Angola, Mozambique, and Zimbabwe have discarded in varying degrees their adherence to Marxist principles of development; South Africa has officially renounced its apartheid system; and Tanzania and Zambia have dismantled significant portions of their formerly socialist economies. In essence, there is a growing consensus among SADC member states that effective regional economic cooperation must be based on a shared commitment to some variant of the liberal capitalist model of development.

SADC's greatest strength is a regional commitment to conflict resolution and to the promotion of shared democratic values (Ohlson and Stedman, 1994). The Cold War's end and the rise of democratization movements have led to the end of civil wars and the holding of democratic elections throughout the region, although an authoritarian trend in Zimbabwe at the beginning of 2006 remains an issue of concern for regional leaders. One of the most important lessons of regional integration theory, which draws upon the success of the European Union, is that the existence of elites with a shared commitment to democracy is the foundation of long-term economic cooperation and development. For this reason, the 1992 Windhoek Treaty (named after the capital of Namibia), which consecrated the launching of SADC, underscored the political dimension of regional relationships and its critical role in the continued expansion of economic cooperation. The leaderships of SADC member states recognize that the fruits of pan-Africanism can only be achieved by the settlement of civil war and the promotion of democracy throughout the African continent. As a result, conflict resolution remains an important cornerstone of the pan-African ideal at the beginning of the twenty-first century.

The Role of Foreign Powers in African International Relations

Many important policies affecting the future of African politics and society are decided in Beijing, Paris, Washington, Berlin, and Tokyo—the capitals of the Great Powers that are significantly involved in Africa at the beginning of the twenty-first century (Aluko, 1987; see also Nielson, 1969). France maintains extensive political-military and economic relationships with African countries, most notably in francophone Africa, those former French and Belgian colonies where, among a variety of factors, French serves as one of the official languages of administration and/or education.[3] The United States often became the most influential political-military actor in the non-francophone portions of the African continent during the Cold War era and increasingly has sought to promote economic links in the post–Cold War era (Schraeder 1994b, 1998). Japan and Germany emerged during the 1980s as extremely involved economic actors and have achieved the status of the second or third most important sources of economic aid or trade for individual African countries (often behind the leading roles of France and the United States) (Schulz and Hansen, 1984; Nester, 1992; Hofmeier, 1994; Brüne, Betz, and Kuhne, 1994; Morikawa, 1997).

Britain's official interest in maintaining privileged colonial ties, once rivaled only by that of France, dramatically waned during the Cold War (Styan, 1996; Bangura, 1983). Economic decline forced British policymakers to make difficult decisions as to where limited economic resources would contribute the most to British foreign policy interests, ultimately leading to the downgrading of British ties with most of its former colonies. In recent years, however, Britain, under the leadership of Prime Minister Tony Blair, has become more active in African international relations, as demonstrated by its leadership role in dispatching peacekeeping troops to Sierra Leone in West Africa. Britain's most noteworthy ongoing involvement with its former African colonies takes place in the context of the Commonwealth of Nations, a loose association of former British colonies that holds an annual summit meeting of heads of state.

Other, traditionally less powerful colonial powers, such as Spain, were never important diplomatic players due to the lack of extensive colonial holdings (Naylor, 1987; Segal, 1989). Weaker colonial powers demonstrated only sporadic interest in their former colonies during times of crisis, such as Belgium in central Africa and Italy in the Horn of Africa (e.g., see Ercolessi, 1994). Portugal, however, has exhibited a renewed interest in strengthening cultural ties with its former colonies and played an important role in promoting the resolution of civil wars in Angola and Mozambique during the 1990s (MacQueen, 1985).

Despite extensive involvement during the Cold War era, most of the former communist bloc countries have drastically reduced their political-military and economic presence on the African continent. The preoccupation of Russian leaders with the economic and political restructuring of the former Soviet Union has precluded any meaningful diplomatic role in Africa (Patman, 1990). Other communist bloc countries that once enjoyed privileged relations with the African continent either completely disappeared (e.g., the former East Germany, which now constitutes part of a reunified Germany) (Winrow, 1990), or became marginalized (e.g., Cuba) due to their pariah status within the international system and a drastic reduction in aid formerly provided by their socialist patrons (Mesa-Lago and Beikin, 1982). The one exception to this trend involves the People's Republic of China (PRC), whose once formidable presence during the 1960s had been transformed by the end of the 1980s into primarily a diplomatic battle with Taiwan as to which capital—Beijing or Taipei—was recognized by African governments as the official seat of the Chinese government (Larkin, 1971; Snow, 1988; Xuetong, 1988). At the beginning of the twenty-first century, however, the PRC economy's burgeoning demand for primary resources (especially oil) and trade outlets has fueled a dramatic expansion of Chinese-African relations, leading some to emphasize the potential dangers that such activities pose for Western, especially US, interests in Africa (Council on Foreign Relations, 2005). (Read more about China in Africa in Chapter 13.)

A variety of middle powers plays varying roles on the African continent. Canada and the Nordic countries, most notably Sweden, demonstrate a strong humanitarian interest, particularly concerning famine relief in the Horn of Africa and Southern Africa (e.g., Stokke, 1989). During the height of the Arab-Israeli conflict, Israel pursued an aggressive policy that exchanged Israeli technical aid for continued or renewed diplomatic recognition of the state of Israel (Peters, 1992; Decalo, 1997). Other Middle Eastern powers, such as Saudi Arabia, pursue religiously based policies regarding the predominantly Muslim states of North and northeast Africa (Creed and Menkhaus, 1986). Iran in particular seeks to foster links with Islamist regimes and movements in Sudan, Egypt, and Algeria; and Iraq's previously expanding relationships with several African countries, most notably Mauritania, were sharply curtailed after Iraq was defeated in the 1991 Gulf War (Lesser, 1993). India and Brazil lead their regions in seeking to expand economic relations with the African continent (Collins, 1985; Dubey, 1990; Karnik, 1988).

The specific impact of foreign powers can be illuminated by analyzing the evolving policies of the two countries—France and the United States—that remain the most active on the African continent. US and French foreign policies were driven by different sets of motivating factors during the Cold War era. US policymakers were principally guided by the ideological interest of containing the former Soviet Union and its communist allies (Schraeder, 1994b). A variety of presidential doctrines, beginning with the Truman Doctrine in 1947 and culminating in the Reagan Doctrine of the 1980s, declared Washington's right to intervene against communist advances throughout the world, including in francophone Africa. As a result, pro-West administrations, such as Senegal under President Diouf, were treated as potential US allies deserving of foreign aid, whereas Marxist administrations, such as Madagascar under Didier Ratsiraka, were isolated. US policymakers also sought special relationships with strategically important regional actors, such as Morocco in North Africa, Ethiopia in the Horn of Africa, and South Africa in southern Africa, that offered special military access rights or maintained important US technical facilities (e.g., telecommunications stations) deemed critical to containment policies in Africa (for example, see Lefebvre, 1991).

French policymakers sought first and foremost to consolidate and promote the *rayonnement* (spread) of the most notable aspects of French culture, including the French language and intellectual traditions (Kolodziej, 1974:479). Also called the promotion of *la francophonie* (a greater French-speaking community), this policy is best represented by the biannual Franco-African summit attended by the leaders of France and francophone Africa, the twenty-third of which was held in Bamako, Mali, in December 2005. Economic interests were perceived by French policymakers as both parallel and integral to the promotion of French culture, as witnessed by the organization of thirteen former French colonies and Equatorial Guinea in the *zone franc* (franc zone). Created in 1947, the franc zone constitutes a supranational financial system in which France serves as the central bank, and a common currency—the Communauté Financière Africaine (CFA) franc—is tied to the French franc and guaranteed by the French treasury. By wedding its fiscal policy to the franc zone, France has sought to preserve monetary stability and French influence throughout francophone Africa (Vallée, 1989).

As long as the United States and France were pursuing fundamentally different but complementary foreign policy interests, Africa remained the chief beneficiary of a complementary Cold War order in which US-French relations tended to be balanced, cooperative, and predictable. Regardless of whether France was led by the conservative partisans of de Gaulle or the socialists of François Mitterrand, French policymakers predictably claimed that historical links and geographical proximity justified placing francophone Africa in France's sphere of influence. The implicit assumption of what serves as the French version of the Monroe Doctrine is that francophone Africa constituted France's *domaine réservé* (natural preserve) or *chasse gardée* (private hunting ground) and therefore remained off-limits to other Great Powers, regardless of whether they were friends like the United States and the other northern industrialized democracies or enemies like the former Soviet Union and other radical powers (quoted in Schraeder, 2000b).

During the Cold War, this conception of francophone Africa was wholeheartedly accepted and even encouraged by US policymakers. Washington in particular expected France and the other European allies to

Only after he committed large-scale atrocities against his own people, including allegedly beating some schoolchildren to death, did France in 1979 finally turn against and depose "Emperor" Jean-Bedel Bokassa, its client ruler in the Central African Republic.

Thomas O'Toole

take the lead in their former colonial territories. As succinctly stated by George Ball, undersecretary of state in the Kennedy administration, the United States recognized Africa as a "special European responsibility," just as European nations were expected to recognize "[US] responsibility in Latin America" (Ball, 1968). According to US policymakers, France emerged as the only European power with both the long-term political will and the requisite military force capable of thwarting communist powers from exploiting instability, prompting some analysts to refer to France as Washington's de facto *gendarme* (policeman) in francophone Africa (Goldsborough, 1978; Lellouche and Moisi, 1979; see also Hoffman, 1967).

The fall of the Berlin Wall marked the beginning of the end of the complementary Cold War order among the Western democracies and its gradual replacement with what is best referred to as a Cold Peace, or rising Great Power competition within the highly competitive economic environment of the 1990s. In the case of France, for example, policymakers were confronted by an intensifying economic crisis on the African continent that created rising pressures for change within the carefully crafted web of economic ties that bound the French economy to those of francophone Africa (Sandbrook, 1993; Callaghy and Ravenhill, 1993). With many of their clients on the verge of financial bankruptcy, French policymakers initially decided to undertake an economic bailout that entailed massive increases in foreign aid. French aid to francophone Africa increased from the already substantial level of $3.7 billion in 1980–1982 to $8.2 billion in 1990–1992—a nearly 120 percent increase during a ten-year period. Once it became clear that the short-term bailouts were insufficient and that projected aid levels were beyond France's fiscal capabilities, French policymakers took the extraordinary step in January 1994 of devaluing the CFA franc by 50 percent. The decision sent shockwaves throughout the CFA franc zone, which had never before suffered a devaluation; it signaled that France's commitment to the cultural imperative of *la francophonie* no longer necessarily took precedence over the pursuit of economic self-interest in an increasingly competitive, post–Cold War world.

In the case of the United States, the end of the Cold War fostered the decline of ideologically based policies in favor of the pursuit of trade and investment (Schraeder, 1998). In 1996, the administration of Bill Clinton unveiled the first formal US trade policy for aggressively pursuing new markets throughout Africa, including in francophone Africa (Department of Commerce, 1996). As discussed in more detail in Chapter 13, the centerpiece of this economic strategy was congressional legislation, the Africa Growth and Opportunity Act (AGOA), passed by both houses of Congress under the prodding of the Clinton White House during its second term in office and subsequently embraced by the administration of George W. Bush. Africa's enhanced economic standing in Washington was perhaps best captured by President Clinton's decision to make a twelve-day presidential visit to Africa in 1998, which included stops in Botswana, Ghana, Rwanda, Senegal, South Africa, and Uganda. For the first time in US history, a sitting US president had led an extended diplomatic mission to Africa, intent on improving US-Africa ties and promoting US trade and investment on the African continent.[4]

The Bush administration's response to the terrorist attacks of September 11, 2001, nonetheless demonstrated the durability of strategic interests in Great Power involvement in Africa. These attacks profoundly influenced US foreign policy as the Bush administration announced a global war on terrorism, including pledges to aid countries threatened by terrorism, that harkened back to the initial stages of the Cold War when the Truman administration underscored the need to aid countries threatened by communism. In the case of the African continent, the Bush administration has focused its efforts on North and East Africa. The microstate and former French colony of Djibouti, for example, emerged in 2003 as the site for the Defense Department's Combined Joint Task Force–Horn of Africa (CJTF-HOA), the primary responsibility of which is to maintain surveillance over the movement of potential terrorist groups in neighboring Eritrea, Ethiopia,

Kenya, Somalia, Sudan, and Yemen. The US-Djiboutian agreement creating the CJTF-HOA includes the housing of more than 1,800 US Special Forces at a US military base in Djibouti—the only such agreement signed with an African country—whose function is to carry out military operations against terrorist groups in the region. Similar anti-terrorism programs include the Trans-Saharan Counter-Terrorism Initiative (TSCTI), which encompasses the countries of Algeria, Chad, Mali, Mauritania, Niger, and Senegal (including the involvement of Morocco, Nigeria, and Tunisia as observer countries) and the East Africa Counter-Terrorism Initiative (EACTI), which includes Djibouti, Eritrea, Ethiopia, Kenya, Tanzania, and Uganda. It is important to note that these three programs are not unique, but rather indicative of the strengthening of US security ties with African countries deemed important to the war on terrorism.

The transformation of foreign policy interests in the post–Cold War era has contributed to the rise of Great Power economic competition throughout Africa, particularly in the highly lucrative petroleum, telecommunications, and transport industries. In the eyes of French policymakers, the penetration of US and other Western companies constitutes "at best an intrusion" and "at worst an aggression" into France's *chasse gardée* in francophone Africa. The seriousness with which this issue was treated at the highest levels of the French policymaking establishment was demonstrated by the public admission of Minister of Cooperation Michel Roussin that a series of meetings had been held on how best to defend French interests, including those within the economic realm, against those of the United States (Glaser and Smith, 1994; see also Védrine and Moïsi, 2000).

Intense competition between the government of the Republic of Congo, Elf-Aquitaine (the French oil corporation), and Occidental Petroleum Corporation (Oxy), a US-based oil company, is an excellent example of the potential future stakes involved in rising US-French economic competition. Desperately in need of nearly $200 million to pay government salaries before legislative elections, newly elected president Pascal Lissouba "naturally turned for help to Elf-Aquitaine (which controls 80 percent of the country's oil production)." When its French manager refused to approve either a $300 million loan or "a request for a $300 million mortgage on the future production of three promising new off-shore oil deposits," Lissouba initiated secret negotiations with the US-based Oxy. An agreement was signed but renounced eight months later by the Lissouba administration due to "intense French pressure" (quoted in Schraeder, 2000b). US-French competition in the highly lucrative petroleum industry is not limited to the Republic of Congo or even US-French relations for that matter, but rather indicative of a more competitive foreign policy environment in which Africa has become an increasingly important source of global oil (e.g., see Klare and Volman, 2004; and Ellis, 2003).

The emergence of economic competition during the Cold Peace has also affected Great Power support for democratization. The end of the Cold War raised expectations that the Western democracies could make democracy and human rights the cornerstones of a new democratic international order that would be consistently applied to all regions of the world, including in francophone Africa. Scholars, activists, and policymakers in both the United States and France increasingly coalesced around the concept of making political democratization a precondition for the improvement of economic and political relations with Paris and Washington. Democracy promotion, however, has never served as the principal foreign policy goal of the northern industrialized democracies. At best it has played a secondary role behind more self-interested foreign policy pursuits. As a result, although democracy promotion has emerged as a more salient foreign policy issue during the post–Cold War era, it nonetheless tends to be compromised when it conflicts with more central foreign policy interests of Paris and Washington (Schraeder, 2002).

In the case of France, the administration of President Mitterrand initially embraced African democratization movements in a much-quoted speech at the 1990 Franco-African summit held in La Baule, France, and warned his counterparts in francophone Africa that future French aid would be contingent on their willingness to promote true democratic change. What became known as the La Baule Doctrine suggested that the promotion of democracy would become the new hallmark of French foreign policy. The bold rhetoric of democratization was nonetheless contradicted by the reality of ongoing foreign aid programs designed to keep pro-French leaders in power (Bayart, 2000; Agir Ici et Survie, 1995). In the case of Cameroon, French aid to the authoritarian regime of President Paul Biya expanded from $159 million in 1990 to $436 million in 1992, the year of the country's first multiparty presidential elections. The primary reason for the dramatic increase in French aid was to ensure Biya's victory, especially as the most popular opposition candidate was John Fru Ndi, an anglophone politician perceived as a threat to French interests in Cameroon. Any misconceptions generated by earlier French rhetoric were resolved at the 1992 Franco-African summit held in Libreville, Gabon. At this meeting, French prime minister Pierre Bérégovoy privately stated that when confronted with the potentially conflicting goals of promoting democracy, ensuring development, and maintaining security, the leaders of francophone Africa were expected to adopt the following order of priorities: above all, security, followed by development, and finally, democratization (Glaser and Smith, 1994:102).

The election of Jacques Chirac as president of France in May 1995 coincided with an increasingly turbulent period in French foreign policy (Marchal, 1995). The growing contradictions in France's democratization policies were shown by the Chirac administration's response to a February 1996 coup d'état in Niger, the first against a democratically elected government in France's former colonies since the beginning of the democratization process in 1990. Despite a 1995 commitment by Minister of Cooperation Jacques Godfrain that France would intervene to reinstate a democratically elected government if a defense treaty had been signed with that country, France refused to intervene in Niger and ultimately decided to work with the military regime headed by Colonel Ibrahim Maïnassara Baré (French, 1996b:A3). Not surprisingly, the democratically elected francophone neighbors of Niger were worried by French inaction. In a throwback to an earlier era of authoritarian rule and highly questionable democratic practices, Colonel Baré announced that there would be multiparty elections in 1996, presented himself as the candidate of the ruling party, and subsequently won the election to the congratulatory toasts of local French diplomats.

Contradictions were also evident in US support for democratization policies. At the very least, punitive measures designed to enforce prodemocracy rhetoric are at best unevenly applied depending on the perceived importance of the African country. The Clinton administration was quick to enforce comprehensive economic sanctions against the mini-state of Gambia when that country's military took power in a coup d'état in 1994, but it refused to impose comprehensive economic sanctions against the military dictatorship of Nigeria that would have affected US access to Nigerian oil, the mainstay of the Nigerian economy (although it did impose a variety of more limited sanctions, such as the suspension of military cooperation). In addition, in the aftermath of the terrorist attacks of September 11, 2001, against the World Trade Center and the Pentagon, the Bush White House had to weigh the benefits of democracy promotion when the pursuit of such a policy would potentially alienate important African allies in the war on terrorism. In the case of Djibouti, for example, a decision to make democracy promotion the principal US foreign policy objective theoretically would have precluded the stationing on Djiboutian soil of the CJTF-HOA. Indeed, all four of Washington's North African allies in the war on terrorism (Algeria, Egypt, Morocco, and Tunisia) lack democratic political systems. "In short," explained one member of the US Embassy in Tunis, "foreign policy is about choosing, and in this case there is no question that the security interest of combating global terrorism with our allies in North Africa is more important than the degree to which the peoples of these countries enjoy democratic forms of governance" (Anonymous interview, January 24, 2003).

Regional variations nonetheless exist. US diplomats have typically been more vocal than their French counterparts in their support for democracy movements in francophone West Africa. The unusually vocal stance of these diplomats is at least partially the result of a self-interested calculation that the United States has little to lose and everything to gain by excoriating pro-French elites who impede the transition to a new political order. The logic of diplomatic competition at the local level is based on perceptions of the democratization process as a zero-sum game—that is, one country's gain is another's loss. From the perspective of local US ambassadors, for example, promoting multiparty democracy is a low-cost strategy with potentially high returns—namely, the replacement of pro-French elites with new leaders potentially more sensitive to US interests. From the perspective of local French ambassadors, the reverse holds true, which explains why French policymakers tend to emerge as protectors of the status quo.

In Benin, for example, President Soglo's victory in the first presidential elections to be held after his country's transition to democracy in 1991 led to the formation of an administration less dependent on France and more interested in promoting closer foreign ties with the United States (Adjovi, 1998). It is precisely for this reason, argue critics of French policies in Africa, that local French diplomats provided significant support to Soglo's authoritarian predecessor, Kérékou, who emerged victorious in the 1996 presidential elections. Although he ultimately accepted the 1996 election results, Soglo remained sharply critical of the "northern countries" (read "France"), whom he at least partially blamed for his defeat at the hands of Benin's former dictator of nineteen years. Regardless of France's ultimate role in the 1996 presidential elections, however, Kérékou's reemergence did not signal a return to the same Beninois-French relationship that existed prior to 1991. The strengthening of several competing institutional actors, most notably a vibrant national assembly, has contributed to growing pluralism in Beninois foreign policy.

Rising competition between the United States and France holds important implications for the dependency-decolonization debate. From the viewpoint of the second generation of African leaders, rising economic competition among the Great Powers provides an opportunity to lessen previously privileged ties of dependence and pursue special relationships and especially economic contracts with countries willing to provide the best offer. Although the ultimate resolution of the "oil war" in the Republic of Congo in favor of France suggests that the ties of dependency are not automatically broken by the end of the Cold War, the Lissouba government nonetheless was able to obtain a better agreement from the French as a result of "playing the American card." In other cases, such as Senegal's decision to offer lucrative exploration rights to US and South African companies at the expense of previously privileged ties with the French oil industry, the second generation of African leaders are successfully utilizing their increased independence within the international system to acquire the best deals for their respective countries, thereby ensuring future electoral victories in democratic political systems where public support—not authoritarian force—increasingly is the key to power.

The UN and International Financial Institutions

The relationship of African countries to the UN and to a host of international financial institutions is critical to understanding the relevance of the decolonization-dependency debate. During the independence era of the 1960s, a variety of factors suggested that membership in the UN was facilitating the ability of the first generation of African leaders to assume greater control over the international relations of their respective countries (Mathews, 1988). In addition to serving as a concrete symbol of African independence, UN membership historically has provided African leaders with an important international forum for promoting African views on a variety of international issues, such as unequivocal support for complete decolonization, opposition to apartheid in South Africa, the promotion of socioeconomic development, and the need for disarmament and attention to regional security. Most important, the UN provides a unique forum for diplomatic negotiations. Financially unable to maintain embassies throughout the world, let alone throughout the African continent, African diplomats take advantage of the fact that almost all countries maintain a permanent mission in New York to carry out the day-to-day business of diplomacy (Mathews, 1988).

In an era in which it has become fashionable for many Westerners, particularly Americans, to criticize their countries' involvement in the UN as providing few if any tangible economic or political benefits, it is important to recognize that UN agencies often play substantial administrative and development roles in many African countries. In several African capital cities, there are a variety of UN offices whose budgets and staffs sometimes approach those of their counterparts within the host government. In Dakar, the capital of Senegal, for example, offices represent a variety of UN agencies, including the United Nations Development Programme (UNDP), the United Nations International Children's Emergency Fund (UNICEF), the United Nations High Commissioner for Refugees (UNHCR), the World Health Organization (WHO), the International Labour Organisation (ILO), and the United Nations Educational, Scientific, and Cultural Organization (UNESCO). Capturing the sentiment of African policymakers during the 1960s, a Senegalese diplomat noted that "these agencies were perceived as critical to the fulfillment of African development goals during the initial independence era, and provided a source of hope especially for those impoverished countries lacking both the resources and the expertise to implement the studies and programs pursued by each of these agencies."[5]

In the aftermath of the Cold War, however, a sometimes vocal segment of African leaders and intellectuals is often apt to associate the UN with foreign intervention and the imposition of Western values. The primary reason for this development is the UN's increased involvement in a variety of largely ethnic-based crises (such as in Sierra Leone, Somalia, and Rwanda), which seemingly have intensified in the post–Cold War era. As succinctly summarized by Zartman (1995a:1–14), these crises often occur against the backdrop of "collapsed states"—the temporary disintegration of the legitimate, sovereign authority of the nation-state that is responsible for maintaining law and order within its territory. This collapse can be complete, as was the case in Somalia when civil war engulfed the country in the aftermath of the overthrow of Somali dictator Mohamed Siad Barre in 1991, or it can entail the breakdown of effective central authority over the majority of the country despite the existence of a ruling regime, as occurred in the case of the Democratic Republic of Congo under the authoritarian rule of Laurent Désiré-Kabila. This perception is due to the replacement of the classic international norms of sovereignty and nonintervention in the affairs of UN member-states with a new set of norms that focus on human rights protection and humanitarian intervention, particularly to save refugees and other peoples threatened by civil conflict and starvation (Deng et al., 1996:5; see also Prendergast, 1996). As aptly noted by former UN Secretary-General Boutros Boutros-Ghali (1992:9), "The time of absolute and exclusive sovereignty . . . has passed; its theory was never matched by reality." Indeed, the UN has undertaken more than twenty peacekeeping missions in Africa, with more than fifteen of these launched in the post–Cold War era.

The series of UN-sponsored military interventions in Somalia from 1992 to 1995 serves as one of the most notable examples of the UN's increasingly interventionist role in African politics and society. At its height, the UN military operation included over 38,000 troops from twenty countries and led to the effective occupation of southern and central Somalia. The intervention was launched in the absence of any official invitation from a legal Somali authority (which, in any case, did not exist), and in direct opposition to heavily armed militia groups who shared a historical mistrust of UN intentions and operations dating back to the colonial era (Hirsch and Oakley, 1995).[6] From the perspective of the UN, the collapse of the Somali state and the intensification of a brutal civil war demanded UN intervention; the conflict was not only spilling over into the neighboring territories of Kenya, Ethiopia, and Djibouti, but it had contributed to the creation of a humanitarian crisis in which approximately 330,000 Somalis were at "imminent risk of death" (Lyons and Samatar, 1995:24).

According to this logic, the UN could justify international intervention, even in the absence of an official invitation by a legally constituted authority, on the grounds of "abatement" of a threat to international peace (Joyner, 1992:229–246).

The Somali case is part of a growing international trend of prompting even internationally recognized governments to accept UN-sponsored humanitarian intervention (Deng, 1993; see also Prendergast, 1996). In the Sudan, for example, a combination of civil war and drought-induced famine, which led to the deaths of over 500,000 civilians since 1986, prompted the UN Office of Emergency Operations in Africa (OEOA) to undertake a humanitarian intervention in 1989 known as Operation Lifeline Sudan (Deng and Minear, 1992). Constituting one of the largest peacetime humanitarian interventions ever undertaken in UN history, Operation Lifeline Sudan was made possible only by mounting international pressure on the Sudanese regime to recognize the scope of the problem and to accept UN-sponsored intervention. Ultimate acceptance, however, did not ensure ultimate happiness on the part of the Sudanese regime. "Even when the initial issues of involvement are resolved, relations between the donors and the recipient country or population are never entirely harmonious," explains a group of specialists on conflict resolution, led by Francis M. Deng, a Sudanese national who served as Special Representative of the UN Secretary General for Internally Displaced Persons. "The dichotomy expressed between 'us' and 'them' becomes inevitable as the nationals feel their pride injured by their own failure and dependency, while the donors and relief workers resent the lack of gratitude and appreciation" (see Deng et al., 1996:11).

African perceptions of eroding sovereignty have been reinforced by the rising influence of international financial institutions in African economies (Mkandawire and Olukoshi, 1995). As Virginia DeLancey discusses in Chapter 5, by the beginning of the 1980s, African leaders were struggling to respond to the effects of a continent-wide economic crisis that combined internal economic decline with mounting international debt. In order to obtain necessary international capital, most African leaders had little choice but to turn to two international financial institutions: the IMF, which issues short-term stabilization loans to ensure economic solvency, and the World Bank, which issues long-term loans to promote economic development. Unlike typical loans that simply require the recipient to make regular scheduled payments over a specific period of time, those of the IMF and the World Bank have included a series of externally imposed demands, typically referred to as "conditionalities," designed to restructure African economies and political systems in the image of the northern industrialized democracies (Callaghy and Ravenhill, 1993).

The emergence of economic conditionalities was signaled by the 1981 publication of a World Bank study, *Accelerated Development in Sub-Saharan Africa: An Agenda for Action.* The conclusion of this report was that misguided decisions of the first generation of African leaders were responsible for the mounting economic crisis. To resolve this crisis, the World Bank and the IMF proposed the linking of all future flows of Western financial capital to the willingness of African leaders to sign and implement structural adjustment programs: economic blueprints designed to radically restructure African economies. Four sets of private sector reforms are characteristic of SAPs: (1) the termination of food subsidies that kept food prices artificially low, effectively discouraging farmers from planting food crops; (2) the devaluation of national currencies to stimulate exports and the domestic production of manufactured products; (3) the trimming of government bureaucracies; and (4) the privatization of parastatals (state-owned corporations). In short, the SAPs embodied the liberal economic consensus of the northern industrialized democracies that Africa's future economic success depended on the pursuit of an export-oriented strategy of economic growth that systematically dismantled all forms of governmental intervention in national economies (Commins, 1988; Campbell and Loxley, 1989).

A second World Bank report published in 1989, *Sub-Saharan Africa: From Crisis to Sustainable Growth: A Long-Term Perspective Study*, heralded the emergence of political conditionalities in IMF and World Bank–sponsored SAPs. In addition to claiming that African countries following IMF and World Bank economic prescriptions were performing better than those that were not, the 1989 report went beyond previous studies by underscoring that the success of economic reforms was dependent on the promotion of "good governance," the creation of transparent, accountable, and efficient political systems patterned after those of the northern industrialized democracies. Simply put, the 1989 report signaled an emerging consensus in favor of making all future flows of Western financial capital contingent on the willingness of African leaders to promote the liberalization of their respective political systems.

The economic and political conditionalities imposed by the IMF and the World Bank have been repeatedly challenged by African policymakers and academics. During the 1980s, the SAPs were criticized for their complete disregard for the political realities African leaders confront. IMF and World Bank economists failed to consider that cutting off government subsidies, one of the above-noted four pillars of private sector reform always included in SAPs, could lead to often violent urban riots. In Sudan, for example, the launching of an SAP in 1985 sparked an urban insurrection that contributed to the overthrow of the regime of Gaafar Mohammed Nimeiri (Harsch, 1989). The implementation of the three remaining pillars of private sector reform also entailed serious political risks, due to their tendency to reinforce short-term economic hardships. The devaluation of the national currency meant an immediate decline in the already marginal buying power of the average citizen, and the trimming of government bureaucracies and the privatization of parastatals triggered significant increases in already high levels of national unemployment. In retrospect, the lack of political sensitivity was because the SAPs were usually formulated by international economists with little (if any) political training or firsthand knowledge of the individual African countries their programs were supposed to serve.

SAPs were also strongly challenged by African policymakers and academics during the 1990s despite the fact that both the IMF and the World Bank had undertaken serious efforts to assess and, when possible, incorporate African sentiments into policy-planning documents. Africans were particularly critical of the consensus of IMF and World Bank economists that economic and political conditionalities were mutually reinforcing and therefore could be pursued simultaneously (Sandbrook, 1993). As demonstrated by Africa's experiments with democratization after the fall of the Berlin Wall in 1989, the creation of democratic political systems complete with institutional checks-and-balances has hindered the implementation of SAPs. Indeed, democratically elected African presidents and congressional representatives often hesitate to enact legislation that will place significant economic burdens on already impoverished populations and thereby potentially contribute to their political demise the next time elections are held.

The end of the Cold War has had a dramatic effect on the role of conditionalities in the African continent's international economic relations. The terms of the debate have shifted away from such Cold War–inspired questions as whether Marxism or an African variant of socialism is favorable to capitalism, or whether single-party or multiparty regimes can better promote the welfare of their respective peoples. Instead, the IMF and the World Bank now consider how to best facilitate the creation of capitalist, multiparty political systems throughout Africa.

The critical dilemma confronting Africa's newly elected democratic leaders is the extent to which they will attempt to work with international financial institutions. If they wholeheartedly embrace SAPs for the future economic health of their societies, they are bound to alienate important actors within their political systems and therefore run the risk of losing subsequent democratic elections. In the case of Benin, for example, the democratically elected government of Soglo was rejected in the 1996 presidential elections after only one term of office, at least partially as a result of his administration's strong support for externally inspired SAPs. In contrast, if democratically elected African leaders refuse to embrace SAPs, they run the risk of losing access to international capital and contributing to the further decline of their economies.

Cautiously optimistic interpretations suggest that reform-minded African leaders and external supporters of change must adopt "realistic, hardheaded" analyses of Africa's economic plight that avoid both the Afropessimism of critics of change and the overly optimistic "cheerleading" stance of those who believe that change can be implemented quickly, smoothly, and relatively free of pain (Callaghy and Ravenhill, 1993). According to this viewpoint, although even the best-intentioned and most reform-minded African leaders may find themselves "hemmed in" by a variety of international constraints that restrict policy choices, they nonetheless are capable of pursuing paths that may lead to economic success over the long term. More pessimistic interpretations from the dependency tradition nonetheless suggest that African countries "desperate for access to international capital" are now "uniquely vulnerable" to the demands of the IMF and the World Bank. "While dependency analysts long argued that international capitalist structures provided the context within which development in Africa occurred," explains Reed (1992:85), "it was only as Africa approached the 1990s that international financial institutions—controlled by the leading capitalist powers and designed to bolster the international capitalist economy—were able to impose policy prescriptions directly upon African governments."

African leaders have sought to curb the impact of economic and political conditionalities by formulating alternative frameworks for development. One of the earliest attempts was the adoption of the Lagos Plan of Action (LPA) at the 1980 OAU Assembly of Heads of State and Government held in Freetown, Sierra Leone. The LPA was not taken seriously in international financial circles due to its contradictory assumption that Western governments and financial institutions would finance the pursuit of self-reliant economic development designed to delink the African continent from the international economic system. In 1989, the ECA published a document, *African Alternative Framework to Structural Adjustment Programmes for Socioeconomic Recovery and Transformation (AAF-SAP)*, that drew at least the grudging acceptance of IMF and World Bank economists. Acknowledging that African leaders were partially responsible for Africa's economic crisis and that some form of economic restructuring was necessary, the 1989 report nonetheless castigated the IMF and World Bank for ignoring the social and political impacts of SAPs. The report specifically called on international donor agencies to promote structural adjustment with a human face: to plan for and respond to the short-term negative social impacts (e.g., rising unemployment) that inevitably accompany the good-faith efforts on the part of African leaders to implement SAPs.

The most recent and far-reaching alternative framework for development advanced by African leaders is the New Partnership for Africa's

Development. The essence of NEPAD is that African countries must undertake economic and political reforms if they wish to attract the foreign capital from the northern industrialized democracies that is deemed necessary to Africa's future development (Hope, 2002). Specifically, African leaders are seeking increases in grant aid (as opposed to loans that must be paid back) and foreign investment and trade from the northern industrialized democracies. In return, they have agreed to establish a peer review mechanism in which African leaders will assess and critique the degree to which African countries are undertaking promised economic and political reforms. Although important hurdles remain (e.g., critics have questioned how Libya and other nondemocratic African countries can take part in the peer review committee), an important step in the NEPAD initiative was educating and seeking the agreement of key northern leaders. To this end, the four major African proponents of the NEPAD initiative (Presidents Abdulaziz Bouteflika of Algeria, Thabo Mbeki of South Africa, Olusegun Obasanjo of Nigeria, and Abdoulaye Wade of Senegal) attended the 2002 annual meeting of the Group of Eight (G8), where they received endorsements for NEPAD and promises of increased aid from the leaders of the eight most powerful northern industrialized democracies: Canada, France, Germany, Italy, Japan, Russia, the UK, and the United States. Although the African Union and the UN have also endorsed NEPAD, only time will tell if rhetoric will be matched by increased flows of foreign capital from the northern industrialized democracies and the strengthening of economic and political reforms on the part of African leaders.

The Changing Equation of Military Intervention

A variety of African security challenges, most notably the emergence of "collapsed states" (Zartman, 1995a) beset by ethnic, religious, and political rivalries, has fostered renewed international debate over the desirability of foreign intervention in Africa at the beginning of the new millennium. The potential military role of the United States, often deemed the "sole superpower" with a responsibility to act, was sharply influenced by a series of US-led military operations in Somalia known as Operation Restore Hope, most notably after eighteen US soldiers were killed and seventy-eight others wounded in October 1993 in a fierce battle in Mogadishu, Somalia (Clarke and Herbst, 1997). The Somali "debacle," as it came to be known, served as the cornerstone of a May 1994 policy directive, Presidential Decision Directive 25 (PDD-25), that announced an extremely cautious US approach to ethnically and religiously based conflicts in Africa. When confronted in 1994 with rising popular demands for US intervention in Rwanda, for example, the Clinton administration, fearful of being drawn into "another Somalia," not only initially blocked the dispatch of 5,500 troops requested by Secretary-General Boutros-Ghali, it instructed administration spokespersons to avoid labeling the unfolding ethnic conflict as "genocide" lest such a label further inflame US public sympathy and demands for US intervention, as was the case in Somalia, or trigger US obligations under international treaties dealing with genocide and its prevention (Jehl, 1994; see also Lemarchand, 1998).

The experience in Somalia also significantly affected the Clinton administration's approach to conflict resolution, most notably by resolving a debate between two currents of thought in the administration. The first emphasized the classic belief that African issues unnecessarily distract the administration and potentially plunge Washington into unwanted domestic political controversies. According to this viewpoint, US involvement (even in terms of conflict resolution) should be restricted to avoid entanglement in "future Somalias" (Cason and Martin, 1993:2). A second, more activist approach also derived from the Somali experience, but underscored that the massive costs associated with Operation Restore Hope could have been avoided by earlier, preventive action. "The choice is not between intervening or not intervening," explained one policymaker at the beginning of the Clinton administration. "It is between getting involved early and doing it at a cheaper cost, or being forced to intervene in a massive, more costly way later" (Cason and Martin, 1993:2). As witnessed by the Clinton administration's cautious approach to the initial stages of the Rwandan conflict, the events of October 1993 in Somalia clearly strengthened the position of those warning against getting too closely involved in "intractable" conflicts in Africa.

The Bush administration entered office in 2001 with a more "realist" vision of international affairs that nonetheless shared its predecessor's maxim of avoiding undue US involvement in African conflicts. This tendency was clearly indicated during the presidential campaign, when Bush noted that the Clinton administration had done "the right thing" in deciding not to intervene in the unfolding genocide in Rwanda in 1994 (French, 2001). Bush administration policy was formalized by Secretary of State Colin Powell, who underscored during his confirmation hearings before the US Senate the need for Africans to "do more for themselves" in the realm of conflict resolution. "In Sierra Leone, Liberia, Angola, the Congo [Democratic Republic of Congo], and elsewhere, this means stopping the killing, taking the weapons out of the hands of children, ending corruption, seeking compromises, and beginning to work in peace and dialogue rather than war and killing," explained Powell. "It means giving the profits from oil and diamonds and precious resources to schools and hospitals and decent roads instead of to bombs, bullets, and feuding warlords" (Powell, 2001). Indeed, according to what could be labeled the "Powell Doctrine" for Africa, African diplomats and military forces, and not those of foreign powers (including the United States), must take the lead in responding to African crises and conflicts.

France, arguably the most militarily active foreign power on the African continent during the Cold War era, also recast its military role at the beginning of the new millennium (Bourmaud, 2000). The evolving nature of French military intervention was best captured by the Chirac administration's response to a series of crises in the Great Lakes region, most notably the emergence and spread in 1997 of a guerrilla insurgency in the Democratic Republic of Congo that successfully sought to overthrow the authoritarian regime of Mobutu. French policymakers perceived the Great Lakes crisis in francophone-anglophone terms: the guerrilla insurgency in eastern DRC was led by Désiré Kabila, who in turn was strongly supported by and allied with the Rwandan government of Paul Kagame and the Ugandan government of Yoweri Museveni. As a result, the French considered Kabila's guerrilla movement to be under Anglo-Saxon influence, and therefore hostile to France. The worst-case scenario envisioned by French policymakers occurred when Kabila's guerrilla army overthrew the Mobutu regime in May 1997 and installed a new government (with Kabila as president) strongly allied with Rwanda and Uganda, which in turn are closely allied with the United States. According to this vision, Kabila's emergence as the president of the Democratic Republic of Congo not only constituted a clear victory for Anglo-Saxon influence at the expense of *la francophonie,* but also raised the possibility that the country might serve as a potential springboard for the further spread of Anglo-Saxon influence throughout francophone Africa, a fear that was dampened after Kabila had a political falling out with his former Rwandan and Ugandan allies, who subsequently launched a second guerrilla insurgency in 1998 designed to militarily overthrow the Kabila regime.

The Chirac administration's attempts at playing a more proactive military role in the Great Lakes region were restrained by a variety of factors, including the lack of interest among the other Great Powers to authorize a UN-sponsored, multilateral military force; the publicly stated promise of the Rwandan government and Kabila's guerrilla forces to militarily engage and inflict heavy casualties on French forces; and the French military's limited military capability to independently move and sustain the large numbers of troops and equipment that would have been necessary for a long-term engagement in such a vast military theater. France's long-term military role in Africa was most dramatically affected by the decision to restructure and downsize the French military that followed in the aftermath of Lionel Jospin's election as prime minister in 1997 and the emergence of a divided government under Chirac's conservative political forces (which led the presidency) and Jospin's Socialist Party and allies (which were responsible for forming a new government). As part of this general reorganization, the decision was made to both downsize the French military presence in Africa and, in some cases, such as the Central African Republic, to eliminate French military bases completely.

The restructuring of French-African military relations is tied to ongoing debates in the French foreign policy making establishment between the so-called *anciens* (the ancients), who favor activist measures (including direct military intervention) to maintain pro-French clients in power, and the *modernes* (the moderns), who emphasize the need to move beyond France's interventionist past in its former colonies (Bourmaud, 2000). At least as far back as February 1994, when the CFA franc was devalued, moves have been afoot to isolate the old-line defenders of France's *chasse gardée* in Africa. No case demonstrated the rising influence of the moderns better than Chirac's rejection of the use of military force to return Henri Konan Bédié to power in Côte d'Ivoire—one of the linchpins of French foreign policy in francophone Africa—after his regime had been overthrown in a December 1999 military coup and replaced with a military regime led by General Robert Gueï. Less than three years later, however, French military intervention in Côte d'Ivoire to prevent the government of President Laurent Gbagbo, who had succeeded Gueï in 2000, from being overturned by a guerrilla insurgency, clearly demonstrated the enduring legacy of the ancients in French foreign policy toward Africa.

The African dimension of an evolving interventionist equation is best captured by two developments. First, a series of successful guerrilla insurgencies fostered the rise during the 1990s of what was often called a "new bloc" of African leaders that includes Isaias Afwerki of Eritrea, Meles Zenawi of Ethiopia, Yoweri Museveni of Uganda, and Paul Kagame of Rwanda (Connell and Smyth, 1998; Ottaway, 1999). Successful in their pursuit of power primarily due to their control over strong, disciplined, and battle-tested guerrilla armies, this new generation of elites shared a commitment to create "responsive and accountable" but not necessarily democratic governments that significantly reordered the foreign policy relationships pursued by their predecessors—although they certainly do not act as a cohesive bloc, as witnessed by the outbreaks of warfare between Ethiopia and Eritrea in 1999 over a disputed boundary. Equally important has been the greater willingness on the part of African regional powers, most notably Nigeria and South Africa, to flex their authority in their regions. Indeed, South Africa's self-anointed role as leader of the "African Renaissance," the strengthening of democratic practices and economic liberalization throughout Africa since the fall of the Berlin Wall in 1989, is part of a conscious effort among South African policymakers to underscore their country's unique position as an intermediary between the African continent and leading foreign powers in all other regions of the world (Crouzel, 2000).

An important outcome of these trends during the post–Cold War era has been the rising tendency of African countries to militarily intervene in their neighbors. The most clear-cut example of this new trend was the expansion of civil conflict in the Democratic Republic of Congo into what foreign observers now commonly call Africa's "First World War." At its height in 2002, this conflict was marked by the introduction of massive numbers of ground troops by at least five African countries: Angola, Namibia, and Zimbabwe, which were fighting on the side of the Democratic Republic of Congo's government, and Rwanda and Uganda, which were seeking to topple that government. Although the individual stakes of African countries contributing troops to this conflict were extremely varied (e.g., see Clark, 2002), together they underscored an emerging reality of African international relations at the dawn of a new millennium: the rising importance of regional military balances of power and the political-military and economic interests of regional actors. Africa, having provided a battlefield for superpower interests during the Cold War, provides another for rising African powers intent on dominating the international relations of their respective regions.

Toward the Future

The end of the Cold War and the rise of democratization movements served as transforming events in the evolution of the international relations of the African continent. These events in turn allow us to draw some tentative conclusions about the dependency-decolonization debate. Although neither approach was completely supported or rejected by the analysis, three trends—the democratization of African foreign policies, rising competition among the Great Powers, and the rising assertiveness of African regional powers—suggest the increased ability of the second generation of African leaders to assume greater control over the international relations of their respective countries. Yet, proponents of the dependency approach can point to the increasingly pervasive nature of intervention on the part of the UN and international financial institutions as supportive of their vision of international relations. Moreover, despite some promising developments related to SADC and ongoing discussions in the OAU about the possible creation of African regional mechanisms to promote democracy and regional security, neither the OAU's pursuit of pan-Africanism nor regional experiments in economic cooperation and integration offer compelling evidence to resolve the dependency-decolonization debate. A common element in all seven of the topics we have discussed, however, is the importance of the democratization process and its impact on the rise of a second generation of African leaders committed to democratic principles. Although it is perhaps too early to tell, one can hypothesize that if democratization succeeds, it will facilitate the peeling away of another layer of dependency and allow the second generation of African leaders to assume greater control over the international relations of their respective countries.

Notes

1. The only remaining territorial questions revolve around the future disposition of Western (Spanish) Sahara (partitioned by Morocco and Mauritania), and Spain's continued control over the enclaves of Ceuta and Melilla, both of which are claimed by Morocco.

2. These countries are Angola, Botswana, Lesotho, Malawi, Mozambique, Swaziland, Tanzania, Zambia, and Zimbabwe.

3. For the purposes of this chapter, francophone Africa includes twenty-five independent states from the following regions: Central Africa (Burundi, Cameroon, Central African Republic, Chad, Republic of Congo, Democratic Republic of Congo, Gabon, and Rwanda); East Africa (Djibouti); Indian Ocean (Comoros, Madagascar, Mauritius, and Seychelles); North Africa or the "Maghreb" (Algeria, Morocco, and Tunisia); and West Africa (Benin, Burkina Faso, Côte d'Ivoire, Guinea, Mali, Mauritania, Niger, Senegal, and Togo). Our definition of francophone Africa therefore is inclusive of both sub-Saharan and Saharan Africa (i.e., "trans-Saharan" Africa or the entire continent) rather than the more exclusionary set of sub-Saharan African countries.

4. The only exceptions to this trend include President George H. W. Bush's one-day visit to Somalia in 1993 while in transit to the Middle East, and President Jimmy Carter's March 29–April 2, 1978, visit to Nigeria.

5. Personal interview, Dakar, Senegal, January 1995.

6. Somali distrust of the UN stems from the decision of that international body to support the reimposition in 1950 of Italian colonial rule over what is currently known as the Republic of Somalia.

Bibliography

Adar, Korwa G., and Rok Ajulu (eds.). 2002. *Globalization and Emerging Trends in African States' Foreign Policy-Making Process: A Comparative Perspective of Southern Africa*. Aldershot, UK: Ashgate.

Adjovi, Emmanuel V. 1998. *Une élection libre en Afrique: La présidentielle du Bénin (1996)*. Paris: Karthala.

Agir Ici et Survie. 1995. *La France à Biarritz: Mise en examen de la politique française (Biarritz 8 et 9 novembre 1994)*. Paris: Karthala.

Ajala, Adekunle. 1988. "Background to the Establishment, Nature and Structure of the Organization of African Unity." *Nigerian Journal of International Affairs* 14 (1):35–66.

Ake, Claude. 1995. *Democracy and Development in Africa*. Washington, DC: Brookings Institution.

Akindele, R. A. 1988a. "The Organization of African Unity and Conflict Situation in Southern Africa." *Nigerian Journal of International Affairs* 14 (1):124–154.

———. 1988b. "The Organization of African Unity: Four Grand Debates Among African Leaders Revisited." *Nigerian Journal of International Affairs* 14 (1):73–94.

Aluko, Olajide (ed.). 1987. *Africa and the Great Powers in the 1980s.* Lanham, MD: University Press of America.

Aly, Ahmad A. H. M. 1994. *Economic Cooperation in Africa: In Search of Direction.* Boulder, CO: Lynne Rienner Publishers.

Amate, C. O. C. 1986. *Inside the OAU: Pan-Africanism in Practice.* New York: St. Martin's Press.

Amin, Samir. 1973. *Neo-Colonialism in West Africa.* Harmondsworth, England: Penguin.

Asante, S. K. B., with David Chanaiwa. 1993. "Pan-Africanism and Regional Integration." Pp. 724–743 in Ali A. Mazrui (ed.). *General History of Africa.* Vol. 8. *Africa Since 1935.* Paris: UNESCO; Oxford: Heinemann; Berkeley: University of California Press.

Ball, George. 1968. *The Disciples of Power.* Boston: Little, Brown.

Bangura, Yusuf. 1983. *Britain and Commonwealth Africa: The Politics of Economic Relations, 1951–1975.* Manchester: Manchester University Press.

Bayart, Jean-François. 2000. "Africa in the World: A History of Extraversion." *African Affairs* 99, no. 395:217–267.

Bischoff, Paul-Henri, and Roger Southall. 1999. "The Early Foreign Policy of the Democratic South Africa." Pp. 154–181 in Stephen Wright (ed.). *African Foreign Policies.* Boulder, CO: Westview.

Blumenfeld, Jesmond. 1992. *Economic Interdependence in Southern Africa: From Conflict to Cooperation?* New York: St. Martin's Press.

Bourmaud, Daniel. 2000. "Nouvelles tendances dans la politique africaine de la France: Réforme institutionnelle et processus de décision." Unpublished paper.

Boutros-Ghali, Boutros. 1992. *An Agenda for Peace: Preventative Diplomacy, Peace-Making, and Peace-Keeping.* New York: United Nations.

Bratton, Michael, Robert Mattes, and E. Gyimah-Boadi. 2005. *Public Opinion, Democracy, and Market Reform in Africa.* Cambridge: Cambridge University Press.

Brüne, Stefan, Joachim Betz, and Winrich Kuhne (eds.). 1994. *Africa and Europe: Relations of Two Continents in Transition.* Münster and Hamburg: Lit Verlag.

Bukarambe, Bukar. 1988. "Regional Order and Local Disorder: The OAU and Civil Wars in Africa." *Nigerian Journal of International Relations* 14 (1):95–111.

Callaghy, Thomas M., and John Ravenhill (eds.). 1993. *Hemmed In: Responses to Africa's Economic Decline.* New York: Columbia University Press.

Campbell, Bonnie K., and John Loxley (eds.). 1989. *Structural Adjustment in Africa.* New York: St. Martin's Press.

Cason, Jim, and Bill Martin. 1993. "Clinton and Africa: Searching for a Post–Cold War Order." *Bulletin: Association of Concerned Africa Scholars,* nos. 38–39 (Winter).

Chazan, Naomi, et al. 1999. *Politics and Society in Contemporary Africa.* Boulder, CO: Lynne Rienner Publishers.

Clapham, Christopher. 1996. *Africa and the International System: The Politics of State Survival.* Cambridge: Cambridge University Press.

Clark, John F. 2002. *The African Stakes of the Congo War.* New York: Palgrave.

Clarke, Walter, and Jeffrey Herbst (eds.). 1997. *Learning from Somalia: The Lessons of Armed Humanitarian Intervention.* Boulder: Westview.

Collins, P. D. 1985. "Brazil in Africa: Perspectives on Economic Cooperation Among Developing Countries." *Development Policy Review* 3 (1):21–48.

Commins, Stephen K. (ed.). 1988. *Africa's Development Challenges and the World Bank: Hard Questions, Costly Choices*. Boulder, CO: Lynne Rienner Publishers.

Connell, Don, and Frank Smyth. 1998. "Africa's New Bloc." *Foreign Affairs* 77 (2) (March/April):80–94.

Council on Foreign Relations. 2005. "More Than Humanitarianism: A Strategic U.S. Approach Toward Africa." New York: Council on Foreign Relations Task Force Report No. 56.

Creed, John, and Kenneth Menkhaus. 1986. "The Rise of Saudi Regional Power and the Foreign Policies of Northeast African States." *Northeast African Studies* 8 (2–3):1–22.

Crouzel, Ivan. 2000. "La 'renaissance Africaine': Un discours Sud-Africain?" *Politique Africaine*, no. 77 (March):171–182.

Davidson, Basil. 1992. *The Black Man's Burden: Africa and the Curse of the Nation-State*. London: James Currey.

Decalo, Samuel. 1997. *Israel and Africa: Forty Years, 1956–1996*. Gainesville: Florida Academic Press.

Deng, Francis M. 1993. *Protecting the Dispossessed: A Challenge for the International Community*. Washington, DC: Brookings Institution.

Deng, Francis M., and Larry Minear. 1992. *The Challenges of Famine Relief: Emergency Operations in the Sudan*. Washington, DC: Brookings Institution.

Deng, Francis M., et al. 1996. *Sovereignty as Responsibility: Conflict Management in Africa*. Washington, DC: Brookings Institution.

Department of Commerce. 1996. "A Comprehensive Trade and Development Policy for the Countries of Africa." *A Report Submitted by the President of the United States to the Congress* (February).

Diop, Momar Coumba, and Mamadou Diouf. 1990. *Le Sénégal sous Abdou Diouf: État et société*. Paris: Karthala.

Dubey, Ajay K. 1990. *Indo-African Relations in the Post-Nehru Era (1965–1985)*. Delhi: Kalinga Publications.

El-Ayouty, Yassin (ed.). 1994. *The Organization of African Unity After Thirty Years*. New York: Praeger.

Ellis, Stephen. 2003. "Briefing: West Africa and Its Oil." *African Affairs* 102 (406):135–138.

Ercolessi, Maria Cristina. 1994. "Italy's Policy in Sub-Saharan Africa." Pp. 87–108 in Stephan Brune, Joachim Betz, and Winrich Kuhne (eds.). *Africa and Europe: Relations of Two Continents in Transition*. Münster and Hamburg: Lit Verlag..

Foccart, Jacques, with Philippe Gaillard. 1995. *Foccart parle: Entretiens avec Philippe Gaillard*. Vol. 1. Paris: Fayard/Jeune Afrique.

French, Howard D. 1995. "Nigeria Comes on Too Strong." *New York Times* (November): E3.

———. 1996a. "France Refuses to Apologize to U.S. for Africa Comments." *New York Times* (October 18): A5.

———. 1996b. "France's Army Keeps Grip in African Ex-Colonies." *New York Times* (May 22): A3.

———. 2001. "In Congo, a Lesson in Where Easy Paths Lead." *New York Times* (January 21): A3.

Gambari, Ibrahim A. 1995. "The Role of Foreign Intervention in African

Reconstruction." Pp. 221–233 in I. William Zartman (ed.). *Collapsed States: The Disintegration and Restoration of Legitimate Authority.* Boulder, CO: Lynne Rienner Publishers.

Gibb, Richard. 1998. "Southern Africa in Transition: Prospects and Problems Facing Regional Integration." *Journal of Modern African Studies* 36 (2):287–306.

Glaser, Antoine, and Stephen Smith. 1994. *L'Afrique sans Africains: Le rêve blanc du continent noir.* Paris: Editions Stock.

Goldsborough, James O. 1978. "Dateline Paris: Africa's Policeman." *Foreign Policy* 33 (winter):174–190.

Gordon, April. 2003. *Nigeria's Diverse Peoples: A Reference Sourcebook.* Santa Barbara, CA: ABC-CLIO.

Grundy, Kenneth. 1985. "The Impact of Region on Contemporary African Politics." Pp. 97–125 in Gwendolen M. Carter and Patrick O'Meara (eds.). *African Independence: The First Twenty-Five Years.* Bloomington: Indiana University Press.

———. 1986. *The Militarization of South African Politics.* Bloomington: Indiana University Press.

Harsch, Ernest. 1989. "After Adjustment." *Africa Report* (May-June):48.

Hirsch, John L., and Robert B. Oakley. 1995. *Somalia and Operation Restore Hope: Reflections on Peacemaking and Peacekeeping.* Washington, DC: United States Institute for Peace.

Hoffman, Stanley H. 1967. "Perceptions, Reality and the Franco-American Conflict." *Journal of International Affairs* 21 (1):57–71.

Hofmeier, Rolf. 1994. "German-African Relations: Present and Future." Pp. 71–86 in Stefan Brüne, Joachim Betz, and Winrich Kühne (eds.). *Africa and Europe: Relations of Two Continents in Transition.* Münster and Hamburg: Lit Verlag.

Hope, Kempe Ronald, Sr. 2002. "From Crisis to Renewal: Toward a Successful Implementation of the New Partnership for Africa's Development." *African Affairs* 101 (404):387–402.

Iyob, Ruth. 1995. *The Eritrean Struggle for Independence: Domination, Resistance, Nationalism, 1941–1993.* Cambridge: Cambridge University Press.

Jackson, Robert, and Carl G. Rosberg. 1982. *Personal Rule in Africa: Prince, Autocrat, Prophet, Tyrant.* Berkeley: University of California Press.

Jehl, Douglas. 1994. "Officials Told to Avoid Calling Rwanda Killings 'Genocide.'" *New York Times* (June 10).

Joyner, Christopher C. 1992. "International Law." Pp. 229–246 in Peter J. Schraeder (ed.). *Intervention into the 1990s: U.S. Foreign Policy in the Third World.* Boulder, CO: Lynne Rienner Publishers.

Karnik, S. S. 1988. "India-Africa Economic Relations: A Select Bibliography." *Africa Quarterly* 25 (3–4):63–110.

Khadiagala, Gilbert M. 1994. *Allies in Adversity: The Frontline States in Southern African Security, 1975–1993.* Athens: Ohio University Press.

Klare, Michael T., and Daniel Volman. 2004. "Africa's Oil and American National Security." *Current History* (May):226–231.

Kolodziej, Edward A. 1974. *French Foreign Policy Under de Gaulle and Pompidou: The Politics of Grandeur.* Ithaca, NY: Cornell University Press.

Korany, Bahgat (ed.). 1986. *How Foreign Policy Decisions Are Made in the Third World: A Comparative Analysis.* Boulder, CO: Westview Press.

Laïdi, Zaki. 1990. *The Superpowers and Africa: The Constraints of a Rivalry, 1960–1990.* Chicago: University of Chicago Press.

Larkin, Bruce D. 1971. *China and Africa, 1949–1970: The Foreign Policy of the People's Republic of China.* Berkeley: University of California Press.

Lavergne, Real (ed.). 1997. *Regional Integration and Cooperation in West Africa: A Multidimensional Perspective.* Trenton, NJ: Africa World Press.

Lefebvre, Jeffrey A. 1991. *Arms for the Horn: U.S. Security Policy in Ethiopia and Somalia 1953–1991.* Pittsburgh: University of Pittsburgh Press.

Lellouche, Pierre, and Dominique Moisi. 1979. "French Policy in Africa: A Lonely Battle Against Destabilization." *International Security* 3 (4):108–133.

Lemarchand, René. 1998. "U.S. Policy in the Great Lakes: A Critical Perspective." *Issue: A Journal of Opinion* 26 (1):41–46.

Lesser, Ian O. 1993. *Security in North Africa: Internal and External Challenges.* Santa Monica, CA: RAND Corporation.

Love, Janice. 2005. *Southern Africa in World Politics: Local Aspirations and Global Entanglements.* Boulder, CO: Westview Press.

Lyons, Terrence, and Ahmed I. Samatar. 1995. *Somalia: State Collapse, Multilateral Intervention, and Strategies for Political Reconstruction.* Washington, DC: Brookings Institution.

MacQueen, Norman. 1985. "Portugal and Africa: The Politics of Re-Engagement." *Journal of Modern African Studies* 23:31–51.

Marchal, Roland. 1995. "La France en quête d'une politique Africaine?" *Politique Etrangère,* no. 4 (winter):903–1116.

Markovitz, Irving L. 1969. *Léopold Sédar Senghor and the Politics of Negritude.* New York: Atheneum.

Mathews, K. 1988. "The African Group at the UN as an Instrument of African Diplomacy." *Nigerian Journal of International Affairs* 14 (1):226–258.

Mesa-Lago, Carmelo, and June S. Beikin (eds.). 1982. *Cuba in Africa.* Pittsburgh: Center for Latin American Studies, University of Pittsburgh.

Mkandawire, Thandika, and Adebayo Olukoshi (eds.). 1995. *Between Liberalisation and Oppression: The Politics of Structural Adjustment in Africa.* Dakar: CODESRIA.

Morikawa, Jun. 1997. *Japan and Africa: Big Business and Diplomacy.* Trenton, NJ: Africa World Press.

Morna, Colleen Lowe. 1995. "Southern Africa: New Era of Cooperation." *Africa Report* 40 (May-June):64–67.

Naylor, Phillip C. 1987. "Spain and France and the Decolonization of Western Sahara: Parity and Paradox, 1975–87." *Africa Today* 34 (3):7–16.

Nester, William R. 1992. *Japan and the Third World: Patterns, Power, Prospects.* New York: St. Martin's Press.

Nielson, Waldemar. 1969. *The Great Powers and Africa.* New York: Praeger.

Nkrumah, Kwame. 1965. *Neo-Colonialism: The Last Stage of Imperialism.* New York: International Publishers.

Ohlson, Thomas, and Stephen John Stedman, with Robert Davies. 1994. *The New Is Not Yet Born: Conflict Resolution in Southern Africa.* Washington, DC: Brookings Institution.

Ojo, Olatunde. 1985. "Regional Co-operation and Integration." Pp. 142–183 in Olatunde J. C. B. Ojo, D. K. Orwa, and C. M. B. Utete (eds.). *African International Relations.* London: Longman.

Olusanya, G. O. 1988. "Reflections on the First Twenty-Five Years of the Organization of African Unity." *Nigerian Journal of International Affairs* 14 (1):67–72.

Omaar, Rakiya. 1994. "Somalia: One Thorn Bush at a Time." *Current History* 93:232–236.

Onwuka, Ralph I., and Amadu Sesay (eds.). 1985. *The Future of Regionalism in Africa.* New York: St. Martin's Press.

Osaghae, Eghosa E. 1995. "The Ogoni Uprising: Oil Politics, Minority Agitation and the Future of the Nigerian State." *African Affairs* 94 (376):325–344.

Ottaway, Marina. 1999. *Africa's New Leaders: Democracy or State Reconstruction?* Washington, DC: Carnegie Endowment for International Peace.

Oyejide, Ademola, Ibrahim Elbadawi, and Paul Collier (eds.). 1997. *Regional Integration and Trade Liberalization in Sub-Saharan Africa.* New York: St. Martin's Press.

Parker, Ron. 1991. "The Senegal-Mauritania Conflict of 1989—A Fragile Equilibrium." *Journal of Modern African Studies* 29:155–171.

Patman, Robert G. 1990. *The Soviet Union and the Horn of Africa: The Diplomacy of Intervention and Disengagement.* Cambridge: Cambridge University Press.

Pazzanita, Anthony G. 1992. "Mauritania's Foreign Policy: The Search for Protection." *Journal of Modern African Studies* 30:281–304.

Peters, Joel. 1992. *Israel and Africa: The Problematic Relationship.* New York: St. Martin's.

Pfister, Roger. 2003. "Gateway to International Victory: The Diplomacy of the African National Congress in Africa, 1960–1994." *The Journal of Modern African Studies* 41 (3):51–73.

Potholm, Christian P., and Richard A. Fredland (eds.). 1980. *Integration and Disintegration in East Africa.* Lanham, MD: University Press of America.

Powell, Colin L. 2001. "Confirmation Hearing by Secretary-Designate Colin L. Powell." Online at www.state.gov/s/index.cfm?docid=443.

Prendergast, John. 1996. *Frontline Diplomacy: Humanitarian Aid and Conflict in Africa.* Boulder, CO: Lynne Rienner Publishers.

Reed, William Cyrus. 1992. "Directions in African International Relations." Pp. 73–103 in Mark W. DeLancey (ed.). *Handbook of Political Science Research on Sub-Saharan Africa: Trends from the 1960s to the 1990s.* Westport, CT: Greenwood Press.

Rooney, David. 1988. *Kwame Nkrumah: The Political Kingdom in the Third World.* New York: St. Martin's Press.

Rusi, Alpo M. 1998. *Dangerous Peace: New Rivalry in World Politics.* Boulder, CO: Westview Press.

Sandbrook, Richard. 1993. *The Politics of Africa's Economic Recovery.* Cambridge: Cambridge University Press.

Schraeder, Peter J. 1994a. "Elites as Facilitators or Impediments to Political Development? Some Lessons from the 'Third Wave' of Democratization in Africa." *Journal of Developing Areas* 29:69–90.

———. 1994b. *United States Foreign Policy Toward Africa: Incrementalism, Crisis and Change.* Cambridge: Cambridge University Press.

———. 2000a. *African Politics and Society: A Mosaic in Transformation.* Boston: Bedford/St. Martin's Press.

———. 2000b. "Cold War to Cold Peace: Explaining U.S.-French Tensions in Francophone Africa." *Political Science Quarterly* 115 (3):395–420.

———. (ed.). 1998. Special edition, "The Clinton Administration and Africa (1993–1999)," *Issue: A Journal of Opinion* 26 (2).

———. (ed.). 2002. *Exporting Democracy: Rhetoric vs. Reality.* Boulder, CO: Lynne Rienner Publishers.

Schraeder, Peter J., with Nefertiti Gaye. 1997. "Senegal's Foreign Policy: Challenges of Democratization and Marginalization." *African Affairs* 96 (385):485–508.

Schulz, Brigitte, and William Hansen. 1984. "Aid or Imperialism? West Germany in Sub-Saharan Africa." *Journal of Modern African Studies* 22 (2):287–313.

Segal, Aaron. 1989. "Spain and Africa: The Continuing Problem of Ceuta and Melilla." Pp. A71–A77 in Colin Legum and Marion E. Doro (eds.). *Africa Contemporary Record: Annual Survey and Documents 1987–88.* Vol. 20. New York: Africana.

Seidman, Ann, and Frederick Anang (eds.). 1992. *21st Century Africa: Towards a New Vision of Self-Sustainable Development.* Trenton, NJ: Africa World Press.

Shaw, Timothy M. 1991. "Reformism, Revisionism, and Radicalism in African Political Economy During the 1990s." *Journal of Modern African Studies* 29:191–212.

Shaw, Timothy M., and Olajide Aluko (eds.). 1984. *The Political Economy of African Foreign Policy: Comparative Analysis.* New York: St. Martin's Press.

Shaw, Timothy M., and Catherine M. Newbury. 1979. "Dependence or Interdependence: Africa in the Global Political Economy." Pp. 39–89 in Mark W. DeLancey (ed.). *Aspects of International Relations in Africa.* Bloomington: Indiana University Press.

Shivji, Issa G. 1989. *The Concept of Human Rights in Africa.* Dakar: CODESRIA.

Snow, Philip. 1988. *The Star Raft: China's Encounter with Africa.* Ithaca, NY: Cornell University Press.

Stokke, Olav (ed.). 1989. *Western Middle Powers and Global Poverty: The Determinants of the Aid Policies of Canada, Denmark, the Netherlands, Norway and Sweden.* Uppsala, Sweden: Scandinavian Institute of African Studies (in cooperation with the Norwegian Institute of International Affairs).

Stremlau, John J. 1977. *The International Politics of the Nigerian Civil War, 1967–1970.* Princeton: Princeton University Press.

Styan, David. 1996. "Does Britain Have an Africa Policy?" *L'Afrique Politique* 1996:261–286.

Suret-Canale, Jean. 1975. *Difficultés du néo-colonialisme français en Afrique tropicale.* Paris: Centre d'Etudes et de Recherches Marxistes.

Vallée, Olivier. 1989. *Le prix de l'argent CFA: Heurs et malheurs de la zone franc.* Paris: Karthala.

Védrine, Hubert, and Dominique Moïsi. 2000. *Les Cartes de la France a l'heure de la mondialisation.* Paris: Fayard.

Villalón, Leonardo A. 1995. *Islamic Society and State Power in Senegal: Disciples and Citizens in Fatick.* Cambridge: Cambridge University Press.

Welch, Jr., Claude E. 1991. "The Organization of African Unity and the Promotion of Human Rights." *Journal of Modern African Studies* 29:535–555.

Winrow, Gareth M. 1990. *The Foreign Policy of the GDR in Africa.* Cambridge: Cambridge University Press.

Wright, Stephen (ed.). 1998. *African Foreign Policies.* Boulder, CO: Westview Press.

Xuetong, Yan. 1988. "Sino-African Relations in the 1990s." *CSIS Africa Notes* 84:1–5.

Young, Crawford, and Thomas Turner. 1989. *The Rise and Decline of the Zairian State.* Madison: University of Wisconsin Press.

Zartman, I. William. 1976. "Europe and Africa: Decolonization or Dependency?" *Foreign Affairs* 54:325–343.

——— (ed.). 1995a. *Collapsed States: The Disintegration and Restoration of Legitimate Authority.* Boulder, CO: Lynne Rienner Publishers.

———. 1995b. "Inter-African Negotiation." Pp. 209–233 in John W. Harbeson and Donald Rothchild (eds.). *Africa in World Politics: Post–Cold War Challenges.* Boulder, CO: Westview Press.

——— (ed.). 1999. *Traditional Cures for Modern Conflicts: African Conflict "Medicine."* Boulder, CO: Lynne Rienner Publishers.

7

Population, Urbanization, and AIDS

April A. Gordon

The twentieth century was the setting for the most explosive growth of human population in history. Whereas it took about 130 years for population to double from 1 billion in the early 1800s to 2 billion in 1930, it took only 43 years for population to double again to 4 billion in 1973. The earth's population passed the 6 billion mark in 2000, and with 76 million to 80 million people being added every year, over 6.5 billion people are alive today. By 2050, population growth will have slowed, but there will still be more than 9 billion people. Most of this growth is occurring among the world's developing countries. By contrast, the world's industrial nations have had, with the exception of the post–World War II baby boom, declining growth rates. In fact, most industrial nations are growing at .5 percent or less a year, and some countries of Europe are actually experiencing negative rates of growth (UN, 2005; Population Reference Bureau, 2005).

A related trend is the revolutionary transition of the world's people from primarily rural agriculturalists to urban dwellers. As of 2003, over 48 percent of the world's people had become urban dwellers (UN, 2003). This change is most advanced in the industrial nations where, in 2000, over 75 percent lived in urban areas. Urbanization in the developing countries is not nearly as advanced; in 2000, only 38 percent were urban (Population Reference Bureau, 2000). However, urbanization is increasing so quickly in the developing world that by 2030 approximately 61 percent of the world's people will be living in cities (UN, 2003).

The problem is that while industrial societies can provide employment and relatively high living standards for most urban dwellers, the opposite is true in developing countries. Jobs do not expand nearly fast enough to meet the need, and relentless poverty rather than improved living standards is the lot of most. Governments, strapped for resources, find it impossible to expand or even maintain the stock of houses, infrastructure, or services under such conditions.

Although population growth rates are high in much of the developing world, the world's highest growth rates are in sub-Saharan Africa. Overall, sub-Saharan Africa's population is growing at a rate of 2.5 percent a year compared with an average growth rate of 1.7 percent in less developed countries as a whole. Consequently, sub-Saharan Africa's population is likely to grow from 705 million in 2005 to over 1.3 billion by 2025 (World Bank, 2005; Population Reference Bureau, 2005). The fastest growing countries in Africa—such as Burkina Faso, Burundi, Chad, Congo, Liberia, and Uganda—will at least triple in size between 2005 and 2050 (UN, 2005).

The growth rate of sub-Saharan Africa's cities is also high, averaging about 4.8 percent a year since 1980. Africa has sixteen of the twenty countries with the fastest rate of urbanization in the world, and the percentage of Africa's population living in urban areas has doubled since 1965—from 14 percent to almost 39 percent today (UN-Habitat, n.d.; Brockerhoff, 2000:7). Most of this growth is occurring in one or two cities within each country rather than being more evenly distributed among cities and towns of varying sizes. One result is that the proportion of urban population living in cities of more than half a million (twenty-eight in 1980 versus three in 1960) jumped from 6 percent in 1960 to 41 percent in 1980, and a third of the urban population lived in cities of 1 million or more (often the capital) (World Bank, 1995:223; 1990:239).

By 2010, there will be at least thirty-three cities in Africa with populations of 1 million or more. Lagos, Nigeria, sub-Saharan Africa's most populous city, will have over 13 million residents (UN-Habitat, n.d.). Lagos is growing so fast that by 2015 it will be the third largest city in the world, with a population of over 23 million people (Brockerhoff, 2000:10). Table 7.1 shows the astonishing rate of urbanization in some of Africa's major cities.

These statistical indicators reveal only the quantitative parameters of Africa's population and urban growth trends. They do not reveal why or how the current situation came to be or what can or should be done about it. There is no consensus on the issues either. For example, there are currently three basic views on the issue of rapid population growth.

One view is that family planning and education are needed to lower birth rates, slow urban growth, and ease population pressure on the land (see Montgomery and Brown, 1990:86). The claim is that family planning is the major reason birth rates have fallen so rapidly in other areas of the Third World ("Reproductive," 1992:11). Also, the fact that Africa has the world's highest birth rates and the lowest rate of contraception usage is

Table 7.1 Urban Growth in African Cities (size in millions)

City, Country	1965	1990	2015
Abidjan, Côte d'Ivoire	.3	2.2	5.1
Addis Ababa, Ethiopia	.6	1.8	5.1
Dar es Salaam, Tanzania	.2	1.4	4.3
Kinshasha, Democratic Republic of Congo	.8	3.4	9.4
Lagos, Nigeria	1.2	7.7	23.2
Luanda, Angola	.3	1.6	4.9
Maputo, Mozambique	.3	1.5	4.7

Source: Martin P. Brockerhoff. 2000. "An Urbanizing World." Population Bulletin 55 (September).

seen as evidence that fertility might fall dramatically in Africa if family planning services were more available (Caldwell and Caldwell, 2002). Studies also show that most urban growth in African cities is due to high birth rates rather than migration; therefore, lowering fertility levels would ease the pressure of growth on cities as well as overall population growth rates (Brockerhoff, 2000:18, 34).

Another view is that economic development is the solution to high rates of population growth. After all, fertility and population growth rates

World Bank

Like most of Africa's large cities, Nairobi has experienced explosive population growth since independence.

fell below African levels in other parts of the world long before the advent of modern contraceptives or family planning services (see Sai, 1988). This suggests that poverty and weak economies are the root causes of high birth rates; family planning under the conditions that exist in Africa can achieve only moderate fertility reductions at best.

The third view, one expressed by some women's groups, is that the emphasis on population growth as a "problem" and birth control as the "solution" puts the blame on women for Africa's development woes by implying they are having too many children. Framing the issue this way may lead to the sacrifice of women's human and reproductive rights in overzealous efforts to achieve population "control." One suspicion is that such programs, if implemented at the expense of women's overall welfare, become a means for the industrialized world to continue to disproportionately benefit from global economic activities that exploit poor countries and degrade the environment (Lutz, 1994:35; Ashford, 1995:7).

Each of these three views has some limited validity, but population issues in Africa are complex, and analyzing current population trends requires some understanding of African history and culture and some understanding of the political and economic constraints on the development of the conditions necessary for a widespread decline of either population growth or urban concentration. Sub-Saharan Africa's population problems are not abstract demographic problems amenable to a technological fix like family planning. Population trends are the result of individual responses to political and economic forces that are both historical and current. The major historical forces still influencing population dynamics include precolonial social institutions (which have survived in modified form to the present day), slavery, and colonialism. Since independence, the fortunes of Africa have been increasingly shaped by highly bureaucratic African states attempting to transform their societies within a global economy in which Africa has faced many disadvantages. It is also true that the extremely high rates of population and urban growth in Africa—far in excess of rates that occurred in industrializing Europe—impose tremendous hardships on struggling countries. It would be irresponsible to ignore the need for conscious efforts to control and manage population as part of an overall development strategy. There is now widespread agreement with this perspective both within and outside of Africa, as will be discussed later in this chapter.

Precolonial and Colonial Periods

Many people unfamiliar with Africa perceive African societies to have been small and village-based, lacking any urban civilization before Europeans came. African scholars have altered this view by describing the many thriving commercial and/or political centers of considerable antiquity in Africa. Along the east coast from Mogadishu to Sofala, numerous commercial towns were developed by Arabs and Africans with a trading network that extended from the interior of Africa to as far away as China. Many miles from the coast in southern Africa, the massive stone ruins of Great Zimbabwe give witness to an ancient, wealthy state that thrived for centuries before the astonished Portuguese set eyes on it in the sixteenth century. In western Africa's Sahel region bordering the Sahara, major cities—Gao, Djénné, and Timbuktu—flourished along the trans-Saharan trade routes. In the forest regions of western Africa, the artistic and religious center of Yorubaland was the city of Ile-Ife, in what is now Nigeria. Kano in Hausaland was a major manufacturing city renowned for its textiles and leather goods. Even the slave trade provided the impetus for the growth of towns such as Kumasi, capital of the Asante in Ghana.

Sub-Saharan African cities never achieved the great size of the major industrial cities of Europe, nor did more than a small minority of the population live in towns or cities. Most retained a horticultural or pastoral way of life. The most likely reason for this is that Africa is so vast that population pressure could be released by migrating to new land rather than through intensification of productive technologies or the adoption of new modes of production. Low population densities, difficulties of transport, and the prevalence of largely self-sufficient communities limited the development of markets for goods and services. This, in turn, along with limited productive capacity, limited the growth of cities.

The Atlantic slave trade played a role, too, by depopulating many regions and promoting ruinous warfare among African communities. The slave trade, plus a growing reliance on cheap manufactured goods from Europe, retarded, if not completely aborted, the industrial development that would stimulate urbanization (Rodney, 1974; Mahadi and Inikori, 1987; Gupta, 1987; Davidson, 1959).

Although data for precolonial Africa are sketchy, there is good evidence that regulation of fertility (childbearing) was a common and accepted practice in most African societies, even those few that were hunter-gatherers such as the San (Bushmen) of the Kalahari. The most common methods of birth regulation involved an approximate one- to two-year period of postpartum abstinence and extended breast-feeding, the latter of which is well known to retard the onset of ovulation once a baby is born. Another custom in many societies deemed it unseemly for a grandmother to become pregnant. Since most females married in their mid-teens, this effectively shortened their childbearing years to the middle or late thirties. Age-grade systems in many countries of eastern Africa often led to later ages of marriage due to late male and female initiation. In Tanzania, males usually married between the ages of twenty-five and thirty. The cost of bridewealth also forced many males throughout Africa to marry fairly late. These practices, among others, resulted in effective child spacing and lowered the number of children born per woman to well below the biological maximum. Polygyny (having more than one wife) made these practices workable, since there was less pressure on a woman to be sexually and reproductively active when there was more than one wife in the household. Along with fairly high mortality rates, regulated fertility (high but not maximum) resulted in slow population growth (Newman and Lura, 1983; Page and Lesthaeghe, 1981; Jewsiewicki, 1987; Valentine and Revson, 1979).

Some scholars contend that the Atlantic slave trade and later colonial policies drastically upset the demographic balance in Africa, promoting both higher birth rates and mortality as well as urban concentration (e.g., O'Brien, 1987; Jewsiewicki, 1987; Page and Lesthaeghe, 1981; Dawson, 1987). Slave raiders sometimes captured whole villages and marched their unfortunate captives to the coast where slave ships awaited them. An estimated 10 to 20 million Africans were lost to the Americas or to death in transport. Untold others lost their lives resisting the slavers or from the economic and social disruption the slave trade caused. Major migrations and wars occurred as a result of people either escaping from slave raiders or pursuing the trade in human flesh themselves. The prime victims of the traffic in slaves were young men and women and children—Africa's aborted reproductive and productive future. The disruptions and mixing of peoples also resulted in a rise in disease, including venereal disease, and higher mortality. In central Africa, venereal and other diseases produced high rates of subfecundity and sterility in such countries as present-day Cameroon, Gabon, Democratic Republic of Congo, and the Central African Republic. With a reduced stock of young reproductive-age women and depleted populations, greater pressures were put on families—on women—to increase their fertility.

In the 1800s and 1900s, colonialism further altered the African landscape. Whereas mercantile capitalism in previous centuries valued Africa for its slaves, newly industrializing capitalism abolished the exploitation of slavery, replacing it with the exploitation of Africa's cheap labor and cheap raw materials. The colonial system incorporated Africa into the emerging global capitalist economy, but Africa did not yield willingly. Unable to secure voluntary labor for plantations, farms, and mines in a continent of self-sufficient farmers and pastoralists, colonial policies such as the hut tax were used to force young males to leave their farms and migrate to towns or other areas where they could earn cash in the colonial economy. Women were usually left in the rural areas to bear and raise children, to farm, or to occasionally earn cash as farm laborers, petty traders, or commodity producers. With fewer men to help with the farm labor, more of the burden fell on women.

Cash cropping, introduced to men by the colonialists to supply desired exports for Europe, also increased women's burdens in the fields. Left to grow most of the food by themselves, women were often compelled to work on their husband's cash crop farms as well. Forced labor, the loss of male migrant labor, and an emphasis on cash cropping all threatened food production. Rising infant mortality and morbidity (disease) due to food shortages were common under the colonial regime (Jewsiewicki, 1987). According to Dawson (1987), mortality rose and population actually declined between 1900 and 1930. The economic pressures created by colonialism created the conditions for higher fertility; children became even more important as sources of farm labor and wages to be remitted to their parents, and high rates of infant and child mortality reinforced the need for high fertility to ensure that some would survive to adulthood.

European Christianity and missionary education also inadvertently encouraged larger families. Missionaries, as well as other colonial agents, promoted Western Victorian ideas of women's "proper role" as dependent wives and mothers rather than encouraging women's productive activities outside the family. Christianity also undermined polygyny in favor of the Western monogamous family. With only one wife to work and reproduce the children necessary for family survival, the old mechanisms of child spacing broke down. Weaning occurred earlier, and postpartum abstinence was increasingly ignored or shortened. Again, the result was higher fertility (Turshen, 1987).

Contrary to the typical pattern in which urbanization (an indicator of "modernization") promotes declining fertility, in Africa the opposite occurred. Primarily male migrants, the inhabitants of colonial towns were now often able to earn the bridewealth payment necessary to acquire a wife at an earlier age. Cultural controls that limited access to wives and hence moderated potential fertility broke down. Because of the expense of maintaining more than one household, monogamy increased in the towns but so did fertility (Dawson, 1987; Turshen, 1987). Retention of rural high fertility patterns also occurred because most migrants retained land or rights to land back in their villages. Residence in cities was usually temporary, as most returned home after some years in the city (Brockerhoff, 2000:18; Montgomery and Brown, 1990:86; El-Shakhs and Amirakmadi, 1986:15–17). Indeed, as mentioned above, much of the growth of urban areas in Africa has been due to high birth rates.

Postindependence Trends

The restructuring of African economies to serve the colonial capitalist economy produced growing populations and migration to cities. These trends mostly reflected hardships imposed on most Africans, not opportunities of modernization and development. After all, extracting Africa's wealth, not promoting economic prosperity for Africans, was the colonial goal. The ensuing poverty and exploitation made families highly dependent on their children both as sources of labor and income and as caretakers when they—the parents—were old.

One would expect that independent Africa, the chains of colonial oppression broken, would embark upon an economic and social transformation that would produce the fabled "demographic transition" to low birth rates and low rates of population growth characteristic of developed countries. According to transition theory, as urbanization and other aspects of modernization grow and families become less dependent on children as a source of labor, smaller families become the "rational" choice of parents. Economic growth should have the effect of altering the pronatalist motivational environment as the costs of rearing children (e.g., educational expenses) increase and new wants (e.g., consumer goods) compete with the desire for children.

None of this occurred in Africa. Unlike the rest of the developing world since 1965, birth rates and population growth remained high in Africa despite declining mortality (especially infant mortality), higher life expectancy, widespread access to formal education, and rising per capita income (World Bank, 1995:213). Even among the urban middle class, usually at the vanguard of the demographic transition, large families remained the norm, and studies showed little motivation for small families or desire to regulate fertility (see Caldwell, 1994; "Reproductive," 1992; World Bank, 1986; Sindiga, 1985; Faruqee and Gulhati, 1983).

The main explanation for sub-Saharan Africa's resistance to the demographic transition is that Africa's disadvantaged position in the global economy has prevented the widespread societal changes necessary for the demographic transition to occur. Most Africans have remained tied to the rural areas even when they live in the city. Traditionally, and even after independence, family survival and prosperity depend on having large families and networks of kin (see Cordell, Gregory, and Piche, 1987; Hyden, 1983). Even now the average number of children per woman in Africa is five—the highest in the world (UN, 2005).

The main question pertaining to Africa is when or whether the expansion of capitalism or other social forces will transform productive and economic and social relations so that large families are seen as less necessary and desirable. The evidence and arguments so far are mixed. On the one hand, some conclude that Africa is beginning its demographic transition. On the other hand, the conclusion is that any demographic transition in Africa will remain limited for decades to come. We will examine each position in turn.

View 1: Africa's Demographic Transition Is Under Way

Evidence for the view that Africa is experiencing its demographic transition (see Caldwell and Caldwell, 2002) is drawn from several kinds of data. For example, recent data show a decline in birth rates and overall population growth along with increased usage of family planning services and contraception. In the mid-1990s, crude birth rates in Africa were forty-four births per 1,000 population; in 2005, the rate had dropped to forty-one. In the mid-1990s, overall population growth was nearly 3 percent per year; this has now dropped to 2.5 percent. This drop of 0.5 percent may look small but its effect on population growth would increase the doubling time of Africa's population from twenty-three to twenty-nine years and lower the overall population size by millions (Population Reference Bureau, 2005:2).

The declines in fertility are not uniform. Moderate to large declines in fertility are most obvious in Mauritius, Seychelles, and some countries in southern Africa. But in most of sub-Saharan Africa birth rates remain above forty, although some notable declines have occurred in a few countries such as Ghana, Gabon, and Zimbabwe, where birth rates are in the low thirties (Population Reference Bureau, 2005). Use of contraception is an important factor in the level of fertility. Those with lower fertility are generally in countries with higher rates of contraception usage, whereas those with the highest rates (around fifty) typically are below 10 percent in contraceptive usage (see Table 7.2).

In the 1990s, surveys in many African countries showed a growing interest in family planning and declining support for large families (Green, 1994:40; Mbacke, 1994:188–189). In East Africa (with the exception of Tanzania), 90 percent of men and women expressed favorable attitudes toward family planning. In Ghana, with the expansion of family planning programs by the government between 1988 and 1993, rising support for family planning, rising contraception usage, and a drop in the number of children desired were reported. In Kenya, for instance, desired family size dropped from seven children in the 1970s to four in the 1990s. Even in Nigeria and Senegal, where birth rates were above forty, desired family size had declined from eight to six children. Studies also suggested a growing unmet need for family planning that resulted in many unwanted pregnancies and abortions (Rosen and Conly, 1998:9–11, 18–19).

Unfortunately, if a demographic transition is under way in Africa, it does not appear to be driven by growing development as has been the pattern elsewhere in the world. Instead, economic crisis seems to be the major motive for smaller families and family planning. In most of Africa, population growth has outstripped economic growth and food production. Estimates are that the average African is 22 percent poorer today than in 1975: 40 percent of Africans live on less than $1.00 per day (Rosen and Conly, 1998:12). With 11 percent of the world's population, Africa pro-

Table 7.2 Crude Birth Rates (CBR), Total Fertility Rates (TFR), and Contraceptive Usage Rates (%), in Selected Countries

Country	Lowest CBR[a]	TFR[b]	Contraceptive Usage[c]
Mauritius	16	1.9	76
Seychelles	18	2.1	—
South Africa	23	2.8	56
Botswana	25	3.1	40
Lesotho	26	3.5	41
Namibia	27	4.2	44
Country	**Highest CBR[a]**	**TFR[b]**	**Contraceptive Usage[c]**
Niger	56	8.0	8
Guinea Bissau	50	7.1	8
Liberia	50	6.8	—
Malawi	50	6.5	31
Mali	50	7.1	8
Angola	49	6.8	6
Sub-Saharan Africa	41	5.6	21

Source: Population Reference Bureau. 2005. *World Population Data Sheet.* Washington, DC: Population Reference Bureau (www.prb.org).

Notes: a. Number of births per 1,000 population in a given year.

b. Estimated average number of births per woman during her lifetime based on current fertility.

c. Percentage of married women using any method of contraception.

duces only 1 percent of the world's goods and services. Formerly, Africans had large families no matter how poor they were. Now, if Africans have more children than they can afford, they are likely to face criticism from others. This has been found in such countries as Kenya, Senegal, Zimbabwe, Ghana, and Nigeria, especially where economic decline and hardship are experienced. In one study in Nigeria, economic hardship was given as the main reason for using contraceptives and delaying marriage. In Kenya, shortage of land was another factor commonly cited for keeping families smaller (Buckley, 1998:A11).

In Caldwell and Caldwell (2002), structural adjustment programs (SAPs) are added as having an impact on the decline in fertility. SAPs and budget constraints led to cuts in public funding for health and education services and the imposition of user fees. These cuts in health care have been imposed at the same time that the AIDS (acquired immune deficiency syndrome) pandemic, which infects and kills mostly reproductive-age people, was rapidly spreading. Along with higher health-care costs, higher edu-

World Bank

Children are a vital economic resource in Africa's extended family systems. Most women want large families, and only a small percentage use modern forms of contraception.

cation costs became a major burden on families. Unmarried females desiring an education and career realized the negative consequences of premature motherhood. All of these trends resulted in a growing demand for contraceptives and lower fertility, especially in urban areas.

To summarize, the evidence, according to view 1, is that "nearly all the traditional supports for high fertility in Africa . . . have been eroding [and] it may be only a matter of time before the fertility transition takes place" ("Reproductive," 1992:8).

View 2: Africa's Demographic Transition Will Be Limited

According to this viewpoint, the declines in Africa's birth and growth rates and studies showing a desire for somewhat smaller families can produce only limited relief from continuing high population growth. For one, most of the declines are limited to a few countries, mainly the more developed, and those with the best family planning programs. Moreover, the declines in desired family size still indicate a preference for large families of at least four to five children, and in some countries—such as the Democratic Republic of Congo, Uganda, Liberia, and Angola—women continue to have an average of seven children (UN, 2005). As long as these trends continue, high rates of growth are guaranteed for the foreseeable future. Many studies also show that men want more children than women do and are less approving of family planning and the use of contraception. This is important because men typically have greater power in reproductive decisions than women do (Rosen and Conly, 1998:18–19). Although this situation might be subject to change through aggressive pro–family planning programs, most countries in Africa do not have such programs. Finally, only 18 percent of African married women use any form of birth control, and when they do, it is to space children or limit their number to the large number—around six—most Africans desire (Rosen and Conly, 1998:9).

Without a major transformation of African societies in which greater economic and political security are available to more people in both urban and rural areas, cultural norms linked to high fertility will persist. As Caldwell and Caldwell (2002) observe, these norms include a respect for high fertility, abhorrence of barrenness, belief that births are needed to reincarnate ancestors, fostering of children, extended family systems, polygyny, and a morally based resistance to contraception.

Family Planning

Whichever view proves to be more accurate depends in part on the degree to which resources and commitment are made to family planning programs. Only since the 1980s have African governments invested much in this area of their countries' development.

One reason for the neglect of family planning is that until recently there has been considerable controversy over the impact of high fertility and population growth rates on Africa. Africans pointed out that most African countries have very low population densities and small populations. To increase the labor force and internal markets and to develop their countries' resources required a larger not smaller population (Goliber, 1985).

By contrast, development agencies and family planning proponents—mostly from capitalist industrial nations—countered that unless rapid population growth was checked, increasing demands for such necessities as food, services, land, and jobs would overwhelm the fragile economies of all but a few African countries (World Bank, 1986, 1989). It was also pointed out that while enormous areas of Africa are sparsely populated and underdeveloped, much of this land is unsuitable for intensive human use without costly investment. And given the current population pressure on land and resources in Africa, severe or even irreversible ecological damage was already undermining the environment upon which Africa's development and future population would depend. Although much of the damage can be attributed to abuses associated with extractive industries and government policies, the expanding poor's need for wood for fuel, water, grazing land, income, or land for crops was also part of the equation. Symptomatic of the environmental damage were extensive deforestation, destruction of wildlife, desertification, and soil erosion in many parts of Africa, as Julius Nyang'oro discusses in Chapter 8. The pressures of population, it was claimed, threaten to reverse Africa's development efforts. Population control measures must be implemented if development is to take place (see Brown and Postel, 1987).

Only since the 1970s have any sub-Saharan African governments expressed concern over their population growth rates or requested assistance in developing family planning services. When the International Family Planning Foundation set up the African Regional Council in 1971, only eight countries were involved: Mauritius, Kenya, Tanzania, Liberia, Ghana, Sierra Leone, Nigeria, and Gambia (Sai, 1988:270). At the 1974 World Population Conference in Bucharest, only three African countries expressed a desire to slow their population growth—Kenya, Ghana, and Botswana. Only half of sub-Saharan countries supported family planning even as a health measure. None provided extensive services (World Bank, 1986:1).

By December 1975, Mauritius, Kenya, Ghana, and Botswana had official policies to reduce growth. A few others, such as Tanzania, Nigeria, and Zaire, issued statements encouraging "responsible parenthood." Notably, Tanzania tried to incorporate population with economic and social planning without an official population policy. This included efforts to promote maternal and child health, birth spacing, increased age of marriage for women (to fifteen years!), and maternity leave (Henin, 1979). By 1976, Africa was receiving 13 percent of UN Fund for Population Activities (UNFPA) funds (Johnson, 1987:263).

African governments' attitudes changed markedly in the 1980s. At the Second African Population Conference, sponsored by the UN at Arusha, Tanzania, in 1984, the watershed Kilimanjaro Programme of Action on Population was adopted. It recommended that population be seen as a central component in formulating socioeconomic development plans. Governments should ensure access to family planning services to all couples and individuals freely or at a subsidized cost. At the UN International Conference on Population held in Mexico in 1985, African population growth was an issue of great concern. Vice president of Kenya Mwai Kibaki discussed the need to stabilize Kenya's population and recommended that stabilizing world population within the next fifty years should be a major commitment. Also in 1985, leaders from forty African countries met in Berlin with World Bank officials to discuss population control (Johnson, 1987:263). By 1986, only Chad, Côte d'Ivoire, Gabon, Guinea-Bissau, and Mauritania did not support family planning. By 1989, on the other hand,

Ghana, Mauritius, Nigeria, Uganda, and Zambia had declared target fertility reductions backed by explicit policies (World Bank, 1989:71).

Interest in population growth was at an all-time high in the 1990s. By 1991 about 60 percent of African governments said their population growth was too high (versus only 30 percent in 1976). Even governments unconcerned about population growth now supported family planning as part of broader maternal and child health care (Green, 1994:34). Seventeen countries had formal population policies; many others were in the process of developing them (Population Reference Bureau, 1993). Symbolically important, the 1994 World Population Conference was held in Africa—in Cairo, Egypt. One hundred and eighty countries, many of them African, agreed to a Program of Action to stabilize world population and to provide universal access to family planning and reproductive health services by 2015 (Ashford, 1995:2, 33).

As discussed above, contraceptive use is increasing in at least some sub-Saharan African countries, especially among more educated urban dwellers. This could be increased if more women had access to family planning services.

The commitment to family planning does seem to be improving. Almost all African countries believe that population growth must be slowed, and they now incorporate family planning into their national health services. Francophone countries have been the slowest to change, but even

April Gordon

A flag in front of a family planning clinic in Swaziland advertises reproductive services for women.

they are changing. For instance, Senegal's family planning program (started in 1991) now reaches even small towns and villages. Contraceptive use rose to 13 percent in 1997 (versus 5 percent in 1986). Burkina Faso increased its number of family planning clinics between 1991 and 1996 from 90 to 750. Improvements have also been reported in Benin, Mali, and Niger (Rosen and Conly, 1998:26–28).

More countries are also recognizing the importance of improving the status of women if family planning is to achieve greater reductions in population growth. As research around the world indicates, substantial fertility declines occur only in countries where most girls attend primary school and efficient family planning programs are widely available (Caldwell and Caldwell, 2002). Ghana's new development plan, Ghana 2020, includes population and family planning goals. Ghana is hoping to reduce its growth rate from 3 to 1.2 percent by 2020. To achieve this goal, it will be vital to improve the status, education, and employment opportunities for women in addition to eliminating discriminatory laws and customs. And as discussed in Chapter 10, a few countries, notably South Africa, have enshrined women's rights, including reproductive rights, in their constitutions.

In part, fertility levels remain high because of the inadequacies of the family planning programs themselves. Except for Kenya and southern Africa, countries do not provide comprehensive family planning services. In Tanzania, for instance, almost half of communities have no family planning services available. Research reveals also that women are more likely to go to clinics that are attractive and well stocked with contraceptive options. If these are available, contraceptive usage increases. Other studies indicate that services are often unavailable or unsuited to the needs of older, unmarried, and sexually active young women. As a result, many of these women use no contraception and put themselves at high risk for HIV infection as well as for unwanted pregnancies (Caldwell and Caldwell, 2002).

Another obstacle Africans face in reducing high fertility levels is that family planning efforts are heavily dependent on external donor and nongovernmental organization (NGO) funding. This reliance on external funding makes Africa vulnerable to cuts in funding determined by outsiders' political agendas. About 25 percent of grant assistance for family planning comes from the UNFPA, but the majority of donor funding comes from the United States. The US Agency for International Development (USAID) accounts for half of all population aid to Africa. Between 1989 and 1996, US-backed funding grew from $72 million to $127 million (Rosen and Conly, 1998:57–60), but US anti-abortion politics have resulted in funding cuts under the former Reagan and current Bush administrations.

In 2001, the US government reinstated the so-called global gag rule, which requires foreign NGOs not to perform or even mention abortion if they want to receive US money for their programs. Among others, two of the most important organizations in Africa, International Planned Parenthood and Marie Stopes International, lost their funding for refusing to go along with US policy. Both groups have had to close clinics in Kenya, leaving thousands of women without services for family planning. In addition, women lost access to cervical cancer screening and childhood immunization services, which the clinics also had provided. The leading family planning organization in Zambia lost 25 percent of its funding. Since family planning clinics also provide many HIV/AIDS services, millions of people have lost access to condoms in at least 29 countries in Africa and to counseling and testing services. In Ghana alone, 700,000 people lost counseling and testing services ("AIDS and Abortion," 2003).

The major issue in high fertility is not access to family planning and contraception, however. Quite simply, African men and women want more children than people do elsewhere in the world. Until this reality changes, it seems unlikely that the demographic transition will reduce fertility much below current levels.

Urban Population Policy

As already discussed, urban population growth from both natural increase (high birth rates) and migration of rural population is continuing at a rapid rate. Due to their poverty, most of Africa's urban dwellers live in slums (World Bank, 2003:122). The large numbers of job seekers combined with stagnant economies in most countries make it impossible for the wage sector to provide enough jobs for all who need them. For this reason, 40 percent or more of an African city's labor force is employed in the informal sector. The oversupply of workers tends to depress wages, making it more difficult to achieve higher living standards (Hope, 1998:353–355). Because the poor have little purchasing power, the private sector fails to respond to their housing or other needs, and government budgets are insufficient to extend most services to more than a lucky minority (see World Bank, 2004).

Urban environments, especially for the poor, are unhealthy to say the least. Lack of access to clean water, air pollution (including indoor air pollution from the use of wood for cooking), airborne lead, raw sewage, and garbage are common problems in overcrowded cities across the continent. On average, an estimated 57 percent don't have basic sanitation, and 20 percent lack safe water. In some cities conditions are far worse. For example, over 80 percent of urban dwellers in Niger, Sierra Leone, and Mali lack basic sanitation (UN-Habitat, n.d.). Even when sanitation and water are available, they may have to be shared among multiple households. For example, in Accra, Ghana, two-thirds of the poorest households with access to a toilet or latrine must share it with more than ten other households. Even among the richest 20 percent of households, 12 percent are sharing toilets with more than ten other households (World Bank, 2003:122).

At the root of these urban problems is Africa's continuing economic and political woes. Economically, Africa has become a marginal player in the global economy. Low foreign investment and government mismanagement and budget cutbacks have made it difficult to reverse urban decline. It is difficult for urban dwellers to improve the conditions in which they live when so many are poor and living in slums (see Hope, 1998). In fact, conditions are expected to worsen. According to the UN, in 2001 over 166 million urban dwellers were living in slums; in the next 25 years, another 400 million people will be moving to the cities with the result that the slum population will double every fifteen years (UN-Habitat, n.d.).

Typically, immigration to cities is the result of rural outmigration. In some cases, however, there is a large increase in the size of rural towns due to an influx of rural dwellers escaping insecurity and violent conflict in the rural areas. Martin Brockerhoff (2000:12–14, 23) discusses two new types of cities sprouting up in Africa under these circumstances. One type is "urban villages"—rural villages that have grown into cities of 200,000 to 400,000, but lack even the most basic services. Another type is the "refugee city." An example of this occurred in Tanzania at the site where refugees from the 1994 genocide in Rwanda fled. Within a few days a "city" of more than 250,000 people had sprung up, becoming Tanzania's second largest city. A similar phenomenon occurred in Eritrea's second largest city, Keren, during the 1990s. Due to civil war in Sudan and the war between Eritrea and Ethiopia, refugees fled to Keren and doubled its population in five years (UN-Habitat, n.d.). Such migration can also be observed in southern Africa. Currently, the near collapse of Zimbabwe's economy as a result of the policies of President Robert Mugabe has led to massive illegal immigration of an estimated 20 percent of Zimbabwe's population to the towns and cities of South Africa, Botswana, and Mozambique (Johwa, 2003).

There is no consensus about what to do, if anything, regarding African urban population trends and the grim realities in the cities. Some free market advocates contend that, however unsalutary urban growth and conditions appear, it is actually more economical to concentrate population and industry than to decentralize in countries of relatively small population size, such as most countries in sub-Saharan Africa. Economies of scale are maximized when businesses have better access to markets and labor, and supportive infrastructure and services are more cheaply provided (Brennan and Richardson, 1986). As incomes and government revenues improve, better housing, services, and so on will increase accordingly. Others add that rapid urban growth is an inevitable consequence of urban economic development and rural stagnation rather than a negative force to be suppressed. Migrants rationally perceive opportunities to be better in the city. Moreover, urban concentration ("primacy") is not excessive in Africa by world standards, as the share of total population in large cities is not usually above 10 percent. Furthermore, primacy tends to fall as countries become more developed (Becker, Hamer, and Morrison, 1994:58–60).

Critics counter that such growth may be economical from the standpoint of the foreign firms that dominate so many African countries, but they perpetuate backwardness and inequality for most of the host countries' people. Intervention and planning are called for in order to promote more balanced and equitable development throughout the country (Rondinelli, 1983). Even those less alarmed by urban concentration concede that urban decentralization could be a desirable by-product of current structural adjustment policies designed to promote rural development, shrink government, and promote exports (Becker, Hamer, and Morrison, 1994:60–61).

While not agreeing on what to do about their cities, most African governments recognize that uncontrolled urban growth is problematic. Consequently, various interventionist strategies have been used throughout the continent to deal with rapid urbanization. They fall into two basic categories: (1) measures to discourage migration to the major cities and (2) policies to improve conditions in the cities. Unfortunately, these two strategies often work at cross-purposes, since improving urban conditions makes cities even more attractive to potential migrants. There are other problems as well, as will be discussed below.

Category 1, discouraging migration, includes efforts to upgrade conditions in the rural areas to prevent outmigration to the cities. In Cameroon, for example, after years of neglect of the rural areas, the government in the 1980s began to pay farmers higher prices, provide more training programs, and increase aid to young farmers. The government invested more in such infrastructural improvements as road building, rural electrification, school construction, and expanded public health centers (Gordon and Gordon, 1988:13). Ethiopia also uses rural development schemes to get people to stay in the rural areas (Brockerhoff, 2000:33). Although rural development is a desirable goal in its own right, rural development projects have not been very successful, nor have they had much effect on migration (Stren and White, 1989:307; Brockerhoff, 2000:33).

Some African governments have tried removing unwanted migrants from the city and destroying squatter settlements as a means of controlling overcrowding and public health hazards. These efforts typically fail because migrants usually return to the city, and their makeshift dwellings are reconstructed on the same or similar sites. Tearing down squatter housing also adds to urban overcrowding by putting even more pressure on available housing (see Morrison and Gutkind, 1982).

A notable recent effort to demolish squatter settlements took place in Zimbabwe in 2005. President Mugabe had the homes of hundreds of thousands of his citizens in urban areas destroyed in a program called "Clean the Filth." The goal was to compel people to return to rural areas by denying them basic services and destroying their homes. The explanation given by the government for this drastic policy was that it was a "city beautification program" (Wines, 2005; HRW, 2005).

Countries such as Kenya, Ethiopia, Tanzania, and Nigeria have attempted resettlement programs as rural development strategies. Some resettlement programs are part of regional development plans designed to promote the growth of towns and cities outside of the one or two main cities. In Ethiopia, industry location policies were used to encourage the growth of medium-sized cities (Brennan and Richardson, 1986). In Cameroon, medium-sized cities were promoted through the decentralization of government activities to regional cities throughout the country (Gordon and Gordon, 1988). Some African countries have built new capital cities as a means of decentralizing their urban populations. Examples here are Abuja in Nigeria, Dodoma in Tanzania, and Yamoussoukro in Côte d'Ivoire. Abuja was designed to reduce pressures on Lagos, Nigeria's largest city, and to promote more migration to Nigeria's sparsely populated interior. So far, these regional development policies have

April Gordon

Poverty and the lack of basic amenities are widespread in many African towns and reflect, among other things, urban bias policies that favor large cities.

had little impact on migration to the largest cities (Brockerhoff, 2000:33–34).

Under category 2, improving the cities, various policies have been tried in an attempt to maintain the livability of overextended cities. Since independence, much of the investment made by African governments has gone to cities to provide essentials like roads, housing, water and electricity, and sewage disposal. There was, in addition, an "urban bias" in government policies that resulted in cheap imported or locally produced food for urbanites and cheap housing for middle-class civil servants. Structural adjustment programs imposed by the International Monetary Fund have forced many governments to cut such subsidies to the cities along with other government spending. Higher prices, declining urban living standards, and deteriorating social services and maintenance of public works followed (White, 1989:5–6; O'Connor, 1991:117).

As discussed above, because cities are growing so rapidly, providing simple housing and basic services has become a major problem. Both the government and most migrants lack the financial resources to provide anything but substandard, squatter housing. New residents to the city are often compelled by their circumstances to settle on unclaimed or unoccupied land and to scavenge for wood, corrugated metal, and other building materials.

In most countries, a "sites and services" policy has become the preferred way to help the urban poor to upgrade their homes and settlements. "Sites" are first cleared for housing; streets and lots are marked off; then "services" such as water points, electricity hookups, and sewage disposal are provided. Residents build on these prepared sites and add improvements as their incomes allow. Because of Africa's economic crisis in the 1980s and 1990s, most governments stopped providing free services to the poor. In some cases user fees were imposed and individuals and communities were required to assume more responsibility to fend for themselves to provide private water connections, self-help housing, and private household electric generators (see Browning, 2002; World Bank, 2003: 122).

Despite the problems in the cities, weak economies, environmental degradation, political conflict, and rapid population growth continue to be forces pushing migration to Africa's cities. Millions see migration to the cities as the best hope they have for a better life. Indeed, cities generally offer their inhabitants better incomes, better services, better nutrition, and less poverty than the places they leave behind. Nonetheless, Africa probably is more urban than it should be based on its current level of economic development. High birth rates guarantee that this growth will continue (Hope, 1998:356). Perhaps, as Brockerhoff (2000:34) concludes, the best way to slow urban growth is to provide women with family planning services, because discouraging migration will almost surely fail.

AIDS in Africa

Complicating the picture of African population trends is AIDS. The statistics on the progression of the disease are staggering. At the end of 1990, the World Health Organization (WHO) estimated that there were 8–10 million people in the world infected with the AIDS virus. Sub-Saharan Africa, with only 10 percent of the world's population, had 25–50 percent of all the AIDS-infected population (Chin, 1990:223). At the Eighth International Conference on AIDS in Africa, held in Marrakech, Morocco, in 1994, the WHO upped the estimated infected population worldwide to over 15 million; the total in Africa had climbed to 10 million ("WHO Address," 1994). In 1999, the WHO estimated that 34 million were living with HIV/AIDS, of which 70 percent (over 24 million) were in sub-Saharan Africa (Population Reference Bureau, 2005:1). (See Map 7.1.)

Current statistics reveal that the situation in Africa is worse not better. In 2005, almost 26 million people were infected, or about 7.3 percent of the adult population. Women are more likely to be infected than men. Almost 57 percent of adults living with HIV in sub-Saharan Africa are women, and these women make up three-quarters of all women worldwide with the disease. Young women fifteen to twenty-four years old are most likely to be infected; for every ten HIV-infected young men there are thirty-six HIV-infected young women (UNAIDS, 2005a).

There are several reasons why HIV/AIDS is so prevalent in Africa. One is the high frequency of sex outside of marriage. Many Africans believe that males are biologically programmed to need sex with many women. Also the mobility of the population, especially the excess of males in urban areas, leads to a high level of casual sex and prostitution among women seeking economic survival and working men who are away from their wives. Another factor is the high level of sexually transmitted diseases in Africa (the highest in the world). Untreated sexually transmitted diseases (STDs) are a high risk factor making HIV transmission easier; and poverty, poor nutrition, and parasitic diseases lower immune systems and promote greater susceptibility to infection (Stillwaggon, 2002; Walker, Reid, and Cornell, 2004:20; Kevane, 2004:183). The low incidence of condom use, even in commercial sex, is another important risk factor since statistics for many countries show that a half or more of prostitutes are HIV positive (in Zimbabwe, 80 percent of prostitutes in major urban areas are reported to be infected with HIV) (Caldwell, 2000:120–125).

Contributing to the problem is the denial and shame associated with AIDS on the part of many Africans. This results in inadequate preventive measures. John Caldwell notes that many Africans refuse to discuss AIDS or acknowledge that family members or friends had died (even prostitutes) of AIDS.

Map 7.1 Estimated Percentage of Adults (15–49) Infected with HIV

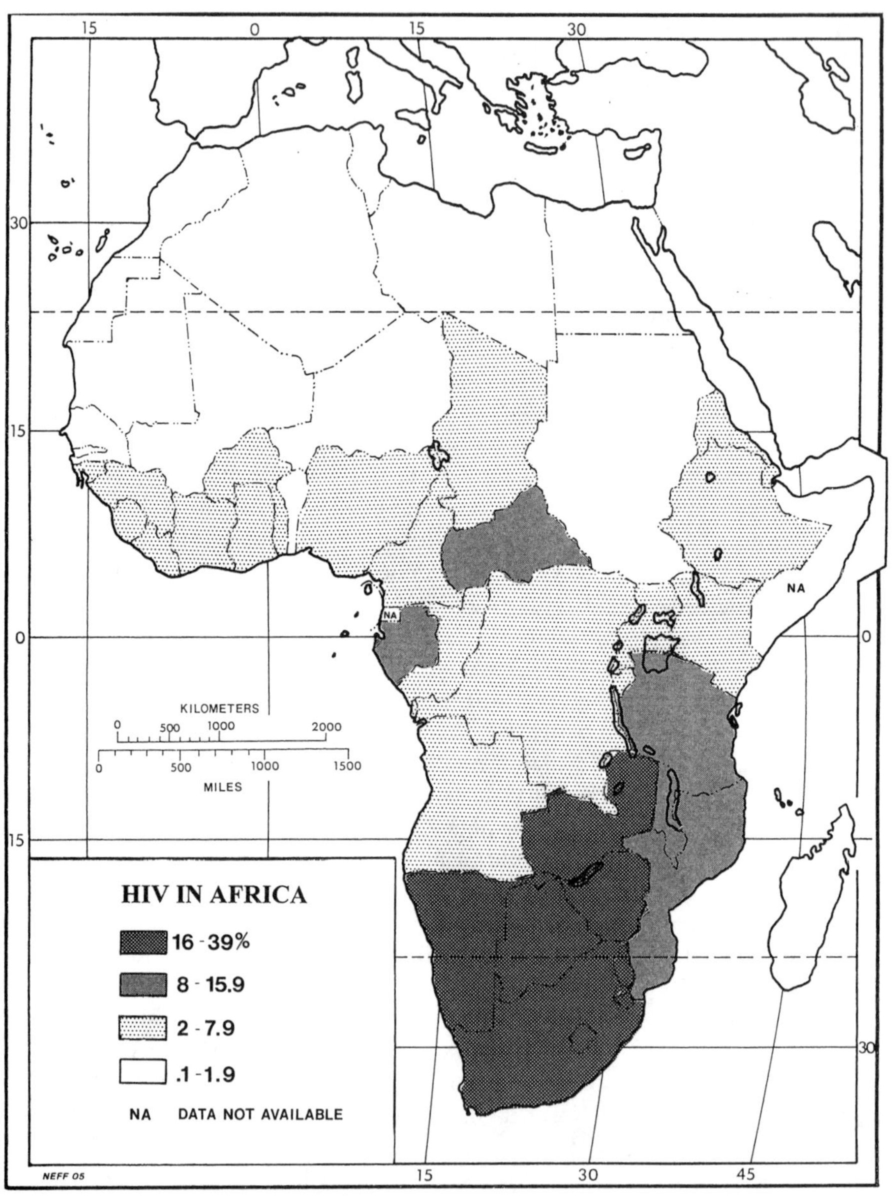

Joint UN Programme on HIV/AIDS (UNAIDS) and World Health Organization (WHO), AIDS Epidemic Update 2004 (Geneva, Switzerland, December 2004) (www.unaids.org).

> The silence exists partly because people have been taught that AIDS is a sexually transmitted disease associated with sexual activity outside of marriage. The church has taught that this is a shameful thing and many believe the infection was a punishment for sin and are reluctant to disclose that any of their relatives bear such witness. (Caldwell, 2000:12)

Many people also refuse to discuss or acknowledge the high prevalence of extramarital sex. Even married couples have poor communication about sexual matters. Many are also reluctant to recognize the reality of widespread adolescent sex, and they believe that providing young people with information about sex or condoms will encourage sexual behavior (Kuchment, 2002; Caldwell, 2000:127–129). For example, in Zambia, one of the countries most affected by HIV/AIDS, government officials argue that monogamy is the only protection against AIDS, and condoms encourage immorality and promiscuity ("Closing the Condom Gap," 1999:8). Many Africans, in fact, hold a negative view of condoms. Exemplifying this attitude is the perception of young Ghanaian women that condoms are associated with "bad girls" and "sex maniacs" (Caldwell, 2000:8).

Government inaction also has contributed to a failure to stop the spread of AIDS. Until recently, most government leaders denied the problem and devoted few resources to education or prevention (other than abstinence), when what is needed is support for condom use, treatment of STDs, and

World Bank

Mothers and their young children in Africa are at high risk of contracting AIDS.

aggressive education efforts. Instead, "millions of people are being allowed to die on the grounds that the only way they can be saved is by adopting a more 'moral' way of life, indeed a way of life that does not conform to their morality" (Caldwell, 2000:131). As a result, young people and unmarried people find it almost impossible to get condoms (or other contraceptives) from health services or family planning clinics (Caldwell and Caldwell, 2002; Caldwell, 2000:123).

Obstruction on the part of many religious leaders is another reason for the ineffectual response to AIDS. Both the Catholic church and many Protestant churches oppose the use of condoms (Kuchment, 2002). In Nigeria, most Christian leaders think AIDS is divine punishment and that it is immoral to give condoms to adolescents, even though most are sexually active. As discussed in Chapter 11, African governments do not wish to antagonize the churches, who can mobilize opposition to them. Confronting the churches on issues they define as dealing with morality is seen by many politicians as risky, so few challenge the churches on these issues (Caldwell, 2000:125–126).

The widespread belief in witchcraft among many Christians and Muslims (see Chapter 11) also prevents behavior change and effective action against AIDS. It leads people to accept a fatalistic view toward death and to believe that the cause of AIDS is malevolent forces or divine punishment (Caldwell, 2000:121, 125–126). Another negative effect of associating HIV/AIDS with witchcraft is the social isolation and even violence against the older women usually accused of witchcraft. Also, families that believe in witchcraft pay large amounts of money for ineffective counseling and treatments from traditional healers. Finally, linking witchcraft and HIV/AIDS hinders efforts to break the silence on the disease and de-stigmatize it (Walker, Reid, and Cornell, 2004:100–101).

Despite the inadequate response of most governments, the majority now are implementing both prevention and treatment policies. A few have made remarkable strides in dealing with the crisis. Once one of the most seriously affected countries, Uganda cut its HIV/AIDS prevalence rate from 13 percent in the 1990s to about 4 percent in 2003 (UNAIDS, 2005a). Uganda's government was the first in Africa to admit it had an epidemic and to ask for help. Since then a cooperative effort involving government, grassroots organizations, and religious groups led to a program to provide AIDS education, urge delay in sexual onset and fewer partners, and promote safe sex. Prevention and treatment of STDs and use of condoms are integral parts of the program. Even "soap operas" on radio and television have characters who promote the use of condoms (Dervarics, 1999:5; "Closing the Condom Gap," 1999:8).

Recent reports indicate that Zimbabwe also has experienced a notable drop in HIV prevalence from 23 percent of its population to 20.5 percent.

In women aged fifteen to twenty-four, HIV rates have dropped almost by half, and among men seventeen to twenty-nine, the drop is about 25 percent. A delay in the onset of sexual activity in young people, a decline in casual sex, and greater condom use are credited for most of the progress that has been made. A relatively educated population, good communications, and the effective work of the health care system in prevention and providing anti-retroviral treatment to the afflicted are also credited by researchers (Cullinan, 2006).

In the predominantly Muslim countries of Senegal and Mauritania, members of the clergy and the government are making bold moves to slow the spread of AIDS. In Dakar, Senegal, prostitutes now get a government card to work legally. They must be tested monthly for STDs and every six months for HIV. Women who test positive for HIV are counseled on safe sex to protect their own health, since contracting an STD could be fatal to them. Punitive measures are avoided since they would only drive prostitution underground. The results of these efforts have been impressive. New STD and HIV infections have fallen and Senegal has one of the lowest HIV infection rates in sub-Saharan Africa. These policies and efforts to promote condom use among the general population have the support of both Islamic and Christian leaders (Schoofs, 1999:B2). Senegal's northern neighbor, Mauritania, also has Islamic clergy involved in AIDS prevention programs that advocate condom use ("Closing the Condom Gap," 1999:8).

It should be emphasized that African governments are not the only ones that have failed to effectively combat the HIV/AIDS pandemic. The late and inadequate response of the international community is also to blame. Indeed, if governments and aid organizations had responded decisively and early to the problem, the infection rates would not have reached the appalling levels we now confront. Only in the past few years do we see significant movements to marshal the resources necessary to fight this disease.

A major advance is the Global Fund to Fight AIDS, Tuberculosis, and Malaria, launched in 2002. Kofi Annan, Secretary General of the UN, urged donor countries to contribute $7–10 billion a year to the effort. Initially, the US response under President Bush was to pledge only $200 million to the Global Fund. Then in his 2003 State of the Union message, Bush promised $15 billion over five years in a new AIDS initiative. He also vowed to ensure anti-retroviral treatment for 2 million infected people. Aid would go to fourteen countries, most of them in Africa (McNeil, 2005; Udoto, 2004). The United States currently provides up to a third of the budget of the Global Fund. Although follow-through on the US commitment for funds and access to cheaper drugs has not been fully realized, these new measures are certainly an improvement on the past.

An interesting question is why the Bush administration became more concerned about the AIDS crisis. Perhaps a major reason is pressure from

Bush's conservative Christian base. As discussed in Chapter 11, several prominent Christian evangelicals—such as Franklin Graham, head of the relief organization Samaritan's Purse—have become convinced that it is their religious duty to fight such evils as poverty, sex trafficking, and HIV/AIDS in Africa (Burkhalter, 2004).

The main problem with the new US AIDS policies is that ideology has sometimes interfered with reality and "best practice" on the ground. In the area of AIDS prevention, for example, the Bush administration has earmarked about 30 percent of its funding to promoting abstinence as the way to prevent infection. USAID, the major US aid and development agency in Africa, is offering grants to faith-based groups to promote abstinence in their prevention programs. The importance of condom use is being ignored and sometimes distorted, due to the fact that many evangelical churches oppose condoms on moral grounds. They ignore the fact that condoms have been shown to be 90 percent effective in preventing HIV infection. The model for many programs is Uganda's "ABC policy," but they are only following A and B—abstinence and be faithful—while ignoring C, use a condom (Kuchment, 2002; Burkhalter, 2004).

Research clearly shows that abstinence-focused programs are misguided. In Uganda's program, abstinence has been shown to be the least effective component of the ABC's. The use of condoms and having fewer sex partners were the most effective. Abstinence also ignores most of the high-risk groups in the AIDS epidemic: sex workers, IV drug users, and gays (Burkhalter, 2004). Moreover, remaining abstinent before marriage and being faithful does not work for many young women in Africa, where in some countries young brides are infected at a higher rate than sexually active unmarried girls. The married girls are infected by their husbands, who may be considerably older than they are (Altman, 2004). Older men who marry young women are likely to be sexually experienced and wealthy enough to afford multiple sex partners, and they typically do not use condoms. Such high-risk sexual behavior frequently results in the man contracting HIV and then passing it to his wife ("Women and HIV," 2004:82–83).

Not all churches hold the conservative line in their AIDS programs. In South Africa, church leaders are campaigning for affordable drugs and ignoring religious prohibitions against condom use. In Namibia, Catholic leaders espouse an "ABCD" policy—abstain, be faithful, use condoms, or face death (Kuchment, 2002).

Recently, the efficacy of ABC policies has been called into question due to patterns of gender inequality in Africa. For instance, Kathleen Cravero, Deputy Executive Director of the Joint UN Programme on HIV/AIDS (UNAIDS), remarks, "We tell women to abstain when they have no right. We tell them to be faithful when they cannot ask their partners to be faithful. We tell them to use a condom when they have no power to do so" (quoted in Crawley, 2004).

Women's lack of power in sexual relations and women's low status in other areas of their lives are closely linked. Illustrating this point, a study of women in Zambia found that only 11 percent of women interviewed believed women had the right to ask their husband to use a condom—even if he is HIV positive or having sex with other women. In Cameroon and South Africa, as many as 48 percent of girls state that their first sexual intercourse was forced (AF-AIDS, 2004). Other studies show that men who batter their partners are more likely to sleep with prostitutes, thus putting themselves and their partners at risk of infection. Battered women are afraid to say no to sex or to ask their partners to use a condom ("Women and HIV," 2004:82–83).

Gender inequality also can affect treatment for women. In Zambia, 70 percent of HIV victims are women, but most of those receiving anti-retroviral drugs are men. Women are taught to ignore their own health needs but to help their husbands if they are ill. Using the same logic, men put themselves first and ignore the needs of their wives if they get sick. A midwife working in a clinic remarked that she sees women bring their sick husbands to the clinic on wheelbarrows, bikes, or even their backs; but she has never seen a man offer as much as his arm to bring his wife in for treatment. Women themselves report that if they were HIV-positive, their husbands wouldn't spend the $8 per month for long-term treatment on them. By contrast, men put themselves first even if treatment costs are a strain on the family's finances ("The Good Wife's Sacrifice," 2004).

Despite more prevention and treatment programs, infections and deaths are increasing in most African countries. It is apparent that it will be a long and difficult battle to bring HIV/AIDS under control in Africa (Goujon, 2005), and even in countries where infection rates have fallen or stabilized, reversals are possible. A recent study in Uganda voiced concern that progress there could be reversed without renewed prevention efforts that focus on condom use. Abstinence and faithfulness alone do not work without condom use because too few people actually practice abstinence or faithfulness. There are also far too few people needing drugs than are receiving them. In 2005, only 500,000 were being treated with anti-retrovirals out of a population of at least 4.7 million who need them (Goujon, 2005), and access is uneven. Whereas about one-third are getting treatment in Botswana and Uganda, no more than 15 percent are receiving drugs in South Africa (UNAIDS, 2005c).

Unfortunately, there are too few countries with effective AIDS prevention programs. Even if more follow in the footsteps of Uganda or Senegal, it will take years to slow or halt the spread of HIV/AIDS in Africa. In the meantime, the demographic effects will be devastating. Sub-Saharan

Africa's overall population growth will be lower and its age structure will be altered as a result of rising mortality, especially in the countries with the highest infection rates (Gregson et al., 1998). In nine countries—Botswana, Central African Republic, Lesotho, Malawi, Mozambique, Rwanda, Swaziland, Zambia, and Zimbabwe—life expectancy has already fallen to below forty years (UNAIDS, 2005b). Higher infant and child mortality add to the problem. One-third of babies born to HIV-infected mothers are HIV-positive; few survive beyond age six (Walker, Reid, and Cornell, 2004:14).

The consequences of the AIDS epidemic go far beyond the direct demographic effects. Most of the victims are young, working-age adults. Thus the labor force that Africa's economic recovery depends upon will be sharply reduced. Many companies are already seeing the effects of HIV/AIDS in growing sickness, absenteeism, and death among their employees, with resulting declines in productivity. In Tanzania, for instance, estimates are that there will be 20 percent fewer workers in 2010 than today, and the mean age will drop from 32 to 28. Remaining workers will be younger, less skilled, and less experienced. Another consequence of AIDS is the growing burden of health care for AIDS patients placed on families, businesses, and health care systems that results in a diversion of scarce resources away from basic care and other needs for the rest of the population (Guest, 2001; "Firms," 2005; Loewenson and Whiteside, 1998:20–21). Virginia DeLancey discusses these and other economic impacts of AIDS in Chapter 5.

The means exist to slow the spread of HIV/AIDS and to treat its victims. The challenge is mobilizing the political will and resources to do the job. That this disease has become the tragedy it is reflects both global and domestic power relationships rather than the inevitable course of the disease. AIDS never had to be the epidemic it has become. In the rich world, there is adequate health care, access to drugs, good nutrition, and effective governments that have controlled both the spread and deaths caused by the HIV virus. In the rich world, AIDS exists, but it is a manageable and treatable disease (Walker, Reid, and Cornell, 2004:7–9). How long before this is the case in Africa as well?

Bibliography

AF-AIDS. 2004. "HIV Prevention and Protection Efforts Are Failing Women and Girls." Online at www.af-aids@healthdev.net (February 10).

"AIDS and Abortion Policy: Pregnant Pause." 2003. *The Economist* (September 27):31–32.

Altman, Lawrence K. 2004. "H.I.V. Risk Greater for Young African Brides." *The New York Times*. Online at www.nytimes.com (February 29).

Ashford, Lori S. 1995. "New Perspectives on Population: Lessons from Cairo."

Population Bulletin 50 (March). Washington, DC: Population Reference Bureau.

Becker, Charles M., Andrew M. Hamer, and Andrew R. Morrison. 1994. *Beyond Urban Bias in Africa.* London: James Currey.

Brennan, Ellen M., and Harry W. Richardson. 1986. "Urbanization and Urban Policy in Sub-Saharan Africa." *African Urban Quarterly* 1:20–42.

Brockerhoff, Martin P. 2000. "An Urbanizing World." *Population Bulletin* 55 (September). Washington, DC: Population Reference Bureau.

Brown, Lester, and Sandra Postel. 1987. "Thresholds of Change." Pp. 3–19 in Lester R. Brown et al. (eds.). *State of the World.* New York: W. W. Norton.

Browning, Kaeren. 2002. "Shanty Towns: A South African Case Study." *Geography Review* (May):2.

Buckley, Stephen. 1998. "Birthrates Declining in Much of Africa." *Washington Post* (April 27):A11–A12.

Burkhalter, Holly. 2004. "The Politics of AIDS: Engaging Conservative Activists." Online at www.af-aids@healthdev.net (January 27).

Caldwell, John C. 1994. "Fertility in Sub-Saharan Africa: Status and Prospects." *Population and Development Review* 20 (March):179–187.

———. 2000. "Rethinking the African AIDS Epidemic." *Population and Development Review* 26 (March):117–135.

Caldwell, John, and Pat Caldwell. 2002. "Africa: The New Family Planning Frontier (Regional Perspectives)." *Studies in Family Planning* (March):76–87.

Center for Reproductive Law and Policy and International Federation of Women Lawyers (Kenya chapter). 1997. *Women of the World: Laws and Policies Affecting Their Reproductive Lives—Anglophone Africa.* New York: Center for Reproductive Law and Policy.

Chin, James. 1990. "Current and Future Dimensions of the HIV/AIDS Pandemic in Women and Children." *Lancet* 336 (July 28):221–224.

"Closing the Condom Gap." 1999. *Population Reports* 27 (April).

Cordell, Dennis D., Joel W. Gregory, and Victor Piche. 1987. "African Historical Demography: The Search for a Theoretical Framework." Pp. 14–32 in Dennis D. Cordell and Joel W. Gregory (eds.). *African Population and Capitalism: Historical Perspectives.* Boulder, CO: Westview Press.

Crawley, Mike. 2004. "Why AIDS Keeps Swelling in Africa." *Christian Science Monitor* (December 1):6–7.

Cullinan, Kerry. 2006. "Researchers Note Sharp Drop in Zim HIV Prevalence." *Mail & Guardian online* (South Africa). Online at www.mg.co.za (February 7).

Davidson, Basil. 1959. *The Lost Cities of Africa.* Boston: Little, Brown.

Dawson, Marc H. 1987. "Health, Nutrition, and Population in Central Kenya, 1890–1945." Pp. 201–220 in Dennis D. Cordell and Joel W. Gregory (eds.). *African Population and Capitalism: Historical Perspectives.* Boulder, CO: Westview Press.

Dervarics, Charles. 1999. "Uganda Beats Back HIV/AIDS." *Population Today* 27 (November):5.

El-Shakhs, Salah, and Hooshang Amirakmadi. 1986. "Urbanization and Spatial Development in Africa: Some Critical Issues." *African Urban Quarterly* 1:3–19.

Faruqee, Rashid, and Ravi Gulhati. 1983. *Rapid Population Growth in Sub-Saharan Africa: Issues and Policies.* No. 559. Washington, DC: World Bank.

"Firms Not Ahead of the AIDS Curve." 2005. *Mail & Guardian online* (South Africa). Online at www.mg.co.za (January 20).

Goliber, Thomas J. 1985. "Sub-Saharan Africa: Population Pressures on Development." *Population Bulletin* 40. Washington, DC: Population Reference Bureau.

"The Good Wife's Sacrifice." 2004. *Mail & Guardian online* (South Africa). Online at www.mg.co.za (March 9).

Gordon, April A., and Donald L. Gordon. 1988. "Cameroon's Urban and Rural Problems: Flipsides of the Same Coin." Paper presented at the Joint Southeast Regional Seminar for African Studies Meeting, "Cameroon Day" Symposium, African Studies Center, University of Florida, Gainesville.

Goujon, Emmanuel. 2005. "UNAids: Prevention Strategies Aren't Working." *Mail & Guardian online* (South Africa). Online at www.mg.co.za (December 8).

Green, Cynthia P. (ed.). 1994. *Sustainable Development: Population and the Environment.* Washington, DC: USAID.

Gregson, Simon, Basia Zaba, Geoffrey P. Garnett, and Ray M. Anderson. 1998. "Projections of the Magnitude of the HIV/AIDS Epidemic in Southern Africa." Pp. 27–60 in Alan Whiteside (ed.). *Implications of AIDS for Demography and Policy in Southern Africa.* Pietermaritzburg, South Africa: University of Natal Press.

Guest, Emma. 2001. *Children of AIDS: Africa's Orphan Crisis.* Sterling, VA: Pluto Press.

Gupta, Dhruba. 1987. "Urbanization in Precolonial West Africa." *Africa Quarterly* 22:27–40.

Henin, Roushdi A. 1979. "Government Approaches to the Population Issue." Pp. 184–199 in Reuben K. Udo (ed.). *Population Education Source Book for Sub-Saharan Africa.* Nairobi: Heinemann.

Hope, Sr., Kempe. 1998. "Urbanization and Urban Growth in Africa." *Journal of Asian and African Studies* 33 (4):345–358.

HRW (Human Rights Watch). 2005. "Zimbabwe: Evicted and Forsaken." No. A1716. Online at www.hrw.org (December 1).

Hyden, Goran. 1983. *No Shortcuts to Progress.* Berkeley: University of California Press.

Jewsiewicki, Bogumel. 1987. "Toward a Historical Sociology of Population in Zaire: Proposals for the Analysis of the Demographic Regime." Pp. 271–280 in Dennis D. Cordell and Joel W. Gregory (eds.). *African Population and Capitalism: Historical Perspectives.* Boulder, CO: Westview Press.

Johnson, Stanley P. 1987. *World Population and the United Nations: Challenge and Response.* New York: Cambridge University Press.

Johwa, Wilson. 2003. "No Barriers Too Great for Zim Immigrants." *Mail & Guardian online* (South Africa). Online at www.mg.co.za (November 16).

Kevane, Michael. 2004. *Women and Development in Africa: How Gender Works.* Boulder, CO: Lynne Rienner Publishers.

Kuchment, Anna. 2002. "Time to Get Religion." *Newsweek International* (February 18): 31.

Loewenson, Rene, and Alan Whiteside. 1998. "HIV and AIDS in Southern Africa." Pp. 13–26 in Alan Whiteside (ed.). *Implications of AIDS for Demography and Policy in Southern Africa.* Pietermaritzburg, South Africa: University of Natal Press.

Lutz, Wolfgang. 1994. "The Future of World Population." *Population Bulletin* 49 (June). Washington, DC: Population Reference Bureau.

Mahadi, Abdullahi, and J. E. Inikori. 1987. "Population and Capitalist Development in Precolonial West Africa: Kasar Kano in the Nineteenth Century." Pp. 62–73 in Dennis D. Cordell and Joel W. Gregory (eds.). *African Population and Capitalism: Historical Perspectives.* Boulder, CO: Westview Press.

Mbacke, Cheikh. 1994. "Family Planning Programs and Fertility Transition in Sub-Saharan Africa." *Population and Development Review* 20 (March):188–193.

McNeil, Jr., Donald. 2005. "A Path to Cheaper AIDS Drugs for Poor Nations." *The New York Times.* Online at www.nytimes.com (January 26).

Montgomery, Mark R., and Edward K. Brown. 1990. "Accommodating Urban Growth in Sub-Saharan Africa." Pp. 74–88 in George T. F. Acsadi, Gwendolyn Johnson-Acsadi, and Rodolfo A. Bulatao (eds.). *Population Growth and Reproduction in Sub-Saharan Africa.* Washington, DC: World Bank.

Morrison, Minion K. C., and Peter C. W. Gutkind (eds.). 1982. *Housing the Urban Poor in Africa.* Syracuse, NY: Maxwell School of Citizenship and Public Affairs.

Newman, James L., and Russell Lura. 1983. "Fertility Control in Africa." *Geographical Review* 73:396–406.

O'Connor, Anthony. 1991. *Poverty in Africa: A Geographical Approach.* London: Belhaven Press.

O'Brien, Jay. 1987. "Differential High Fertility and Demographic Transition: Peripheral Capitalism in Sudan." Pp. 173–186 in Dennis D. Cordell and Joel W. Gregory (eds.). *African Population and Capitalism: Historical Perspectives.* Boulder, CO: Westview Press.

Page, Hilary J., and Ron Lesthaeghe. 1981. *Child-Spacing in Tropical Africa: Traditions and Change.* London: Academic Press.

Population Reference Bureau. 1993. *World Population Data Sheet.* Washington, DC: Population Reference Bureau.

———. 2005. *World Population Data Sheet.* Washington, DC: Population Reference Bureau. Online at www.prb.com.

"The Reproductive Revolution: New Survey Findings." 1992. *Population Reports.* Series M, no. 11 (December).

Rodney, Walter. 1974. *How Europe Underdeveloped Africa.* Washington, DC: Howard University Press.

Rondinelli, Dennis A. 1983. *Secondary Cities in Developing Countries.* Beverly Hills, CA: Sage Publications.

Rosen, James E., and Shanti R. Conly. 1998. *Africa's Population Challenge: Accelerating Progress in Reproductive Health.* Washington, DC: Population Action International.

Sai, Fred T. 1988. "Changing Perspectives of Population in Africa and International Responses." *African Affairs* 87:267–276.

Schoofs, Mark. 1999. "In Senegal, Common Sense Spells Success." *Washington Post,* January 31, p. B2.

Sindiga, Isaac. 1985. "The Persistence of High Fertility in Kenya." *Social Science and Medicine* 20:71–84.

Stillwaggon, Eileen. 2002. "HIV/AIDS in Africa: Fertile Terrain." *Journal of Development Studies* (August): 1–22.

Stren, Richard E., and Rodney R. White. 1989. "Conclusion." Pp. 305–312 in Richard E. Stren and Rodney R. White (eds.). *African Cities in Crisis: Managing Rapid Urban Growth.* Boulder, CO: Westview Press.

Turshen, Meredith. 1987. "Population Growth and the Deterioration of Health: Mainland Tanzania, 1920–1960." Pp. 187–200 in Dennis D. Cordell and Joel W. Gregory (eds.). *African Population and Capitalism: Historical Perspectives.* Boulder, CO: Westview Press.

Udoto, Paul. 2004. "The Global Fund on AIDS, Malaria and Tuberculosis Invites Funding Applications." Online at www.AF-AIDS@healthdev.net (January 17).

UN (United Nations). 2003. "Urban and Rural Areas: 2003." Online at www.esa.un.org/unup.

———. 2005. "World Population Prospects: The 2004 Revision." Online at www.un.org/esa/population/publications.

UNAIDS. 2005a. "AIDS Epidemic Update December 2005 Sub-Saharan Africa." Online at www.unaids.org.

———. 2005b. "Fact Sheet: Africa." Online at www.unaids.org.

———. 2005c. "Regions: Sub-Saharan Africa." Online at www.unaids.org.

UN-Habitat (United Nations Human Settlement Programme). N.d. "State of the World's Cities: Trends in Sub-Saharan Africa." Online at www.unchs.org.

Valentine, Carol H., and Joanne E. Revson. 1979. "Cultural Traditions, Social Change, and Fertility in Sub-Saharan Africa." *Journal of Modern African Studies* 17:453–472.

Walker, Liz, Graeme Reid, and Morna Cornell. 2004. *Waiting to Happen: HIV/AIDS in South Africa.* Boulder, CO: Lynne Rienner Publishers.

White, Rodney R. 1989. "The Influence of Environmental and Economic Factors on the Urban Crisis." Pp. 1–19 in Richard E. Stren and Rodney R. White (eds.). *African Cities in Crisis: Managing Rapid Urban Growth.* Boulder, CO: Westview Press.

"WHO Address to Marrakech Conference." 1994. *Zimbabwe AIDS Information Network News Bulletin* 2 (March):11–12.

Wines, Michael. 2005. "In Zimbabwe, Homeless Belie Leader's Claim." *The New York Times,* November 13, Section 1, p. 1.

"Women and HIV: The New Face of AIDS." 2004. *The Economist.* Online at www.economist.com (November 25).

World Bank. 1986. *Population Growth and Policies in Sub-Saharan Africa.* Washington, DC: World Bank.

———. 1989. *Sub-Saharan Africa: From Crisis to Sustainable Growth: A Long-Term Perspective Study.* Washington, DC: World Bank.

———. 1990. *World Development Report.* New York: Oxford University Press.

———. 1995. *World Development Report.* New York: Oxford University Press.

———. 2003. *World Bank Development Report 2003. Sustainable Development in a Dynamic World: Transforming Institutions, Growth, and Quality of Life.* New York: World Bank/Oxford University Press.

———. 2004. *World Bank Development Report 2004. Making Services Work for Poor People.* New York: World Bank/Oxford University Press.

———. 2005. "World Bank Development Report 2005. World Development Indicators 2005." Online at www.worldbank.org/data/wdi2005.

8

Africa's Environmental Problems

Julius E. Nyang'oro

Most people are now familiar with such terms as *acid rain, the greenhouse effect, ozone depletion, toxic waste, and environmental degradation.* They remind us of a reality we sometimes forget; that is, the fundamental mutual relationship between the environment and humankind. Lynton Caldwell reminds us of this when he describes the two realities in which humans live:

> The abiding reality is that of *earth* the planet—independent of man and his works; the other reality—the transient reality—is that of the *world,* which is a creation of the human mind. The earth and its biosphere form a grand synthesis of complex interactive systems within systems, organic and inorganic, animate and inanimate. The world is the way humanity understands and has organized its occupancy of the earth: an expression of imagination and purpose materialized through exploration, invention, labor and violence. (Caldwell, 1984:8)

This interconnectedness was one of the major issues addressed by the UN Conference on Environment and Development (UNCED) that took place in Rio de Janeiro in July 1992. At this conference, often called the Earth Summit, the global community developed a program of action called Agenda 21, which focuses on promoting both a healthy environment and the development of the world's economies and peoples. Such environmental issues as climate change, conservation of forests, and biodiversity were addressed under the umbrella goal of "sustainable development"[1] (see, e.g., World Bank, 1996). The purpose of sustainable development is to meet the needs of today's people without jeopardizing the ability of future generations to meet their needs (see WCED, 1987). In short, this means protecting the environmental base on which all life, including human life, depends.

The Earth Summit was followed ten years later by the World Summit on Sustainable Development, which met in Johannesburg, South Africa, during August 26–September 4, 2002. The Johannesburg Summit reaffirmed sustainable development as a central element of the international agenda and gave new impetus to global action to fight poverty and protect the environment. The understanding of sustainable development was broadened and strengthened as a result of the summit, particularly the important linkages between poverty, the environment, and the use of natural resources. Significantly, participants at the summit—governments, civil society organizations, and business—made key commitments, targets, and timetables to implement the "Johannesburg Plan," now known as the Millennium Development Goals (MDGs). Above all, the plan committed the world's governments and development institutions to halve by the year 2015 the proportion of the world's people whose income is less than $1 a day and the proportion who suffer from hunger (see www.un.org/millenniumgoals). By making this commitment, the summit was making a pointed connection between the management of the environment and the welfare of the global population. The fact that the conference was held in Johannesburg, South Africa, highlighted Africa's concerns in protecting its environment in the midst of pressures such as globalization, rapid population growth, massive poverty, and economic underdevelopment.

In this chapter we will consider the issue of the environment in Africa. We will look at the interaction between Africans and their environment both in the past and the present. The dilemma for Africans, as for people elsewhere in the world, is how to reconcile human needs (or wants) and activities with sound management of the environment to allow for future sustainability and development. In short, we will examine how Africa is coping with the expectations borne out of the three major environmental summits: Stockholm, Rio, and Johannesburg.

Concern over Africa's environment is not a new phenomenon. As Ayodele Cole (1986) has noted, colonial Africa was endowed with legislation and regulations on environmental health and sanitation, which were sometimes vigorously enforced in both urban and rural areas if it was deemed to be in the best interests of the colonial government. In another example, as early as 1935, E. P. Stebbing wrote a pioneering article to warn the colonial governments about the "encroaching Sahara" as one of the principal environmental problems facing the West African colonies. Stebbing's article was concerned about, among other things, the dwindling fertility of the Sahel as a result of the spread of the Sahara Desert farther south.

Some of the measures undertaken in the Sahel region to alleviate problems arising from the drought of the 1970s, such as the planting of trees and the restricting of animal grazing to protect the thinning grasslands, would have greatly benefited from the historical lessons Stebbing and others addressed more than six decades ago. But as it is, international concern over the Sahel region seems to have assumed significance in the 1970s only when it became apparent that large populations in West Africa were on the verge of starvation because of dwindling rainfall, reduced soil fertility for crop cultivation, and other environmental decay (Eckholm and Brown, 1977).

Yet, it must be added that in comparative terms, the relative neglect of environmental concerns that characterized the Sahel region up to the early 1970s essentially reflected a general neglect of the environment by governments across the globe (Pirages, 1978). In the context of Africa, governments were more concerned with economic growth than with environmental protection, even though economic development had a direct impact on environmental quality (Dixon et al., 1988; Leonard, 1985). Unfortunately, the need for environmental management has until recently been viewed as a constraint on attempts to achieve rapid economic growth. In many cases, this has led to economic growth being achieved at the cost of the environment, which has resulted in irreparable environmental damage (WCED, 1987; Kabeberi, 1988). The viewing of economic development and environmental management as two conflicting objectives raises questions that are central to the concerns about the environment in Africa today (Berntsen, 1995).

The 1972 UN Conference on the Human Environment in Stockholm, Sweden, gave a momentum to a global concern for environmental protection that has helped put environmental management in the forefront of both domestic and international policy. As Caldwell has noted:

> The U.N. Conference on the Human Environment (1972) was a watershed event in human relationships with the Earth. The conference epigram "Only One Earth" symbolized a change in human perception that would become a new factor in the development of ethics and in the evaluation of alternatives in policies affecting the environment. (Caldwell, 1984:1)

The establishment of the UN Environmental Programme (UNEP), with its headquarters in Nairobi, Kenya, should be seen as arising directly from the 1972 Stockholm conference. What should be of significance here is the recognition that the environment in Africa is closely tied to environments elsewhere in the world, and that any attempt at treating one part of the global environment in isolation from the rest would be grossly inadequate (Berntsen, 1995).

The Environment in Africa: Continuity and Change

Geologically speaking, the African continent is an old one. According to Lewis and Berry (1988:36–70), many of the general features of the African landscape have evolved over long geologic periods without being submerged under changing sea levels, without being changed dramatically by glaciation, and without major tectonic upheavals. In comparison, Europe and North America have been affected dramatically by glaciation and tectonic upheavals, which means that they are much younger continents. This difference in geologic history has had serious consequences in terms of current environmental concerns such as soil erosion. According to Lewis and Berry (1988:36), Africa's relative geologic stability has allowed many geologic processes to proceed further in Africa than in the younger continents. For example, in most of the middle, temperate latitudes, much of the soil is of recent origin, often derived from glacial activities. In most of Africa, however, the soils are of ancient origin and have been subject to intensive leaching of nutrients over long periods of time. As a result, African soils tend to lack fertility. This geologic fact means that Africa is actually more vulnerable to human activity than other continents in terms of deforestation, desertification, and soil erosion.

In terms of geographic location, over 75 percent of Africa lies between the tropics, and much of the land beyond the tropics is extremely dry. This land includes the Sahara Desert, which covers most of northern and northwestern Africa, and the Kalahari Desert, which covers large portions of southwestern Africa. About 90 percent of the continent is classified as having tropical climates. This means that the average annual temperatures are relatively high over most of the land. The exceptions to this are the northern and southern edges of the continent, which have a Mediterranean type of climate, and areas of high elevation such as the Kenya highlands, which have relatively cooler temperatures. With most of Africa being tropical, the major factor that distinguishes seasons is precipitation, that is, wet and dry seasons. (See Chapter 2 for additional analysis of the geography of Africa, especially Maps 2.1 and 2.2.)

Over the centuries, humans have adapted their lives and activities to their environment. Certainly this was the case in Africa. As both Thomas O'Toole and Eugenia Shanklin note in Chapters 3 and 9, respectively, Africa is believed to be the first human habitat, going back millions of years. During these vast expanses of time our ancestors were adapting both physically and culturally to the environmental conditions they faced. Most relevant to the study of the African environment in the contemporary period is the shift in human activity from foraging to domesticated food production, which is closely linked to the beginnings of African metallurgy (Austen, 1987:9). However, historical evidence as to what precisely happened in this shift from "savagery to culture" is still lacking and is open to much debate (Austen, 1987:10–16). Domesticated food production has been associated with the increase in population, a more predictable existence, and the establishment of communities. Historians have suggested that by the nineteenth century, Africans had long been organized into large numbers of communities. With the possible exception of a few small groups, such as San (in the Kalahari) and Twa (in the Congo rainforest), the economies of true subsistence had largely disappeared (Lewis and Berry, 1988). Probably the most important thing to note is that humans evolved to conform to their environment and that for the greater part of their existence on earth have constantly been molded by that environment. It seems that over a long period of time, the key to survival was not resistance to change but meeting change with change (or adjustment); otherwise, the human race would not have survived.

The coming of colonialism in Africa significantly changed the nature of existing local or "community" economies that often had complex economic systems to deal with food and other crop production, handicrafts, and trade. For the most part, the economies were localized in specific regions. As Virginia DeLancey notes in Chapter 5, one fundamental change that was initiated during the colonial period and persists today was the creation of a new trading system due to the demand for African raw materials such as palm oil, rubber, ivory, and copper. This, in turn, created tremendous pressure on the African environment to respond to these new and increasing demands. To get a better picture of the overall pressure on the environment in Africa during the colonial and postcolonial periods, this chapter should be read in conjunction with Chapters 5 and 7.

Contemporary Problems of the African Environment

Deforestation

Deforestation occurs when trees are cut down to provide firewood (a primary energy source) and timber, and to free up space for more crop cultivation or grazing land. Other factors relevant to Africa include rapid urbanization, drought, civil wars, oil and mineral extraction, and bush fires (UNEP, 2000b). Lester Brown has argued that

> a sustainable society will differ from the one we now know in several respects. Population size will more or less be stationary, energy will be used more efficiently, and the economy will be fueled largely with renewable sources of energy. (Brown, 1981:247)

Looking at the African environment with regard to maintaining the critical balance between existing forests and human activity, the continent is moving very quickly toward unsustainability. Much of the deforestation—like much other environmental degradation—is the result of large numbers of individuals engaging in decisions that are privately rational but collectively destructive (Bojo et al., 1990).

Human activity in Africa, like elsewhere, has altered the landscape of the earth. Forest clearing is one such activity. Deforestation in the tropics has accelerated dramatically in the years since World War II, but estimates of the area covered by tropical forests and rates of deforestation vary widely, mainly because countries use different measures and definitions of "forest" (Silver with DeFries, 1990:117). In spite of problems of measurement, a UNEP study (1990) revealed that globally speaking, just three countries—Brazil, Indonesia, and the Democratic Republic of Congo (DRC)—contained a major share of the world's tropical forests. Overall, Africa has over 17 percent of the world's forests, and the DRC has over 20 percent of Africa's forests (UNEP, 2000b). There are two basic forest types. The first, closed tropical rainforests, has a relatively tight canopy of mostly broad-leafed evergreen trees sustained by 256 inches or more of annual rainfall. The second, open tropical forests, has a canopy that is not continuous but covers more than 10 percent of the ground. When both types were considered, Brazil contained 26.5 percent of the world total, the DRC 9.2 percent, and Indonesia 6.1 percent (Silver with DeFries, 1990:117).[2]

The UNEP study noted that, globally, closed forests are being destroyed at a rate of about 0.6 percent annually. However, in terms of country variation, the problem seems even more serious. In some countries, such as the DRC, deforestation rates were as low as 0.2 percent a year, but in Côte d'Ivoire they reached 7 percent. Closed forests are thus expected to disappear altogether within twenty-five years in Africa unless effective steps are taken to conserve them. Perhaps the worst case is represented by Madagascar, which in the past few decades has lost more than four-fifths of its rainforest to land clearing (Wells, 1989:162). Current estimates are that forested area per capita will be reduced by 50 percent in Africa in less than twenty years (World Bank, 2000:42).

A major reason for the deforestation in Africa is poverty and economic underdevelopment. Instead of electricity or other modern forms of energy, 90 percent of the population uses fuelwood for cooking in Africa, and wood and brush supply about 52 percent of all energy sources—and the demand is growing (Agyei, n.d.; Anderson, 1987:7). Each year Africa loses woodlands area the size of the Netherlands (Rosen and Conly, 1998:14). These figures by themselves are not astonishing if the continent could devise a system of restoring the stock of trees that are cut down. But, according to Dennis Anderson,

World Bank

Growing land scarcity in Africa is leading to deforestation, soil erosion, and desertification as farmers clear forests or overuse the land in an effort to feed themselves.

World Bank

Commercial logging, as in Gabon, is one factor leading to a rapid loss of forests, including rainforests, in Africa and elsewhere in the developing world.

> the current annual rate of consumption is estimated to exceed the mean annual incremental growth . . . of local tree stocks and forest reserves by the following (rounded) amounts: in Senegal –35 percent (a slight surplus), in the Sahelian countries 30 percent, in Sudan 70 percent, in northern Nigeria 75 percent, in Ethiopia 150 percent, and in Niger 200 percent. (Anderson, 1987:7)

It is generally acknowledged that with the rapid increase in the number of people on the continent and higher rates of urbanization, the need for fuelwood as a source of energy will continue to grow. In fact, urbanization seems to have a direct effect on the loss of forests in Africa, because the spread of deforestation is most noticeable near urban areas. According to Anderson (1987:8), the growth of towns and cities brings about increased demands for fuelwood and charcoal and accounts for much of the decline in tree stocks in the surrounding countryside, often for a radius of 80–160 kilometers or more.

Forest clearing to obtain fuelwood is indeed a major problem; however, fuelwood leads to the degradation of open forests only and plays little part in the destruction of closed forests. The major cause of deforestation in Africa is the clearing of forests for purposes of crop cultivation—the need to expand agricultural land (UNEP, 1990). This problem is also tied to the increase in the number of people. Yet, the UNEP report cautions against generalizations that may not hold:

> Blame should not be laid at the door of shifting agriculture itself. Small strips of forest can be cleared, burnt, planted and left to return to natural forest again, provided the fallow period is long enough. [But] in many places it no longer is. The reasons for this are complicated. Often, as productive, cultivable land becomes scarce, small-scale farmers are pushed into more marginal areas, and shifting agriculturalists onto fragile upland forest areas unable to support their practices. *Fallow periods are then shortened as yields fall and populations increase.* It is estimated that shifting agriculture now accounts for 70 percent of deforestation in Africa. (UNEP, 1990:3; emphasis added)

But the larger point still holds: shifting cultivation is an important agent of deforestation. Shifting cultivation is a practice in which subsistence farmers clear and burn a plot of land in the forest, then grow crops for one or a few years before repeating the cycle. This age-old method of subsistence agriculture recycles nutrients to the soil and maintains productivity without fertilizers, provided the fallow period is long enough to regenerate the forest growth. But, with increasing population and pressure on the land, in many places the fallow period is cut short. Eventually, the soil becomes unproductive, crops no longer flourish, and the trees do not grow back. It is important to remember that once forests are cleared for agriculture, grazing, or logging, there is no guarantee that the trees can grow back. This is the dilemma that many African countries face. Pierre Pradervand, who spent several years traveling through Africa in a quest to understand the dynamics of change on the continent, summarized the deforestation problem as follows:

> By far the most important cause [of deforestation] is the opening up of new land for agriculture. The most striking characteristic of deforestation that emerged in my discussions with the farmers was the speed at which it is taking place. In less than a generation they have seen their wooded environment literally disappear. There does not appear to be another major area of the world where such a transformation has been as rapid and severe. (Pradervand, 1989:37–38)

Deforestation in Africa has also been attributed to structural adjustment programs (SAPs), now ubiquitous on the continent. Here I will give the example of Ghana to illustrate the problem. Since the early 1980s, Ghana has been subject to SAPs as dictated by the International Monetary Fund and the World Bank. Besides other initiatives, SAPs have promoted the export of timber, Ghana's third most important export commodity. A variety of sources (Development GAP, 1993) have shown that major overseas aid and credit packages have been arranged with foreign exchange provided to timber companies to enable them to purchase new materials and equipment. As a result, from 1983 to 1988, timber exports increased from $16 million to $99 million. Such a quick-fix solution to Ghana's need for foreign exchange earnings has contributed to the loss of Ghana's already depleted forest resources. Between 1981 and 1985, the annual rate of deforestation was 1.3 percent, and current estimates are as high as 2 percent. Ghana's tropical forest area is now just 25 percent of its original size (Development GAP, 1993:25).

Cameroon presents another alarming case of deforestation due to logging, and in many cases, illegal logging. Cameroon has the second largest contiguous tract of rainforest in the world after the Amazon Basin. Cameroon's forests are also some of the most biodiverse. Approximately 75 percent of these forests have been logged or allocated for logging concessions. Less than 20 percent have not been logged to at least some extent, and only 6 percent are protected as parks or reserves (World Resources Institute, 2005).

A growing but often underreported source of deforestation is conflict and the disruptions caused by movements of large numbers of people. Africa's civil wars have in some cases produced large numbers of refugees who settle in overcrowded camps, sometimes for lengthy periods of time. Dependent on firewood from the local environment, a devastating loss of trees can occur. As an example, Guinea has an estimated 400,000 refugees and has suffered severe deforestation (World Bank, 2000:242). The most recent example of this problem is in the region of Darfur in western Sudan. There have been armed clashes in Darfur since the late 1980s, stemming in part from conflicts between livestock herders and settled farmers over access to land primarily because of the diminishing fertile kind available to either group. Coupled with problems of state control from the center in Khartoum, environmental problems stemming from deforestation and related issues, the clashes escalated into a large-scale military conflict involving two rebel movements and a militia supported by the government called the *Janjaweed* (see Ali-Dinar, 2004; Department of Public Information, 2004).

Perhaps more important than the causes of deforestation are its effects on people and the environment as a whole. About 75 percent of the population in most African countries are rural dwellers. In terms of subsistence, rural dwellers depend on forests and trees for a long list of essential products: fuelwood, fodder, fruit, nuts, dyes, medicines, and building materials. Fuelwood and fodder alone are in many societies two of the most essential ingredients for survival; without them, rural life would degenerate quickly into a mere struggle for existence (UNEP, 1990). Indeed, in some places this has already come to pass (Timberlake, 1986). Many rural families also depend on tree products for income. Collecting, processing, and selling forest products are often the only ways by which rural women can obtain cash income. In the past, these activities have been called "minor forest industries." But in no sense are they minor. For example, in Egypt's Fayoum province, 48 percent of women work in "minor" forest industries. My own research in Mara region in northeastern Tanzania revealed that in at least 50 percent of the households surveyed, one member of the household was involved in activities related to the forest industry. It is obvious that when forests are depleted, rural families must survive without either the products on which they depend or the incomes they need. Ghana is a good example. An estimated 75 percent of Ghanaians depend on wild foods to supplement their diet. Stripping the forest has led to a sharp increase in malnutrition and disease. For women, the food, fuel, and medicines they harvest from the forest provide critical resources, especially in the face of decreased food production, lower wages, and other economic shocks that threaten household food security (Poulsen, 1990:4).

Deforestation also has negative effects on a host of other environmental problems. For instance, loss of trees is a major factor in land degradation, with serious consequences for food production (which will be discussed below). Desertification, drought, and permanent climate change have also been attributed to the vast loss of tree cover (Rosen and Conly, 1998:14; Development GAP, 1993:25). Deforestation is also largely responsible for the fact that Africa has lost from one-half to two-thirds of its original wildlife habitat (World Bank, 2000:195; Rosen and Conly, 1998:14). Another alarming casualty of deforestation, in association with pollution and soil erosion, is one of Africa's most breathtaking freshwater resources—Lake Victoria, the world's second largest lake. It is reportedly becoming so badly degraded that it could die by 2050 if nothing is done to reverse eutrophication of its waters. Eutrophication is the result of excess nutrients pouring into the lake from local rivers. With the loss of tree cover along the rivers that feed into the lake, there is nothing to prevent sediments and contaminants from washing into the water. Scientists specifically blame "the burning of indigenous forests in Mau and Nandi Hills [Kenya], overgrazing of shallow soils on hill slopes, run-off from fragile soils and plains and gully erosion on escarpment" (Okoko, 2000).

In Madagascar, deforestation is behind a snowballing list of environmental and economic losses—both present and future. In the past forty years, Madagascar has destroyed 50 percent of its forests; the losses are incalculable. Madagascar is one of the richest and most unique ecosystems in the world. It has over 12,000 plant and animal species, many found nowhere else. There is a vast unrealized potential for both ecotourism and bioprospecting. The rosy periwinkle, for instance, provides the basis for some of our most potent anti-cancer drugs. Population growth is a major factor behind the loss of forests in Madagascar. Due to stagnation in agricultural productivity, population growth led to pressures to clear forests for cropland. When yields declined after a couple of years, the land was abandoned or turned to rangeland for cattle. Excessive tree cutting also occurred to provide wood for fuel. Denuded hillsides led to soil erosion. Irrigation of cropland led to damage from sedimentation, clogging of hydroelectric facilities with sediment, and destruction of freshwater and marine ecosystems. Rather than generating sustained economic growth, cutting down forests has left Madagascar poorer than before (World Bank, 2003:165). If such trends are not reversed, the future of Madagascar and its people may be squandered in a destructive race for survival.

Clearly, the present forest situation in Africa is a matter of serious concern. Gunnar Poulsen (1990:4) of UNEP outlined the problem in a report to all African governments. In the report he noted the rapid loss of natural forest resources in Africa, including both flora and fauna. Reforestation efforts compensated for no more than 3.5 percent of the forests being destroyed (although this varies by country), and "forest plantations" did not compensate for the loss of biodiversity. More recently, in UNEP's "GEO-2000" report, tree plantations and agroforestry are mentioned as important to forest rehabilitation in Africa, but it cautions that such efforts are so far in a losing race with the rate of deforestation (UNEP, 2000b).

Desertification

As you can see, forests are part of a complex and delicate ecosystem. When the balance in the ecosystem is altered through human activities such as the cutting down of forests, a chain reaction occurs leading to the deterioration of other parts of the ecosystem. The problem of increased desertification in Africa has been associated with increased deforestation. As Erik Eckholm and Lester Brown have noted, "While 'desertification' has become something of a catch-all word, the problems usually covered by this term involve ecological changes that sap land of its ability to sustain agriculture and human habitation" (Eckholm and Brown, 1977:7).

Lloyd Timberlake (1986) argues that "desertification" more accurately describes the conversion of productive land into wasteland by human mismanagement: "Crops are overcultivated; rangelands are overgrazed; forests are cut; irrigation projects turn good cropland into salty, barren fields" (Timberlake, 1986:59).

In Africa, the declining ratio of mean annual incremental growth of local tree stocks has led to the decreased ability of land to sustain agriculture and human habitation. As with many environmental issues, it is difficult to have an accurate figure on how fast the deserts are spreading in Africa. However, in 1972, the US Agency for International Development estimated that in the years since World War II, 650,000 square kilometers of land once suitable for agriculture or intensive grazing had been forfeited to the Sahara in its southern fringe (Eckholm and Brown, 1977:9). More recent estimates suggest that the problem has become worse. According to new estimates, the continent as a whole is losing an average of 36,000 square kilometers to the desert every year. In 1980 alone, 200,000 square kilometers of arable land were lost (Nnoli, 1990; Skoupy, 1988). The situa-

World Bank

Desertification threatens many areas of Africa, especially the Sahel.

tion seems particularly serious in the Sahel zone.[3] But more countries are increasingly being affected. Notable among the affected areas are Niger, Mali, Burkina Faso, Mauritania, northern Nigeria, northern Ghana, Senegal, Gambia, Chad, Sudan, and Egypt. From this list, it is obvious that desertification has become a major environmental concern in Africa (see BBC News, 2005).

To fully comprehend the nature of desertification in Africa, it is important to discuss the problem in a historical and geological context. We noted earlier that geologically Africa is an old continent. This makes the continent more susceptible to natural processes such as soil erosion. It also makes the soil less fertile, with a diminished "carrying capacity" (ability to sustain human activity). There is, of course, a complex relationship between population and natural/environmental carrying capacity and between population distribution and desertification. The principal point is that, generally speaking, Africa's environment has always been fragile, at least in the last few thousand years (Lewis and Berry, 1988). The argument is usually presented as follows.

In terms of population settlement, Africa seems, at first glance, a vast and empty continent. But on closer inspection, it appears that many countries in Africa are becoming very crowded. Africa has been described as "underpopulated" because its population density is relatively low. Compared with most of Asia, or even Central America, Africa seems uncrowded. Population density, however, is just one side of the population–natural resources balance; land productivity is the other. About 80 percent of the continent cannot be considered arable. Half the potentially arable soils are lateritic and thus unsuited for permanent field crop agriculture. Of the land that is arable, only 7 percent has naturally rich alluvial soils (Revell, 1976; Lewis and Berry, 1988). Skoupy (1988:30) points out that arid and semi-arid regions constitute more than 50 percent of tropical Africa and support more than 35 percent of its population. The drylands of tropical Africa extend over twenty-four countries divided in the following way:

- Largely desert countries with more than 66 percent arid areas: Botswana, Cape Verde, Chad, Djibouti, Kenya, Mali, Mauritania, Niger, Somalia
- Countries with over 30 percent arid and semi-arid areas: Burkina Faso, Ethiopia, Gambia, Mozambique, Senegal, Sudan, Tanzania, Zambia, Zimbabwe
- Countries with below 30 percent arid and semi-arid areas: Angola, Benin, Cameroon, Madagascar, Nigeria, Uganda[4]

It should be obvious that much of Africa's drier land can support only economically marginal, land-extensive uses, such as nomadic pastoralism, or at best only one meager grain crop per year. Thus, there are frequently good reasons why vast, unsettled areas have remained so. It was not by chance that they were left until last. Many regions that are unsettled today are empty precisely because they cannot support sustained settlement.[5]

Using products of modern science and technology such as fertilizer and irrigation may be one way to save the land from the encroaching desert. Certainly, an increase in food production using modern scientific methods would go a long way toward resolving the population problem. However, there is evidence that doing that would only increase environmental degradation. R. E. Tillman (1981) argues that modern technological inputs such as irrigation could improve yields. But this could be achieved only at great financial expense and with high environmental costs and public health risks. As real energy costs rise, so do the costs of irrigated agriculture, which depends on electricity or liquid fuel for pumping and often upon such energy-intensive inputs as fertilizer and biocides—which create environmental hazards of their own. As David Weir and Mark Schapiro point out, this kind of environmental degradation occurs not just in Africa but throughout the Third World:

> Dozens of pesticides too dangerous for unrestricted use in the United States are shipped to underdeveloped countries. There, lack of regulation, illiteracy, and repressive working conditions can turn even a "safe" pesticide into a deadly weapon. According to the World Health Organization, someone in the underdeveloped countries is poisoned by pesticides *every minute.* (Weir and Schapiro, 1981:3)

Pesticides in Africa pose a major toxic waste threat to the environment. In the past forty years, the donor community has provided resources to purchase and use chemical pesticides. The result is a stockpile throughout the continent of more than 50,000 tons of highly toxic and often obsolete pesticides and severely contaminated soils. Almost a third of these pesticides are POPs (persistent organic pollutants) that remain toxic for long periods of time. The POPs have contaminated surface and groundwater and are circulating around the world in our oceans, where they become concentrated in marine food chains. African countries have neither the facilities nor expertise to dispose of these stockpiles (World Bank, 2003:92)

It would seem, therefore, that continuing desertification makes countries in Africa use pesticides and fertilizers that in the long run are dangerous both to the environment and the population. Furthermore, excessive irrigation in dry climates often leads to salinization or alkalinization of cropland, so that much of the available water must eventually be used to flush away salts rather than to irrigate crops.

Finally, the issue of desertification has to be related to the problem of drought, as the two actually go together, the latter preceding the former. Of course, drought may be a result of either natural decline in rainfall or a change in climatic patterns caused by the clearing away of forests (Eckholm and Brown, 1977). In any case, Gordon Wells (1989:148–192), using earth photographs taken by National Aeronautics and Space Administration satellites over the years, presents a devastating picture of the Sahel countries as they have progressively become desert as a result of thirty years of drought conditions (World Bank, 2000:110). From 1968 to the present, rainfall in the western Sahel (i.e., central Chad, coastal Senegal, and Mauritania) has been below the historical mean recorded from 1931 to 1960. Naturally, the environmental repercussion of the long drought is that it has destroyed the ability of the region to sustain its population. Wells (1989:163–164) gives a compelling description of the effects of drought on the environment where Chad, Niger, Nigeria, and Cameroon meet on Lake Chad. In June 1966, Wells reports, satellite photographs from the *Gemini 9* mission showed Lake Chad to be about 22,000 square kilometers; in the lake were numerous islands. A flourishing economy based on fishing and cereal production existed in the lake area, and villages were located on the islands. By the summer of 1985, these cultural patterns had collapsed due to the evaporation of the lake. Photographs taken by orbiting cameras in space indicated the lake had shrunk to only 2,500 square kilometers, although rains in January 1986 increased this to 5,000 square kilometers. Water levels were so low that irrigation projects at the center of regional development plans failed. Thousands of farmers have been forced to leave their land and raise crops or cattle along the receding lake shoreline. Current estimates are that 60 percent of Africa is vulnerable to drought; 30 percent is extremely vulnerable (World Bank, 2000:110). During the 1990s at least twenty-five countries faced severe food shortages as a result of drought (Darkoh, n.d.).

An area experiencing record drought since 1998 is Kenya. Water shortages are occurring in Nairobi (the capital city), as well as in other areas of the country. Power rationing and power outages are problems due to the fact that most of Kenya's power comes from hydroelectric dams built on rivers that are now low. In the countryside, crops are failing, livestock are dying, and some people are starving. Environmentalists blame massive deforestation for the failing rain (African Wildlife Foundation, 2000:3). Indeed, since 1999 countries in the Horn of Africa and parts of East Africa have suffered from drought every year but one. Hardest hit areas in addition to Kenya include parts of Ethiopia, Somalia, and Djibouti ("Famine Spreads," 2006:44).

Soil Erosion and Degradation

Soil erosion, like desertification, is tied in large measure to the problem of deforestation, reflecting the complex interdependence in the ecosystem. As

Cheryl Silver and Ruth DeFries (1990:120) have noted, forests are an important part of the earth system. On a local scale, trees protect the soil from rain and wind that would otherwise wash or blow it away. These two authors further note that despite the image of luxuriant growth in tropical forests, most of the soils that support that growth are remarkably unproductive. This is the case in Africa. High temperatures and rainfall throughout the year encourage leaching of nutrients from the soil, so that few nutrients remain except for those held by the plants themselves.

This naturally calls for better management of topsoils, which includes the need to reduce the clearing of forests. The twin processes of deforestation and soil erosion, especially in tropical Africa, have led to an increased concern to slow down the process. This concern is made more urgent by the nature of Africa's geologic formation, especially its (old) age and its geographic location in the tropics (Lewis and Berry, 1988:iii), which makes the continent more vulnerable to soil erosion. Richard Wagner provides a concise summary of why the cutting down of tropical forests has more serious consequences for the soil than would be the case in temperate rainforests:

> In a temperate rain forest, most of the minerals made available by decomposition of organic litter or disintegration of the parent rock are quickly absorbed by plant roots and incorporated into the vegetation. If you were to stand in an oak-hickory forest in midsummer you would find several inches of slowly rotting leaves covering the rich topsoil, itself black with incorporated humus. Conversely a tropical rain forest has such a continuing high rate of organic litter decomposition that no mineral pool has time to accumulate. Directly beneath the most recently fallen debris is a heavy, clay-containing, mineral soil. As a result of this tie-up of all available minerals in the standing vegetation, the cycling of minerals is rapid and direct. As soon as a leaf falls, it is decomposed and its minerals are absorbed by plant roots and channeled into the growth of another leaf. So tight is this cycling process that those few ions not absorbed by plant roots but leached through the soil into the water table, and then out of the system, are replaced by ions picked up by the tree roots from the slowly disintegrating bedrock below.
>
> When tropical forest is cut, minerals are suddenly released faster than crop plants or the remaining trees are able to use them. They leach out of the system and fertility drops sharply. If the disturbance covers only a few acres, weeds and short-lived successional species quickly invade the area, shield the soil, and begin to restore the balanced mineral cycle. But when very large areas are cleared, this kind of recovery may be impossible. The lateritic nature of the soil also becomes part of the problem. When the forest is cleared, the heavily leached sesquioxides are exposed to high temperatures, and they bake into pavement-hard laterite. Once formed, laterite is almost impossible to break up and areas that once supported lush forest quickly become scrubland at best, supporting only shrubs or stunted trees. (Wagner, 1971:52–53)

Although there are many negative consequences associated with soil erosion, such as the loss of fertility, soil erosion itself is a natural process. As Silver and DeFries (1990) note, without it deltas would not form as soil erodes from the land and travels as sediment through streams and rivers. But the soil exposed in a deforested site generally accelerates the natural process, so much so that some dams in many parts of the tropics have filled with sediment far more rapidly than expected. Indeed, this process could be speeded as high as 100 times above normal. Naturally, the loss of fertility leads to serious land degradation. Because of the connection between deforestation—which is a human activity—and soil erosion, Piers Blaikie and Harold Brookfield (1987:1) have argued that land deforestation should by definition be a social problem, given the fact that purely environmental processes such as leaching and erosion occur with or without human interference. However, for these processes to be described as "degradation" implies social criteria that relate land to its actual or possible uses.

This seems to have been the case in Ethiopia, a country that has suffered the combined effects of drought, famine, and, more important, soil erosion. According to one source, Ethiopia loses an estimated 1 billion tons of topsoil per year (Timberlake, 1986:129). The loss results from overcultivation and lack of forests to provide the natural protection when heavy rains come. In tropical Africa, most rainfall is concentrated in short fierce storms over a few months only. A good example of this concentration perhaps can be gleaned from comparing London (generally known for its rainy and damp weather) and Sokoto in northern Nigeria. Sokoto actually gets 100 millimeters more rain than London, but it falls only in the months of July, August, and September, while in London, the rain is spread throughout most of the year (Timberlake, 1986:66).

The Sokoto/London comparison is important if we are to comprehend the seriousness of soil erosion in many African countries. To return to the case of Ethiopia: as the topsoil is constantly eroded by rain, the process of cultivation itself becomes almost an impossible task. Timberlake tells a dramatic story of this tragedy:

> The people of highland Ethiopia felt the destructive impact of rain on overused soil during one week in May 1984. I was in Wollo Region [in the northeast] then during the third year of drought, and there were suddenly about four days of unseasonal, unexpected, heavy rainfall.
>
> Throughout the region, farmers harnessed up weak oxen and began to sow wheat seeds they had left. But Wollo today is a moonscape of treeless hills and valleys. All the land that an ox can climb or a man stand upon has been cultivated. *Farmers even suspend themselves by ropes to sow hillsides too steep to stand on.*
>
> The rains of May 1984 bounced off this compacted, vegetationless watershed soil. The water ran quickly off in flashfloods, carrying away

> soil and precious seeds towards the lowland deserts to the east, or towards the tide basin to the west. After a night of rain, I looked out from a hilltop to see massive erosion, hills looking as if they had been dynamited, mud and rocks from the fields of hill farmers strewn over the fields of valley farmers. (Timberlake, 1986:21–22; emphasis added)

Obviously, the results of this erosion are devastating in terms of soil fertility. The resulting unproductivity of the land has contributed to the decline in Ethiopian agriculture (Dejene, 1987).

Soil degradation caused by soil erosion, overgrazing, and poor farming practices is reportedly worse in Africa (and some parts of Asia) than anywhere else in the world. Along with Ethiopia, Botswana, Lesotho, Madagascar, Nigeria, Rwanda, and Zimbabwe are suffering the worst problems in this area (Brown, 1998:9; Thomas et al., 2000:86–87). The effects on agriculture, especially food production, are already being felt and are likely to grow worse. This is especially true given the apparent inaction on the part of many African governments to deal seriously with the problem (Brown, 1998:9). Since World War II soil degradation has grown to encompass 850,000 square miles, according to a UN–World Bank study, and has reduced crop yields in Africa by 25 percent (McKenzie, 1999:A4; World Bank, 2000:195). Unfortunately, soil degradation is worsening; at the same time, population is rapidly growing. In the 1990s almost 43 percent of Africans were malnourished (Livernash and Rodenburg, 1998:32). Estimates are that farmers will have to increase food production five times to meet basic food needs by 2050 (Rosen and Conly, 1998:15). But, as Brown laments, "The next generation of farmers will try to feed not the 719 million people of today, but 1.45 billion in the year 2025—and with far less topsoil" (Brown, 1998:9).

Development and the Environment

In Chapter 5 on economic development, DeLancey discusses the problems African governments face in their quest to improve the material conditions of their respective societies. In this chapter, I wish to point to some examples where economic development strategies have negatively affected the environment. The first example is that of cash crops, which are crucial as a source of foreign (hard) currency. The second example relates to the oil industry.

The production of cash crops has been the primary engine for the generation of foreign exchange in most African countries. When the economies of Africa began a backward slide in the 1970s, the World Bank (1981:6–7) advised African countries to continue producing and improving cash crops such as coffee, cotton, tea, and sugar. In many instances, cash crop production has led to misguided government policies that lead to environmental deterioration while yielding few benefits economically. Timberlake analyzes these conflicting goals African countries in general face and makes reference to the specific case of Sudan:

> To describe Africa's crisis as "environmental" may sound odd. . . . What have environmental concerns to do with the fact that in 1985 the entire Hadendawa people of north-eastern Sudan faced extinction due to starvation and dispersal? The Sudanese government, with the help of [foreign aid], has put vast sugar and cotton plantations on its best land along the Nile. It has ignored rapidly falling yields from smallholder farming in the 1970s. It seems not to have noticed that the land—the "environment"—upon which eight out of every [ten] Sudanese depend for their livelihoods is slowly perishing due to over-use and misuse. It invested little in dryland regions where people like the Hadendawa live. So when drought came, these pastoralists and peasants had no irrigated settlements in which to take temporary refuge, no government agencies to buy their livestock, no sources of drought-resistant sorghum seeds ready for planting when the rains resumed. *But neither have the government's investments in cash crops produced money to pay the nation's way through the drought.* The result is starvation and debt: Sudan's external debt in 1985 was estimated at $9 billion. President Nimeiri, overthrown in April 1985, has paid a personal price for leading Sudan to environmental bankruptcy. (Timberlake, 1986:9–10; emphasis added)

The political, economic, and environmental tragedy in Sudan continues even now, although the prospects for people in the war between the North and the South of the country are better than they have ever been since Sudan's independence in 1956.

A related problem is the use of dangerous agricultural chemicals. Of the estimated 25 million agricultural workers poisoned by pesticides every year, 11 million are in Africa, and hundreds of thousands die (Thomas et al., 2000:85). Most of these workers are involved in cash crop agriculture.

Deterioration of the environment in Africa is not confined to cash crop production. The example of the oil industry in Nigeria is presented here to show how widespread the problem is. In one of the rare studies of the ecological results of the oil industry in Nigeria, Eboe Hutchful (1985) notes the complexities involved in developing an oil industry. Oil revenues generated by the mining and selling of oil naturally have increased the capabilities of the Nigerian state, making it possible to finance much-needed development projects. But Hutchful comments that these same processes have generated growing regional inequalities, impoverishment, underemployment, and degradation of the Nigerian environment (Hutchful, 1985:113). Specifically, Hutchful shows that oil-industry activities—exploration, production, refining, and transportation—have caused widespread social and ecological disturbances. These include explosions from seismic surveys; pollution from pipeline leaks, blowouts, drilling fluids, and refinery effluents; as well as land alienation and widespread disruption of the natural terrain from construction of oil-related industrial infrastructure and installations. The areas that have been most affected are the oil-producing areas in three states: Rivers, Bendel, and Cross River (Hutchful, 1985:113–115).

Blowout of rigs is always a risk that oil drilling and exploration carry. Blowouts usually lead to major oil spills such as the one that occurred at the so-called Funiwa-5 location in eastern Nigeria. On January 17, 1980, the Funiwa well, located about 5 miles offshore in the Niger Delta, blew out during operation. Subsequent to the blowout, it took several days for the operating company and the Nigerian authorities to acknowledge the accident and the resulting oil spill, which could not be immediately contained. Although no full account of the accident or its effects ever came to light, the environmental consequences were serious, especially in the ecologically delicate Niger Delta. Hutchful attributes inaction on the part of the government to the enormous influence that foreign oil companies have on the industry. He argues that

> the problem of oil pollution in Nigeria has been exacerbated by the absence of effective regulations and the predatory attitudes of the oil companies. Clearly, as long as the [major oil companies] can maximize the availability of [economic] surplus from oil, the Nigerian state has had little interest in regulating their activities, particularly where such controls may threaten the expansion of production. After many years of widespread exploration and production activities, Nigeria still does not possess a comprehensive or coherent set of anti-pollution legislation. Existing legislation is scattered through a number of statutes limited to specific types of pollution and environment and lacking the backing of detailed regulations. The tendency is to leave considerable discretionary power in the hands of enforcement agencies and corresponding opportunity for the oil companies to evade regulations. (Hutchful, 1985:118)

Hutchful neglected to mention that discretionary power in the hands of bureaucrats also leads to corruption, because offending companies can always buy off their transgressions.

The environmental problems caused by the oil industry in Nigeria have resulted in political conflict between the Nigerian government and the foreign oil companies on the one hand, and the local population, such as the Ogoni people of Rivers state. The Movement for the Survival of Ogoni People, under the leadership of Ken Saro-Wiwa, was established as a vehicle not only for demanding autonomy from the Nigerian state, but also for protesting the environmental hazards caused by the oil spillage and gas flaring that accompany it. The environmental hazards have led to the Ogoni people being net importers of food because of damage to farmland, whereas in years past, the Ogoni had been net food exporters. The crisis of the Ogoni led to the execution of Saro-Wiwa and eight others by the Nigerian government in late 1995 on charges that most of the world saw as trumped up (Osaghae, 1995).

Recently, the Nigerian government in partnership with the major oil companies released the Niger Delta Environmental Survey as part of its development plan for the region. Only time will tell if this signals a genuine commitment to address what are now acknowledged to be the serious ecological and health damages the oil industry has caused (Njoku and Ahiuma-Young, 2000). To date, oil spills, natural gas flaring, and pollution from the oil industry continue to be among Nigeria's major environmental problems (EIA, 2005).

In conclusion, the two examples from Sudan and Nigeria make the important point that what passes as economic development may have serious environmental consequences that may take years, if not generations, to rectify.

Other Issues of Environmental Concern

In our survey of some of Africa's greatest environmental problems, some attention should also be given to the issue of toxic waste dumping in Africa. Although hard data is difficult to come by because most of this trade is underground, what we do know is cause for concern. Most of the trade to African and other poor countries involves hazardous materials such as raw sewage, sludge, incinerated ashes, radioactive wastes, pesticides and other hazardous chemicals, contaminated oils, acids, and poisonous solvents shipped from developed countries. This amounts to about one-fifth of the total traffic to Africa. The governments of some countries in Africa, desperate for foreign trade and hard currency, find accepting such materials a temptation hard to resist. According to some estimates, the financial gains amount to more than the yearly gross domestic product (GDP) of many poor countries (OAU, n.d.; Miller, 1995:87–88). The financial incentives for the industrial waste–producing countries are even greater. Estimates are that the cost for processing these wastes in industrial countries is roughly $3,000 a ton; some African countries have accepted these wastes for as little as $5 a ton (OAU, n.d.).

These wastes are a major threat to the health of millions of Africans and their environment. Most of the people do not even know these wastes are in their midst or the hazards they pose, as the recent case of Somalia demonstrated.[6] In many cases there is poor handling and disposal of hazardous materials, and long-term safety is highly questionable. For example, in a 1981 case in Nigeria, an illegal arrangement between Italian businessmen and Nigerian officials led to the dumping of five shipments of hazardous materials stored in 8,000 drums in a Nigerian citizen's backyard. Some of the drums, containing highly carcinogenic chemicals, were leaking. Luckily, the scheme was exposed and the wastes were removed, but who knows how many such deals are never brought to light (Miller, 1995:88).

Concern over the trade in toxic wastes led to efforts to first control and then to ban the trade altogether. In 1987, for instance, UNEP adopted the Cairo Guidelines and Principles for Environmentally Sound Management of Hazardous Wastes (Miller, 1995:89). In 1988, leaders from the Economic Community of West African States agreed to make it a criminal offense to facilitate dumping dangerous waste and urged developed countries to tighten their regulation of such products. There was an obvious difference of opinion at the conference between those countries (such as Benin) who had accepted such waste (and the money it brought) and those (such as Guinea-Bissau) who were willing to consider regulation (Schissel, 1988:47–49). After other unsatisfactory efforts to regulate the trade in hazardous materials, the Bamako Convention was signed in 1991 by ten African countries who agreed to entirely ban toxic wastes to Africa. A ban was also proposed at the 1992 Earth Summit, but it was blocked by the United States and other industrialized countries. Finally, in 1994, the Basel Convention, which banned the shipment of hazardous wastes from the Organization for Economic Cooperation and Development (OECD) nations to non-OECD nations, was approved. This would have amounted to the end of such shipments from industrial nations to Africa after 1997. The United States was the only OECD country that refused to sign the accord (Miller, 1995:89–94). Despite efforts by the Organization of African Unity (now the African Union) to prevent waste trading by its member countries, some have violated the ban. Among these countries are Benin, Guinea-Bissau, Nigeria, Somalia, and Zimbabwe (OAU, n.d.). To date, an illicit trade in toxic wastes continues, with effects that may not be fully appreciated until a major environmental disaster occurs.[7]

Another issue that warrants some mention is that of wildlife conservation. Africa is rich in biodiversity with more than 50,000 known plant species, 1,000 mammal species, and 1,500 bird species. Its savannahs are home to the world's greatest concentration of large mammals (UNEP, 2000b). Indeed, Africa's spectacular wildlife and game parks are a major attraction in a lucrative tourist industry for some countries and thus play a key role in their economic development efforts. For example, 700,000 visitors spent $400 million in Kenya in 1988 and $510 million in 1994 (Kenya Ministry of Finance, 1995). Tourism-based wildlife viewing also has been important for countries such as Zimbabwe, Botswana, Tanzania, and South Africa.

Lynne C. Rienner

A sign at a national part in Nairobi, Kenya.

Although wildlife is an important source of foreign exchange, there is controversy regarding the killing of wildlife for their fur (e.g., leopards), their ivory (e.g., elephants), or their horns (e.g., rhinos). This concern is understandable. For example, Kenya's elephant population dropped from 165,000 to 16,000 between 1970 and 1990 as a result of poaching (Dickey, 1990:42). Other endangered animals include the black and white rhinos and the mountain gorilla. Since 1950 Africa has lost more than 95 percent of its then estimated 100,000 black rhino; today there are only 2,700 left (World Wildlife Fund, 2000:4). Only 700 mountain gorillas are left (African Wildlife Foundation, 2005).

In 1990, the African elephant was placed on Appendix I of the Convention on International Trade in Endangered Species in order to give it the maximum protection from poaching. In effect, trade in ivory was prohibited in order to eliminate the market for poachers. The results were quite successful; poaching dropped sharply and elephant populations rebounded in many countries, including Kenya. In Tanzania poaching fell from as high as 100,000 elephants a year to less than 100 a year after the ban (see Higgins, 2000:2).

Not all countries, however, view the elephant problem in the same way. Countries such as Zimbabwe, Namibia, Botswana, and South Africa point out that their elephant populations have grown as a result of careful management and control of the poaching problem. These countries have sought

April Gordon

In Zimbabwe, elephant populations were growing until recently. Now, however, political turmoil along with drought and poaching is taking a toll on elephants and other wildlife.

to move the elephant to a less protected status and reopen the ivory trade under carefully monitored conditions. They argue that developing countries need the money that selling ivory on a controlled basis would bring. This money could then be used for conservation purposes, to provide needed revenue for poor communities, and to manage elephant herds more effectively. They point out that growing elephant populations are coming into more conflict with humans by raiding their crops and destroying their property (and sometimes their lives). In essence, the income generated from elephants is "essential to secure political and economic support for conservation at both the local and national levels" (Wildnet Africa, n.d., "Arguments":4).

In 1997—despite the opposition of most African countries and conservationists—Zimbabwe, Botswana, and Namibia were granted a one-time limited permit to sell elephant products, such as ivory. Those opposed to the sale feared that it would open the door to illegal ivory sales due to insufficient safeguards to ensure that only legal ivory was on the market. They also argued that the alleged economic benefits to local people and conservation would not be furthered by opening up the ivory market (Wildnet Africa, n.d., "Case Against"). Three years later, in 2000, Cable News Network (CNN) reported that elephant poaching was on the rise due to the relaxation of the ban. Allan Thornton, chairman of Britain's

Environmental Investigation Agency, called this "the biggest conservation blunder of the 1990s." He and many other conservationists are arguing that the elephant be given back its protected status and that further sales be stopped (Higgins, 2000:1–2).

Even if Africa's large mammals survive, the rest of Africa's biological heritage is at risk throughout the continent. Loss of wetlands and forests, endangered freshwater ecosystems in lakes and rivers, dams, pollution, and overfishing are all contributing to a growing list of endangered species in Africa (UNEP, 2000b). Only time will tell how controversies over the use and conservation of Africa's cherished wildlife heritage will be resolved. Pressures of population on the land, habitat loss, environmental degradation, competing demands for scarce financial resources, and the level of commitment to Africa's natural environment by African officials and citizens will be the decisive variables.

Conclusion

Studying the environment calls for a comprehensive approach that looks at the many-sided aspects of the problem. Our examination of the relationships among deforestation, desertification, and soil erosion certainly makes this point clear. Central to this comprehensive approach, however, is the role of humankind in the use of natural resources and the effects of human activity on the environment. In Africa, human activity can be said to be directed at two related objectives: economic development and human survival. In the last few decades, the attainment of both objectives has become increasingly questionable as economic development has eluded many African countries and as human survival at a very low level has become the order of the day (Danaher, 1994).

Yet, there are many things that African governments can do to alleviate their environmental problem. From an institutional level, my studies at UNEP revealed that no African country had comprehensive national legislation and administrative machinery in the environmental field. (See also UNEP, 1987; Hutchful, 1985:118.) Much of the legislation on the environment was scattered in different areas of concern, such as legislation covering water safely or wildlife preservation (Kabeberi, 1998; Swatuk, 2002a). There have been some positive signs since the 1990s that a commitment to the environment will increase in the years ahead. For one, the international community is recognizing the link between protecting the environment and every other progressive change it hopes to see in Africa. This is related to the idea of sustainable development that was introduced at the beginning of this chapter. The major development lender in Africa is the World Bank. In its 1996 publication on environmentally sustainable development in Africa, the Bank writes, "Caring about the environment in sub-Saharan Africa is not a luxury but a prime necessity" (World Bank, 1996:ix). For sustainable development to occur, issues of the environment, poverty, rapid population growth, and gender equality (among others) must be recognized and addressed because they are all interlinked. This message was reaffirmed by the Johannesburg Summit in 2002. African governments and nongovernmental organizations are beginning to get this message. Africa now regularly holds an African Ministerial Conference on the Environment sponsored by UNEP, the African Union, and the Economic Commission for Africa. Its purpose is to facilitate cooperation between African countries in promoting sound environmental policies (UNEP, 2000a). Regional groups such as the South African Development Community, with its fourteen member countries, are also turning their efforts toward protecting the environment and working toward sustainable development (UNEP, 2000c; Swatuk, 2002b). Countries such as Kenya are developing their own national policies as well (Center for Reproductive Law, 1997). If these efforts are backed by action and resources, African countries may have a chance to preserve their priceless environmental heritage, while using it wisely to benefit their people.

Notes

1. The concept of "sustainable development" has now been popularized in recent discussions about the environment. Such is the case in a study by the World Bank, *Toward Environmentally Sustainable Development in Sub-Saharan Africa: A World Bank Agenda* (1996). Belghis Badri (1994:2), a Sudanese scholar, writes:

> My understanding of sustainable development, as an African scholar, is that it is not a holistic, non-divisible concept. Rather, I can conceive of it as an amalgamation of several indicators that have developed at various stages since the 1960s. . . . To elaborate, our indicators of sustainable development can be explained in terms of social development, economic development, environmental development, political development, intellectual development, women's development and international development.

2. The UNEP study is also discussed in Silver with DeFries (1990).
3. Countries that are generally referred to as forming the Sahel region are Mauritania, Senegal, Mali, Burkina Faso, Niger, and Chad.
4. To get a broader perspective on the drylands problem, note that the drylands in Africa, including hyperarid desert, constitute 1,959 million hectares, or 65 percent of the continent and about one-third of the world's drylands. One-third of these African drylands are hyperarid deserts (672 million hectares), which are uninhabited except in oases. The remaining two-thirds, or 1,278 million hectares, comprise arid, semi-arid, and dry subhumid areas (Darkoh, 1994).

5. Timberlake (1986:39) provides an interesting comparative discussion of this issue. He states: "Whether or not Africa is over-populated, most of it is certainly not *densely* populated. The average population density of Sub-Saharan Africa is only 16 per square kilometer, much less in rural areas. This compares to 100/sq km in China, and 225/sq km in India."

6. On occasion, evidence of toxic waste dumping comes to light in very unpredictable ways. For example, in early 2005, the UN Environmental Programme (UNEP) cited reports that there were indications that hazardous waste, radioactive waste, chemical waste, and other substances in containers which had been dumped on the Somali coastline were damaged by the December 2004 tsunami. In the late 1980s, European companies dumped waste in northern Somalia, but the trend picked up rapidly after the ouster of Somali leader Mohammad Siad Barre in 1991 due to the "stateless" nature of Somalia (Aljazeera, March 8, 2005, online at www.aljazeera.com).

7. See www.ban.org for information on efforts to prevent the trade in toxic wastes and enforce the Basel Convention.

Bibliography

African Wildlife Foundation. 2000. "Virunga Heartland Is Biologically Rich—but Embattled." *African Wildlife News* (Fall):1, 4.

———. 2005. "25 Years of Protecting Africa's Mountain Gorillas." *African Wildlife News* (Spring):4–5.

Agyei, Yvonne. N.d. "Deforestation in Sub-Saharan Africa." African Technology Forum 8. Online at web.mit.edu/africantech/www/articles/deforestation.htm.

Ali-Dinar, Ali B. 2004. "Between Naivasha and Abeche: The Systematic Destruction of Darfur." Paper presented at Sudan's Lost Peace and the Crisis in Darfur Conference. Stichting Instituut voor Nieuwe Soedan (SINS), Amsterdam, The Netherlands. March 27, 2004. Online at www.darfurinfo.org.

Anderson, Dennis. 1987. *The Economics of Afforestation: A Case Study in Africa.* Baltimore: Johns Hopkins University Press (for the World Bank).

Austen, Ralph A. 1987. *African Economic History: Internal Development and External Dependency.* London: James Currey.

Badri, Belghis. 1994. "Sustainable Development: An Analytical Framework for Agenda 21." In UN Non-Governmental Liaison Service (NGLS), *Voices from Africa,* no. 5, Sustainable Development. Geneva and New York: NGLS.

BBC News. 2005. "Aid Funds Finally Flow for Niger." Online at news.bbc.co.uk (July 23).

Berntsen, Thorbjorn. 1995. "Challenging Traditional Growth." *Our Planet* 7 (1):11–12.

Blaikie, Piers, and Harold Brookfield. 1987. "Defining and Debating the Problem." Pp. 1–26 in Piers Blaikie and Harold Brookfield (eds.). *Land Degradation and Society.* New York: Methuen.

Bojo, Jan, et al. 1990. *Environment and Development: An Economic Approach.* Boston: Kluwer Academic Publishers.

Brown, Lester R. 1981. *Building a Sustainable Society.* New York: W. W. Norton.

———. 1998. "The Future of Growth." Pp. 3–20 in Linda Starke (ed.). *State of the World.* New York: W. W. Norton.

Caldwell, Lynton Keith. 1984. *International Environmental Policy: Emergence and Dimensions.* Durham, NC: Duke University Press.

Center for Reproductive Law and Policy and International Federation of Women Lawyers–Kenya Chapter. 1997. *Women of the World: Laws and Policies Affecting Their Reproductive Lives—Anglophone Africa.* New York: Center for Reproductive Law and Policy.

Cole, N. H. Ayodele. 1986. "Environmental Problems and Policies in Africa." Pp. 31–52 in *Environment and Development: Opportunities in Africa and the Middle East.* Conference summary of the World Environment Center, September 25–27, 1985. Nairobi: UNEP.

Danaher, Kevin, ed. 1994. *50 Years Is Enough: The Case Against the World Bank and the International Monetary Fund.* Boston: South End Press.

Darkoh, M. B. K. 1994. "The Deterioration of the Environment in Africa's Drylands and River Basins." *Desertification Control Bulletin,* no. 24:35–41.

———. N.d. "Desertification: The Scourge of Africa." Online at www.cru.uea.ac.uk.

Dejene, Alemneh. 1987. *Peasants, Agrarian Socialism, and Rural Development in Ethiopia.* Boulder, CO: Westview Press.

Department of Public Information, United Nations. 2004. "Killings and Hunger Stalk Western Sudan." *African Renewal Online* (www.un.org).

Development GAP (Development Group for Alternative Policies). 1993. *The Other Side of the Story: The Real Impact of World Bank and IMF Structural Adjustment Programs.* Washington, DC.

Dickey, Christopher. 1990. "The End of the Ivory Trail?" *Newsweek* (April 16):42.

Dixon, John A., et al. 1988. *Economic Analysis of the Environmental Impacts of Development Projects.* London: Earthscan.

Eckholm, Erik, and Lester R. Brown. 1977. *Spreading Deserts: The Hand of Man.* Washington, DC: Worldwatch Institute.

EIA (Energy Information Agency). 2005. "Country Analysis Briefs: Nigeria." Online at www.eia.doe.gov (April).

"Famine Spreads." 2006. *The Economist* (February 4):44.

Higgins, Margot. 2000. "Elephants Face Killing Fields Again." Online at www.cnn.com (December 11).

Hutchful, Eboe. 1985. "Oil Companies and Environmental Pollution in Nigeria." Pp. 113–140 in Claude Ake (ed.). *Political Economy of Nigeria.* London: Longman.

Kabeberi, Janet W. 1988. "Environmental Law in Kenya." Unpublished manuscript, Nairobi University Faculty of Law.

Kenya Ministry of Finance. 1995. *Kenya Economic Survey 1994.* Nairobi.

Leonard, H. Jeffrey (ed.). 1985. *Divesting Nature's Capital: The Political Economy of Environmental Abuse in the Third World.* New York: Holmes and Meier.

Lewis, L. A., and L. Berry. 1988. *African Environments and Resources.* Boston: Unwin Hyman.

Livernash, Robert, and Eric Rodenburg. 1998. "Population Change, Resources, and the Environment." *Population Bulletin* 53 (March).

McKenzie, Glenn. 1999. "Africa's Ailing Soil Struggles for Survival." *The State,* October 17, A4.

Miller, Marian A. L. 1995. *The Third World in Global Environmental Politics.* Boulder, CO: Lynne Rienner Publishers.

Njoku, Jude, and Victor Ahiuma-Young. 2000. "NDES Releases Second Development Action Plan Niger Delta." Online at www.allafrica.com (December 11).

Nnoli, Okwudiba. 1990. "Desertification, Refugees and Regional Conflict in West

Africa." *Disasters: The Journal of Disaster Studies and Management* 14:132–139.

OAU (Organization of African Unity). N.d. "Africa Waste Trade." Online at www.american.edu.

Okoko, Tervil. 2000. "Scientists Move to Save Lake Victoria from Dying." Online at www.allafrica.com.

Osaghae, Eghosa E. 1995. "The Ogoni Uprising: Oil Politics, Minority Agitation and the Future of the Nigerian State." *African Affairs* 94:325–344.

Pirages, Dennis. 1978. *Global Ecopolitics.* North Scituate, MA: Duxbury Press.

Poulsen, Gunnar. 1990. *Report to the Third Meeting of the Committee of Forests and Woodlands (COFAW) of the African Ministerial Conference on the Environment.* Nairobi: UNEP.

Pradervand, Pierre. 1989. *Listening to Africa: Developing Africa from the Grassroots.* New York: Praeger.

Revell, Roger. 1976. "The Resources Available for Agriculture." *Scientific American* 235 (September):165–178.

Rosen, James E., and Shanti R. Conly. 1998. *Africa's Population Challenge: Accelerating Progress in Reproductive Health.* Washington, DC: Population Action International.

Schissel, Howard. 1988. "The Deadly Trade: Toxic Waste Dumping in Africa." *Africa Report* 33 (September–October):47–49.

Silver, Cheryl Simon, with Ruth S. DeFries. 1990. *One Earth, One Future: Our Changing Global Environment.* Washington, DC: National Academy Press.

Skoupy, Jiri. 1988. "Developing Rangeland Resources in African Drylands." *UNEP Desertification Control Bulletin* 17:29–40.

Stebbing, E. P. 1935. "The Encroaching Sahara: The Threat to the West African Colonies." *Geographical Journal* 85:508–524.

Swatuk, Larry A. 2002a. "Rio Minus Ten: The Political Economy of Environmental Degradation." *European Journal of Development Research* 14 (June): 264–275.

———. 2002b. "The New Water Architecture in Southern Africa: Reflections on Current Trends in the Light of 'Rio + 10.'" *International Affairs* 78 (July):507–530.

Thomas, Vinod, Mansoor Dailami, Ashok Dhareshwar, Daniel Kaufmann, Nalin Kishor, Ramon Lopez, and Yan Wang. 2000. *The Quality of Growth.* Washington, DC: Oxford University Press.

Tillman, R. E. 1981. "Environmental Guidelines for Irrigation." Washington, DC: U.S. Agency for International Development.

Timberlake, Lloyd. 1986. *Africa in Crisis: The Causes, the Cures of Environmental Bankruptcy.* Washington, DC: Earthscan.

UNEP (United Nations Environmental Programme). 1987. *New Directions in Environmental Legislation and Administration, Particularly in Developing Countries.* Nairobi: UNEP.

———. 1990. *The Disappearing Forests.* UNEP Environmental Brief No. 3. Nairobi: UNEP.

———. 2000a. "African Ministerial Conference on the Environment (AMCEN)." Online at www.unep.org (accessed December 11).

———. 2000b. "Chapter Two: The State of the Environment—Africa." In *Global Environment Outlook 2000.* Online at www.unep.org/Geo2000 (accessed February 6).

———. 2000c. "Southern African Development Community (SADC)." Online at www.unep.org (accessed December 11).

Wagner, Richard. 1971. *Environment and Man.* New York: W. W. Norton.

WCED (World Commission on Environment and Development). 1987. *Our Common Future.* New York: Oxford University Press.

Weir, David, and Mark Schapiro. 1981. *Circle of Poison: Pesticides and People in a Hungry World.* San Francisco: Institute for Food and Development Policy.

Wells, Gordon. 1989. "Observing Earth's Environment from Space." Pp. 148–192 in Laurie Friday and Ronald Laskey (eds.). *The Fragile Environment. The Darwin College Lectures.* Cambridge: Cambridge University Press.

Wildnet Africa. N.d. "Arguments for Re-opening Trade in African Elephant Products from Southern African States with Healthy and Well-Managed Elephant Populations." Online at www.wildnetafrica.com.

———. N.d. "The Case Against Commercial Trade in Elephant Products." Online at www.wildnetafrica.com.

World Bank. 1981. *Accelerated Development in Sub-Saharan Africa: An Agenda for Action.* Washington, DC: World Bank.

———. 1996. *Toward Environmentally Sustainable Development in Sub-Saharan Africa: A World Bank Agenda.* Washington, DC: World Bank.

———. 2000. *Can Africa Claim the 21st Century?* Washington, DC: World Bank.

———. 2003. *World Development Report 2003. Sustainable Development in a Dynamic World: Transforming Institutions, Growth, and Quality of Life.* Washington, DC: The International Bank for Reconstructions and Development/The World Bank.

World Resources Institute. 2005. "WRI, Cameroon Agreement Cuts Down Illegal Logging." Online at www.biodiv.wri.org.

World Wildlife Fund. 2000. "Rhinos in the Wild: Gaining Ground . . . but Still at Risk." *Focus* 2 (November-December):4–5.

9

Family and Kinship

Eugenia Shanklin

African kinship, marriage, and child-rearing systems are of interest to us in the West for several reasons. First, they are different from our own in intriguing ways. Not only does Hillary Rodham Clinton quote an African proverb—"it takes a village to raise a child"—in her book *It Takes a Village*, but many travelers to Africa have had the experience of handing an edible treat to a child in an African city and watching that child immediately turn to the assembled group of children and share the treat with them. These are cultural differences, differences in the ways in which children are taught. But what do they mean? And how are they instilled in young children? Anyone who has watched Africans raise children has been struck by the emphasis placed on guidance by example. It is the responsibility of all adults—whether in hamlets, villages, or large urban areas—to teach children how to behave, and children watch as properly socialized adults share with the people around them. The meaning is best expressed, perhaps, in a saying of the Kom people of Cameroon, who believe that children, like animals, are born selfish and only become human when they have been taught to share. Children who do not share, who seize a treat and run off to devour it privately, will be ostracized until they can show, at a later time, that they have learned to share with the group. This model of sharing is a widespread one in African societies and one that many Westerners would like their own societies to emulate.

A second reason African systems are of interest to us is that much of what we assume to know about marriage and kinship is what we learn from our own culture and what we often come to believe is just common sense. African systems suggest that our own notions of what is common sense or human nature may be slightly off base when generalized to the rest of the world. Since anthropologists have done most of the investigations of African kinship and marriage, it is important to know, as a colleague recently put it, that "anthropology's purpose is to replace our culture's common sense about Human Nature with profound awareness of the genuine range and variety of human ways around the globe" (Terrell, 2000:10). What we Westerners mean by marriage (monogamy or legitimized mating of one partner of either sex) or kinship (bilateral or bilineal, tracing descent from both parents) are not the norms in Africa, where polygyny (the marriage of one man to more than one woman) and unilineal descent groups (who trace their ancestry through either father or mother) have prevailed, at least until recently.

What implications do these different systems have for the people who live with and within them? Studies of African kinship, in particular, reveal that all or most of the possible solutions to the most basic of questions—how shall humans solve the issues of reproduction (who marries whom and produces children with full rights and privileges), filiation or relatedness (how the offspring are considered to be related to the parents), and responsibility for socialization (rights and obligations of parents and children, as well as who will do the teaching of the child)—are found in African systems, often in surprising ways. One of my Princeton University students once demanded of his classmates, "Why do you Americans believe it is required that each person be given choices?" In Ghana, his land of origin,

April Gordon

In much of Africa, especially in rural areas, the extended family with many children continues to be the norm.

making important choices (whom to marry, where to live) was something to be done by an individual's kin group, not by the individual, especially not by a young, relatively uninformed individual. My student did not consider what Americans think of as freedom of choice as a blessing but rather as a burden. Although in most instances a kinship system is not a microcosm of the society, in Africa, understanding how a kinship system works is one of the best ways to understand how people think. The ideas we take for granted are not necessarily taken for granted in the same ways by other groups. (Philippe Wamba [1999] has published an excellent comparison of his African and American families.)

A third reason African kinship is of interest is that while Africans talk about families in the same way we do, they seem to have in mind something other than our own emphasis on nuclear or conjugal families (families consisting only of parents and their offspring). A number of years ago, while chairing a session at a UN Educational, Scientific, and Cultural Organization (UNESCO) conference (the conference was on a Cameroon disaster that killed nearly 2,000 people and left more than 5,000 homeless, including more than 2,000 orphans), I remarked that Western solutions to such problems—psychiatrists and boarding schools—were being offered for African orphans. I added that, since humans had evolved in Africa, it was likely that during eons of evolutionary history, Africans had come up with their own solutions to human problems. The African solution I heard mentioned most often in conference corridors was "family." As it worked out, the best solution to the problems of the orphaned children (and even adult) survivors was to put them into fictive (that is, made-up) families (Shanklin et al., 2001).

Several older scientists at that conference immediately asked when it had become common knowledge that humans evolved in Africa and what implications this had for contemporary understandings of human evolution. The "Out of Africa" hypothesis began to gain currency in the 1960s and is now fully accepted in anthropology and related disciplines. In effect, it means that all humans alive today had a "great-great-great . . . grandmother" in common. She lived somewhere in Africa between 140,000 and 200,000 years ago. All the different groups we see in the world today sprang from her, our 10,000th great-grandmother, and, in some instances, from those of our ancestors who migrated out of Africa many thousands of years ago carrying this woman's mitochondrial DNA. Recently, this finding has been given further support by explorations of the human genome, which, most geneticists agree, points to a single human "race" with minor differences in skin color, hair form, and the like (Stringer and McKie, 1996; Tattersall, 1998).

The idea that we are all closely related through one African female ancestor may be the most important lesson anthropologists have learned recently about human kinship. Long before the Out of Africa idea was advanced, however, other interesting questions were raised about human marriage and kinship by some of the nineteenth century's most creative thinkers. The questions were usually about the purpose(s) of marriage and why incest taboos are universal—that is, are found in all societies (although what is defined as incest may vary considerably from one society to the next). In the nineteenth century, a number of ideas were advanced—Edward Tylor proposed the idea that "marry out or be killed out" explained why exogamy (marrying out of one's group) was the rule, not endogamy (marrying within the group) (Tylor, 1889). Another idea, E. Westermarck's innate aversion theory (1894), was that siblings raised together develop a dislike for one another that precludes sexuality. Sigmund Freud believed that incestuous impulses must be repressed in order for families, or more broadly society, to exist harmoniously (Freud, 1919); Karl Marx and Friedrich Engels claimed that the invention of private property interrupted the communal bliss of human groups (a fantasy that fueled the film *The Gods Must Be Crazy*) and that the first property was "rights" in women through marriage (Engels, 1942). All these ideas were more or less rejected or disproved by decades of research.

In the middle of the twentieth century, Claude Lévi-Strauss (1949) suggested that the universality of incest taboos was related to the human tendency to form alliances with other groups. One could have sex within the family, say, with one's brother or sister, or one could give a sibling to a neighbor, taking that neighbor's sibling in exchange.[1] Both kinds of unions might produce children. If a brother and sister who had children together experienced hardships, however, they had only themselves to rely on. If a couple in one of those groups that exchanged siblings fell on hard times, they had two sets of built-in allies in the neighborhood—an obvious advantage.

Lévi-Strauss's alliance theory may or may not be the best explanation for why incest taboos exist. What we do know is that most societies forbid some people or categories of people—for example, all those people you call "brother" or "sister"—as marriage partners and approve others, usually others outside the nuclear or immediate family—that is, mother, father, brothers, and sisters. For most (but not all) societies, these rules are based on ideas about who is related to whom—kinship or descent groups, which are culturally invented groups that extend beyond the immediate family (nuclear or conjugal) of mother, father, brothers, and sisters. If people were not to mate randomly or with those closest at hand, rules had to be made to govern which were appropriate mates—incest taboos (you may not mate with . . .) and preferential mating patterns (ideally[2] you should mate with . . .). As will soon become apparent, Africa has been home to all sorts of exceptions, and the brother-sister marriage rule is one of those. In Egypt, during Roman times, brother-sister marriages were common among non-royals, and 15 to 20 percent of all marriages may have been contracted between full siblings (Hopkins, 1980; Scheidel, 1996).

A main difference, it seems to me, between African kinship systems and Euro-American kinship systems is the emphasis placed in Africa on relations between those who consider themselves related by blood. Euro-American systems tend to emphasize relations between husbands and wives—relations created by marriage or in-law relationships (called affinal relations by anthropologists). Many African systems emphasize shared "blood" or consanguineal relations—those between a mother and child or children ("children of one womb," as it is often put), a father and his child or children, and between brothers and sisters. And, too, there is an emphasis in Africa on lineages—groups of people considered to be related to one another consanguineally. This emphasis is an ongoing theme in African kinship studies and one we shall see in different guises in different societies. For example, witness this Azande's statement about brothers and sisters (which Freud, and perhaps Westermarck, would have liked):

> When a boy reaches puberty he may take his sister and with her build their little hut near his mother's home and go into it with his sister and lay her down and get on top of her—and they copulate. His father then begins to keep a watch on them to catch them at this and seizes him and gives him a good hiding and asks him what he means by going after his sister, she is his sister, has he seen people going to bed with their sisters? Then he is afraid. . . . So people say about it that a man begins desire for women with his sisters. So people say that children are like dogs, for a boy will go after his own sister. After they have been stupid for a time, when they grow up they get a sense of shame and whenever they see their sister they do not think of going any more with her to the bush. (Evans-Pritchard, 1974:107)

Notice once again the idea shared by the Azande of eastern Africa and the Kom in west-central Africa that unsocialized children are like animals and must be instructed by peers or elders. This widespread notion about the importance of sharing was built into many African systems, although we know little of the specific details of precolonial kinship and marriage systems. In colonial times, all institutions—kinship, religious, economic, and political—were thoroughly studied by Africanist anthropologists, such as E. E. Evans-Pritchard, who studied the Nuer soon after they were "pacified," as the British put it. Evans-Pritchard's studies of the Nuer and the Azande began the heyday of kinship studies in Africa, and much information was collected by many of the best anthropologists—Colson, Douglas, Forde, Fortes, Gluckman, Goody, Kaberry, Richards, Turner—over the next few decades, until independence. One obvious question we must ask concerning these anthropological studies is, what was their purpose? The answer seems to be that because in stateless societies authority was vested in the lineages, the study of lineages (or, more broadly, kinship) was an administrative key, a way of learning the indigenous rules so that outsiders could govern Africans more efficiently.

In the process of learning how to govern Africans, there were many surprises in store for the learners and even some puzzles that were left over for those who came to the study of kinship decades later. The classic in the field of African kinship was A. R. Radcliffe-Brown and D. Forde's edited volume *African Systems of Kinship and Marriage* (1950). Postcolonial studies have not focused on kinship systems, by and large, but on contemporary problems, many of which were brought about by the disruption of most, if not all, precolonial and colonial practices. Because of this, and because this book emphasizes contemporary issues, after a brief survey of some classic studies of African kinship, I am going to focus my discussion on contemporary holdovers of African kinship systems, on what Basil Davidson (1980) calls similarities between precolonial and postcolonial systems, and on some changes in African families today. In the interests of illuminating some of the contemporary questions and puzzles about African kinship, however, mention should be made of Peter Ekeh's (1990:669) article about studies of African kinship and his contention that social anthropologists emphasized the timeless nature of African kinship, calling it the "latent but fundamental assumption [that] kinship is constant over time in any given society in Africa." This assumption greatly altered perceptions of the history of African societies, Ekeh believes, because anthropologists misunderstood the fundamental (historical, not timeless) basis of African kinship formations in slave trade times—when kinship was used and perhaps altered to enhance protection for individuals against slave raids—and, he further contends, historians have continued to misunderstand African kinship practices in the present. Ekeh thinks African kinship practices continue to be used for protection, now against corrupt political regimes in Africa.

As mentioned, we know little about precolonial times, and what we do know—for example, from travelers' descriptions of long caravans of slaves crisscrossing the continent—suggests severe disruptions of daily (and family) life on almost all levels. Archaeological research into the precolonial, pre–slave raiding era, makes one thing fairly clear: defensive reactions to the slave raiders and their trade led to the formation of kingdoms in places where previously there had been peaceful farming groups (Davidson, 1969, 1980; Ki-Zerbo, 1989; Nkwi and Warnier, 1982). Many such groups probably formed alliances or confederacies to fend off the slave traders; and habits of living, such as valley dwelling, gave way to concealment on the steepest hills. More egalitarian ways of interacting may have given way to authoritarian systems predicated on military discipline. Warfare and slavery had certainly existed in Africa before the Atlantic slave trade began, but the defensive reaction to wide-scale slave hunting may have accelerated, as Davidson suggests, the process of centralizing political institutions that offered some protection, or, as Ekeh suggests, may have strengthened unilineal kinship groups in Africa. As a result, the European colonists who fought, conquered, and divided up African lands among themselves may have found more military kingdoms than existed in pre–slave raiding times.

Davidson mentions three precolonial, colonial, and postcolonial similarities: first, while precolonial African systems may have looked much like those of feudal Europe, there was the important difference that African land ownership systems did not tie people to the land as the European system of serfdom did, because the lineage systems of Africa interposed and prevented the development of small groups of wealthy landowners surrounded by hordes of landless peasants. Second, in Africa, there was a balance, not a monopoly, of weapons power. The feudal lords of Europe had many weapons and could equip a knight in armor on their own behalf, while the rulers of African lands had to attract people by means other than armed threats. Davidson does not add, but I will because so many others mention it so often, that African rulers normally had to attract people to them by their generosity. Third, Davidson says, every group in Africa seems to have a migration story. Most believe that their ancestors migrated in from somewhere else. These similarities or holdovers will become one basis for considering contemporary African family systems after we have examined some classic examples of colonial kinship systems.

African Kinship and Marriage: Precolonial and Colonial Examples

Mating, as we know, is different from marriage, but both are apt to produce children and, for discussions of kinship, children are the crux of the matter. Once a child is born, there is the question of how he or she will be considered to be related to the parents and others (remember that kinship groups are, to some extent, fictitious entities). All cultures affirm the existence of special contributions made by males and females to the reproductive process, although these contributions may be considered very uneven; for example, the Asante believe that a child's blood is contributed only by the mother and that blood determines the child's physical appearance, while the child's spiritual and temperamental dispositions are determined by the father's semen (Fortes, 1950). Most groups divide the contributions of the parents in different ways, often in keeping with the emphasis given in their kinship systems. For instance, groups that trace descent through females (called matrilineal groups) believe that the most important contribution to the fetus is made by the mother; so the matrilineal Asante believe that blood, a most important ritual substance, is contributed by the mother. Groups that trace descent through males, patrilineal groups, often believe that the father's is the most important contribution. The patrilineal Nso' of Cameroon are one of the few groups who believe that both parents contribute equally to the child's formation in the womb (Kaberry, 1969:186).

Daryll Forde (1964) stated the issues arising from mating or parenthood succinctly when he noted that "relations arising from parenthood extend in all societies to form a wider system of kinship" in which inheritance rights, succession rights, and obligations are established. Our bilineal (from both sides) Western system is one way of doing this. That is, kinship is believed to extend from both parents to the child. The more usual African way of doing it is called "unilineal"; that is, one line is emphasized and the other is (almost, but not quite) ignored. Unilineal systems can be extended through the father (patrilineal, inheritance from the father's side) or the mother (matrilineal, inheritance from the mother's side) or through both for different purposes (double unilineal descent, inheritance from both sides but usually of different kinds of property—say, land from the father's side and cattle from the mother's side). Kinship or descent, then, refers to a system in which, for individuals and groups, rights of inheritance and succession and ties of mutual obligation are established on accepted principles (Forde, 1964). A shorter definition of kinship is given by Marvin Harris and Orna Johnson as "relationships based on parentage through descent (consanguineal or 'blood' relations) or through marriage (affinal or 'in-law relations')" (Harris and Johnson, 2000:147).

Anthropological studies have turned up many different examples of kinship systems, but here I am going to follow a lead suggested by Lucy Mair (1979) and concentrate on only the basics, describing some of the classic studies of African groups. Then I return to the question of contemporary holdovers of what may have been the precolonial kinship systems. Mair points out that while the majority of Africans are patrilineal (if one is counting heads or numbers of people), the majority of African societies or ethnic groups are or may have been matrilineal until recently. Although they are more numerous, many of the matrilineal groups in the "matrilineal belt" that extends across central Africa occupy poorer lands and have fewer people than other groups.

Marriage is a concept that has recently undergone dramatic changes in many societies, including US society. Marriage, in Kathleen Gough's (1968) terms, referred to a relationship established between a woman and one or more persons; the relationship ensured that a child born to the woman was accorded full birth rights, provided that the child was conceived and born under certain approved circumstances. Here, Africa provides some flamboyant examples and counterexamples. Many Westerners consider that marriage has something to do with heterosexual domestic mates, but in the Nuer "ghost" marriage or the Nandi female-female marriage, neither gender persuasion nor sexuality is an issue. In both cases, a woman takes as a bride another woman who will bear children (by a man chosen either by the bride or by her new "husband") in the name of a deceased husband. Both result from extreme applications of the unilineal rule found in their patrilineal societies, in which a fertile woman is engaged to bear children in the name of a deceased man who will otherwise not be mentioned in prayers or allowed full privileges in the afterlife.

Probably Westerners see polyandry (the marriage of one woman to more than one man) as the most "exotic" form of marriage that anthropologists have investigated. Polygyny (the marriage of a man to more than one woman) is not uncommon in the world at large, and especially in Africa, but polyandry is uncommon almost everywhere. Once again, Africa provides a fascinating example. In 1949 and 1953, Mary Douglas studied the Lele of the Kasai in what is now the Democratic Republic of Congo. She did not observe polyandry directly, since it had just been outlawed (1947) by the colonial government, but she was told about it by many of her informants who had been participants. The Lele are matrilineal, and the usual form of marriage was for a girl to be betrothed to a man from her childhood on. The match was arranged according to rules of clan membership, in which a man who had "given" a child to his wife could claim a girl of his wife's lineage, either as his own bride or as the bride of a man he might select, usually his sister's son. The second, polyandrous, form of marriage was one in which a woman became the "village wife" and was "married" to the members of an age set group. Male age sets were formed every fifteen years or so, and youths would join up to the age of eighteen through a formal initiation with entrance fees. This group, which in the past had been a military group, would then build a house for its "wife," who might have been captured by them in (past) warfare or, since the banning of warfare, may have, with her parents' collusion, become their captive. Once the village wife had borne daughters, these could be claimed as village wives and, Mair points out, "at the time of Douglas's work, the great majority of village-wives were village grand-daughters" (Mair, 1979:71). The women were not slaves, although there was coercion in some cases; they were formally installed and received gifts at the time of the marriage. Afterward, they were not expected to cook or work in the fields for a while. When they finally settled down, they chose four or five of the ten to twelve men who had formerly been their husbands, and then did farm work and cooking for the smaller number. Eventually, as men moved away from the village or married other wives, the village wife ended up with no more than two or three husbands. Those village wives to whom Douglas spoke pointed out that while some of them had been captured and others had been part of capture by collusion, there was in any event no freedom of choice in Lele marriage. This rather startling example points out another aspect of African marriage and kinship systems: most usually, they are about preserving lineage choices, not individual choices.

A more contemporary definition of marriage, acceptable to Africans and some Americans, might be that marriage consists of the behavior, sentiments, and rules concerned with mating and reproduction in domestic contexts (Harris and Johnson, 2000:135). This definition does not specify either sexual or residential arrangements, but it, like Gough's above and Bronislaw Malinowski's, which follows, emphasizes marriage as being about reproduction. As Malinowski observed, marriage is the licensing of parenthood. That is, the main function of marriage is to legitimize children, but this strikes me as an extremely Western or Euro-American reading. The matrilineal African people I study, the Kom, would disagree strongly with the idea that children *need legitimizing* since, as they say, no child is born without a mother, regardless of whether or not the birth mother is recognized eventually as the "social" mother. Children born into a matrilineal society cannot be "illegitimate" as they can be in a patrilineal society if an acceptable male does not assume responsibility for them. In Kom, should a man decide not to acknowledge a child as his,[3] the woman's father (the child's maternal grandfather) assumes temporary responsibility for the child until a husband comes to marry the mother. Ideally, this is a temporary arrangement, understood much as a driving permit is understood to lead to a driver's license. The child may "need" a father for ritual purposes, usually those involving healing or staying healthy, but it is assumed that the arrangement will not be permanent. A good husband-to-be will also "buy"—five goats for a boy, ten goats for a girl—the children born to his bride in her father's compound whether he fathered them or not, to avoid splitting up the mother and child group. In the (precolonial) times before school fees and hospital bills, this was a more desirable marriage than one with a childless woman (Shanklin, 1983).

Also, and particularly in contemporary Western societies, marriage serves many functions apart from giving rights and privileges to children. In some systems, like our own, marriage gives individuals rights and privileges with respect to each other—for example, the right to claim damages if one partner is injured or to collect pensions upon death. Still, marriage in many African societies is about producing children for a socially approved line of kin, either traced unilineally through the mother's or the father's side, as noted, or traced through both lines, double (unilineal) descent. Two other points about African forms of kinship and marriage before visiting some specific systems very different from our own: first, the forms and definitions of what constitutes African marriage or kinship/descent systems may vary in unexpected ways; second, Africans hate all generalizations about Africa, and indeed the continent seems designed to subvert generalizations about itself.

We can look at three classic (colonial) examples of African systems: the patrilineal Nuer of Sudan, described by Evans-Pritchard; the matrilineal Plateau Tonga of Zambia, described by Elizabeth Colson; and the double unilineal descent groups of the Yakö of Nigeria, described by Forde. Within each, we shall look at relations between brother and sister and at illegitimacy.

The Nuer, about whom Evans-Pritchard first wrote in 1940, are a cattle-herding people of eastern Africa. They have what are known as segmentary lineage systems, based on clan groupings in each territory. In his work on kinship and marriage among the Nuer, Evans-Pritchard (1951:v) described the network of kinship ties within any Nuer community as reducible, ultimately, to a series of marriage unions. Nuer villages are the smallest local groups and, while there are ties to neighboring villages, most activities are carried out within the village community. The strongest ties—economic, feuding alliances—are generally with other members of the village. Further,

> [m]embers of a village are all *mar,* kin, to one another: any villager can trace kinship to every other person in his village, either by a direct kinship tie or through a third person who is in different ways related both to himself and the other person. Furthermore, he can establish kinship of some kind—real, by analogy, mythological, or assumed—with everybody he comes into contact with during his lifetime and through the length and breadth of Nuerland; and this is necessary if he has frequent dealings with them, for all social obligation of a personal kind is defined in terms of kinship. (Evans-Pritchard, 1951:8)

Over and over, Evans-Pritchard stresses the importance not of kinship but of the fact of living together in a small community. He notes, "If a man is not a member of the lineage with which he lives, he makes himself a member of it by treating a maternal link as though it was a paternal one or through affinal relationship" (Evans-Pritchard, 1951:48). Thus, the patrilineal Nuer stress lineage membership above all else, regardless of the links they have to invoke or invent to establish it.

As for relations between brothers and sisters among the Nuer, Evans-Pritchard says that parents do not take an interest in their children's love affairs, but brothers may concern themselves with their sisters' liaisons.

> The only person who may interfere is a brother in an affair of his sister, for her virtue is his responsibility, but he will only do so in certain circumstances. He keeps an eye on his sister and knows who is courting her, but he will only come between her and her lover if he suspects that she is having regular relations with a man without cattle or that she is giving herself to all and sundry.

> It not infrequently happens that a girl becomes pregnant while still unmarried. If the young man has cattle he will be expected to marry her, and if she is not a profligate, he will be glad to do so. If he has insufficient cattle he cannot do so, and though another man will not object to taking her as a wife, he is more likely to take her as a second wife than as a first wife, and he will pay fewer cattle for her bridewealth. It is therefore in the brother's interest to see that this does not happen. It is also in his interest to prevent his sister from becoming a wanton. A man does not expect his bride to be a virgin, but he does not care to marry a jade. A girl of easy virtue may find plenty of lovers but no suitors, and after bearing an illegitimate child is likely to become a concubine for the rest of her life, to the detriment of her family herd. (Evans-Pritchard, 1951:53)

The matrilineal Plateau Tonga of Zambia, formerly Northern Rhodesia, achieve outcomes similar to those among the Nuer—lineage solidarity and close brother-sister relations—by the opposite means: matrilineages and dispersal, not local groupings.

> In pre-European days among the Tonga, political organization as we know it, with an orderly relationship between groups or statuses intermediated through a set of official positions, did not exist. Economic organization was of the simplest. . . . Unused land was a free good, . . . Tonga religion had neither a priesthood nor any hereditary religious officials to give a focus to the general alignment of people in groups. Shrines and their attendant cults were independent of one another. (Colson, 1974:36)

Before David Livingstone passed through in 1853, the Plateau Tonga had no recorded history; in 1950, at the time of Colson's study, they numbered somewhere between 85,000 and 120,000. Colson observes that the most enduring units in Tonga society are the matrilineal clans, which are named, dispersed, exogamous units but not corporate bodies. They do not own property, appoint ritual leaders, or assemble as a group. The corporate groups are much smaller bodies of kinspeople called matrilineal groups; these have a common legal personality, and brothers and sisters share interests in matters of inheritance, succession, vengeance, ritual, and bridewealth compensation. Residence is usually virilocal (that is, patrilocal, with bride and groom residing near the groom's relatives), Colson says, but not otherwise specified. The Plateau Tonga believe that every fully adult man and every fully adult unmarried woman may live wherever they choose. Most people do not remain attached to a single village throughout their lives but may move several times. In daily life, membership within a neighborhood or hamlet may be of more importance than membership within a matrilineal group. If, for example, there is an unoccupied plot in the neighborhood, anyone may choose to take it over. Hunting, fishing, and other work patterns are neighborhood affairs, not just kinship affairs. Kinspeople are involved in a death and must attend the funerals of matrilineage members, but death is also supposed to be a matter for the neighborhood. Each person should die in the neighborhood in which he has his hut and his farms, and if he does not, it is an offense against the land, and his kinsmen will have to pay an animal from their herds—to be consumed by members of the offended neighborhood—in order to send the dead man's spirit back into the neighborhood in which he lived.

Therefore, social groupings among the Tonga are in two categories. The first, the clan and matrilineal group, is reckoned in terms of birth and matrilineal kinship. The second is territorial and determined by choice: neighborhood, village, hamlet, and homestead. In the first, the person's allegiance is settled at birth; in the second, it is settled by marriage if the individual is female, or by choice if the individual is male. All in all, Colson concludes, a dispersed kindred was less vulnerable to local periods of scarcity. Indeed, this is how some matrilineal peoples explain their origins: "So-and-so came here to escape the famine in such-and-such a place. He liked it here and decided to stay. Then others followed him, and now it looks as though we are different from those who stayed in the old area" (Colson, 1974:59).

Certain aspects of paternity are much like the practices mentioned above in matrilineal Kom, and Colson says that approximately 40 percent of women will have had a child before marriage (often by the man the woman expects to marry). "But once her pregnancy is discovered, all marriage negotiations must cease until the child is some months old. Whether the lover marries her or not, he is entitled—and today is forced by legal action—to make a payment which establishes him as the legal father of the child, and his paternity is not altered by the mother's subsequent marriage to another man" (Colson, 1974:65).

Husbands have considerable authority over their wives, although in ways that may not be expected by Westerners. For example, "One of the arguments used to dissuade men from building on their own is the risk they run of beating a wife to death if no one is near to hear her cries and intervene. In a number of instances men have actually done this and have then committed suicide when they saw what they had done" (Colson, 1974:69).

Forde studied the Yakö of Nigeria, among whom the principle of double descent or double unilineal kin-group organization predominates. But "the unilineal tendency itself contains the alternatives of patrilineal and matrilineal reckoning and these are not, as was once assumed, mutually exclusive" (Forde, 1964:86). This system presents some interesting contrasts to those we have just considered, although information on illegitimacy was scarce in the material I consulted. The Yakö during the time of Forde's fieldwork had been tempting fate and the authorities by "acquiring" children in possibly illicit ways, so it may have been the case that the child's provenance was not a matter of grave concern. Between brothers and sisters of one mother, there was a mystical bond in which fertility was invoked; between members of the same patrilineage, there were material economic concerns.

In Yakö society, most older men have more than one wife. Each occupies her own house and has an equal claim on the time, attention, and energy of the husband. The man and his wives are normally a single farming unit, but each unit plants and harvests its own yams, with women acting under the direction of the husband; for lesser crops, the women control their own harvests.

The Yakö believe that physiological paternity gives them a right to social fatherhood, but if there is a disagreement, the rights to the child can sometimes be conferred on the adulterer who actually fathered the child. (This normally happens if a woman has left her husband and is living with another man before marriage money has been repaid and the divorce has been recognized.) Outside the compound in which a person grows up, the patrilineage is the most important corporate group. Patrilineal groups are territorially compact, each having a name and a rule of exogamy. From the patriclan, members can claim rights in building sites, farmland, oil-palm clusters, and planted trees.

The matriclan is not a territorial group, and inheritance is of transferable wealth, especially livestock, currency, or payments made to a woman's kin when she marries. Each child inherits some kinds of property from the

World Bank

Bridewealth and polygyny reflect the vital productive contributions of women to the family. Women kin often work together in the fields and share other work as well.

father and some from the mother, but funerals and disposal of movable property are the responsibility of the matriclan, as is the right to demand compensation in the case of homicide. Fertility too is in the hands of the matriclan, and each matriclan has an associated fertility spirit, which is propitiated by a matriclan priest on important occasions. These matriclans are not territorial groups but cross-cutting ties that extend considerably beyond the local territory—as when, for example, a matriclan helps a young man with the price he must pay for a bride. Forde adds,

> There is usually an intimate relation between a man and his sister's son—the classic relationship which cuts across parental ties in societies stressing matrilineal descent. And among the Yakö this relationship is often converted when opportunity arises into foster-fatherhood, with subsequent adoption of sisters' sons into the patriclan of the mother's brother. (Forde, 1964:113)

Note the importance in all three groups of the principles of lineality, whether through the mother's or father's side or both, and the circumstances in which one or another principle is violated or "fudged" to allow an individual to be included. This lineality and its primary practical outcome—inclusion of nearly all comers—may be one of the most important differences between African kinship systems and others. One lesson learned from the study of lineage systems is that the exclusion of relatives on one side is seldom complete. Of this, Robin Fox says:

> Thus in any society with established unilineal descent groups, an individual usually has important relationships with relatives other than those in his own descent group, the one through whom he gains his descent-group membership. Fortes has called this "complementary filiation." Thus, in a patrilineal society, although a man gains his descent-group status through his father, he is still his mother's child; he therefore has a "complementary" relationship with his mother's agnates [male relatives], and in particular with his mother's brothers. Another way of looking at this is to see it not as a result of "filiation"—of being the child of one's mother—but as resulting from the marriage tie itself. Thus, when a man marries he sets up an affinal relationship between his lineage and that of his wife. His son—this is a patrilineal example—is a member of his lineage and so shares with him in this affinal relationship. Thus the son does not have special relationships with his maternal uncles because they are his mother's brothers, but because they are the brothers of his father's wife. (Fox, 1967:133)

Similarly, questions may be posed about the adaptability of lineage systems in contemporary circumstances; Mary Douglas (1969) asked, "Is Matriliny Doomed in Africa?" and answered that matriliny has exhibited considerable flexibility in urban situations. She concluded that matriliny was no more "doomed" than patriliny, that lineage systems allow a person to call upon a variety of kin ties to enhance life chances and offer opportunities that conjugal or nuclear families do not. This point, first made by Douglas in 1969, is still being debated in the present, nowadays with respect to the impact of globalization on matrilineal systems (Miller, 1996; Peters, 1997a, 1997b).

New Areas of Study and Holdovers from the Past in Contemporary African Societies

Since the golden age of (colonial) anthropological studies of kinship, many new areas of study have arisen (and some have declined). Kinship studies were probably the glory of twentieth-century anthropological studies in Africa because they illustrated better than any other kind of analysis the almost infinite variety of customs that humans invent. But, as Pauline Peters has pointed out (following Fox), where once kinship theory was as central to anthropological theory as the nude was to art, kinship theory has now been chopped into parts: "family, household, relations of production and property, child socialization, group formation, gender relations, sexuality—cannibalized by the changing fashions of ethnographic and theoretical rethinking" (Peters, 1997a:125). Many of these parts have taken on new lives of their own.

Currently, the most illuminating and productive parts of what was kinship theory are the studies of sexuality and gender relations, usually from a feminist perspective (see Chapter 10; and Gordon, 1996; James and Etim, 1999; Yanagisako and Collier, 1987; Van Allen, 2000). These areas have yielded much new data on the subjects of domesticity, family power relations, male-female relations in urban contexts, and the like. For example, one lesson learned from kinship theory is that, like lineage systems in practice, systems of authority in practice—whether characterized as patriarchal or matriarchal—are seldom one-sided. More common in Africa may have been what Judith Van Allen (1972) called a "dual-sex system," in which each sex governed its own affairs and shared power on major decisions, such as who would be king or queen mother. Although dual-sex systems probably were characteristic of many African societies, the patriarchal biases of outside investigators may have caused them to be underreported. A favorite quote from an Asante male elder illustrates the European habit of ignoring the importance of the political role of women: "The white man never asked us this: you have dealings with and recognize only the men; we supposed the European considered women of no account, and we know you do not recognize them as we have always done" (Rattray, 1923:84).

It is likely that more nuanced analyses of the interplay between men's and women's political roles will increase in years to come. Some are already in the literature: for example, Peters (1997b) has focused on women's (once ignored and attacked) authority in matters of inheritance; Kate Crehan (1997) has delineated authority splits between husbands and brothers as important aspects of Kaonde matriliny in Zambia; and I researched a women's rebellion in Kom (Cameroon) in the early 1950s that was usually described (mostly by men) as an anticolonial protest "master-minded" by men (Shanklin, 1990).

Other issues considered critical in earlier kinship studies have been largely sidelined in recent anthropological literature and probably will not be revived. One is the discussion of the variables involved in choice of locality after marriage—in other words, where a couple live after they are married: with the groom's parents (patrilocal), with the bride's parents (matrilocal), with the groom's mother's brother (avunculocal), or separate from either the bride or groom's parents (neolocal). A similarly moot discussion, one that went on for more than a century in anthropology, concerns the functions and correlates of kinship terminology—that is, whether what one calls one's relatives is associated with or determined by the kinds of productive or inheritance systems in effect (Murdock, 1949, 1959). Another area of debate was the question of whether matriliny preceded patriliny. This issue was dropped largely due to the inconclusiveness of the evidence. However, new information on mother-child bonding in mammals, especially primates, may revive this debate around the question of the oldest forms of affiliation, that is, through the mother. The new findings may be either from a feminist or from a sociobiological/evolutionary psychology perspective (see Hrdy, 1999).

An area of interest for those studying contemporary change in kinship customs is that of bridewealth (payment made to a bride's family) or bride service (labor owed to a bride's family). These have long been practiced throughout Africa within practically all types of kinship systems (Bledsoe, 1993; Davies, 1999; Ekong, 1992; Kuper, 1982; Miller, 1999). More interesting than the debates on this subject, although not conclusive, are recent studies of the significance of bridewealth to present-day Africans. For example, Harris and Johnson (2000) report on a study at a South African university in which students were asked their opinion on bridewealth: 88 percent supported the practice (84 percent of men and 90 percent of women). Such prominent people as Nelson Mandela's daughter, Makaziwe, who holds a doctorate in cultural anthropology from the University of Massachusetts, endorsed the practice of bridewealth: "I have no problem with *lobola* (bridewealth). It is to solidify the relationship, to give respect to the woman and the child, so the man can in the future take care of the woman and children" (quoted in Harris and Johnson, 2000:230, after Mwamwenda and Monyooe, 1997).

One area I mentioned above and consider unresolved and perhaps underreported is the importance of brother-sister ties in Africa, regardless of the kind of kinship system practiced. Greater study of this relationship might resolve some of the issues raised in the debate of the "matrilineal puzzle," a debate over whether matriliny presents an insoluble dilemma for men who have to choose between favoring their own offspring or their sister's children (Richards, 1950; Peters, 1997a). Some of the issues relevant to this "matrilineal puzzle" and its reality need further exploration within a feminist theoretical perspective.

Some of these questions or debates may be resolved in the reader's lifetime, others not. Issues that are still very much open to question, like female genital mutilation (FGM) as part of initiation rites (sometimes lineage initiations or marital prerequisites, as among the Yakö, for whom clitoridectomy is a premarital custom), are apt to be debated for many years to come. For interested students, there is a large body of literature on the subject of female genital mutilation, including a discussion in Chapter 10 (see Barstow, 1999; el Dareer, 1982; Hicks, 1993; Jones and Diop, 1999; Lightfoot-Klein, 1989; Sweetman, 1998).

Another area of interest, but one that is only just beginning to be fully discussed, is homosexuality, against which many African societies have severe sanctions. But other societies practiced homosexuality in certain contexts (during adolescence, for example, among the Dahomey), according to Melville J. Herskovits (Murray and Roscoe, 1998), and this entire topic will surely produce a considerable amount of data before its parameters are resolved. A third area of interest, just now being explored, is the connection between witchcraft beliefs and kinship; Peter Geschiere astutely observed that witchcraft is the "flip side of kinship," and his own work (1982, 1997) has given rise to a host of other inquiries. (See Chapter 11 for a more detailed discussion of witchcraft.)

I noted above that kinship was initially studied as an administrative "key" and that anthropologists were looking at the "rules" by which Africa's often stateless societies governed themselves. Davidson explored this point at some length and characterized Africa's political and kinship systems as a "continuum between extremes." They ranged between formative "communities of pioneers" or stateless societies (in which rule by elders was the norm) and centralized societies. Underlying all, "a web of kinship was spun in varying patterns and appearances," and this web "was present in all these societies, the necessary underfabric of their structures" (Davidson, 1969:83). Davidson believed that African kinship systems continued to provide the template for much that went on in African governments at the time he was writing. The influence or resilience of these kinship systems

> differed greatly from people to people, and was increasingly submerged or limited wherever society became deeply stratified, or kings and nobles reinforced their power. Yet even where this happened it did so as a partial process, hesitant and still profoundly moulded by the past. The influence of the kinship structure remained powerful even in defeat. The source of this endurance lay in the power to resolve conflict or promote common action. (Davidson, 1969:83)

It seems to me the question is whether this underlying web of kinship—what Davidson, the historian (and many anthropologists as well), saw as the necessary underfabric of institutional structures—continues to influence the postcolonial era. Have the colonial and postcolonial disruptions destroyed this web, including the safety net associated with it? Or might there be a regrouping, possibly under the contemporary African idiom of family or kinship? The idiom, in my experience, may be ill defined, but it continues to feature inclusiveness as an ideal, at least within ethnic groups and sometimes within regions. This may include in-group solidarity within ethnic groups as well as regions, with its obvious impact on politics. I do not know the answer to this question, and it may be foolish to speculate in light of the highly fragmentary and mixed nature of the evidence to date.

We can look again at some precolonial kinship patterns that have been extended into the postcolonial era. For one, lineage systems prevented development of small groups of wealthy landowners. Second, a balance of weapons power prevented the extremes of coercion. And third, migration stories were found in almost all parts of Africa, suggesting that those who objected to the existing arrangements simply moved on. These three factors probably prevented the development of entrenched interest groups or, more loosely, classes in precolonial Africa, but all have now been violated by conditions in the modernizing, globalizing states of Africa, where the gap between rich and poor has grown enormously in the last few decades and where rulers such as Idi Amin (Uganda) or Mobutu Sese Seko (Democratic Republic of Congo) became pathologically authoritarian and acquisitive before being deposed. Also, the role of the military in staging coups d'état and the current barbarous warlordism in some nation-states indicate that the balance of weapons once in effect has shifted radically. Migration has a continuing role in allowing Africans to escape oppression and seek a better life elsewhere, but the people who once moved on to other parts of Africa are now leaving the continent and the African population altogether, as exemplified by the brain drain of many of Africa's most educated and skilled people to Europe and North America.

Given the corruption of rulers and the weakening of centuries-old institutions by colonial and now postcolonial states, we might question whether traditional kinship systems can survive or cope with the manifold problems

Africans face today. Although there are grounds for pessimism, I think it is much too early to say anything definitive about the current state of affairs. The postcolonial period is only about four decades long, whereas African kinship systems have been in place for thousands of years. Kinship is the means by which Africans coped in the past, and kinship is both intimately intertwined with other institutions that still function in Africa, although perhaps in increasingly limited ways, and facing new challenges for which few precedents exist. As an example of this, remember that an important part of African traditional religion was reverence for the ancestors who managed the affairs of both the living and the dead, through the lineage or kin group. A role for the ancestors is not included in Christianity, nor are the rules for selecting heirs or allocating property left to a kin group. Modern courts and common law, which often exist side by side with "customary law" in African countries, call into question all or most of the previously unchallenged authority of kin groups. Both Christianity and modern Western legal systems pose a challenge, with as yet undecided outcomes, for the future of African kinship systems.

Challenges to Contemporary African Kinship Systems

The effects of colonialism and postcolonial social forces are still under investigation. We can examine some of these under the following three headings: exposure to Western culture (including Christianity, Western education, and capitalist individualism and acquisitiveness); labor migration; and urbanization. All are part of a larger phenomenon—globalization—which results from the expansion of Western capitalism and its values and norms. Globalization has rearranged African social life at all levels, and African kinship systems have not been immune. Although most scholars note the continued resilience of African kinship systems overall, kinship systems are undergoing modifications in response to the new conditions of life in African societies.

In the area of culture, one question is the long-term impact of Christianity on African polygynous marriages. Most research suggests that while monogamy is growing under the influence of Christian ideology (see Gifford, 1998), polygyny has not died out. In many cases it has taken on new forms (fictive monogamy, to some), with many men having sexual relationships and families outside of the monogamous marriage required of Christians. Other cultural influences are Western norms of romantic love, individualism, and consumerism spread by the mass media and Western education. These are affecting gender relations both within and outside of marriage. Especially in cities, a more Westernized African middle class is growing, and the marriages and lifestyles of this class are becoming more similar

World Bank

Although African societies are changing, the role of families passing on valuable skills to their children remains important. In urban Zambia, a self-employed father is teaching his young son to make charcoal burners.

to those of their Western counterparts: more nuclear families and monogamous marriages, more equality in gender relations between husband and wife, and less dependence on the traditional extended family (see Bates, 1989; Bujra, 1993; Ingstad et al., 1992; von Bulow and Sorenson, 1993; Oppong, 1981). This does not mean that Western and African family systems are likely to converge in the near future, but it does indicate that African kinship patterns, like those elsewhere, change and adapt to new conditions.

Other impacts of modern life on African families are more problematic. In both colonial and postcolonial society, migration (primarily of men) to cities away from rural kin has been disastrous, in two ways. For one, it has created a large number of female-headed households in the rural areas, where women often raise their children and do the farming without the help of their husbands. In the cities, too, female-headed households increase, largely as a result of men who are separated from their rural families having sex and children with other women with whom they may not establish a legal or permanent connection. As in the West, the women and children in female-headed households are more likely to be poor than their two-parent counterparts. A second reason is that these complex new sexual dynamics are a major component in the AIDS crisis afflicting Africa, an issue discussed at some length in Chapters 5 and 7.

Urbanization and globalization also promote economic individualism and acquisitiveness. Some scholars have suggested that capitalism has combined with African kinship customs to promote the politics of thievery, corruption, and patrimonialism that afflict Africa and have stunted its political and economic maturation. Recalling the earlier discussion of African notions of the importance of sharing, one can see the roots of the demands placed on Africa's political and economic elites to use their power and wealth to benefit their extended family, village, region, or ethnic group. While consistent with the kinship norms, such behavior undermines Weberian norms of efficiency, impartiality, and rationality expected of modern governments and economies in a globalized world (see Chabal and Daloz, 1999).

Although urbanization is likely to increase, it is unlikely, under current underdeveloped conditions in Africa, to lessen the dependence of most Africans on extended families and ethnic groups. Most studies show that migrants to the city tend to live in quarters close to members of their own kinship or ethnic group, even if mixed with other groups. Kin and ethnic groups in the city support one another, thus making it easier to cope with change and new problems. Most urban dwellers also visit their kin back home regularly and expect to move back to the village at some point. All these things help to reinforce rural-based kinship systems and values (see Peil, 1981; Davison, 1988).

So, although African kinship systems may be changing, they are not dying out. Despite problems and uncertainties, family remains the best hope for most Africans in a changing world. The only thing we can say with certainty is that African families and kinship systems are challenged as never before. But we can expect these dynamic institutions to adapt and respond today as in the past to meet the challenges that lie ahead.

When I began writing this chapter, I asked myself three questions: First, what is new in anthropological studies of African kinship? Second, what can we learn from the twentieth-century classic anthropological studies of African kinship? And finally, why should we care about how Africans do things?

The answer to the first question is that anthropology has moved well beyond the taxonomic and evolutionary concerns of nineteenth- and twentieth-century anthropology and that very little is new under the heading of "kinship studies," but a great deal is being reconsidered and reconfigured to answer new questions, especially about practice. Michael Peletz observes that, since the 1970s, there have been shifts in both methodology and intent; these have included developments in Marxist, feminist, and historical approaches and, in his opinion, have led to the result that

> contemporary kinship studies tend to be historically grounded; tend to focus on everyday experiences, understandings, and representations of gender, power, and difference; and tend to devote considerable analytic attention to themes of contradiction, paradox, and ambivalence. (Peletz, 1995:343)

Ekeh brings to bear a historian's perspective on questions of kinship groupings and their utility in coping with power shifts.

The second question, about what we can learn from the "classic" studies, I answered with two examples of ways in which Africa continues to intrigue and surprise us with its differences in belief and practices. First, we can learn what Africans believe about child-rearing, and -training, for example, how (and why) to teach children to share. Second, from studying varying solutions to similar problems, we could learn something about ourselves and our own assumptions. Here I will add a couple more things we can and have learned: as anthropologists revisit societies studied decades ago, they often must rely on the musings of their illustrious professional predecessors for understanding what went before in the societies they now try to unravel. And, too, as anthropologists and others try to change practices or to understand changing practices, such as ideas about female genital mutilation, studies of kinship and of women's authority in such matters are very helpful in understanding both past and future directions.

My answer to the third question of whether we should care about African ways of doing things involves an equally positive response but a more complicated rationale. Since humans evolved in Africa, studying African responses to social historical disruptions and cataclysmic changes could teach us something about how to deal with such disruptions and changes, whether they occur in our own society or in societies we hope to help with disabling problems of, say, globalization. By way of example, a most interesting notion has been raised by Ekeh (1990), who, in tracing anthropological debates about tribes and tribalism, notes first that "in discarding the terms tribe and tribalism, social anthropology has created a gap in African studies by rendering years of scholarship concerned with the analysis of kinship as virtually irrelevant" and second, explores the proposition that kinship behavior in Africa owes its scope and significance—in both private and public realms—to the weaknesses of the African states, which could not protect individuals against the ravages of the slave trade and (he implies) cannot now protect individuals against the ravages of the contemporary globalizing world or corrupt political leaders in their own states. I think Ekeh's point that there is a valid African (unilineal descent group) solution—unlike the European (statehood formation) solution—to the question of how to protect and maintain both individual and group rights and privileges is a well-taken and intriguing one and that it deserves a good deal more consideration by African and Africanist scholars. Another area Ekeh explores—and I cannot do more than mention here—has to do with more recent usages of terms like *tribe* and *tribalism,* the former discarded now by anthropologists, and the latter used mainly as a term of opprobrium by governments but perhaps misunderstood by social scientists, and used by groups as a basis for morality and thus the protection of individual rights. Returning to Peletz, ongoing studies of new questions and new problems are being conducted by anthropologists who are searching for new answers in such fields as "gender, social inequality, social history, and the entailments of capitalist transformation, modernity, and postmodernity" (Peletz, 1995:367).

In other words, to borrow the delightful title of one anthropologist's article, "Kinship Is Dead! Long Live Kinship!"

Notes

1. Lévi-Strauss's argument was originally stated as a formula for men exchanging women, but the model works either way. Recent primate studies of groups in which females stay put and males are sent out of the group are extremely suggestive.
2. My students always ask what happens if there is no relative in this category; the answer in many societies is that one will be found to "sort of" match. For example, if one is supposed to marry one's father's sister's daughter and the father doesn't have a sister who has an available or marriageable daughter, then a father's sister's daughter's daughter may be chosen instead.
3. This happened most often when the women of a matrilineage would not allow a marriage, usually because of some problems they foresaw with the groom and his matrilineage. Kom men are very proud of their ability to father children and would almost never deny a child who was said to be their own, but they gain rights in the child only by paying brideprice on the mother. If the mother's matrilineage will not allow him to do so, a man has no claim on the child.

Bibliography

Barstow, D. G. 1999. "Female Genital Mutilation: The Penultimate Gender Abuse." *Child Abuse and Neglect* 23:501–510.

Bates, Robert H. 1989. *Beyond the Miracle of the Market.* New York: Cambridge University Press.

Bledsoe, Caroline. 1993. *Nuptiality in Sub-Saharan Africa: Contemporary Anthropological and Demographic Perspectives.* New York: Oxford University Press.

Bujra, Janet. 1993. "Gender, Class and Empowerment: A Tale of Two Tanzanian Servants." *Review of African Political Economy* 56:68–78.

Chabal, Patrick, and Jean-Pascal Daloz. 1999. *Africa Works: Disorder as Political Instrument.* Oxford: James Currey.

Colson, Elizabeth. 1974. "Plateau Tonga." Pp. 36–95 in David M. Schneider and Kathleen Gough (eds.). *Matrilineal Kinship.* Berkeley: University of California Press.

Crehan, Kate. 1997. "Of Chickens and Guinea Fowl: Living Matriliny in North-Western Zambia in the 1980s." *Critique of Anthropology* 17 (2):211–227.

Davidson, Basil. 1969. *The African Genius: An Introduction to African Cultural and Social History.* Boston: Little, Brown.

———. 1980. *The African Slave Trade.* Boston: Little, Brown.

Davies, C. 1999. "Advocacy for Gender Equality: The Case of Bridewealth in Uganda." *Promoting Education* 6 (2):13–15, 37–38, 49.

Davison, Jean (ed.). 1988. *Agriculture, Women and Land: The African Experience.* Boulder, CO: Westview Press.

Divale, William, and Marvin Harris. 1976. "Population, Warfare and the Male Supremacist Complex." *American Anthropologist* 78:521–538.

Douglas, Mary. 1969. "Is Matriliny Doomed in Africa?" Pp. 121–135 in Mary Douglas and Phyllis M. Kaberry (eds.). *Man in Africa.* London: Tavistock.

Ekeh, Peter P. 1990. "Social Anthropology and Two Contrasting Uses of Tribalism in Africa." *Comparative Studies in Society and History* 32 (4):660–700.

Ekong, Julia Meryl. 1992. Bridewealth, *Women and Reproduction in Sub-Saharan Africa: A Theoretical Overview.* Germany: Bon Holos.

el Dareer, Asma. 1982. *Woman, Why Do You Weep?: Circumcision and Its Consequences.* London: Zed.

Engels, Friedrich. 1942. *"The Origin of Family, Private Property, and the State" in the Light of the Researches of Lewis Morgan.* New York: International Publishers.

Evans-Pritchard, E. E. 1940. *The Nuer: A Description of the Modes of Livelihood and Political Institutions of a Nilotic People.* Oxford: Clarendon Press.

———. 1951. *Kinship and Marriage Among the Nuer.* Oxford: Clarendon Press.

———. 1974. *Man and Woman Among the Azande.* London: Faber and Faber.

Forde, Daryll. 1964. *Yakö Studies.* London: Oxford University Press (for the International African Institute).

Fortes, M. 1950. "Kinship and Marriage Among the Ashanti." Pp. 252–284 in A. R. Radcliffe-Brown and Daryll Forde (eds.). *African Systems of Kinship and Marriage.* Oxford: International African Institute.

Fox, Robin. 1967. *Kinship and Marriage.* Harmondsworth, England: Penguin.

Freud, Sigmund. 1919. *Totem and Taboo: Resemblances Between the Psychic Lives of Savages and Neurotics.* Introduced and translated by A. A. Brill. London: G. Routledge.

Geschiere, Peter. 1982. *Village Communities and the State.* London: Kegan Paul.

———. 1997. *The Modernity of Witchcraft: Politics and the Occult in Postcolonial Africa.* Charlottesville and London: University Press of Virginia.

Gifford, Paul. 1998. *African Christianity: Its Public Role.* Bloomington: Indiana University Press.

Gordon, April A. 1996. *Transforming Capitalism and Patriarchy: Gender and Development in Africa.* Boulder, CO: Lynne Rienner Publishers.

Gough, Kathleen. 1968. "The Nayars and the Definition of Marriage." Pp. 49–71 in Paul Bohannan and John Middleton (eds.). *Marriage, Family and Residence.* Garden City, NY: Natural History Press.

Harden, Blaine. 1990. *Africa: Dispatches from a Fragile Continent.* New York: W. W. Norton.

Harris, Marvin, and Orna Johnson. 2000. *Cultural Anthropology.* New York: Allyn and Bacon.

Hicks, Esther K. 1993. *Infibulation: Female Mutilation in Islamic Northeastern Africa.* New Brunswick, NJ: Transaction Publishers.

Hopkins, Keith. 1980. "Brother-Sister Marriage in Ancient Egypt." *Comparative Studies in Society and History* 22:303–354.

Hrdy, Sarah Blaffer. 1999. *Mother Nature: A History of Mothers, Infants and Natural Selection.* London: Chatto and Windus.

Ingstad, Bendicte, Frank Bruun, Edwin Sandberg, and Sheil Tlon. 1992. "Care for the Elderly, Care by the Elderly: The Role of Elderly Women in a Changing Society." *Journal of Cross-Cultural Gerontology* 7:379–398.

James, Valentine Udoh, and James S. Etim (eds.). 1999. *The Feminization of Development Processes in Africa: Current and Future Perspectives.* Westport, CT: Praeger.

Jones, H., and N. Diop. 1999. "Female Genital Cutting Practices in Burkina Faso and Mali and Their Negative Outcomes." *Studies in Family Planning* 30 (3):219–230.

Kaberry, Phyllis M. 1969. "Witchcraft of the Sun: Incest in Nso." Pp. 175–195 in Mary Douglas and Phyllis M. Kaberry (eds.). *Man in Africa.* London: Tavistock.

Ki-Zerbo, J. (ed.). 1989. *General History of Africa.* Vol. 1, *Methodology and African Prehistory.* Paris: UNESCO; and Berkeley: University of California Press.

Kuper, Adam. 1982. *Wives for Cattle: Bridewealth and Marriage in Southern Africa.* London: Routledge and Kegan Paul.

Lévi-Strauss, Claude. 1949. *Les structures élémentaires de la parenté.* Paris: Presses Universitaires de France.

Lightfoot-Klein, Hanny. 1989. *Prisoners of Ritual: An Odyssey into Female Genital Circumcision in Africa.* New York: Haworth Press.

Mair, Lucy. 1979. *African Societies.* Cambridge: Cambridge University Press.

Miller, David. 1999. "Women's Fears and Men's Anxieties: The Impact of Family Planning on Gender Relations in Northern Ghana." *Studies in Family Planning* 30 (1):54–66.

Miller, Doug. 1996. "Matriliny and Social Change: How Are the Women of Rural Malawi Managing?" Online at www.brocku.ca/epi/casid/miller.htm.

Murdock, George Peter. 1949. *Social Structure.* New York: Free Press.

———. 1959. *Africa: Its Peoples and Their Culture History.* New York: McGraw-Hill.

Murray, Stephen O., and Will Roscoe (eds.). 1998. *Boy-Wives and Female Husbands: Studies of African Homosexualities.* New York: St. Martin's Press.

Mwamwenda, T. S., and L. A. Monyooe. 1997. "Status of Bridewealth in an African Culture." *Journal of Social Psychology* 137:269–272.

Nkwi, P. N., and J. P. Warnier. 1982. *Elements for a History of the Western Grassfields.* Yaounde: University of Yaounde.

Oppong, Christine. 1981. *Middle Class African Marriage.* London: George Allen and Unwin.

Peil, Margaret (ed.). 1981. *Cities and Suburbs: Urban Life in West Africa.* New York: Africana Publishing.

Peletz, Michael G. 1995. "Kinship Studies in Late Twentieth-Century Anthropology." *Annual Review of Anthropology* 1995: 343–372.

Peters, Pauline E. 1997a. "Introduction: Revisiting the Puzzle of Matriliny in South-Central Africa." *Critique of Anthropology* 17 (2):125–146.

———. 1997b. "Against the Odds: Matriliny, Land and Gender in the Shire Highlands of Malawi." *Critique of Anthropology* 17 (2):189–210.

Radcliffe-Brown, A. R., and D. Forde (eds.). 1950. *African Systems of Kinship and Marriage*. London: Oxford University Press (for International African Institute).

Rattray, R. S. 1923. *Ashanti*. Oxford: Clarendon Press.

Richards, A. I. 1950. "Some Types of Family Structure Amongst the Central Bandu." Pp. 207–251 in A. R. Radcliffe-Brown and Daryll Forde (eds.). *African Systems of Kinship and Marriage*. Oxford: International African Institute.

Scheidel, Walter. 1996. "Brother-Sister and Parent-Child Marriage Outside Royal Families in Ancient Egypt and Iran: A Challenge to the Sociobiological View of Incest Avoidance?" *Ethology and Sociobiology* 17:319–340.

Shanklin, Eugenia. 1983. "Ritual and Social Uses of Goats in Kom." Pp. 11–36 in Riva Berleant-Schiller and Eugenia Shanklin (eds.). *The Keeping of Animals: Adaptation and Social Relations in Livestock-Producing Communities*. Totowa, NJ: Allanheld, Osmun.

———. 1990. "Anlu Remembered: The Kom Women's Rebellion of 1958–61." *Dialectical Anthropology* 15:159–181; reprinted pp. 133–171 in M. J. Diamond (ed.). 1998. *Women and Revolution: Global Expressions*. Netherlands: Kluwer.

Shanklin, Eugenia, George Mbeh, Columbus Ayaba, and Gilbert Mbeng. 2001. *Beautiful Deadly Lake Nyos: A Research Report on the 1986 Explosion of Lake Nyos and Its Aftermath*. Limbe, Cameroon: Presbook.

Stringer, Christopher, and Robin McKie. 1996. *African Exodus: The Origins of Modern Humanity*. New York: Henry Holt.

Sweetman, Caroline. 1998. *Gender, Education and Training*. Oxford: Oxfam.

Tattersall, Ian. 1998. *Becoming Human: Evolution and Human Uniqueness*. New York: Harcourt Brace.

Terrell, John Edward. 2000. "Doing the Devil's Work in Anthropology." *Anthropology News* (October):10.

Tylor, Edward B. 1889. "On a Method of Investigating the Development of Institutions: Applied to Laws of Marriage and Descent." *Journal of the Royal Anthropological Institute* 18:245–256, 261–269.

Van Allen, Judith. 1972. "'Sitting on a Man': Colonialism and the Lost Political Institutions of Igbo Women." *Canadian Journal of African Studies* 6:165–182.

———. 2000. "'Bad Future Things' and Liberatory Movements: Capitalism, Gender and the State in Botswana." *Radical History Review* 76:136–168.

von Bulow, Dorthe, and Anne Sorenson. 1993. "Gender and Contract Farming: Outgrower Schemes in Kenya." *Review of African Political Economy* 56:38–52.

Wamba, Philippe. 1999. *Kinship: A Family's Journey in Africa and America*. New York: Dutton.

Westermarck, E. 1894. *The History of Human Marriage*. New York: Macmillan.

Yanagisako, S.J., and J. Collier. 1987. "Toward a Unified Analysis of Gender and Kinship." Pp. 14–50 in J. Collier and S. J. Yanagisako (eds.). Stanford, CA: Stanford University Press.

10

Women and Development

April A. Gordon

Since Ester Boserup's (1970) pioneering work on women and development in the Third World, studies continue to confirm her findings that women are not equal beneficiaries with men of the fruits of modernization and development. Studies of women in Africa are consistent in showing that although there have been some gains for women, such as greater educational parity with men or official declarations professing support for gender equality, overall the prospects for women are ominous in many areas. As in other parts of the world, African women have neither the political, legal, educational, nor economic opportunities of their male counterparts. Men in Africa overwhelmingly dominate the institutions of society and have used their positions more often than not to further the control and advantages men have in both the public and domestic arenas.

In discussing the conditions peculiar to Africa that affect women's status and roles, several general factors must be kept in focus. One is that the overall economic and political problems of Africa make life difficult for most African men as well as women. Inequality, oppression, poverty, and lack of opportunity are widespread societal concerns. Nonetheless, women as a group suffer more and have access to fewer resources and opportunities than men do. We must also note that African societies and gender roles are highly diverse; this makes efforts at generalization somewhat tentative and not applicable to every society. Also important is that class as well as gender influences the status and opportunities of individual women. That is, girls born to more elite families will typically have the opportunity to acquire a good education and prestigious career, although they are unlikely to achieve great political or economic power on their own. However, they are prime candidates for marriage to the African men who do wield power and influence. This contrasts dramatically with the modest or nonexistent prospects their peasant or working-class sisters have. The results are that although women as a group suffer from inequality, the interests and perspectives of elite women often diverge from those of poorer women. Last, the forms gender inequality take in Africa reflect indigenous, precolonial, and European influences. European expansion into Africa during the colonial period both undermined sources of status and autonomy that women had and strengthened elements of indigenous male dominance or "patriarchy." At the same time, Western gender ideology and practices that promote male dominance and female dependency have been superimposed on Africa. Since independence, Africa's male leaders have continued to add laminations to the patriarchal structures they inherited from their colonizers, often with the support of Western international investors and donors whose "development" assistance mostly goes to men.

As the following discussion shows, the culmination of precolonial, colonial, and postindependence history has been one of general disempowerment for women. The prospects for women to gain ground economically, politically, and socially will depend on concerted efforts by women themselves, by African governments, and by the international community to ensure that the fruits of development are extended equally to women and men.

Women in Precolonial Africa

Sub-Saharan Africa is a diverse continent whose precolonial history and culture may never be accurately known, since little of it was written down. So it is with considerable caution that we attempt to generalize about gender roles (or anything else) today or in the past. The accuracy of reports on precolonial times must also be questioned, since much of this writing was filtered through the cultural biases and perceptions of European males during the period of slavery or colonialism. Referring to the British, but applicable to other Europeans as well, Dorothy Hammond and Alta Jablow (1970:197) conclude that "four centuries of writing about Africa have produced a literature which describes not Africa but the British response to it. . . . As in a morality play, the British and the Africans are the exemplars of civilization and savagery, respectively." Depictions of women as dominated, servile beasts of burden is an example of the kinds of distortions that have resulted from European ethnocentrism in dealing with African cultures. Moreover, since the 1500s, beginning with the Atlantic slave trade, African societies were increasingly changed by contact with Europeans. Even before most Africans ever saw a white man, the impact of slavery was felt in all parts of the continent. Population movements, wars, disease, loss of productive labor power, and a breakdown of familiar social institutions altered indigenous social patterns (Cutrufelli, 1983:14–16).

Despite problems of the reliability of data, some patterns of gender relationships were prevalent, if not universal, in Africa before the period of European penetration. Politically, for instance, African women in most societies have been influential political actors in informal ways, if not through formal political roles. Women varied from being highly subordinated "legal minors" under the control of their menfolk among groups like the Tswana and Shona in southern Africa to holding positions as chiefs among the Mende and Serbro of Sierra Leone and "headmen" among the Tonga of Zambia. In some societies women even had formal roles in male councils. The figure of the queen mother in many societies of western Africa was very influential, and it was she who selected the king. Women warriors fought for the fon (king) of Dahomey, and powerful warrior queens led their people in battle. Notable examples are Queen Amina of Hausaland, who ruled in the fifteenth and sixteenth centuries, and Nzinga of Angola, who led the earliest and most effective resistance against the Portuguese (Parpart, 1988:208–210).

In addition to such important formal roles as these, women's organizations existed that acted as parallel authority structures to those of males. These included women's courts, market authorities, secret societies, and age-grade institutions (Staudt, 1987:195; Parpart, 1988:208–210). Most generally, parallel authority structures allowed men and women to exercise authority over their own sex and activities. These organizations reflected the sexual division of labor and the different spheres of activity for men and women. There was also recognition that men could best make decisions about men's affairs as could women about their own concerns. One example of parallel male-female organizations was societies that conferred honorific titles upon accomplished members of the community. Both titled men and women had a great deal of prestige and exercised considerable influence. The *ekwe* title, associated with the goddess Idemili, is a case in point. This title is taken by high-status Ibo women of Nigeria, and the most powerful of these women, the *agba ekwe*, reputedly was the most powerful political figure among her people (Amadiume, 1987). In some cases, goddess-focused religions provided a basis for women to control major religio-political functions through societies dedicated to the goddess. Ambrose Moyo, in Chapter 11, points out other religious leadership roles held by women as well as men, such as shaman, diviner, and spirit medium.

Even though women did have these positions of influence and power, males typically had more formal authority positions than females, so a degree of male dominance existed. For most women, power was (and still is) exercised indirectly and informally as sisters, mothers, and wives within the extended family system and was closely associated with women's economic power. Where women had rights to land, animals, labor, and the products of their own or others' labor, their status was higher than if such resources were under male control. Enhancing women's position was the critical role they played in the sexual division of labor within their households. Women were producers: they grew most of the family's food, tended animals, and made tools and other articles used by the family. They cooked, helped construct residences and other buildings, hauled wood, and so on. In many cases, women also sold their surplus in local markets, thus dominating these commercial activities and demonstrating their business acumen. Women were also reproducers in societies where children were wealth, old-age security, and the guarantors that one would be venerated as an ancestor after death and not forgotten. (See, again, Moyo's chapter on religion, in which he discusses the significance of ancestors.) These vital roles were normally translated into high status for women and more autonomy than was typical for women in most regions of the world.

Other manifestations of this relative autonomy and high status of women are seen in marriage customs. Bridewealth, typical in Africa, is a custom that requires a transfer of goods and services from the male's family to that of the bride or to the bride herself. Bridewealth is not to be equated with "selling" daughters. Rather, it indicates the high value attached to women in African society; families must be compensated for the loss of their daughters and the wealth she will bring to her husband's family. Bridewealth not only adds to the prospective bride's sense of her own worth but also provides material benefits for her family. In fact, women often work together both to arrange suitable marriages and to maximize the bridewealth. Traditionally, African women do not take their husband's name when they marry, thus retaining their own identity with respect to their family of origin. Once married, a woman has the right to leave a husband who mistreats her or one with whom she no longer chooses to live. Certain factors, however, discourage this: her family might have to return the bridewealth, or, in patrilineal families, the woman might have to leave her children with her husband and his family. But, unlike in many cultures, a divorced or widowed African woman usually has little difficulty attracting a new spouse, again a tribute to the importance of women and their vital contributions to family and community. (For more on bridewealth and family systems, see Chapter 9.)

Polygyny, a man's right to have more than one wife, has been widely accepted in Africa. Often misunderstood by Europeans as a sign of women's low status, polygyny is more accurately indicative of the centrality of women to the economic well-being of the family. Since family labor was the primary means of accumulating wealth, acquiring women was necessary to family prosperity. By having more than one wife, the family gained not only her productive contributions but also more children.

Women in the family also benefited from the greater prosperity of their households. Additional wives helped each other with tasks, provided companionship (often lacking with husbands), and gave pregnant, nursing, or older women a needed respite from the sexual demands of their husbands.

European Penetration: The Colonial Legacy

By the time outright colonial domination of Africa began in the 1800s, some loss of autonomy for African women may have already occurred. A major reason is that the disease, warfare, and dislocations slavery introduced in earlier centuries put more pressure on women to reproduce and perform maternal functions in order to offset population losses that were occurring (Cutrufelli, 1983:2). Control over women's productive activities in the family may also have intensified.

The record is much clearer on the impact of colonialism. African societies were integrated by force into the expanding global capitalist economy dominated by the European powers. To extract the mineral and commodity wealth of Africa and to ensure a cheap labor supply, radical changes were imposed. The commercialization of agriculture through the introduction of cash crops altered the customary gender division of labor in ways mostly disadvantageous to women. Men were taught to grow new cash crops such as cocoa and coffee for export, while women continued to grow food crops for the family and local consumption. Men were forced into the wage economy to work in the mines, on the plantations, or in town; most women remained in the rural areas, often assuming the responsibilities their absent menfolk could no longer perform. Schooling and the teaching of new skills were made available primarily to males. All in all, although both men and women were exploited within the colonial economy, men gained some access to important resources such as money, skills, land, and education less available to women.

Men also gained political advantages as customary sources of female power were ignored or undermined. Europeans imposed their own prejudices about the proper authority of men over women by dealing only with male leaders. All-male "native authorities" were created in many areas to allow some local government, based on frequently arguable "traditional" or "customary" laws. Tradition was usually interpreted in ways that favored men's control over women, allowing men to gain at women's expense (see Chanock, 1982). For example, as men were provided new commercial opportunities in cash crop agriculture, they began to assert their customary rights to land and the labor of wives in order to accumulate income for themselves; they were not obligated to share this money with their wives. In some cases, this resulted in great wealth for some enterprising men. For instance, among the Beti in Cameroon, some men married many women in order to get virtually free labor from them on their cash crop farms. By custom, women had to help their husbands for little compensation even though these farms were now commercial ventures bearing little similarity to the subsistence family farms of the past (Guyer, 1984). In the Zambian Copperbelt, wives were required to perform their customary domestic services for their husbands in town, although they were unable to claim any share of their husband's income. Unable to get jobs of their own, women often had to support themselves by selling sex, food, homebrew, or domestic services to other men (Langley, 1983:94–95). Not only were women economically responsible for themselves, but the burden of providing for children also fell mostly on women—another matter of custom from precolonial times.

At the same time as their responsibilities were growing, women's rights to land were undermined. Often, the most or the best land was given to the men for cash crops, and there were growing pressures to deprive women of their inheritance rights to land in favor of males in the family (Cutrufelli, 1983:64–69). One of the most damaging colonial land policies for women involved efforts to introduce private ownership of land. In Kenya in the 1950s, the Swynnerton Act was to provide deeds to male heads of households, replacing the African land tenure system that ensured everyone's access to land (Davison, 1988:164–165). Such policies have continued in the postcolonial period. They pose a major threat to the economic well-being of women, since land is the crucial resource for survival among the large numbers of Africans who are small farmers.

Colonial officials and male elders often worked together to get better control of women. Frequently, European officials did not want women in the towns; they wanted only the labor of African men. Therefore, many restrictions were placed on the movement of women (Cutrufelli 1983:22–26). Zambia (then Northern Rhodesia) is a good example of colonial regulation of migratory labor in southern Africa. Rural tribal authorities were given the right to prevent unmarried women and children from moving to the towns, and urban authorities had the power to send those who defied such restrictions back to the villages. Some women did marry or cohabit with men in the towns, but they had no access to wage labor until late in the colonial period (Hansen, 1987:11–13).

Among pastoralists, the introduction of new property and commercial relations also eroded the status of women. Among the Tugen of Kenya and other groups, for instance, women's rights to cattle and the status they once derived from the vital tasks they performed were undermined as men asserted their right to ownership of animals and other property. Ownership rights were redefined in Western commercial terms. This now meant that men, not women, could make decisions and profit from the sale or acquisition of family property. Women themselves became another form of property to be controlled as they lost effective control over their own labor. They had to work for their husbands in order to survive, because they had no rights to own wealth-producing property of their own. Compounding her economic vulnerability, a woman, if divorced, had no right to the wealth she helped her husband acquire through her labor (Kettel, 1986). (See Lovett, 1989, for a good general discussion of gender and the colonial state.)

The Postindependence Period: Dependency and Inequality of Women

In many ways, the problems of women since independence are a continuation of policies and forces set in motion during the colonial period. Although African gender relations were transformed during the colonial period to further European economic and political exploitation of Africa, such distorted and patently unfair practices often continue to be justified by appeals to "African tradition." Despite women's contributions to the struggle for independence and rhetoric in favor of equality for all, the new African states and social institutions are largely Africanized replicas of their colonial predecessors. Advantages men had gained in access to education, jobs, and property enabled them to gain control of most of the wealth, jobs, and leadership positions in newly independent African countries.

Male dominance has been enhanced as many of Africa's new Westernized elites, both male and female, have modeled their own gender roles on those of their Western tutors. These roles are, in turn, disseminated to the masses via education, the media, and many government and women's organizations (cf. Nweke, 1985; Obadina, 1985; Nzomo, 1989; Bujra, 1986). Rather than promoting equal political and economic rights and opportunities for women in their societies, women are often encouraged instead to pursue domesticity and economic subordination to a male, who is "head of the family" (see Schuster, 1982). Male control of formal political power in Western-style political systems is widely portrayed as a natural extension of such male-dominated African institutions as chieftaincies and councils of elders. While this might appear to be consonant with previous gender roles of African societies in which men and women had distinctly different roles in the division of labor, current role expectations are operating in a very different economic and political environment. As in other parts of the world, access to money and other economic resources (e.g., land, businesses, wage jobs, credit) are vital to survival, social mobility, and status.

Moreover, while housewives in the West have a measure of legal protection to compensate for their economic dependency on their husbands, economically dependent women in Africa typically do not have guaranteed rights to their husband's income or property, nor do their children should the husband die or the marriage end in divorce. In addition, male political power is no longer exercised primarily through families and local organizations in which women have leverage in the decisionmaking process. Power is now exercised through the state and bureaucratic institutions whose centralization of power and control of resources are vastly greater than those of the typical decentralized political institutions of the past. In Chapter 4, Donald Gordon discusses how important access to state power and patron-client relationships are in Africa. If women have few positions in the new institutions of power and men are allowed to make the decisions, women risk being politically, economically, and socially marginalized and their interests neglected within their societies.

The minority of Africans who would challenge pervasive male dominance face a double obstacle. Not only must they contend with the structures in their societies that perpetuate existing gender inequality, but the foreign "development establishment" that African nations depend upon for assistance has many of the same biases against women. Western corporations, lending institutions, governments, and development agencies are all male-dominated institutions from male-dominated societies. Gender inequality has been such an inherent feature of Western culture that the discriminatory effect of seemingly "neutral" policies inevitably occurs. Even though more efforts are being made to promote gender equity, most women continue to lack access to the resources necessary to improve their lives and often the lives of their children.

With the above general perspectives in mind, four topics will be looked at in more depth: (1) women in the economy, (2) women and politics, (3) women's groups and gender reform efforts, and (4) prospects for women.

Women in the Economy

Most men and women in sub-Saharan Africa are still employed in agriculture, but this is especially true of women. Estimates are that women do 70–80 percent of the agricultural labor and produce up to 80 percent of the staple food (Gopal and Salim, 1998:177). They also cultivate about half of all cash crops (Jacobson, 1993:67). Despite women's contributions to the agricultural economy, only 7–8 percent own land or have leaseholds to land (Gopal and Salim, 1998:177).

Labor force statistics underrate the amount of work most women perform. According to the World Bank, women work much more than men; an average woman's work day is 50 percent longer than a man's. Women work

World Bank

Women grow most of the food in Africa.

in the fields an average of 1,000 hours per year and spend an additional 3 to 4 hours a day preparing food, cooking, and collecting firewood and water. While their husbands also farm in many cases, during the long slack season men reportedly spend most of the day drinking or visiting friends and relatives (Faruqee and Gulhati, 1983:36–37). Women commonly complain about the inequitable division of labor, that women work while men sit around and tell them what to do, or that women must carry heavy loads (water, wood, children) while the men carry nothing. They also complain that men do not support their families but spend their money on drink, other women, or goods for themselves. Many men even try to claim for themselves money the woman earns herself (Staudt, 1987:206–207). Although the husband may use his income (including that derived from his wife's labor on his farm) to pay off family debts, pay taxes, buy medicine, and offer gifts to his wife, men often spend more on bikes, watches, and radios for themselves. By contrast, women use most of their income for the household and their children (Blumberg, 1995:6–11).

Most women farmers get little help to ease their burdens. As Virginia DeLancey points out in Chapter 5 on African economies, only a small share of investment has gone to rural development in most African countries, and investments that are made go primarily for cash crops, mechanization, extension services, and resettlement projects that mostly help men. More and more women are managing the family farm alone as men turn to other forms of employment. Because farms are likely to be registered to the husband as the sole owner, women are often ineligible for most farm aid available only to farmers with legal title to their land. Even worse, without legal title to the farm, a woman stands to lose everything should her husband die or divorce her (Mulama, 2004a; Picard, 1995:50; Nwomonoh, 1995:176–177).

Not surprisingly, women as well as men are seeking new employment opportunities in the towns. But here too women often find their opportunities circumscribed in part due to women's unequal access to education or training opportunities. The gap between schooling for males and females remains wide and in many cases is worsening as a result of Africa's continuing economic crisis (see Kevane, 2004:143–157). Education is especially low for girls in rural areas where fewer than 25 percent of poor girls are in school (World Bank, 2000:13). Although about 20 percent of girls in Africa go to secondary school, this is only half the number found in the rest of the developing world. Both males and females have been hurt by the drop in government spending in Africa and the increase in school fees (Sengupta, 2003).

While there are educated women in good jobs and professions, most wage jobs for women are in jobs that are, as in the West, typically held by women, that is, nurses, teachers, clerks, and secretaries. Most good jobs are held by men. Uganda is an example of the low representation of women in high-status jobs. Only 2 percent of the female working population is in

April Gordon

In Senegal, the government is trying to encourage families to educate their girls by using the slogan, "I also want to go to school," on billboards such as this one.

administrative, managerial, and professional occupations, and only .05 percent of senior positions in the civil services are held by women (Gopal and Salim, 1998:167).

Wage jobs of any kind are hard for women to obtain, and most find work in the informal (non-wage) sector selling foodstuffs, homebrew, or services (including prostitution) as they did during the colonial period. In fact, women have an estimated 60 percent of informal-sector businesses ("African Leaders," 2004). In Zimbabwe, women's informal sector businesses are 67 percent of the total; in Lesotho, they are 73 percent of the total; and in Senegal, they are 84 percent of the total (Moghadan, 2005:56; World Bank, 2001:121).

Discriminatory laws and cultural practices make it difficult for women to compete economically in agriculture, wage jobs, or business. Typically, women have little access to ownership and inheritance of property or to bank credit. In countries such as Botswana, Lesotho, Namibia, and Swaziland, married women are under the permanent guardianship of their husbands and have no right to manage property on their own (World Bank, 2001:118).

Only since the 1980s have Western development agencies come to realize how their efforts have often hampered rather than helped African women. They erroneously thought that if men were better off, women and general family welfare would improve as well. Instead, it is now recognized that women's economic opportunities and income more often declined while their workloads increased. Examples include Victoria Bernal's (1988) study in northern Sudan and Judith Carney's (1988) study in Gambia; both studies found that irrigation schemes frequently result in men gaining control of, if not always title to, land and production decisions at women's expense. Resettlement schemes also tend to give male farmers land, subsidies, and credit, as in Cameroon (Goheen, 1988) and Zimbabwe (Pankhurst and Jacobs, 1988), although women are required to work on these farms, continue to grow food for their families, and perform other domestic chores such as cooking and child care. In the Zimbabwe study, several women reported how the state marketing board paid their husbands for their cash crops, and how the men then decided how much to give their wives. If women complained about the lack of money, they were beaten. Some women resorted to selling their sexual services to other men to get additional money for household expenses.

To help rectify these inequities, since the 1970s women in development (WID) initiatives have been given more attention. For example, to address the inequities in US development aid, the Percy Amendment passed by Congress requires a "women's impact statement" in every US Agency for International Development (USAID) project in developing countries. USAID now stresses that improving the education and status of women is a key element in its objectives of promoting "sustainable development" in Africa (Green, 1994). The UN, European donor agencies, and most major foundations have developed or expanded women's programs as well (Newland, 1991:124). Beginning in the late 1980s, the World Bank in its publications (see 1989:103–104; 1990; 1996) began to stress the need to promote women's education, health, training, and access to productive resources. In 1987, a Women in Development Division was created, and in 1989 a coordinator for women in development was included in the Bank's four regional complexes, including Africa. More than one-third of all the Bank's 1989 operations in Africa reportedly included actions specifically addressed to women (World Bank, 1990:10).

Unfortunately, as will be discussed below, the gap between men and women is growing. Although some change is occurring, more reforms and assistance for women are needed if the goals of poverty reduction and sustainable development are to be met. (See Gordon, 2001, and Chapter 13 for more on current efforts to promote poverty reduction and development through the Millennium Development Goals.)

Women and Politics

Since independence, women have been excluded from most of the important political positions in African states. Until 2005, there were no women heads of state, and women held only 6–8 percent of the legislative positions in Africa. In half of Africa's states, there were no women at all in cabinet-level positions. Women were only somewhat better represented at local levels of government (Parpart, 1988:8–9; World Bank, 2000:24; Morna, 1995:58).

Although ruling Africa remains largely a male preserve, some dramatic changes are happening that promise to break men's monopoly on power. South Africa's 1994 national elections set the stage for changes elsewhere. For the first time, women won one-fourth of the seats in an African parliament, by far the best record in Africa. After the 1999 South African elections, women's participation increased to more than 30 percent. This progress was the result of the ruling African National Congress party's commitment to ensuring women's representation on party lists submitted to the voters. It also represented the new black majority government's determination to actualize the country's new constitution with its emphasis on gender equality (see "Number," 2004; Center for Reproductive Law, 1997). Uganda also revised its constitution in 1995 and set aside one-third of all councilor seats at the local government level for women (it was ratified in 1997) (Gopal and Salim, 1998:166–167).

In most countries where changes have been made to include more women in public office, efforts have been half-hearted. Most women were not informed about the new opportunities or actively encouraged to enter the political area. Also, because most women have so little access to land, businesses, or well-paying jobs, they usually lack the resources, status, and credibility necessary for successful political candidacy (Gopal and Salim, 1998:173, 177).

There are also cultural barriers to women holding political power. Many Africans, male and female, have accepted the principle of male dominance in society, including in political leadership roles (Mikell, 1997a:341), and few of Africa's male rulers have done much to challenge these views. The typical view has been that male dominance is "natural" or, at least, conforms to African "tradition," neither of which one should attempt to change. For example, when Kenyan women at the UN International Conference on Women in Nairobi in 1985 recommended that women be more equitably represented in parliament, then President Daniel arap Moi responded, "God made man the head of the family [and] challenging that was tantamount to criticizing God" (Staudt, 1987:50; Mikell, 1997a:338–339).

Such attitudes are now changing both among male politicians and average citizens as well. In at least a dozen countries women's representation in parliament, in appointed offices, in judicial positions, and in local and provincial governments is growing. Much of this progress is due to affirmative action efforts by various African political bodies. One example of progress is in parliamentary positions held by women. The fourteen member countries of the regional Southern African Development Community (SADC) have set a goal to achieve 30 percent representation by women in their respective parliaments. Unfortunately, so far only three countries have achieved this goal—South Africa, Mauritius, and Mozambique—but the standard is placing pressure on other countries to improve their efforts in this area (Bengali, 2005; Phiri, 2005). On the individual country level, Rwanda currently stands out as having the highest representation of women in a house of parliament, not only in Africa, but in the world. Almost half of seats in its lower house of parliament are held by women, and women also have gained a third of Senate seats (Lacey, 2005; Longman, 2006:133–160). Despite these examples of progress, women still hold fewer than 10 percent of parliamentary seats and 8 percent of government ministry positions across Africa ("New Strategy," 2004).

Africa's continental-wide political body, the African Union (AU), also is working to promote gender equality in its posts. In 2002, the AU mandated that five of its ten commissioners would be women and that by 2010 half of all seats in AU organ bodies would go to women ("Historical Moves," 2002). On top of this, Gertrude Mongella of Tanzania was selected to be the first female president of the organization ("African Leaders," 2004).

US Department of State

Liberian president, Ellen Johnson-Sirleaf, is the first elected woman president in Africa.

Of enormous symbolic significance to the advancement of women in politics was the election of Ellen Johnson-Sirleaf as president of Liberia in 2005. Johnson-Sirleaf is the first elected woman president in Africa, and she won by a margin of 19 points over her male rival, a popular soccer star.

Such victories are raising questions about what significance more women in government positions will have. For example, has the link between maleness and political office now been irrevocably broken with more female representation to follow? What impact will women actually have on the policies of their countries; for example, will they promote women's equality, will they be less corrupt than men, and will they promote a more peaceful development agenda than their male counterparts have?

On the question of growing female political participation in government, so far there is no great increase in women's representation in most countries. And SADC, which has now raised its goals to 50 percent representation by women in parliament, is unlikely to have most countries reach even the earlier 30 percent goal. Some observers also argue that parliaments in Africa are not where real power lies anyway. Real power is invested in the office of the president in most African countries and among a few loyalists at the upper levels of the executive branch of government. In other words, men still hold a monopoly of power regardless of how many women are in parliament. In Rwanda, for instance, the argument is made that President Paul Kagame has consolidated power in his hands, and few members of parliament—male or female—would dare to challenge him (see Creevey, 2006:169). Women nonetheless are continuing to work to increase their representation in their countries' legislatures. In both South Africa and Namibia, for instance, women's groups are mobilizing for 50/50 representation (Britton, 2006:80–83; Bauer, 2006:91–95).

The second question is what impact women in office have on policies. There is a sentiment among a growing number of Africans that women are more honest and less corrupt than men and might do a better job of governing than men. In both Rwanda and Liberia, where devastating civil wars have disillusioned many citizens with men's use of power, both men and women voted women into office. In Rwanda, there is a perception that women also will be better at reconciliation and forgiveness after the 1994 genocide that claimed an estimated 800,000 lives. In Malawi, Gertrude Mdandawire, elected prime minister in 2004, remarked that men have told her that they had wasted a lot of opportunity for development by electing males in the past, and they were ready to give women a chance to do better (Phiri, 2005).

We won't know for some time whether these perceptions about women are correct. Women's ability to create progressive change is likely to vary from country to country. There is evidence, however, that when women are represented beyond token numbers, they are more likely to address such issues as violence toward women, education and health, and women's rights to land and inheritance (Disney, 2006; Bengali, 2005).

Women have also shown themselves to be capable of performing in areas outside of so-called women's issues. One remarkable example of a woman doing a superlative job in a "man's job" is Dora Akunyele of Nigeria. In 2001, Akunyele was appointed to head NAFDAC, Nigeria's agency for drug enforcement and control, and charged with fighting the country's huge counterfeit drug problem (an estimated 80 percent of pharmaceutical drugs were fakes). In three years' time, Akunyele broke the most powerful Nigerian drug cartel, cleaned up the agency, and reduced the amount of fake drugs in the health care system by 80 percent (Hammer, 2006:33–34).

Women's Groups and Gender Reform Efforts

Despite the progress being made, we must not lose sight of the fact that women still have tremendous barriers to advancement, and they still are not regarded as equal to men. Women remain handicapped by a lack of education, and many do not know the rights they officially have. Even if equitable laws and constitutions are on the books, customary laws that deny women equal rights are frequently followed in practice. In cases where women know their rights, social pressures can prevent them from exercising those rights (Mikell, 1997a:341). Even women in power may be expected to act subordinate to men in order to conform to customs of male dominance. In Rwanda, a female senator admitted that she continues to be deferential to her husband when holding official functions in her home in order to conform to norms of male supremacy (Lacey, 2005).

But women are not passive in the face of their adversities. There are a multitude of women's groups across Africa designed to address women's needs and concerns. One way women are empowering themselves is through grassroots self-help groups often formed by poor, peasant women whose needs are so frequently neglected by government, more elite women's groups, or development agencies. These groups provide vital economic assistance, such as credit for farming or business ventures, or other forms of mutual assistance to members (e.g., child care, piped water). They have their roots in precolonial women's groups where women worked together and provided each other assistance within the extended family network or in age-based groups (Enabulele, 1985; Safilios-Rothschild, 1990). For many women, groups are the only way they can get power or the resources they need because husbands have no power over the group as they do over women as wives. Group solidarity also builds women's self-confidence, and many women have found that their efforts have improved their lives and the welfare of their families and communities (Gordon, 1996:89–100; Kabira and Nzioki, 1993:62–64, 73).

Many women and women's groups have been reluctant, however, to challenge the fundamental gender roles that subordinate women to males, and they extol the sexual division of labor that gives wealth and power primarily to men. Because national women's organizations are controlled by more-educated, middle-class women, their interests and agendas have often diverged from those of the masses of less-educated, often rural women who are struggling to survive and take care of their families. Poor women are facing hardships and inequality that is on a much different level than that of more privileged women. Rather than offend the male ruling establishment or customs in their society, women's groups often tend to be antifeminist, and they concentrate on promoting their interests in securing more access to their husband's income, more advantageous marriage and divorce laws, and education in the domestic arts or beauty and fashion (Bujra, 1986; Staudt, 1987; Kabira and Nzioki, 1993).

Some women's groups have been developing their own brand of feminism, however, which they believe is more responsive to African women's interests. But they have typically sought to avoid identification with Western feminism, which has been painted as un-African and too individualistic (Mikell, 1997b:4). These organizations are growing in number and importance as women are struggling for more rights, opportunities, and economic resources. More groups are using the term *feminist* to describe their activities and goals as they recognize that they need to address their subordination to men. There also is growing awareness that gender equality is needed if national economic and political problems are to be solved. Women are learning that they must challenge the male political leaders and institutions that have limited women and often sought to discredit gender reform efforts (Mikell, 1997b:3–5, 31–32). Elite women are crucial to the success of such efforts, because they have the knowledge of politics, the ability to mobilize women, and the personal resources to convince others of the importance of improving the status of women (Toungara, 1997:61).

Some women's groups are confronting controversial social issues such as sexual harassment, domestic violence, female genital circumcision (or mutilation, FGM), and abortion rights. By far, South Africa leads the way in criminalizing violence against women and in advancing women's reproductive rights. Thanks to women's groups, South Africa's Bill of Rights guarantees all citizens the right to make decisions concerning reproduction and the right to access reproductive health services. In 1996, South Africa passed the Choice in Termination of Pregnancy Act, which guarantees abortion on request during the first trimester of pregnancy. Marital and statutory rape also were outlawed in the Prevention of Family Violence Act (Center for Reproductive Law, 1997:94, 98, 104). Women's groups and women parliamentarians in Kenya and Namibia also are calling for legalization of abortion and for laws to stop rape and domestic violence. Most African governments have restrictive laws on abortion and few penalties for violence against women (Mulama, 2004a; LeBeau, 2001).

One of the most divisive issues is FGM, a procedure that an estimated 2 million girls in twenty-six countries in Africa undergo each year (Crawley, 2005). The custom is so entrenched, however, that in many countries both women and men support the practice. Governments are, therefore, reluctant to ban FGM for fear of driving it underground. Most countries are trying instead to use education to discourage the practice and raise awareness of its harmful effects. In some cases, the support of the clergy (especially Muslim clergy) is being enlisted in order to counter the belief that there is a religious justification for FGM (see Rosen and Conly, 1998:56; Center for Reproductive Law, 1997:165). According to some reports, these efforts are paying off, and there is a growing sentiment among Africans to voluntarily stop the practice (Crawley, 2005).

International pressure and the pressure from women's groups to include women in development planning has helped to raise African men's and women's consciousness to the fact that neglecting women and discriminating against them is hurting the entire development effort. Most African governments have now signed the international accord the Convention on the Elimination of All Forms of Discrimination Against Women (CEDAW).

CEDAW has given women's groups the ammunition they need to push for new measures to promote gender equity at all levels of society (Kevane, 2004:185–189). Legal reform in personal law is one such area where change is needed but often difficult to implement or enforce. As mentioned above, African states have had two kinds of laws, often at odds with each other. Inherited from the West are universalistic, secular, common laws that call for equality before the law for all citizens. Existing alongside such laws are customary laws codified during the colonial period to reflect what were perceived (mainly by men) to be African customs. In Islamic areas, these customary laws are often associated with conservative interpretations of Islamic law or *shari'a*. Customary law and *shari'a* are applied to such areas as marriage, divorce, custody, and inheritance and give men considerable power and privilege over women. Such laws can prevent women from inheriting land or cattle, may allow for arranged marriages of girls without their consent, and often forbid married women from entering into contracts without their husband's approval. In many instances, married women have lost all access to marital property, including their homes, if their husbands died without a will naming them as the beneficiary of "his" property.

Mainly since the mid-1980s, many reforms are being made throughout Africa to address these inequalities. In the 1990s, Ethiopia, Ghana, Zimbabwe, and South Africa enacted new constitutions declaring women's equality and proscribing gender discrimination in such areas as property ownership, employment, or marriage rights. Ghana includes women's right to maternity leave in its constitution, and Ethiopia includes the right of women to plan their families. Both Ghana and Ethiopia also have constitutional provisions against traditional practices harmful to women (Center for Reproductive Law, 1997:154, 165). Countries have been changing their laws to improve women's economic and family rights. In Côte d'Ivoire, polygyny and bridewealth are now forbidden (World Bank, 1986:40). In Islamic Senegal, women can no longer legally be married without their consent, men cannot take additional wives without their first wife's consent, and men can no longer repudiate (divorce) their wives unless a judge grants the divorce (Sow, 1989:34–35). Since 1985, Ghana's Intestate Succession and Property Laws require that all customary marriage and family property be registered and distinction made between self-acquired and family property. If a man dies intestate (without a will), his wife and children now get three-quarters of his property; one-quarter goes to his matrikin (i.e., relatives on his mother's side). Previously among Ghana's matrilineal ethnic groups, most of a man's estate could be taken by his mother's side of the family, leaving his wife and children with little or nothing (Dei, 1994:132–133). Kenya's 1994–1996 national economic program called for joint family decisionmaking on land use and an equal distribution of economic benefits between spouses (Munyakho, 1994:8–9).

Zimbabwe's 1997 Estates Act has been called "revolutionary." A man's surviving spouse and children are automatically his beneficiaries when he dies. The matrimonial home remains with the surviving spouse along with all household goods. A spouse subject to customary law can inherit from a deceased spouse even if he or she dies intestate.

In 1997, the member countries of SADC agreed to reform all laws, constitutional provisions, and social practices that are discriminatory to women. Promoting gender equality would include advancing women's access to productive resources and attacking violence against women (Kevane, 2004:188). Kenya's proposed 2005 constitution also included provisions to guarantee women more property and inheritance rights and discourage widow inheritance, which forces women to marry a male relative of deceased husbands (Mulama, 2004b).

These and similar measures occurring all over Africa represent a growing awareness among African governments that they must develop more equitable laws "to facilitate the development of both men and women" and to avoid "the risk of losing another generation of girls to a life of inequality and powerlessness" (Gopal and Salim, 1998:vi–vii, 109). These legal reforms will be meaningless, however, if they are not enforced and customary law is allowed to take precedence over more equitable statutory (common) laws. In Zimbabwe, despite recent estate reform, women are otherwise still excluded from control over land and cattle, and women's access to economic resources largely remains through men. In legal disputes, judges tend to side with those upholding patriarchal privilege. For example, in a 1999 Supreme Court case in Zimbabwe, the court overturned the right to inherit property that women had gained. The case involved a daughter's claims to her father's estate after her brother evicted her. The (male) judges ruled that "The nature of African society relegates women to a lesser status, especially in the family. A woman should not be considered an adult but only a junior male" (in Kevane, 2004:191). Such cases point out, as Gopal and Salim (1998:102–103) have noted, that "there seems to be an almost impenetrable mental barrier grounded in gender socialization that precludes even liberal male judges from stepping outside the ingrained notions of male superiority and female subservience in marriage."

In conclusion, some countries are making efforts to improve women's rights and opportunities. The rate and extent of change are highly variable across the continent, however, and there is often considerable resistance to reforms that would undermine "traditional" male dominance over the household and male control over economic and political power and resources. Moreover, legal rights, while important, can result in little improvement in women's lives if they are not enforced and if access to education, health and reproductive services, training, and productive resources are not made more available to women as well.

April Gordon

Although computer use is exploding in Africa, it will take a concerted effort to ensure that both girls and boys benefit equally from today's essential communications technologies.

Prospects for African Women

The evidence on the status of women in Africa continues to warrant concern about the future. Although having an education and/or affluent parents or spouses improves women's opportunities, the vast majority of women are limited by both economic underdevelopment and sex discrimination. Consequently, most women will, for the foreseeable future, continue to have a very difficult existence. Most women will have few options but to attempt to survive as subsistence farmers or in the urban informal economy. Policymakers are recognizing, however, that achieving sustainable development will require helping these women to become more productive and empowered members in all areas of social life. As top African economists have noted, gender inequality in education and employment have reduced Africa's economic growth by a stunning 0.8 percent a year since the 1960s (Gender Equity, 2004), and the World Bank (2005) adds that gender equality is essential to reducing poverty and reversing Africa's economic stagnation. Neglecting the talents and skills of women to protect men's privileges is an enormous waste of human resources that Africa—with its vast potential—can no longer afford.

Bibliography

"African Leaders Vow to Promote Gender Equality." 2004. *Xinhua News Agency* (July 9).

Amadiume, Ifi. 1987. *Male Daughters, Female Husbands: Gender and Sex in an African Society.* London: Zed.

Bauer, Gretchen. 2006. "Losing Ground Without Mandatory Quotas." Pp. 85–110 in Gretchen Bauer and Hannah E. Britton (eds.). *Women in African Parliaments.* Boulder, CO: Lynne Rienner Publishers.

Bengali, Shashank. 2005. "Victory a Symbol of Women's Progress." *The Charlotte Observer,* November 20, 26A.

Bernal, Victoria. 1988. "Losing Ground—Women and Agriculture on Sudan's Irrigated Schemes: Lessons from a Blue Nile Village." Pp. 131–156 in Jean Davison (ed.). *Agriculture, Women, and Land: The African Experience.* Boulder, CO: Westview Press.

Blumberg, Rae Lesser. 1995. "Introduction: Engendering Wealth and Well-Being in an Era of Economic Transformation." Pp. 1–14 in Rae Lesser Blumberg, Cathy A. Rakowski, Irene Tinker, and Michael Monteon (eds.). *Engendering Wealth and Well-Being: Empowerment for Global Change.* Boulder, CO: Westview Press.

Boserup, Ester. 1970. *Women's Role in Economic Development.* London: Allen and Unwin.

Britton, Hannah E. 2006. "South Africa: Mainstreaming Gender in a New Democracy." Pp. 59–84 in Gretchen Bauer and Hannah E. Britton (eds.). *Women in African Parliaments.* Boulder, CO: Lynne Rienner Publishers.

Bujra, Jane B. 1986. "Urging Women to Redouble Their Efforts: Class, Gender, and Capitalist Transformation in Africa." Pp. 117–140 in Claire Robertson and Iris Berger (eds.). *Women and Class in Africa.* New York: Africana.

Carney, Judith A. 1988. "Struggles over Land and Crops in an Irrigated Rice Scheme: The Gambia." Pp. 59–78 in Jean Davison (ed.). *Agriculture, Women, and Land: The African Experience.* Boulder, CO: Westview Press.

Center for Reproductive Law and Policy and the International Federation of Women Lawyers (Kenya Chapter). 1997. *Women of the World: Laws and Policies Affecting Their Reproductive Lives—Anglophone Africa.* New York: Center for Reproductive Law and Policy.

Chanock, Martin. 1982. "Making Customary Law: Men, Women, and Courts in Colonial Northern Rhodesia." Pp. 53–67 in Margaret Jean Hay and Marcia Wright (eds.). *African Women and the Law: Historical Perspectives.* Boston University Papers on Africa 7.

Crawley, Mike. 2005. "Africa Spurns Female Circumcision." *Christian Science Monitor.* Online at www.csmonitor.com (April 5).

Creevey, Lucy. 2006. "Senegal: Contending with Religious Constraints." Pp. 151–170 in Gretchen Bauer and Hannah E. Britton (eds.). *Women in African Parliaments.* Boulder, CO: Lynne Rienner Publishers.

Cutrufelli, Maria R. 1983. *Women of Africa: Roots of Oppression.* London: Zed.

Davison, Jean. 1988. "Who Owns What? Land Registration and Tensions in Gender Relations of Production in Kenya." Pp. 157–176 in Jean Davison (ed.). *Agriculture, Women, and Land: The African Experience.* Boulder, CO: Westview Press.

Dei, George J. Sefa. 1994. "The Women of a Ghanaian Village: A Study of Social Change." *African Studies Review* 37 (September):121–145.

Disney, Jennifer Leigh. 2006. "Mozambique: Empowering Women Through Family Law." Pp. 31–58 in Gretchen Bauer and Hannah E. Britton (eds.). *Women in African Parliaments.* Boulder, CO: Lynne Rienner Publishers.

Enabulele, Arlene Bene. 1985. "The Role of Women's Associations in Nigeria's Development: Social Welfare Perspective." Pp. 187–194 in *Women in Nigeria Today.* London: Zed.

Faruqee, Rashid, and Ravi Gulhati. 1983. *Rapid Population Growth in Sub-Saharan Africa: Issues and Policies.* Working Paper No. 559. Washington, DC: World Bank.

"Gender Equity Crucial for Africa's Economic Development." 2004. Xinhua News Agency (May 25).

Goheen, Miriam. 1988. "Land and the Household Economy: Women Farmers of the Grassfields Today." Pp. 90–105 in Jean Davison (ed.). *Agriculture, Women, and Land: The African Experience.* Boulder, CO: Westview Press.

Gopal, Gita, and Maryann Salim (eds.). 1998. *Gender and Law: East Africa Speaks.* Washington, DC: World Bank.

Gordon, April. 1996. *Transforming Capitalism and Patriarchy: Gender and Development in Africa.* Boulder, CO: Lynne Rienner Publishers.

———. 2001. "Women and Sustainable Development in Africa." Pp. 213–237 in Obioma M. Iheduru (ed.). *Contending Issues in African Development: Advances, Challenges, and the Future.* Westport, CT: Greenwood.

Green, Cynthia P. (ed.). 1994. *Sustainable Development: Population and the Environment.* Washington, DC: USAID.

Guyer, Jane I. 1984. *Family and Farm in Southern Cameroon.* Boston: Boston University, African Studies Center.

Hammer, Joshua. 2006. "Healing Powers." *Newsweek* (April 3):30–39.

Hammond, Dorothy, and Alta Jablow. 1970. *The Africa That Never Was.* New York: Twayne Publishers.

Hansen, Karen T. 1987. "Urban Women and Work in Africa: A Zambian Case." *TransAfrica Forum* 4 (Spring):9–24.

"Historical Moves Towards Gender Equality in Africa." 2002. *Africa News Service* (July 15).

Jacobson, Jodi L. 1993. "Closing the Gender Gap in Development." Pp. 61–79 in Lester Brown, Gary Gardner, and Brian Halweil (eds.). *State of the World.* New York: W. W. Norton.

Kabira, Wanjiku M., and Elizabeth A. Nzioki. 1993. *Celebrating Women's Resistance: A Case Study of Women's Group Movement in Kenya.* Nairobi: African Women's Perspective.

Kettel, Bonnie. 1986. "The Commoditization of Women in Tugen (Kenya) Social Organization." Pp. 47–61 in Claire Robertson and Iris Berger (eds.). *Women and Class in Africa.* New York: Africana.

Kevane, Michael. 2004. *Women and Development in Africa: How Gender Works.* Boulder, CO: Lynne Rienner Publishers.

Lacey, Marc. 2005. "Women's Voices Rise as Rwanda Reinvents Itself." *The New York Times.* Online at www.nytimes.com (February 26).

Langley, Philip. 1983. "A Preliminary Approach to Women and Development. Getting a Few Facts Right." Pp. 79–100 in Gerard M. Ssenkoloto (ed.). *The Roles of Women in the Process of Development.* Douala, Cameroon: Pan African Institute for Development.

LeBeau, Debie. 2001. "The Changing Status of Women in Namibia and Its Impact on Violence Against Women." Pp. 185–206 in Ingolf Diener and Olivier Graefe (eds.). *Contemporary Namibia: The First Landmarks of a Post-Apartheid Society.* Windhoek: Gamsberg Macmillan Publishers.

Longman, Timothy. 2006. "Rwanda: Achieving Equality or Serving an Authoritarian State?" Pp. 133–150 in Gretchen Bauer and Hannah E. Britton (eds.). *Women in African Parliaments.* Boulder, CO: Lynne Rienner Publishers.

Lovett, Margot. 1989. "Gender Relations, Class Formation, and the Colonial State in Africa." Pp. 23–46 in Jane L. Parpart and Kathleen A. Staudt (eds.). *Women and the State in Africa.* Boulder, CO: Lynne Rienner Publishers.

Malindi, Grace Margaret. 1995. "Participation of Rural Women in Malawi National Rural Development Program." Pp. 113–131 in Valentine Udoh James (ed.). *Women and Sustainable Development in Africa.* Westport, CT: Praeger.

Meena, Ruth. 1989. "Crisis and Structural Adjustment: Tanzanian Women's Politics." *Issue: A Journal of Opinion* 17 (2) (Summer):29–31.

Mikell, Gwendolyn. 1997a. "Conclusions: Theorizing and Strategizing About Women and State Crisis." Pp. 333–348 in Gwendolyn Mikell (ed.). *African Feminism: The Politics of Survival in Sub-Saharan Africa.* Philadelphia: University of Pennsylvania Press.

———. 1997b. "Introduction." Pp. 1–50 in Gwendolyn Mikell (ed.). *African Feminism: The Politics of Survival in Sub-Saharan Africa.* Philadelphia: University of Pennsylvania Press.

Moghadan, Valentine M. 2005. *Globalizing Women: Transnational Feminist Networks.* Baltimore: Johns Hopkins University Press.

Morna, Colleen Lowe. 1995. "Plus ça Change." *African Report* 40 (January-February):55–59.

Mulama, Joyce. 2004a. "Kenyan Activists Press for Abortion Debate." *Mail & Guardian online* (South Africa). Online at www.mg.co.za (February 5).

———. 2004b. "New Constitution Takes Up Cudgels for Women." *Mail & Guardian online* (South Africa). Online at www.mg.co.za (May 27).

Munyakho, Dorothy. 1994. "Kenyan Women Press for Land Rights." *African Farmer* (April):8–9.

Newland, Kathleen. 1991. "From Transnational Relationships to International Relations: Women in Development and the International Decade for Women." Pp. 122–132 in Rebecca Grant and Kathleen Newland (eds.). *Gender and International Relations.* Bloomington: Indiana University Press.

"New Strategy Promotes Partnerships for Gender and Women's Advancement in Africa." 2004. *Africa News Service* (February 26).

"Number of Women in New SA Parliament up by Ten Percent." 2004. *Sister Namibia* (July):28.

Nweke, Therese. 1985. "The Role of Women in Nigerian Society: The Media." Pp. 201–207 in *Women in Nigeria Today.* London: Zed.

Nwomonoh, Jonathan. 1995. "African Women in Production: The Economic Role of Rural Women." Pp. 171–181 in Valentine Udoh James (ed.). *Women and Sustainable Development in Africa.* Westport, CT: Praeger.

Nzomo, Maria. 1989. "The Impact of the Women's Decade on Policies, Programs and Empowerment of Women in Kenya." *Issue: A Journal of Opinion* 17 (2) (Summer):9–17.

Obadina, Elizabeth. 1985. "How Relevant Is the Western Women's Liberation Movement for Nigeria?" Pp. 138–142 in *Women in Nigeria Today*. London: Zed.

Pankhurst, Donna, and Susie Jacobs. 1988. "Land Tenure, Gender Relations, and Agricultural Production: The Case of Zimbabwe's Peasantry." Pp. 202–227 in Jean Davison (ed.). *Agriculture, Women, and Land: The African Experience*. Boulder, CO: Westview Press.

Parpart, Jane L. 1988. "Women and the State in Africa." Pp. 208–230 in Donald Rothchild and Naomi Chazan (eds.). *The Precarious Balance: State and Society in Africa*. Boulder, CO: Westview Press.

Phiri, Frank. 2005. "Catching Up with Malawi's Female Legislators." *Mail & Guardian online* (South Africa). Online at www.mg.co.za (December 13).

Picard, Mary Theresa. 1995. "Listening to and Learning from African Women Farmers." Pp. 35–62 in Valentine Udoh James (ed.). *Women and Sustainable Development in Africa*. Westport, CT: Praeger.

Rosen, James E., and Shanti R. Conly. 1998. *Africa's Population Challenge: Accelerating Progress in Reproductive Health*. Washington, DC: Population Action International.

Safilios-Rothschild, Constantina. 1990. "Women's Groups: An Underutilized Grassroots Institution." Pp. 102–108 in *The Long-Term Perspective Study of Sub-Saharan Africa*. Vol. 3. Washington, DC: World Bank.

Schuster, Ilsa M. G. 1982. "Marginal Lives: Conflict and Contradiction in the Position of Female Traders in Lusaka, Zambia." Pp. 105–126 in Edna G. Bay (ed.). *Women and Work in Africa*. Boulder, CO: Westview Press.

Sengupta, Somini. 2003. "School Merely a Dream for Many Girls in Africa." *The Charlotte Observer*. Online at www.charlotte.com (December 14).

Sow, Fatou. 1989. "Senegal: The Decade and Its Consequences." *Issue: A Journal of Opinion* 17 (2):32–36.

Staudt, Kathleen. 1987. "Women's Politics, the State, and Capitalist Transformation in Africa." Pp. 193–208 in Irving L. Markovitz (ed.). *Studies in Power and Class in Africa*. New York: Oxford University Press.

Toungara, Jeanne Maddox. 1997. "Changing the Meaning of Marriage: Women and Family Law in Côte d'Ivoire." Pp. 53–76 in Gwendolyn Mikell (ed.). *African Feminism: The Politics of Survival in Sub-Saharan Africa*. Philadelphia: University of Pennsylvania Press.

World Bank. 1986. *Population Growth and Policies in Sub-Saharan Africa*. Washington, DC: World Bank.

———. 1989. *Sub-Saharan Africa: From Crisis to Sustainable Growth: A Long-Term Perspective Study*. Washington, DC: World Bank.

———. 1990. *Women in Development: A Progress Report on the World Bank Initiative*. Washington, DC: World Bank.

———. 1996. *Toward Environmentally Sustainable Development in Sub-Saharan Africa: A World Bank Agenda*. Washington, DC: World Bank.

———. 2000. *Can Africa Claim the 21st Century?* Washington, DC: World Bank.

———. 2001. *World Development Report 2000/2001*. New York: Oxford University Press.

———. 2005. "Regional Briefs: Africa." Online at www.web.worldbank.org.

11

Religion in Africa

Ambrose Moyo

The importance of religion in any attempt to understand African life in all its social, economic, and political aspects cannot be overemphasized. Mbiti's (1969:1) observation that African people are "notoriously religious," consciously or unconsciously, is still true of a large majority of people, urban or rural, educated or less educated. Even those who claim to be atheist, agnostic, or antireligion, of whom there is a growing number, often have no option but to participate in extended family activities, some of which require the invocation of supernatural powers. Religion permeates all aspects of African traditional societies. It is a way of life in which the whole community is involved, and as such it is identical with life itself. Even antireligious persons still have to be involved in the lives of their religious communities, because in terms of African thought, life can be meaningful only in community, not in isolation.

Because of the size of the African continent and the great diversity of religious traditions, with variations even within the same tradition, it would be an impossible task to cover the subject of this chapter in one volume, let alone in one chapter of a book. Consequently, this chapter is a survey of the following three principal religious traditions on the continent: (1) the African indigenous religious beliefs and practices that, for lack of a better term, have been called in Africa scholarship African Traditional Religions (Idowu, 1971); (2) Christianity, including its expressions in the African indigenous Christian movements; and (3) Islam. There are other religious traditions practiced on the continent, such as Hinduism, Buddhism, Judaism, and Baha'i, but they are practiced by small minorities that include few indigenous African people (Barrett, 1982:782).

The study of the Christian and Islamic traditions poses no insurmountable difficulties with regard to our sources of information. Both have their sacred books, namely the Old and New Testaments for Christianity, and the Quran for Islam. The founders of these two traditions, their primary sources, and their geographical origins remain the same for all the adherents of these faiths regardless of the different interpretations. African Traditional Religions have no sacred books, their beginnings cannot be pinpointed, and each of the many traditions is practiced by one African group with no reference whatsoever to the religion practiced by other groups. Each African group exists as a complete social, economic, religious, and political entity with no missionary designs. With the many basic, common elements, there are also some differences in religious beliefs and practices that speak against generalizations. As unrelated and independent as African groups may appear, they nonetheless share some of the same basic religious beliefs and practices. These common, basic features suggest a common background or origin and lead to African Traditional Religions being treated as a single religious tradition, just as Christianity and Islam have many denominations or sects within themselves but continue to be treated as single entities.

Since this chapter is only a survey and an introduction to African religions, the need is to concentrate on the basic, common elements and point out some of the significant differences as we go along.

Perhaps a question may be raised concerning our sources of informa-

Jason Lauré, Impact Visuals

Many African societies have used masks to represent ancestors and other spiritual figures. These dancers are Dogon of Mali.

tion on African Traditional Religions since there are no sacred scriptures or clearly defined and documented dogmas. Indeed, many studies have recently appeared on different aspects of African Traditional Religions, but hardly any of them speak from the tradition they present. They are primarily the works of sociologists, anthropologists, and theologians, many of whom have had little or no experience of these religions as their own faith. Consequently, the African arts, paintings, sculptures, music and dance, myths and rituals, archaeological findings, and oral tradition become extremely important as sources of information. We begin our survey with African Traditional Religions, and the examples used will be drawn from the sub-Saharan region.

African Traditional Religions

Although African Traditional Religions have no sacred books or definitive creeds upon which to base any analysis of these religions, from the sources referred to above, the following religious phenomena seem to be basic and common to most of them: (a) belief in a supreme being, (b) belief in spirits/divinities, (c) belief in life after death, (d) religious personnel and sacred places, and (e) witchcraft and magic practices. This section of the survey will focus on these aspects of African Traditional Religions.

Belief in the Supreme Being

The African perception of the universe is centered on the belief in a supreme being who is the creator and sustainer of the universe. God, as far as the African traditionalist is concerned, is the ground of all being. Humanity is inseparably bound together with all of God's creation since they both derive their lives from God, the source of all life. This strong belief in God appears to be universal in traditional societies. The question to be asked is: How is this God perceived?

Names in African societies tell a whole story about the family—its history, relationships, hopes, and aspirations. African societies have so much to tell about God as they relate to God; hence, each society has many names for the Supreme Being. These names are expressions of the different forms in which God relates to creation. In other words, God in African traditional thought can only be known in the different relationships as expressed in God's names. For example, among my people in Zimbabwe, God is *Musikavanhu* (creator of humankind) and *Musiki/uMdali* (creator), which affirms that God is the originator of all there is. But *Musikavanhu* goes beyond the idea of creator to the notion of the parenthood of God. Hence, God is also designated *Mudzimu Mukuru* (the Great Ancestor). As parent, God is also the sustainer of creation. God's creativity is continuous and is celebrated with every new birth, and each rite of passage is an expression of gratitude to God for having sustained the individual and the community that far. These names also affirm the belief in the continuous creativity of God. Similarly, in the names *Chidziva Chepo* or *Dzinaguru,* God is perceived as the giver and the source of water. Each time it rains, God is sustaining creation in a visible way. This explains, in ceremonies relating to drought, why people appeal directly to God. So also the name *Samasimba* (owner of power/almighty) affirms God not only as the most powerful being but also as the source and owner of all power.

The African traditionalist does not perceive God as some supreme being in merely speculative terms. African thought in general is not given to speculation. That which is real has to be experienced in real-life situations, directly or indirectly. God can, therefore, be real only insofar as God has been experienced in concrete life situations in different relationships with people and the rest of creation. In other words, African traditional thought cannot conceive of God in abstract terms as some being who exists as an idea mysteriously related to this world—distant, unconcerned, uninterested in what goes on here below. African thought can express itself only in concrete and practical terms. Consequently, Africans' view of God can arise only out of concrete and practical relationships as God meets their needs. In that way, they experience God's love and power (see McVeigh, 1974; Mbiti, 1970).

In terms of African thought, there can be only one Supreme Being. Interestingly enough, before the encounter with Christianity, some African societies already had some concept of the Trinity. This seems to have been the case in some African societies, as demonstrated by Twesigye (1987:93) in his research into his people's traditional religions in southern and western Uganda. In an interview with an old traditionalist, Mr. Antyeri Bintukwanga, Twesigye uncovered the following information:

> Before the Europeans came to Uganda and before the white Christian missionaries came to our land of Enkole or your homeland of Kigezi, we had our own religion and we knew God well. We knew God so well that the missionaries added to us little. . . . We even knew God to be some kind of externally existing triplets: *Nyamuhanga* being the first one and being also the creator of everything, *Kazooba Nyamuhanga* being his second brother who gives light to all human beings so that they should not stumble either on the path or even in their lives. . . . *Kazooba's* light penetrates the hearts of people and God sees the contents of the human hearts by *Kazooba*'s eternal light. . . . The third brother in the group is *Rugaba Rwa Nyamuhanga,* who takes what *Nyamuhanga* has created and gives it to the people as he wishes. . . . You see! We had it all before the missionaries came, and all they did teach us was that *Nyamuhanga* is God the Father, *Kazooba* Jesus Christ his son and not his brother as we thought, and that *Rugaba* as the divine giver is the Holy Spirit. (Twesigye, 1987:93)

In traditional societies, God is believed to be eternal, loving, and just, the creator and sustainer of the universe. God's existence is simply taken for granted, hence the absence of arguments for or against the existence of God. Atheism is foreign to African thought. The most widely used name for God among my people is *Mwari,* which means literally "the one who is."

A question often raised is whether God is actually worshiped in African Traditional Religions. Some Western observers have concluded that African people do not worship God but rather have no religion at all, are animists, or worship ancestor spirits or many gods. This issue will be examined in conjunction with the discussion on ancestors and lesser divinities in the next section.

Belief in Divinities and Spirits

The Supreme Being is believed to be surrounded by a host of supernatural or spiritual powers of different types and functions. Their nature, number, and functions vary from region to region, and they may be either male or female, just as God in many African traditions is perceived as being both male and female. The numerous divinities, called *orisha* among the Yoruba in Nigeria or *bosom* among the Akan of Ghana (and sometimes referred to as "lesser divinities" in order not to confuse them with the Supreme Being), are found in most western African traditions but generally not in eastern and southern African traditions. These *orisha* are subordinate to the Supreme Being. They are believed to be servants or messengers of *Olodumare* (God). God has assigned to each one of them specific areas of responsibility. For example, the divinity *Orun-mila* is responsible for all forms of knowledge, and he is therefore associated with divination and the oracle at Ile-Ife in Nigeria. The *orisha* are believed either to have emanated from the Supreme Being or to be deified human beings. Some of the divinities are associated with the sky, earth, stars, moon, trees, mountains, rivers, and other natural elements (see Idowu, 1962).

Perhaps more universal among African traditionalists is the belief in ancestor spirits, called *vadzimu* among the Shona people of Zimbabwe or *amadhozi* among the Zulu/Ndebele traditions. These are spirits of the deceased mothers and fathers who are recognized in a special ceremony, held usually a year after they have died. This ceremony is called *umbuyiso* (the bringing-home ceremony) in Zulu/Ndebele or *kurova guva* by the Zezuru. From that moment, the deceased person becomes an active "living dead" member of the community and is empowered to function as a guardian spirit and to mediate with God and other ancestors on behalf of his or her descendants. Among my own people, it is to these spirits that most prayers and sacrifices are made, but often the prayers are concluded by instructing the ancestors to take the prayers and offerings to

Musikavanhu (creator of humankind) or *Nyadenga* (the owner of the sky/heavens).

The significance of ancestors among Africans has led to the common misconception that these spirits are worshiped. Traditionalists will categorically deny that they worship their ancestor spirits but rather worship God through them. Ancestor spirits are departed elders. African peoples in general have a very high respect for elders. If, for example, one has grievously wronged his or her parents, it would be utterly disrespectful and unacceptable to go directly and ask for forgiveness. One would have to go through some respectable elderly person to whom one would give some token of repentance to take to the parent. Similarly, when a young man and his fiancée decide to get married, the prospective father-in-law will have to be approached by the young man's parents through a carefully chosen and respectable mediator. In the same spirit, a person cannot approach a chief or king directly but must have his or her case taken to the chief through a subchief. Even more so, God—the transcendent, the greatest and most powerful being, the Great Ancestor and creator of all—must be approached through intermediaries. The ancestor spirits are believed to be closest to both their living descendants and to the Supreme Being and are thus most qualified to function as intermediaries.

Ancestor spirits are not the objects of worship. They are guardian spirits and intermediaries. They are believed to be responsible to God for all their actions. As family elders they must be respected, and if not, they too, just like the living elders, can get angry and demand that they be appeased. Quite often, the name of the Supreme Being is not mentioned in petitions; still, it is believed that God is the ultimate recipient of all prayer and sacrifices. Although not worshiped, the ancestors in some traditions are closely associated with the Supreme Being, so much so that it becomes difficult to determine in some of the prayers whether the address is to God or to the ancestor. Take, for example, the following prayer of the Shilluk, who rarely address God directly. Nyikang is the founding ancestor of the Shilluk.

> There is no one above you, O God (Juok). You became the grandfather of Nyikang; it is you Nyikang who walk with God, you became the grandfather of man. If famine comes, is it not given by you? . . . We praise you who are God. Protect us, we are in your hands, and protect us, save me. You and Nyikang, you are the ones who created. . . . The cow for sacrifice is here for you, and the blood will go to God and you. (Parrinder, 1969:69)

One of my Shona informants told me that, as far as the Shona are concerned, God and the ancestors are one; an address to one is an address to the other. This means that even if at times one does not hear the name of God mentioned, it does not mean the people do not worship God. God and ancestors are closely associated and work very closely with each other. For example, they believe that children are a gift of *Mwari* (God) and the *vadzimu* (ancestors). So frequently one will hear the people say *kana Mwari nevadzimu vachida* ("if God and the ancestors are willing"). When faced with misfortune, they will say: *Ko Mwari wati ndaita sei?* ("What crime does God accuse me of?"), or they will say *mudzimu yafuratira* ("the ancestors have turned their backs"; that is, on the individual or family, hence the misfortune) (Moyo, 1987).

There are different categories of ancestor spirits. There are family ancestors, family being understood in its extended sense. These have responsibility over the members of their families only, and it is only to them that the members can bring their petitions, never to the ancestors of other families. Then there are ancestors whose responsibilities extend over the whole tribe and not just over their own immediate families. These relate to the founders of the tribe and are represented by the royal house. These play an active role in matters that affect the entire community or tribe, such as drought or some epidemic. They are called *Mhondoros* (lion spirits) among the Shona people.

Most significantly, ancestor spirits serve as intermediaries. However, there are times when most of the African peoples will pray and make sacrifices to God directly. When, for example, one is in critical danger—face-to-face with some man-eating animal, or when thunder and lightning strike, or drowning—then one would approach God directly.

Belief in Life After Death

Death is believed to have come into the world as an intrusion. Human beings were originally meant to live forever through rejuvenation or some form of resurrection. So, most African peoples have myths that intend to explain the origin of death. There are, for example, some myths that depict death as having come in because some mischievous animal cut the rope or removed the ladder linking heaven, the abode of the Supreme Being, and earth, the abode of humankind. Such a rope or ladder allowed people to ascend to and descend from heaven for rejuvenation. Other myths see death as punishment from God for human disobedience. God and human beings lived together until a tragic event that led to the intervention of death, which then separated God and people.

Despite the loss of the original state of bliss and the intervention of death, it is generally believed that there is still life beyond the grave, that life may take several forms. In some traditions, the dead may be reincarnated in the form of an animal such as a lion, a rabbit, or a snake. In that form one cannot be killed, and if reborn as a lion, one can protect one's descendants from the danger of other animals. Or the person may be reincarnated in one of his or her descendants. In general, people believe there is a world of the ancestors, and when one dies, one goes on a long journey to get to that world. The world of the ancestors is conceived of in terms of this world; hence, people are buried with some of their utensils and implements. That world is also thought of as overlapping with this world, and ancestors are believed to be a part of the community of the living. The terms *living dead* or *the shades* are approximately accurate English renderings of those invisible members of the community (see Mbiti, 1969; Berglund, 1976).

That there is life after death is also affirmed in the belief that a dead person can return to punish those who have wronged him or her while still alive. One of the most feared spirits among the Shona is the *ngozi,* a vengeful spirit that will kill members of the family of the person who wronged the individual while still alive until payment or retribution has been made.

In general, people believe they are surrounded by a cloud of ancestors with whom they must share everything they have, including their joys and frustrations. Their expectation of the hereafter is thought of in terms of what people already know and have experienced. People know there is a future life because they interact with their departed ancestors through spirit mediums.

Religious Leadership and Sacred Places

There are different types of religious leaders in African Traditional Religions. These can be either male or female. Where the tradition has regular shrines for specific deities, there will be some resident cultic officials. At the shrine at Matongeni in Zimbabwe, for example, the priestly community is made up of both males and females, with roles clearly defined. The Yoruba and the Akan have regular cultic officials presiding at the shrines of their divinities. They offer sacrifices and petitions on behalf of their clients. Among most of the Bantu-speaking peoples, heads of families also carry out priestly functions on matters that relate to their families.

Another category of religious leadership, perhaps the most powerful, is that of spirit mediums. These are individual members of the family or clan through whom the spirit of an ancestor communicates with its descendants. They can be either male or female, but most are female. Among these are family spirit mediums and the tribal or territorial spirit mediums such as Mbuya (grandmother) Nehanda in Zimbabwe. The territorial spirits wield a great deal of power, and, to use the example of Zimbabwe, they played a very significant political role in mobilizing people in their struggles for liberation from colonialism. The first war of liberation in Zimbabwe (then Southern Rhodesia) was led by Mbuya Nehanda, a spirit medium who was eventually hanged by the colonial regime. During the time of the second war of liberation, her mediums as well as other spirit mediums worked very closely with the freedom fighters by mobilizing the people and sanctioning the war. The freedom fighters, most of whom claimed to be Marxist-Leninist, soon discovered that they could not wage a successful war without the support of the spirit mediums (Ranger, 1985:175–222; Lan, 1985). Thus, the mediums have political as well as religious roles to play. Through these mediums, people discern the will of the ancestors, get an explanation for the causes of whatever calamities they may be enduring, or obtain advice on what the family or the tribe should do in order to avert similar danger. Mediums are highly respected members of the community from whom people seek advice of any nature.

The other important category of religious leaders is that of the diviner. Again, diviners may be either male or female. Communication with the spirit world is vital for African Traditional Religions. Through divination, people are able to communicate with their ancestral spirits and the divinities. These are consulted in the event of some misfortune, sickness, death, or calamity. They communicate with the spirit world to determine the cause of the problem and to seek possible solutions. There are different methods of divining, using, for example, palm nuts, bones, a bowl of water, wooden dice carved with animals and reptiles, sea shells, or pieces of ivory. Divination would normally be conducted at some location such as a hut set aside for that purpose. In Yorubaland, Ifa divination centered at Ile-Ife is the most famous. The system is very elaborate and uses palm nuts (Awulalu, 1979; Bascom, 1969).

Finally, since religion permeates all aspects of life, the kings and the chiefs also carry out some leadership roles. Where the whole nation or tribe is involved, it is the responsibility of the head of the community to take the necessary action to consult the national or territorial spirits. It is also their duty to ensure that all the religious functions and observances are carried out by the responsible authorities.

With regard to sacred places, reference has already been made to shrines that serve particular divinities such as those among the Yoruba of Nigeria or the Akan of Ghana. Among the Zulus of South Africa, there is a room in each homestead with an elevated portion *(umsamu)* where rituals to the ancestor spirits are performed. The cattle kraal is also associated with ancestors and is therefore an important place for ritual action. Sacred mountains and caves are almost universal among African peoples. They are often associated with ancestors or any of the divinities. Religious officials will ascend these mountains or go into those caves only on special occasions. Such mountains are also often associated with the abode of the Supreme Being. In Zimbabwe, there are several such mountains that serve as venues for prayer and sacrifice, particularly in connection with prayers for rain in cases of severe drought.

Witchcraft and Magic

To complete our study of the African Traditional Religions, it is also necessary to look at the negative forces in these religious traditions. African traditionalists believe that God is the source of all power, which God shares with other beings. The power of the divinities and ancestors, or that derived from medicine, is primarily viewed as positive power to be used for constructive purposes. However, that same power can also be used for destructive purposes, in which case it becomes evil power. Witches and sorcerers represent those elements within African societies that use power for the purpose of destroying life. (In general, witches are female and sorcerers are male.)

Witchcraft beliefs are widespread in Africa even among educated Christians and Muslims. It is generally believed that witches can fly by night, can become invisible, delight in eating human flesh, and use familiar animals such as hyenas or baboons as their means of transport. Witches are believed to be wicked and malicious human beings whose intention is simply to kill, which they do by poisoning or cursing their victims. Witches, sorcerers, and angry ancestor spirits are usually identified as the major causes of misfortune or death in a family.

Magic has two aspects: to protect or to harm. On the one hand, it is used to protect the members of the family, as well as their homestead, cattle, and other property, from witches and other enemies of the family or the individual. On the other hand, magic can also be used through spells and curses to harm or to kill. Beliefs related to magic and witchcraft clearly belong to the category of superstition. They represent ways in which people try to explain the causes of misfortune or social disorders. Misfortune, sickness, or death may also be explained as an expression of one's ancestors' displeasure regarding the behavior of their descendants (see Evans-Pritchard, 1937).

In conclusion, it must be stated that African Traditional Religions continue to influence the lives of many people today, including some of the highly educated as well as many African Christians and Muslims. It must also be pointed out that African religions are not static. Contacts with Christian and Islamic traditions have brought about transformations and syncretism in all three. As Bohannan and Curtin (1995:124) have remarked, "There is an amazingly close overlap between the basic ideas of Islam and Christianity, and of the African religions. Neither Islam nor Christianity is foreign in its essence to African religious ideas"; the reverse is also true. Although Christianity and Islam have added distinct elements to African religions, each has been and continues to be adapted to and shaped by Africa's indigenous religious heritage, as will be shown in the following sections.

Christianity in Africa

Christianity is one of the oldest religions in Africa, and since the 1800s, the number of Christians and Christian churches has expanded rapidly. By some estimates there are 360 million Christians in Africa, a number that may almost double to 633 million Christians by 2025 (Rice, 2004). This makes Christianity the largest religion in sub-Saharan Africa. Recently, growth has been most noticeable in the African Independent Churches (denominations or churches that separated from the European-dominated churches) and in foreign-based evangelical Protestant churches. Since so much has been written on Christianity as a religion, it is not necessary for our purpose to deal with its beliefs, so I will focus instead on the historical development of the religion on the African continent. Special attention will be paid to those aspects that give African Christianity its own identity.

Early Christianity in North Africa and Ethiopia

Christianity in Egypt dates back to the first century. According to the ancient historian Eusebius, writing about A.D. 311, the Christian church in Egypt was founded by St. Mark, author of the second Gospel and a companion of Paul, a tradition still maintained by the Coptic (Egyptian) church. By the end of the first century, Christianity had penetrated into rural Egypt and had become the religion of the majority of the people. Egypt has one of the oldest Christian churches, surpassed perhaps only by Rome in terms of longevity of tradition and continuity in the same locality (King, 1971:1). Recent discoveries of some Christian and non-Christian documents at the Nag Hammadi caves in Egypt show that quite early in the history of Christianity, Egypt had become a center for many different and even conflicting Christian groups and a center for theological reflection and debate (Robinson, 1982). The city of Alexandria was the home of outstanding theologians such as Origen, Cyprian, Clement of Alexandria, and others, whose writings on the different aspects of the Christian faith have influenced the church throughout the ages. The great "heretic" Arius (died A.D. 336), originally from Libya, provoked a controversy that rocked the church for several decades when he taught that Christ was only a human being. The controversy produced two creeds, namely, the Nicene and the Athanasian creeds, which are used together with the Apostles' Creed as definitive statements of the Christian faith throughout Christendom. The two creeds were formulated at the two great councils of Nicaea in A.D. 325 and of Alexandria in A.D. 362. The Athanasian Creed was named after Athanasius, the bishop of Alexandria, who championed the case against Arius.

The recent discoveries from Nag Hammadi show that Egyptian

Christians were very open-minded as they searched for an African Christian identity, welcoming and accommodating new ideas in their search for indigenous expressions of their Christian faith. For instance, in its search for an authentic Christian life devoid of all fleshly desires and serving God through a life of self-denial, prayer, and worship, Egypt was the mother of monasticism. The many caves and the nearby desert provided most ideal locations for ascetic pursuits. Christianity continued to be a vibrant religious tradition until Egypt was conquered by the Muslims during the seventh century. Christianity has survived, although it has been reduced to a religion of a small minority (Robinson, 1982).

Moving south of Egypt, Christianity came to Ethiopia fairly early. The apostle Philip is reported in the Acts of the Apostles to have baptized an Ethiopian eunuch, who returned to his home country to share his newfound faith with his people. Independent evidence dates the coming of Christianity to Ethiopia to the fourth century. With the conversion of the emperor, church and state became united. The Ethiopian Orthodox church, which is one of the most thoroughly African churches in its ethos (Oduyoye, 1986:30), has continued to the present and has maintained close links with the Coptic church.

In "Roman Africa," which comprised the present-day countries of Tunisia, Morocco, and Algeria, Christianity is known to have had a strong following as early as the second century. It produced influential theological thinkers and writers such as Tertullian of Carthage, who was the first person to use the word *Trinity* in his description of the Godhead, and St. Augustine, the bishop of Hippo, whose ideas on such issues as grace, original sin, and the kingdom of God shaped both Western Catholicism and the Protestant Reformation. This church did not survive the Arab conquests, and this area today is almost totally Islamic.

Christianity South of the Sahara

There is no evidence of attempts by the African churches described above to take Christianity south of the Sahara. The earliest such efforts to Christianize the rest of Africa were those of the Portuguese missionaries of the Jesuit and Dominican orders in the fifteenth century who followed Portuguese traders traveling around the coast of Africa on their way to the East, often going into the hinterland of Africa to trade in gold and ivory. In western Africa, Roman Catholic missionaries established Christian communities in Congo and Angola beginning in 1490, but these disintegrated after two centuries, in part because of the slave trade. Missionary work was also started in southern Africa at Sofala (Mozambique). It was from there that Father Gonzalo da Silveira led a group of Portuguese Jesuit missionaries in 1560 to the people of the vast empire of Mwanamutapa in what is now

Thomas O'Toole. Reprinted from Thomas O'Toole, The Central African Republic: The Continent's Hidden Heart *(1986), by permission of Westview Press, Boulder.*

Many Christian churches, such as this cathedral in Bangui, Central African Republic, were built by missionaries during the colonial period.

Zimbabwe. On his way to the capital of the empire, he claims to have baptized 450 persons among the Tonga people. His mission, however, ended with his execution by the emperor, whom he had converted and baptized Christian. This was apparently the result of pressure from the emperor's Arab Muslim trading partners, who feared Christian missionaries would open the door for Portuguese traders to threaten their monopoly. Subsequent Portuguese missionary efforts to the empire by both the Jesuits and the Dominicans were also unsuccessful. Their missionary efforts in eastern Africa suffered a similar fate.

A new phase in the evangelization of Africa was introduced by the rise of the antislavery movement in Europe and the United States in the early nineteenth century. The result was that the British decided to send freed slaves to Sierra Leone, while the Americans sent their freed slaves to Liberia. In both cases, the freed people who had become Christians in their captivity spread Christianity to their fellow black people. Famous among these was Samuel Adjai Crowther, who was missionary to his own people in Nigeria and later became the first African Anglican bishop. The evangelical movement culminated in a missionary scramble for Africa that involved all major denominations in Europe and North America. Famous characters in this process included David Livingstone and Robert Moffat. Many Africans were also involved in these missionary efforts after their conversions, crossing borders in the company of white missionaries or by themselves. As a result of the efforts of such people, Christianity was firmly established in most of Africa by the beginning of the twentieth century (see Sanneh, 1983).

The Rise of New African Christian Denominations

The nineteenth-century missionary activities in Africa were a resounding success, in which almost all major Christian denominations were involved. These activities were facilitated by the support and protection that missionaries received from colonial administrators. Indeed, the Christianization of Africa went hand in hand with its colonization. The missionaries arrived in most countries before the colonialists and learned the language of the local people. They helped the colonialists negotiate and draft the agreements that cheated African chiefs out of their land and its resources. To African nationalists, missionaries appeared to have collaborated with the forces of imperialism. In what is now a famous aphorism, the role of Christian missionaries in the colonization of Africa was once described by Kenyan nationalist leader (and Kenya's first president) Jomo Kenyatta: "When the missionaries came the Africans had the land and the Christians had the Bible. They taught us to pray with our eyes closed. When we opened them they had the land and we had the Bible" (in Mazrui, 1986:149–150). (See the discussions in Chapters 3 and 4 for more information on colonialism.)

Despite its association with colonialism, missionary Christianity had a significant political impact on contemporary Africa. Wherever the missionaries went, they built schools, where a large majority of the first generation of African leaders were educated (see Mazrui, 1986:285–286). These institutions helped create an awareness among oppressed black people that before God they were of equal value with their oppressors, and this inspired many to rise up in defense of their freedom or to liberate themselves. The education black people received from mission schools gave them a sense of pride and value that the colonial regimes were not interested in creating. Many of the missionaries also stood up for some of the rights of black people.

Since independence, the Christian church has continued to expand. Many churches are taking on new, distinctly African forms. Some of these indigenous Christian denominations are radically different in their polity, doctrines, and general ethos from their Western parent churches. These new denominations or churches have often been labeled "African Independent Churches" or, negatively, "sects," but they should be viewed more accurately as authentic African expressions of the Christian faith.

The first of these new denominations appeared in western and southern Africa; thereafter, others emerged in eastern and central Africa.

Researchers have traced the beginnings of these movements back to a Congolese woman named Donna Beatrice, who as early as 1700 claimed to have been possessed by the spirit of St. Anthony. Giving up all her belongings to the poor, she proclaimed a message of the coming judgment of God. She proclaimed that Christ and his apostles were black and that they lived in São Salvador (present-day Angola). For the first time, we have a cry from Black Africa for an indigenous Christ, an expression of a "deep yearning," "the yearning for a Christ who would identify with the despised African" (Daneel, 1987:46). The basic question Beatrice raised and that many of the new African Christian churches have been asking is: "How could the white Christ of the Portuguese images, the Christ of the exploiters—how could he ever help the suffering African, pining for liberty?" (Daneel, 1987:46).

By the 1960s, there were at least 6,000 new denominations or African indigenous churches spread throughout most of Africa, including Islamic Africa (Barrett, 1968:18–36). The reasons for the emergence of the new phenomenon of African Christianity have been many and varied. Some of them began as revival movements within the historical churches and had no intention of breaking away. A good example of this is the Kimbanguist church in what is now the Democratic Republic of Congo (DRC), which was started by Simon Kimbangu, a great healer and prophet. Since his activities were not acceptable to the missionary church, he was arrested shortly after the start of his ministry and tried for subversive activities by the Belgian government. He was sentenced to death, but the sentence was later commuted to life imprisonment; he died in 1951. Today, the Kimbanguist church, officially known as the Eglise de Jésus Christ par le Prophète Simon Kimbangu (the Church of Jesus Christ According to the Prophet Simon Kimbangu), is one of the largest of the new denominations, with followers not only in the DRC but also in other countries in central Africa such as Zambia (see Mazrui, 1986:152–156).

The reasons for the emergence of other African Independent Churches have been discussed extensively (see, for example, Fashole-Luke et al., 1978; Hastings, 1976; Daneel, 1987; Barrett, 1982) and need not detain us here for too long. I shall just highlight some of the major reasons as summarized by Daneel (1987:68–101). First, the African Christians did not find much of an African ethos in the missionary-founded churches. They wanted churches in which they could express their Christian faith in African symbols and images, churches where they could feel at home, so to speak. Christianity as proclaimed by the missionaries was for them not comprehensive enough to meet their spiritual needs; hence, many people even today secretly continue to participate in African traditional rituals. There was no serious attempt on the part of the historical churches to understand African traditional spirituality and culture. Instead, many traditional beliefs and practices were simply labeled "heathen" or "superstitious" and were thus forbidden.

Second, as far as the Africans were concerned, the missionaries and the colonialists were birds of a feather. After all, they shared a common worldview and a common racist perception of the African. The missionaries tolerated and even practiced racial discrimination to the extent of providing separate entries and sections in sanctuaries, and "by so doing [the church] preached against itself and violated human rights" (Plangger, 1988:446). Such contradictions in what people heard missionaries preach and what they practiced contributed significantly to the formation of some of the independent churches.

Third, with the translation of the Bible into African languages, African Christians could now read and interpret the Bible for themselves. They soon discovered, for example, that biblical paragons of faith such as Abraham and David were polygamists. They also found out that the Fifth Commandment demands that parents be honored and that it is the only commandment that comes with a promise, namely, "that your days may be long on earth." For African peoples the "parents" include the ancestor spirits. The translation of the Bible into African languages is thus one of the major contributions by the missionaries to the development of indigenous African Christian spirituality and to the development of African Christian theologies. In the African Independent Churches, the Bible plays a central role, and in some of the churches, one service may have as many as five or six sermons, all of which are biblically based. The tendency in these churches is to be fundamentalistic in interpreting the Bible.

Fourth, indigenous churches are a response to the refusal or slowness on the part of missionaries to relinquish church leadership to the indigenous people; to the missionaries' discouragement of practices such as faith healing, prophecy, and speaking in tongues; and, finally, to missionaries' disapproval of polygamy, ancestor veneration, witches, and traditional medicine.

Some indigenous churches headed by women are a reaction to the male dominance found in Western Christian churches and in African society in general. (See the discussion of male dominance in Africa before and after European expansion in Chapter 10.) For example, spirit possession cults in eastern Africa are dominated by women. They are considered to be the female counterpart of male veneration of lineage ancestors. Again, folk Catholicism in Zimbabwe is a largely feminine popular religion, with an emphasis on devotion to the Virgin Mary, mother of Jesus (Ranger, 1986:42, 52, 58). Women have also been leaders in such movements as Alice Lichina in Kenya, the Nyabingi of Kenya/Uganda, and Magoi's healing/possession movement in Mozambique (Mikell, 1997:26). In southern Africa, women play important roles as healers and diviners, often mixing indigenous beliefs and practices with Christianity. For example, they often rely on "prophecy, speaking in tongues, ecstatic dancing, and laying on of hands rather than herbs to heal" (Gort, 1997:300–301).

In formerly white-ruled South Africa, independent churches were both a refuge from economic, political, and racial domination by whites and a source of resistance to racist government policies. An example is the Church of the Children of Israel founded by Enoch Mgijima. In 1921, the congregation refused to move from land that the white government had designated for whites only. South African troops opened fire, killing 163 defenseless people and wounding 129 others (Davidson, 1989:26).

Because of the variety of factors that led to the emergence of the new denominations, the spiritualities of those denominations take different forms (see Daneel, 1987:43–67). There are basically two types. First, there is what has been called the Ethiopian-type churches. These are essentially protest movements that broke away from the white-dominated missionary churches that tended to align themselves with the oppressive colonial regimes. They identified themselves with the aspirations of oppressed black people and sought to give theological expression and spiritual support to the struggle for liberation. The references to Ethiopia in texts such as Psalm 68:31 were, as observed by Daneel (1987:38), "interpreted as a sign that the oppressed Black people have a specially appointed place in God's plan of salvation." The Ethiopian-type churches are found mainly in southern and eastern Africa, with the majority of them originating toward the end of the nineteenth century and the beginning of the twentieth century. They tend to maintain the same doctrine and church polity as the church from which they broke away, and they even use the same hymnbooks; but they have African leaders. They are nonprophetic movements and do not place a great deal of emphasis on the Holy Spirit and all the extraordinary activities assigned to the Holy Spirit in the other new denominations.

The second kind of new denomination is the spirit-type churches. These are often referred to as Zionist churches because the name Zion often appears in the self-designations of these movements. They are prophetic in character and place a great deal of emphasis on the work of the Holy Spirit, who manifests herself in speaking in tongues, healing, prophecy, dreams, and visions and who helps to identify witches and cast out evil spirits. Their worship services include drums and dancing. They are more concerned with the practical benefits that religion can provide in this world than with other-world salvation. At the same time, they forbid their members to have anything to do with traditional African religion (Morrison, Mitchell, and Paden, 1989:76). Zionist churches include the Aladura or "praying" churches in Nigeria and the Harris churches in Côte d'Ivoire (Ranger, 1986:3).

The new denominations represent a serious attempt to Africanize the

Christian faith by responding concretely to the needs and aspirations of the African people. These movements take the Africans' worldview seriously; for instance, if salvation is to be real, it must include liberation from evil spirits, sickness, and disease. For it to be meaningful and relevant, Christianity must offer protection against black magic, sorcery, and witchcraft, all of which are issues of vital concern to African societies (Kiernan, 1995b:23–25). Except for the Ethiopian-type churches, the other movements are uncompromisingly against participation in the traditional rites and substitute specifically Christian rites to fill the vacuum. The prophet who is inspired by the Holy Spirit, for example, takes the place and assumes the functions of the traditional diviners and spirit mediums; requests for rain are now made directly to God through the mediation of Christian leaders rather than through the tribal spirits mediated by traditional leaders.

According to Jim Kiernan (1995a:118), currently about 30 percent of Africa's population belongs to Zionist and Ethiopian Christian churches, with Zionists being about 80 percent of the total. The Ethiopian churches appeal more to largely poor urban dwellers by helping them to transcend their sense of economic deprivation and personal insecurity and hardship.

In addition to the African Independent Churches, new charismatic, evangelical Protestant churches are growing in popularity in many countries. Many of these churches are associated with mission churches of the Pentecostal variety, such as the Assemblies of God, coming from the United States. These churches are attracting many ambitious, better-educated, younger Africans who want to get rich but find few avenues to success in Africa's stagnant economies (cf. Gifford, 1998). These churches also meet the need many Africans have to explain their misfortune or discredit the success of others by blaming sorcery or witchcraft. Zionist and Pentecostal churches provide support for such beliefs and promise healing and the mobilization of spiritual forces to promote success or counter witchcraft (cf. Kiernan, 1995a, 1995b, 1995c).

Many of the new churches are highly fundamentalist and authoritarian in structure. According to Jeff Haynes, new churches are proliferating usually as a response to some kind of social crisis (1996:174). They are founded by a charismatic leader who claims to have a mystical experience and is regarded as a prophet by his/her followers. The churches are often millenarian, that is, expecting the imminent "end of the world," at which time only believers will be saved. Critical or rational thought is discouraged and dissent from what the evangelist says is viewed as opposing God (Gifford, 1998:178). Such views can give rise to extremist religious movements with tragic results, as recently occurred in Uganda. Early in 2000, leaders of the Movement for the Restoration of the Ten Commandments of God killed at least 924 members of their church, the worst cult killing in modern history.

Cult leader Joseph Kibwetere, a former teacher, public official, and businessman (and devout Catholic), came under the sway of Credonia Mwerinde (allegedly "the real power"). She claimed that the Virgin Mary appeared to her and told her the end of the world was coming. The motive for the mass murder is unclear, but apparently members of the cult became disillusioned and questioned the leaders' authority (and appropriation of members' financial assets) (see Maykuth, 2000).

The Political and Economic Role of Christian Churches

Christian churches play an important and sometimes contradictory role in postindependence Africa. Politically, some churches have aligned themselves with corrupt, authoritarian regimes. For example, many Pentecostal, independent, and evangelical churches in Kenya supported Daniel arap Moi despite his record of antidemocratic and corrupt rule. In Liberia before the 1990 civil war, evangelical and Pentecostal churches backed any government, however oppressive, that promoted evangelism. Worse by far was the actual complicity and direct involvement of some Catholic clergy and lay persons in the 1994 genocide against the Tutsis and moderate Hutu in Rwanda. Church leaders were mostly Hutu and closely tied to the Hutu-dominated government (see Longman, 1998; Gifford, 1998:51–55; Ranger, 2003:116)).

It also appears that many of the churches, especially the new Christian churches, are susceptible to co-optation by the government or to corruption. In Kenya, Archbishop Ondiek of the Legio Maria church was Moi's Minister of Employment; the church was a Moi supporter. In Zambia, the former Chiluba government's antidemocratic and corrupt practices were frequently downplayed or overlooked because Chiluba is an outspoken avowed born-again Christian who put potentially critical Christian leaders in positions of influence in the government (Gifford, 1998:51, 204–205, 216–217). Other church leaders are susceptible to the financial benefits and the prestige that government leaders can bestow on them and their churches (Gifford, 1998:87–88), and those who have benefited from political arrangements (both clergy and lay persons) use the churches to organize opposition to reform. By the same token, politicians at all levels cooperate with church personnel and use the churches to increase their power and seek legitimacy (Longman, 1998:68; Ranger, 2003:116). Paul Gifford's (2004) study of Ghana buttresses these criticisms and concludes that the evangelical churches are for the most part not a force for meaningful political transformation and democratization.

The current economic crisis has had a major impact on the role and forms of Christianity currently spreading in Africa. Many mainline churches and African Independent Churches are failing to attract new members compared to the new Pentecostal and evangelical churches allied with overseas churches. Some of these promote a "faith gospel" promising wealth, health, and happiness. Others promise deliverance from demons and witchcraft. Gifford sees these new churches as a response to the failure of the modernization and development agenda in Africa (Gifford, 1998). With conditions worsening for many Africans and opportunities for advancement in the public or private sectors so limited, religion is seen by many as the best avenue for improving their lives. Indeed, churches with external links often have access to jobs, incomes, and other resources unavailable elsewhere. An additional plus is that many of these churches, especially the faith gospel churches, legitimate the accumulation of wealth as "God's will," thus lessening the risk of the accusation of witchcraft from envious relatives or neighbors. Along with the promotion of sobriety, ambition, education, and hard work, a religious ideology that promotes capital accumulation in Africa could potentially help to accelerate economic growth and development (Gifford, 1998:308–312, 337–348). As Gifford remarks, "Africa's real parallel economy is now that created by Christian activity" (1998:94).

Unfortunately, without major economic and political transformation, beliefs in faith and personal endeavor alone as the means to riches or reliance on deliverance from witches as the cure for social problems are unlikely to work for most of Africa's suffering people. As Terence Ranger (2003:117) argues, "prosperity Christianity" is more about survival than rising to the heights of entrepreneurial success. Magic is often substituted for thrift, and rewards are received for noneconomic reasons. Yet among Africa's impoverished masses, the gospel of prosperity sustains a belief that God won't allow the faithful to perish. The capitalism such faith encourages is mainly "penny capitalism"—that is, informal sector activities among the young and women that prevents starvation. Gifford (2004) echoes these conclusions and adds that with few exceptions, evangelical church leaders do not encourage the hard work ethic, educational attainment, and productive entrepreneurialism necessary for significant economic success or societal development.

It is necessary to mention, however, that some Christian churches, especially the mainstream churches, are advocates for social justice and democracy and critics of corruption (cf. Lungu, 1986; "Churches," 1995). As mentioned above, churches were active in the anti-apartheid struggle in South Africa. In Rwanda, Burundi, and the Democratic Republic of Congo, church leaders have supported political reforms and backed women's and human rights groups. In Burundi, for example, two Catholic bishops were founding members of the main human rights group in the country (Longman, 1998). Moreover, some evangelical missionaries in Africa are playing an important role in addressing human rights and conflict in Africa, such as the civil war in Sudan and the current genocide in Darfur (also in Sudan). Evangelical missionaries are involved in the crusades against AIDS, sex trafficking, and poverty in Africa (Bergner, 2006; Lexington, 2005). It is too early to tell what effects this activism will have on local evangelical churches.

Islam in Africa

Like Christianity, Islam is expanding in Africa. Currently approximately 150–160 million sub-Saharan Africans are Muslims (Quinn and Quinn, 2003). While Muslims can be found in every African country, they are concentrated in areas bordering the Sahara Desert. Islam, which means "submission to God," was founded in the seventh century in Arabia by the Prophet Muhammad. Influenced by Judaism and Christianity, Islam established monotheism and a scripturally based religion first among Arab tribesmen around the towns of Mecca and Medina. Allah (God) revealed to Muhammad how he wanted his followers to live and structure their communities. This revelation is found in the Quran and is believed to be the literal word of God. Muslim Arabs, like Jews, believe they are descendants of Abraham, and they respect the Old Testament and the Prophets. Muslims also revere the New Testament and regard Jesus as a prophet. Muhammad, however, is the last and greatest of the Prophets, and the Quran is God's supreme revelation. Unlike Judaism, both Christianity and Islam are missionary religions; as such they have been the major contenders for the religious allegiance of Africans. Rather than discussing the faith and doctrine of Islam, this study will focus on the historical development of the tradition in Africa and its distinctively African features.

The Spread of Islam: The First Wave

Soon after the death of Muhammad in A.D. 632, his followers embarked on wars of conquest, first among Arabs and then non-Arab peoples in northern Africa and elsewhere. Most of Egypt was taken over by the Muslims by 640. By then, Egypt's rulers supported the Byzantine Orthodox church, while many Egyptians were Coptic Christians who did not accept the Orthodox church's teachings or authority. Many welcomed Arab rule as less oppressive than they had experienced under the Byzantines. The Arabs established themselves initially as a ruling and powerful minority, but Christians were treated as "protected people" *(dhimmi)* who were allowed to practice their faith and regulate their affairs through their own leaders. Still, Christians were second-class citizens required to pay a special tax *(jizya)* in lieu of military service. Nonetheless, educated Christians often

April Gordon

The Great Mosque in the town of Touba is the center of devotion for Senegal's Mouride brotherhood. Amadou Bamba, the founder of the Mourides, is buried here.

held prominent positions in the new Muslim state. Conversion to Islam was gradual. There was some localized persecution and pressure to convert, but most did so for other reasons—for example, attraction to Islamic tenets, commercial advantage, and desire to avoid the *jizya* and second-class status. By the end of the eleventh century, Christianity in Egypt had become a minority religion (Mostyn, 1988:190).

After Egypt, the Arabs moved on to Roman northern Africa, where they defeated the Christians, who were primarily based in the towns, and the Berbers, who had remained untouched by Christianity in the rural areas. J. S. Trimingham observes that

> the North African Church died rather than was eliminated by Islam, since it never rooted itself in the life of the country. Although considerations such as the prestige of Islam derived from its position as the religion of the ruling minority and the special taxation imposed on Christians encouraged change, the primary reasons for their rapid conversion were the less obvious ones deriving from weaknesses within the Christian communities. Among these were Christianity's failure to claim the Berber soul and its bitter sectarian divisions. (Trimingham, 1962:18)

The conversion of the pagan Berbers of northern Africa was a slow process. After their initial military conquests, the Arabs located in the towns. They gradually intermarried with the Berbers, who became increasingly Islamized and Arabized. Many Berbers were incorporated into Arab armies. This period of conquest and gradual Islamization of northern Africa is reported by the great Arab historian Ibn Khaldun:

> After the formation of the Islamic community the Arabs burst out to propagate their religion among other nations. Their armies penetrated into the Maghrib and captured all its cantonments and cities. They endured a great deal in their struggles with the Berbers who, as Abu Yazid has told us, apostatized twelve times before Islam gained a firm hold over them. (Trimingham, 1962:18)

Whereas Islam spread to northern Africa in the aftermath of conquest, the spread of Islam south of the Sahara was primarily the result of peaceful, informal missionary efforts by Arabized Berber merchants who traded manufactured goods from the Mediterranean lands in exchange for raw materials such as gold, ivory, gum, and slaves. They followed the established trade routes, many of which had existed long before the rise of Islam. Wherever they went, Muslims established commercial and religious centers near the capital cities. The Nile River provided access to Nubia, Ethiopia, and Sudan. From Sudan, some of the traders went across to western Africa. The introduction of the camel also made it possible to cross the desert from northern Africa and establish contacts with western and central Africa (Voll, 1982:80; Lewis, 1980:15–16).

Muslim communities were established fairly early in several states in western Africa. In Ghana, for example, already by 1076, there was an established Muslim center with several mosques almost competing with each other (King, 1971:18). By the fifteenth and sixteenth centuries, Islam was the religion of the rulers and elites of many large African states such as the Songhai empire (Voll, 1982:14). (See Map 2.4.) Islam appealed to African elites for several reasons. One was its association with Arab-Muslim civilization and its cosmopolitanism. Islam was also very compatible with or at least tolerant of African religious and cultural practices such as ancestor veneration, polygamy, circumcision, magic, and beliefs in spirits and other divinities. In fact, most African believers were barely Islamized, perhaps observing the Five Pillars of the faith—belief in one God and that Muhammad is his prophet, alms *(zakat)* for the needy, prayer five times a day, fasting during the month of Ramadan, and pilgrimage *(haj)* to Mecca—but often ignoring elements of the *shari'a* (Muslim law) or other Islamic practices (e.g., veiling women), which they found incompatible with local custom (Lewis, 1980:33–34, 60–62; Callaway and Creevey, 1994).

In eastern Africa, Islam was spread by Persian and Arab merchants beginning in the late seventh century. These merchants established coastal trading towns with local Africans all the way down to southern Africa. Through intermarriage and commercial contacts, a unique Swahili language and culture developed. There was little movement of traders or Islam into the interior until the late tenth century, however, because there were few centralized kingdoms to attract them (Lewis, 1980:7). (See Chapter 3 for additional information on this period.)

Islamic civilization contributed much to Africa's own cultural development. Islam is a way of life *(dar al Islam)* affecting all spheres of human activity. It emphasizes literacy and scholarship, traditions that Islam promoted in previously nonliterate African societies. Islam's stress on the community of believers *(umma)* demands the subordination of regional and tribal loyalties that often separated Africans and impeded the growth of larger political units. Islamic law *(shari'a)* as the framework for community life along with Islamic Arab administrative and political structures provided models for Africa's state-builders and gave built-in religious legitimacy to the claims of rulers over the ruled (see Mazrui, 1986:136–137; Davidson, 1991:28–29; Lewis, 1980:37).

The Spread of Islam: The Second Wave

By the eighteenth century in western Africa, Islamic consciousness was spreading from the upper classes to the masses. This new wave of Islamization was being carried by African Muslims through militant mass movements under the religious banner of jihad (holy war). The desire of pious Muslim leaders such as Uthman dan Fodio in northern Nigeria (early nineteenth century) was for social, moral, and political reform. The imposition of more rigorously Islamic theocratic states on lax African believers and non-Islamic peoples was the goal. Jihad thus became a religious justification for wars of conquest and political centralization (Mazrui, 1986:184–185; Voll, 1982:80–81).

The new wave of Islamization was not solely the result of militant movements. Various Sufi (mystical) religious orders or brotherhoods *(tariqas)* dedicated to a more faithful adherence to Islam were at work. One of the earlier ones (sixteenth century) was the Qadiriyya, introduced to the great Muslim center of learning Timbuktu by an Arab *shaikh* (leader) (Lewis, 1980:18–19). In the nineteenth century, the Tijaniyya from Fez, Morocco, gained many followers. The Qadiriyya greatly influenced Uthman dan Fodio, whose jihad movement led to the founding of the Muslim caliphate at Sokoto (Voll, 1982:80–81). (Again, see Chapter 3.)

Sufi brotherhoods under the inspiration of their religious leaders *(marabouts)* were able to mobilize large numbers of people for political and economic as well as purely religious ends. Among these ends was resistance to European imperialism in the nineteenth century. Using the ideas of jihad and the brotherhood of all believers, Muslims were able to organize resistance on a wider scale than African political units or ethnicity would allow (Mazrui, 1986:284). In Senegal, the Mourides transformed jihad into economic enterprise as *marabouts* organized their followers to produce peanuts on brotherhood land. Even today, the Mourides are a major political and economic force in Senegal. They attract many followers for practical reasons but also because of their liberalism in enforcing Islamic law (Voll, 1982:249–250).

In eastern Africa, Mahdism galvanized mass religio-political opposition to European imperialism in the Sudan. The *Mahdi* in Islam is a messianic figure sent by God to save the believers during times of crisis. The Mahdi Muhammad Ahmed and his followers defeated the British at Khartoum in 1885, although the Mahdist forces were eventually defeated (Mazrui, 1986:151–152).

European colonialism and missionary Christianity did not halt the spread of Islam in Africa. In western Africa, colonial rulers made peace with Muslim leaders by protecting their conservative rule over their people and prohibiting Christian proselytizing or mission schools in Muslim areas (Voll, 1982:247). Muslims won many new converts for a variety of reasons. The racism and segregation policies of the Europeans contrasted sharply with the Muslim belief in the equality of believers. Also, in many cases, Muslim army officers under the British and the French treated Africans kindly, dealing with their grievances. They were tolerant in helping fellow Africans adjust African customary law to Islamic law (Zakaria, 1988:203). Indirectly, colonialism promoted Islamic expansion through the introduction of improved communications and rapid social change (Voll, 1982:245). Islam proved able to adjust and change as well as to meet new needs and conditions.

Islam Since Independence

Islamic organizations and practices have undergone remarkable changes in order to cope with Western influences, including Christianity. In some cases the process has involved accommodation and new interpretations of Islam. In other instances, Christianity and Westernization are seen as enemies of Islam and failed experiments, unable to solve Africa's many problems. Such views have spawned a growing number of fundamentalist movements.

Initially after independence, conservative nineteenth-century organizations either died out or transformed themselves. In Sudan, the followers of the Mahdi formed a modern political party that competed in national elections. In Nigeria, also, conservative and reformist Muslims formed political parties, partly in competition with Christians in non-Muslim sections of the country. Few of these political parties, however, were explicitly Islamic. The Mourides of Senegal reorganized and assumed modern economic and political roles to maintain their influence (Voll, 1982:145–250).

The spirit of jihad and forced conversion were largely replaced by a respect for religious pluralism. This was undoubtedly a result of the long history of mutual accommodation between African Traditional Religions and Islam in the past as well as contact with Christianity. In most sub-Saharan African states, Muslims are a minority or, at least, not the only religious community, a fact that tends to reinforce Muslim support for secular states. Muslim leaders readily accepted non-Muslim leaders such as Léopold Senghor (a Catholic), who was president of Senegal for many years. Pluralism is also promoted by the fact that family and ethnic loyalties still take precedence over religious ties for most Africans (Zakaria, 1988:204–205). (See Chapter 9 for more on the centrality of the family in Africa.)

For the masses of Muslim Africans, African traditional beliefs and practices have continued, although with some adaptations to conform to similar practices in Islam. In writing about the Wolof of Senegal, John Mbiti concluded:

> In spite of the impact of Islam, there is still a much deeper layer of pagan belief and observances. . . . Men and women are loaded with amulets, round the waist, neck, arms, legs, both for protection against all sorts of possible evil, and to help them achieve certain desires. Most frequently these contain a paper on which a religious teacher has written a passage from the Koran, or a diagram from a book on Arabic mysticism, which is then enveloped in paper, glued down and covered with leather, but sometimes they enclose a piece of bone or wood, a powder, or an animal claw. (Mbiti, 1969:245)

These are basically African elements, not Islamic, and are practiced by most African groups.

A survey of African indigenous Islamic communities in other parts of Africa also reveals the persistence of African-based practices. Ancestor veneration, the wearing of amulets to ward off misfortune and to protect cattle and homesteads, and beliefs in magic, witchcraft, and sorcery have continued with little discouragement. New elements include the use of charms. Also, as Mbiti (1969:249) observed, "In addition to treating human complaints, the medicine men perform exorcisms, sometimes using Koranic quotations as magical formulae."

African Muslims, as well as African Christians, are seeking to redefine or modify their religion and religious identity in response to modern needs and problems. For many Muslims, this means finding a way to incorporate more orthodox Islamic practices and beliefs into those of their pre-Islamic

African religious and cultural heritage. Moreover, many African Muslims are seeking new religious responses to meet the political, economic, and social problems they are facing. This has led some Muslims to seek a fundamentalist reaffirmation of Islam, often influenced by fundamentalist movements in North Africa and even Iran (cf. Hunwick, 1995; Ilesanmi, 1995; Voll, 1982:250, 337; Brenner, 1993).

Adapting to contemporary concerns, Sufi brotherhoods have been at the forefront in providing new ways to find accommodation between the demands of Islam and popular aspirations, both religious and secular. One such movement is Hamallism, a branch of the Tijaniyya. Hamallism is a social and religious reform movement that stresses the full equality of all people and the liberation of women. It opposes the materialism and corruption of conservative Islamic leaders. Before independence, Hamallists opposed those Muslim leaders who cooperated with French colonialism. Hamallism influenced political leaders like Modibo Keita, former president of Mali, and Diori Hamani, former president of Niger (Voll, 1982:254). On the other hand, anti-Sufi movements such as the Izala in Nigeria and Niger (Movement for Suppressing Innovations and Restoring the Sunna) have attracted many from the urban merchant class with their opposition to *marabouts* and emphasis on individualism and putting wealth into investments (Grégoire, 1993).

In Sudan, Islamic fundamentalists have gained dominant influence over the government. Their efforts to impose the *shari'a* on the entire country, including the non-Muslim south, led to a devastating civil war since 1983 that only recently ended in 2005 (see O'Fahey, 1993). The fundamentalists obliterated previous nonsectarian, modernist Islamic movements such as the Republican Brothers, founded by M. M. Taha. The Brothers sought a reform of Islam in light of modern realities, including advocating the equality of men and women. Taha was executed in 1985 for "heresy" (Al-Karsani, 1993).

Elsewhere, and similar to the new Christian churches that are searching for a more African Christianity, some Muslims are promoting controversial new forms of Africanized Islam. In East and West Africa, the Ahmadiyya movement (originally from India) owes its modest success to its vigorous missionary efforts. The Ahmadiyya translated the Quran into Swahili and other local languages (the first to do so), since most African Muslims do not know Arabic. Currently, there are at least 500,000 Ahmadiyya believers in sub-Saharan Africa. Members are often prominent in government and business circles and more secular. They have made significant efforts to promote the status of women; for example, women are allowed to pray in the mosque with men. The Ahmadiyya are seen as heretical by more orthodox believers (Haynes, 1996:195). Also controversial is the Maitatsine movement. In Nigeria in the 1960s and 1970s Cameroonian Mahammadu

Marwa claimed to be a new prophet of Islam. Marwa was killed along with 100 other people when his followers sparked a violent confrontation with police in the city of Kano in 1980. Rioting by his followers in 1990 left 5,000 people dead (Haynes, 1996:188–191). The Mourides of Senegal have come to revere the town of Touba, where the brotherhood originated, as a site of pilgrimage rivaling Mecca in importance (Mazrui, 1986:151–152).

In recent years, there has been mounting concern about fundamentalist Islamic extremists gaining ground in Africa. These fears have intensified since the terrorist attack on the United States in 2001 and the subsequent launching of the "war on terror." The United States regards Africa as a "breeding ground for terrorism" due to such factors as widespread poverty, failed states, and poor governance by undemocratic and corrupt governments ("Faithful," 2003). To counter this possible threat, the United States has formed a coalition with the governments of nine Saharan states and spent $500 million to combat the spread of jihadist radicalism that could threaten African nations such as Nigeria that provide 15 percent of the United State's oil ("An Awkward Friend," 2005:44).

Despite these fears about Islamic extremists, research shows that African Muslims are mostly moderates, and radical fundamentalism has made few converts in Africa (see Haynes, 1996:212; Sanneh, 1997:214–215). The few civil wars that have occurred that involve Muslims and non-Muslims, such as in Sudan and Côte d'Ivoire, are mainly about oil, land, or political rights rather than religion. Only in Sudan was there an effort to impose an Islamic state or *shari'a* law. In northern Nigeria, where twelve states adopted *shari'a* criminal codes, it was largely in reaction to high crime rates, corruption, and the ineffectualness of Nigeria's secular courts to stem these problems. Reportedly, many Muslims in both Sudan and Nigeria are disillusioned with the results of such efforts to use Islam to solve their problems. Most reject fundamentalism and want to live peacefully with their non-Muslim neighbors (Rice, 2004; "Faithful," 2003).

In fact, the small but growing fundamentalism in their midst divides many Muslims. Some Muslims are secularists and progressive reformers seeking to modernize their societies. Others are traditionalists. Even most fundamentalists are oriented to local issues rather than linked to internationalist Islamic organizations or radical groups like Al-Qaida (see Quinn and Quinn, 2003; Shinn, 2005).

There are some exceptions to this pattern. In Somalia, for example, there are a few radical groups such as Itihad al Islami (AIA), which seeks to establish an Islamic state and has acknowledged terrorist attacks against Ethiopia in the mid-1990s. AIA is believed to have links to Al-Qaida (Shinn, 2005). In northern Nigeria, a small, militant Islamist group started an uprising in 2003 near the Cameroon-Niger border, where it attacked sev-

Map 11.1

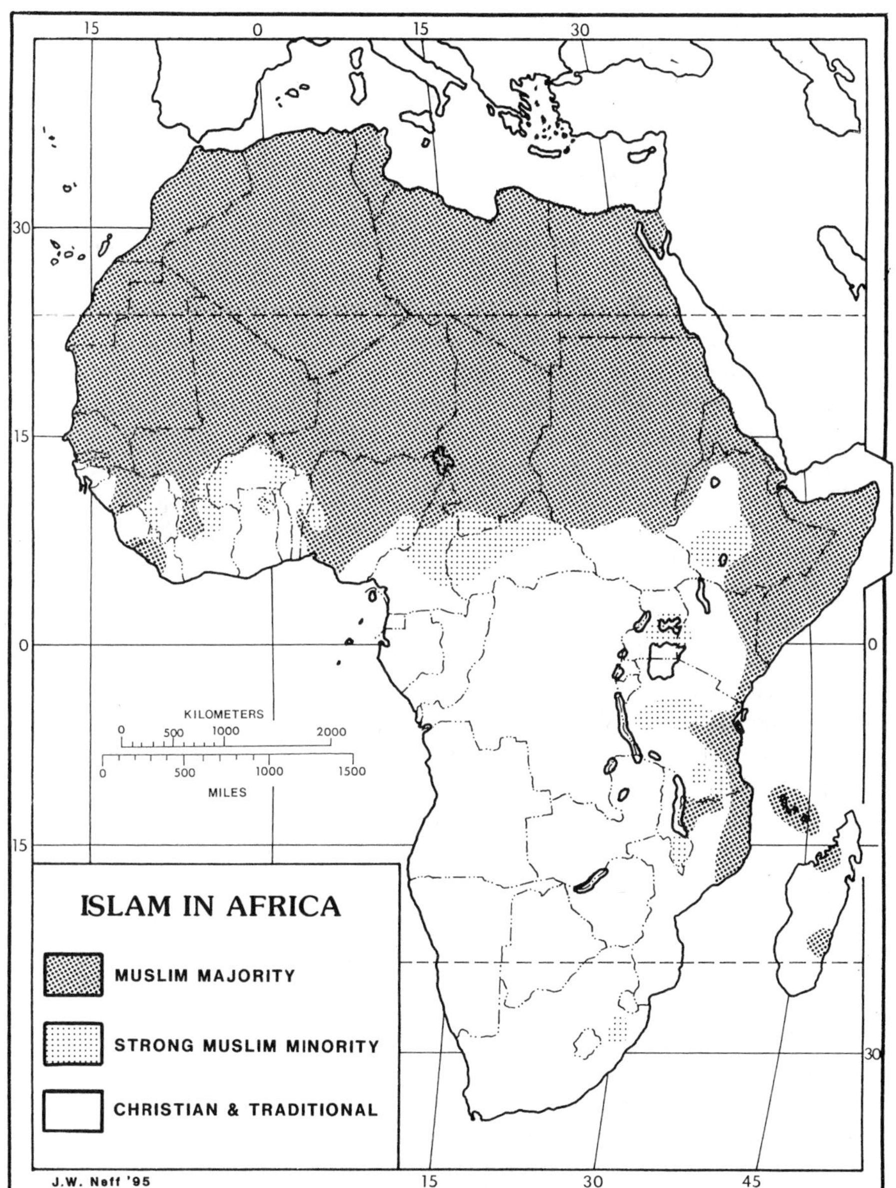
15
0
15
30
30
15
0
15
30
15
30
45
0
KILOMETERS
0 500 1000 2000
0 500 1000 1500
MILES
ISLAM IN AFRICA
MUSLIM MAJORITY
STRONG MUSLIM MINORITY
CHRISTIAN & TRADITIONAL
J.W. Neff '95

eral police stations and patrols. The group, said to be inspired by Al-Qaida, the Taliban in Afghanistan, and the Palestinian resistance movement, was quickly broken up by Nigerian authorities. Its remaining members are in hiding. Like the AIA, the Nigerian militants want to replace the secular state in their country with an Islamic government (Goujon and Abubakar, 2006).

An unfortunate by-product of the war on terror, as well as continuing economic and political problems in Africa, is growing tensions and animosities between Muslims and Christians, especially evangelical Christians. Muslims from Libya, Saudi Arabia, and the Persian Gulf are pouring money into Africa to expand conservative Islam. At the same time, Christian missionaries (mostly from the United States) are pouring money and missionaries into Africa to promote conservative Christianity (Rice, 2004). Extremism can be found among both groups. For example, many Christians regard Islam as the enemy in a virtual war for African souls. Many also see Islam through the lens of the US-led war on terror, which they strongly support and perceive to be a war against Islam. Some Christians even support the war on terror because it is killing Muslims (Rice, 2004). Both Nigeria and Uganda are countries in which growing sectarian clashes have occurred in recent years (Rice, 2004; Gordon, 2003:201–227).

Christians have also formed violent political movements such as the Ugandan Movement for the Restoration of the Ten Commandments of God, discussed earlier in this chapter. Another group in Uganda is the Lord's Resistance Army (LRA) under the leadership of Joseph Kony, who considers himself a prophet. The LRA has been at war with the Ugandan government since 1986. Its goal is to replace the government with one based on Moses' Ten Commandments. The LRA has killed thousands of people and abducted more that 20,000 children, who were forced to fight and kill or become sex slaves to LRA commanders (Cocks, 2003; "Uganda's Child Rebels," 2003). Obviously, any religion in the wrong hands and under favorable circumstances has the potential for violence.

Conclusion

Although it is not possible to do justice to so broad a topic as African religions within the space of a chapter, this survey has, I hope, illustrated the breadth of the continent's religious traditions. Historically, African Traditional Religions and Islam have generally been able to accommodate each other, but there are some strong voices within the Muslim community that have become more critical of the less than rigorous practices of African Islam. African Christian churches, on the other hand, have been openly negative toward African Traditional Religions, but at the same time have found ways of adapting some of their rituals and beliefs so that African Christians could feel at home in new indigenous denominations. The combined efforts of the early missionary and colonial powers to destroy African cultures and religions led to a crisis of identity that, ironically, has promoted the continued practice of African Traditional Religions as a major aspect of African cultures.

Paul Bohannan and Philip Curtin (1995:124) predict that African Traditional Religions will dwindle with development and industrialization. Indeed, conversions to Christianity and Islam are growing steadily. This prediction, however, presupposes that the current economic and political crises of Africa improve and that rural dwellers and the poor in general become situated more securely in the network of relationships and activities we call "modern." Even though African Traditional Religions may dwindle as Africans affiliate with branches of the world's two major religions, Christianity and Islam, Africans will continue to preserve in their new faiths elements of the old, as they have always done.

People will embrace religions they feel speak to their experience and their need for identity and meaning, religions that promise some kind of justice and redress of their existential problems. In Africa, a meaningful religion is one oriented toward promotion of human interests in good health, economic well-being, and human development, as well as managing social relations and easing conflict (Kiernan, 1995b:25). After decades of misrule and economic and political decline, people are seeking solutions to, or at least relief from, suffering, lack of progress, uncertainty, and disruptive social change. The question in Africa, as well as in many other areas of the world, is whether emancipatory and tolerant religions rather than religions of intolerance, repression, and even violence are embraced as people seek to meet their worldly and spiritual needs.

Bibliography

Al-Karsani, Awad Al-Sid. 1993. "Beyond Sufism: The Case of Millennial Islam in Sudan." Pp. 135–153 in Louis Brenner (ed.). *Muslim Identity and Social Change in Sub-Saharan Africa.* Bloomington: Indiana University Press.

"An Awkward Friend for America." 2005. *The Economist* (September 3):44.

Awulalu, J. Omosade. 1979. *Yoruba Beliefs and Sacrificial Rites.* Burnt Mill, Harlow (Essex), England: Longman.

Barrett, David B. 1968. *Schism and Renewal in Africa.* Nairobi: Oxford University Press.

———. 1982. *World Christian Encyclopedia: A Comparative Survey of Churches and Religions in the Modern World 1900–2000.* Nairobi: Oxford University Press.

Bascom, William. 1969. *Ifa Divination: Communication Between Gods and Men in West Africa.* Bloomington: Indiana University Press.

Berglund, Axel-Ivar. 1976. *Zulu Thought Patterns and Symbolism.* London: C. Hurst.

Bergner, Daniel. 2006. "The Call." *The New York Times Magazine* (January 29):40–47.

Bohannan, Paul, and Philip Curtin. 1995. *Africa and Africans.* Prospect Heights, IL: Waveland Press.

Brenner, Louis (ed.). 1993. *Muslim Identity and Social Change in Sub-Saharan Africa.* Bloomington: Indiana University Press.

Callaway, Barbara, and Lucy Creevey. 1994. *The Heritage of Islam: Women, Religion, and Politics in West Africa.* Boulder, CO: Lynne Rienner Publishers.

"Churches Seek 'Critical Distance.'" 1995. *Christian Century* 112 (April 19):416.

Cocks, Tim. 2003. "Spirited Away in the Night by the Lord's Army." *Mail & Guardian online* (South Africa). Online at www.mg.co.za (February 26).

Daneel, M. L. 1987. *The Quest for Belonging: Introduction to a Study of African Independent Churches.* Gweru, Zimbabwe: Mambo.

Davidson, Basil. 1989. *Modern Africa: A Social and Political History.* London: Longman.

———. 1991. *African Civilization Revisited.* Trenton, NJ: Africa World Press.

Evans-Pritchard, E. E. 1937. *Witchcraft, Oracles and Magic Among the Azande.* Oxford: Clarendon Press.

"Faithful, But Not Fanatics." 2003. *The Economist* (June 26):48.

Fashole-Luke, G., R. Gray, A. Hastings, and G. Tasie (eds.). 1978. *Christianity in Independent Africa.* London: Rex Collins.

Gifford, Paul. 1998. *African Christianity: Its Public Role.* Bloomington: Indiana University Press.

———. 2004. Ghana's New Christianity: Pentecostalism in a Globalizing African

Gordon, April. 2003. *Nigeria's Diverse Peoples: A Reference Sourcebook.* Santa Barbara: ABC-CLIO.

Gort, Enid. 1997. "Swazi Traditional Healers, Role Transformation, and Gender." Pp. 298–309 in Gwendolyn Mikell (ed.). *African Feminism: The Politics of Survival in Sub-Saharan Africa.* Philadelphia: University of Pennsylvania Press.

Goujon, Emmanuel, and Aminu Abubakar. 2006. "Nigeria's 'Taliban' Plot Comeback from Hide-outs." *Mail and Guardian* (January 11) (www.mg.co.za).

Grégoire, Emmanuel. 1993. "Islam and the Identity of Merchants in Maradi (Niger)." Pp. 106–115 in Louis Brenner (ed.). *Muslim Identity and Social Change in Sub-Saharan Africa.* Bloomington: Indiana University Press.

Hastings, Adrian. 1976. *African Christianity.* New York: Seabury.

Haynes, Jeff. 1996. *Religion and Politics in Africa.* London: Zed.

Hunwick, John O. 1995. *Religion and National Integration in Africa: Islam, Christianity, and Politics in the Sudan and Nigeria.* Evanston, IL: Northwestern University Press.

Idowu, E. B. 1962. *Olodumare: God in Yoruba Belief.* Ikeja, Nigeria: Longman.

———. 1971. *African Traditional Religion: A Definition.* Maryknoll, NY: Orbis.

Ilesanmi, Simeon O. 1995. "Recent Theories of Religion and Politics in Nigeria." *Journal of Church and State* 37 (Spring):309–327.

Kiernan, Jim. 1995a. "The African Independent Churches." Pp. 116–128 in Martin Prozesky and John de Gruchy (eds.). *Living Faiths in South Africa.* Cape Town: David Philip.

———. 1995b. "African Traditional Religions in South Africa." Pp. 15–27 in Martin Prozesky and John de Gruchy (eds.). *Living Faiths in South Africa.* Cape Town: David Philip.

———. 1995c. "The Impact of White Settlement on African Traditional Religions." Pp. 72–82 in Martin Prozesky and John de Gruchy (eds.). *Living Faiths in South Africa.* Cape Town: David Philip.

King, Noel. 1971. *Christian and Moslem in Africa.* New York: Harper and Row.

Lan, David. 1985. *Guns and Rains: Guerrilla and Spirit Mediums in Zimbabwe.* Harare: Zimbabwe Publishing House.

Lewis, I. M. 1980. *Islam in Tropical Africa.* Bloomington: Indiana University Press.

Lexington. 2005. "Bob Geldof and Bono Have Some Unlikely Friends in America." *The Economist* (July 2):34.

Longman, Timothy P. 1998. "Empowering the Weak and Protecting the Powerful: The Contradictory Nature of Churches in Central Africa." *African Studies Review* 41 (April):49–72.

Lungu, Gatian F. 1986. "The Church, Labour and the Press in Zambia: The Role of Critical Observers in a One-Party State." *African Affairs* 85 (July):385–410.

Maykuth, Andrew. 2000. "Signs of Massacre Went Unheeded." *Christian Science Monitor* (April 2):A20.

Mazrui, Ali A. 1986. *The Africans: A Triple Heritage.* London: BBC Publications.

Mbiti, John S. 1969. *African Religions and Philosophy.* New York: Praeger.

———. 1970. *African Concepts of God.* New York: Praeger.

McVeigh, Malcolm J. 1974. *God in Africa: Conceptions of God in African Traditional Religion and Christianity.* Cape Cod, MA: Claude Stark.

Mikell, Gwendolyn. 1997. "Introduction." Pp. 1–50 in Gwendolyn Mikell (ed.). *African Feminism: The Politics of Survival in Sub-Saharan Africa.* Philadelphia: University of Pennsylvania Press.

Morrison, Donald G., Robert C. Mitchell, and John N. Paden. 1989. *Understanding Black Africa.* New York: Irvington Publishers.

Mostyn, Trevor. 1988. *The Cambridge Encyclopedia of the Middle East and North Africa.* New York: Cambridge University Press.

Moyo, Ambrose. 1987. "Religion and Politics in Zimbabwe." In Kirsten Holst Peterson (ed.). *Religion, Development and African Identity.* Uppsala: Scandinavian Institute of African Studies.

Oduyoye, Mercy. 1986. *Hearing and Knowing: Theological Reflections on Christianity in Africa.* Maryknoll, NY: Orbis.

O'Fahey, R. S. 1993. "Islamic Hegemonies in the Sudan: Sufism, Mahdism, and Islamism." Pp. 21–35 in Louis Brenner (ed.). *Muslim Identity and Social Change in Sub-Saharan Africa.* Bloomington: Indiana University Press.

Parrinder, Geoffrey. 1969. *Religion in Africa.* New York: Praeger.

Plangger, Albert. 1988. "Human Rights: A Motive for Mission." Pp. 441–459 in Carl F. Hallencreutz and Ambrose Moyo (eds.). *Church and State in Zimbabwe.* Gweru, Zimbabwe: Mambo.

Quinn, Charlotte A., and Frederick Quinn. 2003. *Pride, Faith, and Fear: Islam in Sub-Saharan Africa.* New York: Oxford University Press.

Ranger, T. O. 1985. *Peasant Consciousness and Guerrilla War in Zimbabwe: A Comparative Study.* London: James Currey.

———. 1986. "Religious Movements and Politics in Sub-Saharan Africa." *African Studies Review* 29:1–70.

———. 2003. "Evangelical Christianity and Democracy in Africa: A Continental Comparison." *Journal of Religion in Africa* 33:112–117.

Rice, Andrew. 2004. "Evangelicals v. Muslims in Africa: Enemy's Enemy." *The New Republic* (August 9):18.

Robinson, James M. 1982. *The Nag Hammadi Library.* New York: Harper and Row.

Sanneh, Lamin. 1983. *Christianity in West Africa: The Religious Impact.* Maryknoll, NY: Orbis.

———. 1997. *The Crown and the Turban: Muslims and West African Pluralism.* Boulder, CO: Westview Press.

Shinn, David H. 2005. "Islam and Conflict in the Horn of Africa." *Africa News Service* (January 21).

Trimingham, J. S. 1962. *A History of Islam in West Africa.* London: Oxford University Press.

Twesigye, Emmanuel K. 1987. *Common Ground: Christianity, African Religion and Philosophy.* New York: Peter Lang.

"Uganda's Child Rebels: Thou Shalt Not Kill." 2003. *The Economist* (September 6):43.

Voll, John Obert. 1982. *Islam: Continuity and Change in the Modern World.* Boulder, CO: Westview Press.

Zakaria, Rafiq. 1988. *The Struggle Within Islam.* London: Penguin.

12

African Literature

George Joseph

Since 1986, four inhabitants of the continent of Africa have received the Nobel Prize in literature: Naguib Mahfouz (Egypt), Wole Soyinka (Nigeria), Nadine Gordimer (South Africa), and J. M. Coetzee (South Africa). These writers, however, belong to literatures so different that to call them all "African" would seem to refer only to the geographical area where they originate. The work of Mahfouz, who writes in Arabic, belongs to Arabo-Islamic literature, a literature from a cultural space that stretches from Morocco along the Mediterranean across North Africa into the Middle East. The fiction of Gordimer and Coetzee, written in English, belongs to the European settler tradition of South Africa. Soyinka, who also writes in English, combines indigenous Nigerian traditions with those of European literature.

Most accessible to US students are the national literatures written in European languages from countries such as Senegal, Ghana, Nigeria, Cameroon, Kenya, Somalia, and South Africa, but these literatures are only the tip of a very large iceberg. There are written literatures in African languages, such as Hausa, Swahili, Zulu, Wolof, and Arabic (which has put down roots in Africa), as well as many oral traditions. A chapter of this sort can only give the broadest of outlines, and in keeping with the rest of the volume will concentrate on sub-Saharan Africa.[1]

The concept of "literature" most of us hold is of European origin. Typically, literature implies "written letters," but oral traditions in Africa are full-fledged literary traditions regardless of the means of their transmission. I shall use the term *oral literature* to emphasize the links between oral and written literature, while paying careful attention to the specificity of oral traditions.

"Literature" can also imply an artistic use of words for the sake of art alone. Without denying the important role of aesthetics in Africa, we should keep in mind that, traditionally, Africans do not radically separate art from teaching. Rather than write or sing for beauty in itself, African writers, taking their cue from oral literature, use beauty to help communicate important truths and information to society. Indeed, an object is considered beautiful because of the truths it reveals and the communities it helps to build. As someone once said, for an African mask to be beautiful, one must believe in the being for which it stands. The emphasis in this chapter, however, will not be history, ethics, religion, or philosophy but rather the recognized verbal art forms through which the truths of such material are communicated.

African Oral Literature

It is impossible to give a full account of contemporary African authors' debt to oral traditions, not only because much work remains to be done by scholars but also because even a brief account of what is already known is beyond the scope of this chapter. Yet, this debt is widely recognized, and current investigations reveal it to be always greater than previously suspected, even in the case of authors who write in a European language that has few if any visible "Africanisms." In this section of the chapter, I will introduce aspects of African oral literature with which a reader of written African literature should have some familiarity. These include (1) the status, preservation, and transmission of oral literature in African societies and (2) the genres that have so far been identified.

The Status and Transmission of Oral Literature in African Society

Although folklore is defined as traditional customs or tales preserved orally among a people, the status of African oral literature is different from that of the folklore of a people with writing. Folklore in countries such as Italy, France, or England stands as popular literature in opposition to the written productions of an elite and indeed may be influenced by the latter. African oral literature, on the other hand, represents the aspirations of an entire people and ranges from sublime religious ideals to everyday practical advice.

The constants of African oral traditions are transmitted in a variety of ways. In some societies, such as the Dogon (Mali), whom Marcel Griaule studied, any elder who takes the time can learn oral traditions. At the other extreme is the case of the Wolof (Senegal) *griot,* who belongs to a hereditary caste attached to a noble family. The *griot* learns the traditions by heart

Alioune Badara Sissokho

The Wolof *griot* Yoro M'Baye.

from his or her father (there are women *griots*, but with a different store of knowledge) from the time he or she can speak. This information is considered a sacred trust. In precolonial times, a mistake about a family's lineage could mean a *griot*'s life. Since there are a variety of terms to describe the person charged with the oral tradition throughout Africa, we shall use the term *bard* to refer to all of them. Whatever the mode of transmission, it is the elders who are repositories of the treasures of oral tradition, so that it is said, "Every time an old one dies, a library burns down."

Yet, despite careful protection and transmission of the constants of oral traditions, any oral form such as an epic, myth, tale, or praise song can actually be different every time it is performed. (Exceptions would be priestly incantations and prayers, as will be seen below.) A bard will modify his or her material according to the circumstances of the performance. For example, a story will be made less violent if it is performed for a woman. Certain types of information are withheld from foreigners and uninitiated members of a group, while other types of information are communicated only in certain social situations such as initiation rites or other important ceremonies. Stories and myths may always be modified to accommodate recent events, and there are always changes to give pleasure to the audience of the moment. Because a work will change according to these and other such circumstances, it would seem that a bard learns the skeletal structure of a story, myth, epic, or poem and fleshes it out according to fixed formulas that are dictated by the situation. As a result, a poem such as an epic may be very different when a researcher returns or sends someone else to record another version. Furthermore, the written text of an oral performance is a pale reflection of its original, which may have been chanted, sung, or combined with elements of dance and ritual. A true reproduction of a work of oral literature would have to be a videotaped performance, but even such a record creates a false impression of fixed works.

Although the function of oral literature is to provide entertainment and preserve the history, wisdom, and religious beliefs of a society, oral literature takes various forms. The fluidity of the tradition must be kept in mind when reading the following discussion of its relatively fixed characteristics. It should also be kept in mind (1) that the following classification cannot take into account African terms or verbal forms, (2) that our vision of oral literature reflects what researchers have happened to record and informants are willing to give, and (3) that a strict purity of genres is a Western concept. Just as African civilizations tend to be pluralistic in philosophy and religion (they accept the possibility of many versions of truth instead of one), the forms in which they find expression mix poetry and prose, words, dance, and ritual.

Genres of African Oral Literature

Prose tales. Prose in the African oral tradition is that which tends toward ordinary speech as opposed to chanting or singing, although it may contain elements of the latter. Its principal form on record is the tale, which contains elements of myth, legend, and history. Tales, which are generally performed at night by adults, may include mime, dance, and song; may mix animals, humans, and divine beings; and may exist in related groups or cycles, such as the cycle of the hare or the tortoise or the hyena. There is not the same distinction between human, animal, and divine as in Western cultures, since there is a totemic link between humans and animals, both of whom are manifestations of the divine force that pervades the world. In fact, animals often stand in for specific persons, so as not to embarrass the latter or their descendants.

The most widespread theme in this literature is that of the trickster-hero, who recalls the Yoruba (Nigeria) god Eshu-Elegba. (The theme should not be taken to mean that Africans are immoral, since all societies tell tales where cunning overcomes power or advantage.) The trickster may be either a person or an animal. The trickster stands in opposition to the normal order of things. Rather than follow the rules of a society, he gets by on his own cleverness, often against far more powerful opponents. The most common animals in the trickster tradition are the hare (ancestor of the African American Br'er Rabbit in the tales of Uncle Remus), the hyena, the spider, and the tortoise. An example of such a trickster tale is one in which a tortoise challenges both an elephant and a hippopotamus to a tug-of-war and then positions them on opposite sides of a mountain so that they will be tugging against each other. After the resulting stalemate, the two animals gain a new respect for the tortoise.

Tales serve many other functions: they can explain a behavior, such as that of a hen scratching the earth, or a geographical detail, such as the two hills called *les mamelles* outside Dakar, Senegal. The tale pertaining to the latter, by the way, upholds the moral order. The *mamelles* are actually the humps of a hunchbacked wicked woman. One of the humps is her own. Fairies transfer the other hump to her from the back of a kinder woman.

Other tales pose a problem rather than give a clear moral lesson. For example, which of three brothers is the most responsible for saving their father: the first, who magically saw that their father in a distant land was ill; the second, who magically transported the three brothers to their father's side; or the third, who healed their father once they were there?

Tales can also explain the founding of a dynasty, the origins of a people, or the behavior of a god. In these latter cases, tales touch on elements of myth (sacred tales that shape belief) and legend (the stories of heroes and dynasties). Yet, since such elements do not make the tales recognized as authoritative sources of history and religious belief, one must assert that myth and legend in prose form do not have the status of more ceremonial religious poems and formal chanted epics. In other words, tales may use elements from myths and legends without necessarily being the source of those myths and legends.

Myths. Myth may be defined as a "story or a complex of story elements taken as expressing . . . certain deep-lying aspects of human and transhuman existence" (Wheelwright, 1965:538). Most of the prose narrative myths that we have—such as the great Dogon cosmogonic myth that explains how the universe spirals out from a single seed—were collected in conversations between a field researcher and a native informant. While the content of such myths is doubtlessly authentic as far as it goes, we do not necessarily know it in the fullness and in the form that an initiated Dogon audience would accept as sacred and authoritative. Further research may reveal such texts, but it is possible that a developed formal narrative myth constituting the foundation of belief in the sacred will never be revealed to the uninitiated.

Poetry. Poetry in oral literature is distinguished from normal speech by the sustained rhythm and modulation of the voice. It ranges from formal epic chants to informal melodic songs.

Narrative epic. Usually a chanted formulaic narrative that takes several days to perform, the epic tells historical legends dealing with conquerors and founders of a dynasty. Epics such as the *Ozidi* epic of the Ijo of southern Nigeria or the *Mwindo* epic of the Myanga people of eastern Zaire (now Democratic Republic of Congo) involve the entire community in dramatic festivities of music, dance, and poetry. Others, such as the famous *Sundiata* of Mali, may be chanted from beginning to end by a single bard. Sundiata, the legendary founder of Mali, is a shamanistic hero descended from a woman whose totem animal is the magical buffalo of Do. Although he is lame in his early childhood, when he finally walks he has superhuman strength so that he can uproot trees. He is, nevertheless, driven into exile by his brother, and only after a series of magical exploits that reveal his virtue as well as his strength does he return home to reign over the new empire of Mali. An epic of this sort is a source of history and social relations between families. For example, the coronation scene contains a list of the families who are allied to Sundiata and his descendants.

Occupational poetry. There are various forms of lyric poetry that accompany all aspects of life. Occupational poetry consists of poetry that belongs to a group exercising a trade such as farming, fishing, or hunting. For example, the Yoruba *ijala* are songs sung by hunters under the inspiration of the god Ogun of the Yoruba pantheon. They deal with a wide range of subject matter, including human ethics and relations, family lineages, distinguished individuals, mythology, animals, and plants. These are speech-like songs chanted at gatherings for Ogun. Occupational poetry, such as songs of Ewe fishermen and farmers, also includes poems sung during work, not just to relieve drudgery (as do work songs) but also to recall religious functions pertaining to the calling of a group.

Cult poetry. Cult poetry is sung during rituals for the divinities and as an aid in the practice of medicine. It is also used for incantations and as a tool for divination. This poetry, which either invokes or celebrates the forces of nature, contains the most conservative texts of oral literature, since its validity depends on an exact repetition or precise verbal formulas. The human word in this poetry is more than just a sound. It is a powerful act that controls forces of the universe. It is the human word, for example, that calls the force of a divinity to live in a wooden statue or mask.

Cultic chants consist of an enumeration of the characteristics and accomplishments of a divine being and an invocation for help. Consider, for example, this Tanzanian prayer to Ruwa, or God, that accompanies the sacrifice of a bull:

We know you Ruwa, Chief, Preserver.
He who united the bush and the plain.
You, Ruwa, Chief, the elephant indeed,
He who burst forth men that they lived. . . .
Chief, receive this bull of your name,
Heal him to whom you gave it and his children.
(Mapanje and White, 1983:119)

Praise songs. As cultic chants are to divinities, praise songs can be to rulers and other important men and women. Although praise songs serve many functions, such as preserving family history or historical values, their words are believed to empower a warrior about to go into battle by recalling the forces of that warrior's ancestors of whom he is the living representative. Because of their belief in the empowerment of the word, Wolof rulers are known to have gone into battle with encroaching French invaders against overwhelming odds.

The basic units of praise songs are (1) epithets that refer to a town, animal, or other object or event associated with a person or thing praised and (2) the proper name of a person. The latter can be expanded into a genealogy that outlines a whole family history. For example, in the praise song for the Wolof princess Semu of western Africa, instead of naming an important Wolof ruler, the *griot* lists four of his horses and the battlefields on which they died. In this song, a person's forename is usually followed by his or her mother's and father's names. But one can skip one or the other and proceed along either the paternal or the maternal line. Thus, in the song for Semu, the latter is referred to either as Semu Ganka Yaasin Mbaru (Ganka Yaasin being the father and Mbaru a remote paternal ancestor) or Semu Coro Wende (Coro Wende being the mother; see Joseph, 1979).

The following are praise names of the great Zulu chieftain Shaka from the southern tip of the continent:

He is Shaka, the unshakeable,
Thunderer-while-sitting, son of Menzi.
He is the bird that preys on other birds,
The battle-axe that excels over other battle-axes.
He is the long-strided pursuer, son of Ndaba,
Who pursued the sun and the moon.
He is the great hubbub like the rocks of Nkandla
Where elephants take shelter
When the heavens frown . . .[2]

There are many other genres of oral literature that are too numerous to mention. Among them are a wealth of love songs, work songs, and children's songs, as well as the epigrams, proverbs, and riddles that sprinkle African speech. As the Ibo of Nigeria say, "Proverbs are the palm oil with which words are eaten." An example of a riddle is the phrase "a house in which one does not turn around"; the answer is "a grave." There are yet other forms that incorporate acting and dialogue. For example, while a group of Wolof women are pounding millet, one will give the signal and the others will fall into a patterned conversation that follows the preordained plan of a kind of play.[3]

Written Literature in African Languages

Originating not in indigenous oral literature but in the missionary efforts of Islam and Christianity, written literature bore an uneasy relationship to oral traditions. (See Ambrose Moyo's chapter on religion for additional insights into the relationship among African religions, Christianity, and Islam.) African literatures under Islamic influence, such as Wolof, Swahili, and Hausa, were originally written in Arabic script and reflect the spirituality of the Quran—a spirituality sometimes at odds with traditional African cultures. Hausa secular verses in Arabic, for example, worked against sacred praise poetry, which should sing only of the Prophet Muhammad.

Literatures in such languages as Sesuto, Xhosa, Zulu, and Yoruba stand in the shadow of translations of the Bible and books such as John Bunyan's *Pilgrim's Progress.* Early works such as Thomas Mfolo's 1906 *Travelers of the East* came out on missionary printing presses. Yet, as Christianized writers became interested in indigenous oral traditions, they encountered the hostility of their missionary patrons. Thus, works like Mfolo's *Chaka* (Shaka), which is about the famous Zulu hero, did not appear in print until 1925, seventeen years after it was written.

The tension between Euro-Christianity and African traditions is also apparent in the Yoruba novels of the Nigerian chief Fagunwa. In works such as *The Forest of a Thousand Daemons,* Fagunwa, nourished by memories of his grandfather's court and a deep knowledge of Yoruba mythology, evokes a traditional world upon which he imposes references to a Christian God.

Patterns of latent opposition to Islamization or Christianization have given way to outright resistance to colonization in contemporary African writing in African languages. Writers such as Ngugi wa Thiong'o in Kenya and Ousmane Sembene and Cheikh Anta Diop in Senegal call for a literature in African languages as an essential step in "decolonizing the mind." According to Ngugi, it is only "revitalized African languages . . . which will be best placed to give to and receive from the wealth of our common [African and world] culture on an equal basis" (Ngugi, 1990:981). Elsewhere, Ngugi eloquently states the rationale for writing in one's native language:

> In writing one should hear all the whisperings, all the shouting, all the crying, all the loving and all the hating of the many voices in the past, and those voices will never speak to a writer in a foreign language. For us Kenyan writers, we can no longer avoid the question, whose language or history will our literature draw upon. (Zell, Bundy, and Coulon, 1983:434)

Diop and Ngugi see the African writer's situation very much like that of the English or French writer of the Renaissance in the face of Latin cultural imperialism. Just as Renaissance writers had to forge national languages while borrowing from all cultures, so the African writer must encompass the entire range of expression. In Senegal, for example, nationalists are translating major works of literature, arts, and sciences into Wolof. A writer such as the Senegalese Cheikh N'Dao has written his more recent works in Wolof first, before translating them into French, to give freer rein to his creative genius. Sembene increasingly resorts to films in Wolof in order to reach his Senegalese audience. Mazisi Kunene from South Africa writes in Zulu before he translates into English. He has written *Zulu Poems* (1970) and two epics, *Emperor Shaka the Great* (1979) and *Anthem for the Decades* (1981). Although literatures in European languages such as French, English, and Portuguese remain important for the time being, movements such as those in Senegal and South Africa will inevitably change the map of African literature as the production of works in African languages increases.

African Literature in European Languages

The following sections on written African literature in European languages deal with two main themes: (1) the African literary response to European accounts about Africa and (2) the shift in the postcolonial era from responding to European literature to addressing problems of the new African nations. Much of the rest of the chapter is also devoted to naming African authors and works to provide a starting point for newcomers to this literature.

Written African literature in European languages was born in reaction to European colonial writings intended to explain Africa to other Europeans. The Europeans claimed a privileged, objective knowledge about Africa based on extended study, short voyages, or prolonged residence. Some, such as South Africa's Gordimer and Coetzee, consider Africa to be their home. European writings take many forms, including novels such as Joseph Conrad's *Heart of Darkness* (1902), travelogues such as André Gide's *Voyage to the Congo* (1927), and reports to various commercial companies intending to set up operations on the continent. Colonial newspapers are also an important source of European views. Much of this writing paints Africa in terms of extremes. Africans are represented either as noble savages in a picturesque exotic setting or as primitive wild beings suffering from disease, devoid of spiritual and moral qualities, and in need of the civilizing benefits of European colonialism.

Although individual authors have varying positions, they tend to smooth over differences in order to "invent" the concept of Africa as a place with cultural constants. Even distinguished colonial ethnographers such as Leo Frobenius and Maurice Delafosse or intellectuals such as the anticolonialist Gide remained "Eurocentric" (i.e., they "saw" Africa through European cultural biases). They benefited from colonial power, which domesticated the continent for European travel, and, in turn, often used their knowledge and insights to further colonial power. For example, Placide Tempels's *Bantu Philosophy* studies the religion of black Africans in order to facilitate conversion by Catholic missionaries. The French general Louis Leon Ceser Faidherbe wrote distinguished studies of the Wolof (Senegal) with the intention of infiltrating them and subjecting them to French domination.

African Literature in French

Negritude poetry and pan-Africanism as a response to colonial literature. After isolated works such as Bakary Diallo's *Force Bonté,* which sang the praises of the French colonizers, African literature in French came into its own as an alternate voice to European colonial literature in the late 1940s with the founding of the journal *Présence africaine* (1947). Other important works were the publication of Léopold Sédar Senghor's collection of poetry entitled *Chants d'ombre* (1945) and his *Anthologie de la nouvelle poésie nègre et malagache* (1948), which included poems by other African and Afro-Caribbean writers. Senghor's poetry—which also includes *Hosties noires* (1948), *Chants pour Naëtt* (1949), *Ethiopiques* (1956), *Nocturnes* (1961), *Elégie des alizés* (1969), and *Lettres d'hivernage* (1973)—embodies the tenets of the Negritude movement, which was born in the 1930s.[4] At that time, students from francophone African countries and African American writers in exile in Paris discovered their African roots in the context of pan-Africanism.

Pan-Africanism, which ultimately harks back to the late-eighteenth-century effort to return African slaves to the newly created state of Liberia, was forged in a series of congresses held in London, Paris, Brussels, Manchester, Lisbon, and New York between 1900 and 1945. Some of its distinguished early founders included E. W. Blyden and W. E. B. Du Bois. Writings inspired by the pan-African movement continue the European quest for global constants of an African culture and are often inspired by the work of European ethnographers. But, instead of a privileged European narrator, pan-African writings call into question European objectivity by substituting narrators and main characters whose privileged position of authority comes from their identity as Africans. According to "Black Orpheus," Jean-Paul Sartre's preface to Senghor's anthology, such writing turns the tables so that it is the European who is the object of the African's objectifying gaze instead of the other way around.

Negritude defines an African way of being in the world that is antithetical to that of the European. This definition recalls European thinking according to which the European is "intellectual, inventive, violent, steel-hard, and asexual"; by contrast, the African is "emotional, uninventive, at peace with nature, humane, and oversexed" (Owomoyela, 1979:39). But Senghor gives new value to characteristics traditionally attributed to Africans so that "uninventiveness" is attributed to "peace with nature," and what puritanical Europeans consider as "oversexed" is seen as a healthy sensuality. Senghor attempts to give his verse "swing and dance in the rhythms of his native Serer" (Beier, Knappert, and Moser, 1974:141). An example of Senghor's verse is the famous "Black Woman," which establishes a canon of black beauty:

> Naked woman, dark woman
> Firm-fleshed ripe fruit, sombre raptures of black wine, mouth
> making, lyrical my mouth.

Negritude, with its insistence on working out a definition of African cultural identity, made particular sense in the context of the assimilationist policies of French colonialism, which were designed to make Africans culturally into black French people. For some proponents of Negritude, however, the return to cultural roots is not to be confused with cultural isolationism. Although poetry such as Senghor's paints an idealistic picture of African traditions, it owes much to Europe. One sees the influence of the poetry of Paul Claudel and St. John Perse. Sartre's preface to Senghor's anthology, with its emphasis on ways of being and on the gaze of the black underling, places the anthology squarely under the aegis of existentialism. Poems in the anthology such as those of Aimé Césaire reflect the influence of surrealism and Marxism.

Thus, a mixed identity of voice is inherent in Negritude—and, indeed, the entire tradition of written African literature that is the subject of this chapter. As Alioune Diop, the founder of *Présence africaine* (1947), says:

> Neither white nor yellow nor black, incapable of returning entirely to the traditions of our origins or to assimilate ourselves to Europe, we have the impression of constituting a new race of mental mulattoes but a race that has never been revealed in its originality and had hardly ever been aware of it.[5]

The Negritude poets work out their cultural ambiguity in differing ways. Senghor does not attempt to return to a pure state of Africanness but to give new value to traditions and ways of being African in a world in which Africa and Europe are "joined by the navel" (Owomoyela, 1979:41). Senghor has also written essays on various cultural and political subjects; the best known are the three volumes entitled *Liberté I, II,* and *III.*

Other poets, such as Birago Diop (*Leurres et lueurs,* 1967) and David Diop, reject assimilation. David Diop's poetry is particularly forceful:

> My poor brother in the silk-faced dinner jacket
> Squealing murmuring and strutting in condescending drawing rooms
> We pity you. (Quoted in Owomoyela, 1979:45)

The Congolese poet Tchicaya U Tamsi is of a younger generation. Although his poetry inherits its surrealism through Césaire, it is more private and Christian than Césaire's. U Tamsi's collections of poems include *Le Mauvais Sang* (1955; *Bad Blood*), *Feu de brousse* (1957; *Brush Fire,* 1964), *Triche-coeur* (1960; *A Game of Cheat Heart*), *Epitomé* (1962), *Le Ventre* (1964, *The Belly*), and *La Veste d'Intérieur* (1977). U Tamsi's greater freedom is typical of the second generation of African writers.

Owing to the establishment of African literature as a fact by their predecessors, later generations are able to pursue more independent approaches that do not deal directly with issues of assimilation. Such is the case in the poetry of Zairiah V. Y. Mudimbe, whose *Déchirures* (1971) is a collection of love verse.

Fiction from colonialism to independence. Like the Negritude poets, the novelists of the 1950s and 1960s established a point of view that is culturally mixed. Camara Laye represents the beauty and harmony of traditional African culture but also the painful necessity of change. His *L'Enfant noir* (1953; *Dark Child*) is the autobiography of a young man who has made the decision to study in Paris and who laments the loss of a traditional childhood. Yet, for Laye, assimilation should work both ways, as we see in his second novel, *Le Regard du roi* (1954; *Radiance of the King*), where the European Clarence is obliged to learn the ways of his African hosts. Laye's third novel, *Dramouss* (1966; *A Dream of Africa*) warns of the dangers of assimilation without respect for African cultural roots. The novel is an account of the author's return home after six years in Paris. The harmonious traditional society of his childhood is now replaced by a society of violence.

Cheikh Hamidou Kane's philosophical novel *Aventure ambiguë* (1961; *Ambiguous Adventure*) is a more troubling account of assimilation. A family that embodies the essence of traditional African royalty decides to risk sending one of its sons, Samba Diallo, to school in Europe so that he may help his society open up to European technology. The experiment fails, however, when Samba, unable to hold the two cultures together, commits suicide.

Two postcolonial novels by V. Y. Mudimbe also portray the impossibility of holding two cultures together. In *Entre les eaux: Dieu, un prêtre, la révolution* (1973), a priest, Pierre Landu, fails in his attempt to adapt Catholicism and Marxism for what Jonathan Ngate calls an "anti-colonial and ideal view of justice" (Ngate, 1988:13); whereas in *L'Ecart* (1979), Nara goes mad because of his inability to choose between the West and Africa in either love or intellectual activity.

The novels of two francophone Cameroonian novelists, Ferdinand Oyono and Mongo Beti, embody an aesthetic of politically committed realism at odds with the gentler approach of novels such as *L'Enfant noir.* The works of these novelists present a frankly pessimistic view of cultural assimilation in tones of satiric irony that imply a scathing critique of the French colonial civilizing mission. Oyono's tragicomic novels *Une Vie de boy* (1956; *Boy*) and *Le Vieux Nègre et la médaille* (1956; *The Old Man and the Medal*) represent heroes who come to the painful awareness that colonialism and its masters are a sham and that assimilation means humiliation, exploitation, and, in the case of Toundi in *Boy,* death.

Beti also portrays the failure of the colonial system in his novels. *Le Pauvre Christ de Bomba* (1956; *Poor Christ of Bomba*), *Mission terminée* (1957; *Mission to Kala*), and *Le Roi miraculé* (1958; *King Lazarus*) satirize the work of Christian missionaries and French schools. Beti's later novels, written after independence, will be discussed below.

Oyono's and Beti's colonial novels, however, stand in the movement of Negritude as part of the opposition. They represent authentic African voices, but voices that explode not only the myths of the European civilizing mission but also the ethnographic constructions of Africa on which so much of the Negritude movement is based. The satiric realism of Oyono and Beti has been called pessimistic. Although politically committed to the struggle against colonialism, it portrays contemporary Africans as lost and acculturated with no hope for the future because of the disastrous policies of the colonial masters.

Ousmane Sembene and the Afro-Asiatic movement. Like pan-African writers, those inspired by Afro-Asianism also replace the European perspective with an African one. These writers assume the role of conscience of their people. Respectful of African traditions but rejecting the Negritude aesthetic altogether, writers in the Afro-Asiatic movement seek to mobilize their people against European colonial domination through a call to Marxist-inspired political struggle rather than a return to cultural purity. Afro-Asianism, which crystallized at the conference of Bandung, Indonesia, in 1955, marks a coming together of the African struggles for independence with forces generated by (1) movements of Arab and Asian nationalism, (2) the support of the Soviet Union for colonized peoples against Western imperialism, and (3) the newfound independence of China, India, Egypt, and Indonesia.

Sembene embodies the Afro-Asiatic aesthetic in both literature and film.[6] His most important novel is the classic *Les Bouts de bois de Dieu* (1960; *God's Bits of Wood*), which is the story of the successful 1947 Dakar-Niger railroad strike against the French during the colonial period. The author's role as conscience of his people, holding up the way of liberation, is clear in an author's note that precedes the novel:

> The men and women who, from the tenth of October, 1947, to the nineteenth of March, 1948, took part in this struggle for a better way of life owe nothing to anyone: neither to any "civilizing mission" nor to any parliament or parliamentarian. Their example was not in vain. Since then, Africa has made progress.[7]

Other works include the autobiographical *Docker noir* (1956) about the author's experiences as a dock worker in Marseille, *Oh pays, mon beau peuple* (1957), *Voltaïque* (1962; *Tribal Scars and Other Stories*), *L'Harmattan* (1964), *Le Mandat et Véhi Ciosane* (1969; *The Money Order with White Genesis*), *Xala* (1973), and *Le Dernier de l'empire* (1981).

Although *God's Bits of Wood* was successful in Europe, Sembene was dissatisfied because he was unable to reach his own people. Thus, he took advantage of an offer from the Moscow Film School to learn cinema. His first film was *Borom saret,* which tells the story of the driver of a donkey-drawn taxi cart. From that point on, Sembene, the father of African cinema, has converted many of his short stories into films in which he uses native Senegalese languages instead of or along with French. The subsequent work of Sembene spans the entire gamut of African filmmaking—primarily a phenomenon that emerged in former French colonies in Africa—and will be used to represent African cinema in this chapter. His *Emitaï* (1971) and *Camp de Thiaroye* (1988) describe colonialist abuses during and immediately after World War II. *La Noire de . . .* (1965; *Black Girl*) recounts the travails of a maid who is so mistreated by her French master and mistress that she commits suicide.

Other films explore issues in the precolonial past—not to reestablish cultural purity, however, but to make a point about present domination. Sembene's film *Ceddo* (1977) is a study of African resistance to conversion to Islam. This film and *Camp de Thiaroye* are politically so explosive that they have been either banned or edited by censors in Senegal.

Films such as *Mandabi* (winner of a prize at the Venice Film Festival) and *Xala* (1974) are socialist-realist denunciations of abuses in postcolonial Senegalese society. *Xala*—the title means temporary sexual impotence in Wolof—attacks the political, economic, and cultural impotence of the Senegalese black bourgeoisie. This shift from an emphasis on answering European accounts about Africa to a concern to identify problems and issues in contemporary independent Africa is also characteristic of fiction written after French African colonies achieved independence in the early 1960s. Sembene's most recent films in this vein are *Guelwaar* and *Fat'Kine.*

Postcolonial fiction in French. Postcolonial fiction explores many different directions. Two novels of the 1960s stand as a transition between colonial Negritude fiction and later postcolonial fiction, which deals with problems of African society with little or no reference to Europeans.

Yambo Ouologuem's *Le Devoir de violence* (1966; *Bound to Violence*) attacks the ethnographically inspired myths of a harmonious precolonial African culture with a representation of the African past as a series of violent episodes. It presents an even more negative view of the African past than do the ironic Oyono and Beti.

Ahmadou Kourouma's 1968 *Soleils des indépendances (Suns of Independence)* features a deposed African prince who attempts to adjust to conditions in a modern African state. What is striking about this novel is its pluralism. Here there is no authoritative voice or privileged perspective, African or otherwise. Rather, events can be partially, but not entirely, explained by various mutually exclusive perspectives provided by Islamic, European, or traditional African spiritual traditions. The language of the novel, which Africanizes French with expressions drawn from the author's native Mandingo, is probably the most original in African francophone fiction.

Postcolonial fiction explores many different directions. Postcolonial "novels of disillusion" attack the abuses of postcolonial African states: dictatorship, corruption, and misery. This fiction is less clearly didactic in nature. It neither embodies a clear-cut ideology nor does it present authoritative visions of the African past—although the influence of African tradition remains present in many subtle ways. Postcolonial fiction, rather, explores reality in order to open new possibilities. This stance was already prepared by the colonial novels of Beti, Oyono, and Kourouma and is embodied in Beti's later novels: *Perpétue ou l'habitude du malheur* (1974; *Perpetua and the Habit of Unhappiness*), *Remember Ruben* (1974), and *La Ruine presque cocasse d'un polichinelle.* Other writers in this vein are Sony Labou Tansi, whose novels include *La Vie et demie* (1979) and *L'Etat honteux* (1981); Henri Lopes (*Le Pleurer rire,* 1982; *The Laughing Cry*); and Emmanuel Dongala (*Johnny Chien Méchant, 2002; Johnny Mad Dog).*

More recent fiction abandons political agenda altogether for either a variety of inner adventures, such as Ibrahima Ly's *La Toile d'araignée,* or a portrait of the decadence of Senegalese society, as in Abasse Ndione's *Vie en spirale* or Lopes's *Sur l'Autre Rive* (1992).

One of the most prominent writers of the past twenty years is Boris Boubacar Diop, who has written a series of distinguished novels such as *Le temps de Tamango* (1981; *The Time of Tamango*), *Les tambours de la mémoire* (1990; *The Drums of Memory*), *Les traces de la meute* (1993; *The Scent of the Mob*), and *Le cavalier et son ombre* (1997; *The Rider and His Shadow*). He is also the author of several movie scenarios and the founder of the Senegalese newspaper, *Sud.* In 2004 Diop wrote his first novel in Wolof, *Doomi Golo (The Monkey's Kids),* and his *Murambi:Le livre des ossements* (2000; *Murambi: The Book of Bones*) is one of the most prominent products of the project "Rwanda: To Write Against Oblivion" ("Rwanda, écrire par devoir de mémoire"), which Nocky Djedanoum, director of the yearly Fest'Africa festival in Lille, France, started to commemorate the Rwandan genocide of 1994.

Other writers in the project include Monique Ilboudo from Burkina Faso, the Rwandans Vénuste Kayimahe and Jean-Marie Rurangwa, Koulsy Lamko from Chad, the Guinean Tierno Monénembo, the Kenyan Meja Mwangi, Véronique Tadjo from Ivory Coast, Abdourahman Waberi from Djibouti, and Djedanoum (Chad). Writers in the project visited Rwanda and saw firsthand sites of whitened bones that witnessed scenes of genocidal massacre.

Women's writing is an important phenomenon in Africa. Much of it corrects the vision of Africa in men's writing just as African men's writing corrected European accounts of Africa. Women's writing draws back from authoritative positions as it seeks a new language. For example, Mariama Bâ's *Une si longue lettre* (1979; *So Long a Letter*) portrays a woman caught between the rhetoric of the traditional Senegalese family and that of a modern Europeanized feminism as she struggles, first to create her marriage and then to survive it when it turns unexpectedly polygynous. In this first-person narrative, no voice, including the narrator's own, suffices to explain events with authority. There is, for example, no explicit call for monogamy. Bâ's second novel, *Le Chant écarlate* (1981), is similar; it explores the problems encountered by a Frenchwoman in her marriage to a Senegalese man.

Aminata Maïga Ka's two novellas, *La Voie du salut* and *Miroir de la vie* (1985), also present women whose lives diverge from their ways of thinking. Although largely third-person narratives, these pieces taken together artfully reproduce in French the ways of thinking and speaking characteristic of various classes of people. Ka's characters typically fail to cope with the realities that overwhelm them. They turn to suicide and alcohol. Such failures are brought about not only by external events but also by the rhetorics of class, honor, and family in which the characters are trapped. Like the novels of Bâ, these novellas open up new perspectives brought about by women's voices but leave readers to draw their own conclusions.

The most prolific of Senegalese women writers is Aminata Sow Fall, who writes in a more pluralistic vein. Her novels include *Le Revenant* (1976), *La Grève des battus ou les déchets humains* (1979), and *L'Appel des arènes* (1982). These novels not only elaborate a woman's language but also explore the contradictions and blind spots of male discourse. For example, Sow Fall's most recent novel, *L'Ex-père de la nation* (1987), explores the self-deceptive rhetoric of the male narrator, who is a deposed African head of state in prison thinking back over the events of his rise and fall. What seems at first a language of pretension turns out to be a rhetoric of light, transparency, and cleanliness that ironically blinds the narrator to the machinations of power going on inside and outside the presidential palace. Sow Fall artfully reproduces the various French dialects characteristic of different classes of society. Other Francophone women of note include Calixthe Beyala, Ken Bugul, and Myriam Warner Vieyra.

Theater in French. Theater in French has not been a very successful genre in Africa, as opposed to the very dynamic cinematic tradition of Francophone countries. The formal setting of theaters contrasts sharply with the setting of the popular village square where much West African oral literature takes place. The strongest Negritude playwright is Martinique's Aimé Césaire, whose plays *La Tragédie du roi Christophe (Emperor Jones)* and *Une Saison au Congo* are distinguished by a highly original use of French. Another playwright from the early period is Cheikh N'Dao, whose *Exil d'Albouri* dramatizes a moment from the traditional African past.

More recently, however, the African stage has been distinguished by the works of Sony Labou Tansi (*Conscience de tracteur,* 1979; and *La Parenthèse de sang,* 1981) and Nicole Werewere-Liking (*La Puissance de UM,* 1979; and *Une Nouvelle Terre,* 1980). Werewere-Liking's *Orphée d'Afric/Orphée d'Afrique* is a mixed genre, a novel followed by a play. A Cameroonian feminist who wants to bring spiritual healing through African arts, Werewere-Liking has founded Ki-Yi Mbock village, which brings together "resident artists, sculptors, actors and singers who [can] express African spirituality and the rich diversity of African culture" (Smith, 2006:54). Now settled in Ivory Coast, Ki-Yi Mbock's most notable recent endeavor is its Project Hidjingo, which is aimed at taking in and educating youth with a heavy emphasis on therapeutic dance. Werewere-Liking is also a novelist. Her recent novel *Mémoire amputee* won the 2005 Noma Award.

African Literature in Portuguese

Before going on to African literature in English, a word is in order about lusophone (Portuguese) African literature. Poets such as the first president of Angola, Agostinho Neto, the Angolan José Craveirinha, and the Cape Verdean Baltasar Lopes write in the tradition of pan-Africanism. The works of these writers and others are known to English speakers primarily from Mário de Andrade's *Antologia de poesia negra de espressão portuguesa* (1958). Fiction writers include José Luandino Vieira (*Luuanda,* 1963; and *A Vida verdadeira de Domingos Xavier,* 1961; *The Real Life of Domingos Xavier*) and Luís Bernard Honwana (*Nós natanis a cão tinhoso,* 1964; *We Killed Mangy Dog and Other Stories*).

African Literature in English

African writers in English tend to be more independent than those in French because France had a much more centralized policy of linguistic imperialism than did England. Among other policies, France did not promote the translation of the Bible into African languages, as did Protestant England. For this reason, writers in English tend to be more secure in their identity. For example, the best-known Nigerian writer, Wole Soyinka, has said in reference to Negritude, "A tiger does not proclaim his tigritude, he pounces." He goes on to say that what one should expect from poetry is "an intrinsic poetic quality, not a mere name-dropping" (quoted in Zell, Bundy, and Coulon, 1983:491).

As a result, African literature in English has rich traditions in the novel, poetry, and drama. Unlike French, where most writers tend to write in one genre alone, African writers in English practice several genres. The phenomenon is so rich and diverse that it does not yield to so neat a periodization as does French African literature, since novelists of the earlier English African generations already were writing social criticism of African life of the kind common in the third period of French African literature.

Nigerian fiction. Aside from scattered beginnings in the eighteenth and nineteenth centuries (Olaudah Equiano and Phillis Wheatley), Nigerian literature in English took its impulse from two sources. One is the popular tradition of Onitsha novels (named after the market where they were sold) that began in the 1940s. The second is the educational infrastructure provided by the founding of the University College of Ibadan in 1948. Now called the University of Ibadan, this institution had more autonomous policies than later French universities, so that African writers could teach there and establish a closer relationship between African culture and writing in English than could writers who used French.

The best-known and most prolific writer to come out of the Onitsha tradition is Cyprian Ekwensi. Although a man of considerable education, Ekwensi has written popular novels such as *People of the City* (1954), *Jagua Nana* (1961), *Divided We Stand* (1980), and *Motherless Baby* (a novella). He has also written several children's books. Ekwensi's novels feature people from various walks of life but often deal with such issues as prostitution, urban lowlife, and political violence.

The major Nigerian novelist of this early generation is Chinua Achebe, who has also written poetry (*Beware Soul Brothers and Other Poems,* 1972), short stories (*Girls at War and Other Stories,* 1972), and various children's stories. Achebe is a writer from the more learned tradition of Nigerian writing, having completed his studies at the University College of Ibadan in 1953. His great cycle of novels written between 1958 and 1966 spans a period of Nigerian history from the onset of colonialism to the eve of the civil war sparked by the attempt of Biafra to secede from the country in the 1960s.

Like French writers, Achebe—whose statements on the role of the writer in Africa have been published in a collection entitled *Morning Yet on Creation Day* (1975)—originally began to write in order to correct European writings on Africa. He said in a Bill Moyers interview that in college, while reading Conrad's *Heart of Darkness,* he realized that he was not the white hero but "one of the natives jumping up and down on the beach." It was then that he knew that it was time to write another story. Elsewhere he says, "I would be quite satisfied if my novels (especially ones I set in the past) did no more than teach my readers that their past—with all its imperfection—was not one long night of savagery from which the first Europeans acting on God's behalf delivered them" (Zell, Bundy, and Coulon, 1983:345).

Accordingly, Achebe's first novel, *Things Fall Apart* (1958), is the story of the tragedy that the arrival of Christianity and the onset of colonialism represent for the village of Umuofia. Thus, the novel frequently leaves the main character, Okonkwo, in the background in order to give rich descriptions of the traditional village life that is disrupted by the arrival of the Europeans. Achebe alludes to the great life cycles implied in planting and harvesting, getting married and dying, and passing the various ceremonial stages of social promotion.

Achebe's third novel, *Arrow of God* (1964), is set in the 1920s but also deals with the conflict between traditional and modern values. It is the story of the backfire of the project of a village priest named Ezeulu, who sends his son Oduche to the mission school to learn the white man's secrets: Oduche converts to Christianity and kills the sacred python of Ezeulu's traditional African religion.

Achebe's first and third novels recall the literature of Negritude because of their emphasis on African tradition. His second and fourth novels, which deal with conflicts and tensions in modern Nigeria, prefigure novels of contemporary African literature. *No Longer at Ease* (1960) is the story of Okonkwo's grandson, who has difficulties adapting to Nigerian society after he returns from school in England. He falls in love with an outcast woman and succumbs to bribes that ultimately ruin his career. *A Man of the People* (1964) is a satire on the government of Nigeria. The end of the novel, which evokes a military coup, foreshadows the onset of the civil war over the secession of Biafra.

After a period of more than twenty years, Achebe published another novel, *Anthills of the Savannah,* in 1987. This novel describes the power plays and corruption of contemporary African society from the perspective of several narrators, including the president of the country, two of his school friends, and their girlfriends. This kaleidoscopic vision leaves the reader to draw conclusions as to the whys and wherefores of the plot.

Achebe is a master of the English language and draws heavily on classical European as well as Ibo and Yoruba cultures. For example, the title of *Things Fall Apart* is derived from W. B. Yeats's "The Second Coming." The stately English of Achebe's early novels is colored with Ibo-inspired proverbs, whereas in *Anthills of the Savannah,* he reproduces modern spoken Nigerian English, including "pidgin," used by the less educated.

A much more extreme experimentation with English is evident in the works of the non-Ibo novelists Amos Tutuola—whose novels, such as *The Palm-Wine Drinkard* (1952), use speech patterns of the Yoruba language—and Gabriel Okara, who reproduces patterns of his native Ijo syntax in his novels, such as *The Voice.* Ken Saro-Wiwa's *Sozaboy: A Novel in Rotten English* (1985), which portrays army life during the civil war, also experiments with language in its mix of pidgin, broken, and standard English. It is the foundation of Saro-Wiwa's literary reputation, which has been overshadowed by his execution by the Nigerian military regime in 1995 (Killam and Rowe, 2000:257).

Like their French-speaking counterparts, women novelists in Nigeria have been productive, writing in voices different from those of male authors. Flora Nwapa is the first published woman novelist in Africa. Her *Efuru* (1966) and *Idu* (1969) describe the difficulties women encounter as they come to terms with their expected social roles as wives and mothers. Her *Never Again* (1976) is a description of an episode in the Nigerian civil war from a woman's perspective. Nwapa has also published collections of short stories such as *This Is Lagos and Other Stories* (1971) and *Wives at War and Other Stories* (1980). She has founded a publishing house that has published her novel *One Is Enough* (1981) and children's stories, which she hopes will be read by children the world over.

Another major Nigerian woman novelist is Buchi Emecheta, who has been hailed as having given a realistic and complex alternative to the one-sided picture of African women found in male fiction. A sociologist who obtained her training while a single parent supporting five children, Emecheta got her start writing a regular column recording her observations of London society for the *New Statesman.* Her first two novels, the autobiographical *In the Ditch* (1972) and *Second Class Citizen* (1974), detail difficulties of African women in England, whereas *The Bride Price* (1976), *The Slave Girl* (1977), and *Joys of Motherhood* (1979) deal with the difficulties encountered by women as they marry, bear children, or find themselves tools for the ambitions of their male relatives. Other novels deal with the civil war *(Destination Biafra)* and problems in contemporary Nigerian society *(Naira Power* and *Double Yoke).*

Emecheta is a powerful writer whose images are metaphors for deep female experience as well as literal descriptions of traditional African supernatural forces. For example, in *Joys of Motherhood,* the experience of the main character, Nnu Ego, is often explained in terms of water imagery that recalls that she is accursed by her *chi,* a water deity.

Nigerian poetry and theater. Two main forces behind Nigerian literature are the Mbari Club—which is not only a meeting place for writers and artists but also a publishing outlet—and the literary journal *Black Orpheus,* which has published the work of many Nigerian poets in its pages.

Christopher Okigbo (*Heavensgate,* 1962, and *Limits,* 1964) was a poet originally published by Mbari. A posthumous collection entitled *Labyrinths with Paths of Thunder* (1971) came out in London after Okigbo's life was cut short in the civil war. Okigbo, who considered himself a reincarnation of his maternal grandfather—a priest of Idoto—drew on a good background in Western culture as well as the cultures of Nigeria. He has said that his poetic sequence *Heavensgate, Limits,* and *Distances* is "like telling the beads of a rosary; except that the beads are neither stone nor agate but globules of anguish strung together on memory" (Zell, Bundy, and Coulon, 1983:448). An example of his cultural eclecticism is *Heavensgate,* which is written as an Easter sequence conceived as a Catholic mass offered to Mother Idoto.

In his 1965 verse collection, *A Reed in the Tide,* John Pepper Clark, a playwright as well as a poet, calls himself a "mulatto—not in flesh but in mind" (Zell, Bundy, and Coulon, 1983:367). His other verse includes *Poems,* brought out by Mbari in 1962, and *Casualties* (1968).

Clark is also a playwright of distinction whose plays include *Song of a Goat* (1962), *The Masquerade,* and *The Raft.* His *Ozidi* (1966) is based on an Ijo saga. He subsequently published a book-length edition (*The Ozidi Saga,* 1977), which in the oral tradition takes seven days to perform.

Soyinka, who won the 1986 Nobel Prize in literature, is perhaps the best contemporary dramatic poet in English, as well as a distinguished novelist, essayist, and playwright. Soyinka's first verse was published in *Black Orpheus*. His first collection, *Idanre, and Other Poems* (1967), includes the long poem "Idanre," which was written for the Commonwealth Arts Festival of 1965. "Idanre" is a creation myth of Ogun, the Yoruba god of iron, who, with his aspects of creation and destruction, represents human dualism and is for Soyinka the "symbol figure" of his society. Other collections include *A Shuttle in the Crypt* (1971), written during Soyinka's civil war imprisonment, and *Ogun Abibman* (1976), which is a tribute to the African struggle for liberation.

Soyinka's first novel, *The Interpreters* (1965), is the story of a group of university-educated friends who attempt to interpret their role in Nigerian society. The novel has an extremely dense texture of language that recalls James Joyce. *Season of Anomy* (1973) incorporates the myth of Orpheus and Eurydice as it tells the quest of Ofeyi for his abducted mistress, Iriyise, the cocoa princess. The novel is a political allegory of the social ills of modern Nigeria that mixes reality and fantasy, African ritual nature myths, and European archetypes. Soyinka's *Ake: The Years of Childhood* (1981) is an autobiography of his first twelve years.

Soyinka is best known for his more than twenty plays, which use themes concerning African culture and politics as well as the confrontation between Europe and Africa to explore universal constants of the human mind and metaphysical problems of good and evil. Soyinka sets out his views on writing in a collection of essays entitled *Myth, Literature and the African World* (1976). In this work, one of his goals is to establish parallels between a classical Yoruba worldview and the Greek tradition in European literature. His essay "The Fourth Stage" is on the Yoruba concept of tragedy, whereas in "Drama and the African World View," he affirms that the differences of European and African drama result from two different world visions:

> Westerners have a compartmentalizing habit of thought which selects aspects of human emotion and even scientific observations and "turns them into separatist myths." African creativity, on the other hand, results from "a cohesive understanding of irreducible truths." (Zell, Bundy, and Coulon, 1983:52)

Soyinka is a brilliant satirist. In a lighter vein are his early *Lion and the Jewel* (1959), which mockingly chronicles the competition between a polygynous, lecherous village chief and a Europeanized schoolteacher for the hand of a village beauty, and *The Trials of Brother Jero* (1963), which satirizes the syncretistic Christian cults of Nigeria.

Other plays written for important occasions unflinchingly attack popular conceptions. *A Dance of the Forests,* performed to celebrate Nigerian independence in October 1960, criticizes "the myth of the glorious African past, rejecting the Negritude concept that the revival of African culture must be inspired by the African cultural heritage alone" (Beier, Knappert, and Moser, 1974:142). *Kongi's Harvest,* written for the 1966 World Festival of Negro Arts in Dakar, relentlessly satirizes African dictatorships. *The Road* (1965), performed at the Commonwealth Arts Festival (1965), is one of the fullest expressions of Soyinka's tragic view of life.

Works such as the satirical sketches gathered in *Before the Blackout* (1971) and *Madmen and Specialists* (1971) use theater of the absurd techniques to attack the civil war. *Madmen and Specialists,* however, uses the events of the civil war as a context to consider the problem of evil, whereas Soyinka's *Bacchae of Euripides* (1973) combines elements of the Greek play with allusions to public executions on Bar Beach in Lagos during the civil war to conduct a ritualistic exploration of the human mind.

Death and the King's Horseman (1975) is based on historical events in which a district officer prevented the Elesin Oba from committing suicide to follow his king into death. According to Soyinka,

> The confrontation in the play is largely metaphysical, contained in the human vehicle which is Elesin and the universe of the Yoruba mind—the world of the living, the dead and the unborn, and the numinous passage which links all: transition. (Zell, Bundy, and Coulon, 1983:489)

(Soyinka, by the way, served as editor of the distinguished cultural and political magazine *Transition [Ch'indaba].* In 1991 when the magazine was reborn under the editorship of K. Anthony Appia and Henry Louis Gates Jr., Soyinka served as chair of its editorial board.)

Soyinka's *Opera Wonyosi* (1981) draws on Brecht's *Threepenny Opera* and John Gay's *Beggar's Opera* to satirize contemporary Nigerian life. According to Robert MacDowell, Soyinka

> makes use of fascinating devices in his own expressionistic plays; dancing, singing, miming, speeches in verse, flashbacks (sometimes covering eons of time), and characters from the spirit world. He employs techniques familiar at Nigerian festivals, and utilizes any poetic methods which enforce the emotional and intellectual impact of his dramas; in short he has no slavish attachment to the merely naturalistic level of presentation. (Zell, Bundy, and Coulon, 1983:490)

Soyinka is a committed writer but one who has a high conception of his art. At the 1967 African-Scandinavian Writers Conference in Stockholm, he criticized foreign publishers who create reputations for insignificant authors and the African author whom he characterizes as "the most celebrated skin of inconsequence to obscure the true flesh of the African dilemma" (Zell, Bundy, and Coulon, 1983:491). He goes on to say that such a writer

> was content to turn his eye backwards in time and prospect in archaic fields for forgotten gems which would dazzle and distract the present. But never inwards, never truly into the present. . . . The artist has always functioned in African society as the record of the mores and experience of his society and as the voice of vision in his own time. It is time for him to respond to this essence of himself. (Zell, Bundy, and Coulon, 1983:491–492)

Other Nigerian and West African authors. Nigerian authors of the second generation who deserve mention are poets Tanure Ojaide, Odia Ofeimun, Niyi Osundare, and Harry Garuba; the dramatists Femi Osofisan, Ola Rotimi, and Tess Onwueme; and the novelists Kole Omotoso and Festus Iyayi. There is also now a third generation, which includes the poets Afam Akeh, Uche Nduka, Esiaba Irobi, Kemi Atanda-Ilori, and Catherine Acholonu as well as the novelist Wale Okediran.

Nigerian literature dominates West African anglophone writing, but some other notable writers are the Gambian poet Lenri Peters and the Ghanaians Kofi Awooner (poet), Efua Sutherland (playwright), Ami Ata Aidoo (playwright and novelist), and Ayi Kwei Armah (novelist).

East Africa. Important writers from East Africa include the Kenyan short story writer Grace Ogot, who incorporates tribal laws and wisdom in her works; the Ugandan poet Okot p'Bitek; the Kenyan writer Ngugi wa Thiong'o (formerly James Ngugi) and the Somalian novelist and playwright Nuruddin Farah.

Ngugi's novels *Weep Not Child* (1964), *The River Between* (1965), and *A Grain of Wheat* (1967) parallel Achebe's novels in Nigeria in that they trace the history of Kenya from the arrival of the British to modern times. According to Andrew Gurr,

> They start with the alienation of Gikuyu land and end with the alienation of the social and individual psyche of the colonised. The first [novel] begins at a time when the Gikuyu have their land, and the colonial presence is little more than one of missionaries and mission schools, a force which divides the people but does not yet dispossess them. In the second novel they are the dispossessed, tenant farmers, landless laborers or fighters seeking to regain the land which is home. In the third novel the white colonial landlords are going, leaving behind them the traumatized victims of the struggle and the new black landlords who threaten to perpetuate the system of alienation which colonialism set up. (Zell, Bundy, and Coulon, 1983:432)

Ngugi's *Petals of Blood* (1977) is a picture of corruption in modern-day Kenya with flashbacks to the fight for independence. According to Christopher Ricks, the book

> begins with a fire—arson?—in which there are killed three prominent, corrupt figures of the new Kenya. It ends with our knowing exactly what happened and why. But its journey, which has at its heart an actual journey taken by the drought-stricken people of the village of Ilmorog in order to beg for help from the city-world of its MP and of the national conscience, takes it back through all the sufferings of the fight for national freedom. (Zell, Bundy, and Coulon, 1983:433)

Devil on the Cross (1982) was originally written in Kikuyu on leaves of lavatory paper while the author was in prison for a year but under no charges. The novel centers on the heroine Wariinga, who is "fired for refusing to sleep with her boss, and evicted from her shanty for refusing to pay exorbitant rent" (Zell, Bundy, and Coulon, 1983:190). *Matigari* (1987), based upon a Gikuyu folktale, is an allegorical novel criticizing post-independence Kenya.

Ngugi is one of the most powerful writers in Africa today and one of the leading proponents of writing in African languages. (See his *Decolonising the Mind: The Politics of Language in African Literature,* 1986.) His production also includes several plays (*This Time Tomorrow,* 1957; *The Black Hermit,* 1968; *The Rebels,* 1970; *Wound in the Heart,* 1970; and *I Will Marry When I Want,* 1982), short stories (*Secret Lives and Other Stories,* 1975), and critical essays (*Homecoming: Essays on African and Caribbean Literature, Culture and Politics,* 1972; *Writers in Politics, Essays,* 1981; and *Detainees: A Writer's Prison Diary,* 1981).

The cosmopolitan and sophisticated Nuruddin Farah is considered "one of the two or three most important novelists writing in Africa." (Alden, 1995:381). He has written a series of distinguished novels that for the most part trace the evolution and aftermath of the dictatorship of General Siyad Barre (1969–1991). These include novels in the trilogy *Variations on the Theme of an African Dictatorship: Sweet and Sour Milk* (1979), *Sardines* (1981), and *Close Sesame* (1963); as well as *Maps* (1986), *Gifts* (1992), and *Secrets* (1998). *Links* (2003) explores life in the stateless society of Mogadishu. Farah's "novels pinpoint the lethal collusions of family and state authoritarianisms and of tribalism, Islam, and marxism [sic] and feature pioneering studies of the patriarchal subjection of women in the Horn of Africa" (Killam and Rowe, 2000:96). Often considered a post/post writer (postcolonial and postmodern; Alden, 1995:382), Farah "associates multiple viewpoints with tolerance, closure and omniscience with tyranny, and commentators have duly praised his fluid, open-ended narratives, his intricate metaphoric textures, and his nonpartisan, compassionate commitment to human freedom" (Killam and Rowe, 2000:96). As Farah's style develops, he increasingly weaves materials drawn from both African and European frames of reference into a narrative fabric that has a strikingly postmodern quality of "unstitching" itself. (Wright quoted in Alden, 1995:382).

Literature in South Africa. The following account is limited to South African literature, although there is a distinguished literature in other parts of southern Africa such as Zimbabwe (e.g., Wim Boswinkel, Tsitsi Dangaremba, John Eppel, Chenjari Hove, Doris Lessing, Charles Mungoshi, and Yvonne Vera). The following account is also limited to literature written in English because literature in Afrikaans and the other African languages is still not widely accessible to English-speaking readers. Contemporary South African literature is profoundly shaped by the 1948 victory of the Nationalist Party with its platform of apartheid—the policy that different "races"—White, Black, Coloured, and Asian—would develop separately. Although apartheid policies had long existed in the Afrikaner provinces of the British-dominated Union of South Africa, it was not a national policy and the British-dominated Cape Town province had been more tolerant of racial differences. The Nationalist Party held power until 1994, when Nelson Mandela of the African National Congress (ANC) won the 1994 elections that led to the creation of a multiracial republic. One aspect of the apartheid policy was the generalization of a system of passes (internal passports) that strictly regulated the movements of people of different races. The infamous Sharpeville massacre in which 69 Africans were killed and 180 injured originated as a demonstration against the pass laws. Another aspect of apartheid was to make Afrikaans (a Dutch creole language) the language of instruction in schools. This policy inspired demonstrations in the black township of Soweto on June 16, 1976, by students wanting the government to waive the language requirement. A series of riots followed in which many schoolchildren were shot or imprisoned.

The determination of the regime to stay in power through such brutal repression, as well as through constant censorship, led to a fragmentation of South African literature. Writers such as Alex LaGuma and Dennis Brutus were driven into exile and their works—and mention of their works—was banned. White writers such as Nadine Gordimer or J. M. Coetzee were able to flourish and, in the case of Gordimer, even take the censors head on. A group of black writers, such as Matsemela Manaka and Sipho Sepamla, inspired by an anti-apartheid opposition movement called Black Consciousness, managed to stay in South Africa and maintain some measure of literary production in spite of the censorship.

Now that apartheid has ended, one can be guardedly hopeful about the future of South African literature. In June 2006, Cape Town held its first

Book Fair, which revealed a booming, dynamic, and varied (albeit small) publishing industry. In a market almost twenty-five times smaller than the United States, 56 percent of books published come from the UK, with only 28 percent from South Africa (Klein, 2006:1). Nevertheless, according to Marcia Klein, "Publishing has taken off in South Africa as society has changed and writers have looked for new themes beyond apartheid, which previously dominated local writing. There has been an increase in new talent and stories featuring issues like HIV/AIDS. Humour has become a significant element of new South African writing" (Klein, 2006: 1).

Some exiled writers effectively silenced by censorship have managed to find a place in the new market. These include Zakes Mda, Lewis Nkosi, and Rayda Jacobs, who has written all but one of her works since her return to South Africa. However, writers such as Gordimer and Coetzee, who still dominate the South African literary scene in virtue of their Nobel prizes, suffer from problematic postcolonial stances, in spite of the quality of their writings. According to Robert Suresh Roberts, Gordimer's determination to speak for black "Others" at a time when they themselves could not speak has become untenable and even offensive now that the "Others" can speak for themselves (Suresh 2006:633). Coetzee, who according to Suresh, never pretended to speak for the "Other," has been accused of white supremacist tendencies in works such as *Disgrace,* which, according to Mandisi Majavu, laments the treatment whites receive under democracy (Majavu, 2006).

It is also true that, as in all South African economic matters, the publishing industry is dominated by whites, and black writers are struggling to get published. "Where are our young black writers?" asks the young writer Fred Khumalo (Khumalo, 2006:3). Twelve years into democracy, blacks still face huge disadvantages. According to Kwela Books editor Nelleke de Jager, "really talented people have to work at the same time. They don't have the same opportunities as white writers, nor the funding to go and do an MA in Creative Writing and sit and write for three years" (Khumalo, 2006:3). Many black writers are self-publishing or publishing with small presses with very limited marketing. Furthermore, the potential black reading public still suffers from illiteracy fostered by apartheid-era discriminatory educational policies, and writing in national languages such as Zulu or Xhosa is extremely difficult to publish in a market overwhelmingly dominated by English and, to a lesser extent, Afrikaans.

Yet there are hopeful signs. The Department of Education has incorporated the African Literature Association's 100 best books in African literature into its curriculum, and is working to stop black South African writers from going out of print. In Thabiso Sikwane's SAfm radio program "Afternoon Talk" (June 18, 2006), Annari Van der Merwe from Random House (which has the largest market share in South Africa) asserted that publishers are doing their best despite the limitations of the market. She also pointed out that in the absence of a South African writers union, organizations such as the Cape Town–based Center for the Book are very active. (At the Book Fair, for example, the Center for the Book featured a series written by black authors in national languages other than English and Afrikaans.) Nevertheless, these organizations mainly represent white interests because whites still control access to the larger market. Fred Khumalo, in Sikwane's radio program, countered that this white industry is still hampered with myopic vision, but he expressed his confidence that as an educated black readership grows it will create a demand for the stories that black writers have to tell. At this writing in 2006 we share Fred Khumalo's hope. As Khumalo points out, ten years ago such debates did not even exist (Khumalo, 2006:3). Furthermore, there is no longer a strict separation of the reading public into black and white, since people read across color lines.

Olive Schreiner's *Story of an African Farm* (1883) is usually credited with initiating the South African novel in English. According to Killam and Rowe (2000:184), *The Story of an African Farm* received instant recognition, "largely because of its bold criticism of the treatment of women in the Cape colony, its exposé of the general mindlessness and anti-intellectualism there, and its unusual multi-generic form."

Gordimer and Coetzee are considered to be the principal South African novelists in Schreiner's tradition. Nobel Prize–winning Nadine Gordimer's (b. 1923) novels include *The Lying Days* (1953), *A World of Strangers* (1958), *Occasion for Loving* (1963), *The Late Bourgeois World* (1966), *A Guest of Honour* (1971), *The Conservationist* (1983), *Burger's Daugher* (1979), *July's People* (1981), *A Sport of Nature* (1987), *My Son's Story* (1990), *None to Accompany Me* (1994), *The House Gun* (1998), *The Pickup* (2001), and *Get a Life: A Novel* (2005). Gordimer has won prestigious prizes for her novels, including the James Tait Black Memorial Prize, the Booker Prize, the South African CNA (Central News Agency) Award, and the French Grand Aigle d'Or. She received the Nobel Prize in 1991. Her writings also include:

- twelve volumes of short stories, which include *Face to Face* (1949), *Selected Stories* (1975), *Why Haven't You Written? Selected Stories (1950–1972)* (1992), and *Loot and Other Stories* (2003), as well as an edited collection Telling Tales (2004), to which major writers such as Arthur Miller, Es'kia Mphahlele, Gabriel García Márquez, Slaman Rushdie, Margaret Atwood, Günter Grass, John Updike, Chinua Achebe, Amos Oz, Paul Theroux, Michel Tournier, and Njabulo Ndebele have contributed in an effort to raise money to combat AIDS;

- essays on literature and politics, including *The Black Interpreters* (1973), *What Happened to Burger's Daughter; or How South African Censorship Works* (1980), and *The Essential Gesture: Writing, Politics, and Places* (1988);
- *South African Writing Today* (1967) in collaboration with Lionel Abrahams; and
- two books in collaboration with photographer David Goldblatt, *On the Mines* (1973) and *Lifetimes: Under Apartheid* (1986).

Gordimer writes in a realistic vein that explores the "interconnectedness of personal emotion, physical desire, and political conviction and action. . . . Her importance as a writer has been understood mostly to be in her handling of the novel and story forms as political statement: she has developed an idiosyncratic style, moralistic, clear-sighted, wedded in form to the tradition of Tolstoy and George Eliot" (Killam and Rowe, 2000:108).

Gordimer has been criticized for her portrayal of nonwhites as either shady, subaltern characters or sex objects. In this respect she shares the tendency of European colonial writing to portray Africans in terms of extremes. The recognition she has received has also been considered to some extent an ill-gotten gain because of her privileged position as a white middle-class writer able to brave the censors at a time when nonwhite South African writers were forced into silence and/or exile. Furthermore, she has also been considered prejudiced in favor of European forms as opposed to African oral traditions and mythology in her aesthetic criticism of writers such as Flora Nwapa. Nevertheless, Gordimer—aware of the contradictions inherent in her situation and outlook—must be credited with using her position to urge white South Africans to recognize the impossibility of apartheid (Killam and Rowe, 2000:108).

John Maxwell (J. M.) Coetzee (b. 1940), who won the 2003 Nobel Prize in Literature, has been credited with writing the first postmodern novel in South Africa, *Dusklands* (1974), and with introducing an ethical dimension into the style.

> The self-reflexivity of his novels is a means of scrutinizing the assumptions of the discourses that are available to him, . . . while not denying his inevitable imbrication in a tradition of white South African writing; it is also a means of drawing attention to the question of positionality, authority, and agency, always asking "Who writes? Who takes up the position of power, pen in hand?" (Killam and Rowe, 2000:71)

Coetzee has subsequently published nine other novels: *In the Heart of the Country* (1977), *Waiting for the Barbarians* (1980), *Life & Times of Michael K* (1983), *Foe* (1986), *Age of Iron* (1990), *The Master of Petersburg* (1994), *Disgrace* (1999), *Elizabeth Costello* (2003), and *Slow*

Man (2006), as well as an autobiographical memoir, *Boyhood: Scenes from Provincial Life.*

Coetzee, who received a Ph.D. from the University of Texas at Austin, was a professor of English at the University of Cape Town and has also written a distinguished body of critical works, translations, and commentaries on popular culture, and reviews. *White Writing: On the Culture of Letters in South Africa* (1988) is "a collection of critical essays about the European invention of South Africa," whereas *Doubling the Point: Essays and Interviews* (1992) "gathers his major critical writing from 1970 to 1990" (Killam and Rowe, 2000:71). He lives in Australia and has recently become an Australian citizen.

Also of note is the white liberal writer Alan Paton (1903–1988), whose *Cry, the Beloved Country* (1948) and *Too Late the Phalarope* (1953)

> evoke South Africa's human and physical landscapes with a spare and unsparing realism, Hemingwayesque but earnestly moral, biblical in some of its cadences and epiphanies. So close is the fit between the country he depicts and the moral frame through which he views it that South Africa became for many readers inside and outside the country a unique object lesson, an infamous twentieth-century dilemma. (Killam and Rowe, 2000:184)

Just as West and East African writers in European languages began to write in an effort to tell a story about Africa that had been left untold in European colonial writing, nonwhite South African writers in English tell a story that would otherwise remain smothered by apartheid. The earliest of these writers, from the 1920s and 1930s, were often educated in mission schools. They include Thomas Mfolo, whose *Chaka,* mentioned above, was translated into English as well as other languages, and Solomon T. Plaatje (1876–1932), whose *Mhudi* (1930) was expurgated by the mission-controlled publishers. According to Killam and Rowe (2000:184), the novel centers "on the collision between the Matabele nation and the Voortrekkers moving into the interior, and the plight of the helpless tribes caught in the conflict." The novel also shows how the Christianity of sincere and fervent missionaries undermines native cultures.

Later generations of nonwhite writers, often coming from black townships such as Sophiatown, reflect the conditions of their lives under apartheid: Peter Abrahams, whose novels include *Mine Boy* (1946), *Song of the City* (1945), *Path of Thunder* (1948), *Wild Conquest* (1950), *A Wreath for Udomo* (1965), as well as his memoirs *Tell Freedom* (1954); Todd Matshikiza, Ezekiel Mphahlele, Richard Rive, Alex La Guma, and Can Themba, who have published short stories in magazines like *Drum, Zonk!, Afrika,* and *Bona;* and Ezekiel Mphahlele, whose novel *Down Second Avenue* (1959) is an example of autobiographies written by South African writers to denounce the oppression of the white regime.

Nonwhite writers in South Africa such as Bloke Modisane, Lewis Nkosi, Casey Motsisi, and Nat Nakasa have worked against enormous odds including censorship, prison, exile, and the inaccessibility of education. Two of the strongest prose writers in South Africa are Richard Rive and Alex La Guma. Rive's *Emergency* (1964), for example, tells the story of the state of emergency declared by the South African government after the Sharpeville massacre. Like most others, Rive is an urban South African who eschews the pastoralism of Negritude in favor of urban themes—"life in the slums, the consequences of overt protest and the ironies of racial prejudice and color snobbery" (Zell, Bundy, and Coulon, 1983:472). According to Bernth Lindfors, Rive's style is "characterized by strong rhythms, daring images, brisk dialogue and leitmotifs (recurring words, phrases, and images) which function as unifying devices within stories" (Zell, Bundy, and Coulon, 1983:472).

La Guma is also a writer who concerns himself with life in the city, prison, and township. The short story *A Walk in the Night* (1962) tells of Michael Adonis, a colored boy fired from his job and ultimately a fatality of police brutality. And a *Threefold Cord* (1964) is a novel about life in a ghetto bordering Cape Town. Other novels include *The Stone Country* (1967), which tells of life in South African jails; *In the Fog of the Season's End* (1972), dealing with political activism; and *Time of the Butcherbird* (1979), which recounts the forced resettlement of whole communities to other townships. According to Lindfors, La Guma's style is "characterized by graphic description, careful evocation of atmosphere and mood, fusion of pathos and humor, colorful dialogue and occasional surprise endings" (Zell, Bundy, and Coulon, 1983:402).

Unlike these urbanized writers, Bessie Head settled in rural Botswana. She published three novels that make up a kind of trilogy: *When Rain Clouds Gather* (1969), *Maru* (1971), and *A Question of Power* (1974). Of Bessie Head's style Arthur Ravenscroft states, "In *A Question of Power* we are taken nightmarishly into the central character's process of mental breakdown, through lurid cascades of hallucination and a pathological blurring of the frontiers between insanity and any kind of normalcy" (Zell, Bundy, and Coulon, 1983:390). Bessie Head's interest in tradition is reflected in *Serowe: The Village of the Rainwind* (1981), which is a series of interviews conducted among the villagers of Serowe. Also of note are her historical novel, *A Bewitched Crossroad: An African Saga* (1984), and four posthumous texts: *Tales of Tenderness and Power* (1989), *A Woman Alone: Autobiographical Writings* (1990), *A Gesture of Belonging: Letters from Bessie Head, 1965–1979* ed. R. Vigne (1991), and *The Cardinals: With Meditations and Stories* (1993).

In the 1970s and 1980s Black Consciousness poets also wrote important novels. Among these are Mongane Wally Serote's *To Every Birth Its Blood* (1981), and Sipho Sepamla's *The Root Is One* (1979) and *A Ride on the Whirlwind* (1981). Also of note are Lauretta Ngcobo's *Cross of Gold* (1981) and Mbulelo Mzamane's *The Children of Soweto* (1982).

During the last thirty years, experimentation in late and postmodern approaches as well as the intimations of the end of apartheid have inspired a new generation of South African novelists, including Stephen Gray, Ahmed Essop, Sheila Roberts, Peter Wilhelm, Achmat Dangor, and Rose Zwi. Other new voices include Ivan Vladislavic (*The Folly,* 1993), Zoë Wicomb (*You Can't Get Lost in Cape Town,* 1987; *David's Story, 2002*), Mike Nicol (*The Powers That Be,* 1989; *This Day and Age,* 1922; *Horseman,* 1994), Menán du Plessis (*A State of Fear,* 1983; *Longlive!,* 1989), Ellek Boehmer (*Screens Against the Sky,* 1990) (Killam and Rowe, 2000:185), Niq Mhlongo (*Dog Eat Dog,* 2004), and Fred Khumalo (*Touch My Blood,* 2006; *Bitches Brew,* 2006).

Three writers are notable for their representations of urban Cape Town communities. Rayda Jacobs gives a witty picture of the Muslim community in her novels such as *Sachs Street* (2001), *Confessions of a Gambler* (2003), and *Postcards from South Africa* (2004). In his three novels, K. Sello Duiker challenges myths of black sexuality as he contrasts the life on the fringes in the troubled and disturbing shadowy world of Cape Town street culture, male prostitution, and mental illness with life in the affluent suburbs: *Thirteen Cents* (2000), *The Quiet Violence of Dreams* (2001), and *The Hidden Star* (2005). Duiker committed suicide at age twenty-seven in 2005. Duiker's contemporary Phaswane Mpe, who died of HIV/AIDS-related illness in 2004, wrote *Welcome to Our Hillbrow* (2001), which explores the issues of AIDS and xenophobia.

The most prominent writer in this group is the novelist and playwright Zakes Mda (Zanemvula Kizito Gatyeni, b. 1948), who has to date written seven novels: *The Whale Caller* (2005), *The Madonna of Excelsior* (2002), *The Heart of Redness* (2000), *Melville 67 (a novella for youth)* (1998), *She Plays with the Darkness* (1995), and *Ways of Dying* (1995). Mda has also created an important production of plays: *Fools, Bells and the Habit of Eating* (a collection of three plays, 2002); *Love Letters,* in *Let Us Play* (an anthology of plays for young readers and performers, 1998); *Dankie Auntie* (a children's play, 1997) published in *Matatu* 17–18; *The Nun's Romantic Story*, in *Four Plays* (1996); *Four Works* (1993), which includes the plays *Joys of War*, *And the Girls in their Sunday Dresses*, *Banned*, and *The Final Dance*; and *The Plays of Zakes Mda* (1990). *Broken Dreams*, a play on child abuse, AIDS, and tuberculosis (1995), was devised by Mda and the actors, scripted by Mda, and directed by him at the Market Theatre Laboratory, after which it has been performed to more than 400,000 Higher Primary School Students in different parts of South Africa. The work is updated each year. Mda's plays are distinguished by the combination of close scrutiny of social values with elements of magic realism that is even more pronounced in his novels (Killam and Rowe, 2000:161).

Mda, like a number of other contemporary South African writers, has "had to readjust to life after returning from exile, to cope with being placed within a new black elite, and to be witness to problems like political corruption and ineptitude" (Yew, 2002). Other themes of this writing include AIDS; crime; interracial tension beyond the simplistic black is good, white is evil formula; exile and the tension between local anti-Apartheid activists and those returning from exile; the struggle to maintain African tradition against urbanization/modernization; the treatment of job-seeking black Africans from neighboring countries by black South Africans; issues of identity, for example the increasing class mobility of the black population and the resulting sense of identity displacement; homosexuality; and poverty (Swarns, 2002).

Theater in South Africa. Stephen Black (1880–1913) and H. I. E. Dhlomo (1903–1956) stand as the most important pioneers of contemporary South African theater. Black created a style

> characterized by the incorporation of locally understood, topical references updated for each performance, by the development of a range of recognizably South African stock characters such as the colonial maiden, the Boer patriarch, and the gullible native, as well as by skillful exploitation of the growing distinctiveness of South African English. (Killam and Rowe, 2000:82)

Dhlomo, who has been associated with the urban black culture that since the 1930s has been a determining factor of South African history, founded the Bantu Dramatic Society and "sought to view rural tribal history in the light of contemporary urban black experience" (Killam and Rowe, 2000:82). *The Girl Who Killed to Save: Nongqause the Liberator*—the first published play by a black South African—inaugurated an "African-centered, non-colonialist drama [that] should be regarded as a forerunner of the Black Consciousness theater of the late 1970s" (Killam and Rowe, 2000:83).

During the apartheid era (1948–1990), theater in South Africa was shaped either by the state-dominated arts councils that funded white performances or autonomous alternative groups and workshops such as Union Artists, the African Music and Drama Association, Robert McLaren's Workshop '71, The Company (1974), the Market Theatre (1976), and the Junction Avenue Theatre Company (1976). The workshops, which often featured fruitful collaborations between whites and nonwhites, provided a model for theater in South African society after apartheid (Killam and

Rowe, 2000:83). For example, Barney Simon (author of *Born in the RSA,* 1985) collaborated with Percy Mtwa and Mbongeni Ngema to produce *Woza Albert!* in 1980. Mtwa later went on to write *Bopha!* (1986), and Ngema produced *Asinamali!* (1985) and the musicals *Sarafina!* (1987) and *Zulu* (2000).

The dominant figure in such collaborations is Athol Fugard (b. 1932), who was involved in the Serpent Players and the multiracial Space Theatre in Cape Town. Fugard is the most prominent South African playwright,

> largely because of his ability to turn apparently regional and local themes into more universal metaphors for his deeply felt liberal concern with humanity and his existential struggle to understand his own life. Making use of a simple and direct form of neo-realism within a "poor theatre" framework, he combines an actor's sensitivity for dialogue with a designer's eye for the powerful visual images generated during live performance, and he uses these qualities to explore relationships between two or three exquisitely drawn individuals. (Killam and Rowe, 2000:100)

Fugard is important not only as a technical innovator but also as an opponent of apartheid and an eloquent witness to the atrocities of racism and bigotry. For example, *The Blood Knot* (1961), one of the plays he wrote and performed with friends in the black townships around Johannesburg, is a "searing analysis of the psychological consequences of racial division" (Killam and Rowe, 2000:83). Although a white writer, Fugard crosses racial boundaries in workshop productions such as *Sizwe Bansi Is Dead* (1972) and *The Island* (1973), which mark the beginning of his association with actors such as John Kani and Winston Ntshona. The performance of these plays, along with *Statements After an Arrest Under the Immorality Act* (1972), created Fugard's international reputation (Killam and Rowe, 2000). *My Children, My Africa!* (1989) is an eloquent protest against political violence in South Africa. Looking beyond apartheid are such plays as *Playland* (1992), which deals with the need for reconciliation, and *Valley Song* (1996), which portrays the emotional complexities of adjusting to social change. According to Killam and Rowe (2000),

> Fugard's plays, whose sparseness and economy of means owe much to Samuel Beckett, have been a barometer to the social evolution of his country, witnessing with deep sensitivity to the isolation of the human condition and to the myriad injustices of apartheid alike, profoundly responsive to the nuances of South African language use, and uniquely able to encapsulate conflict in scenes of enormous intensity.

While the workshop theaters held out an image of a possible post-apartheid multiracial collaboration, in the late 1960s and early 1970s three companies, inspired by the Black Consciousness movement, reflected a more confrontational stance by blacks but quickly felt the heavy hand of the censor. TECON (Theatre Council of Natal) was banned; the leaders of PET (People's Experimental Theatre) and MDALI (Music, Drama, and Literature Institute) were detained.

Matsemela Manaka and Maishe Maponya are important dramatists of a new generation from the townships that became active after the Soweto riots of 1976. Their work reflects the influence of the "township musical" performed by an all-black cast, and includes *King Kong* (1959) and Gibson Kente's *How Long?* (1971), *Too Late* (1973), and *Sikalo* (1976).

Manaka (1956–1998) founded the Soyikwa Theatre Group, which he used to produce plays that were "unusual for their innovative synthesis . . . of drama, music, dance, painting . . . mime . . . [a]nd forms of African artistic expression long inaccessible to black South Africans" (Killam and Rowe, 2000:84). Manaka's earlier plays respond with satire to conditions of the day such as migrant labor and forced removals (*Egoli,* 1979; *Pula,* 1982; *Children of Asazi,* 1984). Later plays, like Fugard's, look beyond apartheid to develop a "theatre for social reconstruction" (Killam and Rowe, 2000). *Gorée* (1989) symbolically demonstrates "the fusion of European and African cultures, while *Blues Afrika Café* (1990) defines an African identity" (Killam and Rowe, 2000).

Maponya, founder of the Bahumutsi Theatre Group, strikes a shriller protest against the policies and practices of apartheid.

> Remarkable for their abundant theatricality, their indebtedness to Brecht (especially the didacticism of *The Measures Taken*), their innovative uses of gesture and their frequent recourse to improvisation, Maponya's plays supplement dialogue with choral singing, gumboot dancing, and mimed sequences (as in *The Hungry Earth,* 1978), call upon actors to perform multiple roles (as in *Umongikazi/The Nurse,* 1982), and deploy telling juxtapositions of scenes (interrogation and literary recitation in *Gangsters,* 1982). (Killam and Rowe, 2000)

The Marotholi Travelling Theatre, an example of "theater for development," is one of three types of alternative theater that arose during the latter years of apartheid. Manaka's literacy play *Koma* (1986); Doreen Mazibuko's voter-education play *Moments* (1994), and Maponya's Winterveld project with unemployed squatter camp youth all belong to this movement. Workers' theater, a second type of alternative theater that arose during the states of emergency (1983–1987), evolved

> as a collaborative venture between semi-literate factory workers, white intellectuals and experienced theatre practitioners from groups like Junction Avenue, whose plays such as *The Long March, The Sun Shall Rise for the Workers,* and *Comment* sought to mobilize workers and raise political conscience by dramatizing their own experience of the labour

> struggle while at the same time exploiting African cultural sources (gumboot dancing, praise song, the Zulu language). (Killam and Rowe, 2000:85)

Theater-in-education, a third type of alternative theater, involved bringing the classics such as Shakespeare to the townships and rural areas, as well as using theater in various educational projects. According to Killam and Rowe (2000:85), by the end of apartheid with the reallocation of resources and the reorganization of the performing arts councils, "the alternative theatres had become the mainstream, and the state theatres, still wedded to a discredited ideology, found themselves marginalized" and had to seek redefinition, while the return of exiles from abroad and the end of censorship allowed for new kinds of collaboration such as the Johannesburg Civic Theatre opening with the Dance Theater of Harlem.

Exciting new trends in theater are now being set by Sue Pam Grant (*Curl Up and Dye,* 1989), Paul Slabolepzsy (*Saturday Night at the Palace,* 1982; and *Mooi St. Moves,* 1992), and the original experiments such as William Kentridge's Handspring Puppet Company's multimedia adaptation of Alfred Jarry's *Ubu Roi,* in *Ubu and the Truth Comission* (1997, scripted by Jane Taylor). The Grahamstown Festivals of Brett Bailey and the Third World Bunfight's *iMumboJumbo, The Days of Miricale and Wonder,* and *Ipi Zombi* are "amateur township-based performances full of ritual and ceremony which, if nothing else, suggest that there are forms of theatrical performance emerging the like of which has not been seen before" (Killam and Rowe, 2000:85).

South African poetry. The Scotsman Thomas Pringle (1729–1834) is considered the first published South African poet, with such works as *Ephemerides: Or Occasional Poems, Written in Scotland and South Africa* (1828) and *African Sketches* (1834). Writing in the manner of British colonial poets, Pringle is known for his struggles against the oppressive treatment of indigenous people in such poems as "Afar in the Desert"—"one of the most frequently reprinted poems in nineteenth-century Britain" (Killam and Rowe, 2000:230).

In the 1870s and 1880s, a body of poetry grew up around the Kimberley diamond mines (called "digger ballads") and Witwatersrand goldfields (Albert Brodrick, "poet laureate" of the Transvaal). With the creation of the Union of South Africa, the Johannesburg-based Veldsingers including Denys Lefebvre, Francis Emley Walrond, and Alice Mabel Alder, worked to create a distinctively South African poetic tradition centered on the pastoral but also exploiting modernist imagism and symbolism (Killam and Rowe, 2000:215).

In the early part of their careers, William Plomer (1903–1973) and Roy

Campbell (1901–1957) wrote poems attacking racism and created the bilingual literary journal *Voorslag (Whiplash),* which they founded in 1925. They made significant modernist contributions of craft and conscience to South African poetry, but left South Africa because it was not ready for their voices.

In the following decades, the conservative Francis Caery Slater (1876–1958) (*The Centenary Book of South African Verse,* 1925; and *The New Centenary Book of South African Verse,* 1945) dominated South African poetry along with Guy Butler (editor of *Oxford Book of South African Verse,* 1959). Butler, however, belonged to a group of "liberal humanist poets," including Alan Paton, David Wright, Anthony Delius, Roy McNab, and N. H. Bretell, who were critical of rising Afrikaner nationalism and the imposition of apartheid. Many such as Delius and Wright went into exile in response to the censorship imposed on black contributors to *Drum* magazine (Killam and Rowe, 2000:215).

In the wake of the Sharpeville massacre of 1960, South Africa's expulsion from the British Commonwealth in 1981, and the accompanying loss of face for liberal values, poets such as Jack Cope *(Contrast),* Ruth Miller, Sidney Clouts, and Douglas Livingstone concentrated on the craft of poetry in which experimental techniques at times indirectly raised the moral issues of apartheid (Killam and Rowe, 2000:215, 146).

The Black Consciousness movement gave rise to a more confrontational, political poetry that was the hallmark of a new black South African literary tradition in the 1970s. This latter tradition was seriously hampered by apartheid censorship, which had already resulted in the banning and exile of an earlier generation of black poets that included Dennis Brutus, Keorapetse Kgositsile, Mazisi Kunene, Daniel P. Kunene, Kenneth Arthur Nortje, and Cosmo Pieterse. Black Consciousness poets such as Mongane Serote were also driven into exile and there remained a spit between poets outside the country and those inside until the 1990s. Mafika Gwala, a "seminal" theoretician of Black Consciousness, Serote, and Sipho Sepamala are considered the three most important poets of the Black Consciousness tradition. Sepamala is the most prominent, having won the Noma Award for *Third World Express* in 1992.

At the same time, Adam Small and Oswald Mbuyiseni Mtshali were creating a following with poetry that ran parallel to that of the Black Consciousness movement, but came from a different impetus. In 1975 Small, who had previously written in Afrikaans mixed with English, published a collection of English-language poetry. Similarly, Mtshali, in his collection *Sound of a Cowhide Drum,* "offered vivid cameos of black urban life and a measure of protest, but stopped short of suggesting the redefinition of South African reality proposed by Black Consciousness" (Killam and Rowe, 2000:215).

Blac, founded by poet James Matthews, is representative of the black publishing ventures that were launched in the 1970s as a counterweight to the white-run literary magazines and small publishing houses in which black poets of the early 1970s appeared. White poets "who made small reputations while the new black poetry was claiming the stage" included Wopko Jensma, Patrick Cullinan, Don Maclennan, Christopher Hope, Christopher Mann, and "perhaps a dozen more of comparable interest and merit" (Killam and Rowe, 2000:215–216).

Under the pressures of censorship and growing crisis (Durban strikes and the rise of the labor movement, the martyrdom of Steve Biko, the Soweto uprising, and the banning of the Black Consciousness organizations), poetry was disseminated through readings in the townships that found a significant black audience while falling under the radar screen of the white censors. There were also many new poets appearing in the literary magazine *Staffrider.* And poets such as Ingaopele Madingoane, Chris van Wyk, Achmat Dangor, and Donald Parenzee were taking a poetry of protest to the streets of the townships.

In the 1980s, with increased political resistance from organizations such as the United Democratic Front, the Congress of South African Trade Unions, and the ANC, performance poetry became an increasingly popular medium in the townships among poets such as Alfred Qabula, Mi Hlatshwayo, Nise Malange, and Mzwakhe Mbuli. Other significant and powerful political works of poetic protest include Jeremy Cronin's *Inside* (1983), Lesefo Rampolokeng's *Horns for Hondo* (1990) and *Talking Rain* (1993), and Stephen Watson's *Return of the Moon* (1991) (Killam and Rowe, 2000:216).

During the 1990s, women poets added their voice to the tradition. According to Killam and Rowe (2000), South African poetry, beginning as a masculinist, colonial project, has been subverted and remade by black poets; its next remaking may be a feminizing movement as is indicated by Cecily Lockett's anthology *Breaking the Silence: A Century of South African Women's Poetry* (1990). Other women poets include Ingrid de Kok, Kaen Press, Sue Clark, Jennifer Davids, Blossom Pegram (who also published under the name Amelia House), and Lindiwe Mabuza.

Conclusion

African literature is full of threatened promise. For the time being, oral traditions manage to survive despite serious interruptions in time-honored modes of transmission. The children of *griots* go to modern schools before their training in oral traditions is complete. Elsewhere, the attraction to modern life turns attention away from traditions conserving the past.

Written African literature will continue to turn—as it already has—away from a primarily European audience to an African one. As colonialism has receded in time, and problems of the postindependence period have commanded attention, local issues rather than proving an "African" identity to the European world have grown in importance. In addressing these concerns, African writers are incorporating fragile oral traditions into their work to make them accessible to an audience more at ease with oral than with written communication. The choice of language is also changing as writers communicate more often in African languages.

Because of the political and economic instability in Africa discussed throughout this book, African writers have faced and continue to face very real threats of prison, exile, and death. Moreover, writers must make their way through the labyrinth of the Western-dominated publishing market. Despite such obstacles, writers are developing distinct national literatures in both European and African languages. It is already possible to speak of full-blown Nigerian, Senegalese, Cameroonian, and Ghanaian literatures. Other literatures not mentioned in this chapter, such as Zairian and Tanzanian, will also increasingly make their mark. If all goes well, the reader of the twenty-first century will find a rich and highly diverse situation in which the term "African literature" will be as vague a generalization as "European literature" or "Asian literature."

Notes

I would like to thank Emmanuel Obiechina, Ousmane Sene, and Thelma Ravell-Pinto for so kindly reading earlier versions of this chapter, and Wlodzimierz Borejsza-Wysocki for his help in obtaining the photograph of printed African works.

1. For further reading in Arabic-language literature, see Killam and Rowe, 2000; Allen 1982; and Hunwick and O'Fahey, 1994.

2. Trans. Ezekiel Mphahlele, as cited in Beier, Knappert, and Moser, 1974:140.

3. Anthropologist Judith T. Irvine has graciously shared this information with me.

4. Selections from Senghor's poetry have been translated into English as follows: *Léopold Sédar Senghor: Selected Poems* (1964) and *Léopold Sédar Senghor: Prose and Poetry* (1965) (both translated by John Reed and Clive Wake), *Selected Poems/Poésies choisies* (1976; trans. Craig Williamson), and *Selected Poems of Léopold Sédar Senghor* (1977; trans. Abiola Irele).

5. *Presénce afraicaine* 1 (November-December 1947), p. 8. Quoted in Mouralis, 1984:421. My translation.

6. Although the reverse appears in some works, the true order of the author's name is Ousmane Sembene. The reversal in many francophone author's names is due to the fact that in the French schools, the roll was called last name first.

7. Ousmane Sembene, *God's Bits of Wood,* trans. Francis Price (1961) (London: Heinemann, 1983), page facing p. 1.

Bibliography

Bibliographies and Readers' Guides

Arnold, Stephen H., and Milan V. Dimiç. 1985. *African Literature Studies: The Present State/L'Etat présent.* Washington, DC: Three Continents Press.

Berrian, Brenda. 1989. *Bibliography of African Women Writers and Journalists.* Washington, DC: Three Continents Press.

Herdeck, Donald E. (ed.). 1973. *African Authors: A Companion to Black African Writing.* Vol. 1: 1300–1973. Washington, DC: Black Orpheus Press.

Jahn, Janheinz. 1965. *A Bibliography of Neo-African Literature: From Africa, America and the Caribbean.* New York: Praeger.

Jahn, Janheinz, and C. P. Dressler. 1971. *Bibliography of Creative African Writing.* Nendeln, Liechtenstein: Kraus-Thomson.

Jahn, Janheinz, Ulla Schild, and Almut Nordmann (eds.). 1972. *Who's Who in African Literature: Biographies, Works and Commentaries.* Tübingen, Germany: Horst Erdmann Verlag.

Killam, Douglas, and Ruth Rowe (eds.). 2000. *The Companion to African Literatures.* Oxford: James Currey; Bloomington: Indiana University Press.

Swarns, Rachel L. 2002. "South Africa's Black Writers Explore a Free Society's Tensions." *The New York Times,* June 24. Cited in Yew, Leong. 2002. "The New Black Literature in South Africa." In George Landow (ed.). *Postcolonial and Postimperial Authors* (viewed 2006). Online at www.postcolonialweb.org/misc/authors.html.

Yew, Leong. 2002. "The New Black Literature in South Africa." In George Landow (ed.). *Postcolonial and Postimperial Authors* (viewed 2006). Online at www.postcolonialweb.org/misc/authors.html.

Zell, Hans M., Carol Bundy, and Virginia Coulon. 1983. *A New Reader's Guide to African Literature.* New York: Africana.

Oral Literatures

Beier, Ulli. 1966. *The Origin of Life and Death: A Collection of Creation Myths from Africa.* London: HEB.

———. 1970. *Yoruba Poetry: An Anthology of Traditional Poems.* London: Cambridge University Press.

———. 1980. *Yoruba Myths.* Cambridge: Cambridge University Press.

Evans-Pritchard, E. E. (ed.). 1967. *The Zande Trickster.*

Finnegan, Ruth. 1970. *Oral Literature in Africa.* Oxford: Oxford University Press.

Frobenius, Leo. 1937. *African Genesis.* New York: Stackpole Sons.

Griaule, Marcel. 1948. *Conversations with Ogotemmeli.* London: Oxford University Press.

Herskovits, Melville J., and Frances S. Herskovits. 1958. *Dahomean Narrative.* Evanston: Northwestern University Press.

Johnston, H. A. S. 1966. *A Selection of Hausa Stories.*

Joseph, George. 1979. "The Wolof Oral Praise Song for Semu Coro Wende." *Research in African Literatures* 10:145–178.

Mapanje, Jack, and Landeg White. 1983. *Oral Poetry from Africa: An Anthology.* New York: Longman.

Mbiti, John S. (ed.). 1966. *Akamba Stories.*

Oxford Library of African Literature volumes:

Whiteley, W. H. 1964. *A Selection of African Prose.* Vol. 1. *Traditional Oral Texts.*

Written African Literatures in African Languages

Alden, Patricia. 1995. Rev. of Derek Wright. *The Novels of Nuruddin Farah. Modern Fiction Studies* 41.2: 381–383. Online.

Allen, Roger. 1982. *The Arabic Novel: An Historical and Critical Introduction.* Syracuse, NY: Syracuse University Press.

Bertoncini, Elena. 1989. *Outline of Swahili Literature.* Leiden: E. J. Brill.

Gérard, Albert. 1971. *Four African Literatures: Xhosa, Sotho, Zulu, Amharic.* Berkeley: University of California Press.

———. 1980. *African Language Literatures: An Introduction to the Literary History of Sub-Saharan Africa.* Washington, DC: Three Continents Press.

Hunwick, J. O., and R. S. O'Fahey (eds.). 1994. *Arabic Literature in Africa.* Leiden: Brill.

Knappert, Jan. 1979. *Four Centuries of Swahili Verse.* London and Nairobi: Heinemann Educational Books.

Ntuli, D. B., and C. F. Swanepoel. 1993. *South African Literatures in African Languages: A Concise Historical Perspective.* Pretoria: Acacia.

Modern Literatures in European Languages—Criticism

Achebe, Chinua. 1975. *Morning Yet on Creation Day: Essays.* London: HEB.

Awoonor, Kofi. 1975. *The Breast of the Earth: A Survey of the History, Culture, and Literature of Africa South of the Sahara.* Garden City, NY: Anchor Press/Doubleday.

Banham, Martin, Errol Hill, and George Woodyard (eds.). 1994. *The Cambridge Guide to African and Caribbean Theatre.* London: Cambridge University Press.

Beier, Ulli. 1967. *An Introduction to African Literature: An Anthology of Critical Writing.* Evanston: Northwestern University Press.

Beier, Ulli, Jan Knappert, and Gerald Moser. 1974. "African Arts." Pp. 139–145 in *Encyclopaedia Britannica: Macropaedia, Knowledge in Depth.* Vol. 13.

Blair, Dorothy S. 1976. *African Literature in French: A History of Creative Writing in French from West and Equatorial Africa.* Cambridge: Cambridge University Press.

Boehmer, Elleke. 1994. *Altered State? Writing and South Africa.* Sydney: Dangaroo Press.

Booker, Keith M. 1998. *The African Novel in English.* Oxford: James Currey; Portsmouth, NH: Heinemann.

Brench, A. C. 1967. *The Novelists' Inheritance in French Africa: Writers from Senegal to Cameroon.* London: Oxford University Press.

Brown, Duncan, and Bruno Van Dyk (eds.). 1991. *Exchanges: South African Writing in Transition.* Pietermaritzburg: University of Natal Press.

Burness, Donald. 1989. *Fire: Six Writers from Angola, Mozambique, and Cape Verde.* Washington, DC: Three Continents Press.

Chapman, Michael. 1996. *Southern African Literatures.* London and New York: Longman.

Chapman, Michael, Colin Gardner, and Es'kia Mphahlele (eds.). 1992. *Prospectives on South African English Literature.* Johannesburg: Ad. Donker.

Chinweizu, Onwuchekwa Jemie, and Ihechukwu Madubuike. 1980. *Toward the Decolonization of African Literature. Vol. 1: African Fiction and Poetry and Their Critics.* Enugu, Nigeria: Fourth Dimension.

Chipasula, Frank, and Stella Chipasula (eds.). 1992. *The Heinemann Book of African Women's Poetry.* Oxford: Heinemann.

Coetzee, J. M. 1988. *White Writing: On the Culture of Letters in South Africa.* New Haven: Yale University Press.

Cook, David. 1977. *African Literature: A Critical View.* London: Longman.

Cornevin, Robert. 1976. *Littératures d'Afrique noire de langue française.* Paris: Presses Universitaires de France.

Diop, Cheikh Anta. 1974. *The African Origin of Civilization: Myth or Reality.* Edited and translated by Mercer Cook. New York: Lawrence Hill.

———. 1987. *Precolonial Black Africa.* Translated by Harold Salemson. New York: Lawrence Hill.

Draper, James P. (ed.). 1992. *Black Literature Criticism: Excerpts from Criticism of the Most Significant Works of Black Authors over the Past 200 Years.* Detroit: Gale.

Echuero, Michael J. C. 1977. *Poets, Prophets and Professors.* Ibadan, Nigeria: Ibadan University Press.

Egejuru, Phanuel A. 1978. *Black Writers, White Audience: A Critical Approach to African Literature.* Hicksville, NY: Exposition Press.

———. 1980. *Towards African Literary Independence: A Dialogue with Contemporary African Writers.* Westport, CT: Greenwood Press.

Erickson, John D. 1979. *Nommo: African Fiction in French South of the Sahara.* York, SC: French Literature Publishing.

Fuchs, Anne, and Geoffrey V. Davis. 1996. *Theatre and Change in South Africa.* Amsterdam: Harwood.

Gakwandi, Shatto Arthur. 1977. *The Novel and Contemporary Experience in Africa.* London: HEB.

Gérard, Albert. 1986. *European-Language Writing in Sub-Saharan Africa.* Budapest: Akademiai Kiado.

Gikandi, Simon. 1987. *Reading the African Novel.* London: James Currey; Portsmouth, NH: Heinemann.

———. 1991. *Reading Chinua Achebe.* London: James Currey; Portsmouth, NH: Heinemann.

Gleason, Judith. 1965. *This Africa: Novels by West Africans in English and French.* Evanston, IL: Northwestern University Press.

———. 1973. *The Black Interpreters: Notes on African Writing.* Johannesburg: Ravan Press.

Gordimer, Nadine. 1995. *Writing and Being: The Charles Eliot Norton Lectures.* Cambridge: Harvard University Press.

Gurnah, Abdulrazak (ed.). 1993. *Essays on African Writing: A Re-evaluation.* Oxford: Heinemann.

Hale, Thomas A. 1998. *Griots and Griottes.* Bloomington: Indiana University Press.

Harrow, Kenneth. 1994. *Thresholds of Change in African Literature: The Emergence of a Tradition.* Portsmouth, NH: Heinemann; London: James Currey.

———. 1996. *The Marabout and the Muse: New Approaches to Islam in African Literature.* Portsmouth, NH: Heinemann; London: James Currey.

———. (ed.). 1991. *Faces of Islam in African Literature.* Portsmouth, NH: Heinemann.

Irele, Abiola. 1990. *The African Experience in Literature and Ideology.* Bloomington: Indiana University Press.

Jahn, Janheinz. 1961. *Muntu: An Outline of the New African Culture.* New York: Grove Press.

———. 1966. *A History of Neo-African Literature.* London: Faber and Faber.

JanMohamed, Abdul. 1983. *Manichean Aesthetics: The Politics of Literature in Colonial Africa.* Amherst: University of Massachusetts Press.

Jones, Eldred, Eustace Palmer, and Marjorie Jones (eds.). 1991. *The Question of Language in African Literature.* London: James Currey; Trenton, NJ: Africa World Press.

———. 1993. *Critical Theory and African Literature Today.* London: James Currey; Trenton, NJ: Africa World Press.

Julien, Eileen. 1992. *African Novels and the Question of Orality.* Bloomington: Indiana University Press, 1992.

Kannemeyer, J. C. 1993. *A History of Afrikaans Literature.* Pietermaritzburg: Shuter and Shooter.

Kern, Anita. 1980. *Women in West African Fiction.* Washington, DC: Three Continents Press.

Kesteloot, Lilyan. 1972. *Intellectual Origins of the African Revolution.* Translated by A. Mboukou. Washington, DC: Black Orpheus Press.

———. 1974. *Black Writers in French: A Literary History of Negritude.* Translated by E. C. Kennedy. Philadelphia: Temple University Press.

———. 2001. *Histoire de la littérature négro-africaine.* Paris: Karthala-AUF.

Khumalo, Fred. 2006. "Where Are Our Young Black Writers: Paul Ash Speaks to Three Publishers About the Lack of Names, Despite a Publishing Boom in the Country." *Sunday Times.* Special edition for the Cape Town Book Fair (June 17–20).

Killam, G. D. (ed.). 1972. *African Writers on African Writing.* London: HEB.

———. 1984. *The Writing of East and Central Africa.* Nairobi: Heinemann.

Klein, Marcia. 2006. "Read All About It." *Sunday Times.* Special edition for the Cape Town Book Fair (June 17–20).

Klima, Vladimir. 1969. *Modern Nigerian Novels.* Prague: Oriental Institute.

Klima, Vladimir, Frantisek Ruzicka, and Petr Zima. 1976. *Black Africa: Literature and Language.* Prague: Academia Publishing House.

Kurtz, J. Roger. 1998. *Urban Obsessions, Urban Fears: The Postcolonial Kenyan Novel.* Oxford: James Currey; Trenton, NJ: Africa World Press.

Larson, Charles R. 1976. *The Novel in the Third World.* Washington, DC: Inscape.

Laurence, Margaret. 1968. *Long Drums and Cannons: Nigerian Dramatists and Novelists.* London: Macmillan.

Lazarus, Neil. 1990. *Resistance in Postcolonial African Fiction.* New Haven: Yale University Press.

Lindfors, Bernth. 1994. *Comparative Approaches to African Literatures.* Amsterdam: Rodopi.

Lindfors, Bernth, Ian Munro, Richard Priebe, and Reinhard Sander (eds.). 1972. *Palaver: Interviews with Five African Writers in Texas.* Austin: University of Texas Press.

Lo Liyong, Taban. 1990. *Another Last Word.* Nairobi: Heinemann Kenya.

Madubuike, Ihechukwu. 1980. *The Senegalese Novel: A Sociological Study of the Impact of the Politics of Assimilation.* Washington, DC: Three Continents Press.

Maja-Pearce, Adewale (ed.). 1990. *The Heinemann Book of African Poetry in English.* Heinemann: Oxford.

Majavu, Mandisi. 2006. "Review of *No Cold Kitchen: A Biography of Nadine Gordimer.*" Monthly Review. February 9. Online at www.mrzine.monthlyreview.org/majavu090206.html.

Mapanje, Jack, and Landeg White. 1983. *Oral Poetry from Africa: An Anthology.* New York: Longman.

Mayamba, N. 1988. *The East African Narrative Fiction: Towards an Aesthetic and a Socio-Political Uhuru.* Lagos: Cross Continent.

Mazrui, Ali. 1986. *The Africans, a Triple Heritage.* London: BBC.

Miller, Christopher L. 1985. *Blank Darkness: Africanist Discourse in French.* Chicago: University of Chicago Press.

———. 1999. *Nationalists and Nomads, Essays on Francophone African Literature and Culture.* Chicago: University of Chicago Press.

Mortimer, Mildred. 1990. *Journeys Through the French African Novel.* Portsmouth, NH: Heinemann.

Mouralis, Bernard. 1984. *Littérature et développement: Essai sur le statut, la fonction et la représentation de la littérature négro-africaine d'expression française.* Paris: Silex.

Moyers, Bill. 1988. "Chinua Achebe Videorecording." *Bill Moyers' World of Ideas.* Alexandria, VA: PBS Video.

Ndebele, Njabulo S. 1991. *Southern African Literature and Culture: Rediscovery of the Ordinary.* Manchester, UK: Manchester University Press.

Neto, Agostinho. 1979. *On Literature and National Culture.* Luanda: Angolan Writers Union.

Ngara, Emmanuel. 1982. *Art and Ideology in the African Novel: A Study of the Influence of Marxism on African Writing.* London: Heinemann.

Ngate, Jonathan. 1988. *Francophone African Fiction: Reading a Literary Tradition.* Trenton, NJ: Africa World Press.

Ngugi wa Thiong'o. 1981. *Writers in Politics: Essays.* London: HEB.

———. 1986. *Decolonising the Mind: The Politics of Language in African Literature.* Portsmouth, NH: Heinemann.

———. 1990. "Return of the Native Tongue." *The Times Literary Supplement* No. 4,563 (September 14–20):972, 981.

———. 1993. *Moving the Centre: The Struggle for Cultural Freedoms.* London: James Currey.

Obiechina, Emmanuel. 1975. *Culture, Tradition and Society in the West African Novel.* New York: Cambridge University Press.

Ojaide, Tanure. 1997. *Poetic Imagination in Black Africa: Essays on African Poetry.* Durham, NC: Carolina Academic Press.

Okpewho, Isidore (ed.). 1979. *The Epic in Africa: Toward a Poetics of the Oral Performance.* New York: Columbia University Press.

———. 1983. *Myth in Africa: A Study of Its Aesthetic and Cultural Relevance.* Cambridge: Cambridge University Press.

———. (ed.). 1985. *The Heritage of African Poetry: An Anthology of Oral and Written Poetry.* London: Longman.

———. (ed.). 1990. *The Oral Performance in Africa.* Ibadan, Nigeria: Spectrum Books.

———. 1992. *African Oral Literature: Backgrounds, Character, and Continuity.* Bloomington: Indiana University Press.

———. 1998. *Once Upon a Kingdom: Myth, Hegemony, and Identity.* Bloomington: Indiana University Press.

———. (ed.) with Carole B. Davies and Ali A. Mazrui. 1999. *The African Diaspora: African Origins and New World Identities.* Bloomington: Indiana University Press.

———. 2003. *Chinua Achebe's* Things Fall Apart: *A Casebook.* New York: Oxford University Press.

Owomoyela, Oyekan. 1979. *African Literatures: An Introduction.* Waltham, MA: Crossroads Press.

Peters, Jonathan. 1978. *A Dance of Masks: Senghor, Achebe, Soyinka.* Washington, DC: Three Continents Press.

Roscoe, Adrian. 1977. *Uhuru's Fire: African Literature East to South.* London and New York: Cambridge University Press.

Sartre, Jean-Paul. 1963. *Black Orpheus.* Translated by S. W. Allen. Paris: Présence Africaine.

Shava, Pineal Viriri. 1989. *A People's Voice: Black South African Writing in the Twentieth Century.* London: Zed Books; Athens: Ohio University Press; Harare: Baobab Books.

Smith, M. Van Wyk. 1990. *Grounds of Contest: A Survey of South African English Literature.* Cape Town: Jutalit.

Smith, Nicole. 2006. "Werewere Liking-Gnepo (interview)." *Aspire Magazine* (December/January):54–55.

Soyinka, Wole. 1976. *Myth, Literature and the African World.* London: Cambridge University Press.

———. 1990. *Art, Dialogue and Outrage. Essays on Literature and Culture.* 2d ed., edited by B. Jeyifo. London: Methuen.

Suresh Roberts, Robert. 2006. *No Cold Kitchen: A Biography of Nadine Gordimer.* Johannesburg: STE Publishers.

Taiwo, Oladele. 1976. *Culture and the Nigerian Novel.* London: Macmillan.

Traore, Bakary. 1972. *The Black African Theatre and Its Social Functions.* Translated by Dapo Adelugba. Ibadan, Nigeria: Ibadan University Press.

Trump, Martin (ed.). 1990. *Rendering Things Visible: Essays on South African Literary Culture.* Johannesburg: Ravan Press; Athens: Ohio University Press.

Udenta, O. 1993. *Revolutionary Aesthetics and the African Literary Process.* Enugu: Fourth Dimension Publications.

Vera, Yvonne (ed.). 1999. *The Heinemann Book of Contemporary African Women's Writing.* Oxford: Heinemann.

Wauthier, Claude. 1978. *The Literature and Thought of Modern Africa.* London: HEB.

Wheelwright, Philip. 1965. "Myth." P. 538 in *Princeton Encyclopedia of Poetry and Poetics.* Princeton: Princeton University Press.

Wilentz, Gay Alden. 1992. *Binding Cultures: Black Women Writers in Africa and the Diaspora.* Bloomington: Indiana University Press.

Wilkinson, Jane (ed.). 1992. *Talking with African Writers: Interviews with African Poets, Playwrights and Novelists.* London: James Currey.

13

Trends and Prospects

April A. Gordon and Donald L. Gordon

Since publishing the first edition of *Understanding Contemporary Africa* in 1992, we have used this chapter to discuss the question "Where does Africa appear to be heading?" In formulating a response, we have looked at some of Africa's achievements since independence. Especially noteworthy were gains in education, health care, and life expectancy. In the 1990s, we also observed the movement toward democracy and economic reforms after decades of authoritarianism and economic decline. We were cautiously optimistic in 1996 that Africa was headed in the right direction. Many of Africa's leaders were admitting their failures and the need for major reforms. With the active participation of ordinary people in a strong civil society, we felt that a dedicated leadership could build stable institutions suitable to African realities. This would be necessary if Africa was to successfully cope with such challenges as rapid population growth and urbanization, the AIDS crisis, environmental problems, violent conflict, and economic stagnation and debt.

We also noted the need for external assistance. For decades during the colonial period, foreign powers exploited Africa's wealth to advance their own. Since independence, not much has changed. With few exceptions, most African countries have remained impoverished exporters of raw materials to more wealthy industrialized countries. A major difference between now and the colonial period is that rich countries exercise most of their control today as a result of massive African debt. This has allowed Western countries, through such international institutions as the World Bank and the International Monetary Fund (IMF), to use economic and political conditionalities to limit the range of policy choices open to Africans. In reality then, aid has been a two-edged sword. While needed to promote development, aid has often been a tool to promote industrial nations' economic and foreign policy objectives, including shoring up corrupt but compliant authoritarian regimes. Many hoped that the end of the Cold War would make possible a "peace dividend" in which cuts in military spending would be redirected toward lifting countries out of poverty and hopelessness.

In recent years, policy discussions have been moving away from a rigid imposition of structural adjustment and to an emphasis on sustainable development and poverty reduction. These issues are discussed in the text, but here is what the World Bank said in a recent development report: "Poverty amid plenty is the world's greatest challenge. We at the Bank have made it our mission to fight poverty with passion and professionalism, putting it at the center of all the work we do" (World Bank, 2001: v). In another recent publication, the Bank emphasizes that development must be measured in qualitative not just economically quantitative terms:

> Development is about improving the quality of people's lives, expanding their ability to shape their own futures. This generally calls for higher per capita income, but it involves much more. It involves more equitable education and job opportunities. Greater gender equality. Better health and nutrition. A cleaner, more sustainable natural environment. A more impartial judicial and legal system. Broader civil and political freedoms. A richer cultural life. (World Bank, 2000b:xxiii)

In answer to the question posed in the title of a recent World Bank report, "Can Africa Claim the 21st Century?" the Bank's answer is yes, Africa can claim the new century. But this is a qualified yes, conditional on Africa's ability—aided by its development partners—to overcome the "development traps" that kept it confined to a vicious cycle of underdevelopment, conflict, and untold human suffering for most of the twentieth century (World Bank, 2000a:x).

According to the report, overcoming the development traps of the past depends on three factors: increasing political participation and accountable government, changing Africa from a Cold War pawn to a magnet for trade and investment, and utilizing the benefits of globalization and new communications technology to accelerate development (World Bank, 2000a:x).

In our discussion of trends and prospects for Africa, we have chosen to provide updates on the issues discussed in the third edition: poverty reduction, debt relief, trade and investment, aid, and information technology. These issues continue to be crucial to the overall goals of achieving sustainable development (i.e., long-term economic, political, and societal progress) in Africa.

Poverty Reduction

After more than three decades of economic decline in most of Africa, poverty remains a severe and growing problem. In 1990, there were 227 million people in sub-Saharan Africa living on less than $1 a day, the UN's definition of extreme poverty. In 2001, the number increased to 271 million people (UN, 2005:7) and currently stands at 313 million (see Chapter 5). It is shocking that Africa's total income is little more than Belgium's, and thirty-four of the world's forty-eight poorest countries are in Africa. In Africa's poorest countries, a staggering 60–80 percent of people are living on less than $1 per day. In the rest of the developing world, the population in extreme poverty has dropped from 28 to 24 percent. Ghana, Uganda, and Mauritania were among the few countries showing a decline in poverty, but only Ghana's poverty rate (at 29.4 percent) was below 40 percent (World Bank, 2005a; 2005b; 2000a:18; 2001:7, 10, 23–25).

The prospects for alleviating poverty in the near future are not favorable. According to Bank estimates, Africa must increase its GDP by 5 percent a year just to prevent an increase in the number of the poor. Only fifteen countries, including Botswana, Mauritius, and Uganda, had growth this high in the 1990s. Only five countries—Angola, Burkina Faso, Chad, Equatorial Guinea, and Mozambique—currently have the necessary growth rate of 7 percent or better to reduce poverty significantly ("African Trade," 2004). Both current and projected economic growth rates for most countries are at best only 4–5 percent (World Bank, 2005b; 2000a:18). Countries will have to grow at this rate or better for many years to make much of a dent in poverty (World Bank, 2001:274–275).

Despite these grim statistics, the Bank believes that the goal of reducing poverty in Africa is possible. After all, in the 1960s, South Korea had similar rates of poverty but is now a model of development as one of the world's most prosperous newly industrializing countries (NICs) (World Bank, 2000a:12). A key point to remember is that East Asian countries like South Korea achieved their economic transformation in part through policies designed to reduce poverty and promote equity. Growth alone will not ensure that the benefits of growth reach the poor, as the Bank concedes (World Bank, 1997:25).

Unfortunately, Africa now rivals Latin America as the region of the world with the greatest inequality between the rich few and the many poor (World Bank, 2000a:10). Nigeria stands as a striking example of this inequality. In spite of its oil wealth, Nigeria is the thirteenth poorest country in the world, with a gross national income (GNI) per capita of only $390 in 2004 (World Bank, 2004). Most of the oil revenues have ended up in the pockets of a small elite of influential businesspeople and politicians.

Poverty, including child poverty, is increasing in Africa despite years of efforts to promote development.

A recent report revealed that Nigeria has 6 of the world's 100 richest people. All are or were politically influential. One of them, Harry Akande, is the seventh richest person in the world. Two of the six—Ibrahim Babangida and Sani Abacha (now deceased)—were former generals who became presidents of the country as the result of coups and then managed to get fabulously rich; another one, Moshood Abiola, was a wealthy businessman who was elected president then died in jail after being imprisoned by Abacha. These men amassed so much wealth that they could pay off Nigeria's entire foreign debt of $33.5 billion ("Rich," 2000). Inequality of this magnitude is worth pondering in light of the fact that more than 250 million Africans are without access to clean water and more than 200 million lack basic health care (World Bank, 2005b:34; 2000a:10).

Many factors contribute to poverty in Africa including poor governance, external shocks, and AIDS. In many countries an additional factor is violent conflict. In the past fifty years, there have been 186 coups and 26 wars in Africa that together have killed over 9 million people and cost $250 billion dollars (UN, 2005:9; Mitchell, 2004). Approximately a third of African countries are currently experiencing conflict. The World Bank (2005a) estimates that the cost to economic growth each year in the affected countries is 2.2 percent.

The direct costs of conflict do not take into account the indirect costs, which include the illicit plundering of natural resources to fund the continent's most vicious and long-lasting wars, including those in Liberia, Sierra Leone, Angola, and the Democratic Republic of Congo (DRC). In all four countries, so-called blood diamonds, which have been smuggled out of the country and sold in international markets, provided much of the financing for war (Sylla, 2004). Africa's bloodiest civil war is in the DRC, where an estimated 3.8 million people have died. In addition to diamonds, billions of dollars in gold, tin, coltan, timber, and other rare gems and minerals have been sold by various governments, militias, and armies to pay for weapons or for personal enrichment. These weapons, in turn, fuel more violence as the combatants seek more illicit gain (Brummer, 2004; Collins, 2004; "Gold," 2005). One can only imagine how these resources could have been used to promote development rather than more poverty and misery for affected populations. In Angola, suffering from civil war from the 1970s until 2002, over $4 billion in oil revenue disappeared from government accounts in the period of 1997–2002. This sum was equal to the entire amount spent on all social programs in Angola during that same period ("$4 bn," 2004).

A more positive development is the Millennium Development Summit that occurred in 2000. At the summit, 189 nations adopted the Millennium Declaration, which was distilled into eight specific Millennium Development Goals (MDGs, which Virginia DeLancey reviews in Chapter 5). The overall objective is to promote development, human rights, and peace in poor countries. One of the most ambitious goals is to cut by 50 percent the number of people in the world living in extreme poverty by 2015. In 2005, the UN published a report on progress toward meeting the MDGs. With regard to sub-Saharan Africa, the report's sobering assessment was that on its present course Africa will not meet a single target of the MDGs. Of special concern, as mentioned above, is that extreme poverty is actually growing in most of sub-Saharan Africa (see UN, 2005).

For Africa to have any prospects for meeting the MDGs, most observers agree that more must be done to remove Africa's crushing debt burden and to increase trade and aid. We will examine these topics next.

Debt

Africa is the most indebted region of the world and the most aid dependent (World Bank, 2000a:5), and its external debt has grown over the years.

Between 1970 and 2002, Africa received $294 billion in loans and paid back $268 billion. Yet, as Virginia DeLancey notes in Chapter 5, it still owes more than $231 billion. Critics view this high level of debt as an unacceptable "reverse transfer of wealth" from the poorest area of the world to the richest. As countries struggle to service their debt, crucial funds are taken from such vital expenditures as education, health care, and infrastructure. In 2003 alone, African countries paid $15 billion in interest on their debt (Becker, 2004).

IMF and World Bank officials often blame Africa's political leaders for the debt problem. They point to poor management of foreign borrowing and corruption as the main culprits. Although "external shocks," such as rising energy prices, are factors, as are unfavorable terms of trade, one IMF official observed that "African politicians often lived beyond their means, allowing high trade and budget deficits without encouraging savings to cushion their economies." Leaders make things worse by borrowing more money to service earlier debts. This in turn decreases funds available for productive investment, the economy slows, and debt servicing becomes even more difficult (Ligomeka, 2000).

Zambia provides a good example of the debilitating downward economic spiral associated with unsustainable debt. In 1999, Zambia, one of the world's poorest countries, paid $136 million to service its debt to foreign creditors. With 80 percent of its population living in poverty and with one of the world's highest HIV infection rates, debt servicing was the biggest item in the government's budget. That $136 million could have been spent addressing poverty and AIDS. Elsewhere in Africa, governments are forced to spend more on debt repayment than they do on the health and education of their people. Even then they may be unable to meet their debt obligations (Booker, 2000).

In Chapter 5, Virginia DeLancey discussed Africa's debt problems and the measures, such as structural adjustment programs (SAPs), suggested to manage them. Clearly, the prospects for many of Africa's countries are dim unless they can begin investing more of their earnings in improving the lives of their people rather than in making payments into perpetuity on debts they will never be able to repay. Critics contend that SAPs have made debt and poverty worse. Indeed, most debt was acquired between 1985 and 1995 when most African countries were under structural adjustment ("New Study," 2004).

The World Bank acknowledges that mistakes were made with its policies and pledges to make poverty reduction its primary focus in its lending. In June 2004 it replaced adjustment lending with "development policy lending," and it gives countries more freedom to plan and implement their own programs (World Bank, 2006). The Bank is also behind various efforts to promote debt relief.

The Heavily Indebted Poor Countries (HIPC) Initiative is one major proposal to ease the debt burden in the world's poorest countries. Critics argue that the HIPC Initiative is a flawed response to the debt problem. Salih Booker, director of the Africa Policy Information Center, concludes:

> Neither the original nor the "enhanced" version of the HIPC Initiative . . . has succeeded in easing the debt burden of impoverished countries. In fact, the complexities of the HIPC process, and the harsh structural adjustment programs that have accompanied the intervention of international creditors, have served to worsen the debt crisis and hamper the social and economic development of HIPC countries. (Booker, 2000)

The international aid organization Oxfam has also been critical. It has called the debt relief package under the HIPC Initiative a "fraud." Although Zambia's debt was lowered somewhat, the interest it was required to pay actually increased from $136 million to $235 million in 2002. Oxfam figures also showed that in six African countries—Mali, Burkina Faso, Tanzania, Mozambique, Zambia, and Malawi—debt servicing would be greater than spending on basic education even after the countries completed the debt relief program (Denny, 2000). These and other deficiencies of HIPC debt relief have led Kofi Annan, secretary-general of the UN, to conclude that it "does not provide an adequate response" to African debt problems and that "a bolder approach will have to be taken" (Booker, 2000). The World Bank (2006) counters that the HIPC program has provided significant debt relief amounting to $4.4 billion as of June 30, 2005.

Nonetheless, there is a growing movement to cancel Africa's debt altogether. For instance, a 2004 UNCTAD (UN Conference on Trade and Development) study concluded that debt servicing by African countries would make it impossible for them to meet the Millennium Development Goals and that the debt should be cancelled ("New Study," 2004). In 2005, at the G-8 Summit of leading industrial nations in Scotland, Britain's Prime Minister Tony Blair led a crusade for both debt cancellation and increased aid to Africa. "Making Poverty History," Blair pleaded, was possible and both a moral and strategic imperative. In a compromise agreement, the G8 countries vowed to increase their annual aid to poor countries by $50 billion by 2010. An additional $25 billion was included for Africa. Moreover, the debt of the world's eighteen poorest countries was to be cancelled (Editors, 2005:408–409).

Trade and Investment

Debt relief or cancellation is part of a larger strategy for renewed development in Africa. The main rationale for debt relief is to enable African countries to make necessary investments in people and the economy so that Africa will be more competitive in the global economy. The ground rules for poor countries' participation in the global economy are laid out in US-led policies commonly known as neoliberalism or the "Washington Consensus." Among other things, neoliberal reforms require African governments to open up their economies to more foreign investment and trade. Africans are urged to adopt an export-led development strategy, which would consist largely of selling primary products such as agricultural commodities, minerals, and fuels.

There is no doubt that Africa needs more trade and investment. Since 1960, Africa's share of world trade has dropped to only 1.5 percent (USAID, 2005a). Such economic marginalization and the relationship it has to poverty are clear. However, the role of foreign investment is controversial.

The benefit of foreign investment is that it can bring with it much-needed technology, jobs, know-how, and management skills without adding to the debt burden. Unfortunately, despite the huge increase in global trade and investment, little of it has gone to Africa (or to most other less-developed countries). In the 1990s, ten countries received three-fourths of all private investment funds; none of them was in Africa (French, 1998:150–151, 155). In Africa, what foreign investment there is has gone largely toward natural resource extraction, such as oil drilling, farming, logging, and mining. Africa is a treasure house of mineral riches, most of them untapped.

Europe and the United States have long dominated foreign investment in Africa, with mixed results. A new phenomenon is the growing role of Chinese trade and investment. By 2007, China is expected to be the third biggest investor in Africa behind the United States and Great Britain. Of major interest to China is securing oil and mineral resources for its booming economy. Since 2000, trade between China and Africa more than tripled to almost $30 billion in 2005. China now purchases 13 percent of Africa's exports, and in 2004 China had trade deals with forty African countries ("New Scramble," 2004).

China has forty oil agreements with African countries, and about 28 percent of its oil now comes from Africa. Angola is China's second biggest oil supplier, and China has major investments in Sudan as well. Major oil deals with Gabon and Nigeria are also being sought (French, 2005; Johnson, 2006; "New Scramble," 2004).

China is pursuing other ventures in Africa as well. Other trade deals include telecoms and construction deals such as cell phone networks in Kenya, Zimbabwe, and Nigeria and a hydroelectric plant in Zambia. China also has invested in the copper industry and in commercial farms in Zambia and is active in hotel, road, and other big construction projects in Botswana and South Africa. In return, China receives oil, coal, and minerals. African health care workers are receiving Chinese training, and China provides medical equipment and drugs to fight AIDS and malaria. Other support from China has benefited science and technology, education, and agriculture (French, 2005).

The United States finds itself in growing competition with China for oil. Since the terrorist attack on the United States in September 2001 and the launching of the "war on terror," the United States has been seeking non–Middle Eastern and non-OPEC sources of oil. Africa is especially enticing. It already supplies 15 percent of US oil, and this is expected to grow to 25 percent by 2015. Chad, São Tomé and Principe, Equatorial Guinea, and Angola, as well as OPEC-member Nigeria, are major West African points of interest. Oil companies are exploring offshore in the Indian Ocean as well. Oil seems to be a major reason for the Bush administration's heightened interest in addressing Africa's poverty. Walter Kansteiner, US Assistant Secretary of State for Africa, reputedly said that African oil is of "national strategic interest" to the United States—and it is the only American interest in Africa ("Black Gold," 2002).

While revenues from oil and mineral extraction should be a boon to development, in Africa this is rarely the case. Such riches have instead fueled massive waste, corruption, and conflict. It is probably no coincidence that the most corrupt countries in Africa—Chad, Nigeria, Equatorial Guinea, and Angola—are major oil producers. Opportunities for bribes, theft, and patron-client corruption are common, with Africa's people the losers ("Africa's Unending War," 2006; Polgreen, 2005).

To promote trade in commodities other than oil and minerals, the United States is encouraging manufacturing and agricultural exports through the Africa Growth and Opportunity Act (AGOA). Passed in 2000 when Bill Clinton was president, AGOA allows thirty-seven African countries to export about 6,500 products duty-free to the United States. As of 2003, African exports remained less than 2 percent of US imports. Although AGOA resulted in an increase in African exports in some cases, overall results have been mixed (see "No Silver," 2003; "Senegal," 2005).

On the positive side, US trade with Africa increased 37 percent in 2004 to $44.4 billion (USAID, 2005a), and the United States is now the biggest importer of African goods ("US Trade," 2003). Although non-oil-mineral imports have increased, the largest share of US imports under AGOA remains oil and minerals. AGOA also has not engendered a huge increase in US investment in Africa; in 2002, less than 1 percent of US investment was in Africa—a mere $861 million. Sectors such as automobiles in South Africa or information technology in Uganda saw few gains ("US Throws," 2004; "No Silver," 2003; USAID, 2005a).

In some countries, the textiles and apparel sector early on had some spectacular growth in foreign investment. However, the experiences of South Africa, Lesotho, and Kenya indicate how short-lived and partial such gains can be. In 2001, South Africa saw a 21 percent increase in exports in clothing and other goods, and 38,000 new jobs. In Lesotho, eleven new textile factories were built and eight expanded; 15,000 new jobs were created. Lesotho became sub-Saharan Africa's biggest textile exporter to the United States with 31 percent of all textile exports ("Factories," 2005). In 2003, Kenya's textile exports quadrupled, and as many as 150,000 new jobs were expected by the end of that year ("No Silver," 2003; "US Trade," 2003).

In 2005, disaster struck. South Africa's textile industry lost over 150,000 jobs due to competition from cheaper Chinese exports to the United States in spite of duty-free AGOA advantages ("Govt," 2005). Africa's industrial leader South Africa worries that it may lose not only its edge in textiles to Chinese exports, but that it may not be able to compete with cheap Chinese manufactured high-tech products either ("New Scramble," 2004). In Lesotho, most of the factories were owned by Taiwanese and Chinese firms attracted to Africa in order to circumvent US restrictions on Asian clothing imports to the US market. In 2005, six factories were closed, over 6,650 jobs were lost, and the Asian owners fled without warning or paying their workers. With the end of quotas on Asian textiles due in January 2006, exporting from Lesotho was no longer necessary. An estimated 50,000 Lesotho workers could end up losing their jobs ("Factories," 2005). Kenya also fears its textile industry will collapse with the end of quotas (Mugambi, 2005). Indeed, such fears were well founded. The value of Africa's textile and apparel exports to the United States from January to September 2005 fell by 11 percent (Hartlieb, 2006).

Ghana is another textile producer whose domestic textile industry collapsed, a victim of free trade. In Ghana's case, collapse was due to the massive importation of cheap, secondhand clothes from Europe and North America. Ghana's textile industry once supplied 25,000 jobs. Unable to compete with cheap imports, most firms shut down, and only 3,000 of those jobs are left (Crawley, 2004).

Africa also competes in the global economy by selling agricultural products, and some countries are adding fresh fruit, vegetables, and flowers to their traditional agricultural exports. Kenya, for one, is benefiting from exporting fresh flowers, which have become the country's second biggest export and the source of 50,000 jobs (Vasagar, 2006). It is not clear, however, how many countries can successfully exploit this market niche without stealing market share from each other and driving prices down. Far more important to Africa's agricultural producers are ending the damaging quotas and subsidies to farmers in Europe and the United States that prevent African commodities, such as cotton, from being able to compete fairly in world trade ("No Silver," 2003).

The upshot is that Africa continues to be for the most part uncompetitive in the global economy outside of natural resources and agricultural products. This fact raises disturbing questions about the relevance of the neoliberal orthodoxy that free trade is a panacea that can produce sustainable development and sharply reduce poverty in Africa (see "Perils," 2005).

In fact, a UN economic report in 2004 argued that trade liberalization in Africa is insufficient to boost growth or reduce poverty ("African Trade," 2004). This sentiment is shared by others, such as Jeffrey Sachs, director of the UN Millennium Development Project, who maintains that substantially more aid is needed if Africa is to escape its "poverty trap" ("Whatever It Takes," 2005). As William Minter points out, a prosperous and stable Africa requires a mix of public and private investment to promote sustainable and equitable growth. It must also build a more diversified economy, one that ends dependence on raw materials exports. Production needs to be geared for local and regional consumption, not just for overseas export markets, and there should be support for local entrepreneurs, businesses, and investment in human capital (health care, clean water, education) and infrastructure (electricity, ports, roads) (Minter, 2000:203).

Aid

Although the World Bank is convinced that SAPs have produced positive results, they admit that most countries have experienced little or no growth after undergoing structural adjustment (World Bank, 2001:67–69, 189–193). Like Sachs, they now acknowledge that the market alone will not produce development. World Bank President Paul Wolfowitz has joined the chorus of those advocating both debt cancellation and more foreign aid (Andrews, 2005).

As aid advocates point out, in recent years, aid to Africa has actually declined relative to the gross national product (GNP) of donor countries (World Bank, 2001:189–191). Although the US economy was booming during most of the 1990s, US development assistance to Africa dropped from $826 million in 1991 to $689 million in 1997. For 2000, only $305 million in aid was requested for the economy and programs for children, plus $513 million for the Development Fund for Africa (Minter, 2000:201–203). US aid per capita in 1998 was only $19 compared to $32 in 1990 (World Bank, 2000a:236–237). Whether aid will be increased and redirected toward developmental ends (as opposed to political ends as in the past) is critical to Africa's future. As the Bank notes, with effective regional cooperation and donor support in a "coordinated, long-term partnership, . . . Africa could solve its human development crisis in one generation" (World Bank, 2000a:3).

So far this long-term partnership on behalf of African development is not being fully met. As DeLancey discusses in Chapter 5, to reach the commitments made to achieve the Millennium Development Goals, rich countries need to double their development assistance to poor countries to $100 billion with a target of $195 billion by 2015. It is unlikely they will do so. However, most donor countries did promise to increase their aid to .7 percent of their GNP by 2015. In fact, with urging from the United States, Britain, France, Germany, Spain, and others are increasing their aid to this level. However, the United States itself refuses to do so. It is true that the United States has increased its aid to Africa under the Bush administration, and the United States is the largest donor to Africa in dollar terms, but it is next to last after Italy relative to the size of its economy. The United States contributes only .18 percent of its GNP to aid for poor countries (Dugger, 2005; "Where's That Veto," 2005).

The Bush administration has promised to increase aid, but again, the

April Gordon

One of the Millennium Development Goals is to cut by 50 percent by 2015 the number of people without access to clean water. Many Africans must share access to clean water at a community water point with their neighbors.

promises often have gone unfulfilled. For instance, at the Monterrey Summit in 2002, Bush promised to increase US foreign aid by 50 percent over three years, which would have brought the US foreign aid budget to $15 billion by 2006. However, Congress has not allocated the necessary funds. In June 2005, Bush pledged to double official development aid (ODA) to Africa by 2010; in 2004, ODA for Africa was $4.3 billion. When Bush requested a $2.3 billion increase for poverty-related development aid in the 2005 budget, Congress instead cut foreign aid by $2 billion. Similarly, Bush asked for almost $3 billion for his Millennium Challenge Account (MCA), which would provide aid to countries that demonstrate their commitment to good governance and sound economic policies. Congress approved only $1.77 billion (USAID, 2005b:6; "Where's That Veto," 2005). On top of underfunding the MCA, no money was actually granted until April 2005, and that was for only $110 million to Madagascar ("Choosier Approach," 2005). It remains to be seen whether or not the goal Bush has set for $8.6 billion in aid for Africa in 2010 will be met to fund his initiatives to promote education, end hunger, promote trade, and protect Congo's forests (to address global warming) (USAID, 2005a:2).

According to the 2005 Millennium Development Report, if all countries meet their aid commitments, aid will exceed $100 billion by 2010. Although this is a marked improvement from the past, it will still be too little to achieve the MDGs (UN, 2005:37). With Africa already being so poorly positioned to meet the MDGs, this assessment is especially dismaying.

Information Technology

Among the many areas in which Africa lags behind the rest of the world is communications and information infrastructure and technology. While most of the world is traveling "the information superhighway," most Africans do not even have telephones. The statistics at the beginning of the twenty-first century are telling. In the third edition of this book we reported that only 2 percent of the world's telephone users were in Africa, and in Mali, Niger, and the Democratic Republic of Congo, there was only one phone line for every 1,000 people (World Bank, 2000a:154). As for Internet access, as of 2002, only 1.5 million Africans had access to the Internet, and two-thirds of those were in South Africa. In comparison, 25 percent of North Americans and Europeans were using the Internet. Most African Internet users were white South African males who were well educated and associated with NGOs, private companies, or universities (Jensen, 2000:215, 218).

In an increasingly global economy, these figures revealed how truly marginalized Africans, especially the masses of black Africans, have become. How can Africa hope to attract investment outside of natural resources and farming or develop competitive businesses that provide good jobs with such a gap in vital communications technologies? Conceivably, the information gap alone could relegate Africa for decades to the margins of the global economy if not to permanent backwardness.

Luckily, there is recent evidence that Africa's disadvantages in this area may be changing and in some ways may end up being an advantage. For one, being a later starter, Africa can bypass increasingly outdated communications infrastructural investments and adopt the latest technologies—with potentially enormous economic, social, and political benefits.

One trend is that some countries, such as Botswana and Rwanda, are installing the most advanced digital and fiber-optic technologies, bypassing the old telephone line infrastructure found in industrialized countries. As a result, Botswana and Rwanda have among the most advanced communications networks in the world: 100 percent of their main lines are digital. In the rest of Africa, 69 percent of telecommunications lines are digital, which is close to the world average of 79 percent (World Bank, 2000a:154–155; Jensen, 2000:218).

Use of cell phones is also growing rapidly, bypassing the need for expensive land lines. Whereas only six countries had cell phones in the early 1990s, forty-two countries did by 2000 (World Bank, 2000a:154–155; Jensen, 2000:218). At least forty-eight African countries now have cell phone service ("African Internet," 2002:10). Cell phone use is growing so rapidly that Africa now is the first continent in the world with more cell phones than fixed-line phones: 60 million versus 27 million at the end of 2004. Although only 2.8 percent of Africans have access to regular telephone service, 6 percent use cell phones ("Mobile," 2004). Africa's major mobile phone companies, Vodacom and MTN, both South African companies, are busy setting up operations in other African countries such as Uganda, Rwanda, Swaziland, Tanzania, Nigeria, and Cameroon. In 2003, Vodacom had over 8 million customers, while MTN had 6 million ("Ain't No Mountain," 2003:62–63), numbers that have surely grown since then. As fast as cell phone use is expanding, it must be remembered that this is from a very low base and that most Africans still have neither cell phone nor regular telephone service. On the other hand, access to phone service may in fact be considerably greater than these numbers indicate because many Africans in both major cities and many secondary towns now have access to various public phone shops and telecenters or in other ways share phones ("African Internet," 2002:10–11). The demand for and usefulness of phones for personal communication and in business and government are obvious (see "Mo's Show," 2005).

Internet use, while small, is also growing rapidly. In 1995, only four countries were on the Internet, versus fifty in 1999. Access tends to be confined to capital cities, but Internet kiosks, cybercafés, and other public access points are becoming more and more common (for example, in hotels and business centers). Even in small towns, many public phone shops are adding Internet access (World Bank, 2000a:155–156). As of early 2006, there were almost 23 million Internet users in Africa, still only 2.5 percent of the population. This is by far the lowest percentage of any world region (second to last is the Middle East with 9.6 percent). Of sub-Saharan African countries, only five countries exceed 5 percent population penetration: Cape Verde, Mauritius, Seychelles, South Africa, and Zimbabwe ("Internet," 2006).

New information technologies will not be enough by themselves to transform the African continent, but the impact is likely to be as revolutionary there as it is proving to be in other parts of the world. Among the likely benefits are new opportunities for education; information sharing; and marketing African products, services, and newspapers and magazines. Newspapers and magazines from over forty African countries are currently published on the Internet. African governments now have websites, which can make access to government offices and services more available than ever before. These sites also provide opportunities for countries to promote tourism and business opportunities, which could be a boon to trade and investment (USAID, 2005a:7–8; World Bank, 2000a:156–158; Woodward, 2000). Having a website can benefit smaller African entrepreneurs and craftspeople, not just big formal sector firms. For instance, a West African women's cooperative is reported to have a website to help its 7,350 members market their products, monitor export markets, and negotiate prices with overseas buyers (Jensen, 2000:218).

Could information-age technology help Africa gain a stronger position in the global economy and a way to move beyond economic dependence on primary products? Some African countries are trying to exploit the new offshore outsourcing market for information technology services currently dominated by India and the Philippines. For instance, South Africa, Ghana, Senegal, Kenya, Morocco, and Madagascar currently have call centers, although the business is small with only 54,000 jobs in all of Africa ("Kenya," 2005). South Africa is most competitive in this area. In 2003, it had over 38,000 agent positions making both onshore and offshore calls; the number is expected to grow to 70,000–100,000 jobs by 2008. Call centers are also expected to grow from 494 to 939 during this same time period (Rosenthal, 2004; "Into Africa," 2005). Estimates are that British and American firms could save 30–40 percent of the cost of some services by providing them from South Africa ("Into Africa," 2005).

Even Rwanda hopes to benefit. It is trying to move directly into the new knowledge-based service sector economy and thinks this is possible within twenty years. Rwandan officials believe Rwanda could be the

"Dubai of east Africa, providing low-cost offshore banking, data entry, and insurance services for small and medium sized businesses in Europe at a third of the cost" (Woodward, 2000).

Educational opportunities are among the greatest benefits new communications technologies make possible. As budgets for schools, libraries, and teachers are being slashed due to fiscal constraints, satellite communications and the Internet can make classroom instruction, library material, and other educational resources available from the most advanced countries in the world. The World Bank is now offering courses and, soon, degrees in computer science, computer engineering, and electrical engineering through the African Virtual University project. As of 2000, twenty-four African universities were linked to overseas classrooms and libraries via satellite (Jensen, 2000:216). Great Britain is assisting Rwanda's educational system through the Imfundo project. In 2001, it helped the country's educational institutions link up with each other and with government offices. Computer and Internet training will be provided to teachers, and courses will be developed at teacher training institutions. This and other educational programs are geared to a rapid increase in computer literacy in a country where most people have never seen a computer (Woodward, 2000). Such programs are in their infancy and should be a supplement, not a replacement, for African educational institutions. Still, these and other educational links between Africa and the rest of the world will undoubtedly mushroom in the years ahead and can promote greater cooperation and interchange of ideas to the benefit of all.

Conclusion

Africa in the early years of the twenty-first century can point to areas of progress and new economic opportunities. Politically, some countries show progress in consolidating democracy, and some of the continent's worst conflicts appear to be over—such as in Sierra Leone and Liberia. On the other hand, other conflicts—such as in Côte d'Ivoire, Sudan, and the DRC—continue to fester. Since many African states remain fragile, the possibility of state collapse and new military conflicts remains a danger. Overall, the continent continues to struggle with many of the same problems it had in the late twentieth century, and significant progress is likely to remain elusive for most countries—and most of Africa's people—for decades to come.

A factor not discussed often enough in Africa's inability to pull itself up is the devastating brain drain from Africa. Africa's investments in the education of its people are in many cases benefiting the economic advancement of already developed countries more than countries in Africa.

According to the UN's Economic Commission for Africa, since the 1980s more than one-third of Africa's professionals are living in Washington, D.C., and an estimated 70,000 skilled Africans leave the continent every year. This hemorrhaging of brain power has left all of sub-Saharan Africa with only 20,000 scientists and engineers. South Africa, Africa's most industrialized country, has long experienced the emigration of white professionals; now it is losing its black professionals as well. As many as 8,000 black professionals—including nurses, doctors, teachers, and IT experts—are leaving every year. Often lured by higher wages abroad, most are going to the United States, Britain, New Zealand, the Netherlands, or Australia (Nduru, 2004).

Despite all of the negatives, we share the confidence of those who think that with a favorable mix of good leadership, good policies, popular participation, and enlightened support from the international community, there can be progress in Africa. But we do not underestimate how difficult the road ahead will be.

Bibliography

"The African Internet. A Status Report." 2002. Online at ww3.sn.apc.org.

"African Trade Policies 'Applied Haphazardly.'" 2004. *Mail & Guardian online* (South Africa). Online at www.mg.co.za (September 30).

"Africa's Unending War on Corruption." 2006. *The Economist.* Online at www.economist.com (February 3).

"Ain't No Mountain High Enough." 2003. *The Economist.* Online at www.economist.com (November 1).

Andrews, Edmund L. 2005. "For Wolfowitz, Poverty Is the Newest War to Fight." *New York Times.* Online at www.nytimes.com (September 24).

Becker, Elizabeth. 2004. "Debt Relief Deal for Poor Nations Seems to Be Near." *New York Times.* Online at www.nytimes.com (October 1).

"Black Gold." 2002. *The Economist.* Online at www.economist.com (October 24).

Booker, Salih. 2000. "The Myth of HIPC Debt Relief." *Daily Mail and Guardian* (South Africa). Online at www.mg.co.za (December 12).

Brummer, Stefaans. 2004. "SA War Vultures." *Mail & Guardian online* (South Africa). Online at www.mg.co.za (January 16).

"A Choosier Approach to Aid." 2005. *The Economist.* Online at www.economist.com (April 21).

Collins, Clayton. 2004. "When Bullets Fly, Some Firms Swoop In." *Christian Science Monitor,* December 27, p. 13, 16.

Crawley, Mike. 2004. "In Ghana, a Different Kind of 'Casual Friday.'" *Christian Science Monitor,* December 27, p. 4, 7.

Denny, Charlotte. 2000. "Debt Relief Leaves Africa Worse Off." *Daily Mail and Guardian* (South Africa). Online at www.mg.co.za (August 29).

Dugger, Celia W. 2005. "Discerning a New Course for World's Donor Nations." *New York Times.* Online at www.nytimes.com (April 18).

The Editors. 2005. "Global Progress Report, 2006." *Current History* (December):403–410.

"Factories Close: Thousands Jobless in Lesotho." 2005. *Mail & Guardian online* (South Africa). Online at www.mg.co.za (January 18).

"$4 bn Oil Money 'Disappears' from Angola." 2004. *Mail & Guardian online* (South Africa). Online at www.mg.co.za (January 14).

French, Hilary F. 1998. "Assessing Private Capital Flows to Developing Countries." Pp. 149–167 in Lester R. Brown et al. *State of the World.* New York: W. W. Norton.

French, Howard W. 2005. "China's Newest Target: Africa." *Charlotte Observer,* November 20, p. 26A.

"Gold Keeps War in the DRC on the Boil." 2005. *Mail & Guardian online* (South Africa). Online at www.mg.co.za (March 7).

"'Govt Has Failed SA's Textile Sector.'" 2005. *Mail & Guardian online* (South Africa). Online at www.mg.co.za (May 2).

Hartlieb, Thomas. 2006. "Threats Remain to Africa's Growth." *Mail & Guardian online* (South Africa). Online at www.mg.co.za (January 25).

"Internet Usage Statistics. The Big Picture: World Internet Users and Pop Stats." 2006. Online at www.internetworldstats.com.

"Into Africa." 2005. *The Economist* (August 25):52.

Jensen, Mike. 2000. "Making the Connection: Africa and the Internet." *Current History* (May):215–220.

Johnson, Tim. 2006. "China: A Dragon Thirsting for Oil." *Charlotte Observer,* January 18, p. 1P, 6P.

"Kenya Rings in Call Centre Cash." 2005. *Mail & Guardian online* (South Africa). Online at www.mg.co.za (April 9).

Ligomeka, Brian. 2000. "Africa's Debt Due to Bad Management." *Daily Mail and Guardian* (South Africa). Online at www.mg.co.za (December 13).

Minter, William. 2000. "America and Africa: Beyond the Double Standard." *Current History* (May):200–210.

Mitchell, Anthony. 2004. "Poor Markets for Africa's Governments." *Mail & Guardian online.* Online at www.mg.co.za (October 12).

"Mobile Phones the Talk of Africa as Landlines Lose Out." 2004. *Mail & Guardian online* (South Africa). Online at www.mg.co.za (May 5).

"Mo's Show." 2005. *The Economist.* Online at www.economist.com (March 31).

Mugambi, Kaburu. 2005. "Go Beyond Textiles for Agoa, Says US." *The Nation* (Kenya). Online at www.allafrica.com (November 11).

Nduru, Moyiga. 2004. "The Brain Drain Proves to Be Colour Blind." *Mail & Guardian online* (South Africa). Online at www.mg.co.za (February 3).

"A New Scramble." 2004. *The Economist.* Online at www.economist.com (November 25).

"New Study Makes Case for African Debt Write-Off." 2004. *Mail & Guardian online* (South Africa). Online at www.mg.co.za (October 7).

"No Silver Bullet." 2003. *The Economist.* Online at www.economist.com (January 16).

"Oil Boom in East Africa Predicted." 2004. *Mail & Guardian online* (South Africa). Online at www.mg.co.za (April 29).

"The Perils of Following the Free-Trade Route." 2005. *Mail & Guardian online* (South Africa). Online at www.mg.co.za (December 12).

Polgreen, Lydia. 2005. "Chad Backs Out of Pledge to Use Oil Wealth to Reduce Poverty." *New York Times.* Online at www.nytimes.com (December 13).

"Rich Men, Poor Men in Nigeria." 2000. *Daily Mail and Guardian* (South Africa). Online at www.mg.co.za (December 20).

Rosenthal, Beth Ellyn. 2004. "Why the US and UK Are Calling on South Africa Call Centers." *Outsourcing Journal.* Online at www.outsourcing-journal.com.
"Senegal Joins Ghana as Agoa Hub in West Africa." 2005. *Public Agenda* (Ghana). Online at www.allafrica.com (November 11).
Sylla, Coumba. 2004. "Illicit Diamond Trade: Diminishing Returns." *Mail & Guardian online* (South Africa). Online at www.mg.co.za (August 24).
UN (United Nations). 2005. *The Millennium Development Goals Report.* Online at www.unstats.un.org.
USAID (US Agency for International Development). 2005a. *Making Progress in Africa 2005.* Washington, DC: Office of Development and Planning Bureau for Africa.
———. 2005b. *USAID in Africa (Winter).* Washington, DC: Africa Bureau Information Center.
"US Throws a Bone to Africa." 2004. *Mail & Guardian online* (South Africa). Online at www.mg.co.za (January 29).
"US Trade Deal Bringing Mixed Success to Africa." 2003. *Mail & Guardian online* (South Africa). Online at www.mg.co.za (January 9).
Vasagar, Jeevan. 2006. "Caught on the Thorns." *Mail & Guardian online* (South Africa). Online at www.mg.co.za (February 22).
"Whatever It Takes." 2005. *The Economist.* Online at www.economist.com (January 18).
"Where's That Veto Vote." 2005. *New York Times.* Online at www.nytimes.com (November 4).
Woodward, Will. 2000. "Net Brings New Hope to Rwanda." *Daily Mail and Guardian* (South Africa). Online at www.mg.co.za (December 13).
World Bank. 1997. *World Development Report 1997.* New York: Oxford University Press.
———. 2000a. *Can Africa Claim the 21st Century?* Washington, DC: World Bank.
———. 2000b. *The Quality of Growth.* New York: Oxford University Press.
———. 2001. *World Development Report 2000/2001.* New York: Oxford University Press.
———. 2004. "GNI Per Capita, 2004, Atlas Method and PPP." Online at www.worldbank.org.
———. 2005a. "Millennium Development Goals: Sub-Saharan Africa." Online at www.developmentgoals.org.
———. 2005b. "Regional Brief: Africa." Online at www.web.worldbank.org.
———. 2006. "Development Policy Lending." Online at www.worldbank.org.

Acronyms

ACM	African Common Market
AEC	African Economic Community
AGOA	African Growth and Opportunity Act
AIA	Itihad al Islami
AIDS	acquired immune deficiency syndrome
ANC	African National Congress
APPER	Africa's Priority Programme for Economic Recovery
ATR	African traditional religion
AU	African Union
CEDAW	Convention to Eliminate All Forms of Discrimination Against Women
CFA	Communauté Financière Africaine
CITES	Convention on International Trade in Endangered Species
CJTF-HOA	Combined Joint Task Force—Horn of Africa
DRC	Democratic Republic of Congo
EAC	East African Community
EACTI	East Africa Counter-Terrorism Initiative
EC	European Community
ECA	Economic Commission for Africa
ECCAS	Economic Community of Central African States
ECOWAS	Economic Community of West African States
ESF	Economic Support Funds
EU	European Union
FAL	Final Act of Lagos
FGM	female genital mutilation

FRELIMO	Frente de Libertação de Moçambique
GDI	Gender-Related Development Index
GDP	gross domestic product
GEM	Gender Empowerment Measure
GNI	gross national income
GNP	gross national product
HDI	Human Development Index
HIPC	Heavily Indebted Poor Countries
HIV	human immunodeficiency virus
IGAD	Intergovernmental Authority on Development
ILO	International Labour Organisation
IMF	International Monetary Fund
ITCZ	Intertropical Convergence Zone
LDC	less developed country
LPA	Lagos Plan of Action
LRA	Lord's Resistance Army
MCA	Millennium Challenge Account
MDG	Millennium Development Goal
MNC	multinational corporation
MOSOP	Movement for the Survival of Ogoni People
MP	member of Parliament
MPLA	Movimento Popular de Libertação de Angola
NACTU	National African Confederation of Trade Unions
NAFTA	North American Free Trade Agreement
NCNC	National Council of Nigeria and the Cameroons
NEPAD	New Economic Partnership for African Development
NGO	nongovernmental organization
NIC	newly industrializing country
NLTPS	national long-term perspective study
NPC	Northern People's Congress
OAU	Organization of African Unity
ODA	Official Development Assistance
OECD	Organization for Economic Cooperation and Development
OEOA	United Nations Office of Emergency Operations in Africa
OPEC	Organization of Petroleum Exporting Countries
PEPFAR	President's Emergency Plan for AIDS Relief
POPs	persistent organic pollutants
PRC	People's Republic of China
PTA	preferential trade area
RPF	Rwandan Patriotic Front
RTAs	regional trade associations

SADCC/SADC	Southern African Development Coordination Conference. Now Southern African Development Community
SAP	structural adjustment program
SD	sustainable development
SSA	sub-Saharan Africa
STD	sexually transmitted disease
TSCTI	Trans-Saharan Counter-Terrorism Initiative
UAM	Union of the Arab Maghreb
UNAIDS	Joint United Nations Programme on HIV/AIDS
UNCED	UN Conference on Environment and Development
UNCTAD	United Nations Conference on Trade and Development
UNDP	United Nations Development Programme
UNECA	United Nations Economic Commission for Africa
UNEP	United Nations Environmental Programme
UNESCO	United Nations Educational, Scientific, and Cultural Organization
UNFPA	United Nations Fund for Population Activities
UNHCR	United Nations High Commissioner for Refugees
UNICEF	United Nations International Children's Emergency Fund
UN-NADAF	United Nations New Agenda for the Development of Africa
UNPAAERD	United Nations Programme of Action for African Economic Recovery and Development
UPC	Union des Populations Camerounaises
USAID	US Agency for International Development
WCED	World Commission on Environment and Development
WHO	World Health Organization
WID	Women in Development
ZANU-PF	Zimbabwe African National Union—Patriotic Front

Glossary

African Economic Community: a proposed integration of all the economies on the African continent by 2025. The idea was put forth at the Organization of African Unity (OAU) meeting in Lagos, Nigeria, in 1991.

African independent churches: term applied to a diverse range of Christian denominations in Africa that themselves are not part of either the Catholic church or any major Western Protestant organizational structure. As a group, these denominations generally incorporate African ceremonies, icons, and holy sites and often involve charismatic expressions of faith. A few have also had messianic leaders (people who claim to be the Second Coming of Jesus Christ). These churches have grown especially fast in southern Africa.

African traditional religions: a very general term given to indigenous African religious practices that predate the arrival of either Christianity or Islam in their respective areas of the continent. Most of these sets of religious practices are characterized by belief in one supreme being; belief in spirits; belief in life after death; the establishment of sacred places, plants, and/or animals; and belief in the existence of witchcraft and magic. Since the arrival of Christianity and Islam, many African traditional religions have blended with those faiths.

African Union (AU): the fifty-three-member organization founded in July 2002 to replace the OAU (Organization of African Unity) and AEC

(African Economic Community). The goals of the AU are to end conflict in Africa and promote democracy, human rights, and sustainable development. The AU eventually plans to have a common currency and common market, a common defense force, and an organization structure to carry out its missions.

Afro-Asiatic language family: one of the four major families of African languages. This includes mainly the Semitic languages of the North African states, Somalia, and Ethiopia.

Apartheid: Afrikaans word that means "apartness." This is the name given to the system of racial segregation and white superiority put into place in South Africa in 1948. In that year, the largely Afrikaner National Party won a whites-only election, ousting the pro-British government at the ballot box. The apartheid system, which was largely unmodified until 1990, required blacks, whites, mixed-race people, and people of Asian descent to live in separate areas, attend separate schools, and use separate public amenities. Apartheid also banned nonwhites from voting and required blacks to seek governmental permission to live in urban areas and hold urban jobs. Further, all of South Africa's rural areas were racially segregated, with whites given control of 83 percent of South Africa's farmland. The apartheid system also banned interracial marriage and intimate contact, among many other restrictions on public contact between the races and freedom of expression and movement.

Authoritarianism: the political opposite of democracy. Authoritarianism is a general means of governing that does not allow meaningful choices in elections and usually restricts personal freedoms of movement, speech, and assembly. Authoritarian governments may be military governments, one-person dictatorships, one-party systems, or monarchies. Shortly after independence in the era of the late 1950s through the 1960s, most African governments were authoritarian in nature. See *Personal rule.*

Bantu language family: one of the four major families of African languages, also known as the Niger-Congo language family after its birthplace in West Africa. This is by far the largest set of African languages, spoken by the great majority of people in all regions of the African continent. See *Niger-Congo language family.*

Bantu migrations: movements of people starting about 2,500 years ago when population pressures in West Africa began to force people to slowly spread eastward and ultimately southward all across the sub-Saharan region of Africa. These largely agricultural people had developed iron spears, arrows, hoes, scythes, and axes. As a result, the Bantu migrations, which had reached all the way to the southern tip of Africa by at least 1,000 years ago, spread agriculture, iron tools, and the Bantu language family across the vast expanse of the African continent. Today, the majority of Africans are descendants of the Bantu migrations. See *Bantu language family.*

Berg Report: the colloquial name for the 1981 World Bank Report *Accelerated Development in Sub-Saharan Africa: An Agenda for Action.* Written under the supervision of economist Elliot Berg, this document called for the doubling of foreign aid to Africa. More important, it called for African nations to pursue their "comparative advantage" in the world capitalist market, that is, the export of raw commodities. Many Africans and their governments found these recommendations unacceptable in light of their desire to industrialize and export value-added secondary commodities (e.g., the export of cotton is a primary commodity export; the production of textiles is a secondary commodity export). The Berg Report also recommended that the private sector become more involved in African economies and that the public sector take on a more "efficient" (reduced) economic role.

Berlin Conference: a meeting held in 1884 and 1885 in the German capital at which the major European powers with colonial territories in Africa (Britain, France, Germany, Portugal, Spain, and Italy) agreed on a partitioning of the continent into imperial spheres of influence. The current African map is a direct result of the Berlin Conference, whose participants drew these colonial boundaries with little knowledge of and little interest in creating ethnically homogeneous territories. Thus, many of today's African nations have boundaries that split ethnic groups between two or even several nations.

Bourgeoisie: French word for "the middle class." Traditionally, Marxists and other social scientists have used the term to mean shopkeepers, professionals (doctors, teachers, lawyers, etc.), clerks, small- and medium-scale farmers, and small-scale capitalists. Some scholars, on the other hand, use the term as a general reference to a nation's elites.

Bridewealth: the widespread traditional practice of a husband's family compensating a wife's family with cattle or money when a marriage takes place. The theory behind the payment of bridewealth by the husband's family is that the wife's family needs to be compensated in some way for the fertility of their daughter. Only when bridewealth is paid is a marriage considered legitimate. Note how this is the opposite of the Hindu dowry, whereby the daughter's family pays the son's family to marry the woman.

Carrying capacity: a term used by geographers and other students of natural resources to refer to the ability of an ecosystem to support a certain concentration of animal life. For example, a pastureland is said to have exceeded its carrying capacity when too many cattle graze there and the grass is eaten up faster than it can be replenished. Further, both rural and urban areas are assumed to have carrying capacities for a certain number of humans, and if this quantity is exceeded, the area will soon be unable to support human life.

Clientelism: also known as "patron-client networks." Clientelism is a pattern of social interactions in which a powerful "patron" distributes economic, political, and/or social favors to a group of subordinate "clients." The relationship, however, is a two-way street, since if a patron is too harsh on his or her clients, or does not provide enough benefits in exchange for the clients' support, those people will seek a patron elsewhere, thus undercutting the ability of the original patron to wield power by passing out favors. Note that since the passing of favors and acquiescence between patron and client is a two-way relationship, this is not the same phenomenon as dictatorship or despotism.

Coup d'état: the changing of a government through means outside the electoral process. This government overthrow may be either violent (a "bloody" coup) or peaceful (a "bloodless" coup).

Dependency: term given to a relatively loose set of explanations for distorted capitalist development in Asia, Africa, and Latin America. The Dependency School was an influential movement in political economy studies in the 1970s, particularly among scholars of Latin America. According to *dependencistas,* the world capitalist economy is divided into a "core" of leading capitalist states (the United States, France, the United Kingdom, etc.) and a "periphery" of dependent client states (Brazil, Chile, Nigeria, etc.). The economies of these periphery states are mainly serving as sources of raw materials and cheap labor for worldwide capitalist industry, with the cooperation of local elites in the periphery nations who receive political and economic benefits from exploiting local labor and natural resources.

This, according to the Dependency School, is why independent industrialization has remained illusory in the developing world. Critics of the dependency perspective respond that this theory cannot explain why nations such as Taiwan, South Korea, Singapore, and (more recently) Chile and Argentina have developed large industrial and technological sectors that rival the best economic outputs the "metropole" nations have to offer. See *Metropole* and *Neocolonialism.*

East African Community: attempt in the 1970s by the governments of Kenya, Tanzania, and Uganda to form a regional economic union among their three nations, with the ultimate aim of having a common currency, common international trade policies, and no tariffs on each other's goods. This attempt at regional economic integration failed because of political tensions between the three nations caused largely by the economic dominance of Kenya as compared to the relatively weaker economies of Uganda and Tanzania. A new East African community was formed in 1999.

Economic Community of West African States (ECOWAS): attempt of several nations in West Africa to establish regional economic cooperation. Unlike the abortive East African Community, ECOWAS is not an attempt at full economic union among its member states, but is rather a preferential trade area (PTA) in which the participant nations agree to charge each other reduced taxes on the import of goods. ECOWAS also meets periodically to discuss environmental, military, and political issues facing its member states.

Ethnicity: one of the major social and political forces in Africa (and the entire world) and a very general term referring to shared characteristics between similar individuals. Ethnicity can be one or more of the following: a common language, common ancestral ties (bloodlines), a common culture (dress, food, social practices, etc.), a common race, or a common set of religious beliefs.

Foreign debt: debt incurred when a government borrows money from either another government or a bank in another country. The repayment of a foreign debt is usually in the currency of the lender nation. For example, if Malawi's government borrows money from Chase-Manhattan Bank in New York, the bank will expect to be repaid in US dollars, not in Malawi kwatcha.

Foreign exchange: also known as "hard currency," money denominated in a currency that has worldwide acceptance due to the desirability of owning that currency. US dollars, Japanese yen, German marks, French and Swiss francs, and British pounds are examples of foreign exchange. Hard currencies are crucial for African governments, because they are necessary for purchasing imports such as petroleum, automobiles, and machinery. See *Foreign debt.*

Fuelwood: wood that is harvested and burned for cooking purposes. Burning wood is still the major form of energy production in rural Africa. Population density and the cutting of wood for fuel can lead to deforestation.

Great Rift Valley: one of the most important geological features on the planet. It is an extremely long and deep fault line that bisects the entire eastern portion of the African continent. The Rift Valley is home to the major East African lakes, the Red Sea, and an abundance of wildlife unmatched anywhere on earth. Much of the soil in the valley and on its escarpments (sides) is extremely fertile.

Gross domestic product (GDP): measures the total output of goods and services produced by both residents and foreigners in a nation.

Gross national income (GNI): measures the total value of goods and services produced in a country (GDP) plus income received from other countries (such as interest) minus payments to other countries. GNI in some instances, as in recent World Bank statistics, is replacing GNP as a measure of a nation's income and the size of its economy.

Gross national product (GNP): measures the total output of goods and services produced by residents; it includes income residents receive from abroad. Measured yearly, GNP is often used as an indicator of the size of a nation's economy. Another important economic statistic, GNP per capita, is calculated by dividing a nation's GNP by its population. This indicates national income per person.

Homelands: government-designated areas, under South Africa's apartheid system, where the different ethnic groups could live. For the black ethnic groups, the apartheid regime created thirteen homelands, which were supposed to be in areas traditionally occupied by those ethnic groups. The ultimate plan, which was never fully realized, was to move all of South Africa's blacks to these homelands and grant those "nations" independence. Thus, the South Africa the architects of this system planned would ultimately have no black citizens. These homelands were almost all in agriculturally marginal areas and often were not even contiguous. The opposition to the homelands policy was a major component of antiapartheid activity in South Africa. See *Apartheid.*

Hut tax: a tax colonialists imposed on villages to acquire free labor. To provide their colonies with cheap labor, the imperial powers often taxed each village, knowing its people could not pay in currency. Thus, the colonialists "accepted" free labor as payment of the hut tax.

Import substitution: an economic strategy many developing nations follow. The idea behind import-substitution policies is to establish local industries that produce goods that were previously imported (matches, shoes, tools, etc.). Thus, foreign exchange would be saved, since those imports would no longer be required, and hard currency would not have to be spent to acquire them. Unfortunately, when a nation has limited economic resources, following an import-substitution strategy can actually drain foreign exchange, since the focus of industrial output is to produce goods for local consumption and not for export, which could earn even more foreign currency.

Industrialization: a general economic strategy that a country may pursue, along with agriculture and postindustrialism (service and knowledge production). Most economists in the 1950s and 1960s (and even today) assumed that nations should focus their economic resources on industries (cars, textiles, furniture, steel, etc.) rather than agriculture. Unfortunately, for nations that are overwhelmingly rural and poor (the case with almost all African countries), rapid industrialization is especially difficult, and too much of a focus on industrialization can lead governments and businesses to neglect the wealth of knowledge and experience of rural producers. In the extreme, an all-out drive toward industrialization can produce a national neglect of agriculture that can lead to mass hunger and starvation.

Informal sector: general term given to business practices that are outside government regulation and thus immune to taxes. Also known as the black market, many economists estimate that some African nations' economies are taking place largely in the informal sector. While the informal sector can support many lower-middle-class traders and producers, it can also produce extremely wealthy individuals and indirectly weaken a government due to the loss of tax revenue that could otherwise be used in antipoverty and other government programs.

International Monetary Fund (IMF): loosely associated with the United Nations, a bank of last resort that lends money directly to governments, usually to either pay off private bank loans or to fund general government operations. The problem is that the IMF, as any lender would when lending money, puts restrictions on the money's use and, more important, demands that the recipient nation make macroeconomic policy changes, such as reducing the size of government and public debt and scaling back expensive social and antipoverty programs. For this reason, many governments, scholars, and civilians in Africa dislike the IMF, but many nations simply have no economic choice but to accept the IMF's restrictions and policy prescriptions in exchange for the loans.

Intertropical Convergence Zone (ITCZ): the most important meteorological phenomenon for Africa, and the primary rain producer for the continent. The ITCZ shifts seasonally around the equator, thus (ideally) creating a rainy season north of the equator around June and in the south around November. Some nations near the equator even receive two rainy seasons. When the ITCZ "misbehaves," droughts occur in the areas it fails to cover.

Khoisan language family: one of the four major families of African languages. The Khoisan group is characterized by the "click" sounds of many of its consonants. The Khoisan peoples once inhabited large stretches of eastern and southern Africa, but the Bantu migrations and European persecution have reduced the Khoisan to a few scattered pockets in southern Africa's desert regions. Almost all the cave and rock art of southern Africa is attributed to the Khoisan peoples, and their language has influenced some Bantu languages such as Zulu, Xhosa, and Ndebele, which use a subset of the Khoisan "clicks."

Kinship: an anthropological term referring to the patterns of familial relations shared by a group of people. In most African cultures, kinship goes well beyond the traditional Western concept of the "nuclear" family and even extends to the dead and unborn. Kinship is one of the fundamental social structures in sub-Saharan Africa.

Lagos Plan of Action (LPA): a set of general economic goals that most African nations are striving to achieve. Adopted by the United Nations Economic Commission for Africa in 1980, the LPA seeks food self-sufficiency and self-reliance in industry, transport, and communication; human and natural resources; and science and technology. The Lagos Plan of Action can be viewed as an outline of an African declaration of economic independence.

Levirate: a family and marriage practice common throughout Africa. Under the levirate, a man assumes responsibility for his dead brother's widow and children. Conversely, under the "sororate," a woman takes the place of her dead or childless sister. Both these practices are designed to produce children, which is one of the primary reasons for marriage in largely agricultural Africa. Some feminists see both the levirate and the sororate as an onerous burden on women.

Matriliny: a family organization pattern largely confined to the coastal forests of west and central Africa. Under matriliny, family descent is traced through the mother, and a groom usually leaves his family to live with or near his wife's family. Resultant children are also raised with the mother's family and in the mother's village area. This is not the same as matriarchy (rule by women), since in most matrilineal societies formal positions of authority are still largely held by men. See *Patriliny.*

Metropole: an international relations term referring to either the capital city of an imperial power (London, Paris, Lisbon, etc.) or, more recently, to world financial centers of power (e.g., Tokyo, New York, Geneva).

Modernization: a term given to a very broad political-economic concept popular in the 1950s and 1960s among academics and development practitioners. Under the assumptions of modernization theory, increased economic growth in Africa, particularly rapid industrialization, would inevitably lead to the creation of democracy, higher educational standards, and widespread wealth. The assumptions of modernization theory were rooted in the idea that since this was the way the Western world developed, then the same process would inevitably take place in Africa. Of course, the facts that the process of "modernization" took place in the West over a period of several centuries and largely without imperial interference were often overlooked. Still, many of the prescriptions for curing Africa's economic and political troubles still seem based on the ideas of linear development contained in modernization theory.

Multinational corporations (MNCs): a large corporation that has business operations in more than one national territory. Some very large MNCs such as Exxon and DuPont have yearly earnings that are larger than the annual economic output of several African nations. It should be no surprise that MNCs can be very powerful and persuasive economic actors in the developing world.

Nationalism: one of the most fundamental concepts in comparative politics. "Nationalism" can mean different things depending on the context in which the term is used. In the context of African politics and history, nationalism usually denotes the desire and struggle for self-determination and independence among the colonized peoples of the continent. The nationalist era in sub-Saharan Africa started after World War II, when parties and interest groups formed with the goal of full national independence for their colonies. For most countries, the nationalist era culminated in independence in the 1960s, largely under the political leadership of party and interest group heads who had lobbied London and Paris for independence or even had led armed struggles against those European powers.

Negritude: a literary movement of the 1930s among students from francophone African colonies and African Americans in exile in Paris. The Negritude writers consciously filled their works with African motifs, thereby providing a new expression of African ideas and society in written French and English literature. See *Pan-Africanism.*

Neocolonialism: the idea that even after physical and legal colonialism ended in Africa, economic and political dependency on the former colonial power remained. For example, after legal independence in the 1960s, many former British and French colonies in Africa still found themselves in a position to purchase goods from only British and French transnational corporations. Furthermore, in the former French colonies of West Africa, most nations are still dependent on the French franc to support their own national currencies, which gives the French government and banks much economic leverage over those nations. Neocolonialism is similar to the dependency school of thought, which also sees an inexorable, cause-and-effect link between politics and economics. See *Dependency.*

Niger-Congo language family: one of the four major families of African languages. This is also known as the Bantu language family, with its origins in West Africa. As the Bantu migrations spread eastward and westward to encompass almost the entire sub-Saharan region of the continent, the Niger-Congo language family spread as well. Today the majority of Africa's people speak languages with roots in this linguistic family. See *Bantu language family.*

Nilo-Saharan language family: one of the four major families of African languages. This group is largely confined to the northeast and east-central regions of the continent. It is prevalent among the herding and fishing cultures of the area. Examples of groups whose languages have their roots in this family are the Dinka of Sudan and the Tutsi of Rwanda and Burundi.

Organization of African Unity (OAU): a regional supranational organization established in the 1960s, with headquarters in Addis Ababa, Ethiopia. The OAU was the United Nations of Africa, in that its membership included all the independent states on the continent. The heads of all the members came together once a year for a summit meeting, and there were several economic, environmental, and cultural committees within the OAU. Of particular note is the pledge of noninterference in the internal affairs of member nations that all participating countries took. Further, when the OAU was founded, an agreement was reached that there would be no wholesale reconfiguration of the old colonial boundaries inherited by the independent nations. The combination of these two facts limited the effectiveness of the OAU as a truly pan-African entity. Due to the weaknesses of the OAU, it was reorganized under the name African Union (AU). See *African Union.*

Organization of Petroleum Exporting Countries (OPEC): an organization comprising the major oil exporting nations of the world. OPEC is one of the most potentially powerful economic organizations in the history of the planet, owing to industrialization's crucial need for petroleum products. Nigeria, Gabon, and Angola are the three sub-Saharan members of OPEC.

Pan-Africanism: both a literary and political term with similar meanings. In the literary usage, pan-Africanism is a writing style that reverses the late-nineteenth- and early-twentieth-century roles of Africans and Europeans in literature. Here, African writers and their characters critically examine European culture and identity. In the political usage, pan-Africanism can refer to any attempt at creating political solidarity or unity among either African nations or Africans on the continent and living elsewhere (the African Diaspora). Both Kwame Nkrumah, the first president of Ghana, and W. E. B. Du Bois, the African American writer and political activist, are associated with pan-Africanism. See *Negritude.*

Parastatals: government-owned or government-controlled corporations. For example, the postal service in almost all nations is a parastatal. Further, telephone, steel, and electricity-producing corporations are often government-owned or government-operated. Many economists criticize parastatals as wasteful, loss-producing entities. The World Bank and International Monetary Fund are particularly critical of parastatals.

Pastoralism: a form of social and economic organization that depends primarily on the herding of livestock (usually camels, goats, and/or cattle) rather than the cultivation of crops in a fixed area (agriculture). This livestock provides food and also stands as a measure of wealth. Pastoralists often live a seminomadic life by necessity, following shifting rainfall and grass growth patterns. Pastoralism is prevalent in the savannah grasslands and semidesert areas of eastern Africa.

Patriliny: a pattern of family organization practiced by the majority of Africa's people (and the majority of humanity, for that matter). Under patriliny, descent is traced through men, and when a bride marries she goes to live in the groom's village area. Children who are the products of patrilineal marriages are also considered to be primarily part of the father's family line. See *Matriliny.*

Personal rule: a style of authoritarian government prevalent in Africa from the late 1960s to the late 1980s. Under personal rule, the country's leader seeks to identify the state with himself, often placing his face on currency, postage stamps, and in almost every public establishment. The leader may also have stadiums, airports, streets, and schools named after himself. Furthermore, the leader will operate a system of patronage, awarding government contracts, concessions, and bureaucratic posts to his political friends, especially to members of his own ethnic group. Personal rule is a somewhat logical response to the weak state systems and relatively shallow nationalism that existed in Africa immediately after independence. With the emphasis on order rather than freedom, many personal rulers stayed in power for decades. It should be noted that not all these personal rulers were tyrants. On the contrary, one of the more mild-mannered personal rulers, Zambia's Kenneth Kaunda, stayed in power for almost thirty years. In the 1990s, personal rule started to give way to elected democratic governments, but Africa still has not seen the last of this style of authoritarianism. See *Authoritarianism.*

Poaching: the hunting or trapping of animals for food or profit that is prohibited by either national or international law.

Polygyny: the practice of having more than one wife at the same time. In societies that value the production of children, polygyny is widespread, as it is in Africa. Islam puts an upper limit of four on the number of wives one man can have at the same time.

Public sector: a general term given to a government, its employees, and any parastatals that it owns. See *Parastatals.*

Rainforests: closed forest systems that receive an abundant amount of moisture and thus provide a home to an extraordinarily high concentration and diversity of plant and animal life. Since the soil is moist and rather shallow, areas of rainforest that are clear-cut for agricultural purposes are largely unsuitable for farming within a few years. Contrary to widespread popular myth, only a small proportion of Africa is under rainforest, with these areas confined to the coastal regions of the west and to the central inland areas.

Rural sector: a general term given to public and privately held lands and productive activities that take place in rural areas; farming and ranching.

Southern African Development Community (SADC): an alliance formerly known as the Southern African Development Coordination Conference (SADCC) that was originally founded by the nations of southern Africa in an attempt to reduce their economic dependence on the Republic of South Africa. Under British and Portuguese colonial rule, almost all the rail and road transport networks in the region ran in a north-to-south pattern to the ports on South Africa's sea coasts. In the postcolonial era, the apartheid government in South Africa could exert much political and economic leverage on its neighbors by simply threatening to cut off transport routes to the sea. The SADCC was an attempt primarily to break this transport monopoly held by South Africa and, secondarily, was an attempt at regional economic integration and the pooling of technological and educational resources. On the latter two matters it was largely successful. However, when South Africa elected a popular government in 1994, the whole raison d'être of the SADCC changed, and soon thereafter South Africa joined. It is not clear whether the new SADC will become a full-fledged economic community or a vehicle for wider South African domination of the subcontinent, albeit under a black majority government. See *East African Community* and *Economic Community of West African States.*

Spirit mediums: members of a family or village who communicate with the dead. Spirit mediums are part of most African traditional religions and are often very powerful religious and political leaders. In some cultures, spirit mediums are also healers and tellers of the future, which gives them a revered place in public life. See *African traditional religions.*

Squatter settlements: urban or rural lands settled by people who do not hold title.

Structural adjustment programs (SAPs): International Monetary Fund financial assistance programs. When African governments can no longer pay their debts to either private banks or other nations, they often have little choice but to turn to the IMF for financial aid. A condition for this assistance is that the recipient nation adopt a structural adjustment program. The World Bank will sometimes give development grants only when a country agrees to implement an SAP. These economic programs, rooted in neoclassical economic assumptions about public debt, interest rates, inflation, and economic growth, require that the lendee reduce the size of the public sector, cut back on social spending, devalue its currency vis-à-vis hard foreign currencies, raise interest rates to reduce inflation, and lift import restrictions so that foreign goods are more freely available. In the short run, at least, such programs often lead to great hardships on urban dwellers and bankruptcies in the private sector. As such, they are wildly unpopular with rank-and-file citizens and governments alike. See *International Monetary Fund.*

Urban sector: a general term given to government and private institutions located in urban areas and the people who live in cities.

World Bank: a major provider of financial and technical assistance to developing nations. The World Bank is made up of two development institutions, the International Bank for Reconstruction and Development (IBRD) and the International Development Association (IDA). The IBRD focuses on middle-income countries, whereas the IDA deals with the world's poorest countries, most of which are in Africa. The International Monetary Fund (IMF) is the "sister" organization to the World Bank, and they work closely together. See *International Monetary Fund.*

Basic Political Data

Algeria
Capital City Algiers
Date of Independence 5 July 1962
Rulers Since Independence

1. Ahmed Ben Bella, president, 1963–June 1965
2. Col. Houari Boumedienne, president, June 1965–December 1978
3. Col. Benjedid Chadli, president, February 1979–1992
4. Five-member High Council of State (HCS) fulfills the functions of the head of state until January 1994
5. Gen. Liamine Zeroual, president and minister of defense—appointed January 1994
6. Zeroual elected president November 1995–April 1999
7. Abdelaziz Bouteflika, president, April 1999–

Angola
Capital City Luanda
Date of Independence 11 November 1975
Rulers Since Independence

1. Antonio Agostinho Neto, founding president, 1975–September 1979
2. José Eduardo dos Santos, president, September 1979–

Benin
Capital City Porto-Novo
Date of Independence 1 August 1960 (formerly Republic of Dahomey, 1960–1975)
Rulers Since Independence

1. Hubert Maga, president, December 1960–October 1963
2. Col. (later Gen.) Christophe Soglo, president, October 1963–January 1964
3. Sourou Migan Apithy, president, January 1964–November 1965
4. Tahirou Congacou, president, November 1965–December 1965
5. Gen. Christophe Soglo, president, December 1965–December 1967
6. Lt. Col. Alphonse Alley, president, December 1967–July 1968
7. Emile-Derlin Zinsou, president, July 1968–December 1969
8. Lt. Col. Paul Emile de Souza, president, December 1969–May 1970
9. Hubert Maga, president, May 1970–May 1972
10. Justin Ahomadegbé, president, May 1972–October 1972
11. Col. Mathieu Kerekou, president, October 1972–April 1991
12. Nicephore Soglo, president, April 1991–March 1996
13. Mathieu Kerekou, March 1996–April 2006
14. Yayi Boni, president, April 2006–

Botswana

Capital City Gaborone

Date of Independence 30 September 1966

Rulers Since Independence

1. Sir Seretse Khama, president, September 1966–July 1980
2. Quett Masire, president, July 1980–April 1998
3. Festus Gontebanye Mogae, president, April 1998–

Burkina Faso

Capital City Ouagadougou

Date of Independence 5 August 1960 (formerly Upper Volta; renamed Burkina Faso, August 1984)

Rulers Since Independence

1. Maurice Yaméogo, president, April 1959–January 1966
2. Lt. Col. Sangoulé Lamizana, president, January 1966–1980
3. Col. Sayé Zerbo, president, 1980–1982
4. Noncommissioned officers coup, October 1982
5. Maj. Jean Baptiste Ouedraogo, president, January 1983–August 1983
6. Capt. Thomas Sankara, president, Conseil National Révolutionaire (CNR), 1983–1987
7. Capt. Blaise Compaoré, president, CNR, 1987–

Burundi

Capital City Bujumbura

Date of Independence 1 July 1962

Rulers Since Independence

1. (King) Mwami Mwambutsa II, André Muhirwa, 1962–1963. Prime ministers: Pierre Ngendandumwe, 1963; Albin Nyamoya, 1964–1965; Pierre Ngendandumwe, 1965 (assassinated, January 1965); Joseph Bamina, 1965; Leopold Biha, 1965
2. Mwami Ntare V (deposes father, Mwambutsa II, as king); Capt. (later Col.) Michel Micombero, prime minister, July 1966–November 1966
3. Micombero declares Burundi a republic, with himself as president, November 1966–November 1976
4. Col. Jean-Baptiste Bagaza, president, November 1976–September 1987
5. Maj. Pierre Buyoya, chairman, Comité Militaire pour la Salvation Nationale, 1987–1993
6. Melchior Ndadaye, June–October 1993
7. Cyprien Ntaryamire, January–April 1994
8. Interim president Sylvestre Ntibantunganya April–October 1994, president, October 1994–July 1996
9. Ntibantunganya deposed in coup; Pierre Buyoya, interim president, September 1996–June 1998, president June 1998–April 2003
10. Domitien Ndayizeye, president, April 2003–August 2005
11. Pierre Kurunziza, president, August 2005–

Cameroon

Capital City Yaoundé

Date of Independence 1 January 1960 (1960–1961: Republic of East Cameroon; October 1961–1972: Federal Republic of Cameroon, composed of the East—former French trust territory—and West—part of former British trust territory; 1972–: United Cameroon Republic)

Rulers Since Independence

1. Ahmadou Ahidjo, president, May 1960–November 1982
2. Paul Biya, president, November 1982–

Cape Verde

Capital City Praia

Date of Independence July 1975 (in federation with Guinea-Bissau, 1975–January 1981)

Rulers Since Independence

1. Aristides Pereira, president, July 1975–March 1991
2. Antonio Mascarenhas Monteiro, March 1991–March 2001
3. Pedro Verona Rodrigues Pires, president, March 2001–

Central African Republic

Capital City Bangui

Date of Independence 13 August 1960 (1976–1979: Central African Empire)

Rulers Since Independence

1. David Dacko (formerly prime minister), president, November 1960–December 1965
2. Coup led by Field Marshal Jean-Bedel Bokassa, December 1965
3. Bokassa proclaimed "President for Life," March 1972
4. Bokassa crowned emperor, December 1977
5. Bokassa deposed in coup, September 1979
6. David Dacko, president, September 1979–September 1981
7. Gen. André Kolingba establishes military regime, September 1981–1993 (chairman of Military Committee for National Recovery)
8. Ange-Félix Patassé, president, October 1993–March 2003 (overthrown in coup d'état)
9. Francois Bozize, president, March 2003–

Chad

Capital City N'Djaména

Date of Independence 11 August 1960

Rulers Since Independence

1. Ngarta (formerly François) Tombalbaye, prime minister; head of state on independence; president, April 1962–April 1975 (killed in military coup)
2. Gen. Félix Malloum, president, April 1975–1979
3. Hissene Habré, appointed prime minister, August 1978
4. Malloum and Habré resign, March 1979; Transitional Government of National Unity
5. Goukouni Oueddei, president, 1979–1982
6. Hissene Habré, president, 1982–December 1990
7. Idriss Déby, December 1990–

Comoros

Capital City Moroni

Date of Independence 6 July 1975

Rulers Since Independence

1. Ahmed Abdallah, president, July 1975–August 1975
2. Coup led by Ali Soilih, August 1975; president, 1976–1978
3. Ahmed Abdallah, president, reinstated in coup by mercenaries under Bob Denard, 1978–November 1989
4. Bob Denard, November 1989–December 1989 (murdered)

5. Said Djohar, December 1989–1996
6. Mohamad Taki Abdoulkarim, March 1996–October 1998
7. Interim government, Tajiddine Ben Said Massounde, president, November 1998–April 1999 (Massounde deposed in coup d'état)
8. Col. Azzali Assoumani, president, April 1999–

Congo, Democratic Republic of
Capital City Kinshasa
Date of Independence 30 June 1960 (formerly Congo-Kinshasa; named Zaire in October 1971; named Democratic Republic of Congo in May 1997)
Rulers Since Independence

1. Patrice Lumumba, prime minister, June 1960–September 1960
2. Joseph Kasavubu, president, June 1960–November 1965
3. Col. Joseph Mobutu suspends constitution, September 1960. College of Commissioners rules until February 1961
4. Joseph Ileo, prime minister, February 1961–August 1961
5. Cyrille Adoula, prime minister, August 1961–July 1964
6. Moise Tshombe, prime minister, July 1964–October 1965
7. Evariste Kimba, prime minister, October 1965–November 1965
8. Military coup led by Gen. Mobutu Sese Seko, president, November 1965–May 1997
9. Laurent Desire Kabila, May 1997–January 2001
10. Joseph Kabila, January 2001–

Congo, Republic of
Capital City Brazzaville
Date of Independence 15 August 1960
Rulers Since Independence

1. Foulbert Youlou elected president under preindependence constitution, November 1959
2. Military coup, August 1963; Alphonse Massamba-Débat, president, December 1963–4 September 1968
3. Governing National Revolutionary Council, formed September 1968, chaired by Capt. Marien Ngouabi. Maj. Alfred Raoul, prime minister and temporary head of state, September 1968–December 1968
4. Capt. Marien Ngouabi, president, December 1968–March 1977
5. Ngouabi assassinated, March 1977. Col. (later Brig. Gen.) Joachim Yhombi-Opango, president, March 1977–February 1979
6. Col. Denis Sassou Nguesso, president, February 1979–June 1991
7. André Milongo, prime minister, June 1991–August 1992

8. Pascal Lissouba, president, August 1992–October 1997
9. Denis Sassou Nguesso, president, October 1997–

Côte d'Ivoire
Capital City Yamoussoukro
Date of Independence 7 August 1960
Rulers Since Independence

1. Félix Houphouët-Boigny, prime minister, May 1959; president, November 1960–December 1993
2. Henri Konan Bédié, president, December 1993–December 1999
3. Bédié deposed in coup; Gen. Robert Guei, head, Committee of National Salvation, December 1999–October 2000
4. Laurent Gbagbo, president, October 2000–

Djibouti
Capital City Djibouti
Date of Independence 27 June 1977

1. Hassan Gouled, president, June 1977; reelected June 1981, April 1987, and May 1993–April 1999
2. Ismail Omar Guelleh, president, April 1999–

Egypt, Arab Republic of
Capital City Cairo
Date of Independence 28 February 1922
Rulers Since Independence

1. King Farouk to 1952
2. Coup led by Col. Gamal Abdel Nasser and Abdul-al Hakim. Maj. Gen. Neguib, president, June 1953–November 1954
3. Nasser, prime minister, April 1954, president, November 1954–September 1970
4. Col. Anwar Sadat, president, September 1970–October 1981
5. Lt. Gen. Hosni Mubarak, president, October 1981–

Equatorial Guinea
Capital City Malabo
Date of Independence 12 October 1968
Rulers Since Independence

1. Francisco Macias Nguema, president, September 1968–August 1979
2. Military coup led by Lt. Col. Teodoro Obiango Nguema Mbasogo, August 1979
3. Lt. Col. Teodoro Obiango Nguema Mbasogo, president, October 1980–1989

4. Brig. Gen. Teodoro Obiango Nguema Mbasogo, elected president 25 June 1989–

Eritrea

Capital City Asmara

Date of Independence 24 May 1993

Rulers Since Independence

1. Issaias Afwerki, assumes power May 1991; elected president 8 June 1993–

Ethiopia

Capital City Addis Ababa

1. Succession of emperors
2. Emperor Haile Selassie, 1930–September 1974
3. Lt. Gen. Aman Andom, chairman PMAC (Provisional Military Administrative Council) until November 1974
4. Brig. Gen. Teferi Banti, chairman, PMAC. Power actually held by vice chairman, Maj. (later Lt. Col.) Mengistu Haile Mariam and Lt. Col. Atnafu Abate. Banti killed, February 1977
5. Mengistu Haile Mariam, chairman of PMAC, head of state, 1977–May 1991
6. Tesfaye Gebre Kidan, president, May 1991
7. Meles Zenawi, president, May 1991–1995
8. Ngasso Gidada, president, August 1995–October 2001
9. Girma Woldegiorgis, president, October 2001–

Gabon

Capital City Libreville

Date of Independence 17 August 1960

Rulers Since Independence

1. Leon M'Ba, president, 1961–28 November 1967
2. Omar (formerly Albert-Bernard) Bongo, president, December 1967–

Gambia

Capital City Banjul

Date of Independence 18 February 1965

Rulers Since Independence

1. Constitutional monarchy with Dawda Jawara, prime minister, 1965–1970
2. Gambia becomes a republic, April 1970. Dawda Jawara becomes first president, April 1970–July 1994
3. Capt. Yahya A. J. J. Jammeh, proclaimed head of state, July 1994, chairman of the Armed Forces Provisional Ruling Council, 1994–

Ghana

Capital City Accra
Date of Independence 6 March 1957
Rulers Since Independence

1. Constitutional monarchy, 1957–1960; Kwame Nkrumah, prime minister, 1957–1960. Becomes republic, 1960; Nkrumah, president, July 1960–February 1966
2. Lt. Gen. Joseph Ankrah, chairman of National Liberation Council, February 1966–1969. Replaced in 1969 by Brig. Gen. Akwasi Afrifa
3. Competitive electoral politics: Kofi Busia, prime minister, September 1969–January 1972
4. Lt. Col. (later Gen.) Ignatius Kutu Acheampong, chairman, National Redemption Council, replaced by Supreme Military Council, January 1972–July 1978
5. Lt. Gen. Frederick Akuffo, chairman, Supreme Military Council, July 1978–June 1979
6. Flight Lt. Jerry Rawlings, chairman, Armed Forces Revolutionary Council, June 1979–September 1979
7. Dr. Hilla Limann, president, September 1979–December 1981
8. Flight Lt. Jerry Rawlings, chairman, Provisional National Defence Council, December 1981; elected president November 1992–January 2001
9. John Agyekum Kufuor, president, January 2001–

Guinea

Capital City Conakry
Date of Independence 2 October 1958
Rulers Since Independence

1. Ahmed Sekou Touré, president, 1958–April 1984
2. Col. Lansana Conté, president, head of Comité Militaire de Redressement National, Gen. Lansana Conté takes office April 1984; elected December 1993–

Guinea-Bissau

Capital City Bissau
Date of Independence 10 September 1974
Rulers Since Independence

1. Luiz De Almeida Cabral, president, 1974–1980
2. Gen. João Bernardo Vieira, president, Council of State, head of government, 1980; elected president in multiparty elections July and August 1994–May 1999 (Vieira deposed in coup)
3. Gen. Ansumane Mane and Koumba Yala, co-presidents of transitional government, May 1999–January 2000

4. Koumba Yala, president, February 2000–September 2003
5. Henrique Rosa, president, September 2003–

Kenya

Capital City Nairobi
Date of Independence 12 December 1963
Rulers Since Independence

1. Constitutional monarchy, 1963–1964; Jomo Kenyatta, prime minister
2. Kenyatta, president, 1964–August 1978
3. Succeeded by Daniel arap Moi, president, August 1978–December 2002
4. Mwai Kibaki, president, December 2002–

Lesotho

Capital City Maseru
Date of Independence 4 October 1966
Rulers Since Independence

1. Constitutional monarchy under King Motlotlehi Moshoeshoe II
2. Chief Leabua Jonathan seizes power in civilian coup, January 1970–January 1986
3. Maj. Gen. Justin Lekhanya, chairman, Military Council, 1986–April 1991 (military coup)
4. Col. Elias Ramaema, chairman, Military Council, April 1991–April 1993
5. Ntsu Mokhehle, prime minister, April 1993–August 1994
6. King Letsie III dismissed Mokhehle government and assumed role of head of state, August 1994–September 1994
7. Mokhehle resumed post as prime minister, September 1994–
8. King Moshoeshoe II restored to throne with no legislative or political powers, head of state, January 1995–January 1996 (died)
9. King Letsie III resumed throne, February 1996–

Liberia

Capital City Monrovia
Date of Independence 6 July 1847
Rulers Since Independence

1. Until 1944, eighteen presidents
2. William V. S. Tubman, president, 1944–1971
3. William R. Tolbert, 1971–April 1980
4. M. Sgt. Samuel K. Doe, president, People's Redemption Council, 1980–November 1990 (murdered)

5. Amos Sawyer, president, Interim Government of National Unity (IGNU), 1990–1995
6. Transitional executive council, comprising representatives of the former IGNU, the National Patriotic Forces of Liberia (NPFL), and the United Liberation Movement of Liberia for Democracy (ULIMO) form the Council of State headed by David D. Kpomakpor, chairman, IGNU, May 1995–August 1997
7. Charles Taylor, president, August 1997–August 2003
8. Moses Blah, president, August 2003–October 2003
9. Gyude Bryant, interim president, October 2003–December 2005
10. Ellen Johnson-Sirleaf, president, January 2006–

Libya

Capital City Tripoli

Date of Independence 24 December 1951 (from March 1977, named Socialist People's Libyan Arab Jamahiriya)

Rulers Since Independence

1. King Idris, 1951–1969
2. Col. Muammar Mohammed Qaddafi, leader of the revolution, September 1969–

Madagascar, Democratic Republic of

Capital City Antananarivo

Date of Independence 26 June 1960

Rulers Since Independence

1. Philibert Tsiranana, president, 1960–May 1972
2. Gen. Gabriel Ramanantsoa, president, 1972–February 1975
3. Col. Richard Ratsimandrava, February 1975 (assassinated)
4. Gen. Gilles Andria Mahazo, National Military Directorate, February 1975
5. Lt. Comdr. Didier Ratsiraka, president, March 1975–1993
6. Prof. Albert Zafy, president, elected to office February 1993, impeached August 1996, resigned October 1996
7. Adm. Didier Ratsiraka, president, February 1997–May 2002
8. Marc Ravalomanana, president, May 2002–

Malawi

Capital City Lilongwe

Date of Independence 6 July 1964

Rulers Since Independence

1. Constitutional monarchy, Dr. Hastings Kamuzu Banda, prime minister, 1964–1966
2. Banda, president, 1966

3. Banda, "President for Life," July 1971–1994
4. Bakili Muluzi, president, May 1994–May 2004
5. Mingu wa Mutharika, president, May 2004–

Mali

Capital City Bamako

Date of Independence 22 September 1960

Rulers Since Independence

1. Modibo Keita, president, Mali Federation; president, Soudan government, April 1959; president of Mali, 1960–1968
2. Lt. (later Brig. Gen.) Moussa Traoré, chairman of Military Committee of National Liberation, November 1968–June 1979
3. Gen. Moussa Traoré, president, June 1979–March 1991
4. Lieut. Col. Amadou Toumany Toure, acting head of state, March 1991–April 1991
5. Soumana Sacko, prime minister, April 1991–June 1992
6. Alpha Oumar Konare, president, June 1992–June 2002
7. Amadou Tomani Toure, president, June 2002–

Mauritania, Islamic Republic of

Capital City Nouakchott

Date of Independence 28 November 1960

Rulers Since Independence

1. Mokhtar Ould Daddah, president, 1961–July 1978
2. Lt. Col. Mustapha Ould Mohammed Salek, president, Comité Militaire de Redressement National (CMRN), July 1978–June 1979
3. Lt. Col. Ahmed Ould Bouceif, prime minister, April 1979–May 1979 (assassinated)
4. Lt. Col. Mohammed Khouna Haidalla, prime minister, May 1979
5. CMSN (formerly CMRN) forces Salek to resign, June 1979. Lt. Col. Mohammed Mahmoud Ould Louly, president, June 1979–January 1980
6. Haidalla ousts Louly, January 1980. Becomes president, head of state, and chairman of CMSN, 1980–1984
7. Col. Maaouya Ould Sidi Ahmed Taya, chairman of the Military Committee for National Salvation, 1984–; elected president January 1992–August 2005 (overthrown in a coup)
8. Ely Ould Mohammed Vall, president, and a Military Council seize power, August 2005– (elections promised by 2007)

Mauritius

Capital City Port Louis

Date of Independence 12 March 1968

Rulers Since Independence

1. Seewoosagur Ramgoolam, prime minister, 1968–1982
2. Aneerood Jugnauth, prime minister, 1982–

Morocco

Capital City Rabat

Date of Independence 2 March 1956

Rulers Since Independence

1. King Mohamed V, to 1961
2. King Hassan II, March 1961–July 1999
3. King Mohamed VI, July 1999–

Mozambique

Capital City Maputo

Date of Independence 25 June 1975

Rulers Since Independence

1. Samora Moisés Machel, president, June 1975–October 1986
2. Joaquim Alberto Chissano, president, October 1986–February 2005
3. Armando Emilio Guebuza, president, February 2005–

Namibia

Capital City Windhoek

Date of Independence 21 March 1990

Rulers Since Independence

1. Sam Nujoma, president, March 1990–November 2004
2. Hifikepunye Pohamba, president, November 2004–

Niger

Capital City Niamey

Date of Independence 3 August 1960

Rulers Since Independence

1. Hamani Diori, president, 1960–April 1974
2. Maj. Gen. Seyni Kountché, head of state; president, Supreme Military Council, 1974–1987
3. Col. Ali Seibou, president, Supreme Military Council; head of state, 1987–1991
4. Amadou Cheiffou, head, transitional Council of Ministers, 1991–1993
5. Mahamane Ousmane, president of republic, April 1993–January 1996
6. Ibrahim Mainassara Bare, January 1996–April 1999 (assassinated)
7. Provisional government, Maj. Daouda Mallam Wanke, president, April 1999–December 1999
8. Mamadou Tandja, president, December 1999–

Nigeria
Capital City Abuja
Date of Independence 1 October 1960
Rulers Since Independence

1. Alhaji Abubakar Tafawa Belewa, prime minister, 1960–1966; Nnamdi Azikiwe, president, 1963–1966
2. Gen. Johnson Aguiyi-Ironsi, head, Federal Military Government, January 1966–July 1966
3. Lt. Col. Yakubu Gowon, head, Federal Military Government, July 1966–July 1975
4. Brig. Gen. Murtala Mohammed, chief, Supreme Military Council, July 1975–February 1976
5. Lt. Gen. Olusegun Obasanjo, February 1976–October 1979
6. Alhaji Shehu Shagari, president, October 1979–December 1983
7. Maj. Gen. Mohammed Buhari, head of government, December 1983–August 1985
8. Maj. Gen. Ibrahim Babangida, president, August 1985–1993
9. Chief Ernest Adegunle Shonekan, head of government, January 1993–November 1993
10. Gen. Sani Abacha, head of government and commander in chief of the armed forces, November 1993–June 1998
11. Gen. Abdulsalam Abubaker, acting head of government, June 1998–May 1999
12. Olusegun Obasanjo, president, May 1999–

Rwanda
Capital City Kigali
Date of Independence 1 July 1962
Rulers Since Independence

1. Grégoire Kayibanda, president, 1961–July 1973
2. Maj. Gen. Juvénal Habyarimana, president, July 1973–April 1994
3. Dr. Theodore Sindikubwabo, interim president of republic, April 1994–July 1994
4. Pasteur Bizimungu, president, July 1994–March 2000
5. Maj. Gen. Paul Kagame, interim president, March–April 2000; president, April 2000–

Saharan Arab Democratic Republic (Western Sahara)
Capital City None
Date of Independence February 1982 (admitted as fifty-first member of OAU)
Rulers Since Independence

1. Mohammed Abdelaziz, president, 1982–

São Tomé and Principe
Capital City São Tomé
Date of Independence July 1975
Rulers Since Independence

1. Dr. Manuel Pinto da Costa, president, 1975–April 1991
2. Miguel Trovoada, president, April 1991–September 2001
3. Fradique Bandeira Melo Menezes, president, September 2001–

Senegal
Capital City Dakar
Date of Independence 20 August 1960 (14 April 1959–20 August 1960: Mali Federation)
Rulers Since Independence

1. Léopold Sédar Senghor, president, 1960–January 1981
2. Abdou Diouf, president, January 1981–April 2000
3. Abdoulaye Wade, president, April 2000–

Seychelles
Capital City Victoria
Date of Independence 29 June 1976
Rulers Since Independence

1. James Mancham, president, June 1976–June 1977
2. Albert René, president, June 1977–April 2004
3. James Alix Michel, president, April 2004–

Sierra Leone
Capital City Freetown
Date of Independence 27 April 1961
Rulers Since Independence

1. Sir Milton Margai, prime minister, 1961–1967
2. Lt. Col. Andrew Juxon-Smith, chairman, National Reformation Council, March 1967–April 1968
4. Siaka Probyn Stevens, prime minister, April 1968, president, April 1971–October 1985
5. Maj. Gen. Dr. Joseph Saidu Momoh, president, November 1985–April 1992
6. Capt. Valentine E. M. Strasser, head of state, May 1992–January 1996
7. Brig. Gen. Julius Maada Bio, head of state, January 1996–March 1996
8. Ahmad Tejan Kabbah, president, March 1996–May 1997
9. Military coup, led by Maj. Johnny Paul Koromah, chairman of Armed Forces Revolutionary Council, May 1997–June 1997, head of state, June 1997–February 1998

10. Ahmad Tejan Kabbah reinstated as president following intervention of Nigerian-led West African (ECOMOG) force, February 1998–

Somalia
Capital City Mogadishu
Date of Independence 1 July 1960
Rulers Since Independence

1. Aden Abdulla Osman, president, 1960–1967; Abdirashid Ali Shirmarke, prime minister, 1960–1964; Abdirazak Hussein, prime minister, 1964–1967
2. Abdirashid Ali Shirmarke, president, 1967–1969; Mohammed Ibrahim Egal, prime minister, 1967–1969
3. Maj. Gen. Mohammed Siad Barre, president, 1969–January 1991
4. Ali Mahdi Mohammed, president, January 1991–1993
5. No functional government 1993–August 2000
6. Abdikassim Salad Hassan, appointed president of interim government at Arta Peace Conference by broad representation of the Somali clans that compose the Transitional Assembly, August 2000–October 2004
7. Abdulahi Yusuf Ahmed, president of the Transitional Federal government of Somalia, October 2004–

South Africa
Capital City Pretoria
Date of Independence 31 May 1961
Rulers Since Independence

1. Dr. Hendrik Verwoerd, prime minister, 1958–1966
2. B. J. Vorster, president and prime minister, 1966–1978
3. Pieter W. Botha, prime minister, then president, 1978–1989
4. Chris Heunis, acting president, January 1989–September 1989
5. Frederik de Klerk, president, September 1989–May 1994
6. Nelson Rolihlahla Mandela, president, May 1994–June 1999
7. Thabo Mvuyelwa Mbeki, president, June 1999–

Sudan
Capital City Khartoum
Date of Independence 1 January 1956
Rulers Since Independence

1. Ismail al-Azhari, prime minister, 1956
2. Abdulla Khalil, prime minister, 1956–1958
3. Lt. Gen. Ibrahim Abboud, prime minister, 1958–1964
4. Sir el-Khatim el-Khalifah, prime minister, 1964–1965
5. Muhammed Ahmad Mahgoub, prime minister, 1965–1966
6. Sayed Sadiq el-Mahdi, prime minister, 1966–1967

7. Muhammed Ahmad Mahgoub, prime minister, 1967–1969
8. Abubakr Awadallah, prime minister, 1969
9. Field Marshal Gaafar Mohammed Nimeiri, president, May 1969–April 1985
10. Coup, April 1985. Lt. Gen. Abdel Rahman Swar al Dahab, chairman, Transitional Military Council
11. Ahmed Ali el-Mirghani, president, Supreme Council 1986–June 1989 (military coup)
12. Lt. General Omar Hassan Ahmed al-Bashir, prime minister, June 1989–October 1993; appointed president October 1993–

Swaziland

Capital City Mbabane

Date of Independence 6 September 1968

Rulers Since Independence

1. King Sobhuza II, September 1968–August 1982
2. Queen Dzeliwe, regent, August 1982–August 1983 (deposed)
3. Prince Sozisa Dlamini, "authorized person," August 1983
4. Queen Ntombi, regent, August 1983–April 1986
5. King Mswati III, 1986–

Tanzania

Capital City Dar es Salaam (Dodoma is to become the new capital, but many government offices are still in Dar es Salaam)

Date of Independence 9 December 1962 (of Tanganyika); 10 December 1963 (of Zanzibar); Tanganyika joins with Zanzibar to form United Republic of Tanzania in April 1964

Rulers Since Independence

1. Julius Nyerere, prime minister, December 1961–January 1962
2. Rashidi M. Kawawa, prime minister, January 1962–December 1962
3. Tanganyika becomes a republic, December 1962; Julius Nyerere, president, December 1962–November 1985
4. Ali Hassan Mwinyi, president, 1985–November 1995
5. Benjamin Mkapa, president, November 1995–December 2005
6. Jakaya Kikwete, president, December 2005–

Togo

Capital City Lomé

Date of Independence 27 April 1960

Rulers Since Independence

1. Sylvanus Olympio, president, 1960–January 1963
2. Military coup, January 1963, led by Sgt. (later Gen.) Etienne Eyadema. Nicholas Grunitzky, president, 1963–January 1967

3. Col. Kleber Dadjo, chairman, Comité de Réconciliation Nationale (CRN), January 1967–April 1967 (bloodless coup)
4. Gen. Gnassingbé Eyadema, president, April 1967–February 2005 (died in office)
5. Faure Gnassingbe, president February 2005, elected president, May 2005–

Tunisia
Capital City Tunis
Date of Independence 20 March 1956
Rulers Since Independence

1. Habib Bourguiba, prime minister, 1956–July 1957
2. Becomes a republic, July 1957. Habib Bourguiba, president, 1957–1987
3. Zine El-Abidine Ben Ali accedes to the presidency, November 1987–

Uganda
Capital City Kampala
Date of Independence 9 October 1962
Rulers Since Independence

1. Apollo Milton Obote, 1962–1971 (prime minister until 1966; then president)
2. Maj. Gen. Idi Amin, president, 1971–April 1979
3. Yusuf Lule, president, Provisional Government, April 1979–June 1979
4. Godfrey Binaisa, chairman, Military Commission of Uganda National Liberation Front (UNLF) and president, June 1979–May 1980
5. Paulo Mwanga, chairman, UNLF, May 1980–December 1980
6. Obote, president, December 1980–July 1985
7. Coup led by Lt. Gen. Tito Okello of Uganda National Liberation Army; president, July 1985–January 1986
8. Yoweri Museveni, National Resistance Army (NRA), president, January 1986–

Zambia
Capital City Lusaka
Date of Independence 24 October 1964
Rulers Since Independence

1. Kenneth Kaunda, president, 1964–October 1991
2. Frederik Chiluba, president, November 1991–January 2002
3. Levy Mwanawasa, president, January 2002–

Zimbabwe

Capital City Harare

Date of Independence 18 April 1980

Rulers Since Independence

1. Canaan Banana, president and head of state, 1980–1987; Robert Mugabe, prime minister, 1980–1987
2. Robert Mugabe, president, December 1987–

Sources: www.africa-union.org; www.archontology.org; www.wikipedia.org; *Africa South of the Sahara, 1990* (London: Europa Publications, 1989); *Africa Research Bulletin: Political Series* (Exeter: Africa Research, January–September 1991); *Keesing Record of World Events* (London: Longman, January–December 1990 and January–April 1991); *Sub-Saharan Africa, Daily Report* (Washington, DC: Government Printing Office, April 1–November 27, 1991); *Africa South of the Sahara 1995,* Twenty-Fourth Edition Europa Publications Limited (London: Europa Publications, 1994); *The Europa World Year Book 1995* (London: Europa Publications, 1995); *Financial Times International,* March 18, 1996 © 1996 Financial Times Limited; "Benin Vote Surprise," by Nicholas Phythian, Reuters 1996 © 1996 Reuters; "Abdoulkarim Is Elected," by Annie Thomas, Agence France-Presse 1996, © 1996 Agence France-Presse; *Political Handbook of the World 1995–1996* (Binghamton University, State University of New York: CSA Publications, 1996); Central Intelligence Agency, *World Factbook 2000,* www.cia.gov; US State Department, www.odci.gov (accessed 20 November 2000); "Burundi Military Leader Sworn In," *Washington Post,* 12 June 1998, p. A22; "Troops Overthrow Ivory Coast Government," Agence France-Presse, *New York Times,* 25 December 1999, p. A8; Douglas Farah, "Violence Greets Ivory Coast Leader," *Washington Post,* 27 October 2000, p. A24; Norimitsu Onishi, "Dictator Gone, Violence Erupts in Ivory Coast," *New York Times,* 27 October 2000, p. A1; "Ruling Alliance Candidate Elected President of Djibouti," *Times* Wire Service, Los Angeles, 10 April 1999, p. 3; "General Seems to Be Building Toward a Coup in Guinea-Bissau," Agence France-Presse *New York Times,* 24 November 2000, p. A27; "Madagascar President to Quit," International News Digest, *Financial Times,* 6 September 1996, p. 3; "Ex-ruler Elected Madagascar President," *Gazette,* 1 February 1997, p. B8; Norimitsu Onishi, "Nigeria's Military Turns Over Power to Elected Leader," *New York Times,* 30 May 1999, p. A1; Karl Vick, "Rwanda's De Facto Chief Named Nation's First Tutsi President," *Washington Post,* 18 April 2000, p. A30; "Rwandan President Resigns," *Reuters,* 23 March 2000; William Wallis, "Senegal Offers Model as New Leader Sworn In," *Financial Times*, 30 April 2000, p. 10.

Note: The Basic Political Data appendix is based on information gathered from a variety of sources. It should be noted that obtaining completely accurate data on African political events is difficult. Incomplete and conflicting accounts of government actions and dates are common among standard sources, and although all information on independence and on periods of political leadership was corroborated by three or more sources, readers may occasionally find discrepancies in other sources.

The Contributors

Virginia DeLancey is academic counselor in the Program of African Studies at Northwestern University.

April A. Gordon is professor of sociology and coordinator of women's studies at Winthrop University, in South Carolina.

Donald L. Gordon is professor of political science and director of the Richard W. Riley Institute of Government, Politics, and Public Leadership at Furman University, in South Carolina.

George Joseph is professor of French and Francophone Studies and teaches in the Africana Studies Program at Hobart and William Smith Colleges, in New York State.

Ambrose Moyo is senior lecturer and chair of the Religious Studies Department at the University of Zimbabwe, Harare.

Jeffrey W. Neff is associate professor of geography in the Department of Geosciences and Natural Resources Management at Western Carolina University, in North Carolina.

Julius E. Nyang'oro is professor and chair of African and Afro-American Studies at the University of North Carolina at Chapel Hill.

Thomas O'Toole is professor of anthropology in the Department of Sociology and Anthropology at St. Cloud State University, in Minnesota.

Peter J. Schraeder is professor of political science at Loyola University, in Chicago.

Eugenia Shanklin is professor of anthropology at The College of New Jersey.

Index

About the Book

Thoroughly updated to reflect recent events and trends—including Africa and the war on terror, progress and problems in democratization, advances by women in politics, developments in the fight against AIDS, the growing influence of China, the establishment of the African Union, and much more—this new edition of *Understanding Contemporary Africa* treats the range of issues facing the continent in the first decade of the twenty-first century.

The authors provide current, thorough analyses not only of history, politics, and economics, but also geography, environmental concerns, population shifts, family and kinship, the role of women, religious beliefs, and literature. Each topic is covered in an accessible style, but with reference to the latest scholarship. Maps, photographs, and tables of basic sociopolitical data enhance the text, which has made its place as the best available introduction to this diverse and complex continent.

April A. Gordon is professor of sociology and coordinator of the Women's Studies Program at Winthrop University. **Donald L. Gordon** is professor of political science and director of the Richard W. Riley Institute of Government, Politics, and Public Leadership at Furman University.